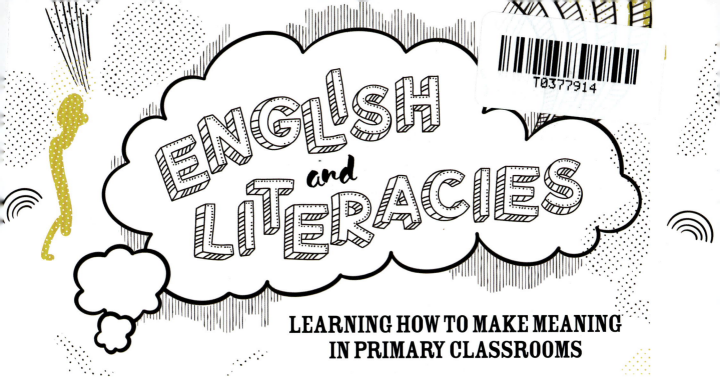

English and Literacies
LEARNING HOW TO MAKE MEANING IN PRIMARY CLASSROOMS

Literacy is too often solely associated with the ability to read and write. Being literate in the twenty-first century means being an empowered receiver, user and creator of diverse text types communicated across multiple and rapidly changing modalities. *English and Literacies: Learning How to Make Meaning in Primary Classrooms* is an accessible resource that introduces pre-service teachers to the many facets of literacies and English education for primary students.

Addressing the requirements of the Australian Curriculum and the Early Years Learning Framework, *English and Literacies* explores how students develop oracy and literacy. Reading, viewing and writing are discussed alongside the importance of children's literature. Taking an inclusive and positive approach to teaching and learning for all students, it explores the creation of texts using spelling, grammar in context and handwriting and keyboarding skills, as well as the need for authentic assessment and reporting. Finally, the text explores the importance of literacy partnerships and how teachers can address literacy challenges across the curriculum.

Each chapter includes case studies that illustrate practical classroom scenarios, reflection questions to encourage further discussion, and Bringing It Together review questions to consolidate learning.

Written by an author team with extensive teaching experience, *English and Literacies* is a fundamental resource for all pre-service and early career primary teachers.

Robyn Ewing AM is Professor Emerita and Co-Director of the Creativity in Research, Engaging the Arts, Transforming Education, Health and Wellbeing (CREATE) Centre, Sydney School of Education and Social Work, Faculty of Arts and Social Sciences at the University of Sydney.

Siobhan O'Brien is a lecturer in the Bachelor of Early Childhood and Primary Degree in the Department of Education at Swinburne University of Technology.

Kathy Rushton is a lecturer in the Sydney School of Education and Social Work at the University of Sydney.

Lucy Stewart is an early childhood and primary educator and consultant.

Rachel Burke is a senior lecturer and applied linguist and teaching English to speakers of other languages (TESOL) educator and researcher in the School of Education at the University of Newcastle.

Deb Brosseuk is a lecturer specialising in language, literacy and literature in the Sydney School of Education and Social Work at the University of Sydney.

Cambridge University Press acknowledges the Australian Aboriginal and Torres Strait Islander peoples of this nation. We acknowledge the traditional custodians of the lands on which our company is located and where we conduct our business. We pay our respects to ancestors and Elders, past and present. Cambridge University Press is committed to honouring Australian Aboriginal and Torres Strait Islander peoples' unique cultural and spiritual relationships to the land, waters and seas and their rich contribution to society.

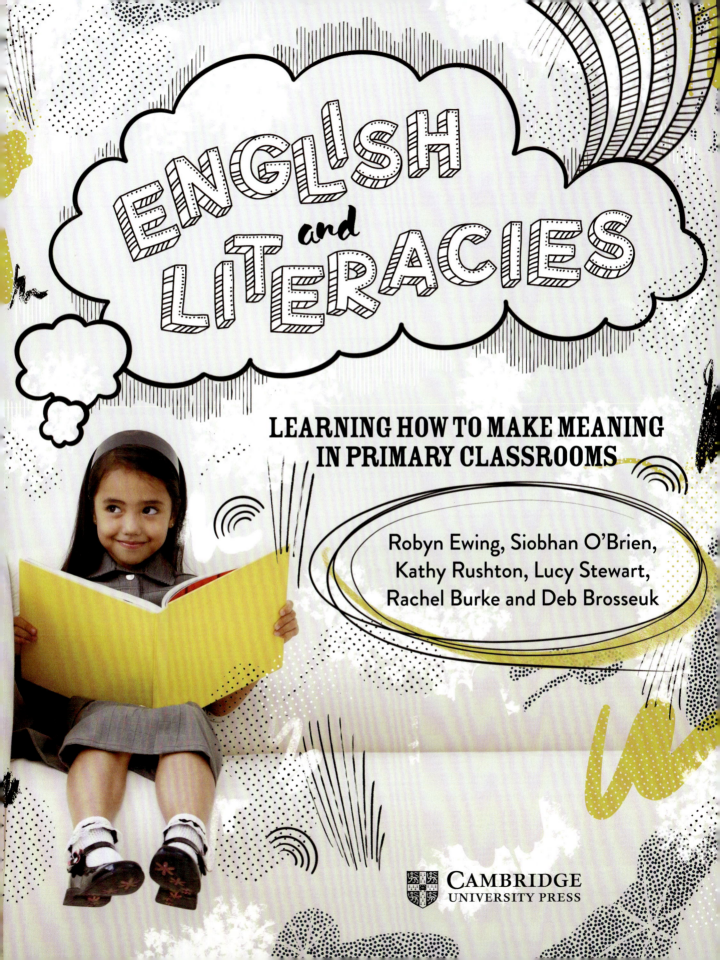

CAMBRIDGE
UNIVERSITY PRESS

University Printing House, Cambridge CB2 8BS, United Kingdom

One Liberty Plaza, 20th Floor, New York, NY 10006, USA

477 Williamstown Road, Port Melbourne, VIC 3207, Australia

314–321, 3rd Floor, Plot 3, Splendor Forum, Jasola District Centre, New Delhi – 110025, India

103 Penang Road, #05–06/07, Visioncrest Commercial, Singapore 238467

Cambridge University Press is part of the University of Cambridge.

It furthers the University's mission by disseminating knowledge in the pursuit of education, learning and research at the highest international levels of excellence.

www.cambridge.org
Information on this title: www.cambridge.org/highereducation/isbn/9781009154031

© Cambridge University Press 2022

This publication is copyright. Subject to statutory exception and to the provisions of relevant collective licensing agreements, no reproduction of any part may take place without the written permission of Cambridge University Press.

First published 2022

Cover designed by Tanya De Silva-McKay
Typeset by Integra Software Services Pvt. Ltd
Printed in China by C & C Offset Printing Co., Ltd, December 2021

A catalogue record for this publication is available from the British Library

A catalogue record for this book is available from the National Library of Australia

ISBN 978-1-009-15403-1 Paperback

Additional resources for this publication at
www.cambridge.org/highereducation/isbn/9781009154031/resources

Reproduction and communication for educational purposes

The Australian *Copyright Act 1968* (the Act) allows a maximum of one chapter or 10% of the pages of this work, whichever is the greater, to be reproduced and/or communicated by any educational institution for its educational purposes provided that the educational institution (or the body that administers it) has given a remuneration notice to Copyright Agency Limited (CAL) under the Act.

For details of the CAL licence for educational institutions contact:

Copyright Agency Limited
Level 12, 66 Goulburn Street
Sydney NSW 2000
Telephone: (02) 9394 7600
Facsimile: (02) 9394 7601
E-mail: memberservices@copyright.com.au

Cambridge University Press has no responsibility for the persistence or accuracy of URLs for external or third-party internet websites referred to in this publication and does not guarantee that any content on such websites is, or will remain, accurate or appropriate.

Please be aware that this publication may contain several variations of Aboriginal and Torres Strait Islander terms and spellings; no disrespect is intended. Please note that the terms 'First Nations', 'Indigenous Australians' and 'Aboriginal and Torres Strait Islander peoples' may be used interchangeably in this publication.

Contents

Authors		xi
Acknowledgements		xiii
Online resources		xv
Introduction		**1**
1	**Literacies learning in the early years: fundamental concepts of text, identities and access to education**	**6**
	Rachel Burke	
	Introduction	7
	Changing definitions of text and literacies	7
	Exploring literate practices in the twenty-first century	11
	The importance of the early years for literacies	19
	Connections between home and school literate practices	22
	Conclusion	24
	Bringing it together	24
	Further resources	24
	References	25
2	**English and literacies education in the Australian context**	**29**
	Siobhan O'Brien	
	Introduction	30
	The Australian Curriculum: an historical perspective	30
	Literacies and being literate in Australian education	35
	Conclusion	43
	Bringing it together	44
	Further resources	44
	References	45
3	**Assessment and reporting**	**48**
	Robyn Ewing and Kathy Rushton	
	Introduction	49
	Understanding key terms and principles	49
	Authentic assessment and its importance	50
	When to assess	51
	Who should assess?	54
	How should we assess?	55
	Reporting assessment results	55
	Planning assessment from the beginning	57

Authentic curriculum-based assessment: examples and case studies	60
Conclusion	67
Bringing it together	68
Further resources	68
References	68

4 Developing oracy: speaking and listening

Siobhan O'Brien

70

Introduction	71
Oracy development prior to school	71
Speaking and listening in the Early Years Learning Framework, Australian Curriculum: English and literacy progression	75
The role of oral narrative in Australian First Nations cultures	83
Instructional strategies for speaking and listening	86
Key issues in speaking and listening in the early primary years	88
Key teaching approaches in speaking and listening for middle to later primary years	93
Conclusion	96
Bringing it together	96
Further resources	97
References	97

5 Learning to be 'literate': exploring contexts, complexities and possibilities for teaching about text

Rachel Burke

100

Introduction	101
Connecting theory with practice	102
A preliminary exploration of ideas regarding literacies development	103
Exploring complexities of literacies teaching: issues of access and inclusion	110
Exploring possibilities for 'weaving' knowledges in literacies learning	115
Conclusion	119
Bringing it together	119
Further resources	120
References	121

6 Reading and viewing

Robyn Ewing

124

Introduction	125
Defining reading and viewing	126
Early experiences: foundations for the reading journey	128

The reading process	131
Phases of reading development	134
A brief history of 'reading' and some related controversies about teaching reading	135
Developing a repertoire of teaching and learning strategies	140
Designing whole-class and small-group activities to facilitate reading development and deep understanding	142
Assessing reading progress and development	144
Important key issues to consider in the teaching of reading	147
Dispelling common myths about learning to read	148
Conclusion	148
Bringing it together	149
Further resources	149
References	150

7 Children's literature as the heart of literacy teaching — 154
Deb Brosseuk

Introduction	155
What is children's literature?	155
Children's literature in curriculum frameworks	156
A vibrant literary vista	160
Setting up, organising and using literary texts in the classroom	162
Curating collections of literary texts	163
Staying up-to-date with literary texts	167
A literary role model	169
Conclusion	173
Bringing it together	174
Further resources	174
Acknowledgement	175
References	175

8 Understanding and responding to texts — 179
Robyn Ewing

Introduction	180
Understanding and responding in the Australian Curriculum	181
Interpreting texts: reader response theory	182
Building understanding through talk: preparing learners to respond through developing context and field knowledge	183
Classroom strategies and approaches to facilitate learners' understandings of and responses to texts	185
Learning important metacognitive skills: 'thinking about thinking'	187

Interpreting images		188
Graphic and semantic organisers		189
Using arts-rich strategies to understand and respond to texts		194
Conclusion		200
Bringing it together		201
Further resources		201
References		202

9 Creating texts

205

Robyn Ewing and Kathy Rushton

Introduction	206
Moving from spoken to written language	207
The joint construction	209
Creating texts across the curriculum	212
Imaginative genres	214
Informative genres	218
Persuasive genres	222
Conclusion	224
Bringing it together	224
Further resources	224
References	225

10 Developing knowledge about language and grammar in context

227

Kathy Rushton

Introduction	228
How knowledge about grammar is developed	228
How knowledge about grammar can be developed at school	231
Making choices to produce texts: field, tenor and mode	233
Conclusion	246
Bringing it together	246
Further resources	246
References	247

11 Working with EAL/D learners: creating positive, inclusive environments, especially for First Nations learners

249

Kathy Rushton

Introduction	250
Learning English: language, literacy and literature	250
Building on learners' cultural, social and linguistic resources	254

Creating positive and inclusive learning environments	257
Always was, always will be Aboriginal land	259
Developing a language-centred classroom	263
Conclusion	268
Bringing it together	268
Further resources	269
References	269

12 Creating positive, inclusive learning environments: working with learners with additional and diverse needs — 273

Lucy Stewart

Introduction	274
Diversity in primary learning environments	274
The importance of positive and inclusive learning environments	279
Key approaches to creating positive and inclusive literacy learning environments	283
Inclusive teaching practices across the primary years	287
Conclusion	292
Bringing it together	292
Further resources	292
References	293

13 Teaching spelling in context — 297

Lucy Stewart

Introduction	298
Key issues in spelling development	298
Connection between spelling and other literacy skills	300
Developing spelling knowledge	301
Stages of spelling development	304
Key approaches to teaching spelling in context in the primary years	307
Learning foci for teaching spelling in context across the primary years	310
Assessment, curriculum and diverse learning needs	315
Conclusion	318
Bringing it together	319
Further resources	319
References	319

14 Publishing texts: developing handwriting and keyboarding skills — 322

Lucy Stewart

Introduction	323

A brief history of handwriting	323
Development of writing and handwriting in young learners	325
Understanding the mechanics of handwriting and keyboarding	331
The role of keyboarding skills in handwriting development	332
Key approaches to teaching and learning handwriting and keyboarding in the primary years	334
Teaching and learning for handwriting and keyboarding across the primary years	338
Assessment, curriculum and diverse learning needs	342
Conclusion	345
Bringing it together	345
Further resources	345
References	346

15 Literacy across the curriculum — 349
Siobhan O'Brien

Introduction	350
Literacy as a general capability in the Australian Curriculum	350
Literacy across the curriculum: strategies and approaches	355
The Australian Curriculum: planning and implementation at the school level	365
Conclusion	372
Bringing it together	372
Further resources	373
References	373

16 Partnerships for literacy — 375
Siobhan O'Brien

Introduction	376
Creating a learning culture	376
Family literacy	379
Parent and caregiver participation in supporting children's reading	382
Literacy learning beyond the classroom learning context	391
Conclusion	395
Bringing it together	395
Further resources	396
References	396

Glossary	400
Book list: children's literature	407
Index	411

Authors

Robyn Ewing AM began her career as a primary teacher and is Professor Emerita and Co-Director of the Creativity in Research, Engaging the Arts, Transforming Education, Health and Wellbeing (CREATE) Centre, Sydney School of Education & Social Work in the Faculty of Arts & Social Sciences at the University of Sydney. A former president of both the Primary English Teaching Association and the Australian Literacy Educators Association, Robyn is a board member of WestWords and a visiting scholar at Barking Gecko. Passionate about the role that arts-rich experiences can and should play in our lives and learning, she particularly enjoys working alongside other educators and artists interested in creative curriculum reform. Robyn has worked in partnership with Sydney Theatre Company since 2009 on 'School Drama', a program aiming to ensure primary teachers have the expertise and confidence to embed drama-rich processes and experiences with quality literature to enhance learners' imaginations and English and literacy learning.

Siobhan O'Brien BEd Hon MEd is a lecturer in the Bachelor of Early Childhood and Primary Degree at Swinburne University of Technology in the Department of Education, and has over 20 years of experience in education, training and development. Siobhan has also worked as a consultant and facilitator with Cambridge Education and Bastow for the Leading Excellence in Classroom Practice course. Her current research area is focused on parent–child engagement and wellbeing with a groundbreaking program titled The Reading WELL (Wellbeing in Everyday Language and Literature), a home reading program that uses books to support self-esteem, body image and resilience.

Dr Kathy Rushton is a lecturer in the Sydney School of Education and Social Work at the University of Sydney. She provides professional learning for teachers and is an experienced TESOL and classroom teacher who has worked in primary and secondary settings, as well as with adults learning English. She is interested in home reading program and literacy, especially with disadvantaged culturally and linguistically diverse communities. Her current research projects include a study of multilingual pre-service teachers and the impact that professional learning has on the development of a creative pedagogical stance that incorporates translanguaging and supports student identity and wellbeing.

Lucy Stewart is an early childhood and primary educator and consultant with experience across a range of early childhood, primary and tertiary settings. She has provided professional development and coaching for the Victorian Department of Education and South Australian Department for Education and contributed to publications in Victoria and the Northern Territory. Lucy continues to work with and advocate for learners with additional needs as well as supporting practice improvement for educators in early childhood settings, specifically in relation to communication, wellbeing, access and inclusion. Lucy is an avid reader, a propagator of plants and a believer in the benefits of dogs and the ocean for wellbeing.

Dr Rachel Burke is a senior lecturer and applied linguist at the University of Newcastle. Rachel's research and teaching focus on linguistically and culturally diverse contexts, with emphasis on strength-based, praxis-driven approaches to education for learners from traditionally underrepresented backgrounds, including people with refugee and asylum seeker experiences. Rachel is privileged to learn from a range of communities and seeks to support collaborative approaches to honouring linguistic diversity. Rachel is a steering committee member of the Refugee Education Special Interest Group (RESIG), a convenor of the Australian Association for Research in Education (AARE) CALD Education Special Interest Group, and a Companion of the UNESCO Chair for Refugee Integration through Languages and the Arts (RILA).

Deb Brosseuk is a lecturer in the Sydney School of Education and Social Work at the University of Sydney. She teaches across the Bachelor of Education Primary program and the Master of Teaching program in English education. Deb's current research interests are focused on exploring pedagogic ways children's literature can be used in the teaching of language and literacy in the early years of formal schooling. She is a proud member of the Australian Literacy Educators' Association and the current co-editor of its practitioner journal, *Practical Literacy: The Early and Primary Years*.

Acknowledgements

We thank and warmly acknowledge the many learners and colleagues who have informed our work, the Cambridge University Press editorial team and those who have contributed through case studies and other resources.

Robyn Ewing warmly thanks the colleagues, teachers and learners she has worked alongside over her career. She is especially grateful to her children, grandchildren and extended family and friends who have taught her so much about meaning-making.

Siobhan O'Brien extends her thanks to the families and children she has taught. Their stories remain a part of her: a narrative quilt that she carries as a rich treasure. She also thanks her colleagues and family for their ongoing love and support.

Kathy Rushton thanks Mary Sanford for sharing the true history of Australia.

Lucy Stewart thanks the families, colleagues and mentors who inspire her to advocate for inclusive and lifelong learning. To her 'furry research assistants', constant companions on her own learning journey through the many hours of work on her first book chapters; and to the learners and future educators, you are the reason I do what I do, thank you.

Rachel Burke is grateful to her many teachers: the people and communities who show her the richness, diversity, and wonder of language.

Deb Brosseuk offers loud, proud, and heartfelt thanks to young learners – and there are many – who helped grow her ideas about children's literature as the centrepiece for literacy teaching and learning. She thanks them for teaching her to listen intently, to let their words affect her, and to give credence and meaning to their literary recommendations.

The authors and Cambridge University Press would like to thank the following for permission to reproduce material in this book.

Figure 1.1: © Getty Images/oxygen, © Getty Images/Photography taken by Mario Gutiérrez, © Getty Images/Alexander Spatari, © Getty Images/Jan Hakan Dahlstrom; **1.2**: © Getty Images/courtneyk; **2.1**: © Getty Images/duncan1890; **3.1**: ship © Getty Images/CSA Images; **3.2**: © Getty images/Print Collector/Contributor; **3.3**: © Getty Images/Sam Feinsilver, © Getty Images/Mayur Kakade; **3.4**: © Getty Images/Traceydee Photography; **4.1**: © Getty Images/PeopleImages; **4.2**, **15.1**, **15.2**, **16.4**, **Table 4.1**, extracts from The Australian Curriculum: English, extracts from National Literacy Learning Progression and extracts from Cross-curriculum Priorities: © Australian Curriculum, Assessment and Reporting Authority (ACARA) 2011 to present, unless otherwise indicated. This material was downloaded from the ACARA website (www.acara.edu.au) as indicated (accessed 20 Nov 2020) and was not modified. The material is licensed under CC BY 4.0 (https://creativecommons.org/licenses/by/4.0/). ACARA does not endorse any product that uses ACARA material or make any representations as to the quality of such products. Any product that uses ACARA's material should not be taken to be affiliated with ACARA or have the sponsorship or approval of ACARA. It is up to each person to make their own assessment of the product; **Figure 6.1**: B. Cambourne & D. Crouch. About the conditions of learning. Accessed at http://www.cambournesconditionsoflearning.com.au/conditions-of-learning-blog-spot; http://www.cambournesconditionsoflearning.com.au; **8.1**: From *Teacup* by Rebecca Young and Matt Ottley. Text copyright © Rebecca Young, 2015. Illustrations copyright © Matt Ottley, 2015. First published by

Scholastic Press, a division of Scholastic Australia Pty Limited, 2015. Reproduced with permission from Scholastic Australia Pty Limited; **p. 191**: © Getty Images/jayk7; **8.4**: The Elements of Drama diagram originally published in *Dramawise Reimagined* copyright © Brad Haseman and John O'Toole, 2017. Reproduced with the permission of Currency Press; **9.10**: dog © Getty Images/Pizzoferrato Photography; **10.2**: glasses © Getty Images/rustemgurler; **10.6**: © Getty Images/Jami Tarris; **10.7**: © Getty Images/Ignacio Palacios; **11.1**: © Getty Image/Grant Faint; **16.2**: © Getty Images/Jose Luis Pelaez Inc; **16.3**: © Getty Images/Cameron Spencer.

Figure 6.1, **Table 16.1** and extracts from the Early Years Learning Framework (including **Tables 13.7** and **14.5**): reproduced under CC BY 4.0 (https://creativecommons.org/licenses/by/4.0/).

Tables 12.2, **16.3**, **16.5** and **16.6**: © 2018 Education Services Australia Limited as the legal entity for the COAG Education Council (Education Council). Cambridge University Press has reproduced extracts of the Australian Professional Standards for Teachers in this publication with permission from the copyright owner. Other than as permitted by the *Copyright Act 1968* (Cth), no part of this material may be reproduced, stored, published, performed, communicated or adapted by any means without the prior written permission of the copyright owner.

Extract from Alice Springs (Mparntwe) Education Declaration: © 2019 Education Services Australia Limited as the legal entity for the COAG Education Council (Education Council). Cambridge University Press has reproduced extracts of the *Alice Springs (Mparntwe) Education Declaration* in this publication with permission from the copyright owner. Other than as permitted by the *Copyright Act 1968* (Cth), no part of this material may be reproduced, stored, published, performed, communicated or adapted by any means without the prior written permission of the copyright owner.

Case studies 7.1 and 7.2 are adapted from examples first published in D. Brosseuk, B. Exley and M. Neumann (2019), 'You know, I could trip and fall onto the track!': inspiring text production, *The Reading Teacher*, 73(4), 453–460, with permission of John Wiley & Sons Inc.

Every effort has been made to trace and acknowledge copyright. The publisher apologises for any accidental infringement and welcomes information that would redress this situation.

Online resources

Additional online resources for *English and Literacies: Learning How to Make Meaning in Primary Classrooms* are freely available at www.cambridge.org/highereducation/isbn/9781009154031/resources. Visit the site to explore weblinks for each chapter and downloadable resources.

Introduction

Children begin to make meaning from the moment they are born. Their emerging abilities to communicate are central to the development of their thinking and imaginations; expression of their feelings and emotions; access to their cultural heritage(s); and growth of their own unique identities. Learning how to mean and becoming literate continues to be critically important in shaping children and young people's life chances. Yet it does not follow the same pattern for all children and cannot be reduced to a simple, linear hierarchy of skills (Ewing, 2020) or a one-size-fits-all approach to teaching those skills. Perhaps because of its centrality to our lives and learning, becoming literate remains a complex and challenging area in education broadly and, particularly in the primary classroom, is riddled with controversy. This book is underpinned by research and practice and reflects our serious commitment to every child's entitlement to a rich and creative English and literacies education in the primary classroom.

Every primary teacher must be knowledgeable about how language works as a resource to make meaning and how we learn to use it; able to teach oracy, reading and viewing and writing using a wide repertoire of appropriate strategies; and possess a love of literature that they are able to engender in learners. They must be able to model and share how to use and create texts (texts used here in its broadest form) in inclusive ways that meet the needs of *all* learners in their care. In time, learners will understand that meaning-making is about the interactions between the speaker, reader or viewer and the text, rather than solely through the text itself. In addition, they will know and experience how different texts will be interpreted differently by different individuals, depending on their experiences, backgrounds and the specific time and place. These understandings will inform their own text creation.

Teaching subject English and helping learners become literate are thus intricately interrelated. Learners in primary classrooms need to work with meaningful texts on relevant and purposeful activities and simultaneously learn about how to use language for multiple purposes in diverse contexts across a range of media. As the English Teaching Association of New South Wales (2004) states:

> English is essentially the study of language as a social and cultural semiotic in its multiplicity of textual forms. Historically, English has been about the shaping of the 'self'. This has meant the promotion of humane values, the enrichment of the imaginative life and the development of aesthetic sensibility through engagement with literary texts. It has also meant a concern with the personal growth of the individual. Today, this includes a kind of self-reflexivity that enables students to understand how their 'self' is located within social and cultural contexts, and constructed through language and text ... Above all, English makes possible the (re)imagining of other ways of being. (n.p.)

At the same time, however, 'literacy' is deemed a general capability in the Australian Curriculum: each subject or discipline area has a specific set of 'literacies'. We frequently talk about 'historical literacy', 'mathematical literacy', 'financial literacy' or 'multiliteracies', for example. It is clear that literacy cannot be characterised as a single or unitary global skill acquired once and therefore for always 'in a lifetime using a "one size fits all" instructional recipe' (Ewing et al., 2016, p. 2). All our children 'must be able to engage in and understand and analyse an ever-increasing range of ways' language and image are shaped, used and applied (Ewing et al., 2016, p. 2).

This book explores the teaching of both English and literacy in the primary classroom. It can therefore be seen as a companion to *Language and Literacy Development in Early Childhood* (Ewing et al., 2016). Written for pre-service and early career primary teachers and interested parents, caregivers and community members, it is based on the following 'passionate creed' (LaBoskey, 1994):

- honouring of the many diverse cultures, ethnicities and backgrounds of learners through providing an inclusive learning environment that builds confidence and self-efficacy
- nurturing the imagination and creativity inherent in all learners
- learners needing to be actively engaged in the meaning-making processes
- developing genuine literacy partnerships with parents, caregivers and the community is critical
- requiring that all forms of authentic literary and information texts play a central role in the English and literacy classroom
- authentically integrating quality creative arts processes and experiences (dance, drama, media, music and visual arts) in the English and literacy program given they are different literacies– different ways of making meaning
- providing adequate time and resources to engage in playful language experiences and activities
- underpinning becoming literate with talking and active listening
- developing dispositions of empathy, risk-taking, experimentation, collaboration and flexibility as important in understanding and creating texts
- enjoying learning to be literate
- realising feedback and assessment should be explicit and authentic and a tool for facilitating progress in learning
- fostering learners' reflective practice for the development of confident literacy learners.

In addition, in terms of resources, we argue that every primary classroom needs to include a reading corner with a rich collection of picture books, novels and poetry, including the learners' writing in self-published books. Non-fiction, information and instructional works, persuasive texts and dictionaries are also important. Dress-ups, puppets and craft areas are also highly recommended. Access to iPads and computers is essential for drafting, editing and, eventually, publishing.

Our book draws on international and Australian research and aligns with both the Australian Curriculum (Australian Curriculum, Assessment and Reporting Authority [ACARA], 2020a, 2020b) and the Early Years Learning Framework (EYLF; Department of Education, Employment and Workplace Relations [DEEWR], 2009). While it centres on the Australian context, we believe many of the topics and issues have relevance for broader international audiences, and the book considers some of the relevant histories and controversies that have dominated English and literacy learning over our years in the field. All chapters include easy access to a range of case studies, weblinks and further reading and resources, as well as opportunities to question and reflect. Key terms and concepts are defined. A list of the literature used throughout the book is also included.

It is not necessary to read the book in a linear fashion: the reader may read chapters of interest in any order and related sections in other chapters are noted where appropriate. However, the chapters are sequenced so that the book intentionally starts with providing a context and overview of the key strategies and instructional approaches presented in the book.

In Chapter 1, Rachel Burke defines what it means to be literate in the twenty-first century as 'being an empowered receiver, user, and producer of diverse text types, communicated across multiple and rapidly changing modalities'. She explores the changing understandings of text, how the foundations required for literate practices begin at the moment of birth, and how inclusive, carefully scaffolded teaching approaches and repertoires are a must for primary classrooms.

Chapter 2 follows with Siobhan O'Brien's careful mapping of the knowledge and understandings of English and literacies education as represented in Australian policy, research and curriculum. Siobhan examines both the EYLF and the Australian Curriculum: English before explaining the literacy capability and the National Assessment Plan – Literacy and Numeracy (National Assessment Program, 2016).

Chapter 3 provides an overview of authentic assessment and effective reporting strategies. Kathy Rushton and Robyn Ewing explain that assessment and reporting should be about facilitating optimal learning for all individuals: assessment as a tool for learning. The chapter provides principles and examples of rich assessment in primary English and literacy, although these principles and terms can be applied in all key learning areas.

How children become competent oral communicators in the home, early childhood and school contexts is discussed in Chapter 4. Siobhan O'Brien also considers the role of story in First Nations Australian cultures before providing a range of teaching and learning strategies educators can use to foster children's speaking and listening.

Some of the possibilities and complexities of recognising the communicative repertoires and resources that learners bring to the classroom are explored in Chapter 5. Rachel Burke examines how to support learners to develop expertise in literate practices in and outside school. She underlines that it is not possible to think about one approach to literacies education, and that different approaches will be relevant in different contexts and at different stages of each learner's journey.

In Chapter 6, Robyn Ewing defines the terms 'reading' and 'viewing' as social practices with meaning at their core. She notes the importance of oral language as a precursor to becoming literate. She then focuses on how children learn to read and how teachers can help through a rich repertoire of reading strategies involving a wide selection of texts and resources. A brief snapshot of the history of reading and its associated controversies is also included.

In Chapter 7, Deb Brosseuk shows how children's literature should be at the heart of English and literacy programs. She demonstrates how teachers can enable primary learners to experience the joy of language, literature and literacy so that they will continue to deeply immerse themselves in quality texts long after they finish their schooling.

In Chapter 8, Robyn Ewing builds on Chapters 6 and 7 to explore how learners can respond in creative ways to all kinds of texts and, in the process, deepen critical understandings of texts that go beyond literal or surface readings.

The importance of ensuring both teachers and learners enjoy creating texts is addressed in Chapter 9. Robyn Ewing and Kathy Rushton look at how substantive conversations need to underpin the development of writing and they investigate different aspects of learning to write within the teaching and learning framework. A range of examples of children's writing are used throughout the chapter to illustrate the concepts discussed.

Learning about grammar in context is explored in Chapter 10. Kathy Rushton shows how understanding grammar is about understanding how language works in a range of contexts and thus informs the choices we make when we are speaking and writing. The works of some contemporary First Nations Australians are used to examine how to develop knowledge about language and grammar in context.

In Chapter 11, Kathy Rushton examines the diversity of Australian primary school communities and how teachers must build on the individual linguistic and cultural resources of every learner. She especially examines the learning needs of those learning Standard Australian English as an additional language or dialect.

Lucy Stewart further explores the diversity of learners in Chapter 12 by focusing on learners with additional needs. She provides opportunities for teachers to reflect on how they can build positive and inclusive learning environments, especially for learners with disability and gifted and talented learners.

Chapter 13 examines the challenges of spelling as both a valuable and complex topic for primary learners. Lucy Stewart looks at the four different kinds of knowledges needed in learning to spell and considers a range of strategies and approaches during the early and later primary years.

A brief account of the history of handwriting begins Chapter 14. Lucy Stewart then provides a rationale for the importance of teaching both handwriting and keyboarding in primary classrooms. She looks at the interrelationships that exist between oral language, reading, and handwriting and keyboarding development; the cognitive and physical components involved to support the teaching of handwriting; and key approaches and teaching strategies to support handwriting development.

Chapter 15 aims to increase knowledge and awareness of why literacy is one of the seven general capabilities in the Australian Curriculum. Siobhan O'Brien considers how the literacy capability is designed to be incorporated into planning and teaching across all key learning areas and the use of strategies for writing genres, including the teaching and learning cycle, tiered vocabulary for word knowledge and vocabulary.

In the final chapter, Chapter 16, Siobhan O'Brien examines the imperative of literacy partnerships and how they support literacy learning. Approaches and strategies that will support teachers in engaging parents with their child's literacy development are a special focus.

It is our hope that this book will enable you to:

- understand the importance of ensuring all children have the time and resources,
- the scaffolding and explicit teaching, and
- the opportunities to engage in imaginative play, wondering, creative exploration, storying, reading and viewing, embodying, enacting, creating, questioning and reflecting. Through these processes they will come to understand multiple ways of meaning-making in our ever changing world.

Enabling children to become deeply literate is perhaps the most important life skill of all.

Robyn Ewing University of Sydney
Siobhan O'Brien Swinburne University
Kathy Rushton University of Sydney
Lucy Stewart Goodstart Early Learning
Rachel Burke University of Newcastle
Deb Brosseuk University of Sydney

References

Australian Curriculum and Assessment Reporting Authority (ACARA). (2020a). Australian Curriculum: English. www.australiancurriculum.edu.au/f-10-curriculum/english

—— (2020b). Australian Curriculum: Literacy. www.australiancurriculum.edu.au/f-10-curriculum/general-capabilities/literacy

Department of Education, Employment and Workplace Relations (DEEWR). (2009). *Belonging, Being & Becoming – The Early Years Learning Framework for Australia*. https://docs.education.gov.au/documents/belonging-being-becoming-early-years-learning-framework-australia

English Teaching Association of New South Wales. (2004). On the relationship between the teaching of English and literacy. www.englishteacher.com.au/about-us/positions-on-english/on-the-relationship-between-english-and-literacy-education

Ewing, R. (2020). Learning to read in the early years: a story of never-ending controversies and contradictions. In B. Marshall, J. Manuel, D. Pasternak, & J. Rowsell (Eds.), *The Bloomsbury Handbook of Reading Perspectives and Practices* (pp. 3–22). Bloomsbury.

Ewing, R., Callow, J., & Rushton, K. (2016). *Language and Literacy Development in Early Childhood*. Cambridge University Press.

LaBoskey, V.K. (1994). *Development of Reflective Practice: A Study of Preservice Teachers*. Teachers College Press.

National Assessment Program. (2016). www.nap.edu.au

CHAPTER 1

Literacies learning in the early years
Fundamental concepts of text, identities and access to education

Rachel Burke

ANTICIPATED OUTCOMES

After working through this chapter, it is anticipated you will be able to:

- consider changing definitions of text and literacies
- reflect on what it means to be literate in the twenty-first century
- explore your own literate identities and practices
- examine the importance of the early years for literacies
- contemplate connections between home and school literate practices
- analyse the nexus between literacies, equity and access to education.

Introduction

From the moment of birth, we are immersed in text. Images, sounds and sensations combine to provide the vast array of sensory input that informs our understandings of the world. Historically, the word 'literacy' was typically associated with the ability to read and write. Yet, throughout our lives, engagement with meaning occurs across a range of modalities, including aural, visual, digital, kinaesthetic and numerical. Being literate in the twenty-first century means being an empowered receiver, user and producer of diverse text types, communicated across multiple and rapidly changing modalities. Foundations for the complex cognitive repertoires, skill sets, sociocultural knowledge and textual understandings required for such literate practices are established in the early years, a period of remarkable growth that forms the basis for a lifetime of textual engagement.

This chapter provides an introduction to some of the fundamental concepts of literacies, commencing with a brief exploration of changing understandings of text and what it means to be literate within the increasingly dynamic and complex communicative environments of the twenty-first century. The chapter explores the importance of the early years in the development of literate practices, and the impact of literacies on lifelong patterns of educational inclusion and attainment, employment, and health and wellbeing. The significance of literate practices to identities and community connections is considered, together with the need for responsive, carefully scaffolded learning experiences that value diverse literate repertoires while offering inclusion in the textual practices embedded within schooling. Overall, the chapter provides a context for the key strategies and instructional approaches presented in the remainder of the book.

Changing definitions of text and literacies

Literacy or **literacies** can be broadly defined as the complex repertoires of cognitive abilities and sociocultural knowledge that we use to engage with text. However, understandings of these repertoires and knowledge, and of text itself, have changed significantly throughout history and vary across and within different cultural contexts. It is important for teachers to be aware of the social, cultural and political factors that impact upon concepts of literacies and text, and the ongoing influences that continue to shape contemporary understandings. As Leu and Kinzer (2000) articulate:

> Literacy, therefore, may be thought of as a moving target, continually changing its meaning depending on what society expects literate individuals to do. As societal expectations for literacy change, and as the demands on literate functions in a society change, so too must definitions of literacy change to reflect this moving target. (p. 108)

Historical interpretations of literacy

Historically, in some parts of the world, literacy has been associated with the ability to read and write printed text. In fact, the English word 'literacy' derives from the Latin term *litteratus* meaning to be 'acquainted with letters or literature', and Harris (1989) states that this term was used in ancient Roman times to indicate scholarliness and familiarity with Latin,

Literacies: may be defined as the various tools we use for engaging with text.

the language of law, governance and academia. For much of history, in many parts of the world, the ability to read and write was largely restricted to those people in governance roles who were charged with interpreting the content of legal and religious documents and relaying information to the wider population (Kern, 2015). While some members of the working classes could read, few had access to books, which were produced by hand and therefore limited in number. In some contexts, the capacity to read and write was a powerful means of control and a defining characteristic of authority (Gee, 2011), being widely considered to indicate higher social standing and intelligence, in what Graff (1981) refers to as the 'Literacy Myth'.

With the advent of hand-operated printing presses featuring movable type in approximately 1440 CE (Wyse et al., 2013), written text became more accessible, and people from different social and economic classes came into more frequent contact with books and other printed materials. Kern (2015) cautions against considering the printing press to be 'the second quantum leap forward after the invention of writing itself' (p. 150), suggesting that such a view is Eurocentric and foregrounds the importance of the technology (which Kern contends existed across the Asian continent prior to its advent in Europe; see also Wyse et al., 2013) rather than the social and cultural circumstances in which the technology successfully contributed to the wider dissemination of printed text. Among the sociocultural conditions that provided a favourable context for facilitating the wider distribution of printed materials were economic factors, with printing identified as a means of profit, the availability of suitable raw materials on which to print text, and the increasing numbers of people who were print literate (Kern, 2015).

Although far from universal, reading became more widespread in many parts of the world due to these and other sociocultural changes, with exposure to new knowledge via printed materials leading to a democratisation of learning and greater access to documents pertaining to education and governance. As Johnson (2015) articulates: 'Increased reading ability among the general population increasingly negated the once essential skill of extensive memorization while simultaneously increasing public demand for text and individuals who could read that text' (p. 111). The wider population was no longer reliant on ruling classes to interpret and convey the written word, and this had important implications for people who were previously dependent on others to access information. In some ways, the impact of these events on popular access to knowledge may therefore be compared to the societal transformation generated by the internet and the advent of digitally accessible text in the late twentieth century.

Print literacy:
the knowledge and competencies required to read and write printed text.

Often referred to as **print literacy**, the repertoire of knowledge and skills required to read and write is central to communication within a society in which printed text is afforded great significance. In recognition of the role of print literacy in facilitating access to education, employment opportunities, social mobility and health care, the United Nations Educational, Scientific and Cultural Organization (UNESCO) established the Experimental World Literacy Program in 1966, declaring literacy to be a fundamental human right. Importantly, print literacy is recognised both as a human right in itself and an instrument for attaining other human rights, such as political, health, legal and economic rights (Read Educational Trust, 2020). While this part of the chapter discusses some of the social and historical factors regarding the reading and writing of printed text, as well as contemporary print literacy rates, it is important to remember that these repertoires do not operate in isolation but are used in collaboration with many other ways of making meaning (New London Group, 1996). We discuss these interrelationships in more detail throughout the chapter and the book.

CONTEMPORARY RATES OF PRINT LITERACY

Print literacy – the ability to read and write – is not one skill or knowledge set but consists of many different **microskills** (Brown, 2001) or underlying resources and repertoires (Freebody & Luke, 1990). Teachers need to be familiar with the various forms of knowledge required to be print literate and understand how these resources interact to allow us to engage meaningfully with text (Freebody & Luke, 1990). Chapter 6 provides a detailed examination of the various repertoires of knowledge required for print literacy, such as understanding the relationships between letters or characters and sounds, knowledge of vocabulary, spelling and word formation, and understanding how textual features vary according to sociocultural context and author intentions. Chapter 6 introduces the four resources, or roles, of the reader framework (Freebody & Luke, 1990) as a way of conceptualising how these different repertoires work together, and the chapter also explores the interrelationships between print literacy and other forms of engaging with meaning, such as oracy, numeracy, visual, digital and intercultural literacy.

Microskills: the underlying resources and repertoires we use to read, view, write, listen and speak (Brown, 2001).

In the twenty-first century, print literacy is more widespread than at any other time in human history (Roser & Ortiz-Ospina, 2018). While it is estimated that only 12 per cent of the world's population could read and write in 1820, by 2016, 84 per cent of people were print literate (Roser & Ortiz-Ospina, 2018). Yet it is important to recognise that there are still large populations of people who are without access to reading and writing in contexts where these forms of engaging with text are central to life opportunities. Of the 16 per cent of people worldwide without print literacy, women and those living below the poverty line are disproportionately represented (Roser & Ortiz-Ospina, 2018). Given the important correlations between print literacy and a range of quality-of-life indicators, including educational attainment, income, health and nutrition, and rates of unemployment, mortality, incarceration and life expectancy (Organisation for Economic Co-operation and Development [OECD], 2017), this continued exclusion from print literacy practices for approximately 16 per cent of the global population is extremely troubling. Importantly, exclusion from print literacy can result from, and continue to perpetuate, social inequalities and injustices.

REFLECTION

1. What would your life be like without print literacy? Think about what opportunities and experiences might be inaccessible. Which professional networks or social events may be closed to you? Would you have other literate practices that might assist you to engage with text? How might your sense of self and identity be affected if you were without print literacy?

2. Take a moment to reflect on the last 24 hours. What forms of print literacy did you engage in during this time? Try to be as specific as possible when describing each task – for example, 'I scrolled through my news feed, scanned for keywords to identify interesting posts … '. Reflect on how various resources (such as recognising symbols, understanding when emotive or persuasive language is used to influence the reader, applying background knowledge to make sense of text, or using contextual clues to help you guess the meaning of unknown vocabulary) allow you to undertake these tasks. Also think about how reading and writing intersect with other ways of making meaning, such as engaging with digital, visual and spoken text.

In Australia, the rates of print literacy are comparatively high, with most Year 5 learners estimated to have achieved 'at or above the minimum standards for reading in 2018' (Australian Institute of Health and Welfare [AIHW], 2020). However, despite this high national attainment of print literacy, there are various populations that are disproportionally represented in lower levels of print literacy achievement. In 2018, learners in Year 5 attending schools in 'remote (85%) and very remote (54%) areas were less likely to achieve at or above the reading minimum' than their peers who attended school in urban centres (96%) (AIHW, 2020). Learners using English as an additional language/dialect (EAL/D) were also marginally 'less likely to achieve at or above the minimum standards in reading (93%)' than their English-language-background peers (AIHW, 2020). Further, Year 5 learners from Aboriginal and Torres Strait Islander backgrounds achieved the reading rate by 77 per cent compared with non-Aboriginal and Torres Strait Islander peers, who achieved the rate at 96 per cent (AIHW, 2020). While there are many complex factors associated with the assessment and reporting of print literacy attainment, it is important for all teachers to be aware of these patterns of achievement and to critically consider issues of equity, inclusion and approaches to education.

Chapter 3 explores issues related to literacies attainment and reporting in Australia, reflects on approaches to literacies assessment and evaluation, and emphasises the importance of responding to the diverse strengths and needs of all learners, including those who are required to make complex transitions between home and school literate practices (Curry et al., 2016; Lee-James & Washington, 2018; Lo Bianco, 2013; Oliver et al., 2021; Wigglesworth & Simpson, 2018). Later in this chapter, we consider the 'home/school connection' and how some learners may be more familiar with the literate requirements of formal schooling and assessment due to similarities with their literate practices at home (Gee, 2011; Heath, 1983; Schleppegrell, 2008). All learners have 'primary' literate practices (Gee, 2011); these **funds of knowledge** (Moll et al., 1992) are unique to their cultural and social communities and reflect complex and interconnected identities related to ethnicity, culture and location (Moje et al., 2004; Moll et al., 1989; Vygotsky, 1978). It is important that teachers recognise and value diverse linguistic and literate practices that may differ from those foregrounded in the schooling system, and that they support learners to make connections with the textual practices required for schooling.

Funds of knowledge: the understandings, practices and resources that each learner develops in their home and communities (Moll et al., 1992). This concept is connected to Vygotsky's social development theory.

REFLECTION

1. Can you remember your own experiences learning to read and write? This may be harder to do if you learnt to read and write as a child, but you may recall having a favourite book or writing your own stories. Were there any routines and events, such as visiting the local library, participating in shared reading or storytelling, or watching books or other print materials being discussed on television or online, that were integral to your experiences? If you learnt to read as an adult, what were some supports that you found helpful?

2. How do reading and writing align with your own funds of knowledge (Moll et al., 1992)? For example, were reading and writing key to your community's literate practices when you were growing up? Or were other ways of communication foregrounded, such as oracy or digital literate practices (which may also involve reading and writing)?

3. What factors and issues do you think might be important to consider when reflecting on the Australian literacy attainment statistics outlined earlier? For example, do you think groups of learners and communities may vary in terms of the communicative practices and literate repertoires that are foregrounded in different contexts, social and cultural expectations and experiences of education (both historically and in contemporary times)? Consider also the variations among learners that may result from factors such as access to the internet and digital resources, and other issues related to equity and inclusion? How do your own experiences learning to be literate shape your understandings?

While we have briefly examined the historical association of literacy with reading and writing printed texts, this way of communication was by no means universal (Thompson, 2015). Many cultures around the world had complex systems for conveying information via visual and oral means that were established over thousands of years and continue to be embedded within the social fabric of society today (Lewis et al., 2014; Thompson, 2015), such as the many languages, dialects and ways of communication used in First Nations Countries and communities across Australia (Malcolm, 2018; WA Department of Education, 2012; see also Chapter 11 for an in-depth consideration of Aboriginal and Torres Strait Islander languages and learning). It is essential for teachers to appreciate that historical communicative practices were varied, that contemporary learners may have diverse language repertoires that differ from those foregrounded in the schooling system, and that these literate practices represent important cultural resources and assets for learning (D'warte, 2014; Fleer & Hammer, 2014; Heath, 1983; Lo Bianco, 2013; Malcolm, 2018; Thompson, 2015).

Exploring literate practices in the twenty-first century

In the twenty-first century, learners are immersed in increasingly complex, textually rich, communicative environments, in which they are required to make sense of combinations of still and moving images, sounds and words in the form of sophisticated and dynamic text types, such as YouTube clips, blogs, pop-up windows, live chat streams, and virtual and extended reality platforms. In many contexts, interactions with print remain important

Texts: may incorporate many forms for conveying meaning, including print, digital, visual, aural, numerical and kinaesthetic elements.

means of engaging with the world, and these interactions are often accompanied by other means of communication (New London Group, 1996; Kress, 2003; Kress & van Leeuwen, 2020; Unsworth, 2006). Contemporary understandings of **text** therefore encompass print, aural, visual, digital, kinaesthetic and numerical mediums, as well as other ways of communicating meaning (Cope & Kalantzis, 2009; Daly & Unsworth, 2011; Kress, 2003; Kress & van Leeuwen, 2020; Serafini, 2012; Unsworth, 2006).

Changing understandings of literate practices are reflected in the UNESCO declaration that:

> literacy as a concept has proved to be both complex and dynamic, continuing to be interpreted and defined in a multiplicity of ways. People's notions of what it means to be literate or illiterate are influenced by academic research, institutional agendas, national context, cultural values and personal experiences … understandings in the international policy community have expanded too: from viewing literacy as a simple process of acquiring basic cognitive skills, to using these skills in ways that contribute to socio-economic development, to developing the capacity for social awareness. (UNESCO, 2006, p. 147)

Multiliteracies: a term coined by the New London Group in the mid-1990s to refer to the many ways in which we engage with the world. 'Multi' means 'many', while literacies are the various tools we use to interpret, utilise, analyse and produce text.

Many of the ideas that shape contemporary understandings of literate practice have their origins in the work of the members of the New London Group, a consortium of leading scholar-practitioners in languages, literacies, cultural diversity and education comprising Courtney Cazden, Bill Cope, Norman Fairclough, James Gee, Mary Kalantzis, Gunther Kress, Allan Luke, Carmen Luke, Martin Nakata and Sarah Michaels. The group met in 1994 in New London, in the United States, to explore the notion of **multiliteracies**, or the various ways of 'reading' the world across multiple modalities and environments. Particular attention to cultural and linguistic diversity, new technologies of communication and changing textual practices in increasingly service-based economies underpinned these new ideas, with the New London Group arguing that proficiency in print literacy – while still essential – was no longer sufficient for a person to qualify as an empowered, critically aware, literate individual (New London Group, 1996). Members of the New London Group, along with other key scholars working in New Literacy Studies (NLS), including Brian Street and Shirley Brice Heath, have advocated for understanding literate practices as socioculturally and contextually dependent and variable, and linked to issues of identities, inclusion and power (Gee, 2005; Heath, 1983; Street, 1993, 2005).

When describing how they arrived at the notion of multiliteracies, the New London Group state:

> We decided that the outcomes of our discussions could be encapsulated in one word – multiliteracies – a word we chose to describe two important arguments we might have with the emerging cultural, institutional, and global order: the multiplicity of communications channels and media, and their increasing saliency. (New London Group, 1996, p. 63)

The group further explained:

> Second, we decided to use the term 'multiliteracies' as a way to focus on the realities of increasing local diversity and global connectedness. (New London Group, 1996, n.p.)

A major premise of sociocultural approaches to literacies is that, in order to be informed and empowered users and producers of text within rapidly changing, digitally mediated, communicative environments, learners require different kinds of literacies or tools for engaging with meaning than children in previous generations (Bearne & Vallely, 2019; Cope & Kalantzis, 2000; Street, 1993, 2003; Unsworth, 2006). For example, while webpages include written text, do we read these texts in the same way that we read printed materials? Many researchers suggest that the resources we use to engage with websites are different and involve more elements typical to visual literacy, including navigational skills and options for engaging with content (Bearne & Vallely, 2019; Simpson et al., 2013; Walsh, 2010). For instance, Walsh (2010) discusses research conducted in the United Kingdom by Bearne and colleagues (2007, in Walsh, 2010), advising that the literacies required to engage with online text suggest 'the navigation of screen-based texts frequently involves "radial browsing" which is quite different from the left-to-right, linear reading of print-based texts' and identifying how learners 'trawl language, image and music as well as highlight key sections to retrieve information' as a way of 'orchestrating the different modes to make meaning' (Walsh, 2010, p. 214). Bearne and Vallely (2019) identify how searching the web 'often means zigzagging back and forth between screens, making sense of the proffered information through a kind of network of ideas', and refer to the work of Kress (2003, in Bearne & Vallely, 2019) when discussing the various choices available to readers when navigating such texts.

Within contemporary means of communication, we have an increasingly complex range of **modes** in which we can share meaning. In fact, many of the technological, visual and media text types common to today's society were unimaginable prior to the twenty-first century. Writing in 2003, Kress advised, 'It is no longer useful to think about a monomodal literacy that exists in isolation from the vast array of social, technological and economic factors in broader society' (p. 1). Many of the texts we encounter on a daily basis are **multimodal**, meaning that they combine two or more ways of communicating. This multimodality is not a new phenomenon; paintings, dance, oral narratives, posters, textbooks and films are all examples of multimodal communication (Bearne & Vallely, 2019; Kress, 2003). These texts require the viewer/reader to have knowledge of various modes of meaning-making in order to draw on their background schema to navigate, create and interrogate the text (Kress, 2003). For example, a performance involving gestures, facial expressions and use of space may be accompanied by audio input such as voice, music and sound effects to convey meaning. Digital multimodal texts, such as animations, slideshows, webpages, video games, and extended and virtual reality platforms, involve increasingly complex ways of communicating meaning (Dezuanni et al., 2015; McTavish, 2014; Valkonen et al., 2020).

Accordingly, 'Being literate involves the understanding of how different modalities are combined in complex ways to create meaning' (Snyder, 2002, p. 3). All learners need to know how to interpret and create multimodal texts for different purposes and audiences and understand how meaning is communicated via the individual modes and multiple modes working together (Daly & Unsworth, 2011; Serafini, 2012; Unsworth, 2006). As Bearne and Vallely (2019) advise: 'The affordances offered by different modes and media, then, influence the way texts are used, returned to, re-viewed or re-read and how they are organised and constructed and the choices made by the reader or composer/writer' (p. 2). Research also indicates that young learners are able to strategically apply and reconfigure literate practices learnt in school to digital platforms used in their home or community contexts, and, conversely, young learners may shape school literate practices using the communicative repertoires they have learnt at home and in their communities (McTavish, 2014).

Mode: the way that something is communicated – for example, written, spoken or performed. Serafini (2012) refers to this as the 'system of signs created within or across various cultures to represent and express meanings' (p. 153).

Multimodal: a text that combines two or more modes or ways of communicating information.

Multimodal texts may present a challenge for some learners as they try to construct meaning from various forms of communication simultaneously. Teachers cannot assume that all learners have equal access to various modes of communication (Dezuanni et al., 2015). Bearne and Vallely (2019) emphasise the importance of not making assumptions about familiarity with digital texts, claiming:

> although many children experience digital texts and environments from a very early age their access to technology varies considerably. There will be differences according to social, cultural, personal and economic factors so that in thinking of how best teachers can respond to the digital experience of their children, focusing on skills is not enough. (p. 2)

Teachers are required to understand the textual practices that learners may bring to the classroom as 'funds of knowledge' (Moll et al., 1992), and make connections between these and other literate practices to actively apprentice learners into navigating and responding to a range of different kinds of text (some examples are shown in Figure 1.1). As you work

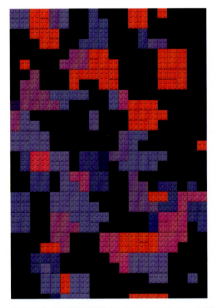

Figure 1.1 Learners will experience various modes of communication across their literacy development

through this book, you will explore, in greater depth, some possibilities for literacies learning across various modalities.

> **REFLECTION**
>
> 1. Think about a multimodal text with which you are familiar – for example, an online, collaborative game. What are the various modes that combine to create meaning in this text type? How do changes in the background music combine with visual images to communicate that you are running out of time or have gained 'new lives', for example? What role does player commentary add to the meaning you draw from the game?
> 2. Which modes of communication were important to your learning during the early years of your education? For example, did your teachers use videos to demonstrate content? Did you access digital learning resources at home? What modes were integrated in these resources (e.g. audio, visual, print or kinaesthetic)? How did you learn to interact with these multimodal texts? Did you receive specific support for navigating and producing these text types?
> 3. To explore the concept of multiliteracies and interrelationships between ways of engaging with meaning, create a mind map of literate practices regarding a particular context you know well – for example, your workplace, a sporting club or a community group. Place the context at the centre of the map and list the various literacies you use to engage with meaning in this setting. As you work on your map, you might notice that many of the repertoires and resources you use to engage in literate practice are interrelated and overlapping, such as print or visual literacy.
>
>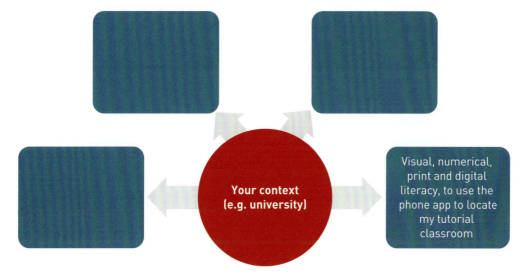
>
> 4. Compare your finished mind map with a colleague's mind map and consider similarities and differences in your literate practices. What do these differences suggest about your ideas regarding literacies, your unique sociocultural circumstances, and your particular linguistic and literate repertoires and identities?

Literacy autobiographies

Our use of literacies – or tools for engaging with the world around us – continues to develop throughout our lives. Different events and experiences will shape how we engage with and create text. Producing a literacy autobiography provides you with an opportunity to consider the importance of literacies in your life, and some of the events, people and experiences that have contributed to your development as a literate individual. You can choose to focus on any form of literacy – for example, you might like to reflect on your experiences developing inter-cultural understandings and ways of navigating similarities and differences between your own world views and other cultural practices. Alternatively, you might focus on a form of digital engagement with text that has provided you with access to social and cultural resources that may have been otherwise inaccessible to you. Whichever focus you select for your literacy autobiography, ensure it is meaningful to you and your life experiences as a literate individual.

The following are some key prompts that may assist you to compose your literacy autobiography:

- Using whichever mode of communication you prefer, briefly describe your chosen literacy (or aspect of your chosen literacy), providing some examples of how it is used in your everyday life.
- Describe why this literacy is important in your life. Think about how your life would be if you were without this particular way of engaging with meaning.
- Now think about experiences or events that have affected your proficiency in this way of engaging with text. Remember, we continue to acquire literacies throughout our lives. For example, if you have chosen to focus on print literacy, you could discuss how commencing university contributed to your development as a writer, introduced new text types, and encouraged you to develop new ways of using language.

You might also consider composing a *multimodal literacy autobiography*, in which you use a range of different ways of communicating meaning. You can choose to organise your text using the structures and stylistic features of autobiographical text types from any communicative context you know. For example, some English and other language contexts feature autobiographies that typically include:

- use of the first person (e.g. 'I', 'me', 'my')
- use of descriptive language to create interest in the story being told
- the discussion of events in a sequence (usually chronological but other options for organising the content, such as using flashbacks, may add impact).

Alternatively, you could organise your text using the *typical stylistic features* of autobiographies (or other relevant text types) that are used in another communicative context you know.

You might like to browse through the Digital Archive of Literacy Narratives (www.thedaln .org) for inspiration.

Question

How might this activity be modified and used in the classroom to assist learners to think about the ongoing nature of literacies learning?

The Australian Curriculum asserts that:

> students become literate as they develop the knowledge, skills and dispositions to interpret and use language confidently for learning and communicating in and out of school and for participating effectively in society. Literacy involves students listening to, reading, viewing, speaking, writing and creating oral, print, visual and digital texts, and using and modifying language for different purposes in a range of contexts. (Australian Curriculum, Assessment and Reporting Authority [ACARA], 2019, n.p.)

It is therefore vital that teachers incorporate a variety of text types in the classroom, and encourage learner exploration of the purposes, structures and features of these literate practices (Derewianka & Jones, 2016). This may involve teachers and learners collaborating to 'mine' each text – whether oral, written, visual, digital and so on – and explore the language and literacies knowledge and resources required to engage with the content (Derewianka & Jones, 2016; Freebody & Luke, 1990; New London Group, 1996; Street, 1993). Learning may be facilitated through focusing on key vocabulary choices, exploring strategies for navigating visual text, verbally modelling communicative interactions and using guided questions to encourage learners to interrogate text (Anstey & Bull, 2009; Derewianka & Jones, 2016; Freebody & Luke, 1990). Of course, each learning context is unique, and teachers need to consider the specific resources, needs and attitudes to education in their classrooms and broader communities.

The chapters in this book explore various aspects of literate practice, reflecting on their role within classroom learning, curriculum content and broader social and cultural contexts, and examine various strategies and resources for jointly 'unpacking' and exploring text with learners. Importantly, as modalities and platforms for communication continue to change, so do the tools we use for engaging with meaning. Learners need to mobilise their communicative resources and adapt their literate repertoires to enable engagement with text and the many different literate practices and technologies that may emerge in the future. As Anstey and Bull (2009) explain: 'A multiliterate classroom aims to empower students to cope with current and future change by developing a repertoire of resources about literacy that they can draw upon and use in any situation' (p. 1).

Visual literacy

CASE STUDY 1.1

Visual literacy refers to the knowledge and repertoires required for engaging with images. This includes the resources we use to interpret and create drawings, charts and graphs, our ability to engage with symbols, letters and characters, and our knowledge of scale, use of colour, perspective and cropping. For example, Whitehead (2009) explains: 'An artist's use of horizontal lines, flying clothes and bending trees and grass to indicate running and speed are not "natural", they are artistic conventions and must be learnt by lots of book sharing and discussions ... ' (p. 71). Learners who have strong visual literacy are able to critically engage with the meanings expressed visually, and, with the required proficiency, can make important connections between the meanings expressed via other modalities, including written or spoken text. These literate resources are also important for asking questions about textual representations, values and agendas, and making connections between compositional choices and author purpose, target audience and social and cultural contexts. ▶ ▶

> ▶ ▶ In 'Beginning critical literacy – young children's responses when reading image and text' (NSW Government, 2021), the NSW Department of Education showcases findings from a study of primary learners' critical engagement with multimodality in illustrated books. Go to the study (accessible at https://education.nsw.gov.au/teaching-and-learning/professional-learning/scan/past-issues/vol-36--2017/its-all-lighted-up--because-this-is-a-happy-ending--beginning-critical-literacy-young-childrens-responses-when-reading-image-and-text-) and read the selected interview questions used by the researchers to guide the learners' engagement with these texts. These key prompts may provide insights into the role of elicitation in facilitating textual engagement.

Questions

As you read the classroom transcripts, consider:

1. How do the learners in this study show their understandings of the use of visual imagery to communicate meaning?
2. What literate resources were learners required to mobilise to engage with these multimodal texts?
3. How might these practices vary in different cultural and social contexts?

CASE STUDY 1.2 — Digital literacy

Digital literacy refers to the resources we use to engage with digitally mediated forms of communication. These resources include not only the functional aspects of managing technology, such as knowing how to access a website or log on to a computer, but, crucially, extend to the critical use of digital texts, including knowing how to evaluate the credibility of online sources, understanding how to synthesise ideas from online sources into other texts, being aware of our digital footprint, and understanding issues regarding privacy, cyberbullying and online safety (Harvey, 2016; Hinrichsen & Coombs, 2013; Kervin et al., 2015; Ladbrook & Probert, 2011; Levy, 2009; McTavish, 2009; Neumann, 2016). As Hicks and Hawley Turner (2013) advise: 'Digital literacy is about more than just adding technology into the teaching we already do' (p. 60).

Dezuanni and colleagues (2015) undertook research in three Queensland preschools in order to investigate strategies for promoting 'digital inclusion' for children and families from low socioeconomic and/or culturally diverse communities, and to examine 'how young children learn through multimodal communication, storytelling and the creative representation of the world using digital technologies' (p. 4). Their research explored the use of iPads for writing, drawing, arts-based learning and dramatic story making, with the study showing that engagement with digital modalities requires learners to employ a range of literate repertoires in order to make meaning (Dezuanni et al., 2015).

Importantly, the researchers were interested in how the digital literacy repertoires developed in preschool might facilitate successful learning when children transitioned into school, noting that the families who participated in the study were 'at risk of being disadvantaged within digital culture and the digital economy' (Dezuanni et al., 2015, pp. 3–4). As with the capacity to read and write, being without the resources to critically engage with digital text represents a significant barrier to accessing information, services and life opportunities in a society where much of the communication occurs via rapidly changing digital technologies (Park et al., 2019). Exclusion from digital texts can therefore deepen existing marginalisation and social inequities.

Among their findings, Dezuanni and colleagues (2015) highlight the important role of teachers in ensuring all learners have the background knowledge and repertoires to engage with digital text types in ways that help them to maximise social, cultural and learning outcomes. Likewise, other researchers exploring the affordances of digital platforms for literacies education report: 'although social participation can be intentionally achieved by children themselves, early childhood education and care (ECEC) professionals and pedagogical practices play a pivotal role, especially when the cultural tools used in learning are new and unfamiliar to children' (Valkonen et al., 2020, p. 447; see also Bearne & Vallely, 2019). In 2020, the Australian Council for Educational Research (ACER) reported that studies conducted in 2017 indicated 46 per cent of learners in Year 6 were unable to engage critically with digital text or determine the best use of software for achieving a particular purpose (ACER, 2020).

The Australian Institute for Teaching and School Leadership's (AITSL) 'Multiple literacy outcomes' resource (available at www.aitsl.edu.au/tools-resources/resource/multiple-literacy-outcomes-illustration-of-practice) explores how digital literacies, as well as other modes of engagement, can support children to interact with text. As you reflect on this case study, consider the role of the teacher in helping to maximise learner outcomes.

Questions

1. What are some of the communicative modes that are used to support the children's engagement with the books?
2. Are there any specific strategies employed to assist all learners to access different modes of communication?

The importance of the early years for literacies

From birth, children observe and participate in various literate practices that are important to their families and communities (Curry et al., 2016; Hill & Diamond, 2013; McTavish, 2014). Sociocultural understandings of literate practice consider relationships between language and 'ways of being in the world' (Gee, 2005, p. 7). As Gee (2005) suggests, 'We continually and actively build and rebuild our worlds not just through language but through language used in tandem with actions, interactions, non-linguistic symbol systems, objects, tools, technologies, and distinctive ways of thinking, valuing, feeling, and believing' (p. 10). Ways of using language and literacies are therefore connected to membership within communities and groups (Gee, 2005, 2011).

Learners will therefore develop particular 'funds of knowledge' (Moll et al., 1992) about communication that are unique to their cultural and social communities, with rich diversity in the literate practices and repertoires existing across and within these groups. As Barratt-Pugh (in Barratt-Pugh & Rohl, 2001) explains: 'Children come from home to early childhood care and education contexts knowing different things about literacy and doing literacy in different ways' (p. 20).

Research identifies the importance of children's participation in literate practices in their homes and communities, showing that literacies learning commences well before formal schooling (Curry et al., 2016; D'warte, 2014; Fleer & Hammer, 2014; Heath, 1983; Hill & Diamond, 2013; Lo Bianco, 2013). When considering connections between the literate practices of home, community and school, researchers remind us that 'there is a need to problematize bounded or unitary conceptions of "home" or "community"' (Pahl & Burnett, in Hall et al., 2013, p. 3; Hull & Schultz, 2001; Lo Bianco, 2013). As Pahl and Burnett articulate: 'Communities may be fluid or transitory or experienced in different ways by different children and literacies may move within and across different locations' (in Hall et al., 2013, p. 3). The need to think about the fluidity of the various contexts in which we communicate is further compounded by what Pahl and Burnett describe as 'the varied ways in which local and global spaces intersect (Massey, 2005)' (in Hall et al., 2013, p. 3), advising that 'we need to see literacy as multisited' (p. 3; see also Hull & Schultz, 2001; Lo Bianco, 2013; New London Group, 1996).

Literate practices are not only fluid and 'multisited' (Pahl & Burnett, in Hall et al., 2013, p. 3), but they are also richly diverse. In some communities, oral language is emphasised and, from a young age, children will be apprenticed into the important spoken text types and social expectations surrounding these forms of communication (Barratt-Pugh & Rohl, 2001; D'warte, 2014; Fleer & Hammer, 2014; Heath, 1983; WA Department of Education, 2012). In cultures where oracy is particularly valued in communication, learners from such communities are likely to have highly developed verbal language resources for gaining, consolidating and articulating new knowledge (D'warte, 2014; Fleer & Hammer, 2014; Heath, 1983; WA Department of Education, 2012). For some learners, print forms may be foregrounded in their homes and communities, and they may have had cloth books as babies, engaged in shared reading, and composed their own books even before they could 'read' and 'write' (Whitehead, 2009). These learners may commence schooling with knowledge of how books 'work', such as understanding that words and images connect, that there is a directionality to reading, that words are spaced and that the story continues on each page (Barratt-Pugh & Rohl, 2001; Whitehead, 2009). In this way, children learn the structures and features of text – regardless of mode – through engagement with the literate practices around them.

In their research into language and literacies learning, Hall and Robinson (in Barratt-Pugh & Rohl, 2001) provide rich descriptions of how young children's participation in everyday activities with their family, such as shopping with a parent, incorporate learning about literate practices. Understanding the purpose and form of a shopping list (whether digital or print), and recognising that items can be counted, added to and deleted from a list, are all important literate understandings. Knowing that products are often contained in packages that feature illustrations, nutritional information, brand names, logos, barcodes and, sometimes, prices are other examples of literacies and numeracy in everyday contexts. If the shopping takes place in a store rather than online, children may also learn that supermarkets include signs and displays and are arranged strategically to encourage customers to purchase items, such as locating lollies in serviced check-out lanes (Barratt-Pugh in Barratt-Pugh & Rohl, 2001).

Children's play activities also involve literate practices, and these communicative interactions form an important basis for ongoing textual understandings (Harden, 2016; Roskos & Christie, 2011). 'Play in childhood and in adult life creates a kind of space and time where we can try things out without having to match up to external notions of correctness and can take risks. During play we can get to grips with things that matter to us alone, build new relationships with other people and even take time out to do nothing at all' (Whitehead, 2009, p. 22). Whitehead (2009) distinguishes between 'play with the matter, or stuff, of language, and play with the meanings encoded, or expressed, in language' (p. 23), noting that the former may include babies' gurgles and babbling, and older children's rhymes and word repetition, and the latter may relate to experimentation with new vocabulary, word play and jokes to use language in creative and humorous ways. Making up stories and games represents another important linguistic and literate practice, with Roskos and Christie's (2011) research illustrating how children's role-play games can encourage an understanding of narratives, plot structure and character development: 'In other words, pretend play stories provide a playful frame for exploring and practicing narrative elements – setting, problem, plot, and resolution – that children can later apply to stories in other contexts, such as oral storytelling and reading and writing stories' (Roskos & Christie, 2011, p. 214).

Community understandings of literate practices

CASE STUDY 1.3

The AITSL 'Community partnerships to improve literacy' resource (available at www.aitsl.edu.au/tools-resources/resource/community-partnerships-to-improve-literacy-illustration-of-practice) provides insights into a community approach to literacies education that connects secondary school learners with kindergarten learners to assist them to engage with text. In this resource, the teacher describes how the program aims to provide learners with a 'love of literacy'.

View the resource online and then answer the following questions.

Questions

As you reflect on this 'community partnership' approach to learning, consider:

1. How is the social and cultural situatedness of literate practice evident in these learners' experiences? For instance, why does a community approach allow for meaningful engagement with text?
2. How is oral language promoted in these learning experiences and used in connection with other forms of literate practice?
3. What elicitation strategies, learning materials and modes for engaging with text are evident in this example?

There is much that teachers can learn from childhood engagement with literate practices, including the importance of a focus on meaning, the need to ensure communication is embedded within a social purpose and context, and the usefulness of authentic materials and props (Harden, 2016; Roskos & Christie, 2007, 2011). Importantly, as Barratt-Pugh (in Barratt-Pugh & Rohl, 2001) explains, the literate practices in childhood are 'carried out as a means to an end and not as an end in themselves. In other words, reading, writing, viewing and information technology are all carried out as a means of getting something done, or finding something out, or just for pleasure' (p. 15).

Connections between home and school literate practices

The different ways that children encounter text in their home communities are not only equally valid, but they are co-constitutive, meaning that strengths in one form of literate practice – for example, ways of using language at home – are an important asset for building textual repertoires and ways with language that may be required for other contexts, such as schooling. However, research indicates that although literate practices outside of schooling contexts are diverse, some formal educational environments may focus on more 'homogenous' literate practices, which 'seem to reflect a particular view of what counts as literacy and, therefore, potentially exclude or disadvantage children who do not share this view, or cannot access these practices' (Barratt-Pugh, in Barratt-Pugh & Rohl, 2001, p. 22).

The literate practices privileged in formal schooling reflect specific knowledge traditions, values and ways of engaging with language that are often viewed as 'common sensical' (Fairclough, 2001) by those who are familiar with these ways with text, but are not necessarily obvious, relevant or relatable to all learners (Curry et al., 2016; Heath, 1983; Hill & Diamond, 2013; Lee-James & Washington, 2018; McTavish, 2014; Schleppegrell, 2008; Schleppegrell & de Oliveira, 2006). The literate practices of formal schooling are privileged, not due to any inherent linguistic superiority, but because of their origins in culturally powerful social contexts. As Lo Bianco (2013) articulates:

> both literate and spoken language forms favoured in schooling are highly selected from what's available in the community, and it is these forms that all students encounter. Naturally they encounter these forms differentially. Some learners encounter these forms as a validation and confirmation of their home cultural life, and others encounter them as a significant marker of discrepancy, a challenge, and, unfortunately quite often, as a major obstacle to their prospects of accessing the curriculum and all its stocks of knowledge and skills. (n.p.)

While participating in formal schooling may mean 'confronting new ways of using language' (Schleppegrell, 2008, p. 21) for many learners (see Rivalland, in Barratt-Pugh & Rohl, 2001; Halliday, 1993), learners with the greatest contrasts between their home and school textual practices may experience increased challenges (Gee, 2011; Heath, 1983). These learners may encounter what Barratt-Pugh (2001) identifies as a 'mis-match between home and other early childhood experiences of literacy', advising that this 'apparent mis-match is not a problem within itself, as literacy in care and education contexts is no more or less valuable than home literacy practices. The problem arises when care and education contexts only value and promote one particular view of literacy which excludes all others' (p. 22).

Accordingly, it is essential that teachers focus on teaching practices for the specific resources, strengths and needs of all learners (Dutton et al., 2018; Heath, 1983; Hill & Diamond, 2013; McTavish, 2014; Moll et al., 1992). Individualised and differentiated literacies instruction, that recognises learners' communicative 'funds of knowledge' (Moll et al., 1992) and helps them to make connections between these resources and the text types and literate repertoires required to engage with schooling and other contexts, is important to disrupting patterns of disadvantage and exclusion (Figure 1.2). As Rivalland (in Barratt-Pugh & Rohl, 2001) articulates,

'Helping children learn how to shift from one literacy context to another is critical if we are serious about providing equal opportunities for children to access literacy and power in the world' (p. 29).

Chapter 5 explores some of the possibilities and complexities of approaches to language and literacies instruction that honour existing linguistic repertoires while simultaneously developing expertise in the specific practices embedded within schooling and other contexts. Informed by the rich corpus of research and resources offered by scholar-practitioners working in a range of sociocultural and educational settings, the chapter considers some ways that teachers can support the complex linguistic and intercultural transitions required of many learners and their families as they shift between linguistic codes of home and school (Curry et al., 2016; Lee-James & Washington, 2018; Lo Bianco, 2013; Rivalland in Barratt-Pugh & Rohl, 2001; Schleppegrell, 2008).

Figure 1.2 Building 'funds of knowledge' encourages literacy development in all facets of learning

Literacy profiles

Literacy profiles are individual learner records that provide an overview of the literate practices that learners undertake outside of school and they can be useful tools for learning about learners' linguistic communities and repertoires. These profiles can take any form, such as a portfolio of learner-produced texts or a list of basic information about languages spoken, community literate practices and learners' interests in particular text types or ways of learning. Literacy profiles are often most effective when teachers, learners, families and communities work together to map each learner's linguistic 'eco-system'. Learners might want to contribute texts, stories, music or YouTube clips to share the languages or different text types that are particular to their communities. Literacy profiles can therefore provide opportunities for teachers and learners to gain new insights into many different communicative ways and literate practices.

Questions

1. Have you considered the role that literacy profiles might play in assisting you to plan for tailored, localised and culturally appropriate learning experiences? Conduct some research into different ways of designing a literacy profile. For example, you could explore the Council of Europe's website regarding literacy profiles for adult learners (see www.coe.int/en/web/lang-migrants/literacy-profiles).
2. How could various modes of communication be integrated into literacy profiles?

3. What aspects of these planning tools might be helpful for designing classroom learning activities?
4. How might literacy profiles act as bridging tools or ways of establishing connections between learners' prior and new linguistic and cultural knowledge, and generating greater involvement of families and communities in the classroom?

Conclusion

This chapter explored some of the fundamental concepts related to literacies, text, identities and access to education. The introductory examination of some historical and contemporary understandings of literacies and text illustrated the fluidity of these concepts and the connections between definitions of 'being literate' and the sociocultural contexts within which communication occurs. The chapter considered the importance of the early years as a time when children form fundamental understandings of text and literate practices, and the significance of these repertoires and resources to sociocultural identities and ongoing learning. Importantly, the chapter contemplated connections between home, community and school textual practices, highlighting the need to ensure all learners' literate repertoires are recognised and valued in the classroom. Finally, in considering the complex cognitive repertoires and sociocultural knowledge required to be informed users and producers of text, the chapter emphasised the importance of providing opportunities for all learners to interact with diverse text types and communicative modalities, and the need to support connections between new and existing literate knowledge and practices.

Bringing it together

To prepare for the discussions presented throughout the remainder of the book, consider the following questions:

1. How do you think teachers might honour the literate repertoires that all learners bring to the classroom, and ensure these repertoires are recognised as important foundations for ongoing learning?
2. Are there any gaps in your own literate practices and knowledge of communicative contexts that might make it difficult for you to understand the differing literate expertise children may bring to the classroom?
3. How might you find out more about literate repertoires that are new to you?

Further resources

Australian Institute of Aboriginal and Torres Strait Islander Studies (AIATSIS)

The Australian Institute of Aboriginal and Torres Strait Islander Studies (AIATSIS) provides information about languages, dialects and literate practices across Australia.

https://aiatsis.gov.au/explore/living-languages

World Literacy Foundation

The World Literacy Foundation provides access to free books and other digital resources for children.

https://worldliteracyfoundation.org

UNESCO

UNESCO works to support global access to all forms of literacy: 'Beyond its conventional concept as a set of reading, writing and counting skills, literacy is now understood as a means of identification, understanding, interpretation, creation, and communication in an increasingly digital, text-mediated, information-rich and fast-changing world' (UNESCO, 2021, n.p.).

https://en.unesco.org/themes/literacy

Digital literacy: what does the research say?

In this 2020 ACER report, various misconceptions about Australian learners' engagement with digital text are explored.

www.acer.org/au/discover/article/digital-literacy-what-does-the-research-say

James Paul Gee on learning with video games

In this short video, Professor James Gee discusses how literacies learning can take place via engagement with online games.

www.edutopia.org/video/james-paul-gee-learning-video-games

References

Anstey, M. & Bull, G. (2009). *Using Multimodal Texts and Digital Resources in a Multiliterate Classroom*. Primary English Teaching Association Australia (PETAA).

Australian Council for Educational Research (ACER). (2020). Digital literacy: what does the research say? www.acer.org/au/discover/article/digital-literacy-what-does-the-research-say

Australian Curriculum, Assessment and Reporting Authority (ACARA). (2019). Australian Curriculum F-10 Curriculum. General capabilities. www.australiancurriculum.edu.au/f-10-curriculum/general-capabilities

Australian Institute of Health and Welfare (AIHW). (2020). Australia's children. Cat. No. CWS 69. AIHW. www.aihw.gov.au/reports/children-youth/australias-children

Barratt-Pugh, C. & Rohl, M. (Eds). (2001). *Literacy Learning in the Early Years*. Taylor & Francis.

Bearne, E. & Vallely, K. (2019). Multimodality. UKLA Occasional Paper. https://ukla.org/wp-content/uploads/Multimodality.pdf

Brown, H.D. (2001). *Teaching By Principles: An Interactive Approach to Language Pedagogy* (2nd edn). Pearson Education.

Cope, B. & Kalantzis, M. (2000). *Multiliteracies: Literacy Learning and the Design of Social Futures*. Routledge.

—— (2009). 'Multiliteracies': new literacies, new learning. *Pedagogies: An International Journal*, 4(3), 164–195.

Curry, D.L., Reeves, E., & Mcintyre, C.J. (2016). Connecting schools and families: understanding the influence of home literacy practices. *Texas Journal of Literacy Education*, 4(2), 69–77.

Daly, A. & Unsworth, L. (2011). Analysis and comprehension of multimodal texts. *Australian Journal of Language and Literacy*, 34(1), 61–80.

Derewianka, B. & Jones, P. (2016). *Teaching Language in Context* (2nd edn). Oxford University Press.

Dezuanni, M., Dooley, K., Gattenhof, S., & Knight, L. (2015). *iPads in the Early Years: Developing Literacy and Creativity*. Taylor & Francis Group.

Dutton, J., D'warte, J., Rossbridge, J., & Rushton, K. (2018). *Tell Me Your Story: Confirming Identity and Engaging Writers*. Primary English Teaching Association Australia (PETAA).

D'warte, J. (2014). Exploring linguistic repertoires: Multiple language use and multimodal literacy activity in five classrooms. *Australian Journal of Language and Literacy*, 37(1), 21.

Fairclough, N. (2001). *Language and Power*. Longman.

Fleer, M. & Hammer, M. (2014). Repertoires of cultural practices for enacting play and learning in a playgroup. *International Research in Early Childhood Education*, 5(1), 42–55.

Freebody, P. & Luke, A. (1990). 'Literacies' programs: debates and demands in cultural context. *Prospect*, 5(3), 85–94.

Gee, J. (2005). *Introduction to Discourse Analysis: Theory and Method* (2nd edn). Routledge.

—— (2011). *Social Linguistics and Literacies: Ideology in Discourses* (4th edn). Routledge.

Graff, H.J. (1981). *Literacy and Social Development in the West: A Reader*. Cambridge University Press.

Hall, K., Cremin, T., Comber, B., Moll, L.C., Hall, P.K., & Moll, L.C. (Eds.). (2013). *International Handbook of Research on Children's Literacy, Learning and Culture*. John Wiley & Sons.

Halliday, M.A.K. (1993). Towards a language-based theory of learning. *Linguistics And Education*, 5(2), 93–116.

Harden, A. (2016). 'Caterpillars and catalysts': a year of literacy learning in an early years classroom privileging dramatic pedagogies. *Australasian Journal of Early Childhood*, 41(3), 20–28.

Harris, W.V. (1989). *Ancient Literacy*. Harvard University Press.

Harvey, M.M. (2016). Recognizing similarities and differences between print and digital literacy in education. *International Journal of Digital Literacy and Digital Competence*, 7(4), 1–16.

Heath, S.B. (1983). *Ways With Words: Language, Life, and Work in Communities and Classrooms*. Cambridge University Press.

Hicks, T. & Hawley Turner, K. (2013). No longer a luxury: digital literacy can't wait. *The English Journal*, 102(6), 58–65.

Hill, S. & Diamond, A. (2013). Family literacy in response to local contexts. *Australian Journal of Language and Literacy*, 36(1), 48–55.

Hinrichsen, J. & Coombs, A. (2013). The five resources of critical digital literacy: a framework for curriculum integration. *Research in Learning Technology*, 21(1), 1–16.

Hull, G. & Schultz, K. (2001). Literacy and learning out of school: a review of theory and research. *Review of Educational Research*, 71(4), 575–611.

Johnson, M. (2015). The invention of reading and the evolution of text. *Journal of Literacy and Technology*, 15(1), 107–128.

Kern, R. (2015). *Language, Literacy, and Technology*. Cambridge University Press.

Kervin, L.K., Verenikina, I., & Rivera, M.C. (2015). Collaborative onscreen and offscreen play: examining meaning-making complexities. *Digital Culture and Education*, 7(2), 228–239.

Kress, G. (2003). *Literacy in the Media Age*. Routledge.

Kress, G. & van Leeuwen, T. (2020). *Reading Images: The Grammar of Visual Design*. Routledge.

Ladbrook, J. & Probert, E. (2011). Information skills and critical literacy: where are our digikids at with online searching and are their teachers helping? *Australasian Journal of Educational Technology*, 27(1), 105–121.

Lee-James, R. & Washington, J. (2018). Language skills of bidialectal and bilingual children: considering a strengths-based perspective. *Topics in Language Disorders*, 38(1), 5–26.

Leu, D.J., Jr & Kinzer, C.K. (2000). The convergence of literacy instruction and networked technologies for information and communication. *Reading Research Quarterly*, 35, 108–127.

Levy, R. (2009). 'You have to understand words… but not read them': young children becoming readers in a digital age. *Journal of Research in Reading*, 32(1), 75–91.

Lewis, M.P., Simons, G.F., & Fennig, C.D. (2014). *Ethnologue: Languages of the World* (17th edn). SIL International.

Lo Bianco, J. (2013). Communication ecology. Primary English Teaching Association Australia (PETAA) Project 40, Essay 4. www.petaa.edu.au/w/Teaching_Resources/Project_40/w/Teaching_Resources/P40/Bianco_essay.aspx

Malcolm, I.G. (2018). *Australian Aboriginal English: Change and Continuity in an Adopted Language*. De Gruyter.

McTavish, M. (2009). 'I get my facts from the internet': a case study of the teaching and learning of information literacy in school and out-of-school contexts. *Journal of Early Childhood Literacy*, 9(1), 3–28.

—— (2014). 'I'll do it my own way!': a young child's appropriation and recontextualization of school literacy practices in out-of-school spaces. *Journal of Early Childhood Literacy*, 14(3), 319–344.

Moje, E.B., Ciechanowski, K.M., Kramer, K., Ellis, L., Carrillo, R., & Collazo, T. (2004). Working toward third space in content area literacy: an examination of everyday funds of knowledge and discourse. *Reading Research Quarterly*, 39(1), 38–70.

Moll, L., Amanti, C., Neff, D., & Gonzalez, N. (1992). Funds of knowledge for teaching: using a qualitative approach to connect homes and classrooms. *Theory Into Practice*, 31(2), 132–141.

Moll, L., Velez-Ibanez, C., & Greenberg, J.B. (1989). *Year One Progress Report: Community Knowledge and Classroom Practice: Combining Resources for Literacy Instruction* (IARP Subcontract No. L-10). University of Arizona, College of Education and Bureau of Applied Research in Anthropology.

Neumann, M.M. (2016). Young children's use of touch screen tablets for writing and reading at home: relationships with emergent literacy. *Computers & Education*, 97, 61–68.

New London Group. (1996). A pedagogy of multiliteracies: designing social futures. *Harvard Educational Review*, 66(1), 60–92.

NSW Government. (2021). Beginning critical literacy – young children's responses when reading image and text. https://education.nsw.gov.au/teaching-and-learning/professional-learning/scan/past-issues/vol-36--2017/its-all-lighted-up--because-this-is-a-happy-ending--beginning-critical-literacy-young-childrens-responses-when-reading-image-and-text-

Oliver, R., Wigglesworth, G., Angelo, D., & Steele, C. (2021). Translating translanguaging into our classrooms: possibilities and challenges. *Language Teaching Research*, 25(1), 134–150.

Organisation for Economic Co-operation and Development (OECD). (2017). *Building Skills for All in Australia: Policy Insights from the Survey of Adult Skills*. OECD Skills Studies. OECD Publishing. www.oecd-ilibrary.org/education/building-skills-for-all-in-australia_9789264281110-en

Park, S., Freeman, J., & Middleton, C. (2019). Intersections between connectivity and digital inclusion in rural communities. *Communication Research and Practice*, 5(2), 139–155.

Read Educational Trust. (2020). *Literacy as a human right*. www.read.org.za/useful-info/literacy-as-a-human-right

Roser, M. & Ortiz-Ospina, E. (2018). *Literacy*. Published online at OurWorldInData.org. https://ourworldindata.org/literacy

Roskos, K. & Christie, J. (2007). Play in the context of the new preschool basics. In K. Roskos & J. Christie (Eds.), *Play and Literacy in Early Childhood: Research from Multiple Perspectives* (2nd edn, pp. 83–100). Lawrence Erlbaum Associates.

—— (2011). The play-literacy nexus and the importance of evidence-based techniques in the classroom. *American Journal of Play*, 4(2), 204–224.

Schleppegrell, M.J. (2008). *The Language of Schooling. A Functional Linguistics Approach*. Lawrence Erlbaum.

Schleppegrell, M.J. & de Oliveira, L. (2006). An integrated language and content approach for history teachers. *Journal of English for Academic Purposes*, 5(4), 254–268.

Serafini, F. (2012). Expanding the four resources model: reading visual and multi-modal texts. *Pedagogies: An International Journal*, 7(2), 150–164.

Simpson, A., Walsh, M., & Rowsell, J. (2013). The digital reading path: researching modes and multidirectionality with iPads. *Literacy*, 47(3), 123–130.

Snyder, I. (2002). Silicon literacies. In I. Snyder (ed.), *Silicon Literacies: Communication, Innovation and Education in the Electronic Age* (pp. 3–12). Routledge.

Street, B. (1993). Introduction: the new literacy studies. In B. Street (Ed.), *Cross-cultural Approaches to Literacy* (pp. 1–21). Cambridge University Press.

—— (2003). What's 'new' in new literacy studies? Critical approaches to literacy in theory and practice. *Current Issues in Comparative Education*, 5(2), 77–91. www.tc.columbia.edu/cice

—— (2005). At last: recent applications of new literacy studies in educational contexts. *Research in the Teaching of English*, 39(4), 417–423.

Thompson, L.W. (2015). Teaching nonliterate adults in oral cultures: findings from practitioners. Commission for International Adult Education. Paper presented at the Commission for International Adult Education (CIAE) International Pre-Conference, 64th, Oklahoma City, OK, 15–17 November.

United Nations Educational, Scientific and Cultural Organization (UNESCO). (2006). *Education For All: Literacy For Life. EFA Global Monitoring Report*. Global Education Monitoring Report Team. https://unesdoc.unesco.org/ark:/48223/pf0000141639

—— (2021). *Literacy*. https://en.unesco.org/themes/literacy

Unsworth, L. (2006). Towards a metalanguage for multiliteracies education: describing the meaning-making resources of language-image interaction. *English Teaching: Practice and Critique*, 1, 55–76.

Valkonen, S., Kupiainen, R., & Dezuanni, M. (2020). Constructing social participation around digital making: a case study of multiliteracy learning in a Finnish day care centre. *Journal of Early Childhood Education Research*, 9(2), 477–497.

Vygotsky, L. (1978). Interaction between learning and development. *Readings on the Development of Children*, 23(3), 34–41.

WA Department of Education. (2012). *Tracks to Two-Way Learning: Understanding Language and Dialect*. http://det.wa.edu.au/curriculumsupport/eald/detcms/navigation/english-as-an-additional-language-or-dialect-for-aboriginal-students/tracks-to-two-way-learning

Walsh, M. (2010). Multimodal literacy: what does it mean for classroom practice? *Australian Journal of Language and Literacy*, 33(3), 211–239.

Whitehead, M.R. (2009). *Supporting Language and Literacy Development in the Early Years* (2nd edn). McGraw-Hill.

Wigglesworth, G. & Simpson, J. (2018). Going to school in a different world. In G. Wigglesworth, J. Simpson & J. Vaughan (Eds.), *Language Practices of Indigenous Children and Youth. Palgrave Studies in Minority Languages and Communities*. Palgrave Macmillan.

Wyse, D., Jones, R., Bradford, H., & Wolpert, M.A. (2013). *Teaching English Language and Literacy*. Routledge.

CHAPTER 2

English and literacies education in the Australian context

Siobhan O'Brien

ANTICIPATED OUTCOMES

After working through this chapter, it is anticipated you will be able to:

- explain the evolution of the Australian Curriculum with a historical perspective
- understand the ongoing policy reform of the Australian Curriculum and the National Assessment Program – Literacy and Numeracy (NAPLAN)
- articulate the context of literacies and being literate in Australian schooling education, while making connections between the Early Years Learning Framework (EYLF) and the Australian Curriculum
- explore the Australian Curriculum: English, and literacy as a general capability
- develop a view of English and the National Literacy Learning Progression that informs the teaching and assessment of learning.

Introduction

Throughout this chapter, you will gain knowledge and understanding of literacies education in the Australian context. This includes insight to Australian education policy and research contexts via the Alice Springs (Mparntwe) and Melbourne Declarations. With a lens focused on the context of curriculum in Australia and the Australian Curriculum, this chapter will guide your knowledge around the policy drivers for curriculum, including the basis of the Australian economic and international benchmarking test, National Assessment Program – Literacy and Numeracy (NAPLAN). The context of the Australian Curriculum and links to the Early Years Learning Framework (EYLF) highlight a crossover between early childhood and primary education and the alignments to the Australian Curriculum.

The development of the Australian Curriculum was a notable milestone achievement for the states and territories, starting from the initial work of ministers for education who were involved the creation of the inaugural Hobart Declaration on Schooling in 1989 (Australian Education Council, 1989). The national curriculum has since become a key driver in Australia's positioning within the Organisation for Economic Co-operation and Development (OECD). This chapter presents insights about literacies education in the Australian context and includes an historical perspective on education policy and the Australian Curriculum. The evolution of the national Declarations on schooling are discussed together with how the goals of education in Australia are defined. The education of young Australians in twenty-first-century learning and the structure of the Australian Curriculum: English and literacy as a general capability are explored. The chapter also presents the National Literacy Learning Progression that is designed to engage all Australians in lifelong learning through the developmental continuum of literacy from emergent to adult.

The Australian Curriculum: an historical perspective

Curriculum: encompasses all the experiences that occur within the school or other learning context. It includes what is intended in syllabus documents (the *intended* or *formal* curriculum), what the teacher implements (the *enacted* curriculum) and what becomes the actuality for the individual learners (the *experienced* curriculum). As well, there are unintended outcomes, often referred to as the *hidden curriculum*.

The Australian Curriculum, Assessment and Reporting Authority (ACARA) was established through many years of national collaboration around the development of goals for schooling, with the fundamental national **curriculum** development work of ACARA guided by the Melbourne Declaration on Educational Goals for Young Australians (Melbourne Declaration; Barr et al., 2008). This process was initially undertaken with the formulation of the Hobart and Adelaide Declarations on Schooling, in 1989 and 1999, respectively (see Australia Education Council, 1989 and Ministerial Council on Education, Employment, Training and Youth Affairs, 1999). From the release of the first phase in 2009, the national curriculum was designed to support twenty-first-century learning. This first phase included the key areas of curriculum learning in English, Mathematics, Science and History. Geography, Languages and the Arts followed in the second phase, and Health and Physical Education, Technologies, Civics and Citizenship, and Economics and Business were completed in the third phase. General capabilities and cross-curriculum priorities were also included in the curriculum design.

Another important aspect of the Australian Curriculum is the inclusion of Aboriginal and Torres Strait Islander peoples' learning. Embedding this in the curriculum was notable because it was the first time that all young Australians would 'learn about the histories and cultures of Aboriginal and Torres Strait Islander peoples' (ACARA, n.d.a). Barr and colleagues (2008) illustrate how embedding Indigenous learnings was significant historically in that 'the commitment to develop a national curriculum reflects a willingness to work together, across geographical and school-sector boundaries, to provide a world-class education for all young Australians' (p. 7), with visibility of their 'contribution to Australia, and of the consequences of colonial settlement for Indigenous communities, past and present' (p. 10), promoting visibility for Aboriginal and Torres Strait Islander peoples to access learning and to achieve success.

Alice Springs (Mparntwe) Education Declaration

The Alice Springs (Mparntwe) Education Declaration of 2019 (pronounced M-ban tua) superseded the Melbourne Declaration and has both some new and remaining components of the Melbourne Declaration. Within the Alice Springs (Mparntwe) Education Declaration, education ministers have agreed that education in Australia will continue to enable all Australians, including Aboriginal and Torres Strait Islander peoples, to achieve their full potential, promote excellence, offer equal access to education and encourage learners to be engaged and informed members of their communities (Education Council, 2019). A renewed commitment to celebrating and learning from Aboriginal and Torres Strait Islander cultures, knowledge and histories is articulated. Addressing the needs of Indigenous Australians is important, because it is known that 'educational outcomes for Indigenous children and young people are substantially behind those of other students in key areas of enrolment, attendance, participation, literacy, numeracy, retention and completion' (Barr et al., 2008). New or revised aspects in the Declaration include explicit emphasis on supporting the well-being, mental health and resilience of young people. The transitions between schooling from early childhood onwards are given further emphasis. The Declaration has two distinct but interconnected goals:

> **Goal 1:** The Australian education system promotes excellence and equity
>
> **Goal 2:** All young Australians become: confident and creative individuals, successful lifelong learners, active and informed members of the community. (Education Council, 2019, p. 4)

It is also important to note that, while the Australian Curriculum is available to all the states and territories in Australia, the primary responsibility for education remains with the government of each state or territory. Since the development of the national curriculum, state-based curriculum authorities have remained active as collaborators in curriculum methodologies within their own states. However, these governing bodies also work in consultation with ACARA and directly with each state or territory's education workforce in ensuring ongoing school improvement and best practice models (e.g. the NSW Education Standards Authority, Queensland Curriculum and Assessment Authority and Victorian Curriculum and Assessment Authority). The work of the state- and territory-based curriculum authorities means that the national curriculum is 'enacted in different ways in different systems and schools; mediations from the intended to the enacted curriculum' across the nation (Lingard, 2018, p. 58).

The Australian Curriculum aims to equip learners with the skills and capabilities required for the twenty-first century. It was designed to be robust in preparing learners as global citizens living in a culturally diverse society to function within a technological and future-focused world. A Curriculum Standing Committee of National Education Professional Association (CSCNEPA, 2007) paper suggests the curriculum's purpose is to 'strengthen civil society and participative democracy, to promote individual development and social cohesion, to develop economic prosperity and environmental sustainability and to prepare students for active global citizenship' (p. 5). Moss and colleagues (2019) also discuss how the curriculum addresses twenty-first-century learning through the interconnected nature of the subject disciplines and cross-curriculum priorities. The emphasis on cross-disciplinary learning rather than fixed subject matter allows for learning to be more dynamic as learners are encouraged to draw their understanding from a broad context of learning areas. Globalisation is combined within the orientations of the **general capabilities** and **cross-curriculum priorities** as they all include a specific lens of globalisation within their context. For instance, the general capabilities identify essential skills for learners to acquire to live and work successfully in the twenty-first century. The cross-curriculum priorities describe the skills, knowledge and understanding that enable effective engagement in a globalised world (ACARA, 2012; Lingard, 2018, p. 61).

General capabilities: within the Australian Curriculum, are the essential skills required for learners to live and work successfully in the twenty-first century.

Cross-curriculum priorities: within the Australian Curriculum, are the skills, knowledge and understandings required to enable effective engagement in a globalised world.

REFLECTION

Access the Alice Springs (Mparntwe) Education Declaration online via www.dese.gov.au/alice-springs-mparntwe-education-declaration and review the Education Goals for Young Australians. What are your thoughts in response to these goals and priorities for young Australians?

Review of the Australian Curriculum 2020–2022

Following on from the Alice Springs (Mparntwe) Education Declaration, the federal, state and territory education ministers agreed to review the Foundation to Year 10 national curriculum (ACARA, n.d.g). This review began in 2020, with a planned release date of 2022. ACARA consulted with key education stakeholders and state and territory authorities to determine the approach and scope of the review. This process involved auditing the Australian Curriculum against international curricula, including those of Singapore, Finland and New Zealand, to ensure that Australian learners are receiving world-class pedagogy with a future-focused vision.

Ongoing policy reform of Australian education

Education policy reform is a global phenomenon, with nationalisation of schooling having occurred across the world over the past three decades (Savage, 2016). In Australia, the nationalisation process is an attempt to produce consistency in schooling approaches and outcomes through the 'development of a national curriculum, standardised national assessments in literacy and numeracy, national standards for teachers and principals, and a revised national model of school funding' (Savage, 2016, p. 833). Ball (1993) talks of this education reform as having influence – policy impacts on the way we run our schools and, ultimately, the society in which we live. The nationalisation reforms in Australia and on an international scale have had effects on curriculum design, assessment and reporting, and on broader staff conditions and salaries. For example, in the 'UK at least (probably also the US, Canada, Australia and New Zealand) the cumulative and general effects of several years of multiple thrusts of educational reform on teachers' work have been profound', with teachers concentrating much more on facets of data collection and assessment and reporting (Ball, 1993, p. 15).

The Australian federal reform processes have further complications as the governance of the education system remains under the control of the states and territories and education policies are determined, ultimately, by the political party in power at the time of policy review. The federal government stipulates a national education policy and also funds national equity programs with grants provided to 'disadvantaged public and private schools across Australia' (Buchanan et al., 2012, p. 97). The success of the policy initiatives is due to the effective role that ACARA plays in implementing them. Savage (2016) suggests that since its establishment in 2008, ACARA has worked in collaboration with the state and territory curriculum agencies, education ministers (federal, state and territory) and other education stakeholders. This has had a significant impact on the changes that have occurred in the historical landscape of political party divisions. ACARA has 'navigated and negotiated the development of these reforms through turbulent political seas, with the make-up of Australian governments swinging heavily towards the Liberal party at federal and state levels in recent years' (Savage, 2016, p. 841).

Other regulatory governance has also been introduced with an emphasis on ensuring the quality of all Australian teachers. These regulatory organisations possess policy development roles and often mediate between the state, territory and federal governments in negotiations. A significant regulatory organisation is the Australian Institute for Teaching and School Leadership (AITSL), which is responsible for the assurance of quality educators within schools and Initial Teacher Education providers, who are closely scrutinised through registration and ongoing accreditation processes (Buchanan et al., 2012). AITSL was also engaged to design and house the Australian Professional Standards for Teachers (APST) and the Australian Professional Standards for Principals.

Some more recent functions of ACARA have included developing the My School website, which 'supports national transparency and accountability of Australia's schools, by publishing nationally-consistent school-level data about every school in Australia' (ACARA, 2020b), and implementing NAPLAN (Savage, 2016).

CASE STUDY 2.1	**A newly graduated teacher applies for teaching positions**

As a newly graduated teacher, Beth is applying for advertised positions in her state. The selection criteria of the roles she applies for ask her to provide her knowledge about the school context and how she will support student learning. Beth sets up a detailed profile for each of the school roles she applies for. To do this, she refers to the My School website to review each school's socioeconomic status and learning outcomes. Beth is also able to search each school's website and locate its school policies and documentation, such as the strategic plan and annual implementation plan. This information gives her insight into the school's goals and priorities.

When she is responding to the selection criteria, Beth refers back to the school profile to inform her application. Beth is offered an interview. The interview panel are very impressed by her specific school-based knowledge and level of preparation. She secures a role and is looking forward to starting in the new school year.

Questions

1. By conducting a thorough research profile of each school, Beth has gained information about their context, goals and learning priorities. How do you think this impacted on her preparation for the interview process?
2. The My School website is primarily designed for parents to research school-based outcomes. Are there other roles the My School information can have in education contexts?

National Assessment Program – Literacy and Numeracy (NAPLAN)

NAPLAN was introduced into all Australian schools in 2008 and is mandatory across all school systems. NAPLAN aimed to establish, and subsequently improve, Australia's world ranking on the **Programme for International Student Assessment (PISA)** scale, a measurement used by the OECD. As part of the national reform, Australia's standardised testing initiative was initiated to ensure the transparency and accountability of the Australian education system.

Programme for International Student Assessment (PISA): measures 15-year-old students' reading, mathematics, and science literacy every three years.

Administered by ACARA, NAPLAN is a large-scale standardised test undertaken annually by students in Years 3, 5, 7 and 9 (Rogers et al., 2019; Rose et al., 2018). The standardised English assessment of literacy is ascertained through three main tests – reading, writing and language conventions (spelling, grammar and punctuation) – and in another test on numeracy (covering algebra, geometry, measurement and problem solving) (ACARA, 2011). The NAPLAN standardised test results were designed to offer an overall indicator of the levels of learners' literacy and numeracy by 'testing the skills deemed important for the twenty-first century' (ACARA, 2011, cited in Rose et al., 2018, p. 871). The NAPLAN results are standardised and offer comparable measures of learner achievement. The standardisation allows for learners in a particular year and school to be compared 'with judgements made about federal funding which is contingent on participation' (Rose et al., 2018, p. 871). The risk here is for pedagogical approaches and authentic curriculum: as schools and teachers become pressured to perform to NAPLAN requirements, they will lean towards 'teaching to the test methods', thus causing 'a very real danger of NAPLAN becoming the de facto curriculum in many schools around the nation for particular students at particular year levels' (Lingard, 2018, p. 63).

NAPLAN is in a process of transitioning to an online adaptive testing format. Federal, state and territory education ministers have agreed that all schools will transition from paper-based tests to computer-based assessments and undertake NAPLAN online by 2022 (ACARA, n.d.f; Thompson et al., 2016). Thompson and colleagues (2016) define the use of terms 'adaptive' or 'tailored' testing in that 'online tests are responsive in real time providing an integrated personalised testing, pedagogy and intervention for each student' (p. 212).

There are two aims of NAPLAN: the first is to drive improvements in learners' outcomes, and the second is increased accountability of schools. There is growing pressure on schools with 'the usage of such data for accountability purposes in relation to some national policies and at state level as well' (Gable & Lingard, 2016, p. 569).

The introduction in 2010 of the federally funded My School website 'makes publicly available the comparative performance of all schools on NAPLAN' (Gable & Lingard, 2016, p. 568). My School has made schools' personalised reports available and, until changes in 2019, parents were 'able to compare their child's school with similar schools or against the national average' (Rose et al., 2018, p. 3).

Literacies and being literate in Australian education

In reviewing the historical policy and practice of education in Australia, Whitehead and Wilkinson (2008) located a strong emphasis on education and schooling from the days of colonisation: 'working-class parents as much as middle-class parents were convinced of the need for literacy, so much so that Australia, like other western countries, was a relatively literate society well before the state intervened in education' (p. 11). With regard to terminology, Green and colleagues (1997) note that the term 'literacy' was not used in Australia until the 1970s, and the fundamentals of learning the English language and grammar use and becoming literate in Australia have a well-debated past (Edwards & Potts, 2008). As schooling opportunities became more accessible to the population, more children were literate. Further populations who migrated to Australia came with aspirational expectations, with the education of their children held as a high priority.

Figure 2.1 Students in Australia in the 1900s

In current times, the central aim of schooling identified within Australian policy has a particular emphasis on the attainment of skills in literacy (reading and viewing, writing, speaking and listening) and also multiliteracies that include information and communications technology (ICT) and communication skills (Green et al., 1997). Hammond (2001) explains how literacy has become central to academic success and necessary for the work and life-based skills required within a community; this is also reflected in policy-level funding initiatives that are focused on learner improvement.

The aim of governments is to ensure that schools and teachers are best prepared to teach through effective evidence-based pedagogy. Whitehead and Wilkinson (2008) indicate that 'literacy, schooling and the production of the compliant citizen are still deeply intertwined' with strong connections between literacy, economics and overall wellbeing (p. 22). Since the early 2000s, there have been numerous literacy initiatives implemented in both the primary and secondary sectors (Hammond, 2001). Funding provisions have included professional development for teachers to enhance their skills, both external and internal to their school, to effectively meet 'the learning needs of the children for whom they are responsible' (Department of Education, Science and Training [DEST], 2005, p. 25).

REFLECTION

Why do you think Australia is a predominantly literate society?

The Early Years Learning Framework (EYLF) and the Australian Curriculum

There are key alignments between the EYLF and the Australian Curriculum that can be noted in the shared vision for education for all Australians. The availability of both the EYLF and the Australian Curriculum provides an impetus for a shared conversation between educators of both early childhood and primary settings that supports the transition of children and their families from early childhood contexts to formalised school settings. The importance of this connection is that the early childhood sector is growing because of increasing numbers of families entering or returning to work when their children are of preschool age. To meet the needs of the sector, state and federal funding is provided, for example, for the Victorian three-year-old kindergarten funding package, the roll-out of which began in 2021. Articulating clear links between the two sectors through policy and pedagogical approaches should enable children to thrive in both learning environments with the support of their families and teachers.

When early childhood settings offer engaging environments, the benefits include increased opportunities for learning and rapid growth and development (DEST, 2005). Because much brain development occurs during preschool years, these 'early experiences affect physical and social development, the ability to learn, the capacity to regulate emotions and the way in which children respond to the external environment in fundamental ways' (DEST, 2005, p. 39). When a child's capacity for learning is met, they will continue to develop after they transition into formalised schooling as the 'early learning experiences, including learning social and pre-literacy and numeracy skills, make the transition to school easier for the child' (DEST, 2005, p. 39). The preschool years support children's development through holistic learning approaches and foster the development of literacy and numeracy, enabling a positive start to school.

The commonalities between the EYLF and the Australian Curriculum are wide-ranging and include a strong alignment to the education goals presented in the Melbourne

Declaration and the Alice Springs (Mparntwe) Education Declaration. Both documents refer to supporting learners in the ever-changing global context and hold accessibility to education for all in the highest regard. The EYLF declares respect for children as competent and resourceful learners from birth. Connor (2015) considers how, like the Australian Curriculum, the EYLF 'gives serious attention to essential elements of high-quality early childhood practice, including play-based pedagogies, strong relationships with children and families and intentional teaching' (p. 3). The EYLF is structured around three interrelated elements – principles, practices and learning outcomes – and the Australian Curriculum builds on these, as articulated within the general capabilities, by:

- respecting the nature of learners at particular stages in their learning lives
- recognising that there is a set of foundational dispositions, knowledge and skills that underpin future learning success
- acknowledging the diversity of starting points that learners bring to next-stage learning
- allowing teachers to connect their pedagogical practices in the first years of school to those used in prior-to-school contexts. (Connor, 2015, p. 15)

REFLECTION

Belonging, Being & Becoming – the Early Years Learning Framework for Australia (EYLF) (Department of Education, Employment and Workplace Relations [DEEWR], 2009) includes principles, practices and learning outcomes for early childhood educators to apply in settings to support young children's learning as well as their transition to school. In what ways do you see that the Australian Curriculum is based on the principles, practices and learning outcomes of the EYLF?

The Australian Curriculum: English – an overview

The Australian Curriculum: English was developed through the *National English Curriculum: Framing Paper* (National Curriculum Board, 2009) and the *Shape of the Australian Curriculum: English* (ACARA, 2010). The Australian Curriculum positions English as a disciplinary area that learners undertake throughout their years of schooling, from foundation through to senior secondary, within which Derewianka (2012) identifies three interrelated elements: 'an explicit knowledge about language, an informed appreciation of literature, and expanding repertoires of language use' (p. 127). As with the continuum of learning, language and text types are presented within the curriculum with regard to age and stage of schooling. For instance, in Year 3 'students are encouraged to engage with narratives, procedures, reports, reviews, poetry and expositions and in Year 10 the extended genres include discussions, literary analyses and transformations of texts' (Derewianka, 2012, p. 131).

In Australian schooling, the study of English aims for learners to be competent in the many forms of communication required to function successfully on a local scale for further education, training and in the workplace, and on a global scale. The study of English in the Australian Curriculum is considered central to all other learning and development. As Australia is a linguistically and culturally diverse country, the study of English fundamentally supports the development of reading and other literacy skills through the engagement of literature that is designed for learners to develop critical literacy that expands the scope of their experience (ACARA, n.d.c).

The Australian Curriculum has embedded a functional approach to language that is 'concerned with how language has evolved in certain ways to enable us to do things in our lives' (Derewianka, 2012, p. 133). Luke (2000) explains how 'Australian approaches to critical literacy have developed a sophisticated metalanguage for students to use in developing understandings of and control over lexicon, sentence-level grammar, and text genres – but a metalanguage that ties language to function, text to context, theme to ideology, and discourse to society and culture' (p. 7).

Functional model of language: considers how spoken and written modes of language enable us to understand the world around us in both school and community contexts; the model explores the textual function of language.

A great deal of work on the **functional model of language** in the Australian context has been undertaken since the 1980s by Professor Michael Halliday and colleagues (in Derewianka, 2012). A functional model describes how language enables us to understand our world, interact and 'create coherent, well-structured texts in both the spoken and written modes (the textual function of language)' – this is primarily concerned with how we can make meaning within school and community contexts (Derewianka, 2012, p. 133).

From a theoretical perspective, literacy is considered a social construct enacted through social practice – that is, through the way we interact and use literacy to function in daily life (Hammond, 2001). To be literate in today's society, we need to be able to critically engage with texts, and interrelate and construct meanings through the various lenses of different groups within society. The pedagogical approaches for achieving this require educators to scaffold learning so that each learner understands the demands of language and builds competency to critically analyse and interpret texts. Hammond (2001) explains that 'such work recognises that the traditional "basic skills", such as word recognition, spelling, comprehension and so on, are indeed crucial to successful literacy development for each individual' (p. 165).

Luke (2000) considers the central role of teachers in learners' literacy development. Further, he suggests that educators need to enable learners to use their existing and new discourse resources for social exchange in the social fields, where texts and discourses matter. These constitute 'the social semiotic "tool kit" that one puts to work in educational, occupational and civic life' (p. 2).

More importantly, 'literacy education, then, is about institutional access and inclusion, and potentially about discrimination and exclusion. It is about setting the conditions for learners to engage in textual relationships of power' (Luke, 2000, p. 2). The policy-level view of system-wide education needs to consider how literacy education can address the needs of all learners and communities.

The Australian Curriculum: English strands

The content knowledge and skills learners are required to acquire through the English curriculum are presented as three interrelated strands: language, literature and literacy (literacy here is apart from the literacy general capability). The strands are developmental in sequence and are designed to support the planning and learning of a cohesive program where 'each strand has its own distinctive goals, body of knowledge, history of ideas and interests, and pedagogical traditions' (National Curriculum Board, 2009, p. 50). This continuum of learning offers learners and teachers opportunities to plan, teach and assess progress. The applied use of evidence-based literacy pedagogical strategies supports learners to progress through the developmental stages of emergent literacy to consolidating understanding and then to become independent and capable learners (National Curriculum Board, 2009).

The language strand

The language strand is focused on learners knowing about the English language and how it works and is presented in the Australian Curriculum as strands, sub-strands and threads (ACARA, n.d.d). Through the content, learners develop their knowledge about the historical foundations of English, including:

- *language variation and change* – looks at the geographical differences of its users and variations in dialect, accent and colloquial use of the English language
- *language for interaction* – the purpose of language and how it enables interaction
- *text structure and organisation* – through communicating effectively, includes the patterns, purposes and skills required for spelling, grammar and punctuation in well-structured sentences and text
- *expressing and developing ideas* – through engaging with text, learners explore how writers use a range of clauses, phrases, 'words and word groups, as well as combinations of sound, image, movement, verbal elements and layout' (ACARA, n.d.d) to portray meaning and influence. The content also covers 'conventions, patterns and generalisations that relate to English spelling, involve the origins of words, word endings, Greek and Latin roots, base words and affixes' (ACARA, n.d.d).

Within the education field in Australia, there has been a renewed focus on the explicit teaching of **phonics and word knowledge**. The Australian Curriculum regards this area of the language strand, 'especially from Foundation to Year 2, as of critical importance' in the way it pertains to reading and word skills (ACARA, n.d.d). During the early stages of phonics and word knowledge, the focus is on developing children's skills to identify sounds in words, letters (graphemes), the spelling of words with teaching of prefixes and suffixes, and meaning strategies. To achieve these skills, learners engage in activities that require listening, reading, viewing, speaking, writing and creating. Phonics screening checks have also been introduced as assessment-based interventions for six-year-olds in many states and territories.

> **Phonics and word knowledge:** the proficiency to identify relationships between letters (the symbols of the written language, graphemes) to the sounds (phonemes) for use with reading and writing (Ewing, 2018, p. 11).

The literature strand

The literature strand is designed to support engagement with literature through the use of texts that include personal, cultural and social topics and issues and also have aesthetic value. Learners develop skills of analysis, interpretation and comprehension so that they are able to understand, appreciate and respond to literature. Learners engage with literary texts, such as 'short stories, novels, poetry, prose, plays, film and multimodal texts, in spoken, print and digital/online forms' and 'include the oral narrative traditions of Aboriginal and Torres Strait Islander peoples, [and] texts from Asia' (ACARA, n.d.d). Within the National

Literacy Learning Progression, the selected texts have both social and artistic value and offer potential for 'enriching the lives of students, [by] expanding their scope of experience' through encounters with the significant experiences of others in narrative and factual form (ACARA, n.d.d). With an informed appreciation of how the English language conveys information and emotion, students also learn the process of how to create and write about imaginative worlds.

Learners develop their knowledge within the following four sub-strands:

- *Literature and context* is designed for learners to engage with and reflect on a text's context. They learn and discuss ideas and viewpoints through the text events, issues and characters drawn from 'historical, social and cultural contexts' (ACARA, n.d.d).
- *Responding to literature* engages and supports learning to 'identify personal ideas, experiences and opinions and discuss' and argue these with others (ACARA, n.d.d).
- *Examining literature* is designed for students to learn how to identify the features of literary texts. They explore how to explain, interpret, discuss, evaluate and analyse stories of various literary genres and 'learn how to compare and appraise the ways authors use language and literary techniques and devices that influence readers' (ACARA, n.d.d).
- *Creating literature* enables students to learn to use their personal knowledge along with exemplars of literary texts to 'develop writing using different forms and genres and for particular audiences. They develop skills that allow them to convey meaning and address significant issues' that heighten their social and community engagement (ACARA, n.d.d). Learners create texts using print, digital and online media.

The literacy strand

The literacy strand is apart from the general capability of literacy and considers the growing repertoire of English usage. Within this strand, learners develop skills that support them to understand and use the English language with accuracy and fluency, both within and outside of school, and for participating in Australian life more generally. For instance, they learn to 'adapt their language use to meet the demands of general or more specialised purposes, audiences and contexts' (ACARA, n.d.d).

The role of the teacher is to embed each strand within teaching and learning in the following four sub-strands:

- *Texts in context* considers how texts relate and 'reflect the society and culture in which they were created' (ACARA, n.d.d). Students learn that texts come from different cultures or historical periods and will have variances in how they narrate, inform and persuade.
- *Interacting with others* has learners engaging with their peers, teachers and the wider community and learning communication skills that support them to use relevant language and to express ideas and key concepts. They also learn how to uphold a point of view when delivering spoken and written presentations.
- *Interpreting, analysing, evaluating* engages and supports students to 'learn to comprehend what they read and view by applying growing contextual, semantic, grammatical and phonic knowledge' (ACARA, n.d.d). They achieve this through exploring the

conventions and structures used in texts that are designed to entertain, inform and persuade audiences.

- *Creating texts* teaches learners how to apply knowledge they have developed in other strands to create a variety of different types of texts, including 'spoken, written and multimodal to entertain, inform and persuade audiences' (ACARA, n.d.d). In developing these texts, they learn the skills required for editing and use a 'handwriting style that is legible and supports sustained writing' (ACARA, n.d.d). They also learn about software programs, to aid their ability to communicate in informative and innovative ways.

English resources and work samples

In the Australian Curriculum: English, a number of work samples and portfolios have been made available by ACARA. These can be referred to by teachers as exemplars of learning. Each portfolio comprises a collection of work drawn from a range of assessment tasks, and each achievement standard is annotated and reviewed by classroom teachers and other curriculum experts. The portfolios are authentic samples of work that allow teachers to moderate and compare samples at different levels of achievement to assist them in making their own judgements about learners' work (ACARA, n.d.e).

REFLECTION

Select a year level from the English work samples portfolios (www.australiancurriculum .edu.au/resources/work-samples/english-work-samples-portfolios), and review the student portfolios for 'above satisfactory', 'satisfactory' and 'below satisfactory' standards. How might these portfolios support your knowledge and understanding of the learning progression in English?

The Australian Curriculum: National Literacy Learning Progression

The Australian Curriculum: English supports learning along a continuum of complexity for learners to develop the skills to 'read, view, speak, write, create, listen to and reflect', attained through critical evaluation and interpretive meaning of verbal, written and multimodal texts (ACARA, 2020c, p. 15). The National Literacy Learning Progression can be used in teaching and planning to support learners to successfully engage with the literacy demands of the Foundation to Year 10 Australian Curriculum. The National Literacy Learning Progression denotes observable indicators aligned to each aspect of literacy. These increase in complexity as the learner progresses and attains each aspect of learning. Teachers are able to refer to the progression points as a tool to assist them with developing needs-based teaching and learning programs for all learners.

The literacy learning progression contains three elements that underpin the development for successful learning. These are speaking and listening, reading and viewing, and writing. Within each element are a series of sub-elements that provide a scaffold for teachers to identify learning needs and abilities and also to make judgements on learning (see Chapters 4, 6, 10, 13 and 14 for detailed discussion of these elements). The sub-elements are:

- speaking and listening – listening, interacting and speaking
- reading and viewing – phonological awareness, phonic knowledge and word recognition and fluency
- writing – handwriting and keyboarding, spelling, punctuation and grammar.

Within each sub-element, distinct levels and indicators are grouped together to form developmental levels. Each level within a sub-element has one or more indicators that is more complex than the preceding level, thus providing the teaching and learning continuum (ACARA, 2020c). Each indicator includes a description about what a learner may say, do or produce. This allows teachers to apply the learning progression to develop specific needs-based learning programs and to set achievable learning goals for individuals. The levels within each sub-element are identified via a letter and number code that indicates an abbreviated name of the sub-element and the developmental level, and these are presented in number order (ACARA, 2020c).

| CASE STUDY 2.2 | A newly graduated teacher prepares for her teaching role |

Beth's school uses the Australian Curriculum for planning and teaching. Before she begins her new role, Beth spends time navigating the English curriculum and the National Literacy Learning Progression and also reviews the work samples on the ACARA website. She notices how the literacy learning progression is focused on supporting literacy development in the early years, particularly in the language and literacy strands, and she can see how this will be helpful for planning and assessment.

Beth then goes to the Scootle website (Education Services Australia, 2021), which is accessible via the Australian Curriculum online, to identify further ways to engage her class with the curriculum.

Questions

1. Beth's research into the Australian Curriculum: English and the National Literacy Learning Progression will stand her in good stead when she beings her teaching role. In what ways (using digital multiliteracies) could she record this information so that it is readily available for her to refer back to in the future?
2. How is Scootle accessed within the Australian Curriculum?
3. What other digital resources have you located that will engage learners with literacy learning?

The Australian Curriculum general capability: literacy

Literacy is one of the seven general capabilities in the Australian Curriculum. The general capabilities are designed to equip young Australians to live and work successfully in the twenty-first century (National Curriculum Board, 2009). Each capability offers teachers and learners opportunities to add depth and richness to learning and supports the development of knowledge, skills and behaviour. Capable learners are able to apply newly acquired knowledge and skills 'in their learning at school and in their lives outside school' (ACARA, 2020a). Literacy is considered an essential skill that is fundamental for further learning and for a productive and sustainable future within a twenty-first-century society where 'literacy involves students listening to, reading, viewing speaking, writing and creating oral, print visual and digital texts and using and modifying language for different purposes in a range of contexts' (National Curriculum Board, 2009, p. 6).

The literacy continuum incorporates two overarching processes: comprehending texts through listening, reading and viewing; and composing texts through speaking, writing and creating. The following areas of knowledge apply to both processes: text knowledge; grammar knowledge; word knowledge; and visual knowledge. These areas of knowledge are further explored in Chapter 15.

On the Australian Curriculum website, the information about literacy as a general capability includes an introduction that describes the nature and scope of the capability, its place in the learning areas, and the elements and sub-elements that underpin the learning continuum (the relevant knowledge, skills, behaviours and dispositions). The literacy general capability is located within the learning continua and the content elaborations of all key learning areas, and is identified with an icon (see Chapter 15, Figure 15.2, for more discussion). When the icon is selected, the literacy capability information provides teachers with pedagogical knowledge and strategies that include supporting learners with items such as word knowledge, the teaching of specific vocabulary, and ideas for comprehending and composing texts. There is an expectation by state and territory education authorities that teachers will use the literacy general capability to teach and assess progress.

REFLECTION

1. Literacy is one of the seven general capabilities in the Australian Curriculum. What is the overall function of the general capabilities?
2. The literacy general capability is located within the content elaborations of all key learning areas (identified with the literacy icon – see Figure 15.2 in Chapter 15). How does this support teachers' planning and pedagogy?

Conclusion

In this chapter, we presented insights and knowledge about the Australian Curriculum, education policy and research contexts via the Melbourne Declaration and the Alice Springs (Mparntwe) Education Declaration. The context for literacy and how it is positioned within Australian education and policy were also discussed, as well as links between the Australian Curriculum and EYLF that highlight the continuum between early childhood education and primary school. Finally, the chapter addressed the Australian Curriculum: English, the National Literacy Learning Progression and literacy general capability, looking at how these are constructed to support young Australians' twenty-first-century learning and lifelong learning along a developmental continuum.

Bringing it together

1. The Australian Curriculum goals are drawn from the Alice Springs (Mparntwe) Education Declaration and the Melbourne Declaration. Who manages these Declarations and what is the goal of this process?
2. In this chapter, links were made between the Australian Curriculum and the EYLF that highlighted the transition between early childhood education and primary school. How do these links support children and families?
3. The Australian Curriculum: English and the literacy general capability are constructed to deliver education to young Australians and support twenty-first-century learning and lifelong learning along a developmental continuum. How does literacy through the National Literacy Learning Progression guide the learners' and teachers' knowledge?

Further resources

ACARA

ACARA is the authority that provides 'advice on, and delivery of, national curriculum, assessment and reporting for all Australian education ministers' (ACARA, n.d.g). ACARA developed the Australian Curriculum, which was introduced to improve the quality, equity and transparency of Australia's education system. The curriculum provides 'teachers, parents, children and the community with a clear understanding of what should be learnt regardless of where they live or what school they attend' (ACARA, n.d.b).

ACARA governs NAPLAN to provide for a consistent measure to determine whether or not learners are meeting important educational outcomes (ACARA, n.d.b). These assessments test learners' knowledge of what is in the Australian Curriculum and inform government, teachers and families as to whether learners are developing the essential skills, such as literacy and numeracy, that they will need in life (ACARA, n.d.b).

ACARA also manages the My School website (www.myschool.edu.au). This is 'a resource for parents, educators and the community to find comparable information about each of Australia's schools' (ACARA, 2020b).

www.acara.edu.au

Australian Curriculum

The national curriculum was introduced to improve the quality, equity and transparency of Australia's education system (ACARA, n.d.b).

https://australiancurriculum.edu.au

Australian Institute for Teaching and School Leadership (AITSL)

AITSL supports school practitioners to improve classroom instruction and the effectiveness of school leaders. It also has responsibility for the APST. AITSL works collaboratively with key professional bodies and guides reform with regard to Initial Teacher Education accreditation and teacher registration.

www.aitsl.edu.au

My School

My School 'supports national transparency and accountability of Australia's schools, by publishing nationally-consistent school-level data about every school in Australia' and NAPLAN (ACARA, 2020b).

www.myschool.edu.au

The Alice Springs (Mparntwe) Education Declaration

The Alice Springs (Mparntwe) Education Declaration contains both new and remaining aspects from the previous Melbourne Declaration, with a renewed commitment to celebrating and learning from Aboriginal and Torres Strait Islander cultures, knowledge and histories. Its aim is to enable all Australians, including Aboriginal and Torres Strait Islander peoples, to achieve their full potential.

www.dese.gov.au/alice-springs-mparntwe-education-declaration

Early Years Learning Framework (EYLF)

The EYLF can be used by educators in early childhood settings to support and nurture children's development from birth to five years and also their transition to school.

www.acecqa.gov.au/sites/default/files/acecqa/files/National-Quality-Framework-Resources-Kit/belonging_being_and_becoming_the_early_years_learning_framework_for_australia.pdf

Scootle

Scootle is an online repository of digital resources that are aligned to the Australian Curriculum (Education Services Australia, 2021).

www.scootle.edu.au/ec/acSubject?name=%22English%22

References

Australian Curriculum, Assessment and Reporting Authority (ACARA). (n.d.a). Aboriginal and Torres Strait Islander histories and cultures. www.australiancurriculum.edu.au/f-10-curriculum/cross-curriculum-priorities/aboriginal-and-torres-strait-islander-histories-and-cultures

—— (n.d.b). Australian Curriculum: About us. www.acara.edu.au/about-us

—— (n.d.c). Australian Curriculum: English. www.australiancurriculum.edu.au/f-10-curriculum/english

—— (n.d.d). Australian Curriculum: English structure. www.australiancurriculum.edu.au/f-10-curriculum/english/structure

—— (n.d.e). Australian Curriculum: English work samples portfolios. www.australiancurriculum.edu.au/resources/work-samples/english-work-samples-portfolios

—— (n.d.f). NAPLAN online. www.nap.edu.au/online-assessment

—— (n.d.g). Review of the Australian Curriculum. www.acara.edu.au/curriculum/curriculum-review

—— (2010). *The Shape of the Australian Curriculum: Version 2.0*. ACARA. https://docs.acara.edu.au/resources/Shape_of_the_Australian_Curriculum.pdf

—— (2011). National protocols for test administration. ACARA. www.nap.edu.au/_resources/2011_National_Protocols_for_Test_Administration_NA.pdf

—— (2012). *The Shape of the Australian Curriculum: Version 4.0*. ACARA. https://docs.acara.edu.au/resources/The_Shape_of_the_Australian_Curriculum_v4.pdf

—— (2020a). Australian Curriculum. General capabilities. www.australiancurriculum.edu.au/f-10-curriculum/general-capabilities

—— (2020b). My School. www.myschool.edu.au

—— (2020c). *National Literacy Learning Progression. Version 3.0*. ACARA. www.lpofai.edu.au/media/kw2lslug/national-literacy-learning-progression-v3-for-publication.pdf

Australian Education Council. (1989). *Australia's Common and Agreed Goals for Schooling in the Twenty-first Century*. Australian Education Council.

Ball, S.J. (1993). What is policy? Texts, trajectories and toolboxes. *Australian Journal of Education Studies*, 13(2), 10–17.

Barr, A., Gillard, J., Firth, V., Scrymgour, M., Welford, R., Lomax-Smith, J., ... & Constable, E. (2008). *Melbourne Declaration on Educational Goals for Young Australians*. Ministerial Council on Education, Employment, Training and Youth Affairs.

Buchanan, R., Holmes, K., Preston, G., & Shaw, K. (2012). Basic literacy or new literacies? Examining the contradictions of Australia's education revolution. *Australian Journal of Teacher Education*, 37(6), 7.

Connor, J. (2015). *Foundations for Learning: Relationships between the Early Years Learning Framework and the Australian Curriculum. An ECA-ACARA paper*. ACARA. https://cpb-ap-southeast-2-juc1ugur1qwqqqo4.stackpathdns.com/global2.vic.edu.au/dist/0/30003/files/2013/06/ECA_ACARA_Foundations_Paper-2cq59mi.pdf

Curriculum Standing Committee of National Education Professional Association (CSCNEPA). (2007). Developing a twenty-first century school curriculum for all Australian students: A working paper prepared for the Curriculum Standing Committee of National Education Professional Association. August.

Department of Education, Employment and Workplace Relations (DEEWR). (2009). *Belonging, Being & Becoming – The Early Years Learning Framework for Australia*. https://docs.education.gov.au/documents/belonging-being-becoming-early-years-learning-framework-australiaf

Department of Education, Science and Training (DEST). (2005). *Teaching Reading: Literature Review. National Inquiry into the Teaching of Reading*. DEST.

Derewianka, B. (2012). Knowledge about language in the Australian curriculum: English. *Australian Journal of Language and Literacy*, 35(2), 127–146.

Education Council. (2019). *Alice Springs (Mparntwe) Education Declaration*. www.dese.gov.au/alice-springs-mparntwe-education-declaration

Education Services Australia. (2021). Scootle. www.scootle.edu.au/ec/p/home

Edwards, D. & Potts, A. (2008). What is literacy? Thirty years of Australian literacy debates (1975–2005). *Paedagogica Historica*, 44(1–2), 123–135.

Ewing, R. (2018). *Exploding SOME of the Myths about Learning to Read. A Review of Research on the Role of Phonics*. NSW Teachers Federation. https://news.nswtf.org.au/application/files/8715/3249/6625/18181_Role_of_Phonics.pdf

Gable, A. & Lingard, B. (2016). NAPLAN data: a new policy assemblage and mode of governance in Australian schooling. *Policy Studies*, 37(6), 568–582.

Green, B., Hodgens, J., & Luke, A. (1997). Debating literacy in Australia: history lessons and popular f(r)ictions. *Australian Journal of Language and Literacy*, 20(1), 6–24.

Hammond, J. (2001). Literacies in school education in Australia: disjunctions between policy and research. *Language and Education*, 15(2–3), 162–177.

Lingard, B. (2018). The Australian Curriculum: a critical interrogation of why, what and where to? *Curriculum Perspectives*, 38(1), 55–65.

Luke, A. (2000). Critical literacy in Australia: a matter of context and standpoint. *Journal of Adolescent and Adult Literacy*, 43(5), 448–461.

Ministerial Council on Education, Employment, Training and Youth Affairs. (1999). *Adelaide Declaration on National Goals for Schooling in the Twenty-First Century*. MCEETYA.

Moss, J., Godinho, S.C., & Chao, E. (2019). Enacting the Australian Curriculum: primary and secondary teachers' approaches to integrating the curriculum. *Australian Journal of Teacher Education*, 44(3), 23–41.

National Curriculum Board. (2009). *National English Curriculum: Framing Paper*. National Curriculum Board.

Rogers, S.L., Barblett, L., & Robinson, K. (2019). Correction to: parent and teacher perceptions of NAPLAN in a sample of independent schools in Western Australia. *Australian Educational Researcher*, 46(1), 203.

Rose, J., Low-Choy, S., Singh, P., & Vasco, D. (2018). NAPLAN discourses: a systematic review after the first decade. *Discourse Studies in the Cultural Politics of Education*, 41(4), 1–16.

Savage, G.C. (2016). Who's steering the ship? National curriculum reform and the re-shaping of Australian federalism. *Journal of Education Policy*, 31(6), 833–850.

Thompson, G., Sellar, S., & Lingard, B. (2016). The life of data: evolving national testing. In B. Lingard, G. Thompson, & S. Sellar (Eds.), *National Testing in Schools: An Australian Assessment* (pp. 212–229). Routledge.

Whitehead, K. & Wilkinson, L. (2008). Teachers, policies and practices: a historical review of literacy teaching in Australia. *Journal of Early Childhood Literacy*, 8(1), 7–24.

CHAPTER 3

Assessment and reporting

Robyn Ewing and Kathy Rushton

ANTICIPATED OUTCOMES

After working through this chapter, it is anticipated you will be able to:

- understand key assessment terms and principles
- articulate and understand the importance of authentic, inclusive assessment processes and practices
- reflect on who should undertake assessment
- consider how and when to assess
- articulate the differences between standardised tests and authentic curriculum-based assessment
- implement a range of strategies and rich tasks to appropriately assess literacy in English and other subjects
- discuss the important relationship between teaching, learning and assessment through a number of classroom examples
- consider effective ways to report to learners and their families.

Introduction

> ... the main purpose of educational evaluation, assessment and measurement should be focused on enabling educators and policy makers to make better informed decisions about how best to help students learn, on the quality of schools as learning communities and on the effectiveness of particular educational resources.
>
> Source: Ewing (2013, p. 52).

As teachers, we are always accountable to learners, parents, the education system we are employed by and the community more broadly for the learning we plan and implement in the classroom. Our goal is to facilitate the learning process for all the individuals in our classrooms, and our effectiveness is most often judged by learners' achievements. While the content in this chapter provides rich examples of assessment in primary English and literacy, the principles and terms discussed apply across all stages of education and key learning areas of the Australian Curriculum.

In Australia, there is much emphasis on high-stakes testing and comparing Australian learners' assessment results with those in other countries, rather than focusing on helping *all* learners reach their potential. In contrast to this approach to assessment, this chapter underlines the complexity of authentic or educative English and literacy assessment. It begins by considering definitions for many of the key assessment terms in use in education contexts, including 'evaluation', 'assessment' and 'measurement'. The importance of implementing inclusive and authentic assessment practices is discussed, along with formative assessment processes (**assessment *for* learning**), summative assessment (**assessment *of* learning**) and assessment as learning strategies.

A range of examples and case studies follow. Each demonstrates the relationship between curriculum and assessment in English and literacy. They also highlight the need to emphasise careful observation and documentation or 'kid-watching', a term that was coined by Yetta Goodman and Gretchen Owoki (2002).

Understanding key terms and principles

'Assessment' is a word that can trigger anxiety for many learners (and sometimes teachers and parents). At its heart, **assessment** should be about making judgements about learners' knowledge, skills and understandings at a particular moment in time to help with appropriate future decision-making and planning of strategies and experiences that will facilitate their further learning. As already mentioned, too often in contemporary education contexts assessment is associated with **tests** and what a learner doesn't know rather than what they do know.

The importance of using **authentic or educative assessment** strategies cannot be overstated. Teachers must always be aware of the ways in which their beliefs and values about learning influence the kinds of judgements they make. For example, the idea that some assessment processes (e.g. teacher-made tests) are subjective and others are more objective (known as **external norm-referenced testing**) is often articulated. In reality, all assessments will be influenced by the world view of the person creating the assessment task.

Assessment *for* learning: tasks that are designed to understand learners' current knowledge and skills to enable the teacher to plan future learning activities and experiences that will meet their needs.

Assessment *of* learning: tasks that are designed to ascertain what a learner knows and understands at the end of a sequence of lessons or unit of work. The Australian Curriculum provides expectations for particular year levels in key learning areas.

Assessment: all informal and formal processes, used by teachers, learners and others, to interpret information about learners' progress. The most important goal of assessment should always be to enhance learning.

Tests: formal, systematic tasks used to gather information about what learners know under strict and uniform conditions. Tests often involve just pencil and paper, but can also be performative.

Authentic or educative assessment: rich and realistic assessment tasks and practices that engage the learner and are linked meaningfully to learning and the curriculum.

External norm-referenced testing: compares the results of an individual learner with so-called 'norms' or 'normal' results of a group of learners of the same age or grade.

REFLECTION

Think about your own experiences with different kinds of assessment tasks.

1. What kinds of assessment tasks do you excel at? Do you know why?
2. Which assessment tasks do you find difficult? Again, why do you think this is the case?
3. Can you remember how you knew you had done well on an assessment task?

Authentic assessment and its importance

Authentic assessment principles resonate with active, learner-centred approaches to teaching and learning (Ewing, 2013). The term 'authentic assessment' originates from the work of Fred Newmann and his colleagues at the University of Wisconsin-Madison during the 1990s. Their work on authentic instruction and assessment provided the basis for the quality teaching (NSW Department of Education and Training, 2003) and productive pedagogies (Education Queensland, 1999) frameworks that were introduced to Australia at the end of the 1990s. Newmann and colleagues (2007) argue that the research on authentic instruction and assessment has 'demonstrated that students who experienced higher levels of authentic instruction and assessment showed higher achievement than students who experienced lower levels of authentic instruction and assessment' (p. viii).

In summary, authentic assessment tasks:

- are meaningful and, where appropriate, reflect real-world tasks
- relate explicitly to the learning goals/intentions
- are often negotiated
- involve judgement, synthesis, problem-solving and application of learning rather than simple factual recall
- engage learners in performing, demonstrating and reflecting
- often provide opportunities for learners to explain their responses
- support taking the time to assess for in-depth understanding rather than merely recalling content
- provide multiple ways to respond rather than rely on a single mode of response
- set explicit standards for tasks based on clear criteria rather than predetermined standards
- promote equity.

Authentic assessment honours learners' cultural and linguistic diversity, provides them with agency and autonomy and engages them actively in both the learning and assessment processes.

Inclusive assessment practices

Inclusivity is an important principle that underpins all literacy and English experiences discussed in this book. Every learner is unique and it is imperative that assessment practices and tasks do not embed inequities by privileging some learners over others. Using **inclusive assessment practices** means that, as teachers, we think carefully about the different backgrounds, diverse linguistic contexts, cultures and special needs of the learners in our care.

Inclusive assessment practices: recognise and honour the diversity of learners and how they learn so that assessment tasks are fair and equitable and do not privilege some learners over others.

> ### REFLECTION
>
> Think about the range of contexts that will affect how learners respond to assessment tasks. Compare, for example, the life worlds of Aboriginal or Torres Strait Islander learners in rural or remote regions with Indigenous learners living in metropolitan centres. How will impoverished learners who attend school without breakfast or lunch cope with assessments? Those learners who have experienced recent trauma, including bushfires, floods or family violence, will face a different set of challenges to learners who speak different languages at home or those who live in more advantaged contexts. How will each of these learners respond to some of the traditional assessment tasks they all face? (See later in the chapter for discussions of NAPLAN and the Best Start Kindergarten Assessment.)

Equitable tasks for all learners

CASE STUDY 3.1

A recently arrived refugee is asked to explain the complexities and nuances of their adopted country's history in a class test. How can they respond to this task in a meaningful way? How would their response compare with someone who has lived in the country since birth? Provide some potential examples of how you, as the class teacher, could vary the assessment task to ensure it was equitable.

When to assess

Teachers are continually gathering information about the learners in their care through systematic observations of learners at play and during discussions or group work, asking questions and listening to children talking and reading, as well as through analysis of learners' writing, other artefacts and test results. They will also look at assessments and teacher comments from earlier years.

Formative assessment

At the beginning of each school year, each term and when starting a new unit of work, teachers will gather diagnostic information (one kind of **formative assessment**) to ascertain the learners' current knowledge, skills and understanding. This may be done using a variety of strategies, such as embodying key concepts, drawing them or making a mind map. Alternatively, benchmarking can be undertaken, with the teacher administering a pre-test. If beginning a unit on imaginative writing, the teacher may precede the unit by asking learners to write a story without providing any scaffolding or input before they start the unit. This will provide information about what the learners already understand about creating an

Formative assessment: plays a pivotal role in the teaching and learning decisions that teachers make. Teachers collect diagnostic information about a learner's needs and abilities (one kind of assessment for learning).

imaginative text. Another example of a formative assessment task is a running record of a learner's reading of an unfamiliar text (see Chapter 6).

In actuality, teachers engage daily in formative assessment strategies during lessons to monitor learners' skills and understandings. This information informs their decisions about next steps and directions for the next learning phase.

In a seminal study, Black and Wiliam (1998) reviewed more than 580 articles about assessment and concluded that formative assessment is most helpful for improving learning because it is ongoing and developmental. Too much attention to marks and comparisons between learners may result in insecurities and unintended messages to the learner about their lack of ability. Oral or written constructive feedback from a teacher or peer about how a response to a task can be improved helps build learner self-belief and resilience. Conducting a writing conference about a written draft that is compared against the negotiated criteria can be helpful before the final draft is completed.

Summative assessment

At the end of a unit or learning experience, the teacher will assess to what extent learners have achieved or understood what was intended. **Summative assessment** tasks need to be designed to best enable learners to demonstrate or articulate what they have learnt.

Optimally, several summative tasks will be undertaken to assist in making this judgement. If the assessment task has been set across the whole grade, opportunities for teachers to discuss expectations using a range of learner responses will help the consistency of teacher judgement when assessing.

It is at these endpoints that **standardised tests** are often introduced to compare learners with others in different contexts thought to be similar in age or gender, for example. As explained earlier, however, it is often unhelpful to make comparisons between learners in different contexts. Kohn asserts (in Harris, 2011) that there is a **hidden curriculum** within the way standardised tests are constructed, with a tendency to privilege shallow, superficial thinking over deeper, more complex thinking, especially if concepts, skills and understandings are mostly assessed through multiple-choice responses.

Norm-referenced tests compare learners' test results with an apparently representative sample of learners. Often these 'norms' have not been updated after significant changes in social contexts that reflect the increased diversity of the learner population. When such tests are then used to publicly rank and compare learners or schools in league tables, they are termed **high-stakes tests**.

High-stakes testing

Despite the preceding statements about high-stakes testing, these are the assessment strategies that are currently most valued in Australia and many other Western countries. In Australia, high-stakes tests are encapsulated by the National Assessment Program – Literacy and Numeracy (NAPLAN). Since 2008, *before* the implementation of the Australian Curriculum, learners have been tested in Years 3, 5, 7 and 9 in reading, writing, language conventions (grammar, spelling and punctuation) and numeracy. While these largely multiple-choice tests (with the exception of the writing test) provide a picture of several

---

Summative assessment: typically occurs at the end of a learning sequence.

Standardised tests: tests that are administered and scored using the same conditions and protocols (e.g. NAPLAN tests).

Hidden curriculum: an unintended consequence within curriculum – for example, a learner who is complimented for sitting quietly may learn that quiet compliance is the desired behaviour.

Norm-referenced tests: compare learners' scores on standardised tests with a so-called representative sample – for example, IQ tests are norm-referenced.

High-stakes tests: tests where there is much at stake for the learner and the educational institution. Results are made public and tables are constructed that rank and compare learners and their schools. For example, in Australia, NAPLAN test scores have been used to compare the results of learners in so-called 'like' schools on the My School website.

narrow aspects of learners' literacy and numeracy skills, including how well they can perform under test conditions, they cannot assess the Australian Curriculum's general capabilities, such as creativity and critical thinking. Learners' achievements in other key learning areas are also not assessed by NAPLAN. For example, the criteria for assessing the writing task do not reward creative ideas or imaginative responses. Rather, more marks are awarded for correct punctuation and spelling. Culturally and linguistically diverse learners, and those from vulnerable socioeconomic contexts, are disadvantaged by these assessment criteria.

NAPLAN has triggered significant controversy since it was developed. The Whitlam Institute (2012, 2013, 2014) has published research in which teachers report that NAPLAN tests cause learners great stress and, as educators, they feel constrained to teach to these tests.

Further, school results are readily accessible through the My School website (www.acara .edu.au/reporting/my-school-website) and, until some changes were made in 2019, it was possible to rank so-called 'like' schools. Parents and caregivers may use the My School website to inform decisions about where to enrol their children. Yet, it can be argued that there is no such thing as a 'like' school (see Blackmore, 2016) and the reporting of learner outcomes through comparing school results is a practice that contributes to the unevenness of schooling outcomes (Ewing, 2020; Mockler & Thompson, 2016). While school results continue to be published and compared, they will carry undue weight within the range of assessment strategies available – more weight, for example, than is attributed to learners' end-of-school achievements. For these reasons, it is important that NAPLAN is regarded as only one snapshot of learner progress in some areas. Some schools are using the data that NAPLAN provides to look at trends to identify strengths and weaknesses in literacy and numeracy in specific cohorts or to provide input when making resourcing decisions.

Ethics, validity and reliability

Ethical assessment is another area that needs to be carefully considered when designing assessment strategies. Assessment tasks must have a high degree of *validity*, and be designed to ensure they reflect what was taught, are appropriate for the particular context and actually assess what they set out to assess. For example, asking a learner to retell a story the teacher has just told or read aloud is one valid way the teacher can understand how well a learner listens responsively. Later chapters will address assessment in different areas of literacy more specifically.

In addition, learners' responses need to be *reliable* or consistent across several different assessment occasions.

REFLECTION

Think about some of the literacy tasks that your reading journey has included.

1. Do you think they accurately reflected what was taught?
2. How appropriate were they for the particular year level?
3. Did you ever feel that an assessment did not reflect your achievements accurately? Why or why not?

Measure: assign a numerical score, grade or level to a task that has an established scale.

Unfortunately, sometimes assessments focus on what is easiest to **measure** or grade rather than what is most important.

When an assessment task has been administered across a number of classes with different teachers responsible for grading, the consistency of teacher professional judgement must be addressed. It is important to bring together the teachers working on the same grade at the school so they can discuss their expectations of responses and how they interpret specific criteria and have opportunities to share how they have assessed individual learner responses.

Who should assess?

Clearly, the teacher is often responsible for assessment, and certainly every teacher regularly collects examples of learners' oral, reading and writing achievements over time. The involvement of others in the assessment process is also highly recommended. Self-assessment and peer assessment provide opportunities for learners to understand the complexity of making judgements alongside how different kinds of assessment work. For these opportunities to be successful, learners must be deeply engaged in the assessment task, understand the learning intention and the criteria that have been developed, and feel they are working in a trusting community where risks are applauded and mistakes welcomed because they facilitate more learning. Learners must be encouraged to reflect on how they have learnt. Parents and caregivers also need to understand the expectations, criteria and purpose of assessment tasks. At times, where appropriate, parents can be asked to reflect on learners' progress.

Peer assessment and self-assessment

Assessment as learning: learners self-assess using a range of different assessment strategies, especially in rich tasks, and reflect on their own learning achievements (Earl, 2013). Peer assessment against explicit criteria can also be an important learning experience.

Peer assessment and self-assessment can be described as **assessment *as* learning**. They encourage and support learners' development of self-directed and self-regulated learning, as well as developing engagement and wellbeing by supporting student agency in their own learning (Timperley, 2011). Using the teacher's explicit descriptive feedback, success criteria and individual goal setting as guides, peer assessment and self-assessment can be both effective and accurate and help to develop self-directed, self-regulated learning.

Learning journals can be an effective way of enabling learners to regularly reflect on what they have learnt and how successful they feel they are at grasping new concepts, skills and understandings. Some reports for parents and caregivers now include space for the learners to provide comments about their progress over the term or semester.

In the later years of primary school, it is of crucial importance for learners to continue to develop the skills needed to regulate and direct their own learning. In these years, learners are asked to consider 'big ideas' outside their own personal experience. If learners are to develop the critical literacy needed to understand and respond to the more abstract and complex texts of the later years of schooling, the language used for particular purposes – for example, to inform, persuade or entertain – must also be understood and analysed.

How should we assess?

Rich assessment tasks are those meaningful and real-world tasks that are educative for the learner, their teachers and family, and the broader school community where appropriate. They are often interdisciplinary. An example is provided here.

Example of a rich assessment task

Saving the planet

In groups of three over the next four weeks:

- identify an issue related to the environment or climate change (e.g. global warming, lack of water, bushfires, flooding, overpopulation, rises in sea levels, extinction of endangered animals)
- undertake some research together
- plan and design an exhibit that represents your findings (e.g. a poster, PowerPoint, video, readers theatre, story, photo journal)
- consider how best to raise awareness of the issue or problem
- demonstrate your understanding of the issue
- discuss alternative actions and what can be done.

This exhibition will be held with your peers and parents/caregivers at the end-of-term celebration.

Cumulative learning portfolios are one example of a rich assessment process that can give the learner quite a lot of control over their own learning. Learners keep a cumulative portfolio over a year (or sometimes longer) for which they select examples of their learning before (formative), during (formative) and after (summative) a particular learning sequence or unit of work. Along the way, the learner, teacher and parent/caregiver can annotate these artefacts to explain their purpose and how they relate to the particular curriculum journey. Learners can reflect on not only what they learnt, but how they learnt. If the cumulative portfolio is an e-portfolio, it can also include audio and video recordings of performative tasks.

Reporting assessment results

Reporting is a part of a teacher's accountability to learners, parents and caregivers, the school community, employers and government. Once again, it is important to think about the kind of reporting that is most useful for different stakeholders. We have already discussed how central explicit and constructive feedback is for the learner. The same importance applies to reporting to parents and caregivers. There are various practices in place for reporting to parents and caregivers, including parent/caregiver–teacher interviews, written reports, gallery showcases of learners' creative works and performances.

Reporting to learners

The most important aspect of reporting to learners is providing explicit descriptive feedback that accurately describes how the learner is meeting the success criteria that have been established and shared before undertaking a task. Offering learners opportunities for peer assessment and self-assessment also allows them to reflect on the learning intentions and success criteria and report on their own individual successes and goals. Reading and writing conferences can help teachers gather information about how learners are progressing and provide timely opportunities for learners to reflect on their progress. As you reflect on some of the examples provided below, think about at what stage reporting to learners would be valuable.

Reporting to families and caregivers

Participating in peer assessment and self-assessment can also prepare learners for three-way conversations with parents and caregivers (Woodward, 1993), when they are given the agency to discuss their work samples and report on their own progress alongside their teacher.

Including parents, caregivers and community members in the planning and implementation of activities undertaken in the classroom can also support a shared understanding about assessment and learner progress.

The Australian Government has mandated using A–E letters on reports to parents/caregivers to represent a grading from outstanding achievement to little or no achievement. Below is an example of a learner's written report.

Halfway through Year 1, Aidan wrote his self-assessment, which was included in his report:

> Terms 1 and 2 of Year 1 has been wonderful because I have learned a lot. I can now use a lot of strategies to solve maths problems. I have also improved my thinking skills. I have tried very hard to improve my reading and I am better at finding answers in texts. I am a kind and caring friend to others. I am taking more responsibility for my learning and I love learning new things.

Examples of current English and literacy assessment strategies

The states and territories employ a range of different assessment strategies and practices. These usually begin in the first year of school. This section provides some examples at the time of writing.

Kindergarten Development Check

In 2020, the Tasmanian Department of Education introduced the Kindergarten Development Check. It is designed to help teachers identify any learner beginning school who may be at risk of not achieving expected outcomes. It is hoped that early identification will enable specific support and, if needed, a specifically designed intervention program.

Best Start Kindergarten Assessment

Since 2010, all children in New South Wales beginning their first year of school (Foundation) in a public school are assessed on their skills in writing, reading, comprehension, speaking, phonics and phonemic awareness, print concepts, counting skills, arithmetic strategies and pattern recognition. The aim is to increase levels of attainment of all learners. The NSW Department of Education website (https://education.nsw.gov.au/teaching-and-learning/curriculum/literacy-and-numeracy/assessment-resources/best-start-kindergarten) provides some further context.

NAPLAN

The Australian Curriculum, Assessment and Reporting Authority (ACARA) website (www.acara.edu.au/assessment) provides past NAPLAN papers and answers in reading, language conventions and writing. It is worthwhile going online to look at some of these, in particular, at the marking criteria for writing.

Phonics Screening Check

The Phonics Screening Check (https://education.nsw.gov.au/teaching-and-learning/curriculum/literacy-and-numeracy/assessment-resources/phonics-screening-check) is a short assessment administered by classroom teachers to assess how six-year-old learners are progressing with synthesising sounds. Each child needs to read 40 individual words on a screen, 20 of which are nonsense words. The Phonics Screening Check has been mandated in England since 2012 and is now mandated in South Australia and New South Wales.

Questions

Examine and reflect on the above examples of some contemporary Australian assessment practices.

1. What main aspects are being assessed using these strategies?
2. How effective do you think these assessment strategies are?
3. Do you think they are meeting the criteria of validity and reliability? Why or why not?

Planning assessment from the beginning

Rather than creating assessments near the conclusion of a unit of study (or relying on the tests provided by textbook publishers, which may not completely or appropriately assess our standards), backward design calls for us to operationalize our goals or standards in terms of assessment evidence as we **begin** to plan a unit or course.

Source: Wiggins & McTighe (1998, p. 8).

Backward design/mapping

So, how do you implement a strategy like backward design that supports the development of authentic curriculum-based assessment? If you follow the suggestions described in the following section, unlike many of the ships that are said to have foundered and disappeared in the seas of the Bermuda Triangle (see Figure 3.1), you will stay right on course!

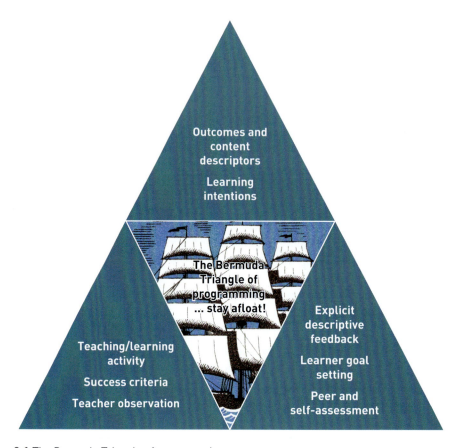

Figure 3.1 The Bermuda Triangle of programming

Planning and moderation

A planning process that results in authentic curriculum-based assessment will include the development of 'learning intentions; success criteria; explicit descriptive feedback; peer and self-assessment and student goal setting' (Fullan & Sharratt, 2012, in NSW Department of Education, 2020) to effectively inform the design and implementation of teaching programs. All teachers are working within a framework provided by their employer that incorporates the national goals for education as realised in the outcomes and content descriptors of the Australian Curriculum (Australian Curriculum, Assessment and Reporting Authority [ACARA], n.d.). As learners progress throughout the years of schooling, it is therefore of benefit to the school community if teachers plan, reflect and evaluate together. The following aspects of planning demonstrate how assessment can be designed as part of any learning program for students at any stage of learning.

Learning intentions

When planning a unit of work, sequence of lessons or single lesson, the teacher must identify the learning goals and make sure they align to the relevant syllabus outcomes, content descriptors and stage of the learners. As a second step in this process, learners should be

Success criteria

When developing teaching and learning activities with relevant learning intentions, it is important to also develop explicit success criteria with the learners. The criteria will be informed by teacher observation of learners' understandings and stages of learning and the content descriptors in the Australian Curriculum. As much as possible, however, these criteria should be negotiated with learners or developed by learners with teacher guidance. The success criteria should relate to the intention of the lesson but be collaboratively developed, discussed and owned by the learners. For example, in the early years, agreeing to leave a space between words or to start a recount by answering the question 'When?' with 'on Friday', 'in the morning' or 'after school' – exemplifies for learners how they can meet the learning intentions.

Explicit descriptive feedback

When the shared learning intentions and success criteria are used as guides, the learning goals will be clear and both learners and teachers will understand what the explicit descriptive feedback will be based on. This is an important aspect of assessment because it helps learners to develop self-direction and self-regulation, where they have control over their own learning. Feedback can be given by peers or the teacher, or developed through individual personal reflection. It is the process by which the individual is able to compare their work and progress in meeting the goals exemplified by the success criteria. In this way, learners are able to understand how successful they have been in meeting goals. Similarly, learners can use the feedback they individually receive, along with the learning intentions and the success criteria, to set their individual learning goals.

Accountability

Accountability is key to developing the trust of parents, caregivers and the community at large. Being ready to discuss and demonstrate the development of each of the learners in your care is an important part of the work of a teacher. There will always be external demands for evidence of learner progress, but daily interaction with the learners will best place you to closely observe their progress.

Record keeping as data for research-informed practice and reporting

Aside from any explicit demands made by your school system, records should be kept to reflect the teaching and learning that is actually taking place in your classroom. This is best done by clearly defining the learning intentions and success criteria for every lesson sequence. Data can be gathered through strategies such as video and audio recording of presentations, learner self-assessment and peer assessment, and careful observation at selected stages in the teaching and learning sequence. These data will allow you to **evaluate** your planning and teaching and at the same time record learners' progress as an embedded part of the learning process.

Evaluation: an umbrella term that stems from *value* and generally refers to making a judgement or estimation about the worth of something. In education contexts, evaluation is often used to refer to the effectiveness of teachers' strategies, activities and experiences or particular resources.

Authentic curriculum-based assessment: examples and case studies

The following three examples and suggestions for designing authentic assessment reflect the principles of authentic curriculum discussed above – there is an explicit and direct relationship to the curriculum that is being taught in the lesson or sequence of lessons and from the outset this is shared with learners. The assessment is also explicitly designed to be responsive to the needs of the cohort of learners that are involved in the learning.

CASE STUDY 3.2 — The Aboriginal soldiers who fought in WWI

In this case study, learners in the final years of primary school are asked to develop knowledge and understandings in both History and English.

Figure 3.2 Anzac soldiers marching to the front, France, 1916

Stage 3 (Years 5 and 6)

Key: Learning intentions (LI); success criteria (SC); assessment 👍

Learning intentions (LI)

In this sequence of lessons, learners will be asked to consider the big ideas relating to the history of Australia as a nation and the contributions of different groups of Australians, in this case Aboriginal and Torres Strait Islander peoples (ACHHK114, ACHHK116) **(LI)**. Embedded in this study is the comparison and analysis of the strategies an author uses to influence readers **(LI)** (ACELY 1801). Learners will be supported to develop self-regulation and self-direction with a focus on peer assessment and goal setting to assist this. **(LI)**

    Curriculum areas: History and English

Type of texts: Reading and comparing a narrative and an historical recount from Rachel Bin Salleh (2019), *Alfred's War*, published by Magabala Books.

Genre/purpose: Writing an historical recount **(LI)**

Subject matter (Field):

History: The contribution and treatment of Aboriginal soldiers from WWI **(SC)**

English: Writing as an historian **(SC)**

Relationship with audience (Tenor): Authoritative stance of an historian dealing with facts **(SC)**

Mode of communication (Mode): Written, distanced in time and space from the reader **(SC)**

Duration: Four lessons

1. Building the field with a video about Australian soldiers in WWI, such as the ABC's *Behind the News* video 'Indigenous ANZACs' (www.abc.net.au/btn/classroom/indigenous-anzacs/10530758). View the video and, in pairs, discuss the information that was shared and use individual whiteboards to record anything that was interesting or puzzling in preparation to pair share with two others.

   👍 Observe/record learners' contributions to their discussions with peers. Are they self-directed and self-regulated in their learning? Ask learners to self-assess their ability to interrogate the text and devise questions to share with peers.

2. Modelled reading: *Alfred's War*, with a focus on comparing the language in the two texts.

   For example:

   Narrative:
   - 'Alfred George lived outside.'
   - 'There were many places Aboriginal people weren't allowed to go.'
   - 'Every year on Anzac Day, Alfred walked to the nearest town for the dawn service.'
   - 'He stayed in the shadows until he heard the lament of the bugle, and then he quietly joined the people gathered in the morning light.'
   - 'He was one of the forgotten soldiers.'

   Historical recount:
   - 'nearly 1000 Aboriginal and Torres Strait Islander boys and men enlisted and fought overseas.'
   - 'prohibited from enlisting in the armed forces on the grounds of their race.'
   - 'despite their bravery and sacrifice, the Black Diggers were not fully recognised by their country or in the communities they returned to.'

   Source: Bin Salleh (2019).

   Compare the language used and how the narrative is more spoken-like, entertaining and easier to read, while the historical recount provides more information in fewer words. **(SC)**

3. Guided writing: focus on developing a text opener (first paragraph) for an historical recount with a focus on the paragraph opener (first sentence in a paragraph) and the sentence openers (beginning of a sentence), to write like an historian (Humphrey et al., 2012).

   Learners use some of the displayed language from the text and, as a group, with guidance from the teacher, begin to jointly construct a text opener. For instance, this paragraph opener ▶ ▶

▶▶ focuses on putting the most important information first in the *sentence opener* position in the first sentence of the paragraph, the *paragraph opener*.

> *In WWI nearly 1000 brave Aboriginal and Torres Strait Islander boys and men, who were at first prohibited from enlisting,* fought overseas but were not fully recognised by their country or communities when they returned. ...

👍 Observe/record learners' contributions to the joint construction. Do they reflect the **(SC)** developed in the modelled reading lesson?

4. Independent writing: in groups/pairs or individually learners write a text opener for the historical recount.

    👍 Learners use a scaffold incorporating the success criteria to write their text opener and to undertake peer and self-assessment. After receiving feedback from the teacher, learners use their participation in peer and self-assessment to set learning goals. (Your feedback, the scaffolds and records of learning goals all form part of recording students' progress.)

Questions

1. Success criteria need to be developed with learners in language they can understand. Using the guide for developing success criteria (SC), imagine you are working with Stage 3 (Years 5 and 6) learners and attempt to write the success criteria using language appropriate for the classroom.
2. Other than a paper record, can you list other appropriate ways for learners to record their goals and to undertake peer and self-assessments to keep a record of their progress?
3. What strategies could you use to further encourage learners to self-direct their learning as a continuance of this series of lessons?

CASE STUDY 3.3 Telling our stories

In this case study, learners invite their parents, caregivers and community members to share in their learning in English and History (Dutton et al., 2018).

Figure 3.3 Family celebrations

Stage 1 (Years 1 and 2)

Key: Learning intention (LI); success criteria (SC); assessment 👍

Learning intentions

Reporting to families is an integral part of the relationship built up between the school and the families and communities of their learners. Examining past family life, especially the histories and cultures of Aboriginal and Torres Strait Islander peoples (ACHHK028), and what has changed or remained the same over time, provides a wonderful starting point for learners to make a connection with their own experiences, families and cultures. By examining the similarities or differences of events from a range of cultures and experiences (ACELY1655), learners are given the opportunity to express themselves in responding to texts.

Curriculum areas: History and English

Type of texts: Reading and responding to a narrative by Jasmine Seymour (2019), *Baby Business*, Magabala Books.

Genre/purpose: Personal response to a text **(LI)**

Subject matter (Field):

History: (SC) Learners explore the histories of Australian families, especially Aboriginal and Torres Strait Islander families, and how they have changed or remained the same over time

English: (SC) Learners express themselves verbally, visually or in writing

Relationship with audience (Tenor): Personal response to engage the listener/viewer/reader **(SC)**

Mode of communication (Mode): Learners' choice of oral, visual or written **(SC)**

Duration: Five lessons

1. Build the field with a video of Aboriginal children singing in several Aboriginal languages, such as one of the resources available on the First Languages Australia website (www.firstlanguages .org.au/resources/marrin-gamu). Confirm that Australians share many languages and invite learners to join in any songs they know or can sing in a language other than English. Then invite learners to ask their families, caregivers or community members if they can teach them a song or poem in any language, that they can then share with the class.

2. Modelled reading: before reading, tell the learners that the book is written by a primary school teacher who is from the Darug people near the Dyarubbin (Hawkesbury) River in New South Wales (www.magabala.com/collections/jasmine-seymour). This is a story about a special ceremony for a new baby at a 'smoking place' where only women and children can go. Read *Baby Business*, with a focus on comparing some of the language in the text and learners' knowledge of their first or second languages or dialects.

    For example:

    Words:

    Gurung – child

    Mudjin – family

    Nura – country

    Wianga – mother

    Yana – walk.

▶ ▶ **Events:** At the smoking place, warm smoke on the:

Feet – connect to country

Chest/heart – to remind you to care for country

Hands – 'take what you need and no more'

Mouth – language on your tongue

Ears – your totem is the bee.

Source: Seymour (2019).

Discuss the language that learners offer and the events in the story. Ask if any learners have seen or remember a ceremony to welcome a new baby into their community or family. Record the language and events from the text for use in the next lesson. **(SC)**

3. Display the words and events from the modelled reading of *Baby Business*. Revisit the song shared in the first lesson and allow any learners who have brought a poem or song from home to share it with the class. Play *The Guardian*'s video showcasing the Noongar version of 'Twinkle, Twinkle, Little Star' (www.youtube.com/watch?v=xLNOH6xowaY) as an example of another Aboriginal language. Refer to the words and events displayed and ask learners to again talk with their parents or caregivers about any special ceremony that their family or community has for newborn babies and if there are any special words that describe the event. Tell learners they will be sharing what they find out about an event for a new baby by using a mime, writing down some words (in any language) or telling the story (in any language) (Dutton et al., 2018).

4. Responding to a text: as a whole class introduce learners to the drama strategy 'mime' (Ewing & Simons, 2016) and display the events listed in *Baby Business*. Choose an event, such as holding the baby's hands in the warm smoke to remind them to only take what they want and not to be greedy. If possible, also display the image and discuss with learners how the mother might feel at that moment, then mime the mother holding the baby, with careful attention to your facial expression. Tell learners you were trying, without words, to let them know how you felt as the mother. Ask learners to try and do the same, to help each other express those feelings. Allow all the learners to participate in miming the same event, discuss their success and then select small groups to prepare and mime one of the other events for the whole class.

At the end of the lesson, remind learners that they will be sharing their own story about a ceremony for a baby by using a mime, writing down some words or telling the story of the event (in any language). Remind them that the audience needs to share in the excitement of the important event, so they have to think about that when they choose how to share their story.

Follow-up: you may also like to share the Community Arts Network (CAN) Noongar lullabies created by Noongar families in 2020 during the COVID-19 pandemic (www.canwa.com.au/project/lullabies).

👍 Observe/record learners' contributions – do they reflect the **(SC)** developed in this lesson? How would you be able to record this lesson as a record of learners progress to share with parents or caregivers?

5. Independent response: in groups/pairs or individually, learners respond to the text by presenting a scene from their own experience, either orally, visually or in writing.

👍 Learners use a scaffold incorporating the **SC** to self-assess and peer-assess and record their success to share with parents/caregivers.

Questions

1. Success criteria need to be developed with learners in language they can understand. Using the guide (SC), imagine you are working with Stage 1 (Years 1 and 2) learners and attempt to write the SC using language appropriate for the classroom.
2. Rewrite the learning intentions (LI) in language that would be suitable to send home to parents and caregivers from a range of diverse cultural and linguistic backgrounds.

Designing assessment for composing texts (Rossbridge, 2017)

CASE STUDY 3.4

In this case study, the process of embedding assessment and reporting at the planning stage is demonstrated through the use of a model and steps for planning in your own classroom.

At the beginning of the school year or term, you will be thinking about how to find out what your learners can already do when composing texts, and then how to develop or adjust your teaching and learning programs to develop these skills further (formative assessment).

Consequently, you will also be wanting to see the learners' progress as a result of the teaching that has occurred (summative assessment).

Below is a model for designing assessment tasks for composing. It can be adapted for a range of contexts. An example has been provided that you could also use as a scaffold to develop and implement your own task. Design or share your task with a colleague. Working with a colleague will create consistency across classes and, more importantly, be the catalyst for getting to know both your learners and colleagues, leading to critical conversations about the upcoming design of teaching.

Using the model

Select a context for composing texts that relates to an upcoming teaching and learning program, particularly in terms of the genre or purpose for composing texts –for example, oral, written, visual or multimodal. Determine when you will implement the pre-assessment task (formative), keeping in mind the support you might provide learners initially in terms of tapping into what they already know. Also decide when you will conduct the post-assessment (summative). This should occur after you have taught the relevant teaching and learning program. Consider whether any adjustments might be made for the post-assessment, such as using a different stimulus.

Decide on features of the task, including the genre and purpose, as well as aspects of register, such as the subject matter, the writers' relationship with the audience and the mode of communication (e.g. oral, written, visual or multimodal).

You will also need to consider the stages in the writing process that will be involved. For example, you may assess the learners' ability to plan and draft, or only the editing and reviewing of a previously written text. It will depend on what you want to find out.

Think about whether you want to apply time constraints. Conditions do not have to resemble those of systemic testing. Great writers tend not to be bound by imposed times!

Finally, think about how you can incorporate learner knowledge and understanding about language into the process. Use a reflections sheet or interview so that you can understand each learner's perception of their own skills and identify the metalanguage learners use as well as their knowledge and understanding about language.

▶ ▶

▶▶ Table 3.1 shows an example of a pre- and post-assessment task.

Table 3.1 Composing texts: pre- and post-assessment task (sample)

Implementation time frame					
Pre: Term 1 Week 1		Post: Term 1 Week 5			
Task features					
Curriculum area/s:	English				
Type of text:	Imaginative		Informative		Persuasive
Genre/purpose:	Literary description – to describe characteristic features of a place				
Subject matter:	Bush/forest path setting				
Relationship with audience:	Storyteller				
Mode of communication:	Oral		Written		Visual
Stage in the writing process:	Plan	Draft	Edit	Review	Publish
Time constraints:	No	Yes			

Steps

1. Read a selection of picture books with strong descriptions of settings from a range of literary genres. Think aloud to highlight aspects of the setting descriptions to learners.
2. Provide learners with an image of a narrative setting (an example image is shown in Figure 3.4). Tell learners they are going to plan and write a draft imaginative description of a setting that would be found at the beginning of a narrative or story.
3. Discuss the purpose of the text. In pairs, learners discuss the image and features they believe would be important to describe to a reader.

Figure 3.4 Example image for learners to discuss

4. Continue discussion by asking the following questions:
- What type of narrative might this setting be found in – for example, adventure, horror, fantasy, realism?
- Why might this setting be important in the beginning of the narrative?
- Who would be your ideal reader?
- How do you want your reader to feel?
- What details do you want to describe for your reader?
- How might you foreshadow what is to come?

5. Learners plan for writing by annotating the image, making notes or drawing on blank paper.

6. Learners independently use the planning to draft their own description.

7. After writing, ask learners to complete an evaluation to identify strengths and goals for their composing.

> Source: This case study was adapted from Rossbridge (2017) and included with permission.

Questions

Using the suggestions and the model lesson, answer the following questions about assessment:

1. How are learners informed about learning intentions and success criteria?

2. Why is it important for a teacher to confirm the assessment process with colleagues?

3. Are there many opportunities for descriptive explicit feedback from the teacher to the learners?

4. How are learners able to effectively and accurately self-assess?

5. Can you identify an opportunity for effective, accurate peer assessment?

6. Are there any opportunities for individual learners goal setting?

Conclusion

This chapter highlighted the need for teachers to embed a balance of diagnostic, formative and summative authentic curriculum-based assessment practices from the beginning of each learning journey. Both assessment of learning and assessment for learning are important and learners should have opportunities to discuss assessment criteria and to self- and peer-assess, because this is how assessment as learning is developed. Teachers should be aware of the need to be inclusive when planning and implementing assessment: assessment goals should focus on equity and social justice and improved learning outcomes for all learners, including those who are disadvantaged or isolated (Ewing, 2012; Reid, 2006).

In any assessment task, the content and concepts being assessed must be valid and contextually appropriate. To be effective, feedback to learners and reporting to parents and caregivers must also be timely and focused. Additionally, assessment tasks must be designed to produce reliable information based on a range of strategies. There is a need to provide multiple opportunities to demonstrate learning and not to rely solely on test results.

Subsequent chapters consider other assessment strategies and examples that resonate with the principles of assessment discussed in this chapter.

Bringing it together

1. Make a list of authentic assessment strategies you have experienced. Which strategies were the most helpful for you?
2. How can you assess for learning as well as assess of learning?
3. How will you know when learning has been most effective?
4. Is it appropriate to compare Australian assessment results with those in other cultures or countries? Why or why not?
5. How can learning be most meaningfully reported to others?

Further resources

Curriculum and assessment

This book includes more discussion about rich assessment tasks and authentic assessment and explores recurrent issues in assessment in Australian education. See, especially, Chapters 1, 4 and 8.

Ewing, R. (2013). *Curriculum and Assessment: Storylines* (2nd edn). Oxford University Press.

Authentic/educative assessment

Chapter 9 in this book provides detail about authentic/educative assessment.

Ewing, R., Kervin, L., Glass, C., Gobby, B., Groundwater-Smith, S. & Le Cornu, R. (2019). *Teaching: Challenges, Dilemmas and Opportunities*. Cengage.

Beyond the script

Useful descriptions of a range of drama strategies that can be used to assess deep understanding, and includes many examples of classroom implementation to support the development of creativity and literacy.

Ewing, R. & Simons, J., with Hertzberg, M. & Campbell, V. (2016). *Beyond the Script Take Three: Drama in the Classroom* (3rd edn). Primary English Teaching Association Australia (PETAA).

My School

It is useful to become familiar with the My School website and how it works. When browsing this website, think about the premises on which it is based.

www.myschool.edu.au

References

Australian Curriculum, Assessment and Reporting Authority (ACARA). (n.d.). Australian Curriculum. www.australiancurriculum.edu.au

Bin Salleh, R. (2019). *Alfred's War*. Magabala Books.

Black, P. & Wiliam, D. (1998). Inside the black box: raising standards in classroom assessment. *Phi Delta Kappan*, Oct, 139–148.

Blackmore, J. (2016). Keynote address. Australian Association for Research in Education, Annual Conference, December.

Dutton, J., D'warte, J., Rossbridge, J., & Rushton,K. (2018). *Tell Me Your Story: Confirming Identity and Engaging Writers in the Middle Years*. Primary English Teaching Association Australia (PETAA).

Earl, L. (2013). *Assessment as Learning: Using Assessment to Maximise Student Learning*. Sage.

Education Queensland. (1999). *Productive Pedagogy*. Queensland Department of Education.

Ewing, R. (2012). Competing issues in Australian primary education: learning from international experiences. *Education*, 3–13, 40(1), 97–111.

—— (2013). *Curriculum and Assessment: Storylines* (2nd edn). Oxford University Press.

—— (2020). NAPLAN 'totally incongruent' with curriculum aims: years of evidence show it must be axed. *Education HQ*, May, 8.

Ewing, R., Kervin, L., Glass, C., Gobby, B., Groundwater-Smith, S., & Le Cornu, R. (2019). *Teaching: Challenges, Dilemmas and Opportunities*. Cengage.

Ewing, R. & Simons, J., with Hertzberg, M. & Campbell, V. (2016). *Beyond the Script Take Three: Drama in the Classroom* (3rd edn). Primary English Teaching Association Australia (PETAA).

Fullan, M. & Sharratt, L. (2012). *Putting Faces on the Data: What Great Leaders Do!* Sage.

Goodman, K. & Owoki, G. (2002). *Kidwatching. Documenting Children's Literacy Development*. Heinemann.

Harris, C. (2011). *The Battle Over Homework* (2nd edn). Corwin.

Humphrey, S., Droga, L., & Feez, S. (2012). *Grammar and Meaning*. Primary English Teaching Association Australia (PETAA).

Mockler, N. & Thompson, G. (2016). Principals of audit: testing, data and 'implicated advocacy. *Journal of Educational Administration and History*, 48(1), 1–18.

Newmann, F., King, B., & Carmichael, D. (2007). *Authentic Instruction and Assessment. Common Standards for Rigor and Relevance in Teaching Academic Subjects*. Iowa Department of Education.

NSW Department of Education. (2020). Student assessment. https://education.nsw.gov.au/teaching-and-learning/student-assessment

NSW Department of Education & Training. (2003). *Quality Teaching: A Discussion Paper*. NSW DET.

Reid, J. (2006). Reading stories: understanding our professional history as teachers. In R. Ewing (Ed.), *Beyond the Reading Wars: A Balanced Approach to Helping Children Learn to Read*. Primary English Teaching Association Australia (PETAA).

Rossbridge, J. (2017). Focusing on assessment and the teaching and learning cycle through whole school professional learning. In H. Fehring (Ed.), *Assessment into Practice: Understanding Assessment Practice to Improve Students' Literacy Learning*. Primary English Teaching Association Australia (PETAA).

Seymour, J. (2019). *Baby Business*. Magabala Books.

Timperley, H. (2011). *Realising the Power of Professional Learning*. Open University Press/McGraw-Hill Education.

Whitlam Institute. (2012). *An Educator's Perspective: The Impact of High Stakes Testing on School Students and Their Families*. University of Western Sydney.

—— (2013). *Parental Attitudes and Perceptions Concerning NAPLAN*. University of Western Sydney.

—— (2014). *The Experience of Education: The Impacts of High Stakes Testing on School Students and Their Families: A Qualitative Study*. University of Western Sydney.

Wiggins, G. & McTighe, J. (1998). What is backward design? In G. Wiggins & J. McTighe, *Understanding by Design*. Association for Supervision and Curriculum Development. https://valenciacollege.edu/faculty/development/courses-resources/documents/WhatisBackwardDesignWigginsMctighe.pdf

Woodward, H. (1993). *Negotiated Evaluation: Involving Children and Parents in the Process*. Primary English Teaching Association Australia (PETAA).

CHAPTER 4

Developing oracy
Speaking and listening

Siobhan O'Brien

ANTICIPATED OUTCOMES

After working through this chapter, it is anticipated you will be able to:

- explain the importance of oral language in becoming literate and identify a range of speaking and listening experiences in prior-to-school and school settings, including in the home environment
- locate speaking and listening in the Early Years Learning Framework, the Australian Curriculum: English and the National Literacy Learning Progression
- reflect on the role of oral narrative in Australian First Nations cultures and consider the implications for the classroom
- consider the key issues in speaking and listening in the early primary years
- apply key teaching instructional approaches and teaching and learning strategies that foster oracy for the early years and later primary years.

Introduction

> Of all the tools for cultural and pedagogical intervention in human development and learning, talk is the most powerful in its possibilities.
>
> Source: Alexander (2008, p. 92).

Many children seem to learn to talk effortlessly – perhaps because they are treated as meaning-makers from the moment they are born. As Alexander writes, talk plays a powerful role in a child's learning and yet, sometimes, once a child can talk, we pay little attention to the ongoing development of speaking and active listening. This chapter begins by focusing on how children become competent oral communicators in the home, in early childhood contexts and at school. The central role of storying and storytelling in learning both language and culture, including the role of oral narrative in Australia's First Nations cultures, is also considered in helping us understand why oracy underpins learning to read and write. This chapter documents how speaking and listening are represented in both the Early Years Learning Framework (EYLF) and the Australian Curriculum: English. Finally, a range of teaching and learning instructional strategies that foster the ongoing development of children's speaking and listening are explored.

Oracy development prior to school

From birth, children are 'communicating beings' who are attempting to make sense of their world (Halliday, 2016, p. 2). As a part of this process, they interact with their closest family members and caregivers to develop neural connections through touch, sound and other sensory stimulation. As the child grows, they continue to respond to being loved, talked with and listened to, and their ability to interact using language grows quickly (Ewing, 2020). The role of family and caregivers in this period is essential to the child's oral language development. Well-developed oral language underpins the process of becoming deeply literate and is critical for children's future life opportunities (Ewing et al., 2016).

Thinking theoretically, Urie Bronfenbrenner's ecological systems theory offers a description of the important role family (and later childcare and school environments) play in the child's development and how their interactions become increasingly complex as they grow. Bronfenbrenner described the context of the child in a series of layers, with his ecological model recognising that specific contexts, labelled as the microsystem, mesosystem, ecosystem and macrosystem, influence and are influenced by a child's interactions (Bronfenbrenner, 1981). Bronfenbrenner describes his ecological theory as resembling Russian nesting dolls because each aspect of the system fits neatly inside the outer systems. The child is placed at the heart of the model, surrounded by the systems that range from the immediate contexts, such as family and schools, to the most outer layer, which includes socio-political and cultural contexts. Bronfenbrenner's model highlights that child development results from the interplay between the child, their family, school, community and society.

Learning to talk

Learning to talk is an ongoing process and is linked to the stages of child development. The skills required to learn language are highly complex and related to semantic knowledge (the meaning of words). The work of Halliday (2004 [1975]) is insightful in this area and considers the social semiotic theory of language and the process of how children learn to make meaning from birth. Halliday (2004 [1980]) believes that language plays a central role in the way a child learns about everyday social and cultural practices. He sees language as constructed through social interaction, rather than as acquired, and identifies three facets of language development: 'learning language, learning through language, and learning about language' (p. 350). When very young children interact with someone and imitate them, it is through this kind of collaboration that they develop new understandings (Vygotsky, 2004).

As the child develops and begins to use their first language, it 'becomes recognizable as language in the adult sense: it gains a "lexicogrammar", an organization in the form of words-arranged-in-structures' (Halliday, 2016, p. 6). Protolanguage comes first and this soon progresses into the first spoken words of the child's mother tongue. Often, early words are approximations and fragments of sentences. For example, after dinner 20-month-old Sami holds out her empty bowl and says, 'More i-cheam Aunty Gina' and it is the adult's role to respond ('You'd like more ice cream, Sami?') – 'with all the grammatical words and morphemes added in place; gradually, the child will incorporate these into his discourse too' (Halliday, 2016, p. 6). Through her systematic observations of children learning to talk, Painter (2006, p. 568) concluded that by about the age of two most of the children she studied were adopting the features of adult language and were able to use language to do things and find out about things at the same time.

It is also important to understand and acknowledge the different cultural and language experiences a young child will have before starting school. Basil Bernstein's (1971, 1990) work on codes is useful in explaining these differences. Families develop ways of speaking that are unique to their family. Sometimes they use words in very specific ways, based on experiences that become part of their vernacular and may not make sense to others. In her conversations with her children and grandchildren, one of the authors of this book would typically end with 'I love you with all my heart'. Other family members have added to this with their own sign-off, like 'I love you with all of my nose'. This is an example of Bernstein's '**restricted code**', as it is highly specific and has a special meaning to one family's history.

In less familiar contexts, language needs to be used in more formal ways that are not tied to a specific situation – in Bernstein's term, more **elaborated codes**, so that our ideas are understood by a broader audience. Over time, then, children need to become familiar with a wide variety of codes so they learn that language is used for a range of different purposes. Knowing when and how to use Standard Australian English – for example, in a formal debate – and when it is more appropriate to talk colloquially – for example, when talking with a best friend – is important. In addition, it is critical that, as teachers, we never devalue, even unconsciously, ways of speaking that are different to our own.

Restricted code: a very specific way of using language in a particular context, often unique to a small group.

Elaborated code: a more explicit or formal way of using language so that the language itself stands on its own rather than being tied to a specific context.

Cambourne's conditions of learning to talk are also very helpful here – see Cambourne and Crouch (2018) and Chapter 6 for more detail.

REFLECTION

The Department of Education Victoria provides a Literacy Teaching Toolkit on its website that features a range of 'Expert literacy videos' (www.education.vic.gov.au/school/teachers/teachingresources/discipline/english/literacy/Pages/expertvideos.aspx). Watch these videos and think about the kinds of literacy experiences your learners might have at home.

1. Does your school value learners' home literacy practices? If so, in what ways?
2. In what ways does your school support learners to bridge the gap between their home and school literacies?

Strategies to support oracy development prior to school

As teachers, we can encourage parents and caregivers to understand the importance of interacting with their children in a variety of entertaining, exploratory, experimental and playful ways. This section suggests some strategies to share with parents and caregivers so they can support the oral language development of their children.

Shared storying/storytelling

Children's oracy development is intrinsically related to their ability to *story* and to the act of *storying* (Campbell, 2013; Lowe, 2002). Lowe (2002) defines storying as a 'meaning-making' activity, 'something that threads between the many separate fragments of information and experience that we encounter' (p. 7). Engaging in storying helps us understand and make sense of events and experiences. It also develops our memories (Egan, 1997; Livo & Rietz, 1986). Young children can tell a story from about the age of three, particularly if they are supported by an adult or older sibling who has shared the experience. Telling stories engages children in an enjoyable activity and, at the same time, helps them find their voice and define who they are (Paley, 1995). Wells (1986, 2009) and Fox (1993) argue that quality conversations, active listening and sharing stories are also essential for children's oral storying and subsequent literacy development.

REFLECTION

1. Was oral storytelling part of your childhood? If so, how was it used? Who was involved?
2. Are you confident telling stories? If so, what kinds of stories do you like to tell? If not, how will you gain confidence in storying as a teacher?

Shared interactive reading aloud

Figure 4.1 Parent reading a story aloud, emphasising the words and discussing the pictures

Shared interactive reading aloud involves a parent, caregiver or older sibling and the child sitting together (Figure 4.1). They look at and discuss the pictures and the more experienced person reads the story aloud, emphasising the words and modelling reading, perhaps pointing at words and adding sound effects where relevant. By interacting and connecting with others, the child develops language skills through sounds and words, hearing stories, observing, listening and responding to questions. Through activities such as shared storying, listening to others reading and observation, children learn language skills via the modelling of the adults and other children (Rogoff et al., 2003). Singing songs and chanting rhymes, tongue twisters and limericks, and engaging in dramatic play experiences using language, sounds and gestures, are all valuable learning experiences. Chapter 6 also discusses these important shared experiences.

Everyday opportunities for developing oracy

Many other opportunities for oral language development occur every day outside the home as families pursue their everyday lives. For example, when grocery shopping parents and children can talk about what is needed when making the shopping list, locating those items in the store, discussing preferred brands and debating whether other items can be added to the shopping trolley. Similarly, they can talk together while travelling to visit friends, when listening to story time and choosing and borrowing books from libraries, and enjoying time playing together in local parks and playgrounds.

The importance of genuine conversations

There has been much research over the past few decades clarifying that it is the dialogue, rather than the word count, that is most important in substantive talk situations. It is clear that genuine conversations, in which the parent and child take turns sharing their thoughts and ideas, are critical in developing children's oracy (see, for example, Romeo et al., 2018).

Within Australia's diverse communities, home settings, interactions and literacy practices vary among different cultures and languages (see, for example, the discussion of celebrating the birth of a baby in different cultures and Noongar lullabies in Chapters 3 and 11). When children learn to speak, it is usually in the first language of their parents. Research shows that learning the English language is not dependent on children speaking English at home, although access to English language instruction will benefit bilingual children's academic progress overall. Access to both English and the home language in early childhood settings will also be important (Dennaoui et al., 2016).

| | 4 DEVELOPING ORACY | 75 |

> **Community support for English language learning** — **CASE STUDY 4.1**

Three-year-old Esra and her family have recently arrived in Australia and do not speak English. The local community is a diverse cultural mix with active community groups. Esra's mother is keen for her children to learn English and to have the best success in learning. She goes to the local library to seek support and finds there are a number of children's story-time sessions and also bilingual books that she can borrow. She also joins a language class to learn English herself. Over time, the family settles well into their new home.

Questions

1. Local support networks are very important for newly arrived families. What does your local community offer for families like Esra's? Conduct an internet search and see if you can locate where children's story-time sessions and different language classes are available. What did your search reveal?
2. Does your local community have a need to create groups and activities for the community to access? If so, what kinds of initiatives could be pursued?

Speaking and listening in the Early Years Learning Framework, Australian Curriculum: English and literacy progression

This section presents how speaking and listening is considered in early childhood through the documents introduced in Chapter 2: the Early Years Learning Framework (EYLF), the Australian Curriculum: English and the National Literacy Learning Progression.

Speaking and listening in the EYLF

The EYLF (Department of Education, Employment and Workplace Relations [DEEWR], 2009) considers that well-developed communication skills are crucial for children because their development is centred around their ability to interact with others and their environment, using gestures and language as forms of communication. Through the developmental stages, we can observe children responding to the world around them in the ways they express their emotions verbally and non-verbally, ask questions, make connections and explore. We can also see this interaction when children are immersed in, and able to express themselves through, art, stories, music, media, dance and performance. Other interactive activities are also valuable – for example, using natural materials such as water, sand and clay as forms of expression. Through engaging with each other, their families and extended community, children also learn how to apply the 'tools to be understood and to describe their learning, ideas and interests' (Verdon et al., 2018, p. 9).

With a strong emphasis on play-based learning as a primary way to develop children's communication and language, the EYLF sets out to ensure that all children have the opportunities to receive the best start in life. The EYLF specifically addresses oracy, speaking and listening, within Outcome 5: Children are effective communicators, with the following contexts and considerations:

- Children interact verbally and non-verbally with others for a range of purposes.
- Children engage with a range of texts and gain meaning from these texts.
- Children express ideas and make meaning using a range of media.
- Children begin to understand how symbols and pattern systems work.
- Children use information and communication technologies to access information, investigate ideas and represent their thinking (DEEWR, 2009, pp. 41–49).

A sense of *belonging* can be enacted when children's first language is valued and acknowledged within the education setting. By incorporating the child's home language, through interaction and ways of communicating, the child is encouraged to continue using both the home language as well as beginning to develop competency and confidence with the use of Standard Australian English. The EYLF notes that 'children's use of their home languages underpins their sense of identity and their conceptual development' (DEEWR, 2009, p. 41). It is also a reflection of our diverse communities: the 2016 Census indicates that more than one-fifth (21%) of Australians speak a language other than English at home, and nearly half (49%) were either born overseas (first generation Australian) or have one or both parents born overseas (second generation Australian) (Australian Bureau of Statistics [ABS], 2017). The most common languages spoken at home, after English, are Mandarin, Arabic, Cantonese and Vietnamese (ABS, 2017). In Australia, there are also more than 250 Indigenous languages, including around 800 dialects 'spoken by the traditional custodians of this land, the Aboriginal and Torres Strait Islander people' (ABS, 2017; Hill et al., 2012).

Teachers' support of children and their families to attain the skills and ability to communicate effectively in both their first language and Standard Australian English, which supports language and interaction in the community, will enhance children's social, emotional and cognitive success. The EYLF encourages teachers to support children to: interact and engage using both verbal and non-verbal language; build communication skills that acknowledge their familiar home/family and community literacies such as cultural cues; and initiate Standard Australian English and home language conversations.

How the EYLF supports literacy development in early childhood

The EYLF supports children to interact verbally and non-verbally with others through encouraging children to:

- respond, using their sensory skills, through exploring and engaging with what they see, hear, touch, feel and taste
- respond with language about play, music and art experiences

- contribute to small and large group discussions
- interact with others (peers and adults) to explore ideas and concepts, and clarify and challenge thinking through asking questions
- express their ideas and emotions to understand and respect the perspectives of others.

The EYLF supports learning and development in children when educators:

- value each child's linguistic heritage and also encourage the continued use of and acquisition of home languages and Standard Australian English
- recognise children's prior learning and continued efforts to communicate and make sense of their experiences both at home and in their communities
- model language use and encourage children to express themselves in a range of contexts and for a range of purposes
- provide, support and engage children in interactions from infant to school transition.

Children engage with a range of texts and gain meaning from these texts when they:

- are encouraged to listen to stories and rhymes and respond to the sounds and patterns heard in speech
- respond with relevant actions, comments and questions to a variety of print, visual and multimedia texts, including questions
- sing and participate in chants, rhymes, jingles and songs as an enjoyable experience
- are introduced to emergent literacy concepts and processes – for example, the sounds of language
- consider the concepts of print, including oral and cultural, and the messages within these
- engage with their own written and constructed texts.

Learning and development in children is promoted when educators:

- create a literacy-enriched environment with displays of print in home languages and Standard Australian English
- provide and read a range of books and other texts that are familiar to the family and community
- tell stories with children and talk about the concepts within the texts
- provide other texts that promote consideration of diverse perspectives
- engage children in conversations and discussions about the meanings of images and texts
- regularly sing songs and chant rhymes and talk about the concepts, such as rhyme, letters and sounds, within these
- provide activities for children in play and explore with words and sounds.

Children are able to express ideas and make meaning using a range of media when settings:

- encourage and engage in play where they can imagine and create roles and scripts
- re-enact well-known stories and symbols of their own culture
- explore the creative arts, including drawing, painting, sculpture, drama, dance and music, to express ideas and make meaning
- use a range of media and experiment with ways of expressing their ideas
- begin to use images, letters and words to convey meaning.

This learning and development in children is promoted when educators:

- acknowledge and build on children's family and community experiences with creative and expressive arts
- provide resources that enable children to express meaning using visual arts, dance, drama and music
- model ways to ask and answer questions during the reading or discussion of books
- provide resources to encourage children to experiment with images and print
- teach children skills and techniques that will enhance their capacity for self-expression and communication.

Children begin to understand how symbols and pattern systems work and this is evident when they are encouraged to:

- use symbols to explore and represent and make meaning such as sounds and patterns in speech, stories and rhyme
- connect their feelings, ideas, words and actions
- predict the patterns of regular routines and the passing of time
- show an understanding of how symbols are a means of communication
- become aware of the relationships between oral, written and visual representations
- begin to sort, categorise, order and compare collections and events
- draw on memory and their experiences to construct meaning using symbols.

This learning and development in children is promoted when educators:

- draw children's attention to symbols and patterns in their environment
- talk about and engage children in discussions about patterns and relationships, including letters, sounds, symbols and systems
- provide access to everyday materials for them to create patterns and to sort, categorise, order and compare
- encourage children to develop their own symbols and systems.

Children use information and communication technologies to access information, investigate ideas and represent their thinking when they are encouraged to:

- identify the technologies used in everyday life
- access images and information to make sense of their world
- design, draw and edit to reflect and compose
- use real or imaginary technologies as props in play experiences to engage with technology for fun and to make meaning.

This learning and development in children is promoted when educators:

- provide access to a range of technologies
- integrate technologies into play experiences
- teach skills and techniques that will encourage children to use, explore and represent their ideas
- encourage collaborative learning with technologies (DEEWR, 2009, pp. 43–47).

REFLECTION

With a strong emphasis on play-based learning to develop children's communication and language, the EYLF addresses oracy, speaking and listening within Outcome 5: Children are effective communicators.

What are the five main ways that Outcome 5 is enacted?

Speaking and listening in the Australian Curriculum

The study of English in the Australian Curriculum is considered central to all other learning and development. The Australian Curriculum: English aims to enable learners to become competent in the many forms of communication required to function successfully in local further education, training and workplace contexts and in global contexts (Australian Curriculum, Assessment and Reporting Authority [ACARA], n.d.). As Australia is also a linguistically and culturally diverse country, the English curriculum fundamentally supports the development of reading and literacy skills through the engagement of literature that is designed for learners to develop critical literacy to expand their scope of experience (ACARA, n.d.). This section focuses on oracy, speaking and listening in the context of the Australian Curriculum: English and the National Literacy Learning Progression.

Often, 'literacy' is defined as consisting of developing skills in reading, writing, speaking, viewing and listening that are appropriate for different purposes and contexts. More recently, however, the concept of literacy has been extended so that the capabilities required for the use and production of information and communication technologies are acknowledged. To achieve an understanding of this broader concept of literacy, learners will need to use language and develop oral language proficiency for both print and multimedia uses.

The Australian Curriculum acknowledges the role that speaking and listening has both inside and outside of school and these skills are embedded in the curriculum to ensure they are explicitly taught. Within the curriculum, the teaching of speaking and listening is addressed in the early years and continues to be consolidated in the later years of schooling. Through engaging in learning, students will develop knowledge and understanding of English use that includes speaking, reading and writing with increasing confidence, accuracy and fluency. Ultimately, the overall goal is the development of sound knowledge and competence in language use for effective listening, speaking, viewing, reading, writing and creating.

Years F–2 content (typically 5–8 years of age)

With the transition to school, and bridging the EYLF, the Australian Curriculum acknowledges that learners bring a range of experiences of language and texts from their home and community that includes diverse cultural perspectives. These valued ways of communication need to be considered as a rich resource upon which to base ongoing language, literature and literacy experiences. Speaking and active listening activities should always be meaningful and appropriate for different contexts.

The curriculum aims to develop these foundation skills and knowledge by providing learners with:

- opportunities to develop language skills
- reading experiences where they engage positively with books
- opportunities to engage through song, rhyme and resources to write and create
- discussions where they talk and interact with others (ACARA, 2009).

Years 3–6 content (typically 9–12 years of age)

In subsequent years, learners continue to consolidate the skills achieved in the early years. They read aloud texts with varied sentence structure and are able to pronounce unfamiliar vocabulary accurately and fluently. They can accurately talk about 'how events, characters and settings are depicted' in texts (ACARA, n.d.). They select and share 'information, ideas and images' from a range of types of text. They express personal opinions based on information in a text (ACARA, n.d.).

Learners are also able to listen carefully to others' views, ask questions to clarify content and 'respond appropriately using interaction skills'. Learners can 'develop and explain a point of view' and 'respond to others' viewpoints' and perspectives. Active contributions to class and group discussions, making presentations and providing feedback' to their peers are also expected (ACARA, n.d.).

Assessment of learning of oracy (speaking and listening) in English is focused on a learner's ability to:

- speak, listen to, read and respond to texts for different purposes and audiences
- speak with accuracy, fluency and confidence in presenting texts.

Chapter 3 also provides details about assessment of speaking and listening.

Table 4.1 presents a document that can be used to plan and assess speaking and listening across the years of schooling. Each of the year levels is presented as a reference for the planning and assessment process with regard to learner achievement.

The National Literacy Learning Progression

The National Literacy Learning Progression was developed to be used by teachers 'to support students to successfully engage with the literacy demands of the Foundation to Year 10 Australian Curriculum' (ACARA, 2020). It provides a comprehensive view of literacy learning concepts and increases sequentially and over time.

The National Literacy Learning Progression presents various observable indicators about the use of Standard Australian English that include 'modes of listening, speaking, reading, viewing, writing and producing texts' (ACARA, 2020). The literacy learning progression was updated in 2020 to provide teachers with a conceptual tool to assist them with developing 'targeted teaching and learning programs for all students working at, above or below year-level expectations' (ACARA, 2020). At the same time, teachers facilitate a shared professional understanding of literacy and numeracy development on a national scale (Roberts, 2020).

Within the National Literacy Learning Progression, there are three specific elements: speaking and listening, reading and viewing, and writing. These elements are further divided into sub-elements, representative 'of evidence-based aspects of literacy development'

Table 4.1 English: speaking and listening sequence of achievement: F–6

	Foundation Year	Year 1	Year 2	Year 3
Receptive modes (listening, reading and viewing)	They listen for rhyme, letter patterns and sounds in words.	They listen to others when taking part in conversations, using appropriate language features and interaction skills.	They listen for particular purposes. They listen for and manipulate sound combinations and rhythmic sound patterns.	They read texts that contain varied sentence structures, a range of punctuation conventions, and images that provide extra information. They listen to others' views and respond appropriately using interaction skills.
Productive modes (speaking, writing and creating)	They identify and describe likes and dislikes about familiar texts, objects, characters and events. In informal group and whole-class settings, learners communicate clearly. They retell events and experiences with peers and known adults.	They interact in pair, group and class discussions, taking turns when responding. They make short presentations on familiar topics.	They explain their preferences for aspects of texts, using other texts as comparisons. They use a variety of strategies to engage in group and class discussions and make presentations.	They contribute actively to class and group discussions, asking questions, providing useful feedback and making presentations.
	Year 4	Year 5	Year 6	
Receptive modes (listening, reading and viewing)	They express preferences for particular types of texts, and respond to others' viewpoints. They listen for and share key points in discussions.	They describe how events, characters and settings in texts are depicted and explain their own responses to them. They listen and ask questions to clarify content.	They listen to discussions, clarifying content and challenging others' ideas.	
Productive modes (speaking, writing and creating)	They understand how to express an opinion based on information in a text. They make presentations and contribute actively to class and group discussions, varying language according to context.	They develop and explain a point of view about a text, selecting information, ideas and images from a range of resources. They make presentations which include multimodal elements for defined purposes. They contribute actively to class and group discussions, taking into account other perspectives.	They explain how their choices of language features and images are used. They make presentations and contribute actively to class and group discussions, using a variety of strategies for effect.	

Source: Modified from ACARA (n.d.).

(ACARA, 2020, p. 4). Populated with indicators, the sub-elements support the developmental levels (see Figure 4.2). For speaking and listening, three elements are presented: listening (LiS), interacting (InT) and speaking (SpK).

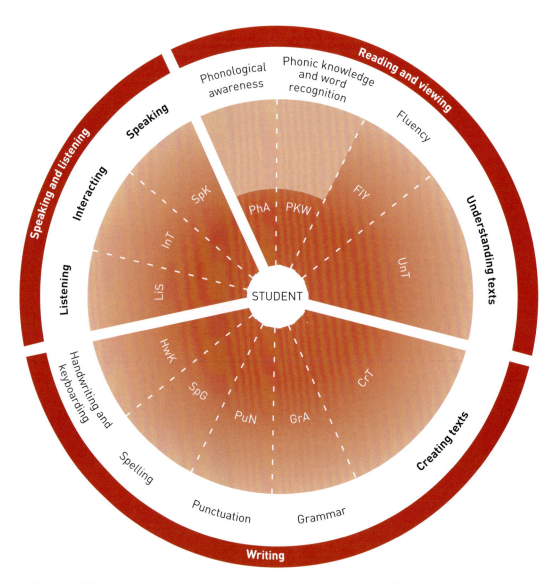

Figure 4.2 Elements and sub-elements of the National Literacy Learning Progression
Source: ACARA (2020, p. 7).

Listening (LiS)

The listening sub-element considers how a student learns to understand and convey meaning from spoken and audio texts. This sub-element supports teaching and learning of the 'increasingly sophisticated language structures of spoken texts used for audiences' and communication purposes (ACARA, 2020). Specific learning area requirements include the use of digital technologies.

Interacting (InT)

The interacting sub-element illustrates how learners become proficient at using language to share information, including pair, group or whole-class oral interactions and also interactions with the wider community.

Speaking (SpK)

The speaking sub-element shows the process of how a learner becomes proficient at language use for expressing and sharing ideas, points of view or responses that are appropriate to audience and required for both formal and informal speaking situations.

REFLECTION

1. In the early primary years, when children are typically 5–8 years of age, the curriculum is designed to provide foundation skills and knowledge through receiving 'a pleasurable and varied experience of literature', with 'the beginnings of a repertoire of listening, speaking, viewing, reading, writing and creating activities and group discussions' (ACARA, n.d.). What are some short-term, mid-term and longer-term strategies you could implement in the classroom to engage children's learning at this stage?

2. In the subsequent primary years, children are 9–12 years of age. In this stage, they are expected to read aloud texts with varied sentence structure, increase their knowledge of unfamiliar vocabulary and be able to 'describe how events, characters and settings in texts are depicted' (ACARA, n.d.). They select and share 'information, ideas and images' from a range of types of text. They express personal opinions based on information in a text. They are able to listen to others' views, ask questions to clarify content and 'respond appropriately using interaction skills'. They also develop and explain 'a point of view and respond to others' viewpoints' (ACARA, n.d.). What are some strategies you could implement in the classroom to engage children's learning at this age and stage?

3. How does the literacy learning progression support planning and assessment of oral language development?

The role of oral narrative in Australian First Nations cultures

This section explores the role of oral narrative in Australian First Nations cultures and provides insight into Indigenous pedagogies, knowledge and cultural practices, such as aspects of culture, art, music, Dreaming and creation stories, and dialogue circles, that develop empathy and understanding.

The Australian Curriculum: English and Australian First Nations peoples

Aboriginal and Torres Strait Islander peoples are acknowledged as the world's oldest continuous living culture. For this reason, the Australian Curriculum: English encourages teachers to prepare lessons to ensure learners come to understand, engage in and appreciate Aboriginal and Torres Strait Islander ways of knowing, being and becoming, including oral storytelling traditions and more recent literature.

Aboriginal pedagogies consider Aboriginal knowledge and cultural practices. These pedagogies are sometimes referred to as 'ways of knowing'. The use and implementation of Aboriginal pedagogies requires a holistic approach that involves explicit planning for both curriculum and pedagogical practices. In Aboriginal and Torres Strait Islander cultures, stories hold the key to the traditions and social ways of Indigenous people and partaking in storytelling is as a way to share and enact values about how to function within a community (MacLean & Wason-Ellam, 2006). The oral culture of First Nations peoples is grounded in the land: their stories are related to country, family, culture and community (MacLean & Wason-Ellam, 2006). This may also indicate a preference of learning style for Aboriginal and Torres Strait Islander learners. For example, the strategy of direct instruction, which involves the use of explicit teaching techniques that are teacher-driven and require the learner to observe and comprehend through cognitive engagement, may not be as effective for some Indigenous learners, who may prefer to learn through watching adults and older siblings. To address learners' needs, teachers need to find out about their cultures, ways of knowing and being so they can plan experiences that value Indigenous knowledge systems and aspects of culture, such as art and music, Dreaming and creation stories, and yarning or dialogue circles.

Dialogue circles help develop oracy, empathy and understanding and are explained below.

Dialogue circles (yarning circles)

A strategy to develop learners' oracy is the practice of dialogue or yarning circles. The circle was traditionally conceived by Aboriginal and Torres Strait Islander peoples to enable communities to work together to come to an agreement. The circle can also act as a teaching and learning strategy for teachers (Queensland Studies Authority, 2010).

A yarning circle provides a context for learners to use spoken language to share experiences or events, generate ideas when introducing new content, reflect on learning or discuss issues in a text (Mills et al., 2013). (See also the discussion of yarning circles in developing community partnerships in Chapter 16.)

The process of a dialogue circle (yarning circle)

A dialogue or yarning circle process includes the following steps:

> The participants sit in a circle, the facilitator introduces the process, all participants are considered equal. A 'power instrument' selected by the group is passed around clockwise and only the person with the item speaks (for example a shell or stone). Everyone listens intently to the person talking. The discussion or debate occurs in sequence and not across the circle. The facilitator allocates time for participants to write thoughts or evaluations, the final round focuses on reflecting. The facilitator ensures everyone leaves the circle feeling calm with no unfinished business. (Queensland Studies Authority, 2010)

REFLECTION

1. Do you think yarning circles would be an effective pedagogical practice in the primary setting? Why or why not?
2. How could yarning circles support teaching and learning in your classroom?

The 8 Ways Aboriginal Pedagogy Framework

Dr Tyson Yunkaporta, with other Aboriginal Elders, researched the ways that Indigenous people learn, culminating in the development of the 8 Ways Aboriginal Pedagogy Framework (Yunkaporta, 2012). The 8 Ways framework reflects how Aboriginal perspectives centre on processes rather than content. 8 Ways is not a 'program' to implement in an education setting; rather, it is a framework that can support teachers to engage with the community. The 8 Ways pedagogies include using stories and symbols and teaching from an aesthetic perspective (Yunkaporta, 2012). The 8 Ways are expressed as eight interconnected pedagogies that involve:

- narrative-driven learning – approaches learning through stories and narrative
- visualised learning processes – uses images and metaphors to support understanding of concepts and content
- hands-on/reflective techniques – uses learning styles such as intra-personal and kinaesthetic skills to develop thinking and learning
- symbols/metaphors – make links to understanding of concepts
- land-based learning – place-based learning that links content to local land and place
- indirect/synergistic logic – uses innovations and understanding by thinking laterally
- modelled/scaffolded genre mastery – models and scaffolds learning (watch then do)
- connectedness to community – noting local viewpoints, learning for community (Yunkaporta, 2012).

REFLECTION

The 8 Ways of learning offer a means for educators to embed Indigenous knowledge systems in their programs.

1. How might 8 Ways shift your pedagogy to use a teaching approach that includes perspectives from Aboriginal and Torres Strait Islander cultures?
2. How does 8 Ways support aesthetic teaching practice?
3. How does 8 Ways promote oracy, speaking and listening practice?
4. How is story sharing articulated through teaching in the classroom in the 8 Ways pedagogy? Consider links to the community, land and local features.

Including aspects of culture, such as art and music, Dreaming and creation stories and dialogue circles, will support and develop empathy and understanding of Indigenous cultures. The implementation of a dialogue or yarning circle is another way to enact this.

5. Would there be any barriers to enacting this process in your classroom?
6. How could you go about establishing dialogue circles as a practice to support oral language development?

Instructional strategies for speaking and listening

When planning and teaching to foster speaking and listening within the teaching program, the use of effective evidence-based practices to support pedagogy is essential. Effective evidence-based practices are the instructional strategies that are used to teach. Research shows that effective literacy learning occurs when schools embed these strategies consistently within their literacy programs (Hattie, 2014). Some examples of evidence-based practices are presented below.

Set a clear learning intention and success criteria

As Chapter 3 explains, setting a clear learning intention that highlights the focus of the lesson will support and optimise learning and ensure learners reach their potential. Negotiating the criteria needed for success is also important. When learners know what they are learning and why they are learning it, the aim and rationale for the lesson is clear and explicit. The learning intention is referred to a number of times throughout the lesson. The success criteria explicitly examine what learners need to achieve in their learning task. For example, if the learning intention is to listen to and comprehend the reading of short texts consisting of a few sentences, the success criteria might be: I can listen to and repeat the words in the sentences.

Explicit teaching practice

Explicit teaching practice is an effective strategy that builds on clear learning intentions. In explicit teaching, the teacher clearly models or demonstrates what is expected to support children with the process of learning the content required for speaking and listening. The explicit focus of the lesson provides the learner with a clear and coherent understanding of what is required for them to undertake in the learning activities. This practice requires the teacher to posses strong content knowledge. An example might be the explicit teaching of one-syllable rhyming words. During the explicit practice, the teacher will need to plan the concepts and activities that ensure the children will know what a rhyming word is. This can be undertaken through songs, books and interactive digital learning apps.

Multiple exposures

Multiple opportunities to be exposed to new ideas or skills allow learners to consolidate their understanding of a topic or learning area. Developing multiple lessons allows children 'to encounter, engage, and elaborate on the new knowledge and skills' through practice (Department of Education and Training [DET], n.d.). In relation to speaking and listening, this could be the use of expressive and receptive language. A teacher may set up a play-based approach with scenarios where children interact and use language to increase their conversational skills over a period of weeks – for example, a play-based activity that models a shopping experience with retail roles or a restaurant that includes the roles of chef and service staff. The learning sessions could focus on particular language use where the children practise greeting people, asking questions and following directions.

Collaborative learning

Collaborative learning occurs when teachers set up learning tasks that require learners to work together in small groups. In a collaborative learning session, all children participate in the learning task. Some learners may have different roles or contribute in various ways – for example, in literature circles each learner chooses a different role to research that is related to a literary text before presenting an activity to the group. To engage learners in a speaking and listening activity like literature circles, teachers need to model strategies that they would like to see in the collaboration. Teachers can also provide prompts that guide the discussions. This scaffolding will enhance the learning and support learners to work collaboratively in groups that function effectively. For further information on evidence-based strategies, refer to the Victorian Education Department's High Impact Teaching Strategies (HITS) (State Government of Victoria, 2019a).

Assessing oral language

Identifying different aspects of learners' oral language and listening skills is important, especially given that they are foundational to the development of reading, viewing and writing skills. A range of skills, including fluency, pronunciation, turn-taking, negotiating meaning through questioning and talking about texts, need to be monitored. It is most likely that your school will have a range of Diagnostic Assessment Tools for English available for assessment purposes. The types of diagnostic tools available will depend on the school's needs. The process of assessment is also set within a school-wide assessment schedule and led by a literacy specialist. For speaking and listening, the assessments will focus on measuring a child's ability and 'understanding of the spoken word, oral language retell, comprehension retell and oral language conversation' (DET, 2019).

An oral language assessment will endeavour to seek information on a child's ability to:

- name objects in a picture or collection
- describe the actions of a character in a picture
- use positional language to describe objects
- engage in conversation with a teacher about a picture prompt so that conclusions can be made about the extent of clarity, utterance, coherence and vocabulary.

One way to monitor speaking and listening progress is to develop a rubric of these skills (see Table 4.2 for an example of a rubric) and to use video recording at different points to capture this range – for example, during a sharing circle, a small-group discussion or a whole-class session.

Table 4.2 Rubric example

Interacting with others			
Descriptor (Victorian Curriculum and Assessment Authority [VCAA], 2021)	**Elaboration (VCAA, 2021)**	**Competency Can the child demonstrate these skills? Y/N**	
Listens to and responds orally to texts and to the communication of others in informal and structured classroom situations using interaction skills, including listening, while others speak (VCELY174)	Listens to, remembers and follows simple instructions		
	Sequences ideas in spoken texts, retells well-known stories, retelling stories with picture cues, and retelling information using story maps		
	Listens for specific things, for example, the main idea of a short statement, the details of a story, or to answer a given question		
	Participates in informal situations, for example, play-based experiences that involve the imaginative use of spoken language		
	Participates in class, group and pair discussions about shared experiences, including shared texts		
	Asks and answers questions to clarify understanding		
Notes			

Key issues in speaking and listening in the early primary years

Speaking and listening in an educative context is central to constructivist theory, in that we learn together and form relationships while also developing cognitive tools (Vygotsky, 1978). Vygotsky's work in this area was extended upon with the term 'scaffolding' as a descriptor for the role of the parent, caregiver or teacher (more knowledgeable other), who provides intellectual support and development. Central to the scaffolding process when a child is learning to talk is that they interact with an adult or older child who provides feedback on their word use (Ewing et al., 2016). To ensure the effective speaking and listening development of children within education settings, it is helpful for educators to have a sound understanding of oral language development and then enact this knowledge with quality instructional practice techniques to ensure that all learners achieve the required outcomes.

Some key issues, areas and concepts for consideration are described in the next section and include information about: expressive and receptive oral language; and pragmatics, phonemic awareness, onset and rime.

Expressive and receptive oral language

Oral language involves both expressive and receptive skills.

Expressive language

Expressive language includes the words, actions, tone, volume, pauses and inflections that we use to express our mood, knowledge and understanding to others. When we apply expressive language skills, we relate to our immediate environment: we describe actions and events, putting words into sentences with grammar use.

Receptive language

Receptive language is the term used for understanding the language expressed by others. This is seen in a child's ability to follow directions or understand a story being read to them by an adult. Children learning to talk often will have more developed receptive language first.

Pragmatics, phonemic awareness, onset and rime

When teachers support children to recognise that words, both oral and written, can be broken down into individual sounds, their oracy and language development will increase. To achieve this, teachers need to have a sound grasp of the following aspects of language development.

Speaking and listening and pragmatics

When individuals interact with others in both formal and informal situations, there are socially constructed rules and cues that guide the communicative process. There is also variance of interaction between different cultures. Often culturally devised, these rules include turn-taking when we speak, and the use of eye contact and body language, such as the distance we position ourselves from one another during a conversation.

These rules or social norms are best described as the *pragmatics of oral language*. Often implicitly learnt, we develop an understanding of pragmatics by simply being immersed in social situations with our families and communities. However, some children require further explicit teaching of pragmatics and social skills to support their understanding of the way language and contexts are used in different settings. This could include voice, sound regulation, greetings and eye contact.

Speaking and listening and phonemic awareness

There are a range of approaches used in schools to teach **phonological awareness**. This section considers how speaking and listening is a part of the process in building phonological and phonemic awareness in younger children. *Phonemic awareness* is a component of phonological awareness and can be defined as the ability to identify and manipulate individual sounds (phonemes) in spoken words.

In current practice, teachers explicitly plan programs that encourage and support learners to develop their phonemic awareness. Hornsby and Wilson (2014) explain that providing opportunities for children to talk, question, experience, inquire, share stories, participate in the shared reading aloud of stories and identify patterns and sounds in familiar texts will

Phonological awareness: the awareness of the sound and structures of language. When developing phonological awareness, children learn to differentiate, identify and locate sounds at the sentence, word, syllable and phoneme (sound) level.

support their learning in context with the world around them. The main aim here is to help children to hear, notice and learn the sounds and patterns in spoken language. This skill also supports further language development, such as vocabulary and reading.

Onset and rime

Onset and rime: the first sound in a one-syllable word (the onset) and the sound of the remaining part of the word (the rime) (Ewing, 2018, p. 10).

Onset and rime describe the phonological units of a spoken syllable. When syllables are split into two parts, the first part is the onset and the second is the rime. The onset contains the vowel and any final consonants. Teaching with resources such as letter cards and images can develop children's understanding and use of onset and rime.

CASE STUDY 4.2 | **Onset and rime in Foundation and Year 1**

Helen is a newly graduated teacher and is looking for ways to engage her foundation and Year 1 class with the use of onset and rime. Onset and rime are described to the learners as the phonological units of a spoken syllable – when syllables are split into two parts, the first part is onset and the second is the rime.

Helen begins a search of the internet to see what sorts of activities are available to support the teaching and learning of onset and rime. She comes across an explicit teaching mini-lesson video and watches the demonstration, differentiated activity, and use of accompanying onset and rime booklets.

Helen decides to teach the onset and rime terminology to her children. She finds that it empowers them and they really enjoy knowing these technical terms. She has also prepared the onset and rime booklets. After the session, the children were excited to be able to share their new words with their parents. The onset and rime learning was increased by these pedagogical strategies.

Questions

Helen found the use of specific terminology supported the learners' interest and awareness of the learning intention.

1. Why do you think this was the case?
2. What does this say about learner agency and learner-centred voice?
3. The onset and rime booklets were able to be easily differentiated. How do you think this supported Helen's teaching at point of need?
4. The shared learning and interaction through the home was very important to Helen. She liked that the children were excited to take their onset and rime booklets home to show their parents. What other opportunities could be developed in the home setting from this learning experience?

Speaking and listening strategies for the early years

This section explores a range of speaking and listening teaching and learning strategies for year levels and stages, including emergent, early primary and later primary. These strategies can be implemented in classroom teaching programs and planning to foster children's oracy skills.

As described earlier, building a rich vocabulary is important for all children. Teachers need to provide opportunities for vocabulary development within their classroom programs to ensure there is always a linguistically rich environment where children are encouraged to learn new words and meanings that build on their existing knowledge and understanding.

To activate this process, teachers role model the use of language by engaging children in purposeful talk and employing the rich vocabulary that has been explored in the learning setting. Providing opportunities to use language in meaningful contexts supports children to develop the confidence to extend their word knowledge. The integration of quality children's literature is a resource that stimulates vocabulary development through reading aloud familiar and new texts. Through these daily shared reading experiences, children build word knowledge and vocabulary development. See Chapters 6, 7 and 8 for more discussion of the important role that quality children's literature plays in the primary classroom.

Circle, sharing or news time

Providing opportunities for learners to share their stories or ideas on a particular topic is very valuable. It is most useful when some structure is introduced to ensure that all learners are engaged. The teacher may organise for different class members to share on different days of the week.

Circle or sharing time may be related to the particular themes being addressed in a unit of work. For example, in a unit about families, learners may be asked to talk briefly about a member of their family who is very special to them. At other times, the established sharing time routine may be used for reflection or evaluation, such as circle time or sharing time.

Active listening

Although listening is the language mode we learn first, it is often the least taught. Consciously making time to talk about the need to listen carefully is important. Reading a descriptive section from a picture book or novel, and then asking learners to draw or map the visual image they created, can be very effective. For example, see the first two pages of Ted Hughes' description of *The Iron Man* as he stands at the top of the cliff (Hughes, 1968).

Rhymes, short songs, chants and poems

Rhymes, short songs, chants and poems also enhance understanding and engage children with the enjoyment of the rhyme, rhythm and sounds of language. Regularly participating in songs and rhyming chants helps children learn phonological awareness (DET, 2020b). Regular practice 'identifying rhyming words, identifying individual sounds and discovering sound-letter patterns' (DET, 2020b) gives children the 'opportunity to share their connections with the rhyming text' (Hornsby & Wilson, 2014). Rhymes and chants are often heard in early years classrooms. Another such strategy, which is often used in later primary years, is choral reading, when multiple voices are heard together.

Think aloud: a strategy where learners share their thought process out loud about a certain point, topic or idea. This supports students with learning concepts being covered in the curriculum.

Think aloud

Teachers can apply the '**think aloud**' strategy to support students with learning concepts being covered in the curriculum. The strategy involves teachers sharing their thought process out loud about a certain point, topic or idea. When modelling strategies for writing, reading, viewing or making mathematical calculations, for example, the teacher can work through the explicit parts of a lesson by verbalising what they are thinking: 'I'm wondering what is going to happen next'; 'Next I will solve the problem by counting on … '; 'If I add this number to the other number … '; and 'I think this is the solution … ' Teachers' tentative use of language is helpful for learners to scaffold their own thinking process.

Modelling through think alouds supports learners by involving them in the articulation of thinking and is identified as an effective instructional tool.

Asking questions

Asking questions that involve learners in more than simple factual recall is very important in all early childhood and primary contexts. While there is a place for factual recall of content knowledge, there is also much need to frame questions to encourage and validate a range of responses that are not simply playing 'guess what's in the teacher's head'. Teachers should plan questions that are focused on investigating learners' understanding of concepts and ideas, but also probe beyond surface understanding. There need to be types of questions that require a precise response as well as questions that invite wonder, reflection, hypotheses or further questions.

When using questioning as a strategy, teachers need to:

- plan the key open questions that will provide a focus for the discussion
- allow learners to have 'thinking time' – there are many occasions when teachers rush a response to something that might require some reflection
- provide a process where all learners have the opportunity to contribute – using think/pair/share is one example of ensuring all learners can respond
- ensure ample opportunities for learners to ask questions of each other and the teacher about the topic, concept or process they are learning about.

See Saxton and colleagues' (2018) *Asking Better Questions* for an in-depth discussion of this important area.

I wonder …

Asking learners to look at images or the covers of picture books, view a documentary or listen to recorded sounds and then document their wondering is also helpful in providing opportunities for them to express their ideas, questions and uncertainties.

Visualising: I can see … I can hear … I can smell …

Reading a section of a story or playing some music while learners have their eyes closed can provide an interesting discussion starter. Through using their senses, children are able to visualise and respond in creative ways. This process will support comprehension and the sequencing of ideas.

Talk moves

As we know, classroom talk can be a 'powerful tool for both teaching and learning' as the 'rich, dialogic supports students' to make sense of new and complex ideas that are explored in the setting. 'Talk moves' is a series of tools teachers can use to scaffold meaningful classroom discussion (NSW Government, 2021).

Positive talk also creates strong classroom communities. Talk moves provides a framework to support this process with prompts for the following strategies:

- wait time
- turn and talk
- revoicing
- reasoning
- adding on
- repeating
- revise your thinking (NSW Government, 2021).

Key teaching approaches in speaking and listening for middle to later primary years

While all the earlier suggested activities should be adapted for use in middle and later primary years (and beyond), the following activities are also valuable.

Choral reading

Choral reading is a strategy where multiple voices read together. As a teaching strategy it promotes thinking and talking, fluency and reading confidence. Following a choral reading session, learners can also discuss the text's meaning. If desired, the reading can be rehearsed and performed. A popular poem for choral reading is Lewis Carroll's 'Jabberwocky' (Carroll, 1871).

Reciprocal teaching

Reciprocal teaching is a strategy that aims to reinforce reading proficiency through speaking and listening via four combined steps – making predictions, clarifying, questioning and summarising – and is most often used with fluent readers (Pilten, 2016). Within the reciprocal teaching steps, learners are encouraged to read, talk and think their way through a selected text and teachers scaffold the talk and discussion between the group members (Palincsar & Brown, 1984).

In the first step, *making predictions*, learners predict what they think the text will present by making assumptions from the heading and some key words related to the main body and supporting ideas. Step 2, *clarifying*, involves learners in making an evaluation of what they have read as a metacognitive process. This step can also include clarification of unknown words, features, concepts or expressions. In step 3, *questioning*, learners form questions related to the text. Through framing questions, learners make judgements about the main idea. This enables them to focus on the content of the text and supports their comprehension. In the fourth step, *summarising*, the discussion centres around identifying the main ideas of the text and explaining why the central points are important, using recalled information. In reciprocal teaching, it is important to explicitly teach the different roles to ensure that learners are confident and competent with the task. For learners with underdeveloped oral language, scaffolding will be required for tasks such as summarising. Other differentiations could include support with generating and asking questions. Items such as sentence starters will also support and enhance the process.

Socratic discussions

The Socratic method is based on the work of the ancient Greek philosopher Socrates. Socratic discussion methods include the use of open-ended questions and a set of reasoning principles to seek a universal understanding (Alexander, 2008; Overholser, 2010). This teaching approach aims to shape children's thinking and engagement in learning through a guided process that encourages self-discovery (Alexander, 2008, p. 92; Calvert & Palmer, 2003).

The Socratic process

The teacher's role is that of an observer or facilitator, but can also include reorienting a discussion if it is going off track or off task.

Before a Socratic discussion can take place, the teacher also needs to model and explicitly cover the importance of turn-taking, eye contact and whole-body listening, to ensure respectful interactions (DET, 2019). An anchor chart noting these factors can be displayed and also used to prompt appropriate behaviours. These could be developed collaboratively with the class during the structured sessions that explore the expectations. Monitors who have specific roles can also use this chart to inform feedback about the session at the conclusion of the discussion (DET, 2019).

To conduct a Socratic discussion, learners are seated in a circle. Unlike in an ordinary classroom discussion, no one person leads the discussion and the participants do not raise their hands to speak. There is also the expectation that all learners will participate. Learners who lack confidence can be encouraged to restate what someone else has said. Learners who dominate may have their responses limited to a set number of contributions (DET, 2019). After a Socratic discussion, learners can reflect on the process and write about the topic covered in the discussion.

Below are some guiding questions that can be used to support a Socratic discussion.

Clarifying questions
- What did you mean by ...?
- Can you explain this point further ...?
- Can you provide an example of ...?

Challenging questions
- Can you come up with a different point of view or perspective?
- Are you assuming anything?

Evidence questions
- What evidence do you have to back this point up?
- Can you provide an example that backs up what you are saying?

Consequential questions
- How would this affect others?
- How would others respond to this?

Text annotation

In a text annotation, learners read a selected text, such as a newspaper report, a diagram, a multimodal or a non-fiction excerpt. The learners make notes or comments from their reading that they would like to raise in the group discussion.

Developing rich discussion skills

To develop rich discussion skills, a list of sentence starters is provided by the teacher to guide learners. Open-ended questions or sentence starters are initially shared and discussed.

Learners can use a prompt as a way of joining the discussion. For example:

- My point of view is …
- What do other people think?
- I disagree with that because …
- I'd like to build on what has been said by adding …
- Can you clarify what you mean by …? (State Government of Victoria, 2019b)

Reflecting upon the discussion could include a self-reflection about the learner's own participation. For example:

- What were my contributions to the group?
- What did I learn about the topic?
- How did the dialogue change my thinking? (State Government of Victoria, 2019b)

Formal talks and speeches

Developing more formal talks or speeches to the class can also be a feature in the later primary years. Care needs to be taken during these events that the teacher is not assessing how well a child can write a speech!

Readers theatre

Readers theatre is an excellent way to help learners develop an understanding of how they can use their voice, intonation, pause and other oral language features to signify different meanings. See Chapters 6 and 8 for more detail.

Accountable talk

Accountable talk refers 'to the type of talk that moves learning forward' and ensures that groups are on task and working towards the desired learning outcomes (DET, 2020a). To achieve this, teachers may need to work hard to establish harmonious relationships using a set of non-negotiable expectations or ground rules. These protocols need to be made explicit to learners, and will support them to 'engage in talk that is accountable and conducive to learning' (DET, 2020a).

Wolf and colleagues (2006) describe three aspects of accountable talk:

1. *Accountability to the learning community* – this means the talk will help others in the group understand and refers to strategies such as paraphrasing, rephrasing, using examples and active listening building.

2. *Accountability to accurate knowledge* – this refers to the use of correct information within a discussion.
3. *Accountability to rigorous thinking* – this promotes logical thinking, reasoning and the ability of learners to explain what they are thinking. Sample ground rules or non-negotiables could be:

   - We will look at the speaker to show we are listening.
   - We will use our facial expressions and body language to show we are listening.
   - We will contribute at least one idea to the group discussion.
   - We will each ask one question during the group discussion.
   - We will build upon what the group members say.
   - We will ask clarifying questions if we are confused.
   - We will thank each other for talk contributions.
   - We will use polite ways to challenge speakers with whom we do not agree.

Explicit modelling of these rules will be important. In addition, the teacher may need to provide scaffolding for those learners who find such situations challenging.

Conclusion

This chapter explained the importance of oral language in becoming literate and how family, culture and society play a part in the process of children developing language skills. The chapter looked at how speaking and listening experiences prior to school impact on children's oracy. We then explored aspects of speaking and listening in the EYLF and the Australian Curriculum: English and the role of oral narrative in Aboriginal and Torres Strait Islander cultures. The consideration of key issues in speaking and listening and the implications for the classroom included key teaching instructional approaches and teaching and learning strategies that foster oracy.

Bringing it together

1. Should oral language be taught independently of other areas of literacy or as a part of the teaching and learning of reading and writing? Why or why not?
2. When working with English as an additional language/dialect (EAL/D) learners, what are some extra considerations required to support oral language development? Where would you find this information in the curriculum?
3. If a child is not reaching the expected milestones of oral language development, what steps could you take to engage further support and specialised information?

Further resources

The Literacy Teaching Toolkit

The Literacy Teaching Toolkit offers ideas and resources to use in teaching programs that are designed to improve outcomes in reading, writing, speaking and listening.

www.education.vic.gov.au/school/teachers/teachingresources/discipline/english/literacy/Pages/default.aspx

First Steps – Speaking and Listening Map of Development

This resource is a valuable guide on the process of oral language development of children.

http://det.wa.edu.au/stepsresources/detcms/navigation/first-steps-literacy

First Steps – Speaking and Listening Resource Book

The *First Steps – Speaking and Listening Resource Book* supports teachers to design lessons for explicit teaching of oral language.

http://det.wa.edu.au/stepsresources/detcms/navigation/first-steps-literacy

Language and Literacy Development in Early Childhood

This book provides pre-service and in-service teachers with an integrated approach to language and literacy learning in early childhood.

Ewing, R., Callow, J. & Rushton, K. (2016). *Language and Literacy Development in Early Childhood*. Cambridge University Press.

References

Alexander, R. (2008). Culture, dialogue and learning: notes on an emerging pedagogy. In N. Mercer & S. Hodgkinson (Eds.), *Exploring Talk in School* (pp. 91–114). Sage Publications.

Australian Bureau of Statistics (ABS). (2017). 2016 Census: Multicultural. Census reveals a fast changing, culturally diverse nation. www.abs.gov.au/ausstats/abs@.nsf/lookup/media%20release3

Australian Curriculum, Assessment and Reporting Authority (ACARA). (n.d.). English: Sequence of achievement, F–6. https://docs.acara.edu.au/resources/English_Sequence_of_achievement.pdf

—— (2009). *The Shape of the Australian Curriculum: Version 2.0*. ACARA. https://docs.acara.edu.au/resources/Shape_of_the_Australian_Curriculum.pdf

—— (2020). *National Literacy Learning Progression. Version 3.0*. www.lpofai.edu.au/media/kw2lslug/national-literacy-learning-progression-v3-for-publication.pdf

Bernstein, B. (1971). On the classification and framing of educational knowledge. *Knowledge and Control*, 3(1), 245–270.

—— (1990). *The Structuring of Pedagogic Discourse: Class, Codes & Control, Volume IV*. Routledge.

Bronfenbrenner, U. (1981). *The Ecology of Human Development: Experiments by Nature and Design*. Harvard University Press.

Calvert, P. & Palmer, C. (2003). Application of the cognitive therapy model to initial crisis assessment. *International Journal of Mental Health Nursing*, 12, 30–38.

Cambourne, B. & Crouch, D. (2018). Cambourne's conditions of learning. www.cambournesconditionsoflearning.com.au/conditions-of-learning-blog-spo

Campbell, V. (2013). Playing with storytelling. In R. Ewing (Ed.), *The Creative Arts in the Lives of Young Children*. Australian Council of Educational Research.

Carroll, L. (1871). Jabberwocky. www.poetryfoundation.org/poems/42916/jabberwocky

Dennaoui, K., Nicholls, R.J., O'Connor, M., Tarasuik, J., Kvalsvig, A., & Goldfeld, S. (2016). The English proficiency and academic language skills of Australian bilingual children during the primary school years. *International Journal of Speech-Language Pathology*, 18(2), 157–165.

Department of Education, Employment and Workplace Relations (DEEWR). (2009). *Belonging, Being & Becoming – The Early Years Learning Framework for Australia*. https://docs.education.gov.au/documents/belonging-being-becoming-early-years-learning-framework-australia

Department of Education and Training (DET). (n.d.). Professional practice. Using high impact teaching strategies to support literacy learning. Professional practice note 9. Victoria State Government. www.education.vic.gov.au/Documents/school/teachers/teachingresources/practice/Professional_Practice_Note_9_HITS.pdf

—— (2019). Diagnostic Assessment Tools in English. Victoria State Government. www.education.vic.gov.au/school/teachers/teachingresources/discipline/english/Pages/date.aspx

—— (2020a). Literacy teaching toolkit: accountable talk. Victoria State Government. www.education.vic.gov.au/school/teachers/teachingresources/discipline/english/literacy/speakinglistening/Pages/teachingpracaccountable.aspx

—— (2020b). Literacy teaching toolkit: phonological awareness. Victoria State Government. www.education.vic.gov.au/school/teachers/teachingresources/discipline/english/literacy/speakinglistening/Pages/litfocusphonological.aspx

Egan, K. (1997). *The Educated Mind*. Chicago University Press.

Ewing, R. (2018). *Exploding Some of the Myths about Learning to Read*. NSW Teachers Federation.

—— (2020). The role of oral language in literacy development. *Practical Literacy*, 25(3), 4–6.

Ewing, R., Callow, J., & Rushton, K. (2016). *Language and Literacy Development in Early Childhood*. Cambridge University Press.

Fox, C. (1993). *At the Very Edge of the Forest: The Influence of Literature on Stories*. Cassell.

Halliday, M.A.K. (2004 [1975]). Learning how to mean. In J. Webster (Ed.), *The Language of Early Childhood (The Collected Works of M.A.K. Halliday, Volume 4.)* (pp. 28–59). Continuum.

—— (2004 [1980]). Three aspects of children's language development: learning language, learning through language, learning about language. In J. Webster (Ed.), *The Language of Early Childhood (The Collected Works of M.A.K. Halliday, Volume 4.)* (pp. 308–326). Continuum.

—— (2016). Language, learning and 'educational knowledge'. In M.A.K. Halliday & J.J. Webster (Eds.), *Aspects of Language and Learning* (pp. 1–15). Springer.

Hattie, J. (2014). *Visible Learning for Teachers: Maximizing Impact on Learning*. Routledge.

Hill, R., Pert, P.L., Maclean, K., Bock, E., Freeman, M., Talbot, L., ... & AIATSIS (2012). Australian Institute of Aboriginal and Torres Strait Islander Studies (AIATSIS) National Native Title Conference, Townsville, 4–6 June.

Hornsby, D. & Wilson, L. (2014). Early literacy is more than phonics. *Practically Primary*, 19(3), 12–15.

Hughes, T. (1968). *The Iron Man*. Faber and Faber.

Livo, N. & Rietz, S. (1986). *Storytelling. Process and Practice*. Libraries Unlimited.

Lowe, K. (2002). *What's the Story? Making Meaning in Primary Classrooms*. Primary English Teaching Association Australia (PETAA).

MacLean, M. & Wason-Ellam, L. (2006). *When Aboriginal and Métis Teachers Use Storytelling as an Instructional Practice. A Grant Report to the Aboriginal Education Research Network, Saskatchewan Learning*. Aboriginal Education Research Network.

Mills, K.A., Sunderland, N., & Davis-Warra, J. (2013). Yarning circles in the literacy classroom. *The Reading Teacher*, 67(4), 285–289.

NSW Government. (2021). Literacy and numeracy. Talk moves. www.education.nsw.gov.au/teaching-and-learning/curriculum/literacy-and-numeracy/teaching-and-learning-resources/numeracy/talk-moves

Overholser, J.C. (2010). Psychotherapy according to the Socratic method: integrating ancient philosophy with contemporary cognitive therapy. *Journal of Cognitive Psychotherapy*, 24, 354–363.

Painter, C. (2006).Preparing for school: developing a semantic style for educational knowledge. Christie, F. (Ed.), *Pedagogy and the Shaping of Consciousness*. Continuum.

Paley, V. (1995). *Kwanzaa and Me: A Teacher's Story*. Harvard University Press.

Palincsar, A.S. & Brown, A.L. (Spring, 1984). Reciprocal teaching of comprehension-fostering and comprehension-monitoring activities. *Cognition and Instruction*, 1(2), 117–175.

Pilten, G. (2016). The evaluation of effectiveness of reciprocal teaching strategies on comprehension of expository texts. *Journal of Education and Training Studies*, 4(10), 232–247.

Queensland Studies Authority. (2010). Dialogue Circles. *Aboriginal and Torres Strait Islander Perspectives – Resources*. www.qcaa.qld.edu.au/downloads/approach2/indigenous_res_dialogue_circ.pdf

Roberts, D. (2020). Using the National Literacy Learning Progression to support student growth. *Practical Literacy*, *25*(1), 38+.

Rogoff, B., Paradise, R., Arauz, R.M., Correa-Chávez, M., & Angelillo, C. (2003). Firsthand learning through intent participation. *Annual Review of Psychology*, 54, 175–203.

Romeo, R., Leonard, J., & Robinson, S. (2018). Beyond the 30-million-word gap: children's conversational exposure is associated with language-related brain function. *Psychological Science*, 29(5), i700–i710.

Saxton, J., Miller, C., Laidlaw, L., & O'Mara, J. (2018). *Asking Better Questions: Teaching and Learning for a Changing World* (3rd edn). Pembroke.

State Government of Victoria. (2019a). High Impact Teaching Strategies (HITS). www.education.vic.gov.au/school/teachers/teachingresources/practice/improve/Pages/hits.aspx

—— (2019b). Socratic discussions. www.education.vic.gov.au/school/teachers/teachingresources/discipline/english/literacy/speakinglistening/Pages/examplesocratic.aspx

Verdon, S., Mackenzie, N., McLeod, S., Davidson, C., Masso, S., Verdon, L., & Edwards-Groves, C. (2018). *Assessment of Children as Effective Communicators in Early Childhood Education and Care: A Literature Review*. Victorian Curriculum and Assessment Authority.

Victorian Curriculum and Assessment Authority (VCAA). (2021). Victorian Curriculum Foundation–10. English. VCAA. https://victoriancurriculum.vcaa.vic.edu.au/english/english/curriculum/f-10

Vygotsky, L.S. (1978). Socio-cultural theory. *Mind in Society*, 6, 52–8.

—— (2004). Imagination and creativity in childhood. *Journal of Russian & East European Psychology*, 42(1), 7–97.

Wells, G. (1986). *The Meaning Makers*. Heinemann.

—— (2009). *The Meaning Makers* (2nd edn). Multilingual Matters.

Wolf, M.K., Crosson, A.C., & Resnick, L.B. (2006). *Accountable Talk in Reading Comprehension Instruction. CSE Technical Report 670*. National Center for Research on Evaluation, Standards, and Student Testing (CRESST). https://files.eric.ed.gov/fulltext/ED492865.pdf

Yunkaporta, T. (2012). *8 Ways Aboriginal Pedagogy from Western NSW*. NSW Department of Education and Training.

CHAPTER 5

Learning to be 'literate'
Exploring contexts, complexities and possibilities for teaching about text

Rachel Burke

ANTICIPATED LEARNING OUTCOMES

After working through this chapter, it is anticipated you will be able to:

- reflect on connections between theories and practices in education
- engage with a preliminary exploration of ideas about how we become literate and consider ways in which ideas about literacies development may inform teaching
- contemplate differential impacts of approaches to literacies education
- consider some complexities and possibilities of education that seek to value different ways with language and support access to powerful literate practices.

Introduction

In Chapter 1, we considered some fundamental concepts regarding literacies and text, and noted how these ideas vary according to cultural context and social, technological and political changes. We explored how, in some cultural contexts, definitions of literacy have shifted from being predominantly associated with reading and writing, to notions of 'literacies' or 'multiliteracies' in the plural, encompassing a broader range of text types, modalities and communicative practices. In the same way that understandings of what it means to be literate vary according to context and are affected by social change, ideas about how we learn to be literate are also fluid and contested. As we emphasise throughout this book, authentic engagement with text – whether it be oral, visual, print, digital, kinaesthetic or a combination of modes – is an active endeavour involving complex and sophisticated cognitive, social and cultural resources. As such, there are many different ideas about how we attain the necessary expertise to impactfully engage with and create text. Further, these ideas are shaped by our own experiences, social and cultural perspectives, and understandings of literate practice.

This chapter explores some of the possibilities and complexities of recognising the important communicative repertoires and resources that learners bring to the classroom, while supporting them to develop expertise in the literate practices that are embedded within schooling and other contexts. An understanding of some of the perspectives, ideas and factors that may impact on literacies learning allows teachers to engage meaningfully with different options for literacies instruction and make informed decisions about their own teaching approaches. However, it is important to remember that there is no one way to think about literacies education and that different contexts may foreground different approaches (Freebody, 2007; Luke, 2000). Even within particular social and cultural contexts, there may be different ideas about how we gain literate expertise, and these ideas may also continue to be affected by new research into human cognition and learning and the arrival of different platforms for communication. As Lo Bianco (2013) advises, we need to take into account the unique complexities of the various 'communication ecologies' that characterise each learning environment, including the structures, expectations and values associated with education, and learners' different resources, strengths and needs.

In considering some of the possibilities and complexities of literacies learning, this chapter also refers to some related theories and approaches. As with many theories, ideas about how we learn to be literate will be interpreted and applied in a variety of ways, and scholar-practitioners may take up modified positions on key arguments or shape teaching approaches across a range of theoretical paradigms. Approaches to literacies education may therefore be eclectic in ideas and understandings, and teachers are encouraged to use this chapter as a springboard for further exploration about these and other theories, approaches and issues.

This discussion is intended to be read in connection with the other chapters of the book, which provide ideas about potential ways to implement different approaches to classroom instruction. Finally, an important reminder is that each approach to literacies learning may impact upon different groups of learners in contrasting ways, depending on social, cultural, historical and contemporary factors (Cazden, 1992; Cope & Kalantzis, 2015; Delpit, 1992, 2006). Accordingly, the chapter emphasises the requirement to maintain professional reflexivity and dialogic approaches to literacies learning. Reflexivity and dialogue with colleagues, learners, families and community members help ensure classroom practices are informed by the understandings and ideas about literacies that are present in the broader linguistic environments in which we live and work.

Connecting theory with practice

Praxis: the meeting point of theory and practice, in which action is informed by theoretical understandings and theoretical understandings are refined and shaped by practice-based evidence.

Everitt (2020) suggests, '**Praxis** is when theory, dialogue, action, and reflection are inextricably linked and mutually inform one another' (p. 102). A theory may be thought of as a carefully considered, evidence-based understanding of how something works. In this chapter, as we explore some of the possibilities and key issues regarding literacies learning, we also consider some of the theories or ideas about how we become literate. These theories may serve two main purposes: to provide evidence-based explanations for what we observe; and to help us plan for how best to assist learners' literacies development. However, it is also important to acknowledge that while theories are based in systematic research and offer us frameworks for planning to assist learners to engage with and learn about literate practices, theories are also hypotheses. Ideas regarding how we develop literacies continue to change, as do the text types and communicative platforms we use in day-to-day life and the research and ideas that may inform our understandings.

It is also important to acknowledge that while theoretical frameworks inform teaching practice, teaching practice, in turn, informs the evolution and refinement of theoretical understandings (Freebody, 2007). This co-constitutive relationship is articulated by Elias and Merriam (1980), who explain: 'Theory without practice leads to an empty idealism, and action without philosophical reflection leads to mindless activism' (p. 4). As you consider some of the possibilities and complexities of literacies learning that are discussed in this chapter, think about how these ideas connect with your own experiences, how they align with the particular curriculum and learning outcomes in an educational context that may be familiar to you, and the connections between these ideas and the literate practices and approaches to teaching and learning that are presented throughout the book.

REFLECTION

Before commencing a discussion of some of the possibilities of literacies learning, it is important to reflect on your present understandings and beliefs. These ideas and values are instrumental in shaping your professional practice. For example, the chapters in this book, while seeking to take a representative approach to the key issues in the field, will necessarily reflect the authors' understandings and experiences of literacies. It is therefore useful for educators to be aware of their own perspectives and ideas as they reflect on various approaches to literacies learning.

1. How do you think we learn to be 'literate'? Revisit the literate practices you described in the mind map reflection task in Chapter 1, and consider which experiences were important to you in developing these capacities.

- Which (if any) of these learning experiences occurred in a classroom or formal learning context and which (if any) occurred outside of school?
- Do you think the necessary learning experiences vary according to the type of literate practices being developed? For example, are different forms of support or input required when gaining proficiency in aspects of digital literacy compared with the experiences required for learning about print or visual texts?

2. Think of a lesson or learning experience that you observed or participated in that you would describe as an example of effective literacies teaching and learning. If you cannot think of a lesson or experience to describe, you might choose a lesson from the Australian Institute for Teaching and School Leadership (AITSL) practice illustrations of the teaching standards (www.aitsl.edu.au/teach/standards):
   - Explain, using whatever mode you prefer (e.g. images, writing or speaking), why you feel this was an effective literacies learning experience. For example, you might reflect on any teaching practices, lesson content or ways of engaging with text that you consider important to facilitating learning.
   - Now consider any aspects of the lesson or learning experience that you might modify for teaching in another context.
   - Finally, consider how your opinions regarding this lesson or learning experience reflect your beliefs about literacies learning.

A preliminary exploration of ideas regarding literacies development

During the twentieth century, a variety of ideas about the development of literate practice emerged, each informed by particular understandings of learning and literacies in the early years. The ideas discussed here illustrate some of the key factors that may be considered when formulating concepts of how we become literate, including biological and cognitive aspects, and environmental and sociocultural influences. Each of these ideas about how we learn to be literate involves certain views and expectations about the nature of literate practice, the roles and resources of learners and teachers, and the ultimate goals and outcomes of literacies instruction. Subsets, variations and alternative approaches to these theories are also considered in other chapters of the book when exploring ideas about how we become proficient in different modalities of communication. It will be helpful to reflect on the discussion of the curriculum context for literacies education in Australia in Chapter 2, to consider the historical contexts in which these ideas first came to prominence. Finally, it is useful to remember that, while the different ways of thinking about how we learn to be literate are described separately here for clarity, some of these ideas and approaches intersect, and practice may be informed by multiple perspectives.

In the early to mid-twentieth century, **maturational theories** of child development became prominent, with psychologist and paediatrician Arnold Gesell's research representing some of the earliest published, large-scale, systematic studies of children's developmental phases

Maturational theories: argue that children need to reach the required level of maturity before commencing reading and writing instruction (Crain, 2010; Oliveira, 2018).

(Fellowes & Oakley, 2014; Oliveira, 2018). This research investigated the biological foundations for developmental milestones. It suggested that, while the environment impacts upon development, biological factors are key and, in most circumstances, all children will progress through the same phases of development, although the pace of the progression might vary between children (Crain, 2010; Oliveira, 2018). It was thought that, 'Any type of instruction that is introduced prematurely would cause the children to be disillusioned and frustrated' (Saracho, 2017, p. 300). Based on this idea, as with other aspects of development, literacy – which was defined as reading and writing printed text – was thought to be something that children would not be ready to undertake until they reached the required level of maturity (Saracho, 2017).

Developmental theories: suggest children's readiness to engage in reading and writing can be accelerated by 'pre-reading' activities (Barratt-Pugh & Rohl, 2001; Fellowes & Oakley, 2014).

Developmental theories in literacies learning were informed by the work of founding educational psychologists such as Edward Thorndike and suggested that, while children's readiness for reading and writing instruction depended on biological maturity, learning experiences can make a difference in accelerating this readiness (Barratt-Pugh & Rohl, 2001; Fellowes & Oakley, 2014). Some proponents of developmental approaches to literacies learning suggested that readiness to read and write could be encouraged through particular 'pre-reading' activities, described by Barratt-Pugh (in Barratt-Pugh & Rohl, 2001) as 'highly structured, sequentially organised, skills-based drills in the form of work books' (p. 2). Fellowes and Oakley (2014) also note that 'perceptual-motor activities' were introduced 'to prepare children for tracking print with their eyes', and tasks associated with the 'recognition and discrimination of shapes, some of which were letter-like' were also used (p. 6). Here, emphasis on the various cognitive aspects of literate practice is evident. As was typical with approaches to literacies instruction in many contexts at this time, reading and writing 'were seen as separate skills taught in isolation through systematic direct instruction' (Barratt-Pugh, in Barratt-Pugh & Rohl, 2001, p. 2).

Emergent literacy: an approach that recognises the importance of children's drawing, talking, singing, playing and engaging with images and print, and the connection between these and other forms of communicative practice, such as reading and writing (Rohde, 2015; Strickland, 1990).

The **emergent literacy** perspective became prominent in the 1960s and 1970s, with developmental and child psychologist and educator Marie Clay's (1982) landmark research regarding children's early engagement with literate practices (Fellowes & Oakley, 2014). Clay coined the term 'emergent literacy' to describe the literate knowledge that children gain by interacting with their environment through talking, drawing, singing, playing and engaging with images and print (Rohde, 2015; Strickland, 1990). In emergent literacy, these practices are considered important precursors to children's learning to engage in other literate practices, such as reading and writing (Barratt-Pugh, in Barratt-Pugh & Rohl, 2001; Fellowes & Oakley, 2014; Mielonen & Paterson, 2009; Saracho, 2017). Strickland (1990) explains that this perspective contrasted with other understandings of literacies learning in which 'Children were considered literate only after their reading and writing began to approximate adult models' (p. 20).

Emergent literacy is informed by the work of physician and educator Maria Montessori, psychologist Jean Piaget and sociologist Lev Vygotsky (1978), who suggested that children's learning is impacted upon by interactions with their environment and through play (Mielonen & Paterson, 2009). These ideas are evident in emergent literacy perspectives that emphasise 'the ongoing development of skill in reading and writing' and 'participation in literacy activities that are meaningful and functional from the child's point of view'

(Mielonen & Paterson, 2009, p. 20). Understandings of the boundaries between 'emergent' and 'conventional' literacies vary, with some scholars suggesting there is no one point at which children transition from emergent to 'real' engagement with text, and that literacies learning should be considered a lifelong endeavour (Alexander, 2005; Fellowes & Oakley, 2014; Neuman & Roskos, 1998). As Whitehead (2007) suggests, this view considers that 'Young children's first investigations of print and their first attempts to use written symbols are ... the earliest stages of literacy' (p. 60).

Within these ideas about how we learn to be literate, several different perspectives may be identified. These perspectives may be understood to be related to what Emmitt and colleagues (2014) describe as 'the deep structure of language (that is, the underlying meaning embodied in language) or the surface structure (that is, the form that language takes: the sounds or letters and words used)' (p. 10). For clarity, these perspectives will be discussed separately; however, as will be considered later, in practice, the boundaries between these perspectives are often far less defined (Emmitt et al., 2014; Stanovich, 1980).

Some approaches to understanding literate practice place greatest emphasis on the cognitive capacities required to engage with text, such as knowledge of relationships between letters and sounds, ability to identify the grammatical parts of speech, and understanding of **metalanguage**. These aspects of literate practice relate to the form that the language takes, although, as parts of language, they are also related to engagement with meaning. Approaches to literacies learning that emphasise cognitive capacities may feature a predominantly '**bottom-up approach**' to engaging with text. Here, the individual units of meaning, such as letters, characters, symbols or sounds, are the initial focus of engagement, followed by words, sentences and paragraphs.

In some contexts, a focus on the cognitive capacities and skills involved in textual practice characterised traditional approaches to literacies instruction, such as those evident in the early years of the massification of schooling, when children were first organised into learning streams based on age and standardised curriculum and assessment measures were introduced (Deschenes et al., 2001; Gao, 2015; Lotherington, 2011). Literacies education in some of these contexts emphasised imitation, practice and drills. On the continuum between teacher-centred and learner-centred instruction, they tended to be associated with teacher-centred approaches, although, as emphasised throughout this book, approaches to teaching and learning may be implemented in varied ways across different learning contexts. Importantly, while these approaches might be associated with aspects of traditional teaching and learning in some settings, they continue to be foregrounded in different ways in many contemporary contexts of literacies instruction.

Understandings of literacies learning that emphasise the importance of environmental factors tend to prioritise meaning-based engagement with text (Barratt-Pugh, in Barratt-Pugh & Rohl, 2001; Fellowes & Oakley, 2014). These perspectives relate to what Emmitt and colleagues (2014) refer to as 'the underlying meaning embodied in language' (p. 10). For instance, 'Whole Language' approaches to instruction, which Fellowes and Oakley (2014) identify as being informed by the emergent understanding of literacies development, 'is an approach to learning that sees language as a whole entity', suggesting that 'writing, speaking, reading, and listening should be integrated when learned' (Patzelt, 1995, p. 1). Some scholars

Metalanguage: the language we use to communicate about language. Examples of metalanguage include 'noun', 'conjunction' and 'metaphor'. It is important to ensure all learners have the opportunity to develop metalanguage for different modalities (Kress, 2003; Unsworth, 2006) – for example, the words 'icon' and 'symbol' may be used to discuss visual text.

Bottom-up approach: describes engagements with text that emphasise working from the individual components of language (e.g. sounds, letters or characters, words, and sentences) up to the overall meaning.

suggest that this focus on meaning-based engagement and integrative use of language is intended to reflect the environments in which we acquire our first language(s) – that is, the language(s) we are exposed to from birth or in early childhood (Patzelt, 1995). Patzelt (1995) suggests that in the 'Whole Language' approach, 'learning is built upon the real experiences and background knowledge of the learner' (p. 1), and that the main principle is that 'The learner should experience language wholly before examining its components (Brockman, 1994)' (p. 1).

Perspectives that emphasise meaning-based engagement with literate practice are often associated with a '**top-down approach**', in which engagement with text commences at the level of overall meaning. In some contexts, 'Whole Language' and 'process' approaches to writing instruction emerged at a similar time (Barratt-Pugh, in Barratt-Pugh & Rohl, 2001). In process approaches to writing instruction, children are encouraged to take ownership of their literate practices, 'making decisions about what to write and how to spell in conjunction with conferences with the teacher' (Barratt-Pugh, in Barratt-Pugh & Rohl, 2001, p. 3). In these approaches, 'children were thought to learn to write through writing (Graves 1983)' (p. 3). Here, particular expectations about the roles of learners and teachers may be identified.

Importantly, in practice, the use of 'top-down' and 'bottom-up' approaches to text may be more nuanced than these distinctions might suggest. Some scholars propose that engaging with text often involves concurrent use of top-down and bottom-up approaches (see Newman, in Luria et al., 2005; Stanovich, 1980), and some teachers emphasise these different orientations to text at different times within a lesson, depending on the purpose and context (Newman, in Luria et al., 2005). In fact, Stanovich (1980) identifies research that suggests a 'third class of theories is formed by those models that posit neither a strictly bottom-up nor strictly top-down processing, but instead assume that a pattern is synthesised based on information provided *simultaneously* from several knowledge sources' (p. 35). As Emmitt and colleagues (2014) assert: 'language is more than any one dimension or perspective. All aspects are interrelated … ' (p. 10).

> **Top-down approach:** describes engagements with text that emphasise working from the overall meaning of text down to the individual components of language, such as sentences, words, sounds, characters or letters.

REFLECTION

To reflect on the 'top-down', 'bottom-up' and 'neither a strictly bottom-up nor top-down' (Stanovich, 1980, p. 35) approaches to engaging with text, think about the literacies learning lesson or experience that you described in the first reflection task in this chapter. Can you identify either top-down or bottom-up approaches – or both – in this learning experience or lesson? To help guide your thinking, consider the following questions:

1. Were there any examples of explicit focus on the individual components of language, such as words, sounds or aspects of punctuation; or, if your chosen learning experience centres on another modality, was there focus on the individual components that make up this form of communication?

2. Were there any examples of meaning-focused engagement with text, such as discussing its purpose and main ideas and/or incorporating opportunities for learners to make connections with background knowledge and experiences?

3. If both top-down and bottom-up forms of engagement with text were evident, was there greater overall emphasis on one approach? For example, was the learning experience framed by communication about overall meaning with specific intervals that focused on individual components? Or was the learning experience mostly focused on individual forms, with some opportunities for the exploration of a text's overall meaning?

4. Is there one of these approaches (top-down or bottom-up or both) that you think may be more beneficial as an orientation to engaging with text in the classroom? If so, what factors have you considered when determining your response to this question, and how might your own learning experiences contribute to your opinion?

Sociocultural approaches: multiliteracies and new literacy studies

In Chapter 1, we explored how the later stages of the twentieth century witnessed growing interest in the **sociocultural** nature of literate practice. The New London Group's notion of multiliteracies – which expanded the understanding of literate practice beyond reading and writing to engage with other modalities, including visual, digital and oral texts – and the approaches embedded within New Literacy Studies, emphasised the importance of the contexts in which communication occurs (Barton, 2001; Cope & Kalantzis, 2009; Kress, 2003; New London Group, 1996; Unsworth, 2006). Key scholar-practitioners working in languages, literacies, cultural and feminist studies, and critical and transformative pedagogies explored ways in which literate practices are related to and implicated in issues of power, access and representation (New London Group, 1996; see also Chapter 1). New Literacy Studies and multiliterate perspectives emphasised the need to focus on critical engagement with the diversified forms of literate practice that were occurring at the end of the twentieth century due to increased global mobility and rapidly changing digital platforms for communication (Kress, 2003; New London Group, 1996).

Sociocultural: approaches to literacies that emphasise the importance of the contexts in which texts are produced and interpreted, engage with texts communicated across a range of modalities and platforms, and suggest that literate practices both reflect and shape social and cultural values.

Sociocultural approaches to literacies education emphasise the need to support learners to develop a diverse range of cognitive, social and cultural repertoires for engaging with text in increasingly complex communicative contexts and modalities. These repertoires are represented in frameworks such as the four resources, or roles, of the reader (Freebody & Luke, 1990), which is discussed further in Chapter 6. The four resources framework has been modified for other forms of literate engagement, including critical numeracy (Watson, 2009) and visual (Serafini, 2012) and digital modalities (Hinrichsen & Coombs, 2013). Kalantzis and Cope (in May & Hornberger, 2008) advise: 'The Multiliteracies framework aims to supplement – not critique or negate – the various existing teaching practices', suggesting that when the four main instructional traditions included in this framework are used strategically, 'each is at least softened, and at best transformed by the others' (p. 207). The four approaches to teaching and learning embedded within the multiliteracies framework are:

- *situated practice* in immersive, text-rich contexts, where learners apply their background knowledge to engage meaningfully with literate practices
- *overt instruction*, where explicit attention to the forms and purposes of text assist learners to develop metalanguage and conscious knowledge of literate practice

- *critical framing*, in which learners analyse constructions, representations, tensions and gaps in text and literate practices
- *transformed practice*, in which learners apply what they have learnt to other contexts (Kalantzis & Cope, in May & Hornberger, 2008).

REFLECTION

In their presentation 'Multiliteracies pedagogy: learning by design' (www.youtube.com/watch?v=5kDoPllbUvQ), Mary Kalantzis and Bill Cope discuss the four main components of multiliterate pedagogies: situated practice, overt instruction, critical framing and transformed practice.

1. Select one of the four main instructional approaches featured in the multiliteracies pedagogy (situated practice, overt instruction, critical framing and transformed practice) and think about:
   - strategic uses of this approach – for example, is this approach suited to providing a meaningful communicative environment for learners, assisting learners to develop metalanguage (language for talking about language) and conscious knowledge of individual aspects of literate practice, or facilitating learner reflection on the social and cultural situatedness of text? Remember that different instructional approaches may be used for various purposes.
   - the roles of the learners and teachers that tend to characterise this approach – for example, does this form of instruction usually feature learner-centred or teacher-centred practice?
   - ways in which this approach may have different impacts on different learner groups depending on their respective 'funds of knowledge' (Moll et al., 1992) or cultural expectations and ideas about literacies and learning.
2. As you reflect on their presentation, also consider why Kalantzis and Cope recommend that teachers should take a range of approaches and not become fixed on one way of instruction. How do you think this advice might assist you to be a responsive, flexible and multidimensional teacher?

In seeking to explore teaching approaches that help learners to expand the repertoires required for critical engagement with text, sociocultural approaches to literacies learning emphasise the importance of forging connections between learners' existing literate repertoires and the textual practices foregrounded in schooling (Gee, 2012). Many of these ideas originate in the work of scholar-practitioners such as Paulo Freire (2007), who criticised 'banking approaches' to learning that construct the teacher as the expert who is responsible for transferring information to novice learners. A major premise of sociocultural ideas is that all learners have 'funds of knowledge' (Moll et al., 1992) that they bring to the classroom, and that these resources may be more or less aligned with the literate practices foregrounded within education (Cazden, 1988; Heath, 1983; Luke, 1994). Evident here are connections with Pierre Bourdieu's (1991) concept of linguistic capital, a form of cultural capital that may offer power to speakers who share the ways with language that are privileged in powerful institutions such as schools.

Crucially, proponents of sociocultural approaches to literacies learning are interested in 'how people, from childhood to adulthood, learn to leverage new school-based (and other public sphere) social languages – in speech, writing, and action – to participate in, and eventually critique and transform, specific sociocultural practices' (Gee, 1999, p. 371). In this way, Barratt-Pugh (in Barratt-Pugh & Rohl, 2001) suggests that sociocultural perspectives of literacies learning 'examine the way patterns of inequality are constructed and maintained, and explore[s] ways of teaching literacy which expose and challenge this inequality, as part of children's developing literacy competence' (p. 4).

The four resources of the reader

Refer to the four resources of the reader framework (Freebody & Luke, 1990). How are some of the main premises of sociocultural understandings of literate practice evident in this framework? For example, consider the following questions:

- Which aspects of the framework are focused on assisting learners to engage with meaning in the text by activating background knowledge of similar text types?
- Which aspects of the framework may facilitate critical engagement with text, in terms of asking questions about gaps, silences and representations?
- Which roles or resources relate to the need to 'decode' and 'encode' text when interpreting and creating meaning?

You might prefer to consider these questions in relation to one of the adaptations of the framework, such as Serafini's work with visual literacy (Serafini, 2012), Hinrichsen and Coombs' (2013) adaptation for digital engagement or Watson's (2009) version for critical numeracy. Watson's adaptation can be found on the Tasmanian Department of Education website (www.tas-education.org/numeracy/critical_numeracy/critical_numeracy.htm).

Curriculum mapping task

In order to reflect on how ideas about literacies learning may impact upon contemporary approaches to instruction, refer to a curriculum that is familiar to you (e.g. the Australian Curriculum, or your state or territory curriculum) and map selected content descriptors or learner outcomes according to the various repertoires that are emphasised in different understandings of how we learn to be literate. For example, while undertaking this task, consider the following questions:

- Are there aspects of the cognitive and social components of literate practices evident in the content descriptors?
- Are there any outcomes that relate to learning about the components of communication, such as parts of language?
- Are there any outcomes that are linked to understanding how texts are shaped according to the contexts in which they are used?

Exploring complexities of literacies teaching: issues of access and inclusion

As discussed throughout this book, literate practices are complex, variable and ever-changing, and teachers are required to implement a range of teaching approaches to meet different purposes and requirements (Cope & Kalantzis, 2015). The importance of responsive instructional approaches to literacies gained visibility through research conducted by scholars such as Shirley Brice Heath (1982), a linguistic anthropologist who undertook a longitudinal study of 300 families from various backgrounds living in working-class communities in the United States. In her research, Heath (1982) identified the complex and established language and literate practices occurring in these homes, and the different ways of apprenticing new family members into these practices. In her paper 'What no bedtime story means: narrative skills at home and school', Heath (1982) provides a powerful overview of the ways in which each family's practices regarding literacies and language aligned or contrasted with the expectations of formal schooling.

Heath's (1982) research explored the impact of these (mis)alignments on children's educational experiences and life opportunities, investigating core patterns of relative advantage and exclusion, and representing one of the earliest studies to highlight how particular groups of learners, such as those from First Nations, migrant, refugee and particular socioeconomic backgrounds, may experience disconnects between home and school literacies. Heath (1982) advises:

> In many cases, their countries and cultures told stories orally and did not rely on written literature dedicated to children. Their patterns of respect for the authority of elders often had little tolerance for talking with their children over books and allowing children conversational time in the presence of adults. (p. 18)

Further, Heath's (1982) research identified how children's communicative behaviours in the classroom were frequently misinterpreted by educators: 'Teachers often interpreted silence from immigrant children as ignorance or resistance' (pp. 18–19). Importantly, this research also identified the transitions in home literate practices that occurred due to urbanised lifestyles and increased employment in manufacturing and service-based work. These lifestyle changes prevented parents and families from having the time to engage in the literate practices that would usually feature in their communicative cultures, with significant implications for children's literacies development and engagement in family and community practices.

Growing evidence of the differential experiences of learner groups highlighted in research by Cazden (1992), Cope and Kalantzis (2009), Delpit (1988, 1992), Heath (1982) and others is indicative of the complexities – and possibilities – of literacies instruction. Lisa Delpit (1988) identifies the need to challenge approaches to literacies learning that assume knowledge of what she describes as 'the culture of power' (p. 280). In an interview about these issues, Delpit (in Teale, 1991) explains:

> Often when we are talking, we leave a lot to the listener to fill in. The more similar the listeners are, the easier it is for that communication to take place. But when you're

talking across cultures, people have different sets of understandings, and you often can't get across your meaning unless you are able to be very explicit. Teaching children who are not a part of the culture of power in a school setting which is part of the culture of power is teaching across cultures. So it is often necessary to be explicit both with what you're trying to communicate and why that information is important to the task at hand. (p. 541)

To treat the forms of literate practice that are privileged in schooling as 'normal', unproblematic or taken-for-granted may inadvertently imply a uniformity of communicative resources among learners that denies the diversity and richness of literate practices across different contexts and cultures (Cazden, 1993). Cazden (1993) advises that treating text types as 'taken-for-granted' with learners whose home and community literate practices may contrast with those foregrounded in schooling, may also 'run the risk of "naturalizing" the new ways, and implying that the learner's previous actions are illogical, stupid, or at least just plain wrong' (pp. 22–23). For all learners, engaging critically with text may provide important opportunities for reflecting on ways that textual expectations vary according to context, therefore assisting with the development of capacities for adapting to new text types and modalities. Cazden (1993) suggests that teachers:

need to discuss, critically, both the old and the new [types of literate practices and texts], and the differences of situational appropriateness of language forms, and often of power relationships among the people who use them. That requires some form of telling – or better, of talking about. This is one example of critical literacy. (pp. 22–23)

REFLECTION

1. Consider potential strategies for supporting learners to explore how text types and features vary according to context. For example, do you think comparing two different texts with the same purpose (e.g. to instruct), but with different levels of formality, types of language or use of modes, might be helpful?
2. What strategic questions or learning tasks might you use to assist learners to compare the various textual features and expectations?
3. Which aspects of these literate understandings relate to 'the deep structure of language (that is, the underlying meaning embodied in language)' and which understandings relate to the 'surface structure (that is, the form that language takes: the sounds or letters and words used)' (Emmitt et al., 2014, p. 10)? Think about how these aspects of language connect to communicate meaning.
4. How do these literate understandings relate to learner outcomes associated with a curriculum that you know, such as the Australian Curriculum, or your state or territory curriculum?

To help you reflect on ways of problematising text, access and read through the lesson plan 'Reading and analyzing multigenre texts', available on the ReadWriteThink website (www .readwritethink.org/search?s=Reading+and+analyzing+multigenre+texts).

As emphasised throughout this book, the literate forms featured in schooling are privileged, not due to any linguistic superiority, but because they originate in powerful social contexts. The literate practices of schooling are an important means of accessing knowledge across the curriculum, and Emmitt and colleagues (2014) remind teachers to 'consider the role of the teacher in identifying various forms of language, including the language of instruction and the language of power used in schools, and in helping students negotiate the use of these forms of language' (p. 61). As Cope and Kalantzis (2009) explain: 'transformative pedagogy is based both on a realistic view of contemporary society (how does schooling offer cultural and material access to its institutions of power?) and on an emancipatory view of possible paths to improvement in our human futures (how can we make a better, more equal, less humanly and environmentally damaging world?)' (p. 9).

The idea of 'apprenticing' learners into the literate practices required for schooling and other contexts is an important concept for teachers, and may be considered in connection with linguist Stephen Krashen's (1982) hypothesis of the 'acquisition/learning distinction' (Delpit, 1992; Gee, 1999). In this theory, Krashen (1982) proposes that developing additional languages in adulthood may involve two different processes: **acquisition** and **learning**. Gee (in Kamil et al., 2000) describes acquisition as being 'a process of acquiring something subconsciously by exposure to models, a process of trial and error, and practice within social groups, which happens naturally and functionally' (pp. 113–114). Krashen (1982) proposes that this process of acquisition is very similar to the way that children acquire **oracy** in their first language(s).

> **Acquisition:** a process that occurs largely naturally and unconsciously, via experimentation, and in informal, social settings (Krashen, 1982).
>
> **Learning:** a conscious process that involves some degree of analysis, instruction or explanation (Krashen, 1982).
>
> **Oracy:** the ability to understand and produce spoken language.

In contrast to acquisition, Krashen (1982) also identifies the role of learning in the development of additional languages in adulthood, which Gee (in Kamil et al., 2000) describes as 'a conscious process gained through teaching and in more formal contexts requiring reflection and analysis' (pp. 113–114). While this instruction can occur in a formal classroom setting or in a more naturalistic context, the conscious explanation of patterns and rules is key. For example, someone who has never been exposed to the English alphabet cannot simply stare at the 26 letters of the alphabet and somehow make the respective connections between the letters and the sounds. This knowledge (the connections between the letters and sounds) must be explained; at the very least, someone must help the reader 'crack the code' to make these connections.

Some scholars suggest that Krashen's (1982) acquisition/learning distinction offers important insights for understanding literacies learning (Delpit, 1992; Gee, 1999). This perspective proposes that, while oracy in our first language(s) tends to be acquired, some other forms of literacies are often *learnt* – at least in part – via a conscious process of instruction (Gee, 1999). While there may be a process of combined unconscious acquisition via exposure and conscious learning via scaffolded instruction evident in language and literacies development, explicit knowledge about how literacies work can assist learners' textual engagement and production in the classroom. This is particularly relevant for learners for whom the literate practices of school may be markedly contrasting to those of home (Delpit, 1992).

Accordingly, some scholars suggest that, while approaches to literacies instruction that seek to mirror the communicative environments of first language(s) acquisition offer text-rich and meaningful contexts for learning, there may be a need to incorporate some elements of explicit instruction (Cope & Kalantzis, 2015). Writing in the 1990s, Cazden (1993) addressed this critical issue when discussing changes from literacies instruction that favoured: 'a past tradition of "bottom up" teaching that emphasized drill on the correct use of small language units' to approaches that 'shifted the teaching focus to meaning and function', including whole language and process-based approaches to writing (p. 4). Cazden (1993) suggests there is a need to consider the complexities of how these approaches may impact on learners, explaining that 'immersion in even the richest literacy activities' (p. 3) may be insufficient, particularly for learners with communicative 'funds of knowledge' (Moll et al., 1992) that vary from the literate practices required for schooling. Accordingly, Cazden (1993) advocates for the usefulness of a middle position between 'acquisition and learning for learners', arguing for a 'whole language plus' approach, in which 'whole language' refers to focus on meaning and 'immersion', and 'plus' refers to '**temporary instructional detours** for attention to component features and cultural differences in language use' (p. 4).

Temporary instructional detours: points within a lesson or learning experience where conscious attention is given to specific parts of the text or language (Cazden, 1993).

REFLECTION

1. What might 'temporary instructional detours' (Cazden, 1993, p. 4) look like in the classroom? How might these detours help to scaffold engagement with text for all learners, including those learners for whom texts and practices of schooling are relatively familiar and those learners for whom these practices are new?

2. Cope and Kalantzis (2015) explain the importance of reflexivity and the 'constant vigilance teachers must have, in order to gauge which pedagogical move is appropriate at different moments of the learning process, for different students, and for different subject matters', advising that, 'The mix and the sequence can always vary, and teachers need to be constantly reading student reactions to each move in order to determine the next best move' (p. 16). How might teachers use Cazden's temporary instructional detours reflexively in response to learner needs?

3. Consider also the Victorian Department of Education and Training's resources on the process approach to writing, which are part of the Literacy Teaching Toolkit (www .education.vic.gov.au/school/teachers/teachingresources/discipline/english/literacy/ writing/Pages/litfocuswritingprocess.aspx). The toolkit includes a section that examines the role of feedback, prompts and strategies for supporting learner writing, and a video of whole-class and small-group instruction exploring the purpose, features and structure of informational reports. As you watch the video, think about the aspects of literate practice (e.g. understanding the text type or focusing on particular aspects of language, such as noun groups and modifiers) that are explored in this lesson. What instructional strategies are used in this example? Can you identify any instances of temporary instructional detours?

CASE STUDY 5.1 — Using the teaching and learning cycle to engage with text

As Derewianka and Jones (2016) explain, 'the language of schooling differs from the language of everyday life. It involves increasingly complex, abstract, and detailed understandings of concepts. It requires students to interact with others in ways that extend, consolidate, and challenge their understanding. And it differs across the areas of the curriculum' (p. xiv). Importantly, Derewianka and Jones (2016) assert that 'this kind of language is not necessarily picked up. It needs to be taught in the context of regular teaching and learning activities' (p. xiv).

There are various frameworks for planning engagement with different text types and modalities within classroom learning, each with the potential to include different approaches to instruction. The *teaching and learning cycle*, which also may be referred to as the *genre curriculum model*, *literacy learning cycle* or *joint construction model*, is a framework that originates in the work of Callaghan and Rothery (1988), and is explored in Chapter 9. Hammond (2001) explains:

> the cycle proposes that in early phases, the teacher takes a more direct role in assisting students to develop the necessary knowledge, understandings and skills, while the students take an 'apprentice' role. As the students develop greater control over the spoken or written genre under focus, the teacher gradually withdraws support and encourages learner independence. (p. 28)

The Victorian Department of Education and Training website provides information about strategic uses of the teaching and learning cycle, including support for EAL/D learner engagement (www.education.vic.gov.au/school/teachers/teachingresources/discipline/english/literacy/Pages/using-the-teaching-and-learning-cycle-with-eald-learners.aspx).

You can also find out more about the VicTESOL Teaching and Learning Cycle Project on its website, including an introduction to the framework, materials and classroom videos (https://victesol.vic.edu.au/index.php/teaching-and-learning-cycle-project/teaching-and-learning-cycle-units-of-work/units-of-work-secondary/#tab-id-2).

Questions

Take time to watch some of the videos, and consider the following questions:

1. Which knowledge, repertoires and understandings about text do the teachers and learners engage during each phase of the framework?
2. Are there any examples of 'temporary instructional detours' (Cazden, 1993) to focus on specific parts of the text or language?

CASE STUDY 5.2 — 'Tracks to Two-Way Learning'

There is a wealth of community-led initiatives and research to support teachers with information and practical approaches to learning about and honouring the rich and varied linguistic and literate repertoires of Aboriginal and Torres Strait Islander peoples (see, for example, Heugh, 2014; Malcolm, 2018; Oliver et al., 2021; Wigglesworth & Simpson, 2018). Community-led initiatives supporting teachers with practical strategies for honouring and building on, rather than replacing learners' existing linguistic repertoires, offer valuable resources to shape classroom practice. To see an example of these initiatives, explore the Western Australian Government's Tracks to Two-Way Learning website (http://det.wa.edu.au/curriculumsupport/eald/detcms/navigation/english-as-an-additional-language-or-dialect-for-aboriginal-students/tracks-to-two-way-learning) (Department of Education and Department of Training and Workforce Development, 2012). This collaboration between communities, teachers, partnership schools, advisers and researchers offers a comprehensive range of supports for learning about and valuing learners' existing literate practices, while building towards expertise in the literacies required for engagement with the school curriculum. Learning modules include: 'Understanding Language and Dialect'; 'Language and Inclusivity'; 'Making Texts Work'; and 'Making a Difference for Learners'.

Questions

Engage with the resources on the Tracks to Two-Way Learning website and answer the following questions:

1. What are some of the key features of a two-way learning environment that are identified in these resources? What understandings about language, culture and education might shape classroom practice in this kind of learning context?
2. What strategies and approaches for honoring learners' 'communication ecologies' (Lo Bianco, 2013) are provided in these resources?

Exploring possibilities for 'weaving' knowledges in literacies learning

Sociocultural understandings of literacies learning emphasise the importance of helping learners make connections between familiar and unfamiliar text types (Cazden, 2006; Cope & Kalantzis, 2015). Cazden (2006) describes connections between familiar and unfamiliar knowledge as '**weavings**', citing Kwek (2005, in Cazden, 2006), who identified references to 'weaving' in philosopher and educator John Dewey's writings, published in 1916. Cazden (2006) explains: 'Weaving names the moments in classroom lessons when explicit connections are made – by teacher or students – across one or another dimension of knowledge. Usually, weavings connect something that is already familiar with new curriculum content. Virtually all theories of school learning stress the importance of such connections' (p. 1).

Weavings: the 'moments in classroom lessons when explicit connections are made – by teacher or students – across one or another dimension of knowledge' (Cazden, 2006, p. 1).

Based on Dewey's writing, Cazden (2006) suggests three main ways of thinking about the facilitation of weavings between various forms of knowledge when working towards curriculum outcomes:

1. cultural connections with learners' background knowledge, understandings from previous learning and world experiences
2. cognitive connections to new learning: 'To paraphrase Dewey, the student is led to utilize prior knowledge to help understand new concept or procedural skills' (Cazden, 2006, p. 5)

3. critical connections, which Cazden describes as 'bi-directional', suggesting: 'Such weaving affects both prior knowledge and the new knowledge or skills' which may have the impact of 'aiding student understanding of the new while also transforming understanding of the more familiar, as Dewey advocates' (Cazden, 2006, p. 5).

CASE STUDY 5.3 — Engaging with advertisements

To illustrate how weavings may be incorporated into literacies learning, Cazden (2006) refers to Jennifer O'Brien's (2001) work in Australia with primary aged learners engaging with representations of gender and motherhood in advertising materials. In this example, the learners considered the advertisements in terms of purpose, structures and features, and identified representations and contemplated target audiences. In researching their own contexts, learners identified alignments and mismatches between the constructions in the advertisements and their own experiences, then produced different advertisements to reflect their own contexts. This example illustrates how learners may use their resources and knowledge from other contexts to shape the literate practices undertaken in connection with curriculum outcomes, and how they may apply their learning about text types and literate practices from the classroom to make sense of the world.

As O'Brien (2001) articulates:

> While students mined the junk mail for representations of mothers, they used questionnaires quite conventionally to gather data, charts to record findings, and reports to present conclusions. When making meaning from the catalogues, students drew on cultural knowledge of Mother's Day acquired in their family and community lives. They were able to use these same resources to question the representations of mothers, to identify gaps, and to suggest possible changes. (p. 52)

Cazden (2006) suggests, 'In weaving terms, O'Brien led her students back and forth between what they already knew from their everyday lives at home and the alternative perspectives and more academic skills in her curriculum' (p. 2).

Question

As you reflect on this case study, think about how the learning experiences described here might align with a framework such as the four resources of the reader (Freebody & Luke, 1990). Which resources and textual repertoires would learners need to engage with to undertake these tasks?

Cazden (2006) identifies three important considerations when evaluating the learning impact of weaving between knowledges. First, teachers need to reflect on the time that is given to discussing and thinking about connections between the resources and knowledge that learners bring to the task, and the academic content they are exploring in the lesson. Second, and relatedly, Cazden emphasises the need to ensure a deep, genuine and thorough engagement with the weaving that is occurring. Finally, teachers are reminded that the resources and knowledge that some learners bring from non-school contexts are not necessarily shared by all learners in the classroom. To this point, Cazden (2006) explains: 'Items from popular culture (music, TV, films) are frequently recommended as a resource for heightening the lesson's "relevance" and "significance", but those very resources will be unhelpful, and may even contribute to a feeling of not "belonging," for those students to whom they are unfamiliar' (p. 13). Cazden (2006) notes that these and other complexities 'serve to suggest the kinds of careful planning and more extended class time that such complex objectives require' (p. 13).

Maximising the learning impact of knowledge weaving and using a range of instructional approaches to provide responsive learning experiences for all learners necessitates knowledge about the learners and their 'communication ecologies' (Lo Bianco, 2013). The dialogic approaches to instruction mentioned at the start of this chapter require teachers to engage with and be advised by families and communities as important sources of information about children's literacies strengths, needs and expectations (Delpit, 1988). As Lo Bianco (2013) advises:

> When we examine the communication ecology of a community, and indeed of an individual child, we can identify the settings, purposes, skills and practices that each community deploys in its communication life, and by which it inducts all new arrivals ... as teachers we draw on it to develop it further by honing the skills and capabilities of its members. There exists a fund of concepts, skills and information to account for the communication environment children are from, in the here and now, and the communication environment teachers and teaching need to support them to acquire for the future. (n.p.)

It is important that teachers reflect on how they might learn about learners' literate practices, particularly those practices that contrast with their own ways of using language, and develop strategies for establishing and maintaining classroom connections with learners' communities. The language profiles discussed in Chapter 1 are one way of engaging with families and communities, and further ideas are included in the 'Further resources' section at the end of this chapter. For example, Urtubey (2019) describes how a school garden offers an inclusive space for learners, teachers and families 'where community members and teachers are all perceived as equal in terms of their assets, knowledge, and contributions' (n.p.). Urtubey (2019) explains: 'An English-speaking colleague told me that conversations with families happen naturally at the garden without the pressure that comes during parent-teacher conferences or behavioral citation meetings' (n.p.).

It is also important to acknowledge that learning about the various communicative resources and literate practices that may be unique to each learner's funds of knowledge (Moll et al., 1992) is not without complexities. Barratt-Pugh (in Barratt-Pugh & Rohl, 2001) identifies the time required to genuinely learn about and engage with diverse literate practices in the classroom, noting the challenges of meeting various requirements related to curriculum and assessment while seeking to authentically 'build on the wealth and diversity of literacy practices that children bring to the early years' (p. 22). Barratt-Pugh also suggests that learning about community practices that may contrast with one's own literate funds 'is linked to trust' and relies on teachers being open to 'becom[e]ing learners' (p. 22). Further, families and teachers 'may feel that a close link between what happens at home and what happens in educational settings is not necessary or wanted' (p. 22). Some parents and caregivers, who have experienced educational disruptions or negative interactions with schooling or are concerned about communicating in the forms of English used at school, may be hesitant to participate. Literate practices are deeply connected to community identities, histories and connections, so sensitivity around these issues is important.

A focus on making connections between existing and new knowledge is a key emphasis in the many approaches to honouring learners' linguistic and literate repertoires and supporting engagement with the literacies required for schooling. Whether these approaches involve 'weaving' (Cazden, 2006, p. 1) different knowledge forms into learning, facilitating joint construction of text types or comparing how these texts may vary across cultural contexts – as in the case of O'Brien's (2001) work with Mother's Day advertisements or providing new spaces for families, learners and teachers to communicate and share knowledge in the school garden described by Urtubey (2019) – they focus on building on, rather than diminishing or overlooking, learners' existing literacies resources. As evident in the resources contained in this book, many of these ideas involve the use of drama, multimodal texts and a wide range of literature to provide opportunities for learners to expand their literate understandings (Emmitt et al., 2014; Ewing & Saunders, 2016). Such approaches 'may give all students the opportunity to express complex cross-cultural understandings in powerful ways' (Haig et al., 2005, n.p.).

For example, writing about learners who are fluent in Aboriginal English, Haig and colleagues (2005) explain that:

> a persuasive text, a combination of image, yarns and information using appropriate genre forms may be more powerful for some audiences than a report or expository essay. Of course, all students should be assisted to learn the more traditional genre forms, particularly those expected in further education, but it is important to remember that there are many ways to communicate ideas and that choices can be made. (n.p.)

These approaches aim to ensure all learners have opportunities to 'see' themselves and others' experiences and ways with language and literacies in the classroom (Sims Bishop, 1990). As Rudine Sims Bishop (1990) advises:

> Books are sometimes windows, offering views of worlds that may be real or imagined, familiar or strange. These windows are also sliding glass doors, and readers have only to walk through in imagination to become part of whatever world has been created and recreated by the author. When lighting conditions are just right, however, a window can also be a mirror. Literature transforms human experience and reflects it back to us, and in that reflection we can see our own lives and experiences as part of the larger human experience. Reading, then, becomes a means of self-affirmation, and readers often seek their mirrors in books. (p. ix)

REFLECTION

In thinking about your own education, reflect on the following questions:

1. Were/are your cultural and linguistic resources, identities and literate practices valued in your various learning environments?

2. As a pre-service teacher, have you thought about how you will incorporate and value learners' cultural and linguistic identities in your classroom?

Conclusion

Literacies education is complex and contextually variable. We continue to form new understandings as sociocultural change and technological advances offer greater insights into human learning and communication. While the theories discussed here are far more complex and contested than can be addressed fully in this chapter, they provide important background information for considering approaches to effective, responsive and inclusive literacies learning. In considering some of the complexities and possibilities for supporting all learners to access and navigate the literate practices embedded within schooling and other contexts, this chapter explored the importance of not assuming universality of these ways with language. Ideas for providing opportunities for learners to consider the ways that different texts are valued in different settings, according to social and cultural factors, and strategies for making connections between different forms of knowledge, were also considered (Cazden, 2006; Cope & Kalantzis, 2009; Delpit, 1988). Ways of facilitating genuine and inclusive engagement with a range of texts and literate practices emphasise the need to develop a variety of instructional approaches appropriate to the specific resources, attitudes and expectations, and learners' strengths, needs and 'communication ecologies' (Lo Bianco, 2013).

Together with the resources contained at the end of the chapter and in the remainder of the book, it is hoped that this discussion may provide a catalyst for further exploration about the complexities and possibilities of honouring the important communicative repertoires and resources that learners bring to the classroom, while supporting them to develop expertise in the literate practices that are embedded within schooling and other contexts.

Bringing it together

1. After reading this introduction to some of the different ideas about literacies learning, and engaging with the various resources and links, take some time to reflect on any strategies or resources that you would like to explore further.
2. Compile a list of professional resources and supports, and input from colleagues, researchers, learners, families and community members, that might help you to develop a range of instructional approaches to literacies education.
3. To extend your understanding of the key themes discussed in this chapter, map your own 'communication ecology' (Lo Bianco, 2013). Using whatever mode you prefer – visual, written, spoken, etc. – think about your membership in different communities and the importance of your shared dialect(s), language(s) and/or cultural understandings to your identities. How do you think your 'communication ecology' has shaped your attitudes to and engagement with education?

Further resources

New Learning Online – Learning By Design

This website provides further information on Kalantzis and Cope's ideas about multiliterate approaches to teaching.

https://newlearningonline.com/learning-by-design

Center for Multicultural Education Boooktalk: Shirley Brice Heath

Shirley Brice Heath (1983) discusses her groundbreaking publication, *Words at Work and Play: Three Decades in Families and Communities*.

www.youtube.com/watch?v=67s_Ve_a_wE

New Learning Online: Lisa Delpit on power and pedagogy

This is an extract from Lisa Delpit's (1988) *The Silenced Dialogue: Power and Pedagogy in Educating Other People's Children*.

https://newlearningonline.com/new-learning/chapter-8/lisa-delpit-on-power-and-pedagogy

VicTESOL – teaching and learning cycle: 1a scaffolding students' literacy: teaching grammar in context

A video on how one teacher structures her 'grammar in context' lesson about houses according to this cycle.

https://victesol.vic.edu.au/index.php/teaching-and-learning-cycle-project/teaching-and-learning-cycle-videos

Victorian Department of Education and Training – strengthening engagement with families from refugee backgrounds

This Victorian Department of Education and Training website about supporting EAL/D learner engagement also includes information about family inclusion.

www.education.vic.gov.au/school/teachers/support/diversity/eal/Pages/ealsupportrefugee.aspx#link3

My language is in my heart and my head: hearing student voices in multilingual classrooms

In this Primary English Teaching Association of Australia (PETAA) resource, Janet Dutton, Jacqueline D'warte, Joanne Rossbridge and Kathy Rushton share a range of ideas to enable learners to harness multilingual and multiliterate repertoires and build on these as they engage with school literature practices.

www.petaa.edu.au/w/Teaching_Resources/PPs/PETAA-PAPER-213.aspx

References

Alexander, P. (2005). The path to competence: a lifespan developmental perspective on reading. *Journal of Literacy Research*, 37(4), 413–436.

Barratt-Pugh, C. & Rohl, M. (Eds.). (2001). *Literacy Learning in the Early Years*. Taylor & Francis.

Barton, D. (2001). Directions for literacy research: analysing language and social practices in a textually mediated world. *Language and Education*, 15(2), 92–104.

Bourdieu, P. (1991). *Language and Symbolic Power*. Polity Press.

Brockman, B. (1994). Whole language: a philosophy of literacy teaching for adults, too! https://files .eric.ed.gov/fulltext/ED376428.pdf

Callaghan, M. & Rothery, J. (1988). *Teaching Factual Writing: A Genre Based Approach*. Disadvantaged Schools Program.

Cazden, C. (1988). *Classroom Discourse: The Language of Teaching and Learning*. Heinemann.

—— (1992). *Whole Language Plus: Essays on Literacy in the United States and New Zealand*. Teachers College Press.

—— (1993). Immersing, revealing, and telling: a continuum from implicit to explicit teaching. Plenary Address, to the Second International Conference on Teacher Education in Second Language Teaching, Hong Kong, 24–26 March.

—— (2006). Connected learning: 'weaving' in classroom lessons. Keynote address, Pedagogy in Practice 2006, University of Newcastle, 18 January.

Clay, M.M. (1982). *Observing Young Readers: Selected Papers*. Heinemann.

Cope, B. & Kalantzis, M. (2009). 'Multiliteracies': new literacies, new learning, *Pedagogies: An International Journal*, 4(3), 164–195.

—— (2015). The things you do to know: a pedagogy of multiliteracies. In B. Cope & M. Kalantzis (Eds.), *A Pedagogy of Multiliteracies*. Palgrave Macmillan.

Crain, W. (2010). *Theories of Development: Concepts and Applications* (6th edn). Pearson Education.

Delpit, L.D. (1988). The silenced dialogue: power and pedagogy in educating other people's children. *Harvard Educational Review*, 58, 280–298.

—— (1992). Acquisition of literate discourse: bowing before the master? *Theory into Practice*, 31(4), 296–302.

—— (2006). *Other People's Children: Cultural Conflict in the Classroom* (2nd edn). The New Press.

Department of Education and Department of Training and Workforce Development. (2012). Tracks to Two-Way Learning. WA Government. http://det.wa.edu.au/curriculumsupport/eald/ detcms/navigation/english-as-an-additional-language-or-dialect-for-aboriginal-students/ tracks-to-two-way-learning

Derewianka, B. & Jones, P. (2016). *Teaching Language in Context* (2nd edn). Oxford University Press.

Deschenes, S., Cuban, L., & Tyack, D. (2001). Mismatch: historical perspectives on schools and students who don't fit them. *Teachers College Record*, 103, 525–547.

Elias, J.L. & Merriam, S. (1980). *Philosophical Foundations of Adult Education*. Robert E. Krieger.

Emmitt, M., Zbaracki, M., Komesaroff, L., & Pollock, J. (2014). *Language and Learning: An Introduction for Teaching*. Oxford University Press.

Everitt, S. (2020). 'Know who they have in front of their eyes': a justice as praxis paradigm for teaching and learning. *Gifted Child Today*, 43(2), 101–107.

Ewing, R. & Saunders, J. (2016). *The School Drama Book: Drama, Literature and Learning in the Primary Classroom*. Currency Press.

Fellowes, J. & Oakley, G. (2014). *Language, Literacy and Early Childhood Education*. Oxford University Press.

Freebody, P. (2007). *Literacy Education in School: Research Perspectives from the Past, for the Future*. Australian Council for Educational Research.

Freebody, P. & Luke, A. (1990). Literacies programs: debates and demands in cultural context. *Prospect: An Australian Journal of TESOL*, 5(3), 7–16.

Freire, P. (2007). *Pedagogy of the Oppressed* (first published in English 1970). Continuum.

Gao, P. (2015). Risen from chaos: What drove the spread of mass education in the early 20th century China? EHES Working Paper No.89. www.ehes.org/EHES_89.pdf

Gee, J.P. (1999). Critical issues: reading and the new literacy studies: reframing the National Academy of Sciences Report on Reading. *Journal of Literacy Research*, September.

—— (2012). *Social Linguistics and Literacies: Ideology in Discourses* (4th edn). Routledge.

Graves, D.H. (1983). *Writing: Teachers and Children at Work*. Heinemann Educational.

Haig, Y., Konigsberg, P., & Collard, G. (2005). Teaching students who speak Aboriginal English. Primary English Teaching Association of Australia (PETAA), Pen 150. www.petaa.edu.au/w/Teaching_Resources/PPs/PEN_150.aspx?hkey=169b5d7e-3ab0-458f-b66b-fcc4375d9521

Hammond, J. (2001). *Scaffolding Teaching and Learning in Language and Literacy Education*. Primary English Teaching Association.

Heath, S.B. (1982). What no bedtime story means: narrative skills at home and school. *Language in Society*, 11, 49–76.

—— (1983). *Ways with Words: Language, Life, and Work in Communities and Classrooms*. Cambridge University Press.

Heugh, K. (2014). Turbulence and dilemma: implications of diversity and multilingualism in Australian education. *International Journal of Multilingualism*, 11(3), 347–363.

Hinrichsen, J. & Coombs, A. (2013). The five resources of critical digital literacy: a framework for curriculum integration. *Research in Learning Technology*, 21(1), 1–16.

Kalantzis, M. & Cope. B. (2008). Language education and multiliteracies. In S. May & N.H. Hornberger (Eds.), *Encyclopedia of Language and Education. Volume 1: Language Policy and Political Issues in Education* (2nd edn, pp. 195–211). Springer.

Kamil, M., Mosenthal, P., Pearson, P., & Barr, R. (Eds.). (2000). *Handbook of Reading Research, vol. 3*. Erlbaum.

Krashen, S. (1982). *Principles and Practice in Second Language Acquisition*. Pergamon Press.

Kress, G. (2003). *Literacy in the Media Age*. Routledge.

Lo Bianco, J. (2013). Communication ecology. The Primary English Teaching Association Australia (PETAA) Project 40, Essay 4. www.petaa.edu.au/w/Teaching_Resources/Project_40/w/Teaching_Resources/P40/Bianco_essay.aspx

Lotherington, H. (2011). *Pedagogy of Multiliteracies: Rewriting Goldilocks*. Taylor & Francis.

Luke, A. (1994). *The Social Construction of Literacy in the Primary School*. Macmillan Education Australia.

—— (2000). Critical literacy in Australia: a matter of context and standpoint. *Journal of Adolescent & Adult Literacy*, 43(5), 448–461.

Luria, H., Seymour, D.M., & Smoke, T. (Eds.). (2005). *Language and Linguistics in Context: Readings and Applications for Teachers*. Taylor & Francis.

Malcolm, I.G. (2018). *Australian Aboriginal English: Change and Continuity in an Adopted Language*. De Gruyter.

Mielonen, A.M. & Paterson, W. (2009). Developing literacy through play. *Journal of Inquiry & Action in Education*, 3(1), 15–46.

Moll, L., Amanti, C., Neff, D., & Gonzalez, N. (1992). Funds of knowledge for teaching: using a qualitative approach to connect homes and classrooms. *Theory Into Practice*, 31(2), 132–141.

Neuman, S.B. & Roskos, K. (1998). *Children Achieving: Instructional Practices in Early Literacy*. International Reading Association.

New London Group. (1996). A pedagogy of multiliteracies: designing social futures. *Harvard Educational Review*, 66(1), 60–92.

O'Brien, J. (2001). Children reading critically: a local history. In B. Comber & A. Simpson (Eds.), *Negotiating Critical Literacies in Classrooms* (pp. 37–54). Erlbaum.

Oliveira, P. (2018). Our proud heritage. true then, truer now: the enduring contributions of Arnold Gesell. *Young Children*, 73(3). www.naeyc.org/resources/pubs/yc/jul2018/enduring-contributions-arnold-gesell

Oliver, R., Wigglesworth, G., Angelo, D., & Steele, C. (2021). Translating translanguaging into our classrooms: possibilities and challenges. *Language Teaching Research*, 25(1), 134–150.

Patzelt, L. (1995). Principles of whole language and implications for ESL learners. https://eric.ed.gov/?id=ED400526

Rohde, L. (2015). The comprehensive emergent literacy model: early literacy in context. *SAGE Open*, January–March, 1–11.

Saracho, O.N. (2017). Literacy and language: new developments in research, theory, and practice. *Early Child Development and Care*, 187(3–4), 299–304.

Serafini, F. (2012). Expanding the four resources model: reading visual and multi-modal texts. *Pedagogies: An International Journal*, 7(2), 150–164.

Sims Bishop, R. (1990). Mirrors, windows, and sliding glass doors. *Perspectives*, 1(3), ix–xi.

Stanovich, K.E. (1980). Toward an interactive-compensatory model of individual differences in the development of reading fluency. *Reading Research Quarterly*, 16, 32–71.

Strickland, D. (1990). Emergent literacy: how young children learn to read and write. *Educational Leadership*, 47(6), 18–23.

Teale, W.H. (1991). A conversation with Lisa Delpit. *Language Arts; Urbana*, 68(7), 541.

Unsworth, L. (2006). Towards a metalanguage for multiliteracies education: describing the meaning-making resources of language-image interaction. *English Teaching: Practice and Critique*, 1, 55–76.

Urtubey, J. (2019). Growing a school community. *Edutopia*. www.edutopia.org/article/growing-school-community

Vygotsky, L. (1978). Interaction between learning and development. *Readings on the Development of Children*, 23(3), 34–41.

Watson, J. (2009). Developing critical numeracy across the curriculum. Critical numeracy. www.tas-education.org/numeracy/critical_numeracy/critical_numeracy.htm

Whitehead, M.R. (2007). *Developing Language and Literacy with Young Children*. Sage Publications.

Wigglesworth, G. & Simpson, J. (2018). Going to school in a different world. In G. Wigglesworth, J. Simpson, & J. Vaughan (Eds.), *Language Practices of Indigenous Children and Youth. Palgrave Studies in Minority Languages and Communities*. Palgrave Macmillan.

CHAPTER 6

Reading and viewing

Robyn Ewing

ANTICIPATED OUTCOMES

After working through this chapter, it is anticipated you will be able to:

- define what 'reading' and 'viewing' mean from your perspective
- understand some of the key enabling processes, conditions and roles that foster emergent reading
- identify strategies, activities and relevant resources used for teaching and assessing reading and viewing in the primary years of schooling
- discuss the history and merits of various approaches to learning to read, along with some of the myths and controversies that have raged in the so-called 'reading wars'.

Introduction

It is a wonderful moment when a child realises that he or she can read! There is no question that becoming a reader is a defining moment in our lives, and most contemporary societies therefore place a lot of emphasis on learning to read. It has been said that reading is to the mind what music is for the spirit (Fischer, 2004). We would argue that reading is also important for the spirit, because being able to read fosters hope and deeply opens up new worlds and possibilities for the reader. It can change our very being, trigger new directions, move us to experience deep wonder, joy and sadness, reveal new understandings about ourselves and others, and inspire us to consider previously unthought-of possibilities. To make the most of our lives, and to succeed in any subject, we need to be able to read for a whole range of different purposes.

Yet how children learn to read has been the subject of much controversy and debate since the early twentieth century. No doubt this is, at least in part, because reading is so important in opening us up to the lives and experiences of others and broadening our understanding of who we are as well as of the diversity of the world we live in. While the first few years of learning to read are critical, it must be recognised that learners need to continue to develop their knowledge about and understanding of reading throughout their lives.

Most of us find it very difficult to remember *how* we learnt to read or the time before we could read. Those who can remember often describe the realisation that they could now read as a kind of 'aha' moment or epiphany. There are still many unknowns about that epiphany and it is probably different for each individual.

Some learners report that they started their first day of school with the expectation that they would be able to read by the end of the day, and felt somewhat dispirited when they didn't manage to achieve this. Learning to read appears to be an effortless and seamless process for some children, while for others it takes longer and can be a struggle. There may be some specific challenges for children and young people from culturally and linguistically diverse (CALD) communities. Different needs will require different approaches and strategies. Sometimes a learner will need to focus more on making sense of what they read, while others will need more work on letter-sound relationships. At times, the process of learning to read causes great anxiety for children, teachers and parents/caregivers.

This chapter initially defines the terms 'reading' and 'viewing' as social practices with meaning-making at their core and makes the point that viewing is defined in curriculum documents as an integral and important part of reading, rather than being separate from it. The chapter includes a brief snapshot of the history of reading and the so-called 'reading wars'. Building on the importance of the development of oral language as a precursor to literacy, as discussed in previous chapters, the chapter then focuses on how children learn to read before moving on to explore how teachers can help children with this learning. The centrality of explicit teacher modelling and scaffolding of the reading process are discussed. Early childhood and primary teachers need to develop a rich repertoire of reading strategies and provide children with a wide selection of texts and resources, coupled with explicit guidance and support, to enable them to meet individual learners' needs at different stages of their reading journey. A range of assessment strategies are also briefly introduced. Finally, a number of common myths about the reading process are considered in light of ongoing debates about reading. Throughout the chapter, the discussion focuses on the need for a balanced approach to learning to read with meaning-making at the centre of the process.

Defining reading and viewing

It is important to define the terms 'reading' and 'viewing' because different understandings of these terms have often underpinned how reading is conceptualised and fuelled ongoing disputes about how teachers, parents and caregivers can best help young children learn to read.

REFLECTION

What are key words that come to mind when you think about the terms 'reading' and 'viewing'? Draw a mind map to represent your understandings of the reading process.

A simple view of reading

Reading has often been conceptualised as developing a set of discrete skills that move from simple to more complex skills and focus first on 'cracking' the print code before turning to comprehension. Described as a 'simple view of reading' (Gough & Tunmer 1986; Hoover & Tunmer, 2018), this conceptualisation separates word recognition processes from language comprehension processes. Learning to read is seen as developing proficiency in a hierarchical set of skills, a 'bottom-up' process that first recognises letter-sound relationships and then moves on to more complex skills through a range of activities (Ewing, 2018). Reading comprehension is seen as the product of word recognition ability and the level of spoken language comprehension.

> **Phonemic awareness:** the ability to focus on, identify and manipulate individual sounds (phonemes) in spoken words (Ewing, 2018, p. 10).

Others (e.g. see Snow et al., 1998) separate out five key components of reading that must be taught explicitly (**phonemic awareness**[1], phonics, fluency, vocabulary and reading comprehension), but often emphasise that letter-sound recognition must be acquired first. Intensive synthetic phonics programs (described in more detail in the next section) are often advocated as the first step.

This approach often stipulates that learners use contrived 'readers' or 'decodable texts' that focus on the blended sounds that have been introduced. Below is an excerpt from the decodable text *Nan and Pap* (Angel, 2005, pp. 1–3), which features the consonant /n/ from *Reading A-Z*:

---

p. 1: 'Nan can nap.'

p. 2: 'Pap can nap.'

p. 3: 'Nan and a pan.'

---

1 Many of the key terms used in this chapter were first included in Ewing (2018) and are used with permission.

Learners are often also encouraged to memorise the most frequent sight words in English because they are often difficult to sound out directly and are used so much. According to the Oxford English Corpus (2006), the 10 most common words in English are: 'the', 'be', 'to', 'of', 'and', 'a', 'in', 'that', 'have' and 'I'.

Later, after achieving these skills first, learners are asked to answer questions about what they have read.

It is difficult to see the centrality of meaning-making in this kind of approach to reading, especially if the learner comes to reading in English when speaking a language other than Standard Australian English as their mother tongue.

A meaning-centred view of reading and viewing

The Early Years Learning Framework (EYLF; Department of Education, Employment & Workplace Relations [DEEWR], 2009) supports the concept of emergent reading as part of children's social, emotional and physical growth. The framework has a broad definition of literacy, describing it as 'the capacity, confidence and disposition to use language in all its forms' and including 'a range of modes of communication including music, movement, dance, storytelling, visual arts, media and drama [alongside] talking, listing, viewing, reading and writing' (DEEWR, 2009, p. 38). Texts are defined as 'things we read, view and listen to and that we create to share meaning' (p. 46).

In concert with the EYLF, the Australian Curriculum: English (Australian Curriculum, Assessment and Reporting Authority [ACARA], 2018) also defines reading as meaning-based: 'processing words, symbols or actions *to derive and/or construct meaning. Reading* includes *interpreting, critically analysing and reflecting upon the meaning of a wide range of written and visual, print and non-print texts*' (our emphasis).

Both of these documents conceptualise reading as much more than the deciphering of a written code – it is clear that learning to read is understood to be about meaning-making and that different kinds of texts, including visual images, are included in their definitions. Viewing or reading images is thus one way we read. The glossary of the Australian Curriculum: English (ACARA, 2020a) also states that, when we view images, we need to: 'Observe with purpose, understanding and critical awareness'.

If learning to read encapsulates 'coming to understand, interpret, analyse and reflect on the world as well as considering new possibilities for how to be in the world' (Ewing, 2018, p. 9), the process of learning to read is about learning how to *mean* in a culture. So, our orientation to reading begins from the moment a child is born. Those children who are born into a language-rich environment of talk, storytelling, reading books aloud, playing with rhyme and rhythm, singing, and impromptu performance using gesture and facial expressions, immediately start to learn about meaning-making with different kinds of 'texts'[2] for different purposes in multiple ways. The kind of text, its purpose, the background of both the reader and the wider cultural context of the community are all embedded in these sociocultural processes (Freebody & Luke, 1990; Luke & Freebody, 1999).

---

2 'Text' is used here in its broadest sense – oral, aural, written, visual, digital.

Along with the Australian Curriculum, the National Literacy Learning Progression is a pathway that includes three elements that reflect interrelated aspects of literacy development: speaking and listening, reading and viewing, and writing (ACARA, 2020b). These are needed if learners are to succeed both at school and in life. As described in Chapter 2, the three elements incorporate sub-elements; for example, in reading and viewing, the sub-elements of phonological awareness, phonic knowledge and word recognition and fluency detail skills that underpin understanding texts. Vocabulary is included within and across all sub-elements. (See Chapter 2 for a detailed discussion on the National Literacy Learning Progression.)

REFLECTION

Can you remember your own early reading journey? Did you enjoy being read to? Can you list your favourite books and characters? Who were your favourite children's authors and illustrators? Why do you think you particularly related to them?

The next section examines the early experiences that provide an excellent foundation for a child's early reading journey. You might like to compare these with your own reflections above.

Early experiences: foundations for the reading journey

Important enablers for learning to read

Research over many decades has demonstrated there are important precursors that, when in place, are enablers for successful early reading. Some of these precursors have already been discussed in detail in earlier chapters. Three key enablers are:

1. a language- and story-rich home environment, where children see all kinds of reading and writing for different purposes modelled and shared by parents, caregivers and other family members (Heath, 1983)
2. frequent and diverse linguistically rich parent–child conversations. Well-developed oral language and a rich vocabulary are crucial foundations for reading, viewing and writing progress. Opportunities for young children to listen to and 'talk' about stories being told and read, play with sound through rhymes and songs, ask questions and engage in storying (Lowe, 2004) and dramatic play, build vocabulary as well as an understanding of how language works.
3. the provision of a range of quality imaginative literature in the home and preschool that is shared, discussed and enjoyed, builds vocabulary and knowledge about grammar and spelling in the child's first language as well as English. As Margaret Meek (1988) so famously wrote, the literary text does a lot of the teaching about what reading is. Wolf (2007) asserts that: 'Decade after decade of research shows that the amount of time a child spends listening to parents and other loved ones read is a good predictor of the level of reading attained later' (p. 82). The number of books in

the home enables a child to self-select material to read and this is also an important predictor in successful literacy learning (Krashen, 2015). (The centrality of quality literature in the reading process is discussed in more detail in Chapter 7.)

With one in six Australian children living in poverty (Australian Council of Social Services [ACOSS], 2018), it is an unfortunate reality that these enablers are not a given for every child. By the time a child starts at school, there is often a highly significant divide between those children who are advantaged by language-rich home contexts and those who are in vulnerable situations (Garcia & Weiss, 2017). This divide means that these extra two enablers are particularly important:

4. language-rich preschool and school experiences, investment in richly resourced early childhood centres, preschools and schools and quality career long professional learning for educators are crucial for *all* children
5. easy access to a wide range of literature and other reading materials in well-resourced school and public libraries (Krashen, 2014; Krashen et al., 2012).

In Australia, there is a need for government to address growing inequities in society to ensure all children's optimal success in becoming literate. Each child deserves to learn to read and, importantly, to read for pleasure, as the International Literacy Association (2018) Children's Rights to Read initiative asserts.

Conditions for language learning and learning to read

Eminent Australian literacy educator Brian Cambourne and his colleagues proposed a set of conditions that help children learn language (Cambourne et al., 1988). These conditions are just as relevant for learning to read and are well summarised in the diagram developed by Cambourne and Crouch (2018), as shown in Figure 6.1. These conditions provide an important checklist for parents, caregivers and teachers.

Conditions and processes for learning to read

Brian Cambourne presents the following descriptions for each of the eight conditions (see Figure 6.1) for learning to read (Cambourne, n.d.):

1. *Immersion* – Surround children with interesting, high-quality children's books and different kinds of text (e.g., charts, labels, newspapers, magazines). Read aloud every day to children, sing to them, play word games, and use movement and dance to generate lively engagement in language, literacy and stories.
2. *Demonstration* – Model reading and writing for children. Let them see you writing notes, letters, stories, recipes, and lists. Make sure they notice you reading to yourself, for pleasure, for information, for directions, for other purposes. Show them how to hold a book, turn the pages, and read aloud.

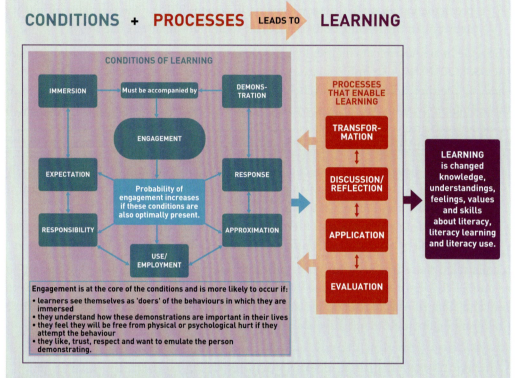

Figure 6.1 Conditions and processes lead to learning
Source: Cambourne & Crouch (2018).

3. *Engagement* – Help children become active learners who see themselves as potential readers and writers. Set up a risk-free environment so they can experiment with language and literacy. Provide easy access to writing and art resources.
4. *Expectation* – Set realistic expectations for language and literacy development. Become familiar with the developmental stages of emergent literacy and support children in appropriate tasks. Expect they will become accomplished readers and writers in their own time.
5. *Responsibility* – Give children choices about books to read. Set up the environment to promote self-direction. Provide children with easy access to books and literacy materials (low shelves, in baskets). Show children how to care for them.
6. *Approximation* – Accept children's mistakes when they are learning to talk, read and write. Congratulate them on their accomplishments. Guide them gently into accuracy and soon they will begin to self-correct.
7. *Use* – Create a climate for functional and meaningful uses of oral and written language. Encourage children to read along with you; help you write notes, letters, and lists; and engage in lots of conversations.
8. *Response* – Listen to children, welcome their comments and questions and extend their use of oral and written language. Celebrate the enormous language and literacy learning that is occurring daily!

Before we discuss the ways teachers can assist children with learning to read, it is valuable to explore what we know about the reading process itself.

The reading process

What actually happens during the reading process? Confident readers bring different sources of information and resources together (Emmitt et al., 2013) to make meaning of any text. They need to develop both constrained and unconstrained skills, and morphemic as well as phonic knowledge, and understand the different roles a reader plays when reading. Three important kinds of knowledge are considered below, each with a brief example:

1. *Semantic information* draws on the reader's existing knowledge, vocabulary, the context and/or experience about the text's field or topic. If there are illustrations or diagrams, the visual cues are also important.

> The teacher is reading from Maurice Sendak's *Where the Wild Things Are* (Sendak, 1963). After Max has dressed up as a wild thing and spoken rudely to his mother, we might use our own experience together with the image and graphophonic knowledge to discuss the next line: 'And he was sent to bed without any _____'

2. *Syntactic or grammatical information* is a reader's knowledge of how the language is structured (e.g. word order, punctuation and understanding of grammar).

> If we read or hear the following sentence: 'There was an old lady who lived in a tiny little _____', we use knowledge of the way English works in terms of word order along our semantic knowledge and letter-sound relationships to predict the word that would be next.

3. *Graphophonic* information (sometimes separated into graphological and phonological) is knowledge about the letters (grapho) and associated sounds (**phonemes**).

> A child comes to a word they don't recognise. They can use the visual clues from the letters and their knowledge of sounds to work out the word: /h/-/o/-/t/

Phonemes: 'The smallest units of a spoken language which can be combined to form syllables and words. In English, there are at least 44 phonemes but only 26 letters (accents may play a role)' (Ewing, 2018, p. 10).

In addition, there may be specific textual information – for example, the message might be conveyed using bold or italic print or large font. Learning how to read information conveyed through graphs, diagrams and charts is also part of the comprehension process.

Paris (2005) has theorised that there is a continuum of constrained and unconstrained skills that children need to develop as they learn to read.

Learning constrained and unconstrained skills

At one end of the continuum are highly constrained skills. Constrained skills include knowing how to write your name, recognising the letters of the alphabet, sight recognition of words used most frequently and knowledge about phonics. They are skills that can usually be acquired relatively easily. At the other end of the continuum are unconstrained skills: those learnt over a lifetime of reading and viewing, such as the building of a rich vocabulary and comprehension. Other skills, such as fluency in oral reading, are placed along the continuum.

While constrained skills are necessary for the development of success in reading and can be more easily assessed, this does not mean they should be overemphasised or taught in isolation, because they are insufficient for the development of complex reading practices (Dougherty Stahl, 2011).

We shall see later that much of the debate about helping children learn to read in English is around how much emphasis teachers should place on 'the alphabetic principle' (Share, 1995), how the sounds connect to the letters and the need to develop phonemic awareness (dividing words into phonemes, the smallest units of sound). In English this is problematic because there is no straightforward one-to-one correspondence between the 26 letters of the alphabet and the (at least) 44 sounds present in most English dialects. In fact, Misty Adoniou (2017) suggests that only 12 per cent of English words can be directly sounded out.

English as a morpho-phonemic system

Given that English has drawn from so many other languages as it has evolved and grown over time, it is important to look at the morphemic (meaning) of words or parts or words *with* the sound system. This is an emerging area of research being led by linguists and educators Jeff and Peter Bowers (Bowers & Bowers, 2017). They have investigated English as a **morpho-phonemic** system and demonstrate that the privileging of phonics in isolation without meaning is highly problematic. They propose a Structured Word Inquiry (SWI) that considers **morphology**, **etymology** and **phonology** being taught together in early reading instruction. Rather than the alphabetic principle, Bowers and Bowers demonstrate 'that letters in English often play no role in representing the sounds of words' (Ewing, 2018, p. 30) because 'English spelling is designed to represent pronunciation *and* meaning' (Bowers & Bowers, 2017, p. 131). As Venezky (1967) explained some decades ago: 'the present orthography is not merely a letter-to-sound system riddled with imperfections, but instead, a more complex and more regular relationship wherein phoneme and morpheme share leading roles' (p. 77).

Interestingly, children find it harder to learn to identify words in 'deep orthographies like English, French, or Danish compared to [those with] a shallow **orthography** like Italian or Spanish' (Seymour et al., 2003, in Bowers & Bowers, 2018, n.p.).

Bowers (2018, in Bowers & Bowers, 2018) systematically 'reviewed all meta-analyses that have assessed the efficacy of systematic phonics' and 'demonstrates that there is little or no evidence that systematic phonics is any better than other common methods used in schools' and none have considered *morphological instruction* (n.p.). Research

Morpho-phonemic: morphemes 'vary widely in their phonological representation across related words. English orthography has evolved to favour consistent representation of morphology over phonology to mark connections in meaning across words' (Ewing, 2018, p. 10).

Morphology: 'The system-enabling morphemes that combine to represent the meaning of words. Every word is either a base, or a base with another morpheme fixed to it' (Ewing, 2018, p. 10).

Etymology: 'The study of the origin and history of words and how their form and meaning changes over time' (Ewing, 2018, p. 10).

Phonology: 'The system by which speech sounds of a language represent meaning' (Ewing, 2018, p. 11).

Orthography: the spelling system that represents a language (Ewing, 2018, p. 11).

undertaken by Bowers and Kirby (2010), Carlisle (2010) and Goodwin and Ahn (2013) has found that morphological instruction was most effective in the youngest and least abled children. Initial reading instruction should therefore be 'designed around the logic of the English writing system – a system that is [morphophonemic] rather than alphabetic' (Bowers & Bowers, 2018, n.p.).

Reader roles/resources

In the 1990s, Peter Freebody and Alan Luke described four inter-related reader roles, or resources, that readers learn to understand and enact or draw on while reading (Figure 6.2): code breaker, text participant, text user and text analyst or critic (Freebody, 2019; Freebody & Luke, 1990; Luke & Freebody, 1999). While combining different kinds of information, a reader is also learning to understand these interrelated roles:

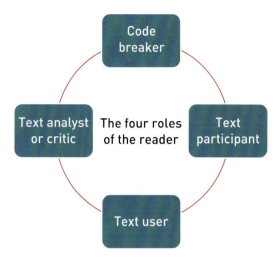

Figure 6.2 The four roles of the reader
Source: Adapted from Freebody & Luke (1990).

- *Code breaker*: involves breaking the code of written text (using **graphophonic knowledge**) as well as visual, gestural, aural and spatial codes.
- *Text participant*: focuses on making meaning and comprehending what is read and viewed, interpreting literal and inferential meanings across vocabulary, grammatical features and other modalities.
- *Text user role*: the understanding of how texts achieve their social and practical purposes for a particular audience, through the choices an author or illustrator makes, including the selection of ideas and the choice of genre (factual, persuasive, procedural, imaginative).
- *Text analyst or text critic role*: the discovery and questioning of the cultural assumptions and world views present in texts, which may in different ways influence, empower or marginalise readers and their communities. This notion of **critical literacy** encourages learners to question and discuss ideas in a story, podcast, video or game, particularly relating to the attitudes embedded about gender, culture and belief systems.

Graphophonic knowledge: 'The knowledge of how letters relate to the sounds of spoken language' (Ewing, 2018, p. 10).

Critical literacy: a questioning and discussing of ideas in a story, podcast, video or game to analyse the attitudes embedded about gender, culture and belief systems.

Over time, and with increasing experience, readers develop more sophisticated ways of using the cues and undertaking each of the roles.

REFLECTION

1. Using your favourite picture book, find an example of how each of the reading cues might work to play a role in making meaning of the text.
2. How would you explain the process of learning to read, incorporating the above ideas?
3. Why do you think there is so much pressure on teachers to teach the constrained skills earlier?

Phases of reading development

While we can consider general stages of reading and literacy development, we need to be mindful that children develop at different rates and stages and move through these phases at their own pace. Individual attributes, family and community experiences, coupled with health and socioeconomic circumstances, make each child's reading journey unique. The general phases of reading development are shown in Table 6.1.

Table 6.1 Phases of reading development

Phase	Reading
Exploratory	• Enjoys listening to books being read aloud • Holds the book and turns pages • Looks at pictures and names objects and characters
Emergent	• Selects favourite books for repeated readings • Memorises the story and joins in as it is read aloud, especially rhyming words and repeated phrases • Understands that print contains meanings • Reads familiar signs and symbols • Knows print in the English language reads from left to right, top to bottom, etc.
Developing	• Retells simple stories • Reads simple texts with support and independently • Asks questions and discusses story ideas and themes • Uses appropriate intonation when reading or pretending to read • Joins in rhyming games • Demonstrates a developing awareness of syllables and sounds of language • Identifies some letters and letter-sound matches • Learns common sight words
Extending	• Reads with fluency and expression • Understands different purposes of texts, such as informative, story, persuasive • Reads independently • Learns about different perspectives in texts • Uses variety of comprehension strategies to make meaning (e.g. makes inferences) • Self-monitors

Source: Adapted from Ewing et al. (2016, p. 120).

REFLECTION

Do you find these suggested phases of reading helpful? What else could you add? Go online or to your university's library to find and explore stages of reading proposed by other researchers.

Having begun to flesh out what happens when we read, the next section provides a brief snapshot of how some of the controversies about teaching reading have been embedded in the history of reading, especially in the twentieth and twenty-first centuries.

A brief history of 'reading' and some related controversies about teaching reading

As Derrick Armstrong (2006, p. 8) reminds us, 'debates about literacy, and in particular the teaching of reading, go to the heart of the role and place of education in our society'. He points out that in many societies, in years gone by, the ruling class deliberately kept citizens illiterate as a way of exerting power and control over them.

'Reading' of symbols in Aboriginal culture dates back many thousands of years but did not evolve in the same way as reading as we understand it in Western cultures, perhaps because the culture of trade within Aboriginal and Torres Strait Islander communities did not require it (Freebody, 2007). As far as we can tell, reading as we know it is only 6000 years old, dating back to the emergence of symbols in 4000 BCE when writing was invented, although in most early civilisations few people were able to read. It is estimated that at the beginning of the nineteenth century in England only about 12 per cent of the population could read and write. Reading aloud was thought to be the most common form of reading. Those in Western civilisations who could read characteristically only owned a few books – the Bible, an almanac and perhaps a devotional book – and these were reread many times. Newspapers and periodicals began to appear in European cultures around 1800 and children's literature and novels began to emerge in the late nineteenth century. As more people began to read silently, there was concern from those in power that this would lead to rebellious thoughts!

Recent estimates show that in 2016 only 10 per cent of young people did not have basic literacy skills (United Nations Educational, Scientific and Cultural Organization [UNESCO], 2020). Nevertheless, there are still 14 per cent of adults over 15 years old who cannot read and write and two-thirds of these are women.

Focusing particularly on reading in Australia, the research project Teaching Reading in Australia, undertaken by Professors Bill Green, Phil Cormack and Annette Patterson (Green et al., 2009), shone a light on how children in Australia were taught to read from the beginning of early white settlement to 1939. The researchers found many examples of both the introduction and later abandonment of methods of teaching reading and argued that successful learning to read was always considered as much more than skills acquisition: the context, the relationship between the teacher and the child, and the reading material all needed to be considered. They also noted that early texts were filled with exhortations about how to behave, so we can deduce that reading was used didactically.

Such approaches to teaching reading have been heavily influenced by different learning theories, some of which are discussed in the next sections.

Reading 'readiness'

In the early 1930s, it was thought that reading 'readiness' was a maturational process and that most children would be ready to learn to read between the ages of six and seven. It was argued that, by this time, a child would have achieved the physical maturation and 'neural ripening' necessary for learning to read (Morphett & Washburne, 1931), regardless of social and cultural factors. Later in the twentieth century, in the 1960s it was thought important to provide children with prerequisite skills for reading, including developing children's gross and fine motor skill development and undertaking activities that focused on auditory discrimination and visual memory.

No doubt this was the rationale for the current legal requirement that all children should begin school by the time they are 6.6 years old in most Australian states and territories. Interestingly, many Scandinavian countries do not begin formal reading instruction until a child is seven or eight years old and Steiner schools follow a similar practice.

The 'look-say' or whole word approach to learning to read

Invented in the 1830s and popular in the 1930s and 1940s, the look-say or whole word method focuses on children learning whole words rather than breaking them down into individual letters or groups of letters. The printed word, often supported by an image, is shown and pronounced and then repeated by the child many times so that, eventually, the child can recognise it by sight. Often the word will also be used in a sentence or phrase to build context. In time, children will build up a sight vocabulary. Flashcard games are often used to help children with learning words in this way.

Phonics-first approaches to teaching reading

Various programs advocating that the mastery of phonics should happen first in the reading process have been in use since the early 1900s. The Ellis method (Reid, 2006), for example, was described in 1922 as beginning with drilling elements that on their own were meaningless to children and proceeded to combine them into words. Along the way, both learners and their teachers were observed to lose interest (Archibald, in Reid & Green, 2004). Most phonics methods usually adopt the simple definition of reading described earlier. These programs assert that letter-sound relationships must be taught first in a prescribed sequence, with small, logical steps. The memorisation of the most frequent sight words is also introduced. Accompanying 'readers', often now called 'decodable readers', have been contrived to concentrate on the words that are introduced at a particular level. It is argued that learners will be able to read these texts accurately after their phonics lessons and that repeated successful readings will lead to automatic **decoding**, word recognition and reading fluency (Frey, n.d., p. 126).

Over the years, many commercial programs have been developed based on the premise that 'intensive phonics taught first is the key to helping all children learn to read' (e.g. Hay-Wingo, Open Court, Jolly Phonics, Ants in the Apple, Words in Colour, Mini-Lit and Multi-Lit) (Ewing, 2018, p. 15).

The most recent iteration of a phonics-first approach in both England and Australia has been seen in arguments that all children must be taught synthetic phonics first.

Synthetic phonics

Cognitive scientists Castles, Rastle and colleagues have recently published a series of articles arguing that initial reading instruction must first concentrate on **grapheme**-phoneme

> **Decoding:** to work out the meaning of words in text, readers combine contextual, vocabulary, grammatical and phonic knowledge effectively (Ewing, 2018, p. 10).
>
> **Grapheme:** 'A single letter or combination of letters that represent a phoneme. Graphemes occur within morphemes and can represent more than one phoneme. In English, 44 sounds and 26 letters offer more than 120 grapheme choices' (Ewing, 2018, p. 10).

correspondences using synthetic phonics because, they assert, English is an alphabetic system in which letters represent sounds (see, for example, Castles et al., 2018; Rastle & Taylor, 2018). Learners start with the smallest units and then learn to blend and synthesise the sounds to form words with consonant-vowel-consonant patterns. Some advocates suggest the learning of individual letter-sound correspondences should be undertaken as early as possible. Meaning is regarded as inconsequential until children have mastered letter and sound correspondence. Sometimes no texts are introduced, but often those texts with a contrived vocabulary are used to reinforce the words that have been taught.

In addition, many of those who privilege synthetic phonics approaches argue that all six-year-old children should be given a synthetics phonics 'check' consisting of 40 words (20 of which are pseudo-words) to ascertain their ability to synthesise sounds. Ewing (2018) notes that 'children must show they are not relying on word meaning or prior experience with the word in order to successfully recode it' (p. 16). Pseudo-words, such as 'thrand', 'poth' and 'froom', are included to 'ensure the children are not using meaning to decode the words' (Ewing, 2018, p. 16). As this is an oral test, some of these words can be pronounced in two different ways – that is, 'thrand/band' but 'poth/both/broth' and 'froom/room/book'. Again, this process will be difficult for those children who are learning English as an additional language or dialect (EAL/D).

These tests have been administered in England since 2012 and are currently mandated in South Australia and New South Wales. Early childhood educators are increasingly feeling pressure from parents to introduce the formalised teaching of phonics and related worksheets in preschool (Campbell, 2015). Such push down to teach reading earlier is often related to parent anxiety about their child being 'ready' to read. As Anderson and colleagues (1985) suggested, however, teachers should teach only the most important and regular letter-sound relationships. Refining and extending learners' knowledge is best done through providing children with many opportunities to read.

Meaning-first approaches

As an alternative to the phonics-first approach, social constructivist theories (e.g. Vygotsky, 1978) and information processing theories (e.g. Atkinson & Shiffrin, 1968) emphasised that meaning-making was at the core of learning to read (and write) and that a learner's social experiences and cultural context would play an important role in how they constructed meaning in their life. These theories have also impacted on reading pedagogy, by asserting that the child must understand the process is about making meaning and be actively involved in the learning process, including the use of the different kinds of information involved when reading – see, for example, early theorists Frank Smith (1978), Marie Clay (1979) and Kenneth Goodman (1968). Don Holdaway (1979) focused on the importance of shared reading with a child before formal schooling, while New Zealander Sylvia Ashton-Warner (1986) emphasised the interactive nature of language and reading in the language experience approach she developed.

Neurological patterns when reading

Recent neurological research at the University of California, Berkeley, in the United States (Deniz et al., 2019) focuses on what happens in the brain when we read stories. The latest interactive maps of the brain predict where different categories of words activate the brain and indicate that we process reading and listening as integrated meaning-making activities rather than in isolated or separate ways: 'We knew that a few brain regions were activated similarly when you hear a word and read the same word, but I was not expecting such strong similarities in the meaning representation across a large network of brain regions in both these sensory modalities' (Deniz, in Anwar, 2019).

It may be useful to read Yasmin Anwar's article 'A map of the brain can tell what you're reading about' (https://news.berkeley.edu/2019/08/19/readingbrainmap) before answering the question below.

Question

What does this new neurological research add to our understanding of reading and viewing?

Language experience approaches

A language experience approach builds children's understanding of the reading process by connecting talking, listening and written language (Dougherty Stahl, 2011). A child can tell or draw their own stories, share their thoughts and ideas about an experience or recall and recount a shared event or a special memory. The parent, caregiver, teacher or older peer acts as a scribe. These stories can be 'read' and reread together. Particular words or phrases may be identified for further discussion. Digital dimensions can also be added.

Whole language

Whole language approaches derive from the theory that talking, listening, reading and writing are all interrelated and need to be integrated authentically. Goodman (1986, 1996) has argued that constructing meaning-making is the most important part of the reading process, so it must be the starting point in learning to read. Each of the cueing systems (semantic, syntactic and graphophonic) are acknowledged as playing an important role in learning to read and teachers respond to the needs of their learners by implementing teaching strategies that use real texts and authentic contexts. There is a strong valuing of the learner needing to be actively engaged in making sense of text.

Structured word inquiry

Approaches that use 'structured word inquiry intervention' (Bowers, 2019; Bowers & Bowers, 2018) demonstrate how well young children and the less able can learn about and understand the logical structure of words and also improve decoding, spelling (Devonshire & Fluck, 2010) and vocabulary knowledge. As discussed earlier, many of the words children use most frequently are not easily sounded out in English. Words such as 'like', 'you', 'the' and 'mother' are multisyllabic and/or multimorphemic. In addition, Anderson (2017) and Anderson and Whiting (2019) have many practical examples of success in classrooms using the structured word inquiry method.

Balanced approaches

A balanced approach draws from all, or a range, of the above approaches to help children learn to read based on the evidence that one single approach cannot meet the needs of all children, or even of one child, at different points in their reading journey. It respects teachers' professional expertise and judgement in making decisions about which strategies from their repertoire best meet the child's learning needs at a particular time.

A balanced approach does not follow a lock-step program. Rather, the teacher responds to the specific needs of the individual (Louden et al., 2005; Spiegel, 1998). Early emergent readers may need lots of time to notice and play with words, and to listen to and identify rhymes and syllables to develop phonological awareness, especially if they have not had opportunities to do these activities at home or in the English language. Tuning in to sounds, identifying initial sounds, alliteration, onset and rime, clapping out the syllables in words, blending phonemes and segmenting words are all important. Learning about phonics – the relationships between letters and sounds – for example, is embedded in reading, sharing and talking about the meanings of words, their origins, word families and patterns.

In the classroom, distinctions between **synthetic phonics**, **analytic phonics** and **embedded phonics** are soon lost because responsive teachers move from analytic phonics to morphology and etymology, to blending the sounds where appropriate, and back to meaning-making. They build children's observations, current understandings and experiences about rhyme, word patterns and syntax in real contexts to develop these further. The interrelationship between morphology, etymology and phonics is made clear.

Learning to read is therefore not a matter of a linear progression from speaking to **recoding** sounds to symbols to learning syllables and words and, finally, to comprehending what these words say and then learning to write. Instead, speaking, listening, reading, writing and viewing must be seen as interconnected parts of an active and ongoing learning process and, ultimately, of social transformation.

As noted, early reading pedagogy should not be characterised by a single paradigm's field of reference. In reality, in the classroom, teachers aim to bring together a range of approaches and strategies to meet the needs of individual children. It has never been helpful to foreground the deciphering of written code as a one-size-fits-all approach to early reading. As Jo-Anne Reid (2006, p. 16) writes, tensions about reading approaches and methods have played out for generations of teachers:

> In the context of often bitter debate about reading methods … many teachers are made to feel inadequate and exposed, less knowledgeable than they would like to be, and vulnerable to tried and true solutions, approaches and strategies that are claimed to guarantee success in reading for their pupils.

Synthetic phonics: a part-to-whole phonics approach emphasising teaching learners to convert letters (graphemes) into sounds (phonemes) (Ewing, 2018, p. 11).

Analytic phonics: an emphasis on larger sub-parts of words (i.e. onsets and rimes, spelling patterns) and phonemes. The starting point is children's known language, but an explicit focus on the components of words, including letter-sound correspondences, follows (Ewing, 2018, p. 11).

Embedded phonics: 'Children are taught letter-sound relationships during the reading of connected text. Since children encounter different letter-sound relationships as they read, this approach will not be a preconceived sequence, but can still be thorough and explicit' (Ewing, 2018, p. 11).

Recoding: 'Translating sound to print, with no associated meaning. Compare with decoding, … which includes meaning' (Ewing, 2018, p. 11).

Reid (2006) urges us 'to teach *children* to read rather than teach *a method of reading*' (p. 16).

Recurring and often unproductive controversies about these different approaches have led to a polarisation, with phonics-first approaches on one side of the debate and so-called whole language approaches on the other. Developing a balance of strategies to teach reading cues and roles, rather than polarising these approaches, is a more productive way forward. It is important to acknowledge that reading is complex and multidimensional and no one approach or time frame will meet the needs of all learners. In light of this, 'Policymakers in educational systems need to carefully consider evidence from different paradigms before making critical decisions' about resourcing and teacher professional learning (Moss & Huxford, 2007, in Ewing, 2018, p. 5).

Developing sophisticated understandings

Too often, once a child has begun to read independently, reading instruction becomes less prioritised in the primary classroom. There are still, however, complex skills and understandings that need to be further developed. Learners need to be encouraged to challenge what they are reading. Louise Rosenblatt (1978) demonstrated that each reader will interpret what they are reading in their own way and depending on whether they are reading for pleasure or to access particular information. A range of strategies can contribute to the development of critical literacies. These include visualisation, making connections, prediction, inferring, monitoring and summarising. These strategies are discussed further in the next section.

REFLECTION

1. What does this brief historical overview suggest to you about the current debates about how to help children learn to read?
2. Can you represent the contrasting beliefs about how reading is best taught?

Developing a repertoire of teaching and learning strategies

This section explores a range of teaching and learning strategies that can form part of a teacher's repertoire when helping children learn to read.

Modelled, shared, guided and independent reading experiences

During different kinds of reading experiences, the teacher takes on varying levels of responsibility as they model the reading process as an expert, share the reading process as pleasurable with learners and support learners to build their confidence about reading independently. Figure 6.3 illustrates the significant role undertaken by the teacher during modelled reading, compared with decreasing teacher responsibility when the learner reads independently (known as the gradual release of responsibility model).

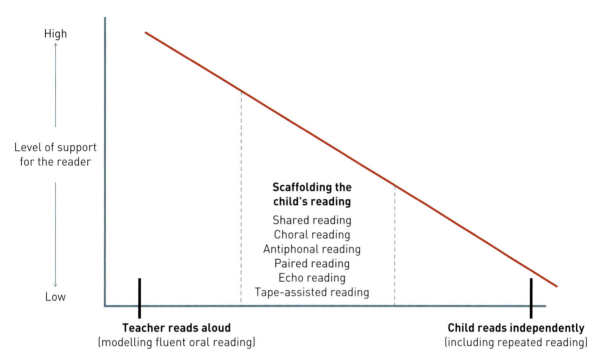

Figure 6.3 Gradual release of responsibility: from modelling to independent reading
Source: Mehigan (2020, p. 24).

Modelled reading

As an expert reader, the teacher, parent, caregiver or more experienced peer models the reading process continuously in the classroom or at home as they read aloud a story or factual text. When reading aloud fluently and with expression to an individual learner or a group of learners, the reader may stop when appropriate to think aloud about what might happen next, comment on an illustration, demonstrate the use of a particular reading strategy or discuss a point of interest (Afflerbach et al., 2008). Such scaffolding of the reading process helps learners develop their knowledge and understanding, almost as though they are apprentices (Rogoff, 1995; Vygotsky, 1978). Modelled reading may be recorded for a child to revisit at a later time.

Shared reading

Shared reading usually involves a group or the whole class reading with the teacher and is modelled on what happens when a parent or caregiver shares a book with a child at home. In the classroom, this works best when an enlarged text or big book is used or the text is projected using an interactive whiteboard with a large screen. Alternatively, a learners can read with a peer for support. Learners are actively engaged, following along with the words, and joining in with familiar parts of the text or with repetitive or rhyming sections. The teacher may pause to discuss vocabulary, print concepts and conventions, highlight rhyming words, ask a question or invite a response.

Shared reading is a strategy that can support the understanding of the interaction between oral language and reading, concepts of print, phonological awareness and phonics. It can also help build vocabulary and understanding of the shared text.

Guided reading

Guided reading often happens in small groups of learners who are all at approximately the same stage of reading. In a guided reading session, the teacher fosters learners' independence by encouraging them to use strategies they already know to read an unfamiliar text. The group may also make some early predictions about the text, relate it to their own experiences, or discuss the plot or the themes raised. The teacher may set a particular purpose for the guided reading session – for example, a focus on a particular strategy or a search for new vocabulary.

Independent reading

Learners also need opportunities to select their own reading preferences from a wide range of texts and to read on their own for a sustained period each day. There are acronyms for different routines in the school day that signal time for independent reading for both learners and the teacher. Examples include *DEAR* (Drop Everything and Read) *Time* and *SSR* (Sustained Silent Reading).

Designing whole-class and small-group activities to facilitate reading development and deep understanding

When engaged in shared, modelled and guided reading, the following whole-class and small-group strategies and experiences can be introduced and modelled by the teacher to facilitate learners' understanding of text. The following strategies are elaborated with examples in Chapter 8 (see pages 183–200):

- 'I wonder' questions
- predicting
- making connections, or intertextuality
- sequencing
- oral and written cloze activities
- drama strategies: embodying and enacting; readers theatre
- metacognitive skills (thinking *about* thinking)
- inferring
- reciprocal teaching
- peer teaching.

Reading and interpreting images

Contemporary images, photos and diagrams are not merely about supporting or complementing printed or digital text: artists carefully use design principles, using colour, light, position, shape and symbol, when they are creating images to share and infer different layers of meaning. Images often play a part in narrating a story. They can be used persuasively to convince us about a particular issue. Often they can challenge or provoke us to reflect on an issue. Learners need time to closely observe and discuss these aspects of images and to share their thoughts so as to understand how meaning can be interpreted in different ways. A particularly valuable resource in this area is Callow's (2013) book *The Shape of Text to Come: How Image and Text Work*. Responding to images is developed in more detail in Chapter 8.

Reading for pleasure

There is clear and consistent research evidence that reading for pleasure enhances children's academic achievement more broadly. Taking time each day to allow learners to make their own choices about what they would like to read at school is important, and also needs to be a priority at home. Research demonstrates that those who read because they enjoy reading, both in childhood and as adults, have higher levels of self-esteem and more understanding of their own lives and those of others (see, for example, Billington, 2020; Organisation for Economic Co-operation and Development [OECD], 2010). Reading for pleasure is also a form of relaxation that is also engaging.

Reading in subjects other than English

Across the Australian Curriculum, reading requires children and young people to have knowledge about the different ways language is used in different subject areas (Derewianka & Christie, 2008). For example, what skills do learners need when reading the report of an experiment compared with reading about an historical event? Learners need to identify different purposes for reading different kinds of text. They must develop confidence with the reading skills and strategies described in the section above (see also Chapter 8), as they relate to different content areas, so that they can understand and interpret documents in History, experiments in Science, ledgers and reports in Economics and Business, and court cases in Legal Studies. The primary classroom provides an important initial context for the teacher to model explicitly how different language choices are made in key learning areas other than English, especially when integrated, or when multidisciplinary units of work span a number of curriculum areas.

REFLECTION

Choose one subject area other than English, and think about the key features to be mindful of when reading in this discipline.

Assessing reading progress and development

CASE STUDY 6.1	Assessing reading programs

Jedda's mother is very worried. She believes it is important for Jedda to progress through the different levels of readers as quickly as possible and is concerned Jedda is in danger of falling behind her peers. Although Jedda is keen to read with her mother each evening, Jedda is not reading at the same level as most of her friends. Jedda's mother makes an appointment to discuss her concerns with the class teacher.

Questions

In role as the class teacher, how would you reassure Jedda's mother? What would you advise Jedda's mother to do?

As discussed in Chapter 3, different kinds of assessment will play an integral role during classroom English and literacy activities. Assessment is not something that is just added on after teaching. Teachers are constantly collecting information about how effectively learners are reading in various situations and for a range of purposes. Earlier in this book, we looked more broadly at the teacher's need to assess for learning, as well as to undertake assessment as learning and assessment of learning (see Chapter 3). Peer assessment and self-assessment opportunities are also important.

Achievement in reading and in other literacy skills is too often measured narrowly. Our emphasis here is on *authentic* (Ewing, 2013) or *educative* assessment (Ewing et al., 2020). It is always important for teachers to identify a child's reading needs and any need for extra support in a particular area as early as feasible. The perception that parents and caregivers sometimes have, that continual screening procedures and reading tests will contribute to the raising of reading standards, is, however, misplaced. Too much focus on ticking off checklists of discrete skills, assigning marks or comparing one child's level of reading with another will send messages to less successful learners that they lack ability or are not doing well. Anxiety can set in. Following are a selection of authentic assessment strategies that can be used to assess learners' reading ability.

Anecdotal observations

Teachers constantly make anecdotal observations to gauge learners' understanding of and engagement in the reading process. They monitor whether learners choose to read in the reading corner, become absorbed in a book as it is read aloud by the teacher or parent/caregiver, ask relevant questions or make connections about what is being read to their own lives and experiences. They will note issues in particular areas for follow-up.

Video and audio recordings of both formative and summative assessment reading activities are helpful tools for teachers in monitoring individual learners' progress and areas in need of further development.

Observational surveys

Marie Clay (2019) created a more formal observation survey to gain detailed information of a child's early literacy knowledge and understanding. The survey includes:

- letter identification
- 'concepts about print' (ability to orient the book, follow the direction of print on the page; use appropriate book vocabulary; engage with content)
- word reading
- hearing and recording sounds in words
- writing vocabulary
- reading a text for a running record.

Many teachers adapt this checklist or develop their own checklists or rubrics to record their assessments of learners' reading progress as they move through different reading phases over time.

Running records or miscue analysis

Running records are another kind of diagnostic reading assessment. They help teachers understand what cues a child is using when reading a text they are not familiar with. Often used during the first few years of school, running records are based on the earlier miscue analysis work developed by Kenneth Goodman (2003; see also Goodman & Burke, 1973) and Yetta Goodman (2008). Adapted for younger children by Marie Clay (2019) and Max Kemp (1987), running records are used when a learner has started to develop some confidence in reading. The teacher chooses a text judged to be at the level that the learner is currently reading with confidence. As the child reads, the teacher records whether the child is reading accurately and what kinds of error they make. Clay (2019) developed a set of conventions that teachers can use and share with other members of their year-level team or with parents and caregivers.

> **Running record:** a diagnostic strategy used to determine a child's use of different knowledge and resources when reading an unknown text.

The record will also show whether the learner is using a variety of cues (semantic, syntactic and graphophonic) to work out unknown words or privileging one kind of cue all the time. Recording the reading enables the teacher to revisit it to analyse what is happening more closely. After the child has finished reading, the teacher may ask some questions about the story to ascertain their level of reading comprehension.

Work samples and artefacts

Reading logs, audio and video recordings, reflective journals, readers theatre performances, literature circle tasks, writing in role as a character and inquiry projects are all authentic tasks used in specific contexts that will provide the teacher, parent/caregiver and learner with information about how an individual learner is progressing. Some teachers will develop rubrics with stated criteria in a particular skill area that all three parties can respond to. Others will benchmark learners before and after a particular unit with a specific focus has been completed.

Traditional 'tests' and high-stakes testing

Historically, standardised tests of learner achievement in reading accuracy, fluency and comprehension have dominated reading assessment. When norm-referenced, these standardised tests are used for comparison with other students. In Australia, the tests administered under the National Assessment Plan – Literacy and Numeracy (NAPLAN) since 2008 have attracted much attention and there are mixed opinions about their efficacy. Such summative assessment can only measure what learners already know (as opposed to what they need to develop further) in fairly technical ways. In addition, these tests mostly benefit those learners who are already achieving well. Many of the standardised tests in Australia are culturally and linguistically biased in favour of Anglo-background, middle-class learners. Care thus needs to be taken to ensure that teachers, schools and school systems do not over-emphasise such assessments and that they use the results in the context of the many other assessment strategies they employ.

Peer assessment and self-assessment

If a trusting classroom environment is developed, learners are more likely to understand that all constructive feedback can be helpful, including their own self-reflection and that of their peers. Reading logs and journals can be scaffolded to support reflective practice. The strategies mentioned above and elaborated in Chapter 8, including literature circles, readers theatre and reciprocal reading, can also help establish opportunities for peer commentary and suggestions.

In their very helpful article, 'Every child, every day', Allington and Gabriel (2012) synthesised research from the past few decades to suggest six elements of reading that each learner needs to experience every day consistently. According to the authors' recommendations, every child must accomplish the following:

- read something they choose
- read accurately
- read something they understand
- write about something that is meaningful personally
- talk with peers about reading and writing
- listen to a fluent adult read aloud (Allington & Gabriel, 2012).

REFLECTION

Choose two assessment strategies with which you are not familiar. Explore these strategies in some detail and think about how you might adapt them to make them work for you. For example, if you choose running records, try to establish the way you would use these to gather information about how an emergent reader was using meaning, structure and visual information cues.

If you agree that it is possible for learners to assess their own reading and that of their peers, think about how you could introduce peer assessment and self-assessment practices in the primary classroom.

Important key issues to consider in the teaching of reading

Commercial reading programs

There are many commercial reading programs available, often with sets of levelled, contrived texts. Caution must be exercised and these programs need to be carefully analysed: they can be at odds with the balanced bespoke approaches and repertoire of strategies we have emphasised in this chapter as necessary to meet learners' individual needs in the context of a literature-rich and text-rich classroom environment. Many of these contrived texts do not make sense beyond the sentence level and nor do they help learners build a rich vocabulary, thus undermining the meaning-making process (see Adoniou et al. (2018) for a further discussion of the issues around so-called decodable texts).

Home reading

Reading together and independently at home needs to be an enjoyable experience for the parent or other caregiver and the child. However, sometimes it can cause great angst. Teachers should encourage parents to read *with* their children rather than insist children read *to* them. Talking together about the text is also very important.

The provision of quality literary texts is central to engaging learners in the reading process throughout their school careers and beyond. Research is clear in showing us that it *does* matter what children and young people read. For example, in a recent study of over 45 000 Spanish young people aged between 11 and 14 years, Jerrim and colleagues (2020) reported that:

> we find little evidence that reading newspapers, comics and magazines have positive benefits for young people's academic achievement … the association between reading books/novels and young people's academic progress at school is quite strong … Our findings have highlighted how, in an increasingly digital world, it is important that young people are encouraged to find time to just sit down and read a good book. (pp. 15–16)

Digital technologies and reading

It is essential that teachers and parents consider the potential role that technology can play in a child's reading, especially given the increasing accessibility of laptops, tablets and smart phones in most schools and homes. There seems to be an ever-increasing number of online programs and apps and, as always, they are of varying degrees of quality. Lisa Kervin (2016) argues that digital play offers new opportunities to develop learners' oracy, reading and writing, as long as the app or program is meaningful and playful. Her research with five young children provides examples of the enabling of creativity some digital technologies provide in authentic contexts, including Pocket Pond, Puppet Pals, Minecraft and iMovie in the early stages of reading; and many other applications can be adapted for more experienced readers.

Dispelling common myths about learning to read

Throughout the chapter, we have touched on a number of myths about learning to read. Sometimes these myths can threaten to undermine teacher professional knowledge. If we are to eliminate the so-called 'reading wars', it is imperative that teachers feel confident about addressing damaging or misleading ideas.

These are some common myths about learning to read:

- Suggesting that teachers and teacher education are solely responsible for any difficulties a child might be experiencing in learning to read. Two of the greatest causes of reading difficulty are poverty and the singular adoption of commercial reading programs designed to simply comply with high-stakes testing.
- Advocating for the simplicity of a one-size-fits-all reading program as necessary for *all* children who are learning to read. Some children take more time to understand the reading process and become confident with the different roles of the reader described in this chapter. There are many reasons why some learners experience difficulty learning to read and teachers need to focus on particular strategies to address those specific needs.
- Privileging the reading of contrived texts with limited vocabulary and sentence structure before the reading of authentic, quality literature. Such contrived texts ignore the importance of meaning-making and often do not engage learners.
- Denying that companies lobbying for government funding to implement specific programs do not make substantial commercial gain from selling their programs to schools, teachers and parents.
- Misrepresenting findings from reports to add weight to arguments about the role of phonics in learning to read. Findings from major reports need to be read carefully and in context.
- Advocating the introduction of more high-stakes tests that will disadvantage EAL/D learners as well as many children in vulnerable or at-risk situations (adapted from Thomas, 2019).

Conclusion

Reading for meaning is critical for learners' success. This chapter acknowledged that reading is a highly complex and multidimensional sociocultural meaning-making process that incorporates viewing. It emphasised that there is no recipe for teaching reading that can be applied to all children to ensure reading success. Teachers are constantly learning new skills to enable access to new kinds of reading. Teaching of reading must be underpinned by a repertoire of sound pedagogical reading practices and strategies that continue throughout the early childhood and primary years and beyond. Although there is much focus on and controversy surrounding learning to read in the early years, a competent reader needs to continue to refine their knowledge, skills and understandings of and about reading and the roles of the reader as they read for different purposes over their lifetime.

Bringing it together

1. Return to your definition of reading and viewing from earlier in the chapter. Would you make any additions or changes to how you now think about reading?
2. What do you understand to be the main issues in the so-called 'reading wars'? Are there commonalities that can be emphasised rather than focusing on differences?
3. How can new digital technologies be used to help learners to develop their reading confidence? What criteria will be important in assessing these resources?
4. Indigo's seven-year-old daughter becomes stressed each night when it is time to read to her mother. In turn, Indigo becomes worried because she knows how important it is to learn to read. She doesn't understand why this daily homework activity causes tension between them when other homework tasks do not. What are some actions Indigo could take to try to resolve this issue?
5. Revisit the myths about learning to read. Have you observed anyone in your placement school advocating one of these myths? How might you respond to them?

Further resources

Australian Literacy Educators' Association (ALEA)

An important professional association for literacy educators. Includes research and professional journals, practical resources, local councils for regular professional learning and annual conferences.

www.alea.edu.au

BookTrust

An extensive UK site that includes resources, reviews and booklists that are very helpful for teachers.

www.booktrust.org.uk

Teaching Reading

Emphasises teachers taking a comprehensive approach to teaching reading in the classroom.

Dombey, H. (2010). *Teaching Reading: What the Evidence Says*. UKLA. https://ukla.org/product/teaching-reading-what-the-evidence-says-2

Foundation for Learning and Literacy

The Foundation for Learning and Literacy has collated a range of resources and school success stories about the evidence base for effective literacy teaching and learning that are useful for teachers and parents.

https://foundationforlearningandliteracy.info

Primary English Teaching Association Australia (PETAA)

PETAA provides quality online learning resources and teacher professional learning. These resources are aligned with the Australian Curriculum.

www.petaa.edu.au

Reading Australia

Curated quality Australian literature along with units of work developed by teachers.

https://readingaustralia.com.au

References

Adoniou, M. (2017). Misplaced faith in phonics and the phonics screening check. *Education Journal*, 313, 25–27.

Adoniou, M., Cambourne, B., & Ewing, R. (2018). What are decodable readers and do they work? The Conversation, 1 November. https://theconversation.com/what-are-decodable-readers-and-do-they-work-106067

Afflerbach, P., Pearson, D., & Paris, S. (2008). How distinctions between reading skills and strategies can improve instruction. *The Reading Teacher*, 61(5), 364–373. www.researchgate.net/profile/P_Pearson/publication/228637376_Clarifying_Differences_Between_Reading_Skills_and_Reading_Strategies/links/541663880cf2fa878ad4018c/Clarifying-Differences-Between-Reading-Skills-and-Reading-Strategies.pdf

Allington, R. & Gabriel, R. (2012). Every child, every day. *Educational Leadership*, 69(6), 10–15.

Anderson, L. (2017). Beyond the word. an orthographic learning journey. http://wordsinbogor.blogspot.com

Anderson, L. & Whiting, A. (2019). Workshop presented at the Australian Literacy Educators Conference, Melbourne, July.

Anderson, R., Hiebert, E., Scott, J., & Wilkinson, I. (1985). *Becoming a Nation of Readers. The Report of the Commission on Reading*. National Institute of Education. http://textproject.org/assets/library/resources/Anderson-Hiebert-Scott-Wilkinson-Becoming-a-Nation-of-Readers.pdf

Angel, V. (2005). *Nan and Pap. A-Z Decodable Series. Reading A-Z*. http://englishworldschool.yolasite.com/resources/raz_d03_nanpap.pdf

Anwar, Y. (2019). A map of the brain can tell what you're reading about. *Berkeley News*. UC Berkeley, 19 August. https://news.berkeley.edu/2019/08/19/readingbrainmap

Armstrong, D. (2006). Future directions in literacy. In R. Ewing (Ed.), *Beyond the Reading Wars*. Primary English Teaching Association Australia (PETAA).

Ashton-Warner, S. (1986). *Teacher*. Touchstone.

Atkinson, R. & Shiffrin, R. (1968). Human memory: a proposed system and its control processes. *Psychology of Learning and Motivation*, 1968(2), 89–195.

Australian Council of Social Services (ACOSS). (2018). Poverty in Australia. www.acoss.org.au/poverty

Australian Curriculum, Assessment and Reporting Authority (ACARA). (2018). *Australian Curriculum: English. Version 8.3*. ACARA. www.australiancurriculum.edu.au/english/pdf-documents

—— (2020a). Elements of Literacy Progression. www.australiancurriculum.edu.au/resources/national-literacy-and-numeracy-learning-progressions

—— (2020b). *National Literacy Learning Progression. Version 3.0*. ACARA. www.lpofai.edu.au/media/kw2lslug/national-literacy-learning-progression-v3-for-publication.pdf

Billington, J. (2020). *Reading Between the Lines: The Benefits of Reading for Pleasure*. Centre for Research into Reading Literature and Society.

Bowers, J. & Bowers, P. (2017). Beyond phonics: the case for teaching children the logic of the English spelling system. *Educational Psychologist*, 52(2), 124–141.

—— (2018). There is no evidence to support the hypothesis that systematic phonics should precede morphological instruction: response to Rastle and colleagues. *PsyArXiv*. https://psyarxiv.com/zg6wr

Bowers, P. (2019). Structured word inquiry. Keynote address Australian Literacy Educators Association, Melbourne, July.

Bowers, P. & Kirby, J. (2010). Effects of morphological instructions on vocabulary acquisition. *Reading and Writing: An Interdisciplinary Journal*, 23(5), 515–537.

Callow, J. (2013). *The Shape of Text to Come: How Image and Text Work*. Primary English Teaching Association Australia (PETAA).

Cambourne, B. (n.d.). About the conditions of learning. www.cambournesconditionsoflearning.com.au

Cambourne, B. & Crouch, D. (2018). Cambourne's conditions of learning. www.cambournesconditions oflearning.com.au/conditions-of-learning-blog-spot/cambournes-model-of-literacy-learning

Cambourne, B., Handy, L., & Scown, P. (1988). *The Whole Story: Natural Learning and the Acquisition of Literacy in the Classroom*. Ashton Scholastic.

Campbell, S. (2015). Feeling the pressure: early childhood educators' reported views about learning and teaching phonics in Australian prior-to-school settings. *Australian Journal of Language and Literacy*, 38(1), 12–26.

Carlisle, J. (2010). Effects of instruction in morphological awareness on literacy achievement. *Reading Research Quarterly*, 45(4), 464–487.

Castles, A., Rastle, K., & Nation, K. (2018). Ending reading wars: reading acquisition from novice to expert. *Psychological Science in the Public Interest*, 11 June. https://journals.sagepub.com/doi/full/10.1177/1529100618772271

Clay, M. (1979). *Reading: The Patterning of Complex Behaviour*. Heinemann.

—— (2019). *An Observation Survey of Early Reading Achievement* (4th edn). Global Education Systems.

Deniz, F., Nunez-Elizalde, A., Huth, A., & Gallant, J. (2019). The representation of semantic information across human cerebral cortex during listening versus reading is invariant to stimulus modality. *Journal of Neuroscience*, 19 August. www.jneurosci.org/content/early/2019/08/16/JNEUROSCI.0675-19.2019

Department of Education, Employment & Workplace Relations (DEEWR). (2009). *Belonging, Being & Becoming – The Early Years Learning Framework for Australia*. https://docs.education.gov.au/documents/belonging-being-becoming-early-years-learning-framework-australia

Derewianka, B. & Christie, F. (2008). *School Discourse. Learning to Write across the Years of Schooling*. Continuum.

Devonshire, V. & Fluck, M. (2010). Spelling development: fine-tuning strategy-use and capitalising on the connections between words. *Learning and Instruction*, 20(5), 361–371.

Dombey, H. (2010). *Teaching Reading: What the Evidence Says*. UKLA. https://ukla.org/product/teaching-reading-what-the-evidence-says-2

Dougherty Stahl, K. (2011). Applying new visions of reading development in today's classrooms. *The Reading Teacher: A Journal of Research-Based Classroom Practice*, 65(1), 52–56.

Emmitt, M., Hornsby, D., & Wilson, L. (2013). *The Place of Phonics in Learning to Read and Write* (Revised edition). Australian Literacy Educators' Association.

Ewing, R. (2013). *Curriculum and Assessment: Storylines* (2nd edn). Oxford University Press.

—— (2018). *Exploding SOME of the Myths about Learning to Read. A Review of Research on the Role of Phonics*. NSW Teachers Federation. https://news.nswtf.org.au/application/files/8715/3249/6625/18181_Role_of_Phonics.pdf

Ewing, R., Callow, J. & Rushton, K. (2016). *Language and Literacy Development in Early Childhood*. Cambridge University Press.

Ewing, R., Kervin, L., Glass, C., Gobby, B., Groundwater-Smith, S., & Le Cornu, R. (2020). *Teaching: Challenges, Dilemmas and Opportunities*. Cengage.

Fischer, S. (2004). *A History of Reading*. Reaktion.

Freebody, P. (2007). *Literacy Education in School Research: Perspectives from the Past, for the Future*. ACER.

—— (2019). What kind of knowledge can we use? Scoping an adequate program for literacy education. In R. Cox, S. Feez, & L. Beveridge (Eds), *The Alphabetic Principle and Beyond: Surveying the Landscape*. Primary English Teaching Association.

Freebody, P. & Luke, A. (1990). 'Literacies' programmes: debates and demands in cultural context. *Prospect: A Journal of Australian TESOL*, 5(3), 7–16.

Frey, R.C. (n.d.). Rethinking the role of decodable texts in early literacy instruction. Thesis. http://mustardseedbooks.org/Freydissertation.pdf

Garcia, E. & Weiss, R. (2017). Educational inequalities at the school starting gate. Economic Policy Institute. www.epi.org/publication/education-inequalities-at-the-school-starting-gate

Goodman, K. (1968). *The Psycholinguistic Guessing Game*. Wayne State University Press.

—— (1986). *What's Whole in Whole Language?* Heinemann.

—— (1996). *On Reading*. Heinemann.

—— (2003). *On the Revolution of Reading: The Selected Writings of Kenneth S. Goodman*. Heinemann.

Goodman, K. & Burke, C. (1973). *Theoretically Based Studies of Patterns of Miscues in Oral Reading Performance. Final Report*. Wayne State University. (Eric Document Reproduction Service No, ED 179 708.)

Goodman, Y. (2008). Retrospective miscue analysis: an overview. Viewed at https://view.officeapps.live.com/op/view.aspx?src=https%3A%2F%2Fwww.rcowen.com%2FWordDocs%2FRMA-OverviewChapter.doc

Goodwin, A. & Ahn, S. (2013). A meta-analysis of morphological interventions in English: effects on literacy outcomes for school-age children. *Scientific Studies in Reading*, 17(4), 257–285.

Gough, P.B. & Tunmer, W. (1986). Decoding, reading, and reading disability. *Remedial and Special Education*, 7, 6–10.

Green, B., Cormack, P., & Patterson, A. (2009). Re-reading the reading lesson: episodes in the history of reading pedagogy. *Oxford Review of Education*, 39(3), 329–344.

Heath, S.B. (1983). *Ways with Words: Language, Life and Work in Communities and Classrooms*. Cambridge University Press.

Holdaway, D. (1979). *The Foundations of Literacy*. Ashton Scholastic.

Hoover, W. & Tunmer, W. (2018). The simple view of reading. three assessments of its adequacy. *Remedial and Special Education*, 39(5), 304–312.

International Literacy Association. (2018). Children's Rights to Read. https://literacyworldwide.org/get-resources/childrens-rights-to-read?_ga=2.31638526.1749477555.1567230912-1933794024.1567230912

Jerrim, J., Lopez-Agudo, L., & Marcenaro-Gutierrez, O. (2020). Does it matter what children read? New evidence using longitudinal census data from Spain. *Oxford Review of Education*, 26(5), 515–533. https://doi.org/10.1080/03054985.2020.1723516

Kemp, M. (1987). *Watching Children Read and Write*. Nelson.

Kervin, L. (2016). Powerful and playful literacy learning with digital technologies. *Australian Journal of Language and Literacy*, 39(1), 64–73.

Krashen, S. (2014). The common core: a disaster for libraries, a disaster for language arts, a disaster for American education. *Knowledge Quest*, 42(3), 37–45.

—— (2015). The great fiction/nonfiction debate. Fact or fiction? The plot thickens. *Language Magazine*, 15(3), 22–27.

Krashen, S., Lee, S., & McQuillan, J. (2012). Is the library important? Multivariate studies at the national and international level. *Journal of Language and Literacy Education*, 8(1), 26–38.

Louden, W., Rohl, M., Barratt-Pugh, C., Brown, C., Cairney, T., Elderfield, J., House, H., Riviland, J., & Rowe, K. (2005). *In Teachers' Hands: Effective Literacy Teaching Practice in Early Years of Schooling*. Australian Government, Department of Education, Science and Training.

Lowe, K. (2004). *What's the Story? Making Meaning in Primary Classrooms*. Primary English Teaching Association.

Luke, A. & Freebody, P. (1999). Further notes on the four resources model. www.readingonline.org/research/lukefreebody.html

Meek, M. (1988). *How Texts Teach What Readers Learn*. Thimble Press.

Mehigan, G. (2020). Effects of fluency oriented instruction on motivation for reading of struggling readers. *Education Science*, 10(56), 23 pp. www.mdpi.com/2227-7102/10/3/56/htm

Morphett, M. & Washburne, C. (1931). When should children begin to read? *Elementary School Journal*, 31(7), 496–501.

Organisation for Economic Co-operation and Development (OECD). (2010). *PISA 2009 Results: Learning to Learn – Student Engagement, Strategies and Practices (Volume III.)*. http://dx.doi.org/10.1787/9789264083943-en

Oxford English Corpus. (2006). Compiled by M. Waite. Corpus ID: 58095914.

Paris, S. (2005). Reinterpreting the development of reading skills. *Reading Research Quarterly*, 40(2), 186–202.

Rastle, K. & Taylor, J. (2018). Print-sound regularities are more important than print-meaning regularities in the initial stages of learning to read: response to Bowers & Bowers (2018). *Journal of Experimental Psychology*, May.

Reid, J. (2006). Reading stories. Understanding our professional history as teachers. In R. Ewing (Ed.), *Beyond the Reading Wars. A Balanced Approach to Helping Children Learn to Read*. Primary English Teaching Association Australia (PETAA).

Reid, J. & Green, B. (2004). Displacing method(s)? Historical perspective in the teaching of reading. *Journal of Language and Literacy*, 27, 12–26.

Rogoff, B. (1995). Observing sociocultural activity on three planes: participatory appropriation, guided participation, and apprenticeship. In J.V. Wertsch, P. del Río, & A. Alvarez (Eds.), *Learning in Doing: Social, Cognitive, and Computational Aspects. Sociocultural Studies of Mind* (pp. 139–64). Cambridge University Press.

Rosenblatt, L. (1978). *The Reader, the Text and the Poem: The Transactional Theory of Literary Work*. Southern Illinois University Press.

Sendak, M. (1963). *Where the Wild Things Are*. Harper & Rowe.

Seymour, P., Aro, M., & Erskine, J. (2003). Foundation literacy acquisition in European orthographies. *British Journal of Psychology*, 94, 143–173.

Share, D. (1995). Phonological recoding and self-teaching: sine qua non of reading acquisition. *Cognition*, 55(2), 151–218.

Smith, F. (1978). *Reading*. Cambridge University Press.

Snow, C., Burns, S., & Griffin, P. (1998). *Preventing Reading Difficulties in Young Children*. National Advisory Press.

Spiegel, D. (1998). Silver bullets, babies and bathwater. Literature response groups in a balanced reading program. *The Reading Teacher*, 52(2).

Thomas, P. (2019). Radical eyes for equity. https://radicalscholarship.wordpress.com/2019/06/10/checklist-media-coverage-of-the-science-of-reading

United Nations Educational, Scientific and Cultural Organization (UNESCO). (2020). Literacy. https://en.unesco.org/themes/literacy

Venezky, R. (1967). English orthography: its graphical structure and its relation to sound. *Reading Research Quarterly*, 2(3), 75–105.

Vygotsky, L. (1978). *Mind in Society. Development of Higher Psychological Processes*. Harvard University Press.

Wolf, M. (2007). *Proust and the Squid: The Story and Science of the Reading Brain*. Harper.

CHAPTER 7

Children's literature as the heart of literacy teaching

Deb Brosseuk

ANTICIPATED OUTCOMES

After working through this chapter, it is anticipated you will be able to:

- understand what children's literature is
- describe the place of children's literature in Australian education documents
- understand why the literature landscape matters
- implement ways to set up, organise and curate children's literature
- know how to stay up-to-date with contemporary children's literature
- understand the importance of becoming a literary role model.

Introduction

Children's literature is the heart of literacy teaching. In the hands of thoughtful teachers, children's literature helps learners of all ages experience, and delight in, language and literacy. In Shelley Harwayne's *Lifetime Guarantees: Toward Ambitious Literacy Teaching*, children's literature is described as a 'trustworthy companion' that can help learners explore new and functional text types, appreciate literary techniques, see different perspectives, question and examine ideas, discover new, creative ways to produce print, visual and digital texts, and imagine possibilities and places beyond their own lifeworlds (Harwayne, 2000, p. 5). It should be no surprise, then, that thoughtful teachers devote their energies to placing children's literature as the centrepiece of their literacy teaching. Teachers want learners to deeply care about language and literacy long after they leave school. Russian pianist and composer Sergei Rachmaninoff once famously said, 'Music is enough for a lifetime, but a lifetime is not enough for music' (University of Cambridge, 2015). And, so, teachers work hard to inspire a lifetime love of literacy in the hearts of learners.

In this chapter we ask: *What is children's literature?* We aim to challenge the traditional idea that children's literature is simply paper-based stories for learners. To do this, we look at what Australia's English curriculum says about literature and literary texts. Then, we reflect deeply on practical ways we can aid learners to find joy in literature and use different literary texts to read silently, read aloud and read with friends; talk about plot, characters and settings; examine word choices; reflect on visual elements in images; see different perspectives; perform readers theatre; and sing. But this is no easy feat. Therefore, to help teachers, the bulk of the chapter offers practical ways to do what evidence-based research tells us, which is to put our trust in literature, and submerge and soak learners in quality literature to best support their efforts to lead literate lives.

> **Children's literature:** a broad range of literature such as picture books, verse novels, short stories and plays, visual and multimodal texts such as book trailers and films, and an assortment of non-fiction that help learners be active, constructive and engaged literacy learners.

What is children's literature?

To help learners lead literate lives, the Australian Curriculum: English asks teachers to use children's literature as a way of teaching learners to talk, view, listen, read, write, respond and create (Australian Curriculum, Assessment and Reporting Authority [ACARA], n.d.a). However, before we can plan to do this, we must understand what is meant by children's literature. Often children's literature is defined as stories written for learners, read by learners and/or written about learners (Jasinski-Schneider, 2016) – a simple, but perhaps too simple, definition. To critically reflect on this, we ask two questions: Is children's literature just a collection of storybooks? Is children's literature just read by learners? While we may answer 'yes' to these questions, we know that learners engage with literature in ways that extend far beyond reading and viewing just storybooks. We also know that adults enjoy sharing children's literature with learners.

Learners engage in a wide array of literature to study the intricacies of language found in literary texts (ACARA, n.d.a). Literary texts include paper-based texts, such as storybooks, Dreaming stories, dramatic television scripts and poetry, and also digital texts. E-literature, or e-lit for short, is paper-based texts that have been digitised for mobile devices such as laptops, smartphones, tablets, smart watches and e-readers. Storybook apps are a good example of e-literature. They take paper-based texts and bring together text and highly interactive visual and audio modes. Popular media services that offer storybook apps include Goodreads, hoopla, Epic! and ComiXology. Interactivity with storybook apps, alongside other sorts of apps like social media, is very much part of many learners' everyday digital literacy practices (Danby, 2020; Frederico, 2017; Ryan et al., 2020). Therefore, to talk about children's literature in the restricted sense of paper-based storybooks is to overlook the ever-evolving digital knowledge and expertise of learners.

Fellowes and Oakley (2020) tell us that when we think deeply about *what* children's literature is, we must also think about what children's literature *does*. In a general sense, children's literature helps learners develop an understanding, appreciation and use of English (ACARA, n.d.a). Literature acts as a linguistic, social, cultural and political artefact, something that learners read, view, discuss and (re)create to better understand themselves and the world in which they live. As learners read, view, discuss and (re)create, there are opportunities for them to act as text analysts, or text critics, picking up on the ideological opinions and viewpoints of authors and illustrators (Luke & Freebody, 1999). Potentially, this can invite self-reflection and stir up a wakefulness of, and emotional sensitivity to, a range of topics – for example, homelessness, bullying, family trauma, immigration, climate change, racism and gender inequities.

And, finally, we must think about *why* children's literature is important. This is where we need to think big! Harwayne (2000) tells us that when we make children's literature the lifeblood of our literacy teaching, we lay a strong foundation for learners to dedicate energies to the mighty 'pursuit of literacy' (p. xiii). As discussed in Chapter 1, being literate is a gateway to personal and social change; it offers opportunities for learners to critically question what they see, to expand their thinking, (re)shape their understandings and take steps towards crafting a more tolerant, compassionate and equitable world. As Short (2012) so beautifully says, children's literature is important because it has 'power to direct and change our lives and world' (p. 17). Therefore, as thoughtful teachers, we must do all that we can to find engaging ways for children's literature to breathe life into the literacy of our learners.

Children's literature in curriculum frameworks

Children's literature is an important part of literacy education in the Australian Curriculum: English Foundation to Year 10 (ACARA, n.d.a). The Australian Curriculum: English is organised into three interconnected strands: language, literacy and literature. The literature strand aims to grow learners' knowledge and understanding of Standard Australian English through 'the study of literary texts of personal, cultural, social and aesthetic value' (ACARA, n.d.a). To achieve this formidable aim, the curriculum provides an overarching statement that encourages teachers to reflect and think deeply about understandings of what literature is and what it looks like within an educational learning context. The Australian Curriculum: English states the following:

> The term 'literature' refers to the past and present texts across a range of cultural contexts that are valued for their form and style and are recognised as having enduring or artistic value. While the nature of what constitutes literary texts is dynamic and evolving, they are seen as having personal, social, cultural and aesthetic value and potential for enriching learners' scope of experience. Literature includes a broad range of forms such as novels, poetry, short stories and plays; fiction for young adults and children, multimodal texts such as film, and a variety of non-fiction. Literary texts also include excerpts from longer texts. This enables a range of literary texts to be included within any one year level for close study or comparative purposes. (ACARA, n.d.b)

This statement draws attention to the wide-ranging forms of literary texts, such as paper print-based texts, as well as visual and multimodal texts. It is through a study of these forms that teachers can aid learners' intellectual capabilities as well as their personal, social and cultural understandings related to the Australian Curriculum's seven general capabilities (ACARA, n.d.c). For example, to achieve greater personal and social capability, and develop responsible decision-making, we can browse anthologist Wendy Cooling's *All the Wild Wonders: Poems of Our Earth* (Cooling & Grobler, 2010) to learn about protecting the Earth for the future. We can also use Dr Sue Pillans' picture book *Cranky Frankie and the Oceans of Trash* (Pillans, 2022) to have reflective conversations around marine debris and ocean plastic pollution, and the need to save Australia's Great Barrier Reef from environmental degradation by ridding it of plastic. And we must not forget about *Dark Emu* (Pascoe, 2018) and *Living Alongside the Animals – Anangu Way* (Wingfield & Austin, 2009) to talk about the sustainable practices of Aboriginal and Torres Strait Islander peoples, both now and in the past.

In addition, through the study of wide-ranging forms of literary texts, teachers can actively promote the skills, knowledge and dispositions set out in the Early Years Learning Framework (EYLF) (Department of Education, Employment and Workplace Relations [DEEWR], 2009). As introduced in previous chapters, the EYLF is designed for early childhood educators who teach learners up to five years of age, and stresses that 'all children experience learning that is engaging and builds successes for life' (DEEWR, 2009, p. 7). Fundamental to the EYLF is the view that learners' lifeworlds are typified by belonging, being and becoming. Experiencing *belonging* is central to learners developing a 'knowing of where and with whom' they belong, whether it be a family, a cultural group, a sporting recreational club or the wider community. *Being* acknowledges the significance of learners' lives, their inherent strengths, interests and capabilities, as well as their participation, agency and voice. Finally, *becoming* reflects learners' ever-changing identities brought about by events and circumstances (DEEWR, 2009). To achieve belonging, being and becoming, the EYLF is arranged under five broad outcomes:

- Outcome 1: Children have a strong sense of identity
- Outcome 2: Children are connected with and contribute to their world
- Outcome 3: Children have a strong sense of wellbeing
- Outcome 4: Children are confident and involved learners
- Outcome 5: Children are effective communicators (DEEWR, 2009).

Literary texts can be utilised to meet the EYLF's personal, social and cultural learning outcomes. Table 7.1 presents a mix of paper print-based, visual and multimodal texts that can

158   ENGLISH AND LITERACIES

be used to encourage talk about themes and ideas in ways that progress learners towards achieving the EYLF outcomes. Icons are utilised as a way of making known different literary text forms and to aid meaning. The icons are explicated below.

Table 7.1 Texts to progress learners towards meeting EYLF outcomes

Picture books	Anthologies	Audio books	Websites	Poems	Music lyrics	Theatre scripts

EYLF outcome	Form	Examples of literary texts	Themes
Outcome 1: Children have a strong sense of identity		*What Riley Wore* (Arnold & Davick, 2019) *The World Needs Who You Were Made to Be* (Gaines & Swaney, 2020) *Student Poem Library* (Red Room Company, 2020) *Just the Way We Are* (Robertson & Shirvington, 2020) *Brave Little Ones* (Zelina & Maczó, 2018)	• Diverse families (sole parent, blended families, same-sex families) • Heritage • History • Inclusivity • Tolerance • Acceptance • Communication • Uniqueness • Respect • Confidence • Courage • Friendship • Belonging • Love
Outcome 2: Children are connected with and contribute to their world		*Arabel and Mortimer Stories* (Aiken, 2019) *Love Makes a Family* (Beer, 2018) *I'm Australian Too* (Fox, 2017) *My Two Blankets* (Kobald & Blackwood, 2015) *The Lost Girl* (Kwaymullina & Tobin, 2017)	• Diverse families (sole parent, blended families, same-sex families, Aboriginal kinship groups) • Diverse family histories (migrant families, refugee families) • Identity • Inclusivity • Tolerance • Acceptance • Kinship • Respect • Belonging

Table 7.1 (cont.)

EYLF outcome	Form	Examples of literary texts	Themes
Outcome 3: Children have a strong sense of wellbeing		*Songs and Lyrics* (Department of Health, 2020) *The Princess and the Fog: A Story for Children with Depression* (Jones et al., 2015) Kenn Nesbitt's Poetry4kids (2020) *What Should Darla Do? Featuring the Power to Choose* (Levy et al., 2019) *Be Kind* (Miller & Hill, 2018)	• Health and safety • Nutrition • Expression • Self-esteem and self-confidence • Self-reflection • Personal actions and consequences • Empathy • Compassion • Feelings • Inclusivity • Kindness • Respect • Identity • Respect • Friendship
Outcome 4: Children are confident and involved learners		*The Gobbledegook Book* (Cowley, 2019) *Papa's Mechanical Fish* (Fleming & Kulikov, 2013) *Here's a Little Poem: A Very First Book of Poetry* (Yolen et al., 2007) *If I Never Forever Endeavor* (Meade, 2011) *The Most Magnificent Thing* (Spires, 2014)	• Imagination • Creativity • Individuality • Curiosity • Responsibility • Experimentation • Reflection • Persistence • Drive • Problem-solving • Respect • Resilience • Cooperation
Outcome 5: Children are effective communicators		*The Enormous Potato* (Davis & Petricic, 1999) *Bedtime Stories (As Told by Our Dad) (Who Messed Them Up)* (Monk, 2020) *Enemy Pie* (Munson & King, 2000) *One* (Otoshi, 2008) *Amelia Bedelia* (Parish & Siebel, 2013)	• Sharing • Teamwork • Anti-bullying • Facing fears • Following rules • Cooperation • Identity • Kindness • Communication • Expression

160   ENGLISH AND LITERACIES

CASE STUDY 7.1   **Noah**

Meet Noah, a five-year-old Preparatory learner. Noah wanted to design an upgraded defence system for the Star Wars starship, the Millennium Falcon. To help Noah see himself as an independent thinker, creative director, open-minded collaborator and bold innovator, picture books provided much of the practical sponsorship and guidance.

When Noah walked into the classroom on Tuesday morning and announced, 'I have an idea', Mr Butler smiled. He knew Andrea Beaty's books *Sofia Valdez, Future Prez* (Beaty & Roberts, 2019) and *Ada Twist, Scientist* (Beaty & Roberts, 2016) had given Noah the confidence to welcome an idea, to care for it and pursue it. Noah happily shared his idea with classmates. He told them about designing an upgraded defence system for the Millennium Falcon. Noah showed his sketched designed solution. Noah's classmates listened as Noah told them in quite practical terms about his design – what he did, why he did it and how it would keep the warship safe. Open-ended questions from Noah's classmates helped him better understand where and why his designed solution was potentially correct or incorrect, flawed or faulty. This time of togetherness sparked capacity for improved design through collaboration and shared reflections.

Question

What EYLF outcomes did Noah meet when interacting with his classmates and talking about his designed solution for the Millennium Falcon's defence system?

A vibrant literary vista

Vista: a vibrant place where language and literature are an important part of the environmental aesthetics to meet the needs and interests of learners.

As thoughtful teachers, we commit to creating a vibrant literary **vista**. When learners enter the classroom, they are met by a vista carefully created to build knowledge, understanding, appreciation and use of English (ACARA, n.d.a). We create the vista because we want to invite learners to engage with and enjoy a wide range of literary texts, such as picture books, fantasy and adventure novels, ballads, haiku and other poems, folk tales, myths and legends, song lyrics and short plays. For instance, if we want learners to engage with witty, wacky and wise characters, then we make available verse novels such as *Kings and Queens* (Farjeon & Farjeon, 2015) or *Poetry Pie* (McGough, 2015). If we want learners to delight in the use of expressive voices, invented dialogue and dramatic role play, then we bring in readers theatre, and take to the stage whimsical characters like Chicken Little, the Pied Piper of Hamelin and the Lazy Cow (Meighan, 2015), as well as grief-stricken Orpheus and foolish King Midas, popular Greek mythological figures (Pugliano-Martin & Pugliano, 2008). And, finally, if we want learners to be intrigued by design, dialogue and visual characterisations, then we bring in graphic novels like Dan Carroll's (2009) *Stick Figure Hamlet*.

When teachers introduce texts such as these, they are well on their way to putting together a vibrant literary vista.

However, creating a vibrant literary vista may not be achieved just because we make available literary texts on bookshelves. Quite the contrary. As thoughtful teachers, we must reflect and think deeply about how we can extend generous invitations to learners to engage with and enjoy different types of literary texts. As a teacher, you will ask yourself:

- How will I provide opportunities for conversations about literature?
- How can learners share their recommendations of funny, interesting, inspiring, sad or thought-provoking literature? Where can I share and display recommendations?
- How will literature be displayed? How can I make it readily accessible?
- How will literature be organised? Should I use plastic baskets, for example?
- How will literature be grouped – by text type, author, topic or interest?
- How will learners know how literature is grouped? Should I use labels, pictures or both?
- How will learners access digital literature such as e-storybooks?
- What computer technologies will I need– for example, iPads or tablets? Where will they be stored?
- Where will literature be enjoyed? What resources are needed to create a cosy reading and viewing space – for example, bean bags, fluffy rugs, lamps, a couch and a smattering of pillows?
- How will I create spaces for different types of reading and viewing? Will they be independent, close buddy or guided group?
- Where can learners perform readers theatre and role play? Where will they take on literary roles in literature circles?
- Where will I meet with learners for individual reading and viewing conferences?
- How will I share information about literature with parents and caregivers?

As a teacher, you will need to ask yourself these questions many times throughout the year. But there is no one *correct answer* to any of them. This is because knowledgeable teachers know that a one-size-fits-all approach does not meet learners' individual interests, inherent strengths and literary needs. For instance, Miss Speolstra knows that her learners love poetry and so she hangs rhymes and chants in surprising places: on the front sliding door; low on the brick wall; above the sink; and on the back of bookshelves. There is even a make-shift stage for budding performing poets! Mr Carlisle has an ongoing art-related literature space where his learners can digitally design and create new book jackets for older literary treasures. A bookmark is also created to accompany each book! And Mrs Kerr knows that her learners much prefer working with theatre scripts on portable lap tables. Learners huddle together and do a table reading (just like in the movies!). In whatever ways teachers choose to create a vibrant literary vista, one thing is certain – it is a lot easier to do beautiful literacy work when learners *choose* to read, write, respond and create with literary texts.

REFLECTION

Learners and their families are well served by thoughtful teachers who give serious thought to creating a vibrant literary vista. This is important because we want learners to learn how to read, write, respond and create, but, most importantly, we want learners to wholeheartedly *choose* to read, write, respond and create. Take some time to look and reflect on what the vista in your classroom says about your values and beliefs around growing learners' knowledge, understanding, appreciation and use of English through literary texts.

Setting up, organising and using literary texts in the classroom

It is a delightful problem to have such an assortment of literary texts that we must think of creative ways to store and display them! But it is too easy just to pop texts on wooden bookshelves and wire bookstands. Teachers have to roll up their sleeves and ask themselves, 'How can we help learners engage with and enjoy texts?' Teachers must think carefully about ways to put texts in the hands of learners. Some teachers put commercially made book boxes on group tables filled with picture books and novels. Depending on learners' interests and abilities, these might include stalwarts such as *Pearl Barley and Charlie Parsley* (Blabey, 2008) and *Who Sank the Boat?* (Allen, 1996), *Charlotte's Web* (White & Williams, 2012), *Matilda* (Dahl, 1988), *The Little Wave* (Harry, 2019) and *Crow Country* (Constable, 2012). To give learners easy access to audio books, teachers can neatly store iPads or tablets on portable charging docks, with headsets neatly positioned on hooks. Some may put in a request to the school registrar for tote trolleys and book bin trolleys, and even soft furnishings, contingent on the facility's budget. Who wouldn't want to get comfortable in a bean bag and read the inspirational lyrics of Destiny Child's 'Survivor', Christina Aguilera's 'Beautiful' or John Lennon's 'Imagine'?

Teachers can also put literary texts in the hands of learners in do-it-yourself kind of ways. Often multinational stores are only too willing to donate out-of-season cardboard display stands. A stand might display chapter book series like Aaron Blabey's *The Bad Guys* (Blabey, 2021), Dav Pilkey's *Dog Man* (Pilkey, 2021) and David Walliams' *The World's Worst Children* (Walliams, 2021) or graphic novels such as Kazi Kibuishi's *Amulet* (Kibuishi, 2018). Sometimes, the local café might have one or two milk crates lying around just waiting to be repurposed as shelving. Or how about upcycling old cardboard archive boxes into spacious organisers? Teachers also might spread delightful verse novels along hanging plastic rain gutters. Yes, rain gutters! Who wouldn't want to select *Inside Out and Back Again* (Lai, 2013), *Like Pickle Juice on a Cookie* (Sternberg & Cordell, 2016) or *Prince Puggly of Spud and the Kingdom of Spiff* (Weston, 2014) from the gutter edge? Teachers seek out these makeshift ways of making literature accessible because they understand the importance of a vibrant literary vista and, quite frankly, it's fun! Other things that could be repurposed for setting up, organising and using literary texts include:

- wicker baskets
- plastic peg baskets and buckets
- plastic laundry baskets
- large flexi tubs
- plastic shoe boxes
- wooden shoe racks
- magazine racks
- cardboard magazine boxes
- dishwasher racks
- cardboard photocopy boxes
- wire book stands
- plastic caddies
- large foil trays
- cardboard archive boxes
- wooden bookends
- clip-on clothes hangers
- under-bed storage containers
- tea chest moving boxes.

Blogs are a fantastic way to find inspiration and new ideas. Abby from Babbling Abby and Deanna from Mrs Jump's Class are favourites. And don't forget about Pinterest and Twitter. Grab a cup of tea and browse the feeds of Teaching Blog Addict, Erica Bohrer and Amy Lemons and scroll through the Instagram hashtags #classroomlibrary, #classroomorganization and #classroomsetup.

REFLECTION

Whichever way you choose to set up and organise literary texts in the classroom, it needs to be at the learners' fingertips. Think deeply and ask yourself, 'How can my classroom walls, shelves, baskets, boxes, windowsills and tables offer learners access to literary texts?'

Curating collections of literary texts

In *Shelf Respect: A Book Lover's Defence* (Austen, 2019), Annie Austen talks about the meaning of literature displayed on a bookshelf. She asks us to reflect and think deeply about what our bookshelves might say. Austen (2019) believes that 'someone's bookshelves are a way of showing you who they are, a presentation of themselves that is at once personal and shared' (p. 10). And so, when we stand in the corner of our classroom and allow our eyes to weave in and out of bookshelves, wicker baskets, storage caddies, wire stands, painted archive boxes, cardboard book boxes and so on, what do we see? Do our collections of literary texts raise questions, reveal new perspectives, inspire acts of kindness, honour second languages, promote a sense of wonderment, pay tribute to long-forgotten literary treasures and encourage cross-curricular exploration? Or do they say something narrower, offering perhaps only a single picture or perspective of the world? Thoughtful teachers review the texts on display in the classroom many times throughout the year to ensure that learners can see a broad representation of life and lifeworlds in literary texts.

To promote an inclusive text experience for learners, teachers carefully curate collections. From within these collections come inspiration for learners to imagine, ponder and think deeply, reflect on different perspectives and notice new, interesting things in their lifeworlds. For instance, learners can stroll suburban streets and run through fields of sugar cane, live inside a body that might not look like their own, meet a divorced father and his new male partner, feel empathy towards someone getting teased, and connect to a different culture and its customs and traditions. Imaginative fiction can trigger self-reflection, bringing new perspectives and opportunities for thoughts and feelings of empathy and compassion (Nikolajeva, 2013; Thexton et al., 2019). While some learners will find these scenarios far-removed from themselves and their lifeworlds, it is hoped they will connect with them in some way and find kinship. But it is imperative that teachers do more than just hastily grab their fair share of literary texts from the library and stack the classroom bookshelves. They must commit time, effort and careful planning to curating collections of literary texts.

To help with this mammoth task, it is useful to ask for assistance from those who know best, such as utilising the expertise of school and community-based librarians. Learners also can be invited to help search for, select and curate collections of literary texts. This joint responsibility is not trivial busywork, but should be approached as informing work. Teachers can learn a great deal about learners' literary interests and favourites, as well as their dislikes. Together, the teacher and learners curate collections that include literary texts that may linger in their minds all through the school day, in the car, tram or bus on the way home and into the night-time. The following sections discuss a few of the many possible ways collections help learners see, think, imagine and wonder.

Literature that honours cultural diversity

The We Need Diverse Books social media movement brought attention to the need for cultural diversity in literary texts (see https://diversebooks.org). This movement raised important questions about the need for learners from diverse cultures to see themselves in texts, and continues to call for texts that inspire thinking and respectful talk about diverse cultures where people, both within and outside the culture, interact with each other. For instance, Mem Fox's beautiful picture book, *I'm Australian Too* (Fox, 2017) can lead to talk about ancestral histories of different families and inclusiveness, as well as acceptance and tolerance. Tamsin Janu's brilliant *Figgy* series (Janu, 2014, 2016) opens learners' eyes to life in Ghana. And it's little wonder that artist, poet and storyteller, and descendent of the Kamlilaroi and Euahlayi people, Gregg Dreise's *Kookoo Kookaburra* (2015), *Mad Magpie* (2017) and *Cunning Crow* (2019) are so well read. For older learners, Nick Earls' *New Boy* (2015) tackles cultural traditions and racism. For more ideas, browse the digital pages of the National Centre for Australian Children's Literature (NCACL, 2019) to access culturally diverse texts, each with links to the Australian Curriculum.

Literature that embraces language diversity

Teachers need to honour not only literature that embraces cultural diversity, but also diversity of language. Sharing memories is one of many ways for sharing literature in the first language of learners. For example, Oscar may tell the class that his favourite childhood series of books follows the antics of a talking cow, or *ko* in Swedish, called Mamma Mu. He proudly reads *Mamma Mu simmar* by Jujja Wieslander (2021) in his native tongue. The melodic sound of the Swedish language is captivating. To embrace Oscar's first language, the teacher and learners might make anchor charts, posters or A5 booklets of key Swedish words from *Mamma Mu simmar*. Tomoko could share the intricacies of Japanese written language by writing her classmates' names in katakana on flashcards. The flashcards can then be fastened together with a metal book ring for ease of viewing.

Another fabulous book for exploring language diversity with learners is *Where Happiness Hides* (Bertini, 2020), which presents the story in various languages such as Polish, Cantonese, Finnish, Italian and Afaan Oromoo. More ways to embrace language diversity in the classroom include:

- stories, rhymes, jokes, comics, riddles, amusing poems and traditional folktales from faraway places
- songs in different languages
- destination guidebooks (e.g. those published by Lonely Planet)
- information books featuring the historical, political and economic background of places within Australia or other countries
- travel brochures featuring popular tourist attractions
- fold-out maps of well-known travel routes.

Literature that encourages reflective talk

Another type of collection is one that can lead to conversations and reflective talk about important matters. Teachers need to teach learners how to put forward honest questions, speak in respectful ways and express their thoughts and opinions without judgement. Reading and viewing picture books such as *The Remember Balloons* (Oliveros & Wulfekotte, 2018) and *The Invisible String* (Karst & Lew-Vriethoff, 2018) can lead to conversations about difficult topics, such as serious illness and coping with feelings of sadness, grief, loss and anger. Many of these themes are also reflected in classic stories like *Storm Boy* (Thiele, 2019) and *His Name Was Walter* (Rodda, 2018). Graphic novels like Shaun Tan's *The Arrival* (Tan, 2006) can lead to reflective talk about what it means to be a refugee. Australian Poetry Slam champion Omar Musa's poems 'My Generation' and 'The Great Displaced' (Musa, 2014) can inspire discussion about homeland, belonging and identity.

Literature that celebrates pursuits and pastimes

When teachers ask learners, 'What are you reading?', it often becomes clear that they are enthusiastic about a particular topic that they want to learn more about. In one teacher's classroom, the learners revealed varying interests through their reading. For Ben, it was learning more about the crazy antics of cheeky blue Wizz (Lee & McKenzie, 2020) or the ill-tempered and utterly selfish Pig the Pug (Blabey, 2020a, 2020b), but for Annastacia, it was following the boarding school explorations of Alice-Miranda-Highton-Smith-Kennington-Jones (Harvey, 2020) that engrossed her. The fast-paced thrilling adventures in Anthony Horowitz's *Alex Rider* (Horowitz, 2021) series were firm favourites with Bailey and Braiden. And Charlotte and her friends loved to read theatre scripts, in particular, those in playwright Ed Monk's *Bedtime Stories (As Told By Our Dad) (Who Messed Them Up)* (Monk, 2020). What a fun script! And so, when learners reveal that they are interested in a topic, this is the teacher's opportunity to collect literature on that topic.

REFLECTION

Learners will benefit from literary texts that meet the needs of their individual pursuits and pastimes. As a teacher, ask yourself, 'How can I learn about my learners' reading pursuits and pastimes?' To aid your understanding about how to uncover learners' interests, reflect on the following questions:

1. What role could individual reading conferences play?
2. How might I informally observe what learners choose to read for pleasure?
3. Would reading for pleasure surveys reveal likes and dislikes?
4. Might learners be keen to post reading interests in a classroom mailbox or on a digital class blog?
5. What role might parents and caregivers play?

Literature that explores home and place

There is something special about home and place that is worth exploration. When teachers explore concepts like belonging and identity and the role they play in shaping our lifeworlds, they often use Jeannie Baker's (2004) picture book *Home* or Nadia Wheatley's (1988) *My Place*. It is important not forget about exploring home and place beyond your own environment. To discover more about crocodiles in Darwin and kangaroos in Canberra, teachers can read aloud Ruth Waters' (2021) *Love from Australia*. Or perhaps learners want to know more about Australian regional towns and cities. Then teachers can turn to Hilary Bell and Matthew Martin's *The Marvellous Funambulist of Middle Harbour and Other Sydney Firsts* (Bell & Martin, 2016) and Alison Lester's (2005) *Are We There Yet?* For exploration of more complex themes, such as isolation and cultural difference and the issues and challenges around displacement, teachers can use Shaun Tan's (2021) postmodern picture book *Eric*.

Other collections

As mentioned earlier, it is important to explore collections alongside learners by inviting them on the adventure of curating collections of literary texts. Learners will happily read, reread and make suggestions when invited to do so. Here are some other types of collections for consideration:

- literature that honours the past
- literature that sparks curiosity and inquisitiveness
- literature that inspires kind-heartedness
- literature that honours art and music
- literature that includes pop-ups and lift-the-flaps
- literature that encourages a love of science, technology, engineering and mathematics (STEM)
- literature that explores feelings and emotions
- literature that explores humanity
- literature that features surreal imagery
- literature that encourages language play
- literature that applauds Australian authors
- literature that teaches us about ourselves
- literature that celebrates world, time and place
- literature that challenges stereotypes
- literature that makes us laugh out loud
- literature that asks bamboozling questions
- literature that features rhythm, rhyme and repetition
- literature that inspires travel to faraway places.

REFLECTION

Run your eyes across your carefully curated collections. What do you see? Do the collections allow learners to engage with literary texts that are representative of 'who is in the world'? Do they encourage learners to see, think, imagine and wonder?

Staying up-to-date with literary texts

Since children's literature is the heart of literacy teaching, teachers need to be familiar with fabulous literary texts. But with the publication of picture books, verse novels, travel blogs, music lyrics, comics, graphic novels, poems, e-books and much more, keeping up is a seemingly impossible task! To help with this gargantuan task, teachers can chat enthusiastically with their colleagues about literature. On placement or in your new school, talk about literature while sipping your morning coffee, warming up your lunch in the staffroom or waiting for the afternoon staff meeting to begin. There is little more exhilarating than sharing your find of vintage Disney comics at a garage sale and reminiscing over the larking about of Mickey, Minnie, Goofy and Pluto with colleagues. Bargain bins at second-hand bookshops, book exchanges or the local opportunity shop can lead to literary treasures.

Still, staying up-to-date with new literature is almost a full-time job. The following sections suggest a few of the many practical ways of keeping up.

Ask learners for recommendations

One way of keeping up with the literature being published is to ask learners for their recommendations. Learners often have strong opinions, and they will happily reveal what they like and do not like. Providing your learners with a basket full of colourful sharpies and asking them to list their favourite literature will almost certainly lead to some lively discussion and debate. The list would most likely roll out the classroom door! And it would no doubt grow over the coming days and weeks. Teachers can share learners' suggestions with others as well. Wouldn't it be grand to see 'Year 2B's Favourite Reads' on the library pin board, or 'Stellar Reads by Year 6' in the school weekly newsletter? Perhaps the school principal can be asked to lend their office door to share learners' suggestions with visitors. No matter the forum of suggestions, they will be of great benefit to learners, colleagues and the wider learning community.

Gratefully accept donations

Gratefully accepting donations from colleagues, learners, parents, caregivers, neighbours and local community groups is a great way of staying on top of literature. It can be exhilarating to rummage through hemp shopping bags and cardboard boxes full of no-longer-wanted literary treasures. Perhaps you might find an old, weathered book of limericks by Edward Lear, a handful of the ever-popular choose-your-own-adventure books, or even a whole series of *Rascal the Dragon* (Jennings, 2004) or *Wicked!* (Jennings & Gleitzman, 1998) books. And what a treat to discover an assortment of picture books, poetry and novels by Australian author and poet Libby Hathorn! It is important to not worry too much about the books' condition or where you might store and display them. And when your collections need refreshing, you can pass these literary delights on to those who are keen to bolster their collections at home or at their local community group.

Make connections in the local community

The local community is a great resource to help us tap into literature. Creating connections with the local librarian or the owner of the local independent bookshop will help keep you up-to-date about literary trends and what people are reading, as well as to see clever ways to organise and display literature. It might also be worth joining emailing lists for local bookshops and libraries, which will often contain information about upcoming book releases, book promotions, guest speakers and in-store author signings. Libraries and many other community spaces also host special events, such as National Simultaneous Storytime (Australian Library and Information Association [ALIA], 2020), book clubs and chapter meetings for literacy associations. These can provide perfect opportunities for teachers and learners to hear and talk about literature that spans across year levels.

Learn from expert organisations

There are wonderful professional organisations in Australia to help teachers stay on top of literature. The Australian Children's Laureate Foundation (ACLF), Children's Book Council of Australia (CBCA) and Reading Australia are not-for-profit organisations whose main purpose is to promote Australian children's literature. A subscription to professional journals is another way to keep in touch with developments in children's literature and new publications. Australian journals offer practical ideas for teaching language and literacy through literature – for example, the Australian Literacy Educators' Association practitioner journal, *Practical Literacy: The Early and Primary Years* (PLEPY), and the high-calibre *Australian Journal of Language and Literacy* (AJLL). Be willing also to share challenging or informative journal articles with your colleagues. These articles can also be talked about at staff meetings.

Peek at authors' social media

Many authors have lively social media accounts, such as on Instagram, Twitter, YouTube and Facebook, and connecting with these is a great way of keeping up with new literature. Sharing buttons makes it easy to peek into authors' literary lives through a simple 'click'. We can visit Emily Gravett's webpage to learn more about her life as an art teacher (Gravett, 2020), and then pop over to her Instagram to see the most delightful drawings of *Cyril and Pat* (Gravett, 2019). Perhaps most excitingly, when we search the hashtag #Operationstorytime on Instagram, Facebook, Twitter and YouTube, we can see Eva Chen, Jan Brett, Dav Pilkey, Peter H. Reynolds, Oliver Jeffers, Todd Parr and many more authors doing fun read-alouds. And we must not miss Mo Willems (2020), author of *Don't Let the Pigeon Drive the Bus!*, create his lunchtime doodles. Keep an eye out for the questions-in-live Instagram and Facebook feature, which provides learners with opportunities to ask questions of their most-loved poets and authors.

A literary role model

If we want learners of all ages to deeply care about literature, and devote their energies to viewing, reading, responding to and creating an assortment of literary texts, then we must be literary role models and show learners that we are enthusiastic about literature. When learners settle down with their chosen picture book or graphic novel during independent reading time, the teacher must settle down too, sitting quietly and reading the works of a favourite author. Learners then see that teachers also are devourers of literature and, even more importantly, that they respect and cherish literature. Teachers should also make time to have literary conversations and talk about what they have viewed and read. For example, the teacher might draw attention to the things that entertained, bewildered, excited and even bothered and disappointed them in the texts they read, making comments and asking questions (e.g. 'I was totally annoyed about … ', 'Why would the author/illustrator do that?' or 'I loved it when … '). Being a literary role model is an important part of being a thoughtful teacher and of literacy teaching.

LAUNCH

CASE STUDY 7.2

Literature can help learners of all ages to think deeply, express opinions, make guesses or, in five-year-old Sebastian's case, deal with problems. Sebastian's problem was simple. He was bothered by the hungry ibis birds that made their way to the eating space at lunchtime. 'Those ibis birds are real pesky,' Sebastian announced, 'You know … they wait to get our food.' Mrs Bryant nodded and asked, 'What can you do about it?' Sebastian shrugged his shoulder and replied, 'I don't know.'

▶ ▶

▶▶ What role might children's literature play in helping Sebastian solve his problem of removing the pesky ibis birds from his lunchtime eating space?

To help Sebastian understand the complexity of what might be involved to solve his problem, Mrs Bryant introduced the literacy pedagogical framework LAUNCH. LAUNCH is an acronym for ways of working:

(L) Latch onto an idea.
(A) Ask questions and search for answers.
(U) Use your creativity.
(N) Never be afraid to fail.
(C) Collaborate and cooperate with your classmates.
(H) Have a blast.

The aim of LAUNCH is to stimulate expectations of being curious and creative, to take risks, to aim big and to not be afraid to fail (many times!). To help with this, Mrs Bryant harmonised LAUNCH ways of working with children's literature.

(L) *What Do You Do with an Idea?* (Yamada & Besom, 2014)

(A) *Rosie Revere, Engineer* (Beaty & Roberts, 2013)

(U) *The Dot* (Reynolds, 2003), *Ish* (Reynolds, 2004) and *Sky Color* (Reynolds, 2012)

(N) *The Most Magnificent Thing* (Spires, 2014), *If I Never Forever Endeavor* (Meade, 2011) and *The Book of Mistakes* (Luyken, 2017)

(C) *Beautiful Hands* (Otoshi & Baumgarten, 2015) and *When Pencil Met Eraser* (Kilpatrick et al., 2019)

▶▶

(H) *The Cow Tripped Over the Moon* (Wilson & Wood, 2015)

Source: LAUNCH artwork by Dr Sue Pillans, www.drsuepillans.com

It is important to note that LAUNCH themes can also be complemented by literature more suited to older learners. Literature with a more sophisticated rule of LAUNCH themes might include Meg McKinlay's (2017) *A Single Stone*, Tim Minchin's (2014) *Storm* and Charlie Mackesy's (2019) *The Boy, the Mole, the Fox and the Horse*. Also be sure to explore books, short stories and anthologies by Australian authors such as Ursula Dubosarsky, Anita Heiss, Libby Gleeson, Oliver Phommavanh and Damon Young for evidence of LAUNCH themes.

Now back to Sebastian.

Sebastian found the picture books delightfully entertaining, but, most importantly, they helped him better understand themes such as persistence, failure, hope and resilience. And so, to heighten Sebastian's awareness of ideas, Mrs Bryant read the Independent Publisher's Gold Award book, *What Do You Do with an Idea?* (Yamada & Besom, 2014). Questions for philosophical discussion and critical reflection included:

- What is an idea?
- What makes an idea significant?
- What makes an idea creative?

Rosie Revere, Engineer (Beaty & Roberts, 2013) encouraged Sebastian to search for answers by asking questions. When book character Rosie asked herself if she could build a gizmo to help her Aunt fly, this question was a tricky one, but worth her attention. Mrs Bryant told Sebastian that, like Rosie, his idea was deserving of attention too. Questions for philosophical discussion and reflection included:

- Is there ever only one answer?
- Where can we look for answers?
- Who could help us look for answers?

To develop Sebastian's creativity, the class read three books from Creatrilogy by Peter Reynolds: *The Dot* (2003), *Ish* (2004) and *Sky Color* (2012). These books showed Sebastian how to harness creative thinking by tinkering, experimenting, recording, playing, trying out ideas and finding solutions. Questions for philosophical discussion and reflection included:

- Where can we be creative?
- Do you think creativity is about new ideas and solving problems?

To show Sebastian that it is okay to fail, the class also read *The Most Magnificent Thing* (Spires, 2014), *If I Never Forever Endeavor* (Meade, 2011) and *The Book of Mistakes* (Luyken, 2017). When Sebastian's three-dimensional designed solution to stop the ibis birds from gathering in the eating space completely fell apart, his disappointment was clear. As Sebastian sat beside Mrs Bryant, trying to control his juddering voice, he ever-so-softly said, 'Mrs Bryant, it's so broken.' Mrs Bryant reminded Sebastian that failure is an opportunity for new ways of trying. Questions for philosophical discussion and reflection included:

- What does it mean to fail?
- Is there such a thing as a failed idea?
- Is there such a thing as perfection?

The picture book *Beautiful Hands* by Otoshi and Baumgarten (2015) inspired Sebastian to use his hands to explore the possibilities of alternative materials and different construction methods. Sebastian's classmates' hands helped Sebastian too! This time of togetherness forced Sebastian to think critically about his designed solution and explain the *what*, *how* and *why* of his design to his classmates. This triggered a mixing of thinking, new ideas and clever design, just like in the picture book, *When Pencil Met Eraser* (Kilpatrick et al., 2019). After new designs, more design failures, and even more playing and tinkering, Sebastian produced a designed solution to stop the peskiness of the ibis birds. Questions for philosophical discussion and reflection included:

- What makes a good collaboration?
- How do you know when your collaboration is going well?
- Can sharing ideas help our own ideas to grow?

The CBCA's Book of the Year, Tony Wilson's *The Cow Tripped Over the Moon* (Wilson & Wood, 2015) reminded Sebastian to have a blast. After all, learning has to be fun. Questions for philosophical discussion and reflection included:

- How can you measure your success?
- Can you have a blast, even when you fail?

Question

What children's literature could you use to help learners in higher year levels think big, be curious, take risks and fail well? Teachers working in higher year levels might explore literature with a more sophisticated rule of LAUNCH themes, such as Shaun Tan's *The Lost Thing* (Tan, 2000).

Conclusion

Children's literature is an important part of literacy education in Australia. Literature is in the reflective conversations we have, in the theatre scripts we read, in the poems we recite, in the lyrics we sing, in the short stories we write, and in the postmodern picture books we share. Thoughtful teachers use literature as a trustworthy companion to encourage learners' talking, viewing, listening, reading, writing, responding and creating. They work hard to collect a wide range of literature forms, including print-based, visual and multimodal texts. An array of literature forms helps learners delight in language and better understand text structure and organisation, as found in verse novels, short stories, comics, graphic novels, poetry anthologies, and much, much more. Thoughtful educators teach a love of literature so that learners can begin their journey into the 'world of literate people' (Harwayne, 2000, p. 111), and, most importantly, to make a long-lasting impact on the literacy lives of learners.

Bringing it together

1. What role does children's literature play in your literacy teaching?
2. In what ways will you use children's literature to accomplish the goals set out in the Australian Curriculum?
3. How can you set up and organise children's literature to meet the diverse needs and interests of your learners?
4. Who can help you stay informed about children's literature, both in your school community and beyond?
5. Where can you find expert information related to children's literature?

Further resources

Australian expert literacy organisations

Grab a cup of tea, get comfortable and explore the digital pages, teacher journals, recommended resources and professional development events of the following:

- Australian Association for the Teaching of English: www.aate.org.au
- Australian Children's Laureate Foundation: www.childrenslaureate.org.au
- Australian Literacy Educators' Association: www.alea.edu.au
- Primary English Teaching Association Australia: www.petaa.edu.au
- Reading Australia: https://readingaustralia.com.au

Children's Book Council of Australia (CBCA)

To discover award-winning Australian literature, visit the website of the Children's Book Council of Australia and browse its winning, shortlisted and notable book lists.

https://cbca.org.au

Prime Minister's Literary Awards

Another great place to discover award-winning literature is the Prime Minister's Literary Awards. Each state also has literary awards; see, for example, the NSW Premier's Literary Awards.

www.arts.gov.au/pm-literary-awards

www.sl.nsw.gov.au/awards/nsw-premiers-literary-awards

Australian Library and Information Association

Parents, caregivers and other important family members can be invited to celebrate reading and literacy on the Australian Library and Information Association National Simultaneous Storytime.

www.alia.org.au/nss

National Centre for Australian Children's Literature (NCACL)

Explore the collections of authors' and illustrators' creative works digitalised in the National Centre for Australian Children's Literature (NCACL).

www.ncacl.org.au/collections-2

LAUNCH

To learn more about the literacy pedagogical approach LAUNCH, go to the journal article:

Brosseuk, D., Exley, B. & Neumann, M. (2019). 'You know, I could trip and fall onto the track!': inspiring text production. *The Reading Teacher*, 73(4), 453–460. https://doi .org/10.1002/trtr.1865

Acknowledgement

Case studies 7.1 and 7.2 are adapted from examples first published in Brosseuk, Exley and Neumann (2019) with permission of John Wiley & Sons Inc. The LAUNCH artwork in Case study 7.2 was provided by Dr Sue Pillans.

References

Aiken, J. (2019). *Arabel and Mortimer Stories (A Puffin Book)*. Puffin Books.

Allen, P. (1996). *Who Sank the Boat? (Paperstar)* (Illustrated edn). Puffin Books.

Arnold, E.K. & Davick, L. (2019). *What Riley Wore* (Illustrated edn). Beach Lane Books.

Austen, A. (2019). *Shelf Respect: A Book Lovers Guide to Curating Book Shelves at Home*. Sphere.

Australian Curriculum, Assessment and Reporting Authority (ACARA). (n.d.a). Australian Curriculum: English. www.australiancurriculum.edu.au/f-10-curriculum/english

—— (n.d.b). Australian Curriculum: English. Key ideas. https://australiancurriculum.edu .au/f-10-curriculum/english/key-ideas

—— (n.d.c). Australian Curriculum: General capabilities. www.australiancurriculum.edu .au/f-10-curriculum/general-capabilities

Australian Library and Information Association (ALIA). (2020). ALIA National Simultaneous Storytime 2021. www.alia.org.au/nss

Baker, J. (2004). *Home*. Greenwillow Books.

Beaty, A. & Roberts, D. (2013). *Rosie Revere, Engineer*. Harry N. Abrams.

—— (2016). *Ada Twist, Scientist (The Questioneers)* (Illustrated edn). Harry N. Abrams.

—— (2019). *Sofia Valdez, Future Prez (The Questioneers)* (Illustrated edn). Harry N. Abrams.

Beer, S. (2018). *Love Makes a Family*. Dial Books.

Bell, H. & Martin, M. (2016). *The Marvellous Funambulist of Middle Harbour and Other Sydney Firsts*. University of New South Wales Press.

Bertini, A. (2020). *Where Happiness Hides*. Dirt Lane Press.

Blabey, A. (2008). *Pearl Barley and Charlie Parsley* (Illustrated edn). Front Street, Inc.

—— (2020a). *Pig the Slob (Pig the Pug)* (Illustrated edn). Scholastic Press.

—— (2020b). *Pig the Tourist (Pig the Pug)* (Illustrated edn). Scholastic Press.

—— (2021). *The Bad Guys in They're Bee-Hind You! (The Bad Guys #14)*. Scholastic Paperbacks.

Brosseuk, D., Exley, B., & Neumann, M. (2019). 'You know, I could trip and fall onto the track!': inspiring text production. *The Reading Teacher*, 73(4), 453–460. https://doi.org/10.1002/trtr.1865

Carroll, D. & Shakespeare, W. (2009). *Stick Figure Hamlet*. CreateSpace Independent Publishing Platform.

Constable, K. (2012). *Crow Country* (Original edn). Allen & Unwin.

Cooling, W. & Grobler, P. (2010). *All the Wild Wonders: Poems of Our Earth*. Frances Lincoln Children's Books.

Cowley, J. (2019). *The Gobbledegook Book*. Gecko Press.

Dahl, R. (1988). *Matilda*. Puffin.

Danby, S. (2020). New texts, new kids, new ways of thinking: engaging young children with digital texts in the home. In B. Exley & A. Woods (Eds.), *Literacies in Early Childhood: Foundations for Equity and Quality* (pp. 162–175). Oxford University Press.

Davis, A. & Petricic, D. (1999). *The Enormous Potato*. Kids Can Press.

Department of Education, Employment and Workplace Relations (DEEWR). (2009). *Belonging, Being & Becoming – The Early Years Learning Framework for Australia*. https://docs.education.gov.au/documents/belonging-being-becoming-early-years-learning-framework-australia

Department of Health. (2020). Songs and lyrics. www1.health.gov.au/internet/publications/publishing.nsf/Content/sugar-drinks-toc%7Esugar-drinks-6-songs-lyrics

Dreise, G. (2015). *Kookoo Kookaburra*. Magabala Books.

—— (2017). *Mad Magpie* (Illustrated edn). Magabala Books.

—— (2019). *Cunning Crow*. Magabala Books.

Earls, N. (2015). *New Boy*. Penguin Australia.

Farjeon, E. & Farjeon, H. (2015). *Kings and Queens*. Puffin Books.

Fellowes, J. & Oakley, G. (2020). *Language, Literacy and Early Childhood Education* (3rd edn). Oxford University Press.

Fleming, C. & Kulikov, B. (2013). *Papa's Mechanical Fish*. Farrar, Straus and Giroux (BYR).

Fox, M. (2017). *I'm Australian Too*. Scholastic Australia.

Frederico, A. (2017). Digital literature for children: texts, readers and educational practices. *Nordic Journal of ChildLit Aesthetics*, 8(1). https://doi.org/10.1080/20004508.2017.1285551

Gaines, J. & Swaney, J. (2020). *The World Needs Who You Were Made to Be*. Thomas Nelson.

Gravett, E. (2019). *Cyril and Pat* (Illustrated edn). Simon & Schuster Books for Young Readers.

—— (2020). Emily Gravett – Home. www.emilygravett.com

Harry, P. (2019). *The Little Wave*. University of Queensland Press.

Harvey, J. (2020). *Alice-Miranda in the Outback: Alice-Miranda 19*. Penguin eBooks.

Harwayne, S. (2000). *Lifetime Guarantees: Toward Ambitious Literacy Teaching*. Heinemann.

Horowitz, A. (2021). *Alex Rider: Anthony Horowitz 10 Explosive Missions. Action Adrenaline Adventure*. Walker Books.

Janu, T. (2014). *Figgy in the World*. Scholastic Australia.

—— (2016). *Figgy and the President*. Scholastic Australia.

Jasinski-Schneider, J. (2016). *The Inside, Outside, and Upside Downs of Children's Literature: From Poets and Pop-ups to Princesses and Porridge*. University of South Florida Library. https://scholarcommons.usf.edu/childrens_lit_textbook

Jennings, P. (2004). *Rascal the Dragon*. Penguin.

Jennings, P. & Gleitzman, M. (1998). *Wicked!* Puffin Books.

Jones, L., Edwards, M., & Bayliss, L. (2015). *The Princess and the Fog: A Story for Children with Depression*. Jessica Kingsley Publishers.

Karst, P. & Lew-Vriethoff, J. (2018). *The Invisible String* (Illustrated edn). Little, Brown Books for Young Readers.

Kenn Nesbitt's Poetry4kids. (2020). Welcome to Poetry4kids.com. www.poetry4kids.com

Kibuishi, K. (2018). *Amulet #1-8 Box Set*. Graphix.

Kilpatrick, K., Ramos Jr, L.O., & Blanco, G. (2019). *When Pencil Met Eraser* (Illustrated edn). Imprint.

Kobald, I. & Blackwood, F. (2015). *My Two Blankets* (Illustrated edn). HMH Books for Young Readers.

Kwaymullina, A. & Tobin, L. (2017). *The Lost Girl*. Walker Books.

Lai, T. (2013). *Inside Out and Back Again* (Reprint edn). HarperCollins.

Lee, A. & McKenzie, H. (2020). *Do Not Open This Book*. Scholastic Press.

Lester, A. (2005). *Are We There Yet?* (Gift edn). Kane/Miller Book Pub.

Levy, A., Levy, G., & Kaiser, D. (2019). *What Should Darla Do? Featuring the Power to Choose*. Elon Books.

Luke, A. & Freebody, P. (1999). A map of possible practices: further notes on the four resources model. *Practically Primary*, 4(2), 5–8.

Luyken, C. (2017). *The Book of Mistakes*. Dial Books.

Mackesy, C. (2019). *The Boy, the Mole, the Fox and the Horse* (Illustrated edn). HarperOne.

McGough, R. (2015). *Poetry Pie*. Puffin Poetry.

McKinlay, M. (2017). *A Single Stone*. Candlewick.

Meade, H. (2011). *If I Never Forever Endeavor* (Illustrated edn). Candlewick.

Meighan, J. (2015). *Fairytales on Stage: A Collection of Children's Plays Based on Famous Fairy Tales (On Stage Books Book 2)*. JemBooks.

Miller, Z.P. & Hill, J. (2018). *Be Kind* (Illustrated edn). Roaring Brook Press.

Minchin, T. (2014). *Storm*. Orion.

Monk, E. (2020). *Bedtime Stories (As Told by Our Dad) (Who Messed Them Up)*. Playscripts Inc. www.playscripts.com/play/2874

Munson, D. & King, C.T. (2000). *Enemy Pie*. Chronicle Books.

Musa, O. (2014). *Parang*. Penguin Group Australia.

National Centre for Australian Children's Literature (NCACL). (2019). Welcome to the NCACL Cultural Diversity database. www.ncacl.org.au/resources/databases/welcome-to-the-ncacl-cultural-diversity-database/#

Nikolajeva, M. (2013). Picturebooks and emotional literacy. *The Reading Teacher*, 67(4), 249–254. https://doi.org/10.1002/trtr.1229

Oliveros, J. & Wulfekotte, D. (2018). *The Remember Balloons* (Illustrated edn). Simon & Schuster Books for Young Readers.

Otoshi, K. (2008). *One* (Later printing edn). KO Kids Books.

Otoshi, K. & Baumgarten, B. (2015). *Beautiful Hands*. Blue Dot Press.

Parish, P. & Siebel, F. (2013). *Amelia Bedelia* (Anniversary edn). Greenwillow Books.

Pascoe, B. (2018). *Dark Emu* (Illustrated edn). Scribe US.

Pilkey, D. (2021). *Dog Man: From the Creator of Captain Underpants (Dog Man #1)*. Graphix.

Pillans, S. (2022). *Cranky Frankie and the Oceans of Trash*. Van Haren Publishing.

Pugliano-Martin, C. & Pugliano, C. (2008). *Scholastic Greek Myth Plays (Best Practices in Action)* (Illustrated edn). Scholastic Teaching Resources (Teaching Strategies).

Red Room Company. (2020). *Student Poem Library. Red Room Poetry.* https://redroomcompany.org/student-poems

Reynolds, P.H. (2003). *The Dot. (Creatrilogy)*. Candlewick.

—— (2004). *Ish. (Creatrilogy)*. Candlewick.

—— (2012). *Sky Color (Creatrilogy)*. Candlewick.

Robertson, C. & Shirvington, J. (2020). *Just the Way We Are* (Illustrated edn). ABC Books.

Rodda, E. (2018). *His Name Was Walter*. HarperCollins.

Ryan, M.L., Emerson, L., & Robertson, B.J. (Eds.). (2020). *The Johns Hopkins Guide to Digital Media (2014-03-20)* (2nd edn). Johns Hopkins University Press.

Short, K. (2012). Story as world making. *Language Arts*, 90(1), 9–17. www.jstor.org/stable/41804370

Spires, A. (2014). *The Most Magnificent Thing* (Illustrated edn). Kids Can Press.

Sternberg, J. & Cordell, M. (2016). *Like Pickle Juice on a Cookie* (Illustrated edn). Harry N. Abrams.

Tan, S. (2000). *The Lost Thing*. Lothian.

—— (2006). *The Arrival* (Illustrated edn). Arthur A. Levine Books.

—— (2021). *Eric*. Templar Publishing.

Thexton, T., Prasad, A., & Mills, A.J. (2019). Learning empathy through literature. *Culture and Organization*, 25(2), 83–90. https://doi.org/10.1080/14759551.2019.1569339

Thiele, C. (2019). *Storm Boy: The Illustrated Story*. New Holland Publishers.

University of Cambridge. (2015). Music. Cambridge Digital Library. https://cudl.lib.cam.ac.uk/collections/music/1

Walliams, D. (2021). *The World's Worst Children 3: Fiendishly Funny New Short Stories for Fans of David Walliams Books*. D. Walliams (Edition Ed.). Harper Collins.

Waters, R. (2021). *Love From Australia* (Illustrated edn). Little Hare Books.

Weston, R.P. (2014). *Prince Puggly of Spud and the Kingdom of Spiff* (Illustrated edn). Razorbill.

Wheatley, N. (1988). *My Place*. Walker Books.

White, E.B. & Williams, G. (2012). *Charlotte's Web* (Illustrated-Media tie-in ed.). HarperCollins.

Wieslander, J. (2021). *Mamma Mu simmar*. Natur & Kultur.

Willems, M. (2020). *Don't Let the Pigeon Drive the Bus!* Scholastic Inc.

Wilson, T. & Wood, L. (2015). *The Cow Tripped Over the Moon*. Scholastic.

Wingfield, E. & Austin, E. (2009). *Living Alongside the Animals – Anangu Way*. IAD Press.

Yamada, K. & Besom, M. (2014). *What Do You Do with an Idea?* (9th print edn). Compendium Inc.

Yolen, J., Peters, A.F., & Dunbar, P. (2007). *Here's A Little Poem: A Very First Book of Poetry* (Illustrated edn). Candlewick.

Zelina, G. & Maczó, H. (2018). *Brave Little Ones*. Independently published.

CHAPTER 8

Understanding and responding to texts

Robyn Ewing

ANTICIPATED OUTCOMES

After working through this chapter, it is anticipated you will be able to:

- articulate how 'understanding' and 'responding' are defined in the Australian Curriculum: English
- consider how reader response theory accounts for the two-way transaction between the author's or illustrator's intention(s) and the reader's interpretation
- reflect on the different ways that teachers can model responding to and interpreting texts
- explore the importance of building understanding through rich classroom talk about text, including field knowledge, predicting, questioning and inferring
- introduce a range of metacognitive skills and strategies that can be used to understand and respond to spoken, digital, multimodal and visual texts, including retelling, summarising, analysing, generalising and evaluating
- discuss how images can be interpreted
- understand the importance of graphic organisers, peer teaching and arts-rich activities in enabling creative and critical responses to and reflection about texts.

Introduction

This chapter builds on Chapters 6 and 7 by exploring in more detail a range of concrete strategies and activities that teachers can introduce in the classroom to facilitate the deepening of learners' understanding of different kinds of spoken, written, digital, multimodal and visual texts. In this chapter, we again refer to all kinds of texts (oral, written, digital and multimodal), so 'text' is used here in its broadest sense.

Through building an understanding of the author's or illustrator's intentions in creating a text, and responding thoughtfully in diverse and inclusive ways to what they listen to, read or view, learners become more deeply literate: they relate new ideas and understandings to their own contexts and experiences, develop confidence in constructing meanings and, where appropriate, challenge assertions that are made. Learners can also use authors' expert models when developing their spoken and digital presentations and undertaking their own writing.

This chapter begins with a case study that illustrates how learners can respond to texts in creative ways facilitated by the class teacher. It moves to briefly examine reader response theory before exploring the importance of building learners' understandings through talk and teacher modelling to ensure learners have both context and field knowledge. A range of classroom strategies and approaches are then considered that may facilitate the different ways that learners can respond to texts. Through such responses, learners build critical understandings of texts that go beyond literal or surface comprehension. A particular emphasis is placed on metacognitive and creative arts-rich strategies that can be adapted for imaginative, instructional and information texts.

CASE STUDY 8.1   **Understanding and responding to *Where the Forest Meets the Sea***

Year 1 learners at a suburban Sydney school are studying the environment and are reading Jeannie Baker's (1987) *Where the Forest Meets the Sea.* The story is about a boy and his father who explore a magical place where the forest meets the sea and there are many reminders of the past.

The children carefully studied each of the different collages of the beach and the forest. They discussed the beauty of this environment and how Aboriginal people have lived there and cared for the environment for more than 60 000 years. The final opening of the picture book superimposes images that suggest this natural setting may be destroyed through 'modern' apartment buildings and boats and other symbols of Western civilisation. The boy asks: *But will the forest still be here when we come back?*

The children discussed whether it would be a good thing or a bad thing to allow this kind of construction to go ahead here. The teacher then stepped into the role of a property developer who proposed to build a new resort on this land. Afterwards, the teacher divided the class into small groups to represent different members of the community (the council, people who have lived here for many years, business people and shop owners, and conservationists).

The children, in role as members of these groups, discussed the pluses and minuses of the resort proposal. Then a town meeting was convened where each group shared their comments about the proposal.

Later, the children wrote in role to the developer to share their opinions and thoughts on the proposed resort.

Questions

1. Why do you think the teacher used these role-playing strategies with her class?
2. How might the teacher assess the children's learning after the unit has concluded?

Understanding and responding in the Australian Curriculum

The National Literacy Learning Progression in the Australian Curriculum defines texts broadly as:

> A means for communication. Their forms and conventions have developed to help us communicate effectively with a variety of audiences for a range of purposes. *Texts* can be written, spoken or multimodal and in print or digital/online forms. Multimodal texts combine language with other systems for communication, such as print text, visual images, soundtrack and spoken word as in film or computer presentation media. (Australian Curriculum, Assessment and Reporting Authority [ACARA], 2021)

In the reading and viewing element of the progression, the *understanding texts* sub-element is defined as:

> how a student becomes increasingly proficient in decoding, using, interacting with, analysing and evaluating texts to build meaning. Texts include components of print, image, sound, animated movements and symbolic representations. This sub-element is organised into three subheadings: comprehension, processes and vocabulary. (ACARA, 2021)

In the speaking and listening element, the *interacting* sub-element is defined as:

> how a student becomes increasingly proficient at active listening, strategic and respect-ful questioning and using language to share information and negotiate meaning and outcomes. Students interact across an increasing range of curriculum contexts and purposes in pair, group or whole-class oral interactions. This sub-element focuses on the development of two-way interaction processes to clarify and create understanding. (ACARA, 2021)

The *comprehension* sub-element sets out a progression. Initially, the learner:

- demonstrates interest in texts
- recognises illustrations in texts
- recognises some icons or symbols from the environment (familiar logos). (ACARA, 2021)

The learner progresses and, finally:

- reads and views sophisticated texts (see *text complexity*)
- interprets symbolism in texts, providing evidence to justify interpretation

- derives a generalisation from abstract ideas in texts
- critically evaluates the use of visual elements in multimodal texts on the same topic or with similar purposes
- integrates existing understanding with new concepts in texts
- analyses the credibility and validity of primary and secondary sources
- evaluates the style of a text
- evaluates the use of devices such as analogy, irony and satire
- analyses how authors manipulate language features, image and sound for a purpose (to create humour or playfulness)
- analyses bias in texts
- explains assumptions, beliefs and implicit values in texts (e.g. that economic growth is always desirable)
- evaluates the social, moral and ethical positions taken in texts. (ACARA, 2021)

These definitions and progressions emphasise using, interacting with, analysing and evaluating texts to make meaning. They resonate strongly with the roles of the reader (Freebody & Luke, 1990; Luke & Freebody, 1999), as discussed in Chapter 6. Although described separately, all roles interact with each other. Learners need to be able to articulate how and why we read for different purposes and why we respond in different ways at different times.

Interpreting texts: reader response theory

Reader response theory is underpinned by social constructivist theory (Vygotsky, 1978), as outlined in Chapter 6. It emphasises that readers bring their own contexts, knowledge and experiences to any text they are listening to, reading, viewing and responding to. Reading and viewing texts is thus always a transaction between the speaker, writer or artist and the reader and should always be a reflective and creative meaning-making process. Readers and viewers may agree with the ideas or assertions made in a text or image, relate them to their own experiences or question, and even challenge, the assumptions made.

An important theorist in this area, Louise Rosenblatt, suggested that the reader constructs meaning from a text within a particular social context (Rosenblatt, 1978, 1985). They might be listening to the radio or reading a novel alone, or they could be in class listening to the teacher reading a serial text and subsequently discussing it. Alternatively, they could be sharing their thoughts in a book club context or perhaps in a computer chat room or on Zoom. The opportunity to share responses with others will affect how the reader constructs meaning.

Benton and Fox (1987) discuss a range of different kinds of responses that encourage learners to ask questions and share their ideas, opinions and feelings when reading literature. In time, learners come to understand that there are usually multiple possible interpretations of any text rather than just one (Rosenblatt, 1985). Benton and Fox suggest a range of strategies that will be helpful in understanding and responding to narratives:

- predicting what will happen
- considering what events have led to the current dilemma, event, situation or issue
- visualising how the character will react or is currently feeling at a particular moment in a story

- interacting with the events as they unfold or reacting to the character's personality, actions or emotions in a particular situation
- evaluating how well the author's style and linguistic choices have suited their purpose and engaged the reader.

Each of these strategies will involve learners in substantive conversations. The next section considers the important role of these conversations in building understanding of texts.

Building understanding through talk: preparing learners to respond through developing context and field knowledge

The importance of rich, substantive classroom talk or dialogue about all texts cannot be overstated and has already been discussed at length in Chapters 4, 6 and 7. This section explores valuable strategies involving talk to enable learners to build information about a text's context and relevant knowledge about the subject matter. Learners may also benefit from an introduction to key vocabulary. The processes of teacher and peer modelling, predicting, questioning and inferring are introduced. These are all useful for helping learners move beyond simple literal or surface comprehension to making inferences and developing critical literacies.

Teacher and peer modelling

Using 'think alouds' and appropriate questions and comments during shared reading experiences, teachers can model how they personally respond to and interrogate texts as they read. For example, the teacher might reread or rephrase a particularly dense paragraph aloud, instead of silently as they would usually do. They might ask a question about a term or action used in an instructional text; pause at a particular point in a story to recap or respond to what has happened so far; or provide a quick oral summary after reading an information text about a particular topic. This kind of explicit modelling makes it clear to learners how important it is to respond to a text while they are reading and how this process can further deepen their understanding of the text itself.

Similarly, providing learners with opportunities to discuss and reflect on their responses to books that have been read in whole-class contexts, or in small groups or individually, enables peer modelling. Literature circles and readers theatre are two strategies that incorporate peer modelling and are discussed later in the chapter.

'I wonder' questions

By generating 'I wonder' questions about a story, a poem or a factual text, learners are encouraged to use the information they have gleaned initially from an image or the cover or title of a text to think deeply about possibilities. The teacher may provide an initial suggestion: *I wonder why he is looking at the sky …* or *I wonder when this story is set …* Learners are then invited to contribute their wonderings. These wonderings can be listed on the interactive whiteboard to return to later for further consideration.

Predicting

One of the most important abilities readers need to develop is the ability to make plausible predictions about what might come next in a text and to be able to justify why they think this could eventuate. At a critical moment in a story, learners need to be encouraged to share what they think might happen next and perhaps articulate their reasoning for these predictions. When undertaking a science experiment, they can first be asked to hypothesise about what might happen during the process. Learners can also be asked to enact or depict what might happen next as suggested in the section about drama.

Making connections: text-to-self, text-to-text and text-to-world

Intertextuality: the relationships between literary texts.

When learners are able to relate what they are reading and viewing to their own experiences and cultural background (often called 'text-to-self'), or reference it to another story or situation ('text-to-text' or **intertextuality**) or to a particular historical or recent event ('text-to-world'), this connection helps their understanding and interpretation of the text or image. Once again, teachers need to model this process out loud when modelling reading or sharing a book. The connections can be discussed and then represented through drawing or writing. For example:

- reading *Storm Boy* (Thiele, 2019) might lead learners to initially discuss their own experiences of the Coorong or another long and windswept beach (text-to-self)
- reading about the relationship between Billy and his childhood friend Ollie in *Ollie's Odyssey* (Joyce, 2016) might remind a child of *The Velveteen Rabbit* (Williams, 1922) (text-to-text)
- reading Libby Gleeson's *Red* (Gleeson, 2012) evokes the reality of climate change issues (text-to-world).

Exploring friendship

The picture book *Lost and Found* (Jeffers, 2005) explores the developing friendship between a boy and a penguin that arrives at his door one day. The teacher and children may share some ideas about what makes a good friendship in their own experience (text-to-self). They may also think about other stories they have shared that highlight friendship as an important theme and discuss the similarities and differences (text-to-text). Some examples might include:

- *Amy and Louis* (Gleeson & Blackwood, 2006)
- *Pearl Barley and Charlie Parsley* (Blabey, 2007)
- *Henry and Amy* (King, 1998)
- *The Duck and the Darklings* (Millard & King, 2014).

Later they may discuss why friendships are important more generally in people's lives and communities (text-to-world).

Building a repertoire of quality literary texts with themes that resonate with your learners will be an important resource for future classes.

Questions

1. What other books would you add to the above list?
2. What other activities might you explore to deepen the learners' connections with these texts?

Classroom strategies and approaches to facilitate learners' understandings of and responses to texts

This section considers a range of classroom strategies that can facilitate learners' understandings of and responses to texts.

Sequencing

Ordering the events in a recount or a story can be helpful for emerging readers. Story maps and storyboards help the reader to map out and logically sequence the structure of the story or the steps in a procedure (Figure 8.1). Similarly, when looking at a recipe, discussion about how the recipe orders the ingredients before the making process can be undertaken. Sequencing the steps can be done orally as a whole-class group, in small groups or individually.

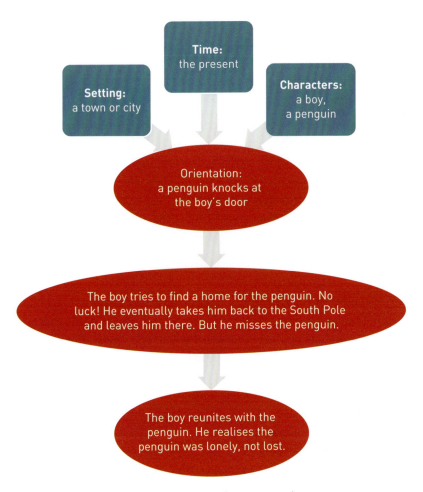

Figure 8.1 An example story map for *Lost and Found* (Jeffers, 2005)

Key images or text excerpts can be jumbled up for learners to sequence. Learners can be asked to provide a reason for the sequence they have created. In some cases, there are multiple ways the images or excerpts can be sequenced other than the way they have been sequenced by the author or illustrator.

Oral and written cloze activities

Cloze activity: the omission of key words or phrases in a text to enable learners to make a meaningful selection.

Leaving out key words or even phrases in a paragraph or poem to be added by the listener or reader is called a **cloze activity**. Learners need to use their prediction skills and understanding of word order to add what makes sense to come next. Cloze can be used in fiction or non-fiction texts. While engaged in shared reading with the class, the teacher may stop at a strategic moment and ask learners to provide the missing word. This can help learners use their understanding of the text so far to predict what comes next. At the same time, learners might also be thinking about how the teacher is using inflection and intonation.

For example, see the omissions in the nursery rhyme below:

Hey diddle diddle, the cat and the fiddle
The cow jumped over the _____.
___ little dog _____ to see such fun
And the _____ ran away with the spoon.

Sometimes in a written cloze activity, a selection of words may be listed for the learner to choose the appropriate word.

Once the text being used for close study has been shared, a similar process can be implemented when learners are reading with reading buddies. They can take it in turns to read a page, stopping at important moments to enable their partner to join in. Such an activity helps the development of fluency. An excerpt from a shared story can also be used as a written cloze activity.

Visualising

Being able to imagine what is happening while listening, viewing or reading is an important skill in deepening understanding for both emergent and experienced readers. Visualising also heightens our emotions and helps us identify with the report, the plot, the character, the setting or the situation. Visualising can be aided when readers discuss, draw or embody the images they have created in their minds.

Often it can also be useful for the teacher to read a section of a picture book, a description of a character or setting without displaying the accompanying illustrations, and ask learners to depict the images they have imagined.

The following is a powerful example of a paragraph that can be read without showing the images and then asking the children to visualise *The Iron Man* (Hughes, 1968):

The Iron Man came to the top of the cliff. Where had he come from? Nobody knows ... Taller than a house ...

Inferring

Being able to read 'between the lines' or **infer** beyond the literal meaning of a text is an important skill and one that can take some time to develop. Inferential comprehension can be especially challenging for multilingual learners who are learning English for the first time, because English has some very dense colloquial expressions (e.g. 'It's time for this class to pull up their socks' does not mean the children need to bend down and pull up their socks!).

Learners need to be encouraged to make intuitive predictions about what is meant by a text but not explicitly stated. To do this, they draw on clues in the text or image and on their own experiences. Sharing thoughts and ideas and engaging in the drama processes referred to in the next section can be helpful for making inferences. Other art forms can also be effective in helping learners make inferences in response to different texts (see 'Using arts-rich strategies to understand and respond to texts' later in the chapter).

Infer: extract something from evidence in a text not made explicit. Inferential comprehension is the ability to understand the underlying or deeper meaning(s) of a text as opposed to its literal meaning.

Learning important metacognitive skills: 'thinking about thinking'

Metacognition refers to being aware of our thinking and learning processes and being able to articulate them. These metacognitive processes include monitoring, summarising and assessing how well we have understood something. Each is discussed briefly in this section.

Metacognition: awareness of our thinking and learning skills and processes.

Monitoring

A learner who is able to monitor whether they understand what they are listening to, viewing or reading, and can pinpoint what they do not understand, will be able to begin to address the gaps in their understanding.

REFLECTION

Consider the following scenario.

You are introducing the story *Ollie's Odyssey* (Joyce, 2016) to your class when eight-year-old Meka raises his hand and comments: 'I'm not sure what "odyssey" means.'

How might you address Meka's comment?

You might explain it immediately or ask other learners. Alternatively, the meaning might be explored through looking ahead in the book with the class, exploring any clues that are available on the cover or even by relating it to another story. Whichever strategy is selected, it will be important to check back with Meka to ensure that he is now able to articulate the meaning in his own words.

Are there other strategies you could use here?

Summarising

Helping learners to identify and succinctly summarise the main ideas and themes in an oral or written text and articulate these in their own way is an important skill. In the same way, being able to discard superficial comments or information or and less important elements is useful.

Assessing understanding

As discussed in Chapters 3 and 6, teachers and learners should engage constantly in a variety of authentic formative assessment strategies to ensure learners have understood key concepts, vocabulary, events or procedures. Many of the suggested activities in this chapter can become assessment tools in themselves and provide valuable information about where a learner is doing well and where more assistance may be needed.

Interpreting images

Images, photos and diagrams are not merely about supporting or complementing printed or digital texts or self-expression – for example, think about how images play a powerful role in advertising and marketing. Kalantzis and Cope (2006) suggest that making meaning visually is growing increasingly significant because the viewer can see the whole meaning all at once. Instagram, for example, has both image and text, but the image is more privileged.

Artists and illustrators carefully choose well-established design principles, including colour, light, position, shape and symbol, when creating images to share different layers of meaning. Images may play part of the narrative role in a story, or they may be used to persuade us about a particular issue, encourage us to purchase a product, and challenge or provoke us to reflect on an issue. Learners need time to closely observe and discuss these aspects of images and share their thoughts to understand how meanings are being communicated through the design and how they might be interpreted in different ways.

A whole visual grammar has been developed to provide a language for discussion of visual images (see Kress & van Leeuwen, 1996). A particularly valuable resource in this area is Callow's (2013) book, *The Shape of Text to Come: How Image and Text Work*.

The reflection below uses an image from the picture book, *Teacup*, to explore how Matt Ottley has communicated meaning about the sea through his choice of design, position and use of light and colour.

REFLECTION

Consider Figure 8.2, concentrating on the image itself rather than the text.

1. Without knowing the whole story, what thoughts or emotions does the image evoke for you? What grabs your attention first? Why?
2. Why do you think these particular colours have been selected by the illustrator?
3. Why do you think the boat is positioned where it is?
4. What other aspects of the image are important for you?

Figure 8.2 A double-page spread from *Teacup*
Source: Young & Ottley (2015).

Graphic and semantic organisers

Graphic and semantic organisers are tools that learners can use to examine a text and then map the relationships in it. They can help readers focus on learning new concepts and reflect on how they can be related to other concepts.

Such tools include the following:

- Venn diagrams provide a visual way to organise the synergies and contrasts between two sources of information. For example, learners could first list the characteristics of two main characters in a story and then map the similarities and differences on a Venn diagram.

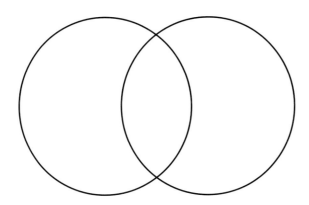

- Mind maps or concept maps are an excellent visual way to find out what a learner understands about a particular concept. For example, before introducing the book *Just One Bee* (Bertini et al., 2020), which highlights the important role bees play in the environment, learners could construct a simple mind map of what they know about bees (Figure 8.3).

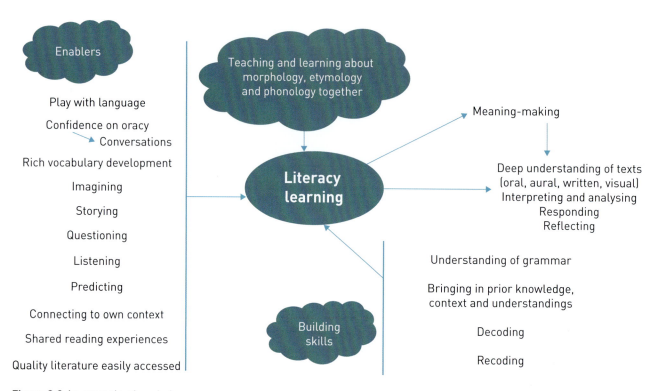

Figure 8.3 An example of a mind map

- Plus, Minus, Interesting (PMI) is a critical thinking tool that was developed by Edward de Bono (1988) to look at the positive or advantageous aspects of a situation alongside the negatives or disadvantages and other elements that are of interest before making a decision. Table 8.1 is a PMI chart developed by a family after listening to David Attenborough's suggestions for addressing the world's environmental problems in the Netflix documentary *A Life on Our Planet* (Attenborough, 2020).

Table 8.1 PMI chart for *A Life on Our Planet* (Attenborough, 2020)

Plus +	Minus –	Interesting
Slow the rate at which the global population is growing	Some Western countries with ageing populations need population growth	By 2100, the population is expected to reach 11 billion people
Raise people out of poverty	Wealthy people may need to reduce their standard of living	In 2100, the planet will be four degrees Celsius warmer, meaning parts of the Earth will be uninhabitable

Table 8.1 (cont.)

Plus +	Minus −	Interesting
Improve access to healthcare globally	The population will increase	
Enable children, especially girls, to stay in school for as long as possible	Delay in young people entering the workforce	
Shift to renewable energy	Workers in fossil fuel industries will lose their jobs	Morocco now generates 40% of its needs from renewable energy
Return some areas to the wild	Some farmers will lose their land	If no-fish zones were implemented over a third of the world's oceans, we would have all the fish we would need

- Word clouds visually highlight the most frequently used words in a text.

Peer teaching

As discussed earlier, there are many activities that can be used to help foster deep understanding of literary texts. Learners gain much from planning a presentation to share their ideas with each other. They benefit from giving and receiving constructive feedback and from self-evaluating and peer-evaluating such opportunities. Valuable peer-teaching activities are reciprocal teaching and literature circles.

Reciprocal teaching

The practice of reciprocal teaching encourages teachers and members of a small reading group, or group members working collaboratively, to talk about a text they are reading. Individuals might read part of the text, talk about it and think aloud about a key issue as they progress through the text. Through dialogue about the text that is scaffolded by the teacher or discussion leader, learners will jointly construct meanings. Four notable skills fostered through reciprocal reading are predicting, clarifying, questioning and summarising (Palincsar & Brown, 1984). See also Chapters 4 for more details about reciprocal teaching.

Literature circles

In literature circles, small groups of learners work together to explore a picture book, a chapter from a novel or a poem in depth. Literature circles can be designed in different ways, but usually each learner in a group reading a particular literary text is designated a role or chooses a role to explore the text from a particular perspective. Roles include the:

- *discussion leader/director* – leads the group discussion through selecting important questions for discussion
- *text connector* – makes connections with the themes or events in the story
- *word wizard/vocabulary enricher* – chooses some unfamiliar words to explore in depth
- *artful artist* – visually represents a critical moment or event or character
- *profiler* – profiles the main character(s)
- *summariser* – effectively summarises key events and major themes
- *literary luminary* – locates key literary devices that build meaning.

After each group member has spent some time researching their particular role, they share their understandings with the other members and lead the group to focus on their individual role. This may involve discussing the features of the main characters, examining the author's crafting of the language itself, learning vocabulary, exploring the plot structure or making connections between their own life experiences and the story. There are many online and text-based resources that suggest a myriad of ways literature circles can be organised in the classroom (see, for example, Simpson, 2014).

Responding through oral presentation

Oral presentations can be a very useful way to both assess and challenge learners' understandings of ideas or concepts and to ask them to respond in ways that take them beyond the initial text.

| 8 UNDERSTANDING AND RESPONDING TO TEXTS | 193 |

Demonstrating understanding through oral presentation

CASE STUDY 8.2

This case study provides three scenarios that demonstrate the importance of using oral presentations to demonstrate deep understanding.

Expressing understanding of risk-taking

Five-year-old Asher and his Foundation class were learning about risk-taking through watching and listening to the story *Rose Meets Mr Wintergarten* (Graham, 1992) on YouTube (www.youtube.com/watch?v=dewmK5K_CdU).

Afterwards, Asher had to think about what risk-taking involves and then to upload two videos of himself: one describing what risks Rose had to take in the story and the second explaining what risks he had taken during the week.

Question

Listen to the story *Rose Meets Mr Wintergarten* on YouTube. How would you respond to these two tasks?

Oral presentation to express preferences about how children learn best

When the COVID-19 pandemic resulted in remote learning for school children at times during 2020, a Year 3 class had been studying argument texts and listening to a debate about whether it was better to learn face-to-face or remotely. They were asked to make an oral presentation on Zoom about their preference. Jordan (8) developed an oral presentation about his preference for learning remotely. His talk was illustrated with several video clips showing how learning from home enabled him to look after his vegetable garden, spend more time with his family and helped to protect his grandparents from the virus.

Questions

1. Undertake this activity yourself. What do you think about the merits of learning remotely versus learning at school?
2. How would you respond to the task?

Peer teaching through oral presentations

A Year 5 class was studying space using inquiry-based learning. Each learner had to choose a concept to research and then present an explanation of the concept to the whole class, using PowerPoint or another resource. Timothy (10) chose to look at Einstein's theory of relativity. Each class member then responded with questions or comments. The teacher was able to assess both Timothy's understanding of the concept alongside how well his classmates had understood his explanation through their questions and comments.

Question

What would be the key assessment criteria for this task?

Using arts-rich strategies to understand and respond to texts

As Ewing (2019, p. 16) writes, there is an ever-increasing and substantial body of research and writing, both in Australia and internationally, that demonstrates how arts-rich strategies and processes embedded across the curriculum can transform teaching and learning. This has been particularly noteworthy in the English and literacy classroom (see, for example, Bamford, 2006; Catterall, 2009; Deasy, 2002; Ewing, 2010a, 2010b; Ewing & Saunders, 2016; Martin et al., 2013; Winner et al., 2013). This section explores how responding through arts-rich processes and experiences can foster learners' development and deep understanding of texts.

REFLECTION

1. Have you considered the importance of learners using the arts to respond to texts and enabling deep understanding?
2. Are you confident in introducing arts-rich strategies in the English classroom?
3. Are there skills and processes you need to develop in the arts disciplines?

Developing deep understanding through creative arts pedagogies

Developing a broad understanding of creative arts pedagogies enables teachers to plan and implement learning experiences that engage and challenge learners to ask difficult questions, represent their thoughts, and combine new ideas and understanding with prior knowledge to create alternative possibilities (Latham & Ewing, 2018). The conditions that effectively foster creative responses in the classroom, while also enhancing learners' self-esteem and self-worth, include:

- ensuring adequate space and time for deep exploration and investigation
- setting tasks that are genuinely collaborative so that learners exchange ideas about the tasks and their own views and are pushed to use their higher-level thinking skills in discussion
- encouraging the expression and representation of ideas in a range of different media
- providing learners with opportunities to engage in dialogue about their ideas, to disagree with each other and justify their perspectives
- planning authentic interdisciplinary integration of subject areas via topics that are meaningful and relevant to the learner (see, for example, Gibson & Ewing, 2020).

While each arts discipline has distinctive knowledges, skills and understandings, common to all are creative 'processes that include play, design, experimentation, exploration, communication, provocation, use of metaphor, expression or representation, and the artistic or aesthetic shaping of the body or other media' (Ewing, 2010a, p. 16). These arts-rich processes can play an important role in fostering learners' imaginations and creativities before, during and after reading, and help them to think critically, express themselves creatively and respect others' perspectives.

The next sections explore how arts-rich strategies and processes can foster deep responses to texts.

Responding through embodying and enacting: drama-rich strategies

Many drama strategies and processes are useful for responding to and, consequently, deepening our understanding of what we read. At the core of educational drama are **embodiment** and **enactment**.

Both embodiment and enactment enable us to 'walk in someone else's shoes' to understand different perspectives and points of view. Representing a concept, an idea or an emotion with our whole bodies or enacting what happens next, with the whole class, in a small group or individually, can strengthen our capacity to predict and infer while reading (see Ewing, 2010b; Ewing & Saunders, 2016; Ewing & Simons, 2016; O'Toole & Dunn, 2015 for an introduction to and definitions of these strategies).

While there are many different ways of representing the building blocks or elements of drama, here we include a diagram (Figure 8.4) that was developed by Haseman and O'Toole (2018).

Embodiment: physically representing an idea, concept, emotion or character.

Enactment: actioning an event, a moment in time or a character's reaction to a dilemma.

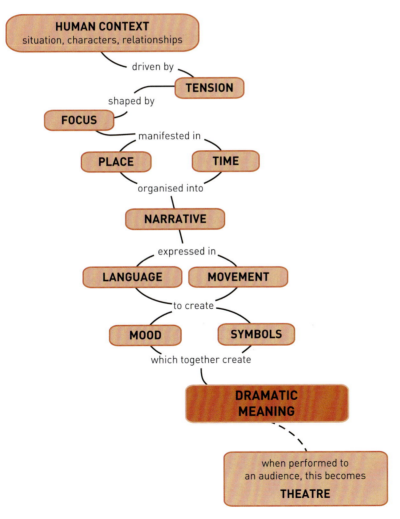

Figure 8.4 The elements of drama
Source: Haseman & O'Toole (2018).

CASE STUDY 8.3 — Building field knowledge through embodiment

Before beginning a unit of work on the Stolen Generations using *The Burnt Stick* (Hill, 1996), the teacher asks learners to stand in a circle facing outwards and to nominate a word that encapsulates the feeling that coming home from school evokes (for example, 'freedom', 'comfortable' or 'relaxing'). She then asks them to embody that word while they say it one by one around the circle. The teacher asks them to think about how their bodies have interpreted the emotion of coming home.

The teacher then asks the learners to embody the feeling that they would experience if they were suddenly taken away from their home and were told they may never see their home again (for example, 'lost' or 'distressed'). They repeat the earlier process, nominating the word and embodying the emotion. The teacher asks them to think about how their bodies have interpreted the emotion of being taken from home.

Finally, they are asked to move from the embodiment of being at home to the embodiment of being taken away and then back to being at home as the teacher claps 10 slow beats on a tambourine or using clapsticks.

Later, learners and teacher discuss the two contrasting experiences.

Learners can reflect on the process of embodiment and how it helps their understanding of Aboriginal and Torres Strait Islander children's despair when they were forcibly removed from their families and homes.

Question

Try the embodiment activity. Does the drama process of embodiment help to deepen understanding of such a complex concept? Why or why not?

REFLECTION

There has been increased focus on the Stolen Generations in Australia over the past two decades. The taking of Aboriginal and Torres Strait Islander children from their parents over several generations has caused huge intergenerational damage and much sorrow, which continues despite the 2008 Apology to the Stolen Generations by then Prime Minister Kevin Rudd. How did you respond to the embodiment activity above? Did it help you understand a little about how these children might have felt? Often they never returned to their homes or saw their families again.

Readers theatre

Readers theatre is a particular type of drama strategy that seamlessly integrates speaking, listening, reading and writing (Ewing et al., 2016; Hertzberg, 2009). To conduct readers theatre in the classroom, scripts are developed or adapted from a poem or a narrative the teachers and children are using for close study, and the focus is on using the voice expressively, considering pitch, pace, tone and pause together with facial expression, limited gesture and movement, to highlight meaning. Because these oral performances are based on familiar texts, they develop learners' confidence in reading aloud and improve fluency as well as deepening their understanding of a text. Learners work collaboratively in groups to practise the performance of their script.

Often the teacher will write the script, but as learners become more confident and experienced with readers theatre, they can develop their own scripts. Learners will need a number of sessions to rehearse their reading and think about words they want to emphasise and where they will pause or make some kind of gesture or movement. They can annotate the text to help their memory of these decisions and perhaps also note where a sound effect or percussion instrument might be used for added emphasis. Research has demonstrated that readers theatre can improve both fluency and reading for meaning (see, for example, Mraz et al., 2013; Young et al., 2019). Readers theatre can be used as a guided reading group activity. It has been effectively used with multilingual learners who are learning English as an additional language or dialect (EAL/D) as it builds content and vocabulary knowledge (Hertzberg, 2012).

Excerpt from a readers theatre based on *Cyclone* (French & Whatley, 2016)

Storyteller 1: Darwin, December 1974
Storyteller 2: Pile the presents by the tree
Storyteller 3: Though clouds spiral out at sea. [make spirals in the air]
Storyteller 1: Wind snarls, [snarling noise]
Storyteller 2: skies weep grey [rain sounds]
Storyteller 3: But Santa's sleigh is on its way! [bells]
Storyteller 1: How can wind hurt Christmas Day?
Storyteller 2: Ignore the storm
Storyteller 3: as rain pelts down [heavier sounds of rain]
Storyteller 1: on parties across Darwin town. [party sounds]

Frozen moments, still images and freeze frames

In this activity, learners are asked to depict a critical moment in the story or historical event as a freeze frame (or as a depiction, frozen moment, still image or tableau). There is no movement or dialogue – it is a moment in time captured for close study just as we capture a special or celebratory moment through a photo. The learners are asked to think about their feelings at that point and the teacher or a peer may lightly tap them on the shoulder to hear what their thoughts or feelings are (called 'tapping in'). This moment can be drawn or captured on camera and learners may use the image as a trigger to write about their response. (More detail about frozen moments can be found in Ewing & Saunders, 2016 and Ewing & Simons, 2016.)

Role on the wall

This drama strategy helps learners build a character profile through brainstorming the character traits of one of the main characters. In Figure 8.5, the teacher and children have developed a chart to represent the gorilla's character in Anthony Browne's *Gorilla* (Browne, 1987).

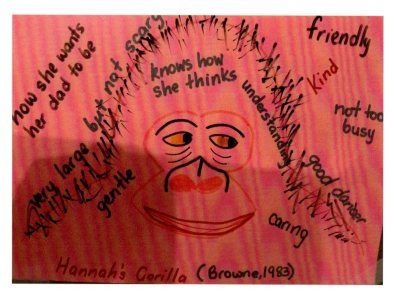

Figure 8.5 An example of a 'role on the wall' co-created by the author with a Year 2 class for the gorilla's character in *Gorilla* (Browne, 1987)

Puppetry

Puppets are another way to respond to a text and are often very popular with younger children, especially those who are not so comfortable with speaking up in front of the class. Being able to express their thoughts and feelings through a puppet (which can be easily made from junk materials) can be a turning point in children's confidence with oracy.

Responding and interpreting texts through movement and dance

Movement and dance are underused in many primary classrooms, yet there is emerging research documenting that involvement in movement and dance can enhance learners' language development and confidence (see, for example, Deans et al., 2017; Rieg & Paquette, 2009). Further developing the concept of embodiment discussed in the drama section above, learners can individually or in small groups:

- initially walk in role as a particular character, then extend this to moving in the way they envisage a particular character might move
- 'dance' how they see or interpret particular concepts, emotions or contexts in literature, science, history or geography
- retell a story or a particular moment in a story or a sequence of events through dance and still image, then draw and describe what they have created.

Responding to text through visual arts

Drawing, sculpting, collage and other visual arts are very important ways of responding to language in texts and organising our symbolic representation of what we read and listen to. Yet visual arts are too often only used in the early years of school or as an activity after writing has been completed. Mackenzie's (2011, 2017) research suggests it should often be the other way around: embodiment first, followed by visual representation and writing later. Figure 8.6 shows a Year 1 learner's representation of Peterboy's 'spiderling fingers' as he searched for 'a scrap of wonderfulness' to put the light back in his grandfather's eyes in *The Duck and the Darklings* (Millard & King, 2014).

Understanding and responding through music

Anita Collins' (2014) review of research about the importance of music for children cites ongoing research into the benefits of learning music, especially learning a musical instrument. Researchers (e.g. Dammann, 2009; Wandell et al., 2009) have found that those who learn music for at least two years acquire language and the rules of language more effectively than those who do not study music for at least this amount of time. It is strongly asserted that the study of music provides 'insight into the development of language processing in the brain' (Patel, 2008, cited in Collins, 2014). In addition, other research has argued that musical rehearsal nurtures the development of both attention skills and the individual's executive functioning, which includes the ability to predict consequences as well as emotional responses (Jonides, 2008).

Figure 8.6 A child's representation of 'spiderling fingers' in *The Duck and the Darklings* (Millard & King, 2014)

In her chapter on 'Leading with music', Millie Locke (2020) demonstrates interdisciplinary activities that engage children in responding to literature or global social justice issues through music-making. She reminds us that music is a way of making meaning and a language in itself. Locke demonstrates the importance of enabling children to develop active listening skills and to explore themes, characters and events through music-making and movement. She provides practical activities to help children respond to narrative and images through creating musical accompaniments using their voices or percussion instruments.

Understanding and responding through writing

There are many different kinds of writing that learners can use to rehearse or reflect on their understanding of a text and make a response. The kind of response made will be influenced by many factors, including the learner's experience, confidence with writing and knowledge of the area or story. Ewing's (2002) evaluation of research about creative writing for the NSW Department of Education and Training concluded that opportunities for learners to engage deeply with quality children's literature provided exemplary models for their own creative writing. Written responses to texts include:

- reading logs or reading response journals to give learners opportunities to record and reflect on their reading choices and their responses to their reading
- writing in role from a particular character's point of view to encourage learners to think about and explore a different perspective. Writing in role is often most powerful after using some of the embodiment strategies discussed earlier.
- retelling the story from another perspective, perhaps after storytelling, depicting the most critical moments through a series of still images, or using puppets, to foster the development and understanding of multiple perspectives

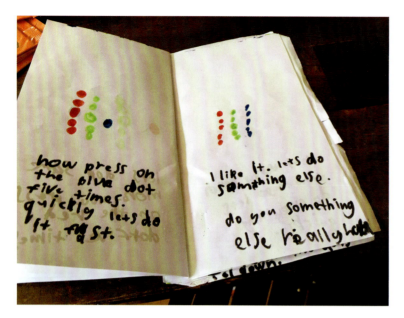

Figure 8.7 An excerpt from Timothy's book modelled on Tullet's (2010) *Press Here*

- writing an alternative ending to take the reader's response beyond the author's resolution. See, for example, Rebecca Solnit's (2020) retelling of the 'Cinderella' story in *Cinderella Liberator*.
- making a book or writing a poem modelled on an expert writer's use of structure or design. In Figure 8.7, Timothy, aged five, has written his own version of Hervé Tullet's (2010) *Press Here*.
- writing a letter to the author (or to one of the characters) to allow children to explain and share their favourite moments in a story or their favourite characters
- responding through writing a story or poem with a related theme – for example, after studying *Prayer for the 21st Century* (John Marsden, 1997), an individual or class can write their own wishes for the world in couplets modelled on the structure in Marsden's meditation.

'Doing a book to death': a caveat when exploring responses to texts

When helping children explore different responses to texts, teachers must take care not to 'do a book to death', as author Nadia Wheatley reminds us (personal communication with author). They must be careful they never take away the joy of the responding to a story, poem, information text or image. When we, as teachers, give learners questions to answer, background information about the context or the author, or activities to follow up with, the intention should always be to further contribute to their curiosity, understanding and enjoyment.

Conclusion

This chapter explored a variety of ways teachers can foster learners' deep understanding of texts through exploring different ways of responding to them. The teaching and learning strategies and processes discussed here are by no means exhaustive. We encourage you to continue to build your knowledge about strategies and experiences. One of the most important takeaways from this chapter is the importance of developing a rich repertoire of engaging strategies and experiences. Sharing different ways to respond to texts will help deepen learners' understandings of texts and also build their awareness of the complex and multidimensional nature of literacy.

Bringing it together

1. Were you familiar with the different strategies described in this chapter for nurturing learners' deep understanding of a broad range of texts? Invest time in researching those you are less knowledgeable or less confident about to ensure you develop a repertoire of strategies that you can adapt to meet the needs of individual learners in your care.
2. Examine the evidence that supports the potential role the arts can play in English and literacy (Ewing, 2010a, 2010b, 2019). Choose one of the art forms discussed in this chapter that you need to learn more about. How can deep understanding and meaningful responses to texts be enhanced using this art form?
3. How can the media arts be employed to foster children's deep understanding of texts?

Further resources

Reading Australia

Developed by the Copyright Agency, the Reading Australia website hosts resources for early childhood, primary and secondary teachers, including units of work and a list of over 270 books chosen by a panel from the Australian Society of Authors to celebrate the work of leading Australian writers and illustrators.

https://readingaustralia.com.au

The School Drama Book and Companion

Taken together, these resources provide the rationale for using drama-rich pedagogy with literature to develop deep understanding as well as a range of units to adapt for the classroom. An overview of drama devices with video clips also demonstrates how these can be used in the classroom.

Ewing, R. & Saunders, J. (2016). *The School Drama Book: Drama, Literature and Literacy in the Creative Classroom*. Currency Press, and its companion multi-touch book, *The School Drama Companion: A Collection of Devices* (available from iTunes).

From drawing to writing

Provides evidence for the importance of drawing and its role in the development of writing in early childhood classrooms.

Mackenzie, N.M. (2011). From drawing to writing: what happens when you shift teaching priorities in the first six months of school? *Australian Journal of Language & Literacy*, 34(3), 322–340.

WestWords

WestWords (WW) is a literature and arts organisation based in western Sydney. Its work is underpinned by a deep understanding of the importance of literature and literacy in its broadest sense to change the life chances of children and young people. The WW website offers a comprehensive online program of workshops and information about professional learning for teachers as well as residencies in schools and support for writers.

www.westwords.com.au

Book Trust UK

Dedicated to supporting teachers and parents to excite children about reading, the UK-based BookTrust website provides helpful units of work and resources for teachers.

www.booktrust.org.uk/about-us

References

Attenborough, D. (2020). *A Life on Our Planet*. Netflix Original Documentary.

Australian Curriculum, Assessment and Reporting Authority (ACARA). (2021). Australian Curriculum Literacy Progression. www.australiancurriculum.edu.au/resources/national-literacy-and-numeracy-learning-progressions/national-literacy-learning-progression/writing/?subElementId=50747&scaleId=0

Baker, J. (1987). *Where the Forest Meets the Sea*. Walker Books.

Bamford, A. (2006). *The Wow Factor: Global Research Compendium on the Impact of the Arts in Education*. Waxmann Verlag.

Benton, M. & Fox, G. (1987). *Teaching Literature 9–14* (2nd edn). Oxford University Press.

Bertini, A., Lamond, M., & Nielson, C. (2020). *Just One Bee*. Dirt Lane Press.

Blabey, A. (2007). *Pearl Barley and Charlie Parsley*. Puffin.

Browne, A. (1987). *Gorilla*. Walker Books.

Callow, J. (2013). *The Shape of Text to Come: How Image and Text Work*. Primary English Teaching Association Australia (PETAA).

Catterall, J. (2009). *Doing Well and Doing Good by Doing Art: The Long-Term Effects of Sustained Involvement in the Visual and Performing Arts during High School*. Los Angeles Imagination Group.

Collins, A. (2014). Neuroscience, music education and the pre-service primary (elementary) generalist teacher. *International Journal of Education & the Arts*, 15(5). www.ijea.org/v15n5

Dammann, G. (2009). Hearts and minds. *New Statesman*, 138(4964), 32–33.

De Bono, E. (1988). *De Bono's Thinking Course*. BBC.

Deans, J., Meiners, J., Young, S., & Rank, K. (2017). Dance: art embodied. In C. Sinclair, N. Jeanneret, J. O'Toole & M.A. Hunter (Eds.), *Education in the Arts* (3rd edn). Oxford University Press.

Deasy, R. (Ed.). (2002). *Critical Links: Learning in the Arts and Student Academic and Social Development*. Arts Education Partnership.

Ewing, R. (2002). *Focus on Literacy: Writing Evaluation. Report for NSW Department of Education and Training*. University of Sydney.

—— (2010a). *The Arts and Australian Education: Realising Potential*. AER 58. ACER. https://research.acer.edu.au/aer/11

—— (2010b). Literacy and the arts. In F. Christie & A. Simpson (Eds.), *Literacy and Social Responsibility: Multiple Perspectives* (pp. 56–70). Equinox Publishing.

—— (2019). *Arts-rich Pedagogy and Becoming Deeply Literate*. Drama Australia.

Ewing, R. & Saunders, J.N. (2016). *The School Drama Book: Drama, Literacy and Literature in the Creative Classroom*. Currency Press.

Ewing, R. & Simons, J., with Hertzberg. M. & Campbell, V. (2016). *Beyond the Script* (3rd edn). Primary English Teaching Association Australia (PETAA).

Freebody, P. & Luke, A. (1990). Literacies programs: debates and demands in cultural context. *Prospect*, 5, 7–16.

French, J. & Whatley, B. (2016). *Cyclone!* Scholastic Australia.

Gibson, R. & Ewing, R. (2020). *Transforming the Curriculum through the Arts* (2nd edn). Palgrave Macmillan.

Gleeson, L. (2012). *Red*. Allen & Unwin.

Gleeson, L. & Blackwood, F. (2006). *Amy and Louis*. Scholastic.

Graham, B. (1992). *Rose Meets Mr Wintergarten*. Walker Books.

Haseman, B. & O'Toole, J. (2018). *Dramawise Reimagined: Learning to Manage the Elements of Drama*. Currency Press.

Hertzberg, M. (2009). *Readers Theatre to Improve Comprehension and Fluency. e:update 009*. www.petaa .edu.au/PDFs/PETAA_Docs/PPs-open/171F.pdf

—— (2012). *Teaching English Language in Mainstream Classes*. Primary English Teaching Association Australia (PETAA).

Hill, A. (1996). *The Burnt Stick*. Puffin.

Hughes, T. (1968). *The Iron Man*. Faber and Faber.

Jeffers, O. (2005). *Lost and Found*. Harper Collins.

Jonides, J. (2008). Musical skill and cognition. In M. Gazzaniga (Ed.), *Learning Arts and Brain: The Dana Consortium Report on Arts and Cognition* (pp. 11–17). NY Dana Consortium.

Joyce, W. (2016). *Ollie's Odyssey*. Atheneum/Caitlyn Dlouhy Books.

Kalantzis, M. & Cope, W. (2006). The contemporary significance of visual meanings. https:// newlearningonline.com/literacies/chapter-11/the-contemporary-significance-of-visual-meanings

King, S.M. (1998). *Henry and Amy*. Scholastic.

Kress, G. & van Leeuwen, T., 1996. *Reading Images: The Grammar of Visual Design*. Routledge.

Latham, G. & Ewing, R. (2018). Conversation about poetry. In G. Latham & R. Ewing, *Generative Conversations for Creative Learning Reimagining Literacy Education and Understanding*. Palgrave MacMillan.

Locke, M. (2020). Leading with music. In R. Gibson & R. Ewing (Eds.), *Transforming the Curriculum through the Arts* (2nd edn). Palgrave Macmillan.

Luke, A. & Freebody, P. (1999). Further notes on the four resources model. Reading Online. Available through the Australian Literacy Educators Association at www.alea.edu.au

Mackenzie, N.M. (2011). From drawing to writing: what happens when you shift teaching priorities in the first six months of school? *Australian Journal of Language & Literacy*, 34(3), 322–340.

—— (2017). Draw, talk, write (and share). https://noellamackenzie.com/2019/10/22/draw-talk-write

Marsden, J. (1997). *Prayer for the 21st Century*. Lothian Books.

Martin, A.J., Mansour, M., Anderson, M., Gibson, R., & Leim, G.A.D. (2013). The role of arts participation in students' academic and nonacademic outcomes: a longitudinal study of school, home, and community factors. *Journal of Educational Psychology*, 105(3), 709–727.

Millard, G. & King, S. (2014). *The Duck and the Darklings*. Allen & Unwin.

Mraz, M., Nichols, W., Caldwell, S., Beisley, R., Sargent, S., & Rupley, W. (2013). Improving oral reading fluency through readers theatre. *Reading Horizons: A Journal of Literacy and Language Arts*, 52(2). https://scholarworks.wmich.edu/reading_horizons/vol52/iss2/5

O'Toole, J. & Dunn, J. (2015). *Pretending to Learn: Helping Children Learn through Drama*. Drama Web Publishing.

Palincsar, A. & Brown, A. (1984). Reciprocal teaching of comprehension-fostering and monitoring activities. *Cognition and Instruction*, 2, 117–175.

Patel, A.D. (2008). Science & music: talk of the tone. *Nature*, 453(7196), 726–727.

Rieg, S.A. & Paquette, K.R. (2009). Using drama and movement to enhance English language learners' literacy development. *Journal of Instructional Psychology*, 36(2), 148ff. https://go.gale.com/ps/ anonymous?id=GALE%7CA204682056&sid=googleScholar&v=2.1&it=r&linkaccess=abs&issn =00941956&p=HRCA&sw=w

Rosenblatt, L. (1978). *The Reader, the Text, the Poem: The Transactional Theory of the Literary Work*. Southern Illinois University Press.

—— (1985). The transactional theory of the literary work: implications for research. In C. Cooper (Ed.), *Researching Response to Literature and the Teaching of Literature: Points of Departure* (pp. 33–35). Ablex.

Simpson, A. (2014). Responding to literature: talking about books in literature circles. PETAA Paper 197. Primary English Teaching Association Australia (PETAA).

Solnit, R. (2020). *Cinderella Liberator: Fairytale Revolution*. Vintage Classics.

Thiele, C. (2019). *Storm Boy: The Illustrated Story*. New Holland Publishers.

Tullet, H. (2010). *Press Here*. Chronicle Books.

Vygotsky, L.S. (1978). *Mind in Society: The Development of Higher Psychological Processes*. M. Cole, V. John-Steiner, S. Scribner, & E. Souberman (Eds.), Harvard University Press.

Wandell, B., Dougherty, R.F., Ben-Shachar, M., Deutsch, M.K., & Tsang, K. (2009). Training in the arts, reading, and brain imaging. In C. Asbury & B. Rich (Eds.), *Learning, Arts, and the Brain: The Dana Consortium Report on Arts and Cognition* (pp. 51–60). Dana Press.

Williams, M. (1922). *The Velveteen Rabbit*. Simon and Schuster.

Winner E., Goldstein, T., & Vincent-Lancrin, S. (2013). *Art for Art's Sake: The Impact of Arts Education, Overview*. OECD Publishing.

Young, C., Durham, P., Miller, M., Rasinski, T., & Lane, F. (2019). Improving reading comprehension with readers theatre. *Journal of Educational Research*, 112(5), 615–626. https://doi.org/10.1080/0 0220671.2019.1649240

Young, R. & Ottley, M. (2015). *Teacup*. Scholastic Australia.

CHAPTER 9

Creating texts

Robyn Ewing and Kathy Rushton

ANTICIPATED OUTCOMES

After working through this chapter, it is anticipated you will be able to:

- explain how learners move across the spoken-written mode continuum and back again
- understand and implement the process of joint construction of text
- use different components of the teaching and learning model, including building field knowledge, modelling and joint construction, when helping learners create different kinds of written texts for a range of purposes and contexts across the curriculum
- identify particular features of different kinds of written texts, including imaginative, informative and persuasive genres.

Introduction

Writing can be a magical experience (Adoniou, 2018): we can gain deep satisfaction and enjoyment from putting pen to paper or fingers to laptop. We can lose ourselves in expressing our feelings, needs and expectations in a journal, or perhaps in creating an imaginative story or poem, recounting an experience, writing an informative text about a favourite place or animal, expressing our ideas in an opinion piece about an issue in current affairs or having fun compiling a travel guide.

Sometimes, however, learners report that writing at school is boring, stressful or even formulaic. In some writing programs, a number of recipe-like steps can make learning to write seem like an exacting formula that must be followed.

This chapter stresses the importance of both teachers and learners as *writers* (Graves, 1983) as they create, either together or individually, a range of different texts for different purposes and become a community of writers. After considering a parent's account of her daughter's experience of learning to write, we look at how substantial dialogue always needs to underpin the development of writing. The interrelationship between speaking and writing is then considered, using the mode continuum. We then explore the different aspects of learning to write within the teaching and learning framework, including the importance of building learners' field knowledge, teacher modelling to break down the features of different kinds of texts, joint construction and independent writing. Throughout the chapter, we use a range of examples of children's writing to illustrate different kinds of texts and emphasise that creating texts can and should be enjoyable.

REFLECTION

What can you remember about how you learnt to write? What kinds of texts did you choose to write first?

The *creating texts* sub-element of the Australian Curriculum's National Literacy Learning Progression describes how:

> students become increasingly proficient at creating texts for an increasing range of purposes. Students' writing moves from representing basic concepts and simple ideas to conveying abstract concepts and complex ideas, in line with the demands of the learning areas. (Australian Curriculum, Assessment and Reporting Authority [ACARA], 2021)

Learners gradually learn how to craft ideas for different purposes and for a range of different audiences, adding visuals or diagrams when appropriate. Over time, they build a rich vocabulary. This chapter shows how teachers enable learners to consider and create a variety of text forms and how they are structured.

Moving from spoken to written language

Interview with a parent — CASE STUDY 9.1

I have a daughter, who struggled at school. She is now 15 and home-schooled. She started school in Kindergarten, but as time went on she struggled more and more. She went to a very middle-class school, which was very different to my daily experience as an educator working in schools in south-western Sydney, where students were often highly supported and valued for what they brought to school, for their diversity. My daughter didn't fit in because a lot of her peers came to school reading quite well, it was a very affluent community and she was seen as somebody different who couldn't be helped. As a parent and an educator, I believe that all students can be helped and I guess crunch time came when, in Year 4, the teacher, with all good intentions, asked if my daughter could bring a set of headphones to school so she could sit in the computer area and work on the phonics program. That was about the only thing they saw they could do for her, but I saw it as something bigger than my daughter and her needs – it was a reflection of the overall pedagogy which was being implemented in the classroom. She had a lovely teacher in Year 3 who would get everyone writing on their own, albeit with no modelling or joint construction. She would sit side by side with my daughter and work with her, but I don't think that really helped because she became reliant. There is a responsibility to ensure that all students can communicate orally in a range of situations, not just where there is high support.

Since moving to home schooling early in Year 4, writing is now my daughter's favourite thing to do. It's developed slowly over time and she's positive about it and enjoys it, particularly story writing. I modelled writing for her – I wrote in front of her, I talked about how to write. We talked a lot about everything we were going to write about. I gave her choices that she was interested in, we did lots of planning and drawing as a part of planning. I remember if drawing happened at school, it was after writing, but we used it to develop and categorise vocabulary and to label things. I did a lot of modelling until I felt she was interested and engaged and then I would slowly hand it over and we would move into joint construction. She could have done this in a school classroom if she'd had a chance to practise. For instance, by working in a small group; telling a friend; writing on a small whiteboard; writing on Post-it notes.

The best way to teach writing in any classroom, especially challenging ones, is to first talk about what you're writing about, use pictures, use images, play games, develop vocabulary and make sure students actually know the content they are going to write about before they write – the field knowledge. Then *don't* say, 'OK good, you've got the vocabulary, we've watched a video, we've read a book, we've done a picture now go and write'. No! There needs to be other steps before independent writing. Model what the writing would look like and pull it apart, deconstruct it and then give students some understanding about the grammatical features, and after that apply that knowledge in jointly writing together.

Questions

1. What were some of the issues this young learner was finding difficult in the classroom situation?
2. What are the key things that this parent emphasised in helping her daughter enjoy learning to write? Can you relate these to what should be happening in the classroom?

Helping learners to move from spoken-like to more written-like language can only take place through oral interaction with texts. The texts that we talk about may include a wide range of digital texts, including websites, databases, emails, text messages, emojis, online gaming sites, movies, books, diagrams, maps … in fact any text that can be created and then viewed, read or written. This is important for teachers to remember, so that they avoid creating a false dichotomy between texts that belong in school and texts that don't. Rather, the texts we read, view or write about at school should help to develop learners' knowledge and understanding about the world and the texts that they will encounter there (Ewing et al., 2016). This process must include the teacher and parent or caregiver as expert guides in helping learners to choose quality texts and to understand how texts are created. The talk around texts should be about the choices authors, designers and illustrators make to engage, inform and persuade their readers and viewers.

The mode continuum

All language use can be represented on the mode continuum (Figure 9.1). This continuum is a very useful framework for teachers to use when planning and programming the teaching of speaking and listening and how they relate to reading and writing. With this framework, which shows the progression from most spoken-like to most written-like language, talking about texts can be seen as an interim discourse, one that supports the development of meta-language – that is, the language used to talk about language. By talking about texts, learners have opportunities to develop their understandings and to incorporate the use of words and structures from the written texts into their oral interactions and then into their own writing.

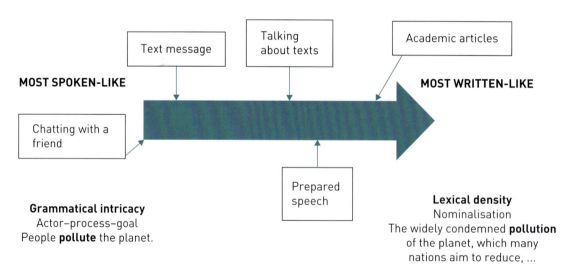

Figure 9.1 The mode continuum

Written language

As illustrated in Figure 9.1, written language is defined as lexically dense because the most written-like language needs to condense its message and therefore uses more lexical items, or content words. Especially in informative texts, this is often achieved in English through the use of nominalisation – turning words into nouns (e.g. 'pollute' becomes 'pollution'). The noun can then be described in an extended noun group, using adjectives such as 'harmful, destructive', adjectival phrases such as 'of the planet' and clauses such as 'which many nations aim to reduce'. This extended noun group is now packed with information and can be used as a sentence opener to focus the reader's attention in a paragraph opener, which helps to develop a cohesive, informative text. Both written and spoken language are on the mode continuum and some prepared speeches may be more lexically dense than some written texts, like a text message between friends, which is more often like spoken language. As the content or subject matter of texts becomes more dense and abstract in the later years of schooling, texts are more difficult to read, not necessarily because of the use of technical language or unusual vocabulary, but rather because the texts are more lexically dense and therefore require more effort to make meaning from (Halliday, 1985).

Spoken language

When learners begin to develop literacy, the emergent stage, which is usually in the early years of schooling or for some children even earlier (Ewing et al., 2016), the texts they read or view and start to write themselves often feature more spoken-like language patterns that support the development of literacy. Young learners are supported to 'read along' with a parent or caregiver. When the language is familiar, rhyme and rhythm help to develop fluency in reading and aid prediction; and pitch, pause, emphasis, intonation and pronunciation also help to make links to the patterns of word groups and clauses and the punctuation in the written text. As opposed to lexically dense written texts, spoken language is defined by its grammatical intricacy (see Figure 9.1). Oral language exchanges often take place in a physically close context where the participants are known to each other, so many text messages and emails are also spoken-like because technology can be used to provide a similar personal bridge. Texts that use fewer words that carry meaning are therefore spoken-like texts. The use of emojis in text messages demonstrates this, as they are easy to read and understand.

So both written and spoken language are on the mode continuum, and as learners proceed through the years of schooling, they will need support to understand and create the more written-like, abstract and challenging texts they will encounter.

The joint construction

Creating texts through **joint construction** is ideally a daily part of the teaching and learning cycle where the teacher is able to explicitly develop learners' understanding of all aspects of writing for a particular purpose and audience in the particular genre that is the focus of the joint construction (sometimes also called 'guided writing'). Jointly constructed texts are not models; rather, they are texts that are developed jointly between teacher and learners through oral language exchanges and shared writing. The teacher begins to hand over (Gibbons, 2002) control of the process to the learners in a safe, inclusive manner where

Joint construction: supports learners to jointly compose a text through both oral interaction with their teacher and peers and by sharing a pen or keyboard in the creation of a text. Also known as *guided writing*.

participation and engagement are key. The teacher is the guide because they have the knowledge about the structure and grammatical features of the genre and can act and work with learners as they make choices together.

Once a genre focus has been made by the teacher, a sequence of joint constructions can guide learners through the stages, phases and grammatical features 'at all levels of the text from word, group, sentence, paragraph' through to the whole-text level (Derewianka, 2011, p. 11), as outlined in Table 9.1.

Table 9.1 Sequence for a joint construction

TEXT
STAGE/PHASE
PARAGRAPH
CLAUSE COMPLEX (Sentence)
CLAUSE
GROUP
WORD
MORPHEME

Source: Adapted from Derewianka (2011).

Zone of proximal development: a term coined by Vygotsky (1978) to describe the distance between a learner's potential development with adult or older more experienced peer support or scaffolding and their developmental level independently.

Scaffold: support for learners to achieve a complex task that is gradually removed as learners experience success.

Teaching and learning cycle: the cycle for creating a written text that includes building the field; deconstructing a modelled text; jointly constructing a text; and independently constructing a text.

During the joint construction, teachers hand over control to learners at the site of the **zone of proximal development** (Vygotsky, 1986) and they also provide support for learners in choosing and using appropriate vocabulary, punctuation and spelling. When the focus is on the purpose and audience for the text, and on its meaning, learners are more easily able to actively engage in sharing their ideas, as the support and guidance provided by the teacher and their peers can ensure success for all learners. The joint construction will develop through spoken language if the learners' attention is focused on the text's meaning and on their language choices, as they share ideas, words, a pen or a keyboard. While the focus of the joint construction is on writing, the teacher provides a **scaffold** by encouraging oral language interaction between the learners and between the teacher and learners. The goal of the joint construction is to provide a high level of cognitive challenge and also support (Hammond & Gibbons, 2001) by maintaining a focus on meaning.

Preparing for the joint construction: the teaching and learning cycle

It is important to understand that the **teaching and learning cycle** (Figure 9.2) is a cycle, not a linear highway, so in the course of developing a sequence of lessons or a unit of work, this cycle will roll along and be repeated. A whole text and all of its features do not need to be developed in one lesson. Instead, aspects of the text should be addressed in a series of lessons, with many opportunities to build the field, deconstruct and jointly construct aspects of the focus text, interspersed with sessions when learners work together to independently construct texts.

Field building

During field building, learners are supported to develop knowledge about the subject matter and the audience and purpose of the text they will be creating. If the text is a multimodal text, such as a film, a cartoon strip or a picture book, they will need support with how the subject is realised visually as well as verbally. To develop knowledge about the field, learners might undertake a guided viewing of a film or website or a modelled reading of a text, and they might also engage in drama strategies like 'walking in role' or 'conscience alley' (Ewing & Saunders, 2016a; Ewing & Simons, 2016). Drama strategies can be used to develop empathy and understanding of the perspectives of characters in novels and picture books, and also of people and events in history. This preparation can also utilise learners' first languages to support understanding of the subject matter and how the English language expresses ideas about it, developing vocabulary and metalanguage relevant to the focus text (see the section 'Identity texts' in Chapter 11).

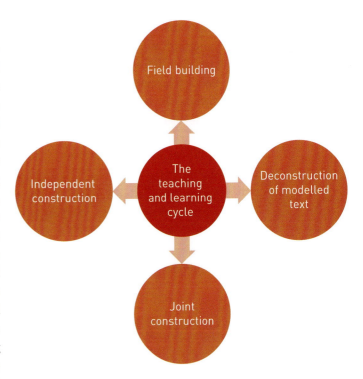

Figure 9.2 The teaching and learning cycle
Source: Adapted from Rossbridge & Rushton (2015).

It must be emphasised that sometimes learners will write solely for themselves. They may wish to record or reflect on an experience or respond to something to refer to later, or they may wish to use writing to work through an idea. In some classrooms, learners have a journal for this kind of writing.

On other occasions, it will be important for learners to share their writing draft with a peer and/or the teacher. Introducing some peer and self-editing processes can be helpful for editing.

Modelled reading/viewing: text deconstruction

The next step is to use a text to model the text that learners are going to create. It needs to reflect the subject matter or field, but, more importantly, it should be an example of the genre that will be created. For instance, a story or narrative could be used to build the field of what life is like in a city but, to describe a city factually as an example of the built environment, a factual description will need to be modelled and deconstructed. This will allow the teacher to deconstruct the text and to point out the structure, grammatical features and vocabulary that will support learners in their writing.

Joint construction

The third step, the joint construction, is a time for talking as learners now have developed ideas about the field, the subject matter and the language choices that best suit the audience and purpose of the text they are going to write. Whether writing is undertaken with pens or keyboards, it is a time for sharing ideas orally and beginning to write. The writing could be paragraph and sentence openers for an information report, dialogue for a narrative, or the factual or literary description of an event, character or person. The aim of the joint construction is to provide guided opportunities for learners to compose a text. The activity of writing includes keyboarding, handwriting, spelling and punctuation, but in the joint construction the focus is on the cognitive function of composition.

Independent construction

The final step in the teaching and learning cycle is independent construction. The most important thing to remember about independent construction is that it does not mean learners have to work alone. Working in groups or pairs can further support learners to develop their ideas or build on their understandings about the text they are writing. Allow learners to choose whether to work alone or in groups and then keep the cycle going and repeat … and repeat … and repeat!

Creating texts across the curriculum

The general terms 'informative', 'persuasive' and 'imaginative' are often used to categorise the types of texts that learners need to read, view or write; however, to support learners to make appropriate choices when reading or writing a text for a particular purpose, it is necessary to be more explicit. The purpose of a text, or the genre, is defined by the structure and the grammatical choices made to achieve its purpose. Therefore, while the teaching of subject English in primary schools includes the development of literacy and language, it is also necessary to develop learners' understandings about the genres that are used in all subjects, from Mathematics to Art, History, Geography and Science. Every time a teacher reads, views or writes a text with learners, a genre appropriate to the subject area is being modelled and the teaching and learning cycle needs to be implemented. Prior to learners writing any text independently, the field should be built and its purpose, audience, structure and grammatical features explored through modelled reading and text deconstruction, and then used in a guided writing lesson to develop a joint construction, in the process described in the preceding section (Rossbridge & Rushton, 2015).

Genre

The texts we use, and the meanings we make with language, are influenced by factors external to language itself. Together these factors make up the context in which language is being used. The features of the context that influence and shape the language we use include:

Genre: the social purpose of an oral or written text.

Register: the register of a text is made up of the field (what is happening), tenor (who is taking part) and mode (the role of language) (Halliday, 1985).

- the type of social purpose, or **genre**, of the text
- specific aspects of the immediate context, or **register**, of the text (Humphrey et al., 2012, p. 6).

Genres are the product of particular cultures and they develop through social interaction in particular cultural contexts and situations (Martin & Rose, 2008). It is therefore easy to see why some people are more familiar with certain genres than others, depending on their day-to-day purposes for using language. For instance, most people are familiar with recipes, stories and advertisements, which could be categorised as informative, imaginative and persuasive texts, respectively. However, an explanation of nuclear fission is also an informative text, far removed from a recipe for meatballs, so it is important to be explicit about the features of genres learners will need to write. Genres can be defined by **expression**. As demonstrated in Figure 9.3, comparing just the sentence openers and use of verbal groups in these short excerpts from a procedure and an explanation illustrates why it is important to explicitly teach the appropriate features of a range of genres if the purpose of the text is to be effectively achieved.

Expression: the language used for the intended audience.

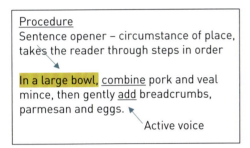 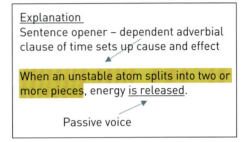

Figure 9.3 Genres can be defined by expression

Choosing and using quality texts across the curriculum

Reading and writing cannot be separated and, as shown in this chapter, developing literacy is underpinned by talking and listening. It is therefore vital to choose a range of authentic texts to develop all aspects of writing. (See also Chapters 6, 7 and 8 for further discussion of the importance of quality texts.) For instance, when describing characters or settings in a narrative an author can, and perhaps should, include an opinion: 'a long-legged teen'; 'a generous smile'; 'a lovely day'; 'a mysterious ever-changing desert'; and 'a lush rainforest'. In contrast, when describing the real world, we try to present facts rather than opinions: 'a 16-year-old nearing 180 cm'; 'a sunny day'; 'an arid desert'; and 'a humid rainforest'. In a comparison like this, the focus might be on the choice of adjectives, supporting learners to differentiate between opinion and factual adjectives and how to make choices appropriate for the audience, purpose and particular context of the text.

The key to choosing texts is to be clear about their purpose by using the framework provided by field, tenor and mode. The language to express ideas about the subject, to set the right tone for the audience and to develop a cohesive text, will all be addressed. (Field, tenor and mode are discussed in more detail in Chapter 10.) It is then important to decide what the text offers. Some questions to ask are:

- Does it help to develop knowledge about the field?
- Is it a good model to deconstruct?
- Is it a great stimulus for a joint construction?
- Does it offer useful vocabulary or ideas?

Even more important is to consider what your learners' strengths and understandings are and how they can be further developed. In the following example, learners had been writing literary descriptions of characters using a range of quality children's texts. In this example, learners read the wordless picture book, *Mirror*, by Jeannie Baker (2010).

The picture book tells two stories: one about a family in an inner-city suburb in Sydney and the other about a family in Morocco. The stories are displayed side by side in the book and the pictures are wonderfully detailed collages that invite close inspection because of their vibrancy. In this lesson, the teacher wanted to demonstrate the difference between a literary and a factual description. As the learners all shared the experience of living in an inner-city suburb in Sydney, it was relatively easy for them to factually describe what the suburb was like, and because of their previous work with a range of quality literary texts, they were also able to use more lyrical, literary language to describe Morocco, which for them was a distant and unexplored place.

The learners offered their suggestions of descriptions and the teacher encouraged and guided the use of language, but all the recorded suggestions were made and amended by the learners themselves. This was a joint construction of dot points for learners to use as a starting point for writing either a literary or factual description (Figure 9.4). Some learners then worked on their own and wrote both texts, others worked together in pairs and some worked in small groups. The teacher walked around the room, providing assistance, and the learners had access to the joint construction and the stimulus text while they wrote independently.

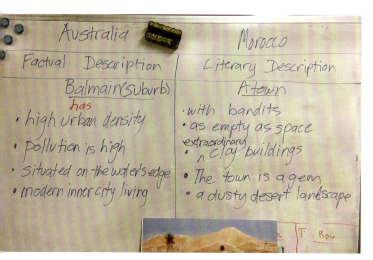

Figure 9.4 Language to describe place

Imaginative genres

Writing imaginatively is an important part of the primary curriculum. Learners can explores possibilities, thoughts and feelings through a story or poem. Writing in this way can enable us to make sense of and reflect on new experiences, work through an issue or dilemma, or connect our ideas with those of others.

Many of us make sense of our world through sharing stories, so it is not surprising that many learners enjoy creating imaginative stories about their lives and the lives of others.

REFLECTION

Think about a way you have used a story to make sense of something that happened today.

1. Who did you share this story with? Did you share it differently with several people? Why?
   Are you a natural storyteller? Do your family tell lots of stories?
2. Now consider: do you enjoy listening to others tell stories?

As discussed in Ewing and colleagues (2016), sharing stories usually begins before school with oral storying (Lowe, 2002), often shared with an adult, older sibling or peer. It can provide a window for parents, caregivers and teachers into the learner's imagination (Fox, 1993). Further, Fox reminds us how important it is to immerse children in talking and listening, including oral storytelling, because these activities foster their ability to tell stories. Confidence in sharing a story and listening actively to the stories of others enables the development of narrative writing. It helps learners think about narrative conventions: how story is located in time and space through some kind of orientation for the reader; who the story is about and how these characters develop; the plot or series of events usually sequenced chronologically; and from whose perspective the story is told. Once these conventions are learnt, learners can explore and experiment with them.

| **The Luperian's eye (Jordan Buultjens, Year 3)** | **CASE STUDY 9.2** |

Here I am, getting carried to the wild beast's nest. I can hear the dragon's fiery breath, inches away from me, about to blast me to smithereens. The leaves of the trees are curling around me, like an invisible hand is tying me up. It raises its head, about to breath white-hot flames, to kill, when …

Chapter one: A wild, wild, beastly creature

It all started when I was walking silently in the ghostly forest. My father, the chief of the bandicoon tribe, said I wasn't allowed to play there after hours, but my curiosity had overcome me, even though I knew why I wasn't allowed to play here.

The reason was …

Questions

1. Do you think Jordan's story opens well?
2. What features can you identify as typical of a narrative?
3. What kinds of stories do you think Jordan has read that have influenced his writing style?

The most successful imaginative writing (e.g. fictional stories and poems) often starts for learners with play and lots of storying (Lowe, 2002). Vygotsky (2004) suggested that dramatic play is an expression of our imaginations and provides the basis for creativity. He also suggested that drawing and storytelling provide excellent follow-on activities after play. Some children place themselves in the story, sometimes at the centre, creating and playing in a fictional world.

For example, Noah (aged 6; see also Figure 9.5) wrote:

I once saw a little speckle of
lite and it shode me all its
avencher that it went.
I woneted to go on those
invenchers that he went.
Soon I pacet what
at I needed …

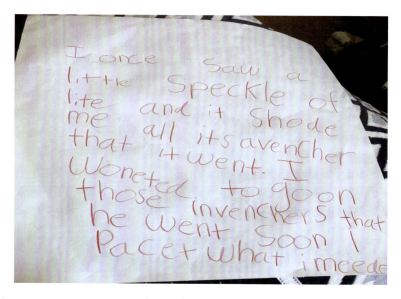

Figure 9.5 'A little speckle of lite', Noah (aged 6)

It is clear that the rich heritage of listening to stories read by his parents and teachers has influenced Noah's desire to write and he is already demonstrating a rich vocabulary.

At other times a learner might use a much-loved fairy tale or other story as the starting point. They might create new adventures or write alternative endings. After Timothy and his brother played at imitating fantasy creatures inspired by their reading, Timothy created 'Ugly Sluggly' (Figures 9.6 and 9.7).

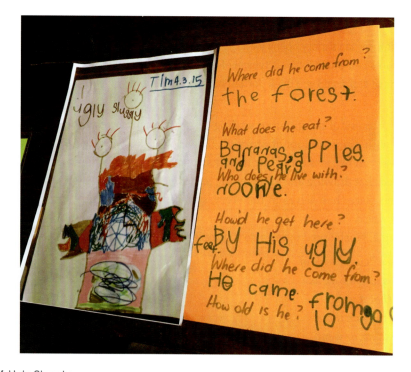

Figure 9.6 Ugly Sluggly

After drawing Ugly Sluggly, Timothy described his character's features. Mackenzie and Veresov's (2013) research has confirmed that those children encouraged to draw their stories during their first year at school were able to create more complex stories than if they only used writing.

When asked about writing imaginatively, Timothy commented about the importance of the visual for him:

> Imagination is ... in your mind ... it's when you think of stuff that is not actually real ... I think of things I know and then I make up other things like them. I like writing stories because it's fun and you get to make up things. (Timothy, aged 6)

Figure 9.7 Creating Ugly Sluggly

As discussed in other chapters and in the earlier section on creating factual texts, embedding arts-rich activities in the teaching of imaginative writing, whether a story or poem, is an excellent way to slow down the process and ensure learners have enough time to think creatively (Cremin & Myhill, 2013; Ewing & Saunders, 2016a; Gibson & Ewing, 2020; Nesbit & Hane, 2007). Key events or moments in a story can be depicted as frozen images or a tableau. These frozen moments can be unfrozen and dialogue added, which can be recorded. Later, these embodied images can be represented visually. Learners can role walk as a particular character or a character can be hot-seated to probe their feelings at a particular time.

When enabling learners to write imaginatively in the classroom, teachers must provide these opportunities to feel, look, listen, explore and sift through a range of ideas and potential characters and storylines. Latham and Ewing's (2018) conversation about poetry includes a discussion that a Year 2 teacher had about the purpose of poetry, using a number of contemporary poems. An early career teacher also shared her emphasis on sensory experience when encouraging her learners to write poetry. For example, she tipped a basket of colourful autumn leaves into the centre of the learning circle and gave her class time to look, smell, feel, drop them and scrunch them up. The class talked together about all the things they noticed about autumn leaves before they moved as leaves. Only later did they write about them. Georgia Heard (1989) uses poetry to help learners discover new ways of saying things and overcome the use of what she calls 'overused' words. She believes poetry can be the way forward for struggling readers and writers.

This time to investigate, read, think, talk, embody, draw and play with how words are organised in texts is an important precursor to imaginative writing. Understanding that writing often takes a number of drafts, and involves sharing with others and editing, is also important for success. This process can be fun, as renowned fantasy writer Ursula Le Guin (2017) wrote:

> I like the dances of meaning words do with one another, the endless changes and complexities of their interrelationships in a sentence or a text, by which imaginary worlds are built and shared. Writing engages me in both these aspects of words, in an inexhaustible playing, which is my lifework. (p. 52)

When encouraging learners to write creatively, teachers can also help learners 'think about new or divergent ways of expressing ourselves through written text by stretching more conventional ways of writing' (Ewing et al., 2015, p. 108). This can be through exploring how expert writers experiment with expression, as well as sharing our own writing as teachers. As Biesta (2013) suggests, writing imaginatively can help develop our identities. Figure 9.8 shows the first pages of a child's story that was inspired by *The 27th Annual Hippopotamus Race* (Lurie, 1989).

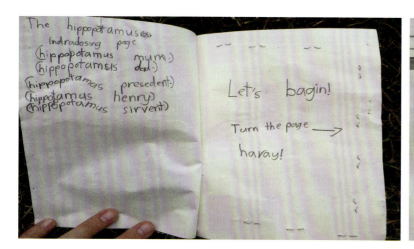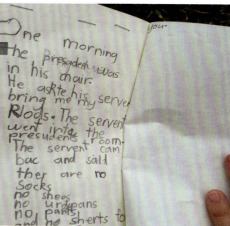

Figure 9.8 Excerpts from a child's story inspired by Lurie's (1989) *The 27th Annual Hippopotamus Race*

> **REFLECTION**
>
> Donald Graves (1983) talks about how important it is for teachers to be readers and writers.
>
> 1. Do you see yourself as a writer? If not, why not? If yes, what kind of writer are you?
> 2. Are you motivated to write imaginatively? What are your strengths as a writer? Are you successful in communicating your ideas? Are you functionally adequate? Are you versatile?

Text opener, paragraph opener and sentence opener: (theme of clause) are used to create cohesive texts.

Passive voice: shifts the focus of the clause by removing the actor – for example, 'Zombies *attacked* ... ' (active voice) becomes 'The attack *was* by Zombies ... ' (passive voice).

Nominalisation: the process of turning conjunctions, adverbs, adjectives and verbs into nouns (e.g. *nominalise* (verb); *nominalisation* (noun)).

Informative genres

Creating cohesive informative texts requires the use of grammatical features to concisely package and present information. Some of the features that develop cohesion are **text openers, paragraph openers** and **sentence openers**, which are used across a text to focus the reader's attention. Similarly, cohesion can be achieved visually by foregrounding an element of a diagram or image. **Passive voice** and **nominalisation** are also used to form noun groups that can be used as sentence openers. In Figure 9.9, Timothy (now in Year 5) informs us about an animal, the Nanos Thery, he has created after carefully researching the features it would need in a desert environment.

The Nanos Thery

Text opener: this first paragraph in the text introduces the subject

The Nanos Thery or _Salvos Mimmalis_, is an inhabitant of the Gibson and Tanami deserts. It gets its name from the greek words for 'dwarf' and 'dog' due to its small doglike appearance with long legs, small head and long tail. It doesn't usually hunt in groups. This Omnivorous Mammal lives in a burrow, and has adapted to the harsh environment of the Australian desert over many thousands of years. (Tim)

Paragraph opener: this first sentence introduces the topic of this paragraph

Sentence openers: focus on the subject (theme of clause)

Figure 9.9 Introduction to a factual text created about an imaginary animal

Unlike imaginative literary genres, which may focus on a playful and even disruptive use of language to engage and entertain the reader, in factual genres the focus is on providing information in a concise, clear way that informs the reader. In the contemporary context, where 'fake news' and photoshopped images flood our electronic devices with alternative 'facts', it is vital that learners are made aware of language choices that seek to persuade rather than inform.

For instance, the answer to the question, 'What is a boxer?', may be: 'A boxer is a medium to large, short-haired breed of dog, originally developed in Germany for bull-baiting'. The answer gives information, as does this alternative answer: 'A Boxer is an energetic, intelligent, athletic, loyal breed with a sweet and playful temperament that makes it a good choice for families with young children' (The Spruce Pets, 2020).

However, the word choices of 'loyal, sweet, playful' and 'good choice for families with young children' attempt to persuade the reader that, while the boxer was bred to be aggressive and strong, it is suitable for family life. These are two very different answers, for the same audience but with a different purpose.

When writing informative texts, there is often a lot of information that needs to be presented in a cohesive and clear way. As noted, grammatical features that support the development of cohesion and help to focus the reader's attention across a text include the use of text, paragraph and sentence openers. The visual equivalent of these is **salience**, which is the way the viewer's eye is drawn to an aspect of an image. This can be achieved through foregrounding an element by using size, colour, sharpness of focus or placement and framing (Humphrey et al., 2012, p. 155).

Salience: the elements of an image that stand out and draw the viewer's attention.

The informative texts in the following sections all have the boxer (Figure 9.10) as the subject matter, or field, but each of the genres uses a range of features to achieve its purpose.

Figure 9.10 An image of a boxer

[Annotation on image:]
Salience: most prominent part of the image
Placement: centre
Framing: use of one colour as background adds to the prominence of the dog

Describing

Descriptive texts help create a clear visual image of the person, animal or object. Make a list of all the descriptive information that is provided about the boxer in Figure 9.11.

> The boxer *is* an energetic, intelligent, athletic, and loyal dog breed with a sweet and playful temperament that makes it an ideal companion. Boxers often get along very well with children and possess an instinct to protect the family, making them wonderful family dogs despite their history as fighting dogs. Boxers have become incredibly popular in the United States, but the breed dates back to 16th-century Europe.
>
> (The Spruce Pets, 2020)

Sentence openers focus on the topic

Use of extended noun group to describe. Use of timeless present tense and relating verbs in a simple sentence using the adjectival phrase *'with a sweet and playful temperament'* and adjectival clause *'that makes it an ideal companion'*.

Figure 9.11 Factual description – grammatical features

Instructing

Instructional texts include recipes and how-to manuals. How does the structure in Figure 9.12 differ from the earlier factual writing about the boxer?

How to train a boxer puppy:
1. <u>Attach</u> the leash at home before the first walk.
2. <u>Use</u> the leash with the puppy for one to two hours every day.

Use of action verbs in imperative (bossy) mode and active voice, instructing the reader on how to do something.

Figure 9.12 Instructional text – how to train a puppy

Explaining

Explanations are also informative texts, but instead of describing or instructing, their aim is often to explain how something works or why something has developed in a certain way (Figure 9.13).

How dogs were developed by humans

Wolves <u>were tamed</u> as humans about 15 000 years ago. The wolves which were chosen were the ones that were most compatible with humans. Breeds <u>have been developed</u> to hunt, to protect and to act as companions.

Extended noun groups package information.

Use of passive voice supports continued focus on the topic in the sentence opener.

Sentence openers focus on the topic.

Figure 9.13 Explanation – how dogs were developed by humans

Recounting

Recounting may involve developing a factual recount – for example, using the picture book *Diary of a Wombat* by Jackie French (2002) as the model. After reading the text with the class, the story was modelled and deconstructed, and then joint constructions were developed about the boxer, Ruby, using the same pattern of language as in the picture book. The joint construction in Figure 9.14 has an intertextual reference – 'a bad nut' – to Roald Dahl's (1964) *Charlie and the Chocolate Factory*, demonstrating how a range of texts can be used to support writing.

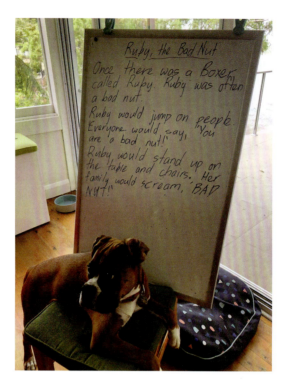

Figure 9.14 An example of a joint construction about Ruby after modelling

The final independent production was a book, *Ruby's First Year* (Figure 9.15). In this case, the field varied but the genre was the same as the modelled text.

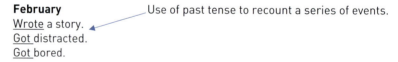

Ruby's First Year by Lucy McGuinness

Figure 9.15 A recount of Ruby's first year

The final genre included in this chapter is persuasive texts, which are used for stating strong opinions with the aim of convincing others of a particular point of view.

Persuasive genres

There are a range of text types that are written to convince a reader to follow a particular point of view. Persuasive texts include discussion that rehearses different arguments in a fairly balanced way, argument that is much more the presentation of one perspective, advertisements that present a very clear and one-sided directive, and opinion pieces written to the editors of newspapers. For success in writing persuasively, the writer needs to bring knowledge and understanding of structuring factual texts and choose an opening that focuses on the subject, together with the ability to engage the reader through expressing feelings and using emotive language.

Once again, in developing a discussion or argument text, listening to information about the issues and talking together about the issues as a whole class or in small groups, is an important beginning. Debating the issues, even informally, can also provide the basis for a written text. Drama strategies like conscience alley (Ewing & Saunders, 2016a) can help learners rehearse different points of view and develop confidence in considering a range of perspectives. Afterwards, developing notes using the Plus, Minus, Interesting (PMI) scaffold can also help clarify alternative viewpoints (see Chapter 8 for more about PMI).

Whether it is a discussion piece or an argument that is being produced, the writer needs to begin with either an overview of the different perspectives or a statement clearly outlining the position they will take. A series of statements or emotive arguments will follow, often bolstered by evaluative comments.

Argument genre

CASE STUDY 9.3

Using the understandings gained from the earlier sections of this chapter, examine the argument below written by Timothy, now in Year 5.

Why adults should choose to run their houses with solar energy

Solar energy is definitely a clean, renewable energy. It takes up little space and you can even have solar panels on your house. They can also save you money greatly. For example, if you can have more than enough energy to run your house, you can send the energy back to the grid and get credits so that you don't have to pay as much in other bills or you can also store up as much energy as you want in a battery if you have too much!

Even if you only power a few things with solar energy, it will definitely still help you economically and might even make your house worth more if you want to sell it. When you have solar panels, you can control them to do whatever you want – to this appliance, to these power points and to which rooms. It can be a very helpful tool and will excel your house fabulously.

Think about the world now. There is global warming, sea level rise, less rain and lots of natural disasters. We need to have a good turnaround so that we can live freely again. Solar energy is the best idea! You don't need any extra space, solar panels are easy to install compared to other renewable energy, and can save you money.

Questions

1. What features do you notice that are typical of the argument genre?
2. Do you think the author has convinced us that adults should use solar energy in their homes?
3. What else does the author need to do to ensure they have made a strong argument for choosing solar energy in the home?

Conclusion

Creating texts should be an interesting and enjoyable component of the primary classroom. This chapter introduced the mode continuum, which demonstrates the progression of most spoken-like to most written-like forms of language along a continuum. It can be used as a framework when planning and programming as it clearly demonstrates the relationship between the teaching of speaking, listening, reading and writing. The teaching and learning cycle then set out a series of cyclical processes that teachers and learners can engage in when creating written texts in all key learning areas. These strategies highlight the interrelationship between meaningful classroom conversations, the building of rich vocabularies and the sharing of authentic texts in a range of genres when fostering children's understanding of creating texts for different purposes and audiences. The chapter strongly suggested that, as teachers, we need to be writers too, so that we can genuinely model what it means to write.

Bringing it together

1. Reflect on the suggestion that you need to be a writer to help learners create texts. How do you respond to that suggestion? You might like to use Julia Cameron's (2021) suggestion that spending 5–10 minutes each day writing in stream-of-consciousness mode is a way to gain confidence as a writer and help you write more often.
2. Which genre of writing do you feel most comfortable creating? Why do you think this is the case? What implications does this have for you, as a teacher, in scaffolding the creation of texts in other genres?
3. Which genres will you need to explore in more detail when preparing to help learners understand their purpose?

Further resources

The School Drama Companion

This multi-touch book is designed as a companion text to *The School Drama Book*. It showcases 24 key drama devices and how-to videos, providing an overview of each device and guidance on how to use them in the classroom.

Ewing, R. & Saunders, J. (2016b). *The School Drama Companion. A Collection of Devices*. www
.sydneytheatre.com.au/education/teacher-learning/the-school-drama-companion

The ABC of Australian Poetry

A collection of Australian poetry compiled by Libby Hathorn, including longtime favourites alongside her own poetry and poems of other contemporary poets.

Hathorn, L. (2010). *The ABC of Australian Poetry: A Treasury of Poems for Young People*.
Harper Collins.

Grammar and Meaning

An essential reference about the social purpose, grammatical features, structure, phases and stages of a range of genres.

Humphrey S., Droga, L. & Feez, S. (2012) *Grammar and Meaning: New Edition*. Primary English Teaching Association Australia (PETAA).

Critical conversations about text

Watch a joint construction being developed with a group of learners and read the PETAA paper that describes the preparation for the joint construction.

PETAA Paper 196, 'The critical conversation about text: joint construction'. www.youtube .com/watch?v=WByszvdMWm4

Conversations about Text 2

Each chapter in this book provides examples of classroom practices to develop the teaching and learning cycle for factual and persuasive genres.

Rossbridge, J. & Rushton, K. (2011) *Conversations about Text 2: Teaching Grammar using Factual Texts*. Primary English Teaching Association Australia (PETAA).

References

Adoniou, M. (2018). Where has all the magic gone? Keynote address, Primary English Teaching Association Australia Conference, Canberra, 19 October.

Australian Curriculum Assessment and Reporting Authority (ACARA). (2021). National Literacy Learning Progression. www.australiancurriculum.edu.au/resources/national-literacy-and-numeracy-learning-progressions/national-literacy-learning-progression/writing/?subElementId=50747&scaleId=0

Baker, J. (2010). *Mirror*. Walker Books.

Biesta, G. (2013). *The Beautiful Risk of Education*. Routledge.

Cameron, J. (2021). *The Artist's Way. A Spiritual Path to Higher Creativity* (Revised edn). Random House.

Cremin, T. & Myhill, D. (2013). *Writing Voices: Creating Communities of Writers*. Routledge.

Dahl, R. (1964). *Charlie and the Chocolate Factory*. Puffin.

Derewianka, B. (2011). *A New Grammar Companion for Teachers* (2nd edn). Primary English Teaching Association Australia (PETAA).

Ewing, R., Callow, J., & Rushton, K. (2016). *Language and Literacy Development in Early Childhood*. Cambridge University Press.

Ewing, R., Manuel, J., & Mortimer, A. (2015). Imaginative children's literature, educational drama and creative writing. In J. Turbill, G. Barton & Brock, C. (Eds.), *Teaching Writing in Today's Classrooms. Looking Back to Look Forward*. Australian Literacy Association.

Ewing, R. & Saunders, J. N. (2016a). *The School Drama Book: Drama, Literacy and Literature in the Creative Classroom*. Currency Press.

—— (2016b). *The School Drama Companion. A Collection of Devices*. www.sydneytheatre.com.au/education/teacher-learning/the-school-drama-companion

Ewing, R. & Simons, J., with Hertzberg. M. & Campbell, V. (2016). *Beyond the Script Take Three: Drama in the Classroom*. Primary English Teaching Association Australia (PETAA).

Fox, C. (1993). *At the Very Edge of the Forest: The Influence of Literature on Story-telling by Children*. Cassell.

French, J. (2002). *Diary of a Wombat*. Houghton Mifflin.

Gibbons, P. (2002). *Scaffolding Language, Scaffolding Learning: Teaching Second Language Learners in the Mainstream Classroom*. Heinemann.

Gibson, R. & Ewing, R. (2020). *Transforming the Arts through the Curriculum*. Palgrave Macmillan.

Graves, D. (1983). *Writing: Teachers and Children at Work*. Heinemann.

Halliday, M. (1985). *An Introduction to Functional Grammar*. Edward Arnold.

Hammond, J. & Gibbons, P. (2001). *Scaffolding: Teaching and Learning in Language and Literacy*. Primary English Teaching Association Australia (PETAA).

Hathorn, L. (2010). *The ABC of Australian Poetry: A Treasury of Poems for Young People*. Harper Collins.

Heard, G. (1989). *For the Good of the Earth and Sun: Teaching Poetry*. Tandem Library.

Humphrey, S., Droga, L., & Feez, S. (2012). *Grammar and Meaning*. Primary English Teaching Association Australia (PETAA).

Latham, G. & Ewing, R. (2018). A conversation about poetry. *Generative Conversations for Creative Learning Reimagining Literacy Education and Understanding*. Palgrave MacMillan.

Le Guin, U. (2017). *No Time to Spare. Thinking about what Matters*. Houghton Mifflin.

Lowe, K. (2002). *What's the Story? Making Meaning in Primary Classrooms*. Primary English Teaching Association.

Lurie, M. (1989). *The 27th Annual Hippopotamus Race*. Penguin.

Mackenzie, N. & Veresov, N. (2013). How drawing can support writing acquisition: text construction in early writing from a Vygotskian perspective. *Australasian Journal of Early Childhood*, 38(4).

Martin, J. & Rose, D. (2008). *Genre Relations: Mapping Culture*. Equinox Publishing.

Nesbit, M. & Hane, J. (2007). 'Ditto': the creative process in dance and writing. *Teaching Artist Journal*, 5(2), 94–103.

Rossbridge, J. & Rushton, K. (2015). *Put It in Writing. Context, Text and Language*. Primary English Teaching Association Australia (PETAA).

The Spruce Pets. (2020). *Boxer: Dog Breed Profile*. www.thesprucepets.com/breed-profile-boxer-1117944

Vygotsky, L. (1986). *Thought and Language*. MIT Press.

—— (1978). Socio-cultural theory. *Mind in Society*, 6, 52–8.

—— (2004). Imagination and creativity in childhood. *Journal of Russian and East European Psychology*, 42(1), 7–97.

CHAPTER 10

Developing knowledge about language and grammar in context

Kathy Rushton

ANTICIPATED OUTCOMES

After working through this chapter, it is anticipated you will be able to:

- recognise how knowledge about grammar is developed in a range of contexts
- recognise the importance of the mode continuum in supporting learners' understandings about grammatical choices
- identify some of the choices speakers and writers make to produce effective oral and written texts
- identify how grammatical choices in any text, written or spoken, are defined by the audience and purpose of the text – the genre.

Introduction

Grammar is a way of describing how a language works to make meaning within a particular culture (Derewianka, 2011). In short, learning about grammar is learning about how language works in a range of contexts and this informs the choices we make when speaking and writing. For many of us, language itself is not often the focus of the many events and encounters that make up our daily lives, as most often our exchanges – even our text messages, which are written versions of oral language – are exchanged in a familiar context with others whom we know well. For instance, the traditional nursery rhyme and song: 'Ring-a-ring o' roses, A pocket full of posies, A-tishoo! A-tishoo! We all fall down', and the accompanying dance and gestures, are familiar to many people; but for those who are not familiar with them, there are many questions that need answering: What is a ring of roses? What is a pocket of posies? Why do we say 'A-tishoo'? What is it all about? ... The simple dance and the words that direct the movement are not usually explored for any deeper meaning as they are sung in a context where the focus is on movement and the words of the song are ancillary to the activity. Yet this is how much of our language develops – we learn to use language to satisfy our curiosity, hunger, need for companionship and a myriad other needs and desires, even including dance moves.

Anyone speaking a language, dialect, Creole or pidgin has learnt how to use the grammar of that language ... and that includes you! However, for teachers it is not enough to just use the building blocks of language, the grammar; teachers need to be able to reflect on and talk about how language works and to help learners to do the same. As noted in earlier chapters, talk about language and how language is used is referred to as *metalanguage*. The main context in which knowledge about language and grammar is developed is through learning to interact orally with speakers of a language. That context is the one in which most young children develop their first language/s. They do not receive instruction about how to speak, but develop language through interaction in response to their needs. This early development of language, protolanguage, evolves as the child's needs develop. The linguistic needs of a young child include the expression of their desires, such as demand, command, greet, observe and play (Ewing et al., 2016; Halliday, 2004; Painter, 2006). Infants express these desires through sounds and gestures, which they eventually redefine through their experiences interacting with others as they develop their first language or mother tongue.

How knowledge about grammar is developed

Is it 'in the holidays' or 'on the holidays?' I always get those two mixed up. How can we tell which word to use? It's all about why we need that particular little word, and what job it's doing for us. It's about grammar ...

> *Whadda ya mean grammar?*
> *Well grammar is all about making the right choice to make your meaning clear.*
> *Got it. So, if grammar means me making a choice that makes things really clear I'm choosing 'in' cause the holidays are a coupla weeks long. So when I want to tell someone what I did when I was on holiday, I'll choose 'in'.*

> *That's it! And if, for instance, you wanted to say which day in the holidays you went skate-boarding, you'd say: I went skate-boarding 'on' Saturday 'in' the holidays.*
> *Wow! I don't know why everyone goes on about grammar – it's so easy, ya just have to choose.*

When a child first enters an educational setting, connections are built with their understandings and experiences in oral language and elaborated in the first educational focus on the development of metalanguage. For instance, in the first year of schooling, young children are taught to make connections to their use of language in a variety of contexts and the explicit purposes of that language use, such as statements (greet, observe, play), commands (command, demand, play), questions (greet, demand, play) and exclamations (demand, command, play) (ACARA, n.d.). For some children, this might be the first time that the use of language is discussed, but for others it may be a familiar topic at home. Whatever the case, young learners enter school knowing how to use many of the grammatical resources their language offers and some will even be able to discuss many aspects of how their language works, even if they are not yet literate in that language.

The school years are focused on the development of language, but also on literacy and developing knowledge about literature (ACARA, n.d.). To help learners to build on their existing linguistic resources and to develop new knowledge and understandings about language, literacy and literature, it is important for teachers to recognise the differences between spoken and written language. These differences are best summarised by using the concept of the mode continuum, which was introduced in Chapter 9, and indicates the range of grammatical choices speakers and writers make to produce effective oral and written texts. All grammatical choices made to produce a text, whether written or spoken, are defined by the audience and purpose of the text – the genre. The years of schooling privilege a range of 20 or more genres (Humphrey et al., 2012, p. 199), which are broadly categorised as imaginative, persuasive and informative texts (see Chapter 9).

To begin the literacy journey through schooling, learners must begin to explore the audiences and purposes of these genres and teachers need strategies that will engage, challenge and scaffold their learners. To achieve this, learners should be encouraged to play with new ideas, especially the most challenging ones they will encounter, as play is based on choice and collaboration, two ways of scaffolding learning experiences to be both challenging and supportive (Hammond, 2001). A pedagogy that supports the development of language and literacy needs to be strongly focused on choice, and on using quality children's literature, because this brings a third voice (Saxby, 1993) into the classroom. Every learner's world is expanded by hearing the voice of an author and, in this way, many diverse voices can enter the classroom. Quality texts not only encourage learners to read interesting and engaging content, but they also exemplify the effective use of language and therefore provide great models for writing.

The demands related to writing a range of genres are limited in this chapter to examples of three imaginative genres (literary description, recount and narrative) and one informative genre (factual recount). These genres are relevant to all the years of schooling and allow us to explore the work of some contemporary Australian authors, most of whom are First Nations Australians, while looking at how to develop knowledge about language and grammar in context.

Elaborated and restricted codes

The development of language/s in the home is the basis for further learning. For some young people, the transition from home to school is a seamless one, but for others the transition is linguistically confronting because the way language is used in the school may vary greatly from the way it is used in the home. In short, it is not the language/s that are spoken in the home that are key to educational success; rather, it is the way language is used (Bernstein, 1990). As Halliday (2004) has pointed out, children are socialised in the home and the use of language is part of this socialisation.

The development of a child's language is related to the social context in which it is learnt (Ewing et al., 2016; Painter, 2006; Williams, 2000). The development of an orientation towards an *elaborated code* (Bernstein, 1990; see also Chapter 4) may begin in the earliest years at home and then be further developed in educational settings through interactions with both texts and individuals. However, for children who have not been supported in the early years, the pedagogic practices in schools are crucial in supporting the development of an elaborated code.

A *restricted coding* orientation works well in familiar contexts but will be a barrier to educational success if an elaborated coding orientation is not also developed. This coding orientation hinges on the ability of the individual to make appropriate linguistic choices relating to contexts and genres. The individual needs to be able to identify the purpose and the audience of any written or oral text and then make the appropriate grammatical choices. Those who can do this may not even be aware of their ability as this knowledge is acquired through use and interaction.

There are serious implications for teachers' pedagogy here, as teaching learners about making these choices appropriately can only be effective if learners are allowed to interact and choose language and texts in a range of contexts for a range of purposes and a range of audiences. Bernstein's coding theory (Bernstein, 1990) provides a way of examining how social advantage is realised in the personal language development of some children. It also provides a framework for understanding why some children can be assisted to develop an elaborated code by supporting oral language, especially in interaction about texts they have read or viewed. When teachers help learners to identify the relationships between context, audience and purpose in all the texts they encounter, individual learners will be supported to make appropriate linguistic choices (Dutton et al., 2018; Rossbridge & Rushton, 2010, 2011).

The mode continuum

The mode continuum was introduced in Chapter 9. Here we explore it further in relation to the reading journey through primary school. In the early years of primary school, many of the texts children first learn to read are written forms of oral language, such as poems and rhymes and the repetitive text in many picture books for young readers. Reading more spoken-like, grammatically intricate text is easier because it echoes our daily use of oral language and is therefore familiar to us. Most importantly, teachers need to identify the structure and grammatical features of texts by distinguishing the key difference between spoken and written language. This is best described as the *lexical density* or *grammatical intricacy* of a text (Halliday, 1985; see also Figure 10.1). Lexical density is developed by including more lexical items, or content words, in each clause. It is this that differentiates written-like texts from more spoken-like texts, which usually have fewer lexical items in each clause. Grammatical items are the words that are not absolutely necessary to make meaning – for example, asking 'Would you like eggs for breakfast?', as opposed to saying just: 'Eggs?' In the latter query, tone of voice, punctuation and context clearly convey the meaning, without the inclusion of grammatical items (Derewianka, 2011; Halliday, 1985; Humphrey et al., 2012).

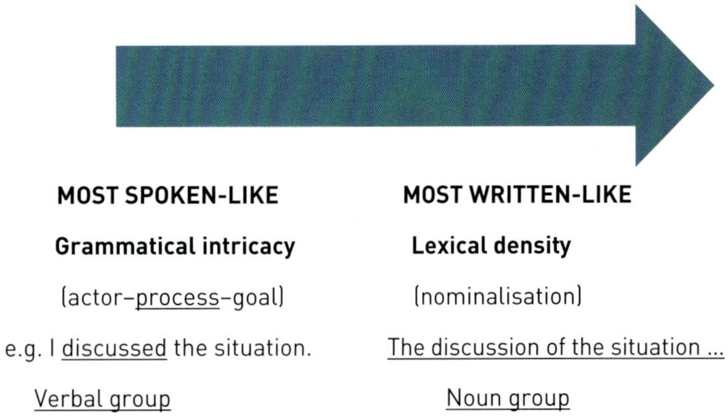

MOST SPOKEN-LIKE

Grammatical intricacy

(actor–process–goal)

e.g. I discussed the situation.

Verbal group

MOST WRITTEN-LIKE

Lexical density

(nominalisation)

The discussion of the situation …

Noun group

Figure 10.1 The mode continuum

As learners move through the years of schooling, they are presented with more lexically dense texts. The more complex texts that learners are required to read in the later primary years and in secondary school present challenges, as they include new knowledge in a range of subjects and a wider range of imaginative genres in English. However, lexical density is not established by the use of more complex vocabulary. Instead, it is achieved in the way that the language is organised. In Figure 10.1, in the examples 'I discussed the situation' and 'The discussion of the situation …', complex ideas are presented in writing in the form of nouns that can then be modified.

To take this further, we can look at some modifications. For instance, 'The heated discussion of the situation, which went on for hours' is a noun group built around the lexical item, the main noun 'discussion', and includes the pre-modifying adjective 'heated' and two post-modifiers – an adjectival phrase 'of the situation' and an adjectival clause 'which went on for hours'. This packs lexical items into a noun group, which can be moved around in the clause. When teachers are able to deconstruct texts in this way, it is possible for them to support learners to reflect on the choices they make when writing or speaking and to discuss the choices an author or illustrator have made.

How knowledge about grammar can be developed at school

Too often, grammar is seen as a set of rules that need to be obeyed. This attitude towards grammar, when combined with a lack of knowledge about how language really works, can result in a deadening pedagogical approach to this aspect of language learning. There are many textbooks and worksheets that offer learning about grammar as tick-a-box activities – for example, underlining the nouns and circling the verbs in sentences. Many learners silently ask, 'Why? Why? Why? What is the point of this?' Sadly, the answer is often that the books are being used because somebody bought them or the teacher is planning to assess the learners' ability to identify parts of speech. Whatever the situation, these types of activities in no way support learners to develop knowledge about the relationships between context, audience and purpose and between field, tenor and mode.

Developing knowledge about grammar needs to happen in context and the curriculum provides many opportunities for this as learners develop knowledge across the subject areas and explore the specific use of genres and language. While the framework of imaginative, persuasive and informative texts may be of help in thinking generally about the main purposes of a range of texts, it is not of much use in supporting young learners to make effective grammatical choices. For instance, the structure and choice of grammatical features in an imaginative text like narrative are completely different from those of an informative text, such as a recipe; but, similarly, a recipe is completely different to other informative texts, such as information reports, procedural recounts or explanations (Humphrey et al., 2012; Rossbridge & Rushton, 2011, 2015). It is therefore of vital importance for both teachers and learners to be able to identify the genre of a text, and not only the purpose, audience and structure, but also the language choices that establish the field, tenor and mode (see the next section).

The most valuable pedagogical contexts include reading and discussing modelled texts or responding to texts during a joint construction, also sometimes referred to as *guided writing* (Ewing et al., 2016; see also Chapter 9). In the classroom, reading and responding to quality children's literature and other texts, with support to identify the structure and features of a range of subject-specific written genres, will help learners to develop the elaborated coding orientation that will benefit their learning throughout their schooling (Humphrey et al., 2012; Rossbridge & Rushton, 2014, 2015). The remainder of this chapter provides examples of how knowledge about grammatical features can be developed by reading and viewing quality texts and responding to them by writing a range of relevant genres. At the heart of these activities is the opportunity for learners to read, view and listen to well-constructed texts and to jointly discuss choices in writing a range of genres.

REFLECTION

1. Think about your own experiences in a classroom or any teaching and learning strategies you have heard or read about. Choose one effective strategy that is suggested for developing knowledge about language and literacy. Can you place the strategy on the mode continuum?
2. Think about the language learners use to engage in the strategy and whether it is more spoken-like or written-like. Use these prompts to help you evaluate and place the activity on the mode continuum. Does the strategy:
   - support the development of oral or written language
   - help learners to identify any of the relationships between context, purpose and audience
   - help to develop effective individual language choices? How?
3. Could you make any changes that would further develop the learners' use of metalanguage and knowledge about language?

Making choices to produce texts: field, tenor and mode

The three lenses for examining any text are the *field*, or subject matter; the *tenor*, which is the meanings that indicate the relationship between the author and audience or between participants within the text; and the *mode*, or choices made to produce a cohesive text appropriate to the context, audience and purpose (see Figure 10.2). These three lenses are appropriate for examining oral and written texts as well as the myriad of visual texts that modern technology affords us (Rushton & Callow, 2018).

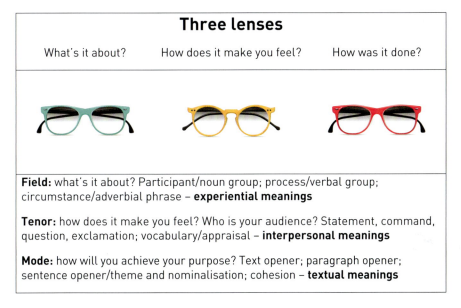

Figure 10.2 Field, tenor and mode

For learners to move beyond literal meanings and develop inferential comprehension, they must be able to make critical responses to modelled texts. A critical response explores inferences about participants and events in the text and also explores the author's stance. This is important in every subject and essential in challenging contexts, like History, when even the choice of a simple pronoun such as 'we' or 'they' in primary sources can suggest the stance of the author. For example, the choice of terms like 'settlement/invasion' or 'terrorist/freedom fighter', alongside the choice of 'we' or 'they', can reveal the author's position with regard to interpreting historical 'facts'. Understanding and analysing grammatical choices can support learners to understand literal and inferential meanings in a text. A close examination of the grammatical features of a text provides the reader with a framework for examining the development of a character and reveals inferential meanings in the text.

Thus, by identifying and discussing the author's choices at group and word level, many inferential meanings may be revealed. In the resolution of *The Lost Girl* by Ambelin Kwaymullina (Kwaymullina & Tobin, 2017), the author chose the verbal groups 'huddled; saw; followed; saw' to track the lost girl's actions and emotions as she uses the clues given to her by 'mother nature' to find her way back to her people. The use of the two action verbs 'huddled' and 'followed', and the repeated use of the sensing verb 'saw', position the girl as an active protagonist who uses her senses to overcome the complication of being lost. By utilising her own abilities as a sensor, she keeps the traditions of her people by looking to her country for clues that will keep her safe.

Understanding these inferences from the text will help young children to see more than just the literal story – for example, in *The Lost Girl*, they also learn about Aboriginal cultural beliefs and traditions. Explicit reference to the choices an author makes, even just at group or word level, can support learning even for very young readers and writers. Becoming familiar with the levels of text and how they are realised can support analysis of the texts that learners are reading or writing at any stage of schooling. Table 10.1 provides a reference point for teachers to ensure that all levels of text are made explicit to learners across subjects and at all stages of schooling.

Table 10.1 Levels of text

Level of text	Description
Text	Genre, purpose, audience, structure
Paragraph	How are paragraphs used to organise the text? Text opener; paragraph opener/topic sentence
Clause complex	Sentences in written texts – how are they structured? Simple, compound, complex Sentence opener/theme of clause
Clause	Basic unit of meaning usually contains a verbal group
Group	Participant/noun group; process/verbal group; circumstance/adverbial prepositional phrase
Word	Do vocabulary choices enhance field, tenor and mode in the chosen genre?
Morpheme	Smallest unit of meaning (e.g. shoe shoe**s**; ability **dis**ability Prefixes, suffixes

Source: Adapted from Derewianka (2011, p. 11).

In the following examples, some key grammatical features are examined and suggestions are made for supporting learners to develop knowledge at all levels of text. This grammatical knowledge provides learners with resources for viewing, reading, writing, listening and speaking.

REFLECTION

Explore the Australian Curriculum outcomes and content descriptors that you are using in the classroom and identify those that relate to the teaching of grammar.

Choose a stage of learning and, using Table 10.1, examine which levels of text should be taught at each stage.

Field: the subject matter – what's it about? Experiential meanings

The expression of meanings related to the field, or subject matter, is developed through the choices of processes (verbal groups), participants (noun groups) and circumstances (adverbials). Together, these three resources consider experiential meaning, answering the questions: *What's happening?* (process); *Who's involved?* (participant); and *When?*, *Where?* and *How?* (circumstance). As these questions are often used to prompt responses during modelled reading, by taking one further step learners' grammatical knowledge will also be developed. Using this lens, learners can find the answers they want by examining the groups and words in the text.

Processes/verbal groups

Verbal groups answer the question: *What's happening?* A verbal group can include one word or several words that help to develop the meaning and the tense of the verb. Consider the way meaning changes when modal verbs and auxiliary verbs are included with the main verb. In these examples, the verbal groups are underlined: I <u>swim</u>; I <u>was</u> <u>swimming</u>; I <u>will swim</u>; I <u>might swim</u>; I <u>must swim</u>; I <u>could have been swimming</u>. There are several types of verbal groups, including action, sensing, relating and saying verbs/processes. The *action verbs* are ones that can be 'seen' – for example, run, jump, sit, follow, build, break, drive and type. *Sensing verbs* are verbal groups that express what happens in the heart or the head – for example, see, think, love, hate, wonder, decide and remind. *Saying verbs* help to express what is said – for example, mutter, murmur, say, shout and bellow. *Relating verbs* are those that link two things and often they are expressed using the auxiliary verbs 'to be' or 'to have' – for example, 'It is a bird, it has wings'. In English, the auxiliary verbs help form the tense and, when they are used with a main verb, they are included as part of the verbal group (see Table 10.2 for examples).

Table 10.2 'To be' and 'to have'

Auxiliary verbs			
Person	**Singular**	**To be**	**To have**
First	I	was, am, will be	had, have, will have
Second	You	were, are, will be	had, have, will have
Third	He, she, it	was, is, will be	had, has, will have
Person	**Plural**	**To be**	**To have**
First	We	were, are, will be	had, have, will have
Second	You	were, are, will be	had, have, will have
Third	They	were, are, will be	had, have, will have

Another important thing to know about verbal groups is that some verbs are irregular and do not conform to the normal formation of past tense as in regular verbs like 'lov<u>ed</u>', 'hat<u>ed</u>' and 'decid<u>ed</u>'. Irregular verbs have their own discrete forms for the past tense and include very familiar verbs – for example, bring/<u>brought</u>; swim/<u>swam</u>; think/<u>thought</u>; go/<u>went</u>; eat/<u>ate</u>. Online search engines will provide lists of irregular verbs that can be brought to learners' attention as needed – for example, when recounting the event of a swimming carnival, the verbs 'to bring', 'to swim', 'to go' and 'to eat' would be a useful focus.

The other possible inclusions in verbal groups are adverbs and modal adverbs, and the modal verbs: might, must, would, could, should, ought, may and can. The use of modal adverbs and verbs is a wonderfully concise way to alter the meaning of a verbal group – for example, 'I am going', 'I might be going', 'I'm probably going' and 'I should be going' (Derewianka, 2011; Humphrey et al., 2012; Rossbridge & Rushton, 2010).

As the teacher, introducing your learners to quality texts (Ewing et al., 2016) will make it easy to choose a focus for modelled reading. If you also think ahead to what learners might be writing in conjunction with the text, it will support you to make useful and relevant choices. The genre you decide on will guide your choice and help you to evaluate the qualities of the text you have chosen. For instance, in *Little Bird's Day* (Morgan & Malibirr, 2019), the well-known Aboriginal author of *My Place*, Sally Morgan, and Johnny Warrkatja Malibirr, a Yolŋu man from Arnhem land, tell a beautiful story in words and pictures that describes Little Bird's day in the bush. Young learners can make connections to their own daily routine and will benefit from hearing and reading the verbal groups used to describe what happens during the day. If learners are introduced to this rich vocabulary during a modelled reading, they will be able to choose some of these words to use in their own literary recount of the story or in a factual recount of their own daily routine.

One way to introduce verbal groups is to create a cline focusing on one or more words from the text. Using a cline enables the learners to sort words using a criterion suggested by the teacher. In the example of a cline in Figure 10.3, the synonyms for 'eat' are displayed in a range from the tiniest 'bite' to the biggest 'feast'. If all the verbal groups are displayed and learners are given opportunities to read the text independently after the modelled reading, they will be able to choose some of the words to support the joint construction of the cline. Later, working in pairs or groups, learners might also like to create their own clines. Most importantly, there is a purpose to learning about verbal groups, as learners will be using them in their own writing. They will also have learnt how verbal groups can inform a reader about the happenings in a text, and also about the country as seen through the eyes of two Aboriginal people.

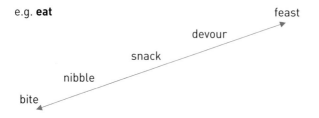

Figure 10.3 A vocabulary cline

Participants/noun groups

Younger learners can be supported to develop noun groups to orally describe characters, settings or events in a range of imaginative and informative texts (Rossbridge & Rushton, 2010). Noun groups are groups of words that may include pre-modifiers, like adjectives and demonstratives, and post-modifiers, like adjectival prepositional phrases and adjectival clauses. Noun groups are also a major resource available to writers to develop cohesive texts that focus the reader's attention across a text when they are positioned as sentence openers, which are especially important in persuasive genres. Older learners will be reading and writing longer, more complex texts, and the use of nominalisation will be the key to them developing more lexically dense written-like texts (Humphrey et al., 2012, p. 144). The ability to nominalise – that is, to present information as a 'thing' – is especially useful when the text requires detailed explicit description or is abstract – for example, 'the environmental pollution'; 'the discontent'; 'the inevitable decline of the empire'. Learning about noun groups is therefore one of the basic building blocks in developing cohesive texts for any learning stage.

The easiest starting point for identifying participants in a text is to ask: *Who?* or *What?* This is in juxtaposition to the processes/verbal groups in a text discussed in the preceding section, which answer the question: *What's happening?* Table 10.3 gives examples of how information can be grouped around nouns by using pre-modifiers (adjectives in front of the noun) and post-modifiers (adjectival phrases and clauses after the noun).

Table 10.3 The noun group

Pre-modifiers				Noun	Post-modifiers	
Determiners (**Which one?**): Articles: *a, an*	Demonstratives/ pointers: *this, that*	Possessives (pronouns/ adjectives): *my, her, their, your*	Adjectives: (**How many?**) Quantity/numbering: (**What like?**) Opinion, factual, comparative: (**What kind?**) Classifying:	**Main noun/ thing:**	Adjectival (prepositional) phrase: e.g. **with**, **at**, **in**	Embedded adjectival clause: **Who:** ☺ people **Which:** things **That:** ☺ people and things
The			*first, ancient, sailing*	**ships**		, **which** *just reached the shore,*
	Those		*two brave Macassan*	**men**	**at** *the water's edge*	, **who** *wanted to come ashore,*
	These		*two Aboriginal*	**Boats**	**with** *carved prows*	, **that** *were made from an ancient tree,*

There are many ways learners may enjoy responding to texts. *Once There Was a Boy* (Leffler, 2016), for example, is a deeply moving story of love, betrayal and friendship written and illustrated by Dub Leffler, an Aboriginal man descended from the Bigambul and Mandandanji people of south-west Queensland, who grew up in a small town near Tamworth in New South Wales. The orientation of this text suggests that the boy lives in an ancient boat and the illustration suggests a prow that looks something like a Viking ship. Using the structure of the noun group as a guide, the teacher and learners could jointly construct some descriptive noun groups. These noun groups might describe the beautiful setting of the boy's island home, using ideas and words from the text, learners' suggestions and contributions from the teacher. All contributions can be incorporated and developed into a descriptive noun group that is used in a written sentence or orally. The pattern shown in Figure 10.4 demonstrates how a noun group can be built around a noun in a joint construction. Using the possible structure of a noun group that includes both pre-modifiers and post-modifiers, with prompts such as 'Which one?', 'How many?', 'What like?' and 'What kind?', and trigger words such as 'with', 'at', 'in', 'who', 'which' and 'that', as shown in Table 10.3, will support learners to develop complex noun groups to enrich both their oral language and their writing.

Building noun groups: seven noun groups
1. **Boat**
2. the **boat**
3. the two **boats**
4. the two ancient **boats**
5. the two ancient Aboriginal **boats**
6. the two ancient Aboriginal **boats** *with* carved prows
7. the two ancient Aboriginal **boats** *with* carved prows, *that* were made from an ancient tree,

Figure 10.4 Building noun groups

Learners who rely too heavily on their own oral language when writing may describe the boy's home with these three simple sentences, indicative of oral language: 'His home was a boat. It had a carved prow. It was made from an ancient tree.' These sentences may be replaced by a more written-like simple sentence with a complex noun group (underlined): 'The boy's home was <u>an ancient boat with a carved prow, that was made from an ancient tree</u>.' By jointly constructing some descriptive noun groups, learners are supported to develop detailed descriptions and at the same time practise the very useful skill of building noun groups with embedded adjectival clauses. This is the beginning of understanding one of the ways of developing more lexically dense texts by starting to understand the clause patterning that helps to create a range of sentence types.

Before, during or after reading, dramatic responses to this text, such as using conscience alley, sculpting or walking in role (Dutton et al., 2018; Ewing & Simons, 2016), would be very appropriate to support understanding of the characters' motivations and feelings and the development of inferential comprehension. As *Once There Was a Boy* is so visually rich, it would also be appropriate to use a range of visual responses, such as retelling or recounting the story as a short film or in a cartoon style with illustrations and captions, or just by selecting one scene or character to represent visually. Similarly, using a pattern like that in the following example, learners can be supported to jointly construct noun groups to respond to the inferred meanings of a visual text. In this case, it could be a predictive response to the cover of the book before reading.

10 DEVELOPING KNOWLEDGE ABOUT LANGUAGE AND GRAMMAR IN CONTEXT   239

The _____ boy who, _____,	
What is he like?	*How does he feel?*
lonely	hoped a boat would arrive
solitary	wished he could swim like a dolphin
thoughtful	wondered what it was like to live under the sea

Learners can use the ideas and vocabulary that have been jointly constructed to develop noun groups to use in their own sentences to respond to the text. This is also an opportunity to deconstruct a visual text to support learners in creating their own visual texts while demonstrating how the three lenses of field, tenor and mode are useful in exploring both verbal and visual texts (Humphrey et al., 2012) – see Figure 10.5.

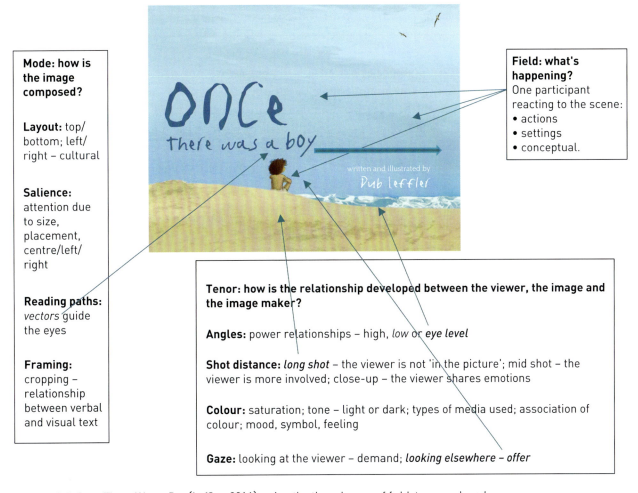

Figure 10.5 *Once There Was a Boy* (Leffler, 2016), using the three lenses of field, tenor and mode

Circumstances/adverbial prepositional phrases

Adverbial prepositional phrases describe the circumstances surrounding the verbal group. All prepositional phrases are made up of a preposition and a noun group that is *not* a participant in the clause. The prepositions that start prepositional phrases are usually very short single words like 'with', 'in', 'from', 'on', 'off', 'by', 'up', 'at', 'until' and 'near'. Teachers of young readers often prompt with questions like 'When?', 'Where?' and 'How?', and these questions are often answered by a circumstance/adverbial prepositional phrase that gives the information requested – for example: 'When? *In* the afternoon'; 'Where? *At* the beach'; and 'How? *With* a lot of laughter'. Adverbs can also provide this information, but single-word adverbials are included in the verbal group. The circumstance/adverbial prepositional phrase can always be identified by the following:

- The group answers a question like 'When?', 'Where?', How?', etc.
- It adds more information to the verbal group.
- Like a kangaroo, it can hop around in the clause, as in the following example.

'I have breakfast *in the morning*. *In the morning* I have breakfast.'

Circumstances/prepositional adverbial phrases are not part of the processes/verbal groups or participants/noun groups; rather, they can be placed anywhere in the clause or sentence. It might help learners to differentiate between adverbial prepositional phrases, as opposed to adjectival prepositional phrases, by likening them to kangaroos that can hop around in the clause to give the listener or reader a lot of information about time, place, manner, duration, frequency and accompaniment (Derewianka, 2011; Humphrey et al., 2012; Rossbridge & Rushton, 2010, 2011).

Figure 10.6 Adverbial phrases are like kangaroos – they can hop around

If the prepositional phrase cannot be moved and it is clinging on behind a noun (like a koala), then it is an adjectival prepositional phrase and is part of the noun group which is the participant in the clause, and it is a post-modifier. The prepositional phrase is a post-modifier in the noun group and is acting like an adjective to describe the noun. It is helping to answer a different question: 'Who?' or 'What?', as shown in the following example.

Figure 10.7 A prepositional phrase is like a koala – it clings behind a noun

'The koala *with* the strong claws   is clinging   *to* the branch.'
PARTICIPANT   PROCESS   CIRCUMSTANCE

Q. **Who** is clinging to the branch?
A. The koala ***with the strong claws*** **(adjectival)** is clinging to the branch.

Q. **Where** is the koala clinging?
A. The koala *with* the strong claws is clinging *to the* **branch (adverbial)**.

The Lost Girl by Dr Ambelin Kwaymullina — CASE STUDY 10.1

Dr Ambelin Kwaymullina is a novelist, illustrator and Aboriginal law academic who comes from the Palyku people of the Pilbara region of Western Australia. Her extended family includes many well-known storytellers, including her mother, Sally Morgan. In the resolution of her picture book *The Lost Girl* (Kwaymullina & Tobin, 2017), the girl finds her way back to her people by following a crow through her country. In a modelled reading, after discussion of the two action verbs 'huddled' and 'followed' and the sensing verb 'saw', the girl's relationship to her country and culture may be further revealed by examining the *many circumstances of place* that answer the question 'Where?' and **the one circumstance of time** that answers the question 'When?' She is positioned in the landscape as a girl who uses her senses to motivate her actions:

> The afternoon grew colder. She huddled beneath an overhanging rock, pressing herself into a hollow that had trapped the warm air of the day. Then she saw a crow flying in the sky, flapping from tree to tree and calling 'Caw! Caw! Caw!' The girl followed the crow ... through the trees and over the rocks and up the hills ...
> until **at last** she saw the glow of her people's campfires in the distance.
>
> Source: Kwaymullina & Tobin (2017).

Question

When you ask the questions, 'When?', 'Where?' and 'How?', can you find both the phrases and the words in a text that answer the questions?

Similarly, in *Going to the Footy* (Coombes, 2019), every page of the simple text answers the implicit question: 'How?' The statement on the first page is: 'Everyone is going to the footy'. On each page that follows, an illustration accompanies a circumstance of manner: 'On a plane. In a canoe. On a bus. In a car.' The accompanying illustrations show the many ways that Tiwi people travel to the footy. Debbie Coombes' mother and grandfather are from the Tiwi Islands and they taught her how to paint, so the colourful illustrations give an insight into Tiwi culture as the reader explores the many different forms of transport that are used. It is easy for young learners to make a personal connection to this text and as the sentence on each page is only one circumstance of manner, it is a text that provides rich opportunities for discussion and a wonderful springboard for writing about the learners' own experiences of transport.

Tenor: the relationship between the reader and writer – who is your audience? Interpersonal meanings

Tenor is about audience and interpersonal meanings. Through this lens, learners can examine texts to see how their own or an author's choices position a viewer or reader. In the earliest years, young learners' attention is drawn to the main resource for tenor, the speech functions: statement, command, exclamation and question. Building on oral language intonation, emphasis and pause, the speech functions are identified by the punctuation that marks the written forms. The use of modality, including modal adverbs and verbs, is another resource for developing the relationship between the author and the reader or viewer. When developing tenor, the question to ask is: What word works best in this text with this purpose? Therefore, expanding vocabulary is best developed through reading, writing, talking, listening and the repetitive use of vocabulary in appropriate contexts.

In their very useful text *Grammar and Meaning*, Humphrey and colleagues (2012) summarise the appraisal system, which is a framework for examining tenor and vocabulary:

> Evaluative vocabulary, or more specifically, vocabulary expressing attitude, refers to the resources writers and speakers use to make positive and negative evaluations of a range of phenomena. Expressions of attitude can be divided into three categories, according to whether they:
> - express feelings to build up empathy and suspense (e.g. in stories, *affect*)
> - make moral judgements of people's behaviour (*judgement*)
> - assess the quality of objects such as literary or artistic works, people's appearance or other natural or man-made phenomena (*appreciation*). (p. 101)

Knowledge of the appraisal system is useful in imaginative texts and of special relevance to persuasive texts, such as speeches, discussions and expositions, and even historical recounts or biographies. Through this lens, learners can examine texts to see how their own or an author's choices position a viewer or a reader, as shown in the following example.

Statement: 'My uncles furl sails and haul ropes and ready the spears and canoes.'

Command/Exclamation: 'Watch, Jalak, lower your spear and strike!'

Question: 'What if, like him, I stay?' (Rawlins et al., 2018)

Waves: factual description setting for stories

CASE STUDY 10.2

Donna Rawlins, an Australian writer, illustrator and teacher, wrote the picture book, *Waves* (Rawlins et al., 2018), which is about the peoples who have come across the waves to Australia over the past 50 000 years. It includes 15 stories that take us up to Abdul's voyage in the 2000s. Heather Potter and her husband Mark Jackson have illustrated the stories and each story comes with a short factual description of the historical context in which it is set. For instance, part of the background to this story states: 'Jalak and his people were sailing from Sulawesi, Timor and other nearby islands to trade with the Yolgnu people of "Marege" (northern Australia) for hundreds of years' (Rawlins et al., 2018). The inclusion of these two types of text (factual and imaginative) provides a rich ground for comparison, especially for learners in the later years of primary school.

In Jalak's story, for instance, some words like 'lumbering', which is used to describe the boat in which he is travelling, could easily be replaced by 'big' or 'slow', a fact that provides a starting point for discussion about the author's purpose and whether it was achieved. Similar choices the author has made in describing the journey on board the 'lumbering perahu' are 'towering'; 'furl'; 'ready'; 'at last'; 'crystal waters'; 'strike'; 'bitter'; 'the distant shore'; 'rich and important'; 'the deadly sea'; and 'enchanted'. Using the appraisal framework and understandings about the use of speech functions, a modelled reading of a short text like this can be compared to the accompanying short factual account of the same events, revealing the differences in tenor through the choices of vocabulary. In the story of Jalak, for example, there is a repetition of the question, 'What if ... ?', which is used to provoke an emotional response in the reader by building 'empathy and suspense (eg. In stories, affect)' (Humphrey et al., 2012, p. 101). In contrast, the factual account uses terms like 'some archaeologists say' and 'there is certainly evidence', which are meant to assure the reader about the facts presented rather than move the reader emotionally.

Question

Why is it important to identify the individual genres that are grouped under the umbrella terms 'persuasive', 'informative' and 'imaginative'?

By using teaching strategies like modelled reading and text deconstruction, learners can be supported to compare texts and explore tenor. Comparing stories with historical recounts or news reports about important events or significant people will reveal how the author's choices vary according to purpose and audience. Looking through the lens of tenor, it is possible to see how the reader or viewer is positioned and what strategies the author has employed to engage, persuade, entertain or move them. This is an especially important aspect of informative historical texts and persuasive texts, as perspective and opinion are expressed and best analysed through the lens of tenor.

Mode: the subject nature of the text and the role language plays within it – how will you achieve your purpose? Textual meanings

Mode is about textual meanings and how the author will achieve their purpose. For older learners, including those in secondary and tertiary settings, mode becomes possibly the most important lens through which to view a text. The texts learners need to read and write increase in lexical density as the subject matter they engage with becomes more sophisticated and challenging. Reading and writing longer texts is supported if the reader or writer has a clear understanding of how a cohesive text is developed. Even young learners are aware of the role of conjunctions but are often not aware that they can indicate time, manner, cause and so on (Derewianka, 2011). Providing suggestions of a range of conjunctions and text connectives suitable for particular purposes can instantly improve learners' writing if they often write using their oral language as their main resource. This sort of writing is often characterised by run-on sentences and interspersed with conjunctions like 'and', 'then' and 'because'. Cohesion may also be achieved through the use of reference, deletion, substitution and collocation; however, a focus on thematic choice and nominalisation may be of the most value in supporting young readers and writers.

Text opener, paragraph opener and sentence opener

The theme or sentence opener is most often the subject – 'the bit before the verb' in a clause – and the choice of sentence opener helps to develop cohesion across a text, especially if the choice of paragraph opener or topic sentence is also previewed in the text opener or opening paragraph. The sentence opener can be described as the starting point from which experiences unfold as it helps to coherently organise meanings across a text. The sentence opener is often a participant (noun group), but it may also be a process (verbal group), in instructions like recipes, or a circumstance (adverbial). If a circumstance is chosen as the sentence opener, it is often because the text is organised in a particular way – for example, a historical recount organised around time may often have circumstances (marked themes) as sentence openers (e.g. '*In* the latter part of his reign … '; '*At* the end of the century … '; '*In* 1788 … ').

Sometimes, to focus on a particular phenomenon, it is necessary to use nominalisation to convert a verb, an adjective, an adverb or even a conjunction into a noun. This enables writers to develop a noun group in a thematic position as a sentence opener (Humphrey et al., 2012, p. 155). This process is possibly the most important textual resource for developing lexical density. It condenses information and organises abstract ideas into packages in which a 'thing' can be modified using pre-modifiers, post-modifiers and the framework of the noun group.

CASE STUDY 10.3 *Young Dark Emu: A Truer History*

Bruce Pascoe, the author of *Young Dark Emu: A Truer History* (Pascoe, 2019), lives in Victoria and has Bunurong, Tasmanian and Yuin heritage. In this book, he uses the diaries of non-Aboriginal explorers who saw Aboriginal people living, working and eating in their own lands before the invasion of Europeans had developed into the settlements that brought strange people and animals into Aboriginal people's lives. What those explorers saw and reported were wonderful sights, some of which, like the Brewarrina fish traps in New South Wales, are still in existence. For learners studying history, this text offers an accessible way to read and comprehend primary sources and to

10 DEVELOPING KNOWLEDGE ABOUT LANGUAGE AND GRAMMAR IN CONTEXT — 245

understand how the history of Australia did not start in the eighteenth century. For instance, quotes from Charles Sturt's diary are contextualised in a historical recount by Pascoe, and in the excerpt that follows, the sentence openers have been italicised and underlined to demonstrate how they guide the reader through the text:

> *Charles Sturt* was a good bushman and a great writer.
> *In 1844*, he led …
> *When Sturt's party* reached …
> *They* continued …
> *His journal* records …
> *Sturt* was looking …
> *Sick and weary and with horses stumbling with hunger, thirst and fatigue*, Sturt was amazed to find …
> *He* was …

Source: Pascoe (2019).

If this text was shared in a modelled reading, it would provide some wonderful examples of how to organise a text cohesively by using a range of resources to summarise the text in the sentence openers. There are also some examples of very descriptive expanded noun groups, such as: 'an expedition to Australia's centre, which was hampered by difficulty' and 'a large settlement of Aboriginal people'. These noun groups are built around the noun/nominalisation 'expedition/ settlement'. Learners could be supported to jointly construct a historical recount as a class by first preparing some topic sentences for paragraphs that recount this episode in Sturt's journey. Learners could then be guided to ensure that the sentence openers are well developed and that attention is paid to all levels of text, including the opening paragraph, the text opener, as well as the paragraph and sentence openers.

Question

Could you give even very young children a range of sentence openers to help them with their writing?

REFLECTION

Choose a text in a particular subject area as the context for developing knowledge about one aspect of grammar that is foregrounded in your chosen text. Evaluate your choices using this checklist:

1. Is the text a rich, quality text when the three lenses of field, tenor and mode are used to examine it?
2. Have you analysed your chosen text by referring to the examples given in this chapter?
3. Have you decided in which genre learners will be writing when they respond to the text?
4. How will modelled reading of the text support the joint construction of your chosen genre for responding to the text?

Conclusion

Knowledge about grammar is developed through reflection and discussion of texts, both visual and verbal. While students have learnt to use grammar as they developed their first language, whether that is English or another language, they might not have reflected on that use. For teachers, knowledge about the mode continuum is essential, as it supports the identification of the grammatical choices learners make. Some learners will use only their own oral language as their main resource for writing, while others will also have the benefit of interaction with a wide range of texts, both oral and written. Producing effective oral and written texts is dependent on choice and appropriate choices will be defined by the audience and purpose of a text. As teachers, we need to understand the importance of grammar, introduce learners to a wide range of quality texts and support them to respond to, deconstruct, discuss and jointly construct texts. These experiences will enable learners to explore how a wide range of grammatical features are appropriately chosen for a particular context and inform and enhance their own writing.

Bringing it together

1. Choose a text from your favourite subject, then use the lenses provided by field, tenor and mode to explore the grammatical features that are foregrounded in that text. Which features are both relevant to the subject and suitable to discuss with learners at a particular stage of learning?
2. During which daily reading and writing activities would you choose to talk with learners about making grammatical choices in context?
3. Begin to explore the grammatical features that are foregrounded in a range of quality texts, suitable for both subjects and stages of learning. Starting with the examples in this chapter, develop a list of resources as the basis for rich discussions about grammatical features.

Further resources

A New Grammar Companion

An excellent support for teachers with many useful examples of grammatical features in context and ideas for planning and programming to teach grammar in context.

Derewianka B. (2011). *A New Grammar Companion for Primary Teachers*. Primary English Teaching Association.

Grammar and Meaning

Contains wonderful resources, especially the appendices, which outline the social purpose, structure and language features of the genres that would be taught across the curriculum.

Humphrey, S., Droga, L. & Feez, S. (2012). *Grammar and Meaning: New Edition*. Primary English Teaching Association.

Investigating Model Texts for Learning

Provides a range of analysed models for teaching reading and writing across the curriculum.

Humphrey S. & Vale E. (2020). *Investigating Model Texts for Learning*. Primary English Teaching Association Australia (PETAA).

Conversations about Text 1

Teachers share their expertise teaching grammar in context using quality children's literature. Chapters are organised around straightforward descriptions of grammatical features and each chapter gives classroom examples.

Rossbridge, J. & Rushton, K. (2010). *Conversations about Text 1: Teaching Grammar using Literary Texts*. Primary English Teaching Association Australia (PETAA).

Conversations about Text 2

Each chapter in this book is organised around a genre, with sub-headings focusing on reading, writing and building the field through oral language. Many practical examples exemplify the teaching of a wide range of genres across the curriculum.

Rossbridge, J. & Rushton, K. (2011). *Conversations about Text 2: Teaching Grammar using Factual Texts*. Primary English Teaching Association Australia (PETAA).

The critical conversation about text

This Primary English Teaching Association Australia (PETAA) paper provides a brief but detailed examination of a how a joint construction is developed, accompanied by a video showing how it was done in a real classroom.

Rossbridge, J. & Rushton, K. (2014). The critical conversation about text: joint construction. PETAA Paper 196. Primary English Teaching Association Australia (PETAA).

Put It in Writing

In this PETAA resource, a selection of genres are explored and analysed using quality texts. The text is organised into the broad categories of informative, imaginative and persuasive with explicit reference to genres and stages.

Rossbridge, J. & Rushton, K. (2015). *Put It in Writing*. Primary English Teaching Association Australia (PETAA).

References

Australian Curriculum, Assessment and Reporting Authority (ACARA). (n.d). Australian Curriculum: English. www.australiancurriculum.edu.au/Search/?q=cultural%20identity

Bernstein, B. (1990). Elaborated and restricted codes: overview and criticisms. In *The Structuring of Pedagogic Discourse. Volume 4: Class, Codes and Control* (pp. 94–130). Routledge.

Coombes, D. (2019). *Going to the Footy*. Magabala Books.

Derewianka, B. (2011). *A New Grammar Companion for Teachers*. Primary English Teaching Association.

Dutton, J., D'warte, J., Rossbridge, J., & Rushton, K. (2018). *Tell Me Your Story: Confirming Identity and Engaging Writers in the Middle Years*. Primary English Teaching Association Australia (PETAA).

Ewing, R., Callow, J., & Rushton, K. (2016). *Language and Literacy Development in Early Childhood*. Cambridge University Press.

Ewing, R. & Simons, J., with Hertzberg. M. & Campbell, V. (2016). *Beyond the Script Take Three: Drama in the Classroom*. Primary English Teaching Association Australia (PETAA).

Halliday, M.A.K. (1985). *Spoken and Written Language* (pp. 61–67). Deakin University Press.

—— (2004). Three aspects of children's language development: learning language, learning through language, learning about language. In J.J. Webster (Ed.), *The Language of Early Childhood. M.A.K. Halliday* (pp. 308–326), Continuum.

Hammond, J. (Ed.). (2001). What is scaffolding? *Scaffolding Teaching and Learning in Language and Literacy Education* (pp. 1–14). Primary English Teaching Association Australia (PETAA).

Humphrey S., Droga, L., & Feez, S. (2012). *Grammar and Meaning: New Edition*. Primary English Teaching Association Australia (PETAA).

Humphrey, S. & Vale, E. (2020). *Investigating Model Texts for Learning*. Primary English Teaching Association Australia (PETAA).

Kwaymullina, A. & Tobin, L. (2017). *The Lost Girl*. Walker Books.

Leffler, D. (2016). *Once There Was a Boy*. Magabala Books.

Morgan, S. & Malibirr, J.W. (2019). *Little Bird's Day*. Magabala Books.

Painter, C. (2006).Preparing for school: developing a semantic style for educational knowledge. In F. Christie (Ed.), *Pedagogy and the Shaping of Consciousness*. Continuum.

Pascoe, B. (2019). *Young Dark Emu: A Truer History*. Magabala Books.

Rawlins, D., Potter, H., & Jackson, M. (2018). *Waves*. Walker Books.

Rossbridge, J. & Rushton, K. (2010). *Conversations about Text 1: Teaching Grammar using Literary Texts*. Primary English Teaching Association Australia (PETAA).

—— (2011). *Conversations about Text 2: Teaching Grammar Using Factual Texts*. Primary English Teaching Association Australia (PETAA).

—— (2014). The critical conversation about text: joint construction. PETAA Paper 196. Primary English Teaching Association Australia (PETAA).

—— (2015). *Put It in Writing*. Primary English Teaching Association Australia (PETAA).

Rushton, K. & Callow, J. (2018). A gallery of practices – mobile learning, language, literacy and the arts (K-6). In *Mobile Technologies in Children's Language and Literacy*. 12 October, 29–49. https://doi.org/10.1108/978-1-78714-879-620181003

Saxby, M. (1993). Children's literature: what to look for in a primary reading program. In L. Unsworth (Ed.), *Literacy, Learning and Teaching: Language as Social Practice in the Primary School* (pp. 55–91). Macmillan.

Williams, G. (2000). The pedagogic device and the production of pedagogic discourse: a case example in early literacy education. In F. Christie (Ed.), *Pedagogy and the Shaping of Consciousness* (pp. 88–122). Continuum.

CHAPTER 11

Working with EAL/D learners
Creating positive, inclusive environments, especially for First Nations learners

Kathy Rushton

ANTICIPATED OUTCOMES

After working through this chapter, it is anticipated you will be able to:

- support learning about English language, literacy and literature while respecting and building on the dialects and languages learners bring to school, as well as those of Aboriginal and Torres Strait Islander peoples
- create a positive and inclusive learning environment that foregrounds language
- develop a language-centred classroom by identifying some resources and strategies that build on learners' cultural, social and linguistic resources while supporting the development of English language and literacy and exploring English literature.

Introduction

Many Australian classrooms reflect the diversity of Australian communities and the children from those communities come to school possessing a range of experiences with literature and the English language and literacy (Ewing et al., 2016). As teachers, we aim to build on the individual linguistic and cultural resources of each of our learners, whether they are monolingual, or are identified by an educational system as a learner with a language background other than English (**LBOTE**) or as one who is learning Standard Australian English (SAE) as an additional language or dialect (**EAL/D**). This is a challenge for teachers because over 350 languages are now spoken in Australia (Eades, 2013; Lo Bianco & Slaughter, 2017) and, especially in urban areas, the population is becoming increasingly multilingual and multicultural (Chik et al., 2019; D'warte, 2014). Children in some communities may share in a rich oral cultural heritage. In some Aboriginal and/or Torres Strait Islander communities, for instance, children do not have English as a first, or even second, language, but they may come to school speaking one, two or even more languages and dialects (Ewing et al., 2016). Some parents and caregivers are not literate in their first language or in English, while others speak one or more languages or dialects. While some homes have no books, other homes have many books, often in more than one language or dialect, and these are shared with children.

> **LBOTE:** language background other than English.

> **EAL/D:** English as an additional language or dialect.

While being bilingual is in itself supportive of learning in all aspects of the Australian Curriculum (Cummins, 2000, 2005), some learners from socially and economically disadvantaged communities, especially Aboriginal and Torres Strait Islander learners or refugee learners, may be experiencing the intergenerational trauma that results from dispossession and poverty. These learners may require specific support to build on their linguistic and cultural resources or to develop academic proficiency in English (Dutton & Rushton, 2018a, 2020; D'warte, 2014), particularly if their educational experiences have not provided the support they needed. This is especially true in some regional and remote areas where children 'have found themselves in the charge of a newly graduated monolingual teacher who has never had sole responsibility for a class, has never had contact with remote Aboriginal children, and has no training in teaching English to speakers of other languages' (Moses & Yallop, 2008, pp. 52–53). The challenge for teachers in all educational settings is to respect and strive to understand the cultural and linguistic resources each child brings to school and to build on those resources. In this chapter, the focus is on literacy and oral language development for bilingual learners, but all semiotic systems, including Auslan, the language of the deaf community, should be recognised and respected as a first language – that is, the language that is the basis for developing literacy in any language.

Learning English: language, literacy and literature

The Australian Curriculum (Australian Curriculum, Assessment and Reporting Authority [ACARA], n.d.) and the Australian Professional Standards for Teachers (APST; Australian Institute for Teaching and School Leadership [AITSL], 2017) both recognise the diversity of Australian classrooms, but because there is a focus on standardised testing for all learners at regular points throughout their schooling, teachers often feel pressured to teach to the test. This may too often result in classrooms that are English-only zones (Dutton & Rushton, 2018b). The creative, engaging practices that develop inclusive classrooms and learner wellbeing often give way to a focus on English in monolingual classrooms. This is an understandable but false dichotomy, as the practices that engage and enrich also support the development of the first language or dialect and are the ones that will best develop learner engagement and, as a result, both language and literacy (Cummins, 2000, 2005; D'warte, 2014). Teachers with specialist qualifications in teaching English to speakers of other languages (**TESOL**) take a pedagogical stance that provides both cognitive challenge and high support for students learning English, learning through English and learning about English (Hammond, 2006; Hammond et al., 2018).

TESOL: teaching English to speakers of other languages.

A Vietnamese Australian parent talks about her 10-year-old daughter	**CASE STUDY 11.1**

Mira is fluent in Vietnamese as well. She can read Harry Potter in Vietnamese. I am very happy to see how she has developed both Vietnamese and English fluently. A lot of work for me as a mother, but I can see that what I have tried to do to keep her mother tongue has been worthwhile. I believe that she will be very grateful to us as her parents who are committed to keeping her bilingual.

We read Vietnamese books every day, and my daughter has been doing very well at school. There is no problem with her English. Mira has written many stories and poems in English – read her award-winning story *A New Life* [see later in this chapter].

I want her to be proud of her origins, her identity and language. You may know that Vietnam has recently been severely hit by flooding and storms. My daughter has created a website to raise funds and she has also sold her books to raise money for kids in Central Vietnam. Even though she was born and raised in Australia, you can see that she has developed her own bond to Vietnam.

Questions

1. How do you think this Vietnamese Australian learner has been able to develop both her languages – Vietnamese and English – while living in an English-speaking country?
2. As a classroom teacher, how could you help and encourage bilingual or bidialectal learners to develop both their first language or dialect and English?

Language

For learners developing SAE as an additional language or dialect, oral interaction is the most vital component (Ewing et al., 2016). Young learners may find it fairly easy to communicate in a familiar context, such as the playground. Through play and daily interactions within familiar settings, many young learners are able to develop enough control over the language to interact successfully. This is described as developing basic interpersonal communication skills (**BICS**), but the ability to interact in a familiar context can sometimes hide the lack of development in cognitive academic language proficiency (**CALP**), which is a much slower process and usually takes around seven years (Cummins, 1986).

BICS: basic interpersonal communication skills.

CALP: cognitive academic language proficiency.

This much slower process includes the development of understandings about the structures of language and appropriate vocabulary. Basic interpersonal communicative skills may develop, with a heavy reliance on gesture and intonation to make meaning in a shared physical context (Ewing et al., 2016). However, as a learner moves through educational contexts, learning becomes more reliant on reading and writing about more complex, abstract ideas. This requires a more complete mastery of language and literacy than that needed to interact orally in a shared physical space.

For instance, abilities like classifying, evaluating and inferring (Painter, 1996) are necessary for success in educational contexts and can be developed and used in either first or additional languages or dialects. However, one factor that may impact negatively on learning in an additional language is the loss of the first language in the early years of schooling. This is known as subtractive bilingualism (Collier & Thomas, 2001) and it has a negative impact, as learners who are given the opportunity to develop literacy in their first language or dialect are more easily able to extend their understandings to an additional language or dialect (Cummins, 1981). Bilingual learners may be advantaged academically if they have support in developing both languages or dialects (Cummins, 1981; Krashen, 1992) because they are then able to develop the skills and understandings that are needed to handle the more abstract and decontextualised ideas that challenge them in the later years of primary school.

Literacy

When bilingual learners begin to develop literacy in English or in their first language, register is especially important, as their cultural and linguistic experiences may be different from those of monolingual English speakers. Derewianka (2011) notes that: 'Any particular combination of field, tenor and mode [see the definitions and examples provided in Chapter 10] in a situation is referred to as the "register". By being aware of the genre and register, we are able to predict the language choices that would be typical of that situation' (p. 6). This is because the context in which language is used and the structure of the text, including, for example, gestures, groups, words or even placement of an image, can support prediction about the meaning of a text. Any text, whether it be visual, oral or written, may still be viewed through the three lenses of field, tenor and mode (Halliday, 2004), and together these three aspects of text make up the register.

Reading patterns in languages other than English

English is read horizontally, from top left to bottom right, on a page or screen, and the placement of images accommodates this reading path. Not all languages follow this pattern – for example, Chinese characters are traditionally read vertically from top to bottom, and right to left, starting on the right side of the page, so the placement of images will follow the reading path just as they do in English (Figure 11.1).

Figure 11.1 Reading patterns for Chinese characters are different to reading patterns for English characters

Questions

1. Choose a subject, relevant to the Australian Curriculum, and compare how images are placed on a website and in a book for an informative, imaginative or persuasive text. What is made salient in the images? (See also Chapters 8 and 10 – pages 186 and 239.)
2. Does the placement of images echo the choice of sentence openers in the verbal text?
3. Why do you think the images are supportive or disruptive of the verbal text that accompanies them?

As learners build up their familiarity with a range of texts and develop their knowledge and understandings, they are supported in both their reading and writing. Being able to predict requires a connection between personal experiences and the text, whether it is being viewed, read, heard or written (Ewing et al., 2016). The social purposes, or genres, of the texts that are read, viewed or written in primary educational contexts should be deconstructed and jointly constructed in a continuous teaching learning cycle, which includes field building and independent construction (Myhill et al., 2013; Rossbridge & Rushton, 2014). In this way, cultural knowledge and literacy are developed simultaneously because learners are given opportunities to interact orally and in writing with their teachers and peers. It is vital that bilingual learners are introduced to a wide range of literature that will support the development of vocabulary and also provide opportunities to explore the structure and grammatical features of the genres that are related to all primary subjects (see Chapters 8 and 10).

Literature

Choosing and using quality children's literature in the classroom will not only engage young learners but also provide the models of language that will support the development of vocabulary and knowledge about the curriculum (see Chapter 7). However, some steps can be taken that will especially support bilingual learners. The first, and most obvious, step is to make sure the texts are inclusive. When choosing any text, identify the perspective from which it was written. Who are the 'we' or 'us' of the text? Is everyone in your class included? (Alton-Lee, 2003; Dutton et al., 2018; D'warte, 2014: Ewing et al., 2016).

Using the four resources model (Freebody & Luke, 1990) as a framework (as discussed in Chapters 6 and 8), consider what opportunities the text provides to explore the roles of text analyst, text user, text participant and text decoder (see Table 11.1). With the framework provided by this model of reading and the model of language provided by Halliday (2004), it is possible to develop questions and prompts that will support bilingual learners.

Table 11.1 Questions for deconstructing a modelled text

	Field	Tenor	Mode
Text decoder	Are there any patterns across the text (see Chapter 10)?	Are vocabulary choices made to persuade, inform or entertain?	Is there a pattern in the paragraph and sentence openers?
Text participant	Have I read or viewed any other texts about this subject?	How is the author positioning me? Am I being informed, persuaded or entertained?	How is this text structured?
Text user	What is my response to this text?	What does the text require from me?	What is the purpose of this text?
Text analyst	What choices has the author made about sentence structure, groups and words to develop the field?	Who is the assumed audience of this text? What is the author's point of view?	How do the author's choices relate to the field and the purpose of the text?

Building on learners' cultural, social and linguistic resources

Building on social and cultural resources

Through interaction with oral and literary texts, speakers become familiar with their purpose and structure. English speakers who hear the sentence openers 'Once upon a time ... ', 'First take the ... ' or 'Ovens are used ... ', for example, can usually successfully predict that the text that will follow is a narrative, instruction or explanation. A few words can therefore support prediction about the purpose, audience, field, tenor and mode of a text because 'meaning does not reside solely in the words and structures of the text, but is constructed in the course of a transaction between the text and the reader' (Gibbons, 2002, p. 80). This knowledge is developed through many interactions with the world and with texts, and the ability to draw on this knowledge is described as *schema theory*. For English-speaking learners, and especially for those learning English, it is important to introduce a range of texts, both oral and written. Texts such as songs, poems and rhymes support understanding of the relationship between emphasis, pause and intonation and how they relate to punctuation (Ewing et al., 2016). Similarly, knowledge of traditional written tales and stories forms the basis of the cultural knowledge that supports interaction with literature at all stages of life. For instance, the Cinderella story of rags to riches is suggested to have followed the Silk Road from China thousands of years ago, and many versions of the story have been told and retold in many media up to this day. For a different retelling, see Rebecca Solnit's (2020) *Cinderella Liberator: Fairytale Revolution*.

Talk in the classroom can be focused on producing an oral text, such as in debating or public speaking, and the focus for these activities is most often on English language (see also Ewing et al., 2016, Chapter 5). However, even these activities can be seen as ranging from monologue to dialogue 'as a cline from language in action to language as reflection' (Martin & White, 2005, p. 28).

The other type of talk is best described as ancillary to an activity, being the language used most often in a classroom when learners are collaborating on a task. The task can be anything from playing a sport to independently completing a written task in groups. It is during these activities, when talk is used as a process to support completion of a task and not as a performance, that learners can be encouraged to use their first languages or dialects, even if they are reading or writing in English. Differentiating between talk as performance or process can help teachers in deciding when to strongly encourage learners to use all their linguistic resources and to support each other in developing understanding of curriculum concepts as well as literacy in English.

Building on linguistic resources

Deconstructing a modelled text

Some of the questions used to deconstruct a modelled text, in this case one produced by a primary school learner, are used here to demonstrate what the learner may have drawn from her wide reading of literature in both of her languages.

CASE STUDY 11.2 — Excerpts from an award-winning story by Mira Nguyen, age 10

A New Life

Excerpts from an award-winning story by Mira Nguyen, age 10

> **Mode/text user:** What is the purpose of this text?

Zain Ibrahim stared at the open window, the howling wind blowing into his face. Vivid images of bombs, exploding Syria away appeared in Zain's mind. He saw his father, running for his life. It made his heart ache just thinking about it. Then Zain saw the desperate eyes of his father, and he was gone. 'That horrible war!' he shouted, uncontrollably, tears seeping down his rosy cheeks. 'I would be living a happy life in Syria if it wasn't for it!' …

'Zain!' whispered Zain to himself. 'C'mon, be sensible!' Zain took a deep breath and closed his eyes, trying to calm himself down. But the pictures of war drifted back into Zain's mind. He remembered his shout of glee when he saw land. He remembered the contentment. But that contentment has proved Zain wrong. Norway was mundane. The horrible Norway with its chalky, lifeless mountains and ceaseless snow, making a burden on Zain's back, his spine shivering through the howling wind. Well, that's what Zain thought. Everyone thought Norway's mountains were scenic. Everyone thought it was lucky to live in Norway. Everyone apart from Zain Ibrahim …

'Why did there have to be war in the first place?'

> **Mode/text analyst:** how do the author's choices relate to the field and purpose of the text?

He glowered at the window, it's blinds flapping through the frosted wind. Zain's eyes stayed, glaring at the window, his anger bubbling furiously in his stomach. But then he stopped. Zain stopped glaring at the window. His lips formed a tiny smile, his eyes staring at the window in shock, yet delight. For a few seconds, he seemed transfixed, unable to move or speak, his gaze fixed upon the scene outside the window. The dark sky twinkled with the lights of trillions of stars and the moon shone brilliantly, he saw the never-ending mountains flow across Norway, but the one spotlight was different: The Northern Lights. Luminous lights danced across the sky as Zain witnessed the natural spectacle of colour and grace … For the first time in Norway, Zain was happy. More than that. Way more. He pushed the blinds away from the window, coaxing the lights to burst with colour, with happiness ….

> **Tenor/text decoder:** are vocabulary choices made to persuade, inform or entertain?

'Zain?'

It was Zain's mother … 'Isn't it beautiful?' whispered Zain, his eyes glued to the twinkling stars and vivid lights. His mother didn't say anything, but Zain felt a small nod. He felt warmth trickle into his skinny body. His **mother**'s warmth. The warmth and tenderness that made Zain change his future. 'Mum,' Zain whispered. 'Can we live in Norway for the rest of our lives?' Zain's mum just smiled, but he could tell it was a yes. He could tell that his mum was surprised. He could tell that his mum was bursting with happiness. Zain felt his hands press against the shiny, burnished glass. *'It was just a window'* was what Zain thought. 'No Zain,' whispered his mum, reading Zain's thoughts. Zain looked up at his mother in surprise. His mother looked into Zain's chestnut-brown eyes as Zain gazed into his mother's hazel ones. 'It's *your* window Zain!' said his mother softly. 'To *your* happiness, to *your* freedom, to *your* dreams, *your* future.'

> **Field/text participant:** have I read or viewed any other texts about this subject?

Figure 11.2 Excerpts from an award-winning story by Mira Nguyen, age 10

Read the excerpts from Mira's story, *A New Life*, and answer the following questions.

Questions

1. What are some films, children's picture books or novels that Mira might have viewed or read to inform her about the plight of refugees?
2. Choose one or more quality children's literary texts. Can you identify some good examples of the narrative structure and features that could be used to further support Mira's writing?

Mode/text user: what is the purpose of this text?

To entertain but also to move the reader to consider the plight of refugees.

Mode/text analyst: how do the author's choices relate to the field and the purpose of the text?

Mira has followed the structure of the narrative and in almost every sentence informs the reader about the setting and the character's inner thoughts as he reacts to each phase of the plot development. For instance, the use of a physical action by the main character is also a metaphor for his changing feelings: *He pushed the blinds away from the window, coaxing the lights to burst with colour, with happiness … .*

Tenor/text decoder: are vocabulary choices made to persuade, inform or entertain?

The vocabulary choices are meant to move the reader emotionally, but also to inform and state a point of view about war and the status of refugees – for example, *vivid images of bombs; the desperate eyes of his father …*

Field/text participant: have I read or viewed any other texts about this subject?

This is a very sophisticated text and many adults would have trouble writing this well. It indicates that Mira, although she may be a born storyteller, has probably interacted with many stories. Mira has structured her text very well, inviting the reader into the action in the text opener paragraph in which she establishes the setting and situation where we meet her main character, Zain. She also establishes for the reader how the character feels and how these feelings have developed as a reaction to his history and the current setting in which we meet him.

Language gives every person access to culture, so being bilingual or multilingual allows access to more than one culture and the stories and literature that are an expression of it. Supporting speaking, listening, reading and writing for young learners in the first dialect or language adds to rather than detracts from understandings about English literature and the development of literacy.

Creating positive and inclusive learning environments

Understanding how students' existing communicative repertoires might better support new language development has led to a shift in new pedagogies focused on what students already know and can do as the basis for language learning, in contrast to conventional teaching models centred on what students lack. This pedagogical reorientation better accords with contemporary theories of learning that emphasize the importance of building on students' prior knowledge and capabilities ...

Source: Slaughter & Cross (2020, p. 8).

All learning does not happen at school and the very best teachers aim to support learners to build on what they bring to school and to help them to feel that school is a place where they belong. For teachers, this must start with respecting diversity and then continue to developing an understanding of identity and how to connect with the families and communities of their learners. This requires teachers to be vigilant about developing self-directed independent learners by providing a classroom environment in which risk-taking is encouraged. Teachers cannot be expected to be familiar with the cultural and linguistic heritage of all the learners they might teach, but all teachers can develop a classroom environment in which identity and diversity are explicitly addressed and respected. For many learners, it is a risk to reveal their true identities if they feel that school is not a place where they belong.

Developing resilient, confident learners

A school and classroom environment that supports resilience, confidence and success must be, by definition, one that also works closely with families and communities. Supporting students to become self-regulated, self-directed learners must be built on the learners' own confirmation of their identity, which, in turn, means an explicit recognition of language and culture. If the teacher has the linguistic or cultural resources of a dialect of English or a language other than English, they can use those resources with all learners regardless of the learners' language backgrounds (Dutton & Rushton, 2018a, 2018b; D'warte, 2014).

Asking learners to bring a story from home is a simple first step in supporting them to bring their language and culture into the classroom. Retelling the story can be either in English or the first language or a dialect, or using both languages if the learner is given the agency to choose. In this way, a bridge can be built between communities, families and the school even if the teacher does not have the linguistic and cultural knowledge to fully support the learner. Developing activities like this positions the learner as the expert and helps them to confirm their place in the school and the wider society. As one teacher comments: 'It also empowered the child to promote their language and to teach others ... Students are becoming teachers ... of a myriad of languages building confidence and relationships. Yanu (until next time), Primary teacher (Garingai language)' (Dutton et al., 2018, p. 128).

Redefining 'us': connecting with communities

In research on linguistic repertoires, primary and secondary learners were positioned as 'linguistic ethnographers' (D'warte, 2014) as they explored their use of language at home and at school. The focus of the research activity was to provide opportunities for teachers and learners to explore the use of language in their classroom, school or community to identify who 'we' are by focusing on their use of language. By exploring language as researchers, learners participated in an authentic real-world task in which they explored not only reading, writing, talking and listening, but also the symbols, signs and gestures that they used to communicate. This also provided an opportunity to compare cultural differences and similarities, and promoted intercultural understanding, as an obvious way to make connections between the community, the families and the school.

All learners can participate in such research activities (see Figure 11.3), whether they are monolingual, bilingual or multilingual, literate or illiterate, or have only words or phrases in a language. It is also an activity that encourages talk as process. The process starts with a discussion and, as learners explore their use of language, they develop metalanguage (i.e. the language to talk about language) and have opportunities to make connections between the language/s they or their peers use. Learners can also use their own language or dialect in the process of discussing the research. This takes place as they discuss how they will undertake and record their research and whether they will use photography, audio or visual recordings, or observations. As they develop their research questions about the purpose of their research and what and how to collect information, they are developing language and literacy.

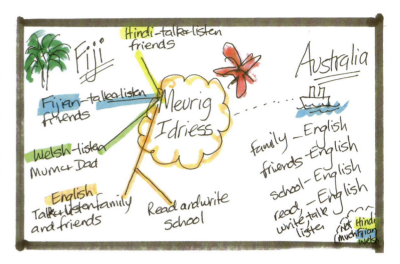

Figure 11.3 A learner's example of researching their language

Individual learners can also be encouraged to create a language map to show their own use of language in response to prompts like: 'How do I communicate?', 'Where do I use language?', 'When do I use language?' and 'With whom do I communicate?' (Dutton et al., 2018). For teachers, this provides an excellent way to identify the language resources of each of the learners, and is a great activity for the beginning of the school year or term. It also provides a visual expression of language use, which young learners may find to be a great starting point for a discussion about their own language use.

REFLECTION

1. Who is the 'us' of your classroom and how is it confirmed every day?
2. How will you identify and build on all of your learners' linguistic and cultural resources?

Always was, always will be Aboriginal land
Bidialectalism and the importance of the home language

Many Aboriginal and Torres Strait Islander learners may come to school speaking one or more Indigenous languages, creoles or dialects, but not English, while others may speak a creole, a dialect of English or an Aboriginal English, and yet others may come to school speaking SAE. In short, some Aboriginal and Torres Strait Islander learners may need support in the development of SAE as another dialect and others may need support in learning SAE as an additional language; but all Aboriginal and Torres Strait Islander learners will need to be included in the classroom through recognition of their language and culture. It is important to remember that the Aboriginal and Torres Strait Islander peoples of Australia have always been multilingual. When Captain Arthur Phillip was claiming the lands of Australia for the British crown in the late 1700s, there are estimated to have been at least 250 distinct Aboriginal languages, each with their own dialects, being spoken in Australia (Schmidt, 1990).

The first or home language of an Aboriginal or Torres Strait Islander learner may be several languages or dialects, creoles and pidgins. A creole, like 'Kriol', is now the first language of many young children in remote areas. However, the majority of Aboriginal people live in cities and regional areas rather than remote areas (Reeve, 2012), so many people speak one of the dialects, referred to as Aboriginal English, that have developed since the invasion of their lands and the removal of children from their families. Speaking traditional languages was prohibited up until the late twentieth century and, as Eades (2013) notes, 'The historical development of Aboriginal English is fascinating because it demonstrates how Aboriginal people have adapted their ways of communicating to English' (p. 79). It is a marker of the resilience of Aboriginal and Torres Strait Islander peoples that, even though they were often removed far from their traditional lands and families, some of their languages survive. It was in contexts like these that creoles and pidgins developed, as people of different language groups were thrown together and children were unable to speak or learn their traditional languages. Aboriginal English, 'the name given to dialects of English which are spoken by Aboriginal people and which differ from Standard English in systematic ways' (Eades, 2013, p. 79), was developed in this context.

Traditionally, Aboriginal and Torres Strait Islander peoples have expressed curiosity and a willingness to interact interculturally and linguistically with newcomers, and before Europeans settled in Australia, the Macassans and the Dutch had already had contact with Aboriginal and Torres Strait Islander peoples. Trade took place between Indigenous peoples across thousands of kilometres of Australia (Sutton, 1988) and the cultural practices of many Aboriginal and Torres Strait Islander peoples meant that marriage took place across language groups. Aboriginal English may include words and grammatical structures borrowed from traditional languages and the choice to use Aboriginal English is a purposeful one for many Aboriginal people. For instance, Aboriginal poet Lorna Munro writes: 'I am the gulf, the bay and the cove. I bin 'ere long-time' (cited in Leane, 2020, p. 9). Munro has chosen to use Aboriginal English to establish the Aboriginal ownership of the land and her own relationship to her people. As Eades points out, Standard English is 'simply the dialect of English which is spoken by the more powerful, dominant groups in society' (Eades, 2013, p. 78). Many of the dialects of English spoken in Britain or the USA developed in this way, changing over time, but carrying some of the features of the languages that were spoken by particular groups of people in the past. Aboriginal English belongs to Australia and is a unique and valid way to communicate.

Always was and always will be a multicultural, multilingual country

The Uluru Statement

Voice. Treaty. Truth.

Our Aboriginal and Torres Strait Islander tribes were the first sovereign Nations of the Australian continent and its adjacent islands, and possessed it under our own laws and customs. This our ancestors did, according to the reckoning of our culture, from the Creation, according to the common law from 'time immemorial', and according to science more than 60,000 years ago.

Source: Uluru Statement (2021).

Across all states and territories of Australia, many Aboriginal and Torres Strait Islander people have been dispossessed, their lands stolen and their children removed, but even in this challenging context they have also been able to maintain their links to their land and cultural heritage (Ewing et al., 2016). For example, generations of people from Pemulwuy's homeland, the Bediagal lands, which are in the Georges River area in the centre of Sydney, are still living on their traditional lands, although they remained unnoticed until the industrialisation of the area in the 1960s: 'This has been the transformative process of resilience in conditions of stress, trauma and change: drawing on the past to create new futures' (Goodall & Cadzow, 2009, pp. 278–279).

Aboriginal and Torres Strait Islander children may not always find 'their lives, social values and language patterns reflected in the texts that they encounter at school' and, in fact, they may be excluded by the perspectives taken in some texts (Bishop, 2003). It is therefore vital that as many links as possible are made between the cultural heritage of Aboriginal and Torres Strait Islander learners and their community, especially if their language is at risk or they are not living on Country with direct links to their traditional cultural and linguistic community and their Elders. Linda Tuhiwai Smith (1999) states: 'By "naming the world" people name their realities' (pp. 157–158) and it is therefore vital to offer Indigenous learners as many opportunities as possible to use Aboriginal and/or Torres Strait Islander dialects, creoles and languages and to support them to identify and discuss the lands and languages that belong to the First Nations peoples of Australia.

It is through ceremony, story, song and dance that Aboriginal and Torres Strait Islander culture has been kept alive for millennia, making these the oldest continuous living cultures in the world. In 1839, at the Mission school in Wellington, New South Wales, the Reverend Watson wrote in his journal that when the Wiradjuri children were 'able to read so as to understand, their attention becomes excited; they begin to feel a pleasure in the employment, and never appear to be wearied with it' (Van Toorn, 2006, p. 35). Reading, as well as telling and listening to stories, has been part of Aboriginal and Torres Strait Islander cultures for almost 200 years, and stories and culture are inextricable, as are engagement and the affirmation of identity and culture. Engaging with Aboriginal and/or Torres Strait Islander languages, cultures and stories gives all teachers and learners a shared cultural focus as Australians. Aboriginal and Torres Strait Islander peoples have protected their land and are now reviving, teaching, reading and writing, using their languages (Regan & Troy, 2014). It is through shared stories that we can build intercultural understanding and respect in our classrooms.

The rich and varied cultural resources of Australia's First Nations

Aboriginal and Torres Strait Islander ways of communicating, learning and making meaning are becoming better understood as Aboriginal and Torres Strait Islander researchers and academics share their understandings with the wider Australian community. This is especially important in schooling (Hogarth, 2020). From their earliest interactions with English speakers, Aboriginal and Torres Strait Islander peoples have expressed their wish that their children receive an education that encompasses both worlds. The concept of two-way schooling was developed by Aboriginal Elders to describe the kind of schooling learners received at Northern Territory schools like Yirrkala and Yipirinya, which included Aboriginal education in language. Two-way schooling described a concept that was opposite to the one-way schooling that taught English only with a curriculum that did not include Aboriginal knowledge and culture (Ewing et al., 2016). One key connection between cultures is story and story sharing, which is recognised as one of the 8 Ways of Aboriginal learning (Yunkaporta, 2009). Other aspects of the 8 Ways include links to the community and land, non-verbal expressions such as maps, symbols and images, and, most importantly, the deconstruction and reconstruction of learning. Some means to implementing these 8 Ways of learning are demonstrated in this chapter. They include deconstructing a modelled text; language mapping; encouraging translanguaging; developing identity texts; and sharing stories in Aboriginal and Torres Strait Islander languages. Bringing Indigenous languages and stories into the classroom is the best way for most non-Indigenous teachers to start the journey of two-way learning, and today there are many wonderful examples of books that use Aboriginal languages and share Aboriginal and Torres Strait Islander stories (Ewing et al., 2016). The list in Table 11.2 exemplifies the wide range of suitable resources now available for teachers.

Table 11.2 Resources exemplifying Aboriginal languages

Title	Author	Featured use of Aboriginal language
Cooee Mittigar	Jasmine Seymour & Leanne Mulgo Watson (2019)	Both author and illustrator are Darug women from the Boorooberongal people of the Dyirabun-Hawkesbury region of New South Wales, using Darug language with translations.
Guwayu, For All Times – A Collection of First Nations Poems	Red Room Poetry Edition. Jeanine Leane (2020)	Aboriginal poets writing in English, Aboriginal English and other Aboriginal languages
Mamang	An old story retold by Kim Scott, Iris Woods and the Wirlomin Noongar Language and Stories Project (Woods & Scott, 2011)	Prize-winning author and Noongar academic Kim Scott helps to tell a traditional story in Noongar language with direct translation and English translation.

Table 11.2 (cont.)

Title	Author	Featured use of Aboriginal language
Moli Det Bigibigi	Karen Manbulloo (2019)	Written in Kriol with English translation.
Our Little Yuin	Children of Little Yuin Aboriginal Preschool (2015)	A story by preschool children using Yuin language and English.

REFLECTION

1. How will you inform yourself about the traditional owners of the lands on which you teach?
2. How will you share knowledge about Aboriginal and Torres Strait Islander cultures and languages while meeting the demands of the curriculum?

Developing a language-centred classroom

Translanguaging

Translanguaging (Li, 2014) describes a view of language that gives all linguistic resources equal validity and is realised in the classroom by giving agency to individual learners who are encouraged to choose when and where to use any, or all, of their language resources. This is a change from the way many classrooms are viewed, because students who are learning the dominant language of the school are encouraged to become self-directed and self-regulated learners in their use of language. Some schools and classrooms are very diverse, with learners speaking many different languages or dialects, while other schools may have a majority of learners from the same language background (Dutton & Rushton, 2018b, 2020; Dutton et al., 2018). Whatever the context, research has shown that all learners, spanning those who are monolingual to those who are multilingual, will benefit both academically and socially when translanguaging is implemented in the classroom (Dutton & Rushton, 2020).

Language is key to culture, so an inclusive classroom is best developed by encouraging learners to express themselves using all of their language resources. Supporting oral interaction and discussion using both the first (L1) and additional language (L2) or dialect supports the development of language. This is because the interactions are of a higher order than highly contextualised daily interactions, with the communication in and around the completion of tasks or about abstract concepts being learnt in a range of curriculum areas.

When choosing strategies and activities to support the development of language and literacy, the first step is to recognise the range of ability and interests of the learners in the class. By choosing open-ended learning activities, the teacher is able to make continuous formative assessments of the learners while providing them with choice. By choosing activities and comprehension questions like those in Case study 11.3, learners have ample opportunities to use all their linguistic resources in discussing and responding to the text they have read. They will have opportunities to develop metalanguage and to read and respond to texts in several ways, if encouraged to use a language of their choice.

CASE STUDY 11.3 Example Comprehension Contract

We have been using the Comprehension Contract as part of our regular guided and independent reading program for the past two terms. After explicit teaching on how to complete each of the activities, the learner work samples offer excellent insight into the children's comprehension, so much so that this has become a key formative assessment tool for our Year 3 teaching team.

Source: Primary teacher.

Year 3 Comprehension Contract

1. Choose a book, or a story from The School Magazine, and write a review to share with your classmates. Charlotte's Web – Chapter 1,2,3,4,5,6,7,8,9,10,11,12,13,14,15,16,17,18,19,20,21,22 (each number links to a reading of that chapter).

2. Find two or more books or stories written by the same person. Draw a storyboard for each book and compare: was anything similar? (e.g. ideas, characters, places, events, structure of the story, words?)

3. Read a story, then find a book that is about something real that was in the story (like a story about a dog and a book or online article about real dogs). Talk to someone about which one you enjoyed reading the most and tell them why.

4. Check your class's book reviews and read a book or an article that someone has recommended, then post your own comments.

   [Some opportunities for translanguaging]

5. Write a list of any new words you've read that are interesting or puzzling. Find someone and tell them about one of your new words. Make up a sentence using one of them OR look up the word and see what it means (use a dictionary). Do you know any other words that mean the same thing (use a thesaurus)?

6. Find a play or poem that you like and read it out loud with someone else (look in 'The School Magazine').

7. Choose a story and turn it into a readers theatre using your own words. Have one narrator and two characters.

8. Read a story and draw a picture of your favourite character from the story. Write a caption underneath that explains why it is **your** favourite. Add a speech bubble and a thought cloud to your image that helps us understand what the character thinks and feels.

9. Write a story or a report about something real. You can make a book, draw a cartoon, make a film or write a poem.

10. Find a book you liked reading and answer **one** of these questions to share with the class during the 'comprehension contract discussion'. Post your answer for your classmates to read. Read their answers and make a comment.

Figure 11.4 Year 3 Comprehension Contract

Read the Comprehension Contract in Figure 11.4 and answer the following questions:

1. How long did it take the story to happen?
2. Are there parts of the story that took a long time to happen but were told about quickly or in a few words? Are there parts that happened very quickly, but took a lot of space to tell about?
3. Where did the story happen?
4. Which character interested you the most?
5. Was there anyone who doesn't appear in the story but without whom it couldn't have happened?
6. Who was telling (narrating) the story? Do we know? And how do we know?
7. Is the story told in the first person (and if so, who is this person)? Or is the story told in the third person, by someone we know about in the story, or by someone we know or don't know about outside the story?
8. Think of yourself as a spectator. With whose eyes did you see the story? Did you only see what one character in the story says, or did you see things sometimes as one character saw them, and sometimes as another, and so on?

Source: Adapted from Chambers (1993).

Question

Can you identify any other translanguaging opportunities in this contract?

Identity texts

Another way to support learners to use all their language and cultural resources is by developing an identity text. An identity text is any oral or written text or representation of a learner's personal story or any other family or community story that a learner chooses to share (Cummins, 1981; Cummins et al., 2015). The important factor here is that the learner has agency both in choosing the story and choosing the language or languages in which to tell it. For disadvantaged learners or those who speak a marginalised language or dialect, developing identity texts provides an opportunity to create an authentic link between the school and the community.

To develop identity texts in the classroom, learners could first be asked to bring a story to school and then to share that story with their peers. Starting with a modelled text, drama strategies like walking in role, conscience alley and advance/detail (see Chapters 6, 8 and 10 for more information) can then be used to help learners develop understandings about how a narrative evolves and the aspects of the story that make it engaging and entertaining. Using picture books can provide a visual and verbal model of the amusing or important events and issues in a family story (Dutton et al., 2018); some good choices include *Remembering Lionsville* by Bronwyn Bancroft (2016), *As I Grew Older* by Ian Abdulla (1993), *Isabella's Bed* by Alison Lester (2007) and *Island Born* by Junot Diaz (2018). The chosen text should be deconstructed to demonstrate the stages, grammatical features and language choices that make the narrative engaging (see Chapter 10). Learners can collect their story from home in any way they choose, but they need to be reminded that retelling the story in an accurate and engaging way is part of the task.

Using the advance/detail storytelling strategy (Ewing & Simons, 2016, p. 82) will support both talking and listening skills as the listener can use hand signals or just words: 'advance' to continue with the story or 'detail' to continue, for example. Careful listening is as important as the retelling because the partners will then need to retell each other's story with another pair. Another important aspect of developing identity texts in this way is the agency that learners need to enjoy in choosing the story and developing the scripts. The criteria developed through deconstructing a text will guide the choice, but the groups should work collaboratively to choose for themselves which story will be the first to be made into a readers theatre script (see Chapters 6 and 8).

Throughout these activities, learners are engaged in talking and listening and they also have many opportunities to use translanguaging strategies and to reflect on language choices with their peers. There are also many opportunities for the development of metalanguage as learners discuss their stories at all levels of text from whole text to sentence, group and word. Furthermore, as learners begin to develop their scripts, they move along the mode continuum from spoken to written language. The dialogue of the characters is direct speech, in any language, but the narrator's role will differ as it will be the more written-like aspect of the readers theatre script. The narrator will use the third person, as opposed to the first person of the characters, and the intonation and emphasis that the narrator may use to describe a character's feelings will be very different from the character expressing their feelings in direct speech (Dutton et al., 2018; Humphrey et al., 2012; Rossbridge & Rushton, 2010).

As the groups begin to develop their scripts, peers and the teacher can provide support with word choice and spelling, but each learner should be encouraged to write their own role. To make the script coherent, it will be necessary for the learners to collaborate, whatever their level of capability. Collaboration will encourage discussion and therefore the development of metalanguage, literacy and opportunities for translanguaging. In this context, the most capable learner in English literacy will not necessarily be the most able in the chosen language other than English. Learners will be able to experience true collaboration and equality as each learner brings their own linguistic and cultural knowledge to the task. By developing identity texts as readers theatre scripts, the four macro skills of reading, writing, talking and listening are all addressed, and opportunities are provided for translanguaging and developing comprehension, knowledge and understanding of the purpose, structure and language features that make up a successful narrative. Perhaps most importantly, identity texts provide an authentic link between the school and the community.

One way to develop identity texts

- Develop criteria for assessing the literary value of a story.
- Conduct a modelled reading of an identity text that uses a language other than English.
- Use drama strategies such as walking in role, conscience alley and advance/detail to illustrate how to tell and dramatise a story.
- Ask learners to talk to family and friends in their communities, to bring a story from home and to be ready to use another language.

- Use the advance/detail drama strategy to retell the story in pairs and then have pairs pair share and retell their partner's story.
- Ask the groups of four (two pairs) to then use the criteria for assessing the literary value to choose the story to develop a readers theatre script (Table 11.3 shows a useful narrative scaffold for a readers theatre script).
- Collaboratively develop a readers theatre identity text using learners' first languages.
- Record the presentations and/or invite parents and community members to view the presentations.

Source: Adapted from Dutton et al. (2018).

Table 11.3 Narrative scaffold for readers theatre script

Stage	Character (1) Character (2) Narrator (1) Narrator (2)	Narrator tells the story: describes the scene; character's actions or feelings; events Character speaks directly: dialogue in any language
Orientation	N1	
	C1	
	C2	
	N2	
	C1	
	C2	
Complication	N1	
	C1	
	C2	
	N2	
	C1	
	C2	
Resolution	N1	
	C1	
	C2	
	C1	
	C2	
	N2	

REFLECTION

What are some of the ways you can provide opportunities for translanguaging while meeting the demands of the curriculum?

Conclusion

All non-Indigenous Australians are privileged to live in a country that is home to the oldest, continuous living cultures in the world. This provides us all with a unique opportunity to define what it means to be Australian, by honouring and exploring the many lands, cultures and languages of the First Nations Aboriginal and Torres Strait Islander peoples of Australia. Supporting learners to learn English, learn about English and learn through English (Halliday, 2004) does not mean that the many Australian languages or learners' first language or dialect should be ignored. Rather, it is only by respecting and identifying all of a learner's cultural and linguistic resources (Cummins et al., 2015; D'warte, 2014; Li, 2014; Slaughter & Cross, 2020) that a positive and inclusive learning environment can be created. This is of vital importance for any learner who finds themselves in a marginalised or disadvantaged group in society, and especially for learners whose traditional or first language is under stress (Eades, 2013; Ewing et al., 2016; Hogarth, 2020; Yunkaporta, 2009).

The development of a classroom that foregrounds language is the best way to provide the support that learners need. This means that after each learner's linguistic and cultural resources are identified, opportunities are provided for them to use their languages and discuss their lives and cultures in the classroom while they are achieving the goals of the curriculum (Dutton et al., 2018; Ewing et al., 2016; Rossbridge & Rushton, 2010). By promoting learner agency and making authentic links to families and communities, teachers are better informed for identifying suitable resources and choosing strategies that build on learners' strengths while supporting the development of English language and literacy.

Bringing it together

1. How will you ensure that your classroom is inclusive of all the cultures and languages that are represented among the lives of Australians?
2. How can we best honour the rich cultural traditions of the First Nations peoples of Australia?
3. What teaching and learning strategies best describe a language-focused classroom?

Further resources

Designing Learning for Diverse Classrooms

This Primary English Teaching Association Australia (PETAA) publication provides support for teachers with a diverse range of learners to design learning activities that focus on language and literacy development.

Dufficy, P. (2005). *Designing Learning for Diverse Classrooms*. Primary English Teaching Association Australia (PETAA).

Tell Me Your Story

A PETAA resource promoting language and literacy through strategies that identify learners' cultural and linguistic resources and implement strategies to build on them.

Dutton, J., D'warte, J., Rossbridge, J. & Rushton, K. (2018). *Tell Me Your Story: Confirming Identity and Engaging Writers in the Middle Years*. Primary English Teaching Association Australia (PETAA).

Beyond the Script Take Three

Using quality children's literature, this text offers descriptions of drama strategies and examples of drama in practice in classrooms.

Ewing R. & Simons, J., with Hertzberg. M. & Campbell, V. (2016). *Beyond the Script Take Three: Drama in the Classroom*. Primary English Teaching Association Australia (PETAA).

Teaching English Language Learners in Mainstream Classes

A PETAA book that discusses the development of language and literacy for EAL/D learners and provides a range of strategies for use in mainstream classrooms.

Hertzberg, M. (2012). *Teaching English Language Learners in Mainstream Classes*. Primary English Teaching Association Australia (PETAA).

Put It in Writing

Provides a range of strategies for promoting talk and developing literacy using informative, persuasive and imaginative texts.

Rossbridge, J. & Rushton, K. (2015). *Put It in Writing*. Primary English Teaching Association Australia (PETAA).

References

Abdulla, I. (1993). *As I Grew Older*. Omnibus.

Alton-Lee, A. (2003). *Quality Teaching for Diverse Students in Schooling: Best Evidence Synthesis*. Ministry of Education. www.educationcounts.govt.nz/publications/series/2515/5959

Australian Curriculum, Assessment and Reporting Authority (ACARA). (n.d.). Australian Curriculum: Student diversity. www.australiancurriculum.edu.au/resources/student-diversity

Australian Institute for Teaching and School Leadership (AITSL). (2017). Australian Professional Standards for Teaching. www.aitsl.edu.au/teach/standards

Bancroft, B. (2016). *Remembering Lionsville*. Allen & Unwin.

Bishop, R. (2003). Changing power relations in education: kaupapa Māori messages for 'mainstream' education in Aotearoa/New Zealand. *Comparative Education*, 39(2), 221–238. www.jstor.org/stable/3099882

Chambers, A. (1993). *Tell Me: Children, Reading and Talk*. Primary English Teaching Association Australia (PETAA).

Chik, A., Benson, P., & Moloney, R. (Eds.). (2019). *Multilingual Sydney*. Routledge.

Collier, V. & Thomas, W. (2001). Literacy programs in prison: ideas about purpose, culture, and content. *Journal of Correctional Education*, 52(2), 68–73.

Cummins, J. (1981). Four misconceptions about language proficiency. *Bilingual Education, NABE Journal*, 5(3), 31–45. https://doi.org/10.1080/08855072.1981.10668409

—— (1986). Empowering minority students: a framework for intervention. *Harvard Educational Review*, 56(1), 18–36.

—— (2000). *Language, Power and Pedagogy: Bilingual Children in the Crossfire*. Multilingual Matters.

—— (2005). A proposal for action: strategies for recognizing heritage language competence as a learning resource within the mainstream classroom. *The Modern Language Journal*, 80(4), 585–592.

Cummins, J., Hu, S., Markus, P., & Montero, M.K. (2015). Identity texts and academic achievement: connecting the dots in multilingual school contexts. *TESOL Quarterly*, 49(3), 555–581.

Derewianka, B. (2011). *A New Grammar Companion for Primary Teachers*. Primary English Teaching Association.

Diaz, J. (2018). *Island Born*. Bloomsbury.

Dufficy, P. (2005). *Designing Learning for Diverse Classrooms*. Primary English Teaching Association Australia (PETAA).

Dutton, J., D'warte, J., Rossbridge, J., & Rushton, K. (2018). *Tell Me Your Story: Confirming Identity and Engaging Writers in the Middle Years*. Primary English Teaching Association Australia (PETAA).

Dutton, J. & Rushton, K. (2018a). Poets in the making: confirming identity in English. *Scan: The Journal for Educators*, 37, 117–129.

—— (2018b). Confirming identity using drama pedagogy: English teachers' creative response to high-stakes literacy testing. *English in Australia*, 53, 5–14.

—— (2020). Using the translanguaging space to facilitate poetic representation of language and identity. *Language Teaching Research*. Sage. https://doi.org/10.1177/1362168820951215

D'warte, J. (2014). Exploring linguistic repertoires: multiple language use and multimodal activity in five classrooms. *Australian Journal of Language and Literacy*, 37(1), 21–30.

Eades, D. (2013). *Aboriginal Ways of Using English*. Aboriginal Studies Press.

Ewing, R., Callow, J., & Rushton, K. (2016). *Language and Literacy Development in Early Childhood*. Cambridge University Press.

Ewing, R. & Simons, J., with Hertzberg. M. & Campbell, V. (2016). *Beyond the Script Take Three: Drama in the Classroom*. Primary English Teaching Association Australia (PETAA).

Freebody, P. & Luke, A. (1990). Literacies programs: debates and demands in cultural context. *Prospect: An Australian Journal of TESOL*, 5(3), 7–16.

Gibbons, P. (2002). *Scaffolding Language, Scaffolding Learning: Teaching Second Language Learners in the Mainstream Classroom*. Heinemann.

Goodall, H. & Cadzow, A. (2009). *Rivers and Resilience: Aboriginal People on Sydney's Georges River*. University of New South Wales Press.

Halliday, M.A.K. (2004). Three aspects of children's language development: learning language, learning through language, learning about language. In J.J. Webster (Ed.), *The Language of Early Childhood: M.A.K. Halliday* (pp. 308–326). Continuum.

Hammond, J. (2006). High challenge, high support: integrating language and content instruction for diverse learners in an English literature classroom. *Journal of English for Academic Purposes*, 5, 269–283. doi:10.1016/j.jeap.2006.08.006

Hammond, J., Cranitch, M., & Black, S. (2018). *Classrooms of Possibility: Working with Students from Refugee Backgrounds in Mainstream Classes*. New South Wales Department of Education.

Hertzberg, M. (2012). *Teaching English Language Learners in Mainstream Classes*. Primary English Teaching Association Australia (PETAA).

Hogarth, M. (2020). A dream of a culturally responsive classroom [online]. *Human Rights Defender*, 29(1), 34–35. https://search-informit-com-au.ezproxy.library.sydney.edu.au/documentSummary;dn=062718599881553

Humphrey, S., Droga, L., & Feez, S. (2012). *Grammar and Meaning: New Edition*. Primary English Teaching Association.

Krashen, S. (1992). *Fundamentals of Language Education*. McGraw-Hill.

Leane, J. (Ed.). (2020). *Guwayu, For All Times: A Collection of First Nations Poems*. Magabala Books.

Lester, A. (2007). *Isabella's Bed*. Lothian.

Li, W. (2014). Who's teaching whom? Co-learning in multilingual classrooms. In S. May (Ed.), *The Multilingual Turn: Implications for SLA, TESOL and Bilingual Education* (pp. 167–190). Routledge.

Little Yuin Aboriginal Preschool. (2015). *Our Little Yuin*. Shooting Star Press.

Lo Bianco, J. & Slaughter, Y. (2017). Language policy and education in Australia. In T. McCarty (Ed.), *Encyclopedia of Language and Education, Language Policy and Political Issues in Education, vol. 1* (pp. 449–461). Springer. doi.1007/978-3-319-02344-1_33

Manbullo, K. (2019). *Moli Det Bigibigi*. Pan Macmillan.

Martin, J. & White, R. (2005). *The Language of Evaluation: Appraisal in English* (pp. 26–38). Palgrave Macmillan.

Moses, K. & Yallop, C. (2008). Questions about questions. J. Simpson & G. Wigglesworth (Eds.), *Children's Language and Multilingualism: Indigenous Language Use at Home and School* (pp. 30–55). Continuum International Publishing Group.

Myhill, D., Jones, S., Watson, A., & Lines, H. (2013). Playful explicitness with grammar: a pedagogy for writing. *Literacy*, 47(2), 103–111.

Painter, C. (1996). The development of language as a resource for thinking: a linguistic view of learning. In R. Hasan & G. Williams (Eds.), *Literacy in Society* (pp. 50–57). Addison Wesley Longman.

Reeve, R. (2012). Indigenous poverty in New South Wales major cities: a multidimensional analysis. *Australian Aboriginal Studies Journal of the Australian Institute of Aboriginal and Torres Strait Islander Studies*, 1, 19–34.

Regan, C. & Troy, J. (2014). Blackwords and 'reciprocal recognitions'. *Australian Aboriginal Studies*, 1, 119.

Rossbridge, J. & Rushton, K. (2010). *Conversations about Text: Teaching Grammar Using Literary Texts*. Primary English Teaching Association Australia (PETAA).

—— (2014). Critical conversation about texts. PETAA Paper 196. Primary English Teaching Association Australia (PETAA). www.petaa.edu.au/imis_prod/w/Teaching_Resources/w/Teaching_Resources/PPs/PETAA_Paper_196___The_critical_conversation_.aspx

—— (2015). *Put It in Writing*. Primary English Teaching Association Australia (PETAA).

Schmidt, A. (1990). *The Loss of Australia's Aboriginal Language Heritage*. Aboriginal Studies Press.

Seymour, J. & Mulgo Watson, L. (2019). *Cooee Mittigar*. Magabala Books.

Slaughter, Y. & Cross, R. (2020). Challenging the monolingual mindset: understanding plurilingal pedagogies in English as an additional language (EAL) classrooms. *Language Teaching Research*, 25(1), 1–22.

Smith, L.T. (1999). *Decolonizing Methodologies: Research and Indigenous Peoples*. University of Otago Press.

Solnit, R. (2020). *Cinderella Liberator: Fairytale Revolution*. Vintage Classics.

Sutton, P. (Ed.). (1988). *Dreamings: The Art of Aboriginal Australia*. Viking Penguin Books Australia Ltd.

Uluru Statement. (2021). Uluru Statement from the Heart. https://ulurustatement.org

Van Toorn, P. (2006). *Writing Never Arrives Naked: Early Aboriginal Cultures of Writing in Australia*. Aboriginal Studies Press.

Woods, I. & Scott, K. (2011). *Mamang*. UWA Publishing.

Yunkaporta, T. (2009). Aboriginal pedagogies at the cultural interface (Doctoral thesis, James Cook University, Australia). http://eprints.jcu.edu.au/10974

CHAPTER 12

Creating positive, inclusive learning environments
Working with learners with additional and diverse needs

Lucy Stewart

ANTICIPATED OUTCOMES

After working through this chapter, it is anticipated you will be able to:

- reflect on the complex and diverse needs of learners within English and literacy learning environments
- describe the importance of creating positive and inclusive learning environments
- draw upon relevant policies and guiding documents to support continued understanding of inclusive learning environments
- understand the impact of early childhood and primary experiences on early and long-term English and literacy learning outcomes
- identify some of the key approaches to supporting learners in positive and inclusive learning environments
- understand a range of teaching strategies to support inclusion in the literacy learning context.

Introduction

Australia's classrooms are a rich tapestry of cultures, experiences and backgrounds. This chapter explores the diversity of learners in schools and provides opportunities for teachers to reflect on building positive and inclusive learning environments. A range of diverse needs and approaches will be explored, including learners with disability, and gifted/talented and English as additional language/dialect (EAL/D) learners in alignment with the Australian Curriculum (Australian Curriculum, Assessment and Reporting Authority [ACARA], 2018).

Diversity in primary learning environments

One of the many challenges facing teachers in primary learning environments is to ensure that each and every learner has equitable access to all learning opportunities across the curriculum (Westwood, 2018). With the increasingly diverse backgrounds and needs of learners in Australian schools, there are many factors that teachers need to consider in order to ensure the inclusion of all learners (Graham et al., 2018). Arthur and colleagues (2014) suggest traditional literacy pedagogies can sometimes overlook or devalue the diversity of family literacy practices and this can lead to equity issues, especially for those learners from disadvantaged or at-risk backgrounds and for bilingual and First Nations Australian learners.

Diversity: acknowledging and understanding the uniqueness of every individual, including the dimensions of race, gender, ethnicity and sexual orientation, while, at the same time, valuing our interdependence as human beings.

While there are numerous definitions of **diversity**, it essentially encompasses the unique characteristics of each learner that make them different from other learners (Hyde, 2013). These differences cover a wide range of abilities and disabilities, gifted and talented, and learning difficulties. Diversity also encompasses cultural, language, family and socioeconomic backgrounds. It can include Aboriginal and Torres Strait Islander learners, learners from refugee and asylum-seeker backgrounds and children living in rural or remote areas. Vulnerable children, learners who have experienced childhood trauma and children with health care needs are other examples of the intricate and complex experiences and backgrounds of learners in Australian classrooms. Learners may also be a part of one or more of these categories, because they are not 'mutually exclusive' (Westwood, 2018).

Inclusive learning environments: learning environments where all learners feel they belong and are supported socially, emotionally, intellectually and academically.

While diversity adds to the rich tapestry of the culture of each learning environment, it presents challenges for teachers to ensure that each learner is supported within an **inclusive learning environment**. As English and literacy are key strands within the Australian Curriculum, understanding how backgrounds and additional needs affect learning is increasingly important. It is essential that teachers understand the learners they teach (Australian Institute for Teaching and School Leadership [AITSL], 2020). Each learner has individual strengths and talents, as well as needs for support. This individuality calls for differentiation within the curriculum (Graham et al., 2018).

Examples of diversity in Australian primary school settings

A range of terminology and varying degrees of experiences result in a wide array of individual needs in classrooms, which is why it is so important for the teacher to know the individual learner and understand their learning needs.

Table 12.1 shows some examples of individual experiences and needs.

Table 12.1 Individual learner needs

• Vision impairment	• Socioeconomic disadvantage
• Hearing loss/impairment	• Cultural background
• Intellectual or cognitive disability	• Family background
• Physical disability	• Aboriginal and/or Torres Strait Islander background
• Dyspraxia	
• Complex medical needs	• English as additional language/dialect (EAL/D)
• Specific learning disability	
• Learning difficulties	• Vulnerable children
• Dyslexia, dyscalculia, dysgraphia	• Remote or rural learners
• Attention deficit hyperactivity disorder (ADHD)	• Out-of-home or kinship care
	• Refugee, asylum seeker or migrant background
• Autism spectrum disorder (ASD)	
• Gifted/talented	• Childhood trauma
• Communication needs	• Gender
• Specific language impairment	• Challenging behaviour
• Mental health disorders	• Oppositional defiance disorder (ODD)

Note that some additional needs may also be classified as a disability.

Sources: ACARA (2018); Department of Education and Training (DET, 2019); Graham et al. (2018); Nationally Consistent Collection of Data on School Students with Disability (NCCD, 2019); Westwood (2018).

Questions

1. Reflect on your previous experiences and understanding of diversity. Consider whether the information provided in this chapter so far has broadened your understanding. If so, how?
2. Consider the implications for supporting learners who experience one or more of these additional needs and how this might add both value and complexity to the literacy learning environment.

The impacts of diverse and additional needs on literacy learning

Many learners will experience difficulties in the primary school environment across developmental domains. Learners who experience difficulties can lose motivation and confidence in their ability to complete tasks (Westwood, 2008). It is important to note that there can be behavioural consequences from a lack of success and engagement in the classroom (Hyde, 2013). Learners may evade tasks to avoid feeling they are struggling and, ultimately, this means they do not practise skills, creating a cycle of failure for the learner (Westwood, 2008). This can, in turn, lead to negative attitudes towards themselves as learners and learning more generally and disruptive behaviours may result (Westwood, 2008). It is essential that teachers see the learner, not just the behaviour, and have an awareness of what the behaviour might be communicating.

Another element of particular importance is the long-term potential effect that difficulties in early literacy development may have on learners' life experiences. Research has shown that learners with low reading skills in the early years can experience ongoing literacy problems throughout their schooling (Westwood, 2008). Prior (2013) highlighted the restrictions and missed opportunities that an inability to read and write can cause beyond the school years: illiteracy can be associated with other disadvantages, including mental health and social issues, vulnerability, unemployment and a higher risk of antisocial behaviour and subsequent links with justice systems. Ultimately, maintaining the confidence and motivation of all learners in the literacy learning context is a major challenge for teachers (Westwood, 2008).

Vulnerable learners

Vulnerable learners in English and literacy classrooms can be overlooked because they may not fit into the categories highlighted by the Australian Curriculum or they are seen as learners with challenging behaviours (Harris, 2016). An alarming number of learners are vulnerable and/or affected by trauma. Vulnerability can be multifaceted and complex, often involving family stressors such as unemployment, homelessness, disability, addiction, family violence, health problems, economic hardship and trans-generational trauma (Roberts, 2015). Child protection services, out-of-home or kinship care and the justice system may also be involved. As a result, learners can experience vulnerability across the physical, social-emotional, cognitive and language domains of development, affecting their engagement, participation and learning in the literacy classroom (Australian Early Development Census, 2019).

Childhood trauma and vulnerability

One in five learners starting school are developmentally vulnerable, and among Aboriginal and Torres Strait Islander learners, the figure is twice this (Early Learning, Everyone Benefits, 2016, in Harris, 2016). According to Kezelman and colleagues (2015, in Upton et al., 2015), childhood trauma affects five million adults in Australia, showing the continuing effects of trauma in later life.

Childhood trauma and vulnerability can result in a range of long-term impairments, including to education and the achievement of full educational potential (Upton et al., 2015). Developmental trauma can have far-reaching effects on a child's learning and development yet is often overlooked. Trauma may be the result of a significant incident; however, it is more likely to be a repetitive experience. Some of these experiences can include domestic violence, poverty, abuse, neglect, serious illness and lack of emotional attachment from a parent (Harris, 2016).

Trans-generational trauma can also impact on young learners by affecting the ability of a parent or caregiver to respond to the emotional needs of their children. This can occur in learners with refugee backgrounds, where violence, isolation, loss of home, family and community can affect the next generation through trauma-affected parents and other family members. This experience is, unfortunately, also shared by First Nations Australians as a result of colonisation and the Stolen Generations (Harris, 2016).

Trauma in the early years impacts upon brain development in young learners, affecting concentration, attention, memory and daily functioning. It can affect behaviour and ability to learn in the classroom environment (Harris, 2016). Learners can experience delays across a number of developmental domains, difficulties with regulation and executive functioning, as well as in developing relationships with peers and adults.

Questions

1. What does vulnerability mean to you?
2. What might vulnerability look like in learners in your literacy classroom?

A strong relationship can also be seen between poor literacy and social disadvantage (Buckingham et al., 2013). Social disadvantage can include a number of interacting factors that result in disadvantage. These factors may vary between states and territories (and localities) within Australia, but some common examples are low parent education levels, long-term and short-term unemployment, poor internet access, low engagement in work or study, child maltreatment and prison admissions (Vinson et al., 2015). According to the Australian Early Development Index (AEDI) survey in 2009, 13.9 per cent of children in the lowest socioeconomic quintile in their first year of school were classified as developmentally vulnerable in relation to language and cognitive skills (Buckingham et al., 2013).

Some examples of the diverse nature of populations within learning environments have been discussed. Further detail is now explored in relation to learners with disability, and gifted/talented and EAL/D learners in alignment with the Australian Curriculum (ACARA, 2018).

Disability

Almost 20 per cent of school students in Australia receive an adjustment on the basis of disability (NCCD, 2020, in AITSL, 2020). The *Disability Discrimination Act 1992* provides specific definitions of disability; however, broader categories are used for the purposes of the Nationally Consistent Collection of Data on School Students with Disability (NCCD). These categories include physical, cognitive, sensory and social-emotional (NCCD, 2019).

A range of additional needs affect some or all aspects of literacy learning. Specific learning disabilities, such as dyslexia and dysgraphia, affect handwriting, spelling, writing, reading fluency and comprehension (Devine, 2015; McCloskey & Rapp, 2017; Prunty & Barnett, 2017). Specific language impairments can impact upon oral language development and, subsequently, phonological awareness, often with later reading and spelling difficulties (Cordewener et al., 2012).

There are some additional needs that might not be initially associated with literacy development but, due to the need to develop phonological knowledge, language and auditory issues may have longer-term effects on spelling development. Learners with hearing impairment or loss can experience delays (in comparison with their same-age peers) in oral language development, specifically vocabulary, reading and spelling skills (Westwood, 2018). This might also include articulation issues (such as in children born with a cleft palate) and expressive and/or receptive language developmental delays. Autism spectrum disorder (ASD), auditory processing issues and developmental coordination disorder (DCD) or dyspraxia can affect speech and physical movement and, in turn, the development of the mechanics of handwriting (Devine, 2015; McCloskey & Rapp, 2017; Prunty & Barnett, 2017; Westwood & Graham, 2003).

Gifted and talented learners

There is no universally accepted definition of gifted and talented learners. However, a key feature that can be observed in these learners is a characteristic or skill that is significantly above average for their age and expected level of development (ACARA, 2018). For example, a gifted and talented learner may develop language skills significantly faster than typical development; they may show exceptional creativity or have the capacity to recall information at an extraordinary level (Jarvis, 2013). Many gifted and talented learners may possess high intelligence and age-appropriate social and emotional skills. Others, however, may demonstrate a particular aptitude in one area, although their physical and emotional skills may not develop at the same rate (Westwood, 2018).

The educational profile of a gifted and talented learner may be diverse and uneven. While a learner demonstrates exceptional skills in one area, they may require support in another (Jarvis, 2013). Being a gifted and talented learner does not preclude experiencing difficulties in the classroom and, specifically, English and literacy learning. Gifted and talented learners can experience learning difficulties and disabilities, such as dyslexia, ADHD and processing disorders (Wormald, 2015). These learners are sometimes referred to as 'twice exceptional' because they are identified as gifted in one or more areas, but also are identified as have a learning disability or difficulty (Jarvis, 2013).

Gifted and talented learners can demonstrate underachievement and perfectionism (Westwood, 2018) and will have variations in their 'giftedness' across curriculum areas. As with learners with disabilities, they have strengths and abilities as well as individual learning needs (ACARA, 2018).

English as additional language/dialect (EAL/D) learners

English as additional language/dialect (EAL/D) learners have a language or dialect other than English as their first language (sometimes referred to as their 'home language') and need 'support to develop proficiency in Standard Australian English' (ACARA, 2018). Some examples of these learners include Aboriginal and/or Torres Strait Islander learners, learners who have immigrated to Australia and international learners from non-English-speaking countries. They can also include learners who are born in Australia but English is not spoken in their home environment (this can include families who use Auslan) and learners from refugee backgrounds (ACARA, 2018).

The needs of EAL/D learners in English and literacy learning are explored in detail in Chapter 11; however, it is important for teachers to be aware of the needs of all learner backgrounds when creating positive and inclusive learning environments. For example, some Aboriginal and Torres Strait Islander learners are particularly at risk of experiencing language and literacy challenges, and the reasons for this are complex and diverse (Prior, 2013). The *Closing the Gap Report* found that one in four First Nations learners in Years 5, 7 and 9 experience challenges with reading (Australian Government, 2020). Environmental factors, such as poor school attendance, absence of cultural connection in the classroom and lack of skilled teaching in remote areas, may affect English and literacy learning, rather than the cause being lack of an individual's ability (Prior, 2013). In addition to attendance, school readiness is also a predictor of literacy difficulties and language ability in the primary years. Some learners from Aboriginal and/or Torres Strait Islander backgrounds may also be at-risk in the early childhood years (Main & Konza, 2017).

In a context where literacy provides access to opportunities and acts as a protective factor, inclusive educational settings for Aboriginal and Torres Strait Islander learners is essential and, as such, is explored further in Chapter 11.

REFLECTION

1. Consider your experiences so far in working with children. Have you worked with learners with disabilities, EAL/D learners, gifted and talented learners or vulnerable learners?
2. Reflect on how this chapter adds to your knowledge base. Are there any areas you need to find more information about?

The importance of positive and inclusive learning environments

Positive and inclusive learning environments seek to ensure equitable access for and inclusion of each learner and their educational needs (Westwood, 2018). An inclusive learning environment caters to the needs of all learners across an increasingly diverse learner population. Children at all ability levels, learners with disabilities and learners from low socio-economic backgrounds, diverse cultures, race, language or family backgrounds are valued for their unique talents and abilities and what they can contribute.

Inclusion begins with removing the barriers between children with additional needs and participation in mainstream learning environments. Learners should be provided with access to mainstream schools, unless there is a significant need for the learner to require a specialist school environment (Carrington et al., 2016).

Relevant legislation, frameworks and policy documentation

Anti-discrimination is not only a human right but also a legislative requirement in Australia. Australian learning environments and educators are guided by key legislative and policy documents in terms of what constitutes inclusion and how it can be enacted in their context. On an international level, the United Nations Convention on the Rights of the Child (United Nations, 1989) is clearly reflected in a number of curriculum frameworks across Australia, highlighting the importance of children's right to education that maximises their abilities but also shows awareness and respect for their diverse backgrounds (Department of Education, Employment & Workplace Relations [DEEWR], 2009).

The *Disability Discrimination Act 1992* and the *Disability Standards for Education 2005* (the Standards) provide the legal requirements for educators and schools to ensure that learners are not discriminated against on the basis of disability. The Standards require all schools and teachers to ensure the equitable access and participation of learners with disability, including consultation with the learner and their families/guardians to provide 'reasonable adjustments' to enable this access and participation (ACARA, 2018). While this legislation does not mandate inclusion in educational settings, the Australian Curriculum and the United Nations Convention on the Rights of Persons with Disabilities 2006 (Article 24) 'identifies the universal right to inclusive education' (Duncan et al., 2020; Poed et al., 2020).

Particularly in the early years of school, it is important for teachers to understand the impact of a learner's early childhood experience. In the early childhood years, inclusion is valued and represented through the Early Years Learning Framework (EYLF) (DEEWR, 2009). The key values of belonging, being and becoming provide the foundation for early childhood practice. The EYLF guides teachers to enact the rights of all children to have access to education, focus on maximising their abilities and respect for family, culture, languages and identities as per the UN Convention on the Rights of the Child. Importantly, it embeds in children's earliest education and care experiences the importance of their rights to be active participants in matters that affect them (DEEWR, 2009).

The EYLF, as a national framework, may directly inform educators or be used to complement state and territory frameworks on early childhood education. The EYLF also supports the Alice Springs (Mparntwe) Education Declaration (Education Council, 2019), which, as discussed in earlier chapters, is the most recent educational vision of all Australian governments for children and young Australians, supporting all Australians to become active and informed citizens, confident and creative individuals and successful learners as well as providing for 'improved outcomes for Aboriginal and Torres Strait Islander young people' (DEEWR, 2009, p. 5).

The Australian Children's Education and Care Quality Authority (ACECQA) has developed the National Quality Framework (NQF) and National Quality Standard (NQS). These outline the importance of inclusive learning environments and practice in early childhood education and care, placing particular emphasis on the value of strategic inclusion plans and reconciliation action plans in early childhood services across Australia (Livingstone, 2018).

Teachers not only have a legal responsibility to support the development of positive and inclusive learning environments, but they have also an ethical and professional responsibility. In early childhood education and care, the Early Childhood Australia (ECA) Code of Ethics outlines the ethical requirements of educators in relation to their work with children

(ECA, 2016). The Code of Ethics is informed by both the UN Convention on the Rights of the Child (United Nations, 1989) and the UN Declaration on the Rights of Indigenous Peoples (UN General Assembly, 2007). The ECA Code of Ethics draws attention to the responsibilities of teachers to promote inclusive practice, equity and a sense of belonging (ECA, 2016).

Primary teachers are also required to align with the Australian Professional Standards for Teachers (APST) in order to maintain professional registration and ongoing accreditation (AITSL, 2017) (see Table 12.2). Qualified early childhood teachers in Victoria are also required to register and provide evidence of the APST, although this requirement may differ between states and territories (Victorian Institute of Teaching [VIT], 2021).

Table 12.2 Examples of APST linked to inclusive learning environments

Standard	Description
Standard 1 – Know students and how they learn	
1.1	• Physical, social and intellectual development and characteristics of students • Demonstrate knowledge and understanding of physical, social and intellectual development and characteristics of students and how these may affect learning.
1.2	• Understand how students learn • Demonstrate knowledge and understanding of research into how students learn and the implications for teaching.
1.3	• Students with diverse linguistic, cultural, religious and socioeconomic backgrounds • Demonstrate knowledge of teaching strategies that are responsive to the learning strengths and needs of students from diverse linguistic, cultural, religious and socioeconomic backgrounds.
1.4	• Strategies for teaching Aboriginal and Torres Strait Islander students • Demonstrate broad knowledge and understanding of the impact of culture, cultural identity and linguistic background on the education of students from Aboriginal and Torres Strait Islander backgrounds.
1.5	• Differentiate teaching to meet the specific learning needs of students across the full range of abilities • Demonstrate knowledge and understanding of strategies for differentiating teaching to meet the specific learning needs of students across the full range of abilities.
1.6	• Strategies to support full participation of students with disability • Demonstrate broad knowledge and understanding of legislative requirements and teaching strategies that support participation and learning of students with disability.
Standard 7 – Engage professionally with colleagues, parents/carers and the community	
7.1	• Meet professional ethics and responsibilities • Understand and apply the key principles described in codes of ethics and conduct for the teaching profession.
7.2	• Comply with legislative, administrative and organisational requirements • Understand the relevant legislative, administrative and organisational policies and processes required for teachers according to school stage.

Source: AITSL (2017).

REFLECTION

1. Reflect on your understanding of diversity and the professional and ethical responsibilities of teachers. Consider whether the information provided in this section has deepened your understanding of the learners in your classrooms and your responsibilities as a teacher. If so, how?

2. Consider APST 7.2: Comply with legislative, administrative and organisational requirements. Understand the relevant legislative, administrative and organisational policies and processes required for teachers according to school stage (AITSL, 2017). Review your understanding of the legislation, policies and professional requirements of inclusive learning environments. Reflect on how this aligns with your knowledge so far and with your teaching philosophy.

3. The APST provide the benchmark for teacher practice. Reflect on your knowledge and understanding of these standards.

Barriers to and benefits of inclusive learning environments

One of the many challenges facing teachers is ensuring that each and every learner in their learning environment has equal access to all opportunities across the curriculum. Here we discuss the barriers that may make achieving this difficult. We also discuss the benefits of inclusive learning environments for both learners and teachers (Carrington et al., 2016; Westwood, 2018).

One significant barrier to positive and inclusive classrooms has been identified as teacher attitudes, particularly in relation to the practicality of implementation of inclusive education (Vaz et al., 2015; Westwood, 2018). Studies have shown that, while the provision of support to teachers positively affected attitudes, a number of concerns still had considerable impact on teacher attitudes; in particular, the balance of providing time and accommodations to learners with additional learning needs without disadvantaging other learners (Carrington et al., 2016; Vaz et al., 2015; Westwood, 2018).

The specific disability and level of need of individual learners can have an impact on teacher attitudes. Teachers have expressed concerns around the viability of inclusion of learners with complex and/or severe disabilities and what learning would be feasible in these learning environments (Vaz et al., 2015). The child's specific learning needs may also have an impact on teacher attitudes. For example, Woodcock (2013) found that teachers maintained positive attitudes towards learners with specific learning disabilities. However, the presence of behavioural and emotional problems affected how positive they felt about inclusion – the more severe the behavioural or emotional need, the less positive teachers felt about inclusion (Vaz et al., 2015; Westwood, 2018).

Professional learning for teachers is a key issue to address in terms of attitudes towards inclusion. If teachers have not worked with learners with additional needs and have limited prior knowledge of diverse backgrounds and what these look like in practice, training to support teachers to create inclusive environments is essential (Westwood, 2018). Teachers who perceive that their competence and training in relation to teaching learners with additional needs is insufficient will have a less positive attitude towards creating an inclusive environment (Vaz et al., 2015; Westwood, 2018).

Despite the challenges of creating positive and inclusive learning environments, there are some significant benefits to this approach. Westwood and Graham (2003) observed increased positive attitudes within peer groups, additional resources that were beneficial for all learners, and benefits of the personal attributes of learners with disabilities to the learning environment. Research conducted with teachers about their perceptions of inclusive practices showed that they saw valuable opportunities for all learners' understanding of values, including acceptance and empathy (Carrington et al., 2016).

Key approaches to creating positive and inclusive literacy learning environments

The approaches to creating any learning environment are wide and varied. Graham and colleagues (2018) posit the concept of 'Sustainable Learning' as a way to view inclusive practices in classrooms. This addresses the learning of all learners, 'teaching that matters' and ways to create 'learning that lasts' (Graham et al., 2018, pp. 9, 11), highlighting the continued focus on the broader aspects of learning environments for all learners and their unique backgrounds and abilities. In the next section, the approaches explored could also be considered 'traits' of positive and inclusive literacy learning environments rather than approaches on their own.

Building positive relationships

Building positive relationships with children and families is particularly foundational in early childhood practice. These relationships are essential for children's sense of belonging and for achieving the best outcomes for children (DEEWR, 2009). It has also been shown that the value of positive relationships between teachers and learners is being increasingly recognised in the early years of schooling, particularly in relation to learning and social outcomes for at-risk learners (Carrington et al., 2016).

According to theorist Urie Bronfenbrenner, positive relationships are powerful to the point of supporting a learner to succeed despite the impacts of their individual situation and/or environment (Hayes et al., 2017). The development of positive relationships between learners and teachers, all adults working with a learner, and the learners and their peers is essential in supporting positive and inclusive learning environments and best outcomes (Hayes et al., 2017). Research also supports the necessity of these relationships in the early years of schooling for Aboriginal and Torres Strait Islander learners in order to provide consistency, connection and a sense of belonging (Zubrick et al., 2006, in Carrington et al., 2016). Chapter 16 looks in more detail at creating school–family–community partnerships.

Building a culture of inclusion

Literacy learning environments (and broader school environments) play a vital role in advocating for inclusive education. Support from the school community helps create a culture of inclusion, where the school is in a position to problem-solve any challenges as a community (Carrington et al., 2016).

In order to build an inclusive literacy learning environment, learners need to feel a sense of belonging, including connections with peers and teachers. Teachers can model inclusive practices through literacy learning and a culture of respect and learning that provides for the participation of all learners (Robinson & Truscott, 2014). Learners need to be able to see themselves in the selection of literary texts shared in the classroom and to relate to the themes in the units of work that are implemented.

CASE STUDY 12.1   'But my friends will notice'

Louis is a learner in Year 3 at the local primary school. He has recently been assessed and diagnosed with ASD. Louis is very interested in technology and is building confidence in forming friendships and working collaboratively with his peers. However, during writing experiences, Louis becomes frustrated and often will not complete the task. The report from his educational psychologist has recommended the use of voice-to-text apps on the iPad. Louis is very keen to try this, but after the first instance he was reluctant to try it again, saying this was 'because his friends will notice'.

Questions

1. Reflect on this scenario. Is there a culture of inclusion in this learning environment?
2. As a teacher, how would you support Louis to continue using the voice-to-text apps to enable his writing development?
3. Consider technology as an assistive tool and as a tool for learning. How could you integrate both into the literacy learning environment?

High expectations for every learner: strength-based approach and growth mindset

A key principle of the EYLF is: 'High expectations and equity' (DEEWR, 2009, p. 12). It calls for educators to believe in each learner's capacity to learn and develop regardless of their unique abilities and circumstances. This principle highlights the importance of families and teachers around the child maintaining high expectations (not the same expectations) for each learner. Collaboration between learners, families, communities and other professionals and organisations, in order to support the inclusion, participation and equitable access to educational success for each individual learner (DEEWR, 2009), is critical. The Australian Curriculum outlines the importance of high expectations for each learner and of teachers understanding the current level of each learner and that every learner learns at a different rate (ACARA, 2018).

This is echoed in the strength-based approach, promoted in early childhood settings in Victoria through the Victorian Early Years Learning and Development Framework (VEYLDF) (Department of Education and Early Childhood Development [DEECD], 2012).

The strength-based approach informs practice and also acts as an approach to writing Transition to School Statements to support learners' positive transitions to school. The use of strength-based language when thinking about and communicating learning intentions and goals provides a lens that focuses the teacher on what a learner *can do* rather than what they cannot do (DEECD, 2012). A focus on what the learner can do and how teachers support that learning is the essence of high expectations for every learner.

As discussed earlier in the chapter, learners' beliefs about themselves impact upon their learning. The concept of a growth mindset evolved out of research into the consequence of praise and types of praise provided to learners by teachers on learner motivation and performance (Mueller & Dweck, 1998). This early research found that praising a learner's intelligence had a more negative consequence than expected. Learners were more focused on performance rather than learning and, when not successful, these learners were found to have developed less persistence, enjoyment and, ultimately, lower performance on other tasks. Importantly, when asked about intelligence, the learners who were praised for effort were more likely to see intelligence as a trait to improve, while the learners praised for intelligence believed intelligence to be a fixed trait (Mueller & Dweck, 1998).

REFLECTION

1. Reflect on your own beliefs around intelligence. Do you believe intelligence is a fixed trait or something that can grow and evolve with effort? As a teacher, where do you sit on the spectrum of a fixed versus a growth mindset?
2. Think about your current practice. How often do you use descriptive, explicit feedback? Consider how you could increase this in relation to literacy learning. Rather than praising a learner with 'well done' or 'that was really clever', consider ways that you could provide feedback on a learner's persistence and effort in working on a task.
3. Is a strength-based approach similar to any other approaches you are familiar with or is it something new to you? Consider the role of the language you use to think about learning, describe learning and communicate this learning to learners and their families.

Collaborative approach

A collaborative approach to supporting learning is beneficial for all learners and, particularly, for positive and inclusive environments. A collaborative approach is represented in literature in various ways: as social pedagogy (Petrie, 2011), multidisciplinary approaches, partnerships with families and professionals (e.g. the VEYLDF) and 'problem-solving teams (PSTs)' (Williamson & McLesky, in Westwood, 2018).

As an example, PSTs include all teachers involved in supporting the learner as well as the inclusion support team within the school setting, the learner, parent/family/guardian and any other professionals who work with the learner (e.g. occupational therapist, psychologist or paediatrician) (Westwood, 2018). This team meets to use their expertise and knowledge about the learner to agree on goals and teaching approaches that are most suitable and consistent for the learner and to solve any problems that may arise (Westwood, 2018).

Multidisciplinary teams working around learners have been shown to be successful when teachers are supporting learners across multiple cultural interfaces, such as in Aboriginal and/or Torres Strait Islander communities in regional and remote areas (Kearney et al., 2014). Building relationships between family and communities can maximise opportunities for educational success (Kearney et al., 2014).

Ongoing professional learning for educators

Inclusion is a humanitarian, legal, ethical and professional responsibility for schools and teachers to enact. While the benefits of inclusive practice outweigh the barriers, the complexities of teaching in diverse learning environments are by no means easy for teachers. The constantly changing landscape of education and the backgrounds and needs of learners requires teachers to have the capacity and motivation to develop their teaching practices (Graham et al., 2018).

The effects of teacher self-efficacy and attitudes towards inclusion have been explored previously in the chapter; however, it is important to highlight that not everything can be provided in pre-service training. Ongoing professional learning and implementation of training into practice are essential in building teacher capacity (and thus positive attitudes) towards inclusion (Vaz et al., 2015; Westwood, 2018).

Opportunities to observe high-quality inclusive practices from an experienced teacher have also been highlighted as valuable forms of professional learning (Forlin & Chambers, 2017, in AITSL, 2020). In addition to observation, the use of video case studies and collaboration with other educators are also valuable practices that can be implemented into whole-school contexts (AITSL, 2020).

Supportive transitions

Supportive transitions are important for learners to feel safe and secure. Research shows the impact a positive transition to school has on a learner's later outcomes, making it imperative to ensure that these transitions are as successful as possible (DET, 2017).

Whether this involves transitions that occur throughout the day (e.g. start of the school day, moving from class to class) or larger transitions (e.g. from preschool to primary school and primary school to secondary school), this can be a challenging experience for all learners, but particularly for learners with disability (Pitt et al., 2019).

Supportive and successful transitions draw upon the positive relationships that have been built and the collaborators in the child's learning and development (DET, 2017). Each learner's experience of transitions will vary, as will the level of support they require. Some learners may need support transitioning between daily routines, while others may need a higher level of support for the significant transitions (such as change between educational contexts). Teachers play a key role in helping learners with change by working together with families, the learner and their support team and acknowledging change, while also reducing the potential for confusion, uncertainty and anxiety (AITSL, 2020; DET, 2017).

Universal Design for Learning

The Universal Design for Learning approach takes into account the diversity of contemporary learning environments and the premise that knowledge, understanding and learning can be achieved in multiple ways. The approach is based on the key principles of multiple ways to represent knowledge to engage learners and enable them to show their understanding (Capp, 2017). While empirical evidence for the efficacy of this approach is still developing, it does provide food for thought about literacy learning environments, how literacy learning is represented and assessed, and how learners are engaged. Universal Design for Learning is seen as a more flexible, creative approach to teaching and learning that lends itself to the inclusion of a diverse range of learners (Capp, 2017).

Inclusive teaching practices across the primary years

Teaching practices and strategies across the primary school years that are beneficial for learners with additional needs can prove to also be effective for all learners in the environment (AITSL, 2020).

Direct and learner-centred teaching methods

Inclusive learning environments require flexible and adaptable teachers who are able to address the needs of all learners through effective teaching strategies (Westwood, 2018). Direct teaching and learner-centred teaching are often perceived as being opposite approaches – that is, a teacher's philosophy must be one or the other. However, striking a balance between the two may be the best way to support the diversity of learners in literacy learning environments (Westwood, 2018).

Learner-centred teaching can be highly beneficial in enabling learners to be responsible for leading their own learning, allowing them to engage with their interests and develop important literacy skills (Westwood, 2018). However, it is important to note that not all learners benefit from this type of teaching all the time. Learner-centred approaches can, at times, be detrimental for some learners and widen the gap of inequality, particularly in relation to the core early literacy skills (Andersen & Andersen, 2017).

Direct teaching can also provide benefits for all learners at different stages, but particularly those with learning difficulties, including specific learning disabilities, intellectual disabilities and ASD (Westwood, 2018). In order to be effective, direct teaching should be interactive, where the teacher engages skilfully with the learners throughout the lesson. The key challenge for teachers is finding a balance between these two approaches in order to be responsive to the needs of each learner.

Effective assessment strategies

Effective assessment strategies are a key component in inclusive teaching practices. Ongoing formative assessment informs pedagogical decisions and also is a means of ensuring teaching practices are effectively addressing the needs of learners (Graham et al., 2018).

Summative assessment and other formal standardised assessment tools play an important role. Formal diagnosis of illness or disability through standardised assessment tools (such as cognitive assessments) may be helpful in relation to applications for funding and special consideration in later schooling. It is the formative assessment data, however, that allow teachers to be most responsive to the learner. See more discussion about assessment in Chapter 3.

Supporting individual needs

Individual Education Plans

Individual Education Plans (IEPs; sometimes also referred to as Individual Learning Plans) are common practice in Australia (Westwood, 2015). Their design may differ between states and territories. The IEP specifies any modifications, accommodations and additional supports a learner may need to enable equitable access and participation in the learning environment (ACARA, 2018; Westwood, 2015).

IEPs are developed and reviewed by student support groups (SSGs), including the learner, their family, relevant teachers and inclusion support within the school context. Other professionals may also be involved, depending on the learner and their individual needs (Association for Children with a Disability, 2020).

Environmental support

Individual needs can be supported through making physical adjustments to the learning environment. A learner with limited mobility, fine or gross motor impairment (such as in dyspraxia or cerebral palsy) may benefit from adjusted furniture to aid mobility and tools to enable holding pencils and using keyboards to type written material. The use of enlarged text and hands-on materials can benefit all young learners, but also be of particular benefit to learners with visual impairments (AITSL, 2020).

Multisensory materials and learning spaces

As explored in other chapters, multisensory learning is valuable for all learners and is particularly beneficial for the inclusion of learners with different learning needs (Oakley, 2017). The use of materials that have visual and auditory elements, such as spoken information accompanied with written notes, captions on films and the use of hand signal or some sign language, can benefit learners with different sensory impairments (Westwood, 2018).

Digital technology

Access to digital technology supports a range of learner needs. Providing increased opportunities for learners to develop skills using digital technology can enable them to learn more autonomously, when needed, to suit their own learning goals. For example, gifted and talented learners can use digital technology as a way to continue developing their interests and learning independently (Westwood, 2018). Assistive technology will be discussed further later in the chapter.

Trauma-informed practice

In order to support the needs of individuals and groups of learners, a range of teaching practices can be implemented. As discussed earlier in the chapter, childhood trauma and vulnerability affect a significant number of learners in Australian classrooms. Trauma-informed practice can not only support these learners but can also be beneficial for all learners in the learning environment.

There are numerous resources available but, as a starting point, some key practices and strategies to keep in mind within the literacy classroom are as follows (Harris, 2016; Statman-Weil, 2015):

1. Focus on building relationships with learners and families. Building a secure base and sense of trust is not always easy for young learners (and families), so a welcoming and inclusive learning environment built upon positive relationships is an important foundation.

2. Create a safe and predictable environment, including consistent daily routines. This might include a daily schedule, using resources such as visual schedules, so that learners are aware of what is happening for the day and feel safe and secure within the routine. This may also mean being aware of a need for additional support during transitions or other difficult periods during the day.

3. Where possible, let learners know when there will be a change to routine or an extraordinary event. The provision of this information ahead of time can support learners to feel secure and prepare themselves for potentially triggering events. Giving advance notice when trusted teachers will be absent, when loud noises such as fire drills are planned or that a visitor is coming to the classroom for an incursion can provide learners with an opportunity to ask questions and seek assistance. While this is not always possible, lessening the impact of such instances can support learners to feel secure in the environment and therefore focus on their learning.

4. Support positive behaviour and self-regulation – this will look different in every classroom. For example, if a learner finds it challenging to sit in a large group, resulting in disruption, consider whether listening to instructions or watching from a quiet space may be more comfortable for them. Sometimes, being flexible and open-minded enables teachers to support positive behaviour choices that, despite being different from other learners in the group, may better support the engagement of all learners. This can also include providing descriptive feedback when positive behaviours are demonstrated.

5. Ensure developmentally appropriate choices are available. Making developmentally appropriate experiences and tasks available to all learners is an essential component of building a sense of agency and belonging in the classroom. It is important that all learners feel they have the ability to learn and have choices within that learning. Differentiation is vital in all classrooms, but is particularly important for developmentally vulnerable learners.

▶ ▶

6. Remember that not all strategies work for all learners. Supporting all learners in the learning environment can be emotionally, mentally and physically taxing for teachers, but continuously learning and employing a range of strategies are important parts of teacher development and are also beneficial to learners. Relying on the same strategies with every group of learners may not be successful.
7. Remember that the behaviour is the behaviour, not the child. Challenging behaviour in the literacy environment can be disruptive to learning, but the behaviour is often a communication, particularly in children who have experienced trauma. Look at the events before the behaviour occurred for triggers in order to ultimately support a secure, inclusive and engaging learning environment.

Reasonable adjustments to tasks

The Australian Curriculum provides for the implementation of reasonable adjustments to support learners to access and participate in learning (ACARA, 2018). These adjustments differ from learner to learner and should be regularly reviewed. Reasonable adjustments take into account recommendations for the individual learner as well as the views of the learner and their family and other caregivers. The adjustments should support participation and progress as well as the independence of the learner. They also need to take into account how other learners may be affected (ACARA, 2018). Some possible adjustments include using additional teaching strategies, such as different ways of delivering instructions (e.g. simplified sentences, including visual reminders), as well as maintaining routines and predictability to assist attention and concentration (DET, 2020b).

Some examples of reasonable adjustments in literacy learning might include allowing for extra reading time, using peer tutoring or small-group work to build reading skills and including practical tasks to build other skills rather than employing purely reading-based tasks (DET, 2020a). Reasonable adjustments to writing might include the use of assistive technology and different alternatives to assessment, such as oral presentations instead of written submissions (DET, 2020b).

Assistive technology

Assistive technology can be used to support the participation and enhance the learning of a wide range of learners. It can be used to extend gifted and talented learners and to support and extend learners with disability and from other diverse backgrounds (Collins, 2016; Oakley, 2017). Technology as a tool for learning, more specifically inclusive education, can be explored through three categories – skill-building, emancipating and meaning-making (Oakley, 2017). Applications (apps) and software programs have been used to support different areas of literacy learning. Many of these focus on skill-building, including through games and drills for skills, such as letter-sound correspondence, sequencing skills and alphabetical knowledge. While providing much needed repetition, many of these apps are close-ended and limiting. Technology that enables more open-ended and collaborative tasks for literacy development is needed (Oakley, 2017).

Technology that assists and includes learners in the literacy context steers away from a focus on decoding and encoding skills and focuses on empowering the learner to participate in text-based opportunities with the use of particular tools. Tools such as speech-to-text and text-to-speech through tablet apps and computer software, as well as text-scanning pens such as the C-Pen reader, can remove the barrier of words on the page and enable participation in the learning of deeper literacy skills and processes (Oakley, 2017; SPELD Victoria, 2021). E-texts and libraries, such as those available through Vision Australia, can also provide opportunities for learners to independently engage with texts (Vision Australia, 2021).

Finally, the use of technology and pedagogy should include all learners in opportunities for meaning-making. The use of digital tools, including PowerPoint or Google slides to enable digital story creation, digital storybooks to support comprehension skills and a combination of these with voice-to-text software, can allow learners to co-create texts together. Audio and video recording allows learners to contribute in multisensory ways to their creations (DET, 2020b; Oakley, 2017).

Virtual reality, augmented reality, mobile technology and mind-mapping tools are a few more examples of the constantly evolving technology available to learners. However, it is vital that they are used appropriately and that teachers invest time in learning how to best support learners with assistive technology (Oakley, 2017).

The investment in technology in schools is still an area questioned, after the Organisation for Economic Co-operation and Development (OECD) found a number of factors that may inhibit successful learning through the use of technology (OECD, 2015, in Oakley, 2017). Some contributing factors of this lack of evidence for learning successfully included the design of the software, pedagogical approaches and technology skills of learners and teachers (Oakley, 2017). Caution is also advised in relation to purchasing technological tools. Undertaking some research into how to use tools and whether they are appropriate tools to meet the inclusive needs of the particular learners is recommended (SPELD Victoria, 2021).

Learner with dyslexia reluctant to use assistive technology

CASE STUDY 12.2

Layla is in Year 5 and has been diagnosed with a specific learning disability with impairments in reading, writing and spelling. Layla has an IEP in place that has details of adjustments to her learning to enable her full participation in the learning environment. One of these adjustments is the provision of a C-Pen to use in the classroom, particularly when she needs to read large amounts of text. Despite having this tool, Layla does not want to use it. She says, 'It doesn't even work and the other kids will think I'm dumb'. Layla's parents are very keen for her to start using the C-Pen in the classroom and are becoming frustrated that it is not being used.

Questions

1. Consider the different factors at play in this scenario. Based on your learning in this chapter, why do you think Layla is not using the technology that has been provided to assist her?

2. As a teacher, how would you develop Layla's sense of belonging and inclusion in the learning environment? What collaborations may need to take place to ensure this?

Conclusion

Access to equitable educational opportunities is a fundamental human right. Throughout this chapter, examples have been provided to explore the complex and diverse landscape that is the literacy learning environment across Australia. Inclusive educational environments are essential in enabling participation of all learners regardless of ability, disability or background.

The barriers to and benefits of inclusion in the literacy learning environment were described. It was emphasised that, while challenging, inclusion is fundamental in ensuring the educational opportunities for all learners through teaching practices, approaches and understanding of the diversity of the needs within any classroom.

As each learner is an individual, so is every teacher. Reflection and awareness of what is known and not known about learners and their needs in order to continue learning and growing as teachers is not only a legal requirement but also a vital professional responsibility.

Bringing it together

1. In what ways can diverse learning needs impact on literacy learning?
2. Consider the importance of ongoing professional learning in creating positive and inclusive literacy environments. Reflect on whether there are any areas or goals for your own professional learning related to inclusion. If there are, what actions will you take?
3. Contemplate the following scenario. You are working in a Year 4 classroom. You are aware that one learner is gifted and talented. You observe this learner during literacy experiences and other experiences that involve writing. They often become anxious and upset or complain of a stomach-ache and not being able to complete the task. What do you need to find out about this learner to best support their participation in the classroom?
4. Assess your own digital technology skills. Do you feel confident in using a range of devices and applications (such as sound recording or voice-to-text)? If you had a child who needed to use a C-Pen, would you be confident in supporting them to use it in the classroom? Why or why not?
5. Consider your current placement experience. Are you aware of all the learning needs and developmental levels of each learner? Are there learners who have IEPs? If you are not sure, how might you find out about or assess for this information?

Further resources

Every Kid Needs a Champion

In this Ted Talk, Rita F. Pierson emphasises the importance of adapting teaching to suit each learner, regardless of their background, and maintaining high expectations. Sometimes it takes just one teacher to make a difference to a learner's best outcomes.

www.ted.com/talks/rita_pierson_every_kid_needs_a_champion?language=en

Inclusive education means all children are included in every way, not just in theory

This article by Kathy Cologon (2015) from The Conversation website further explores some of the common misunderstandings of inclusion, including research demonstrating better outcomes for learners included in mainstream schools.

https://theconversation.com/inclusive-education-means-all-children-are-included-in-every-way-not-just-in-theory-45237

Breaking down inclusion barriers and myths

This article on the ACECQA website by Rhonda Livingston (2018) provides some interesting perspectives on misconceptions that exist about inclusion, particularly in the early childhood context.

https://wehearyou.acecqa.gov.au/tag/inclusion

Four things students with vision impairment want you (their teachers and friends) to know

This is an article published on The Conversation by Melissa Cain and Melissa Fanshawe (2019) featuring the voices of learners and mothers/academics in relation to the perceptions and experiences of learners with vision impairment.

https://theconversation.com/four-things-students-with-vision-impairment-want-you-their-teachers-and-friends-to-know-115377

References

Andersen, I.G. & Andersen, S.C. (2017). Student-centered instruction and academic achievement: linking mechanisms of educational inequality to schools' instructional strategy. *British Journal of Sociology of Education*, 38(4), 533–550. doi.10.1080/01425692.2015.1093409

Arthur, L., Ashton, J., & Beecher, B. (2014). *Diverse Literacies in Early Childhood: A Social Justice Approach*. Australian Council for Educational Research.

Association for Children with a Disability. (2020). Student Support Groups. www.acd.org.au/student-support-groups

Australian Curriculum, Assessment and Reporting Authority (ACARA). (2018). Australian Curriculum: Student diversity. www.australiancurriculum.edu.au/resources/student-diversity/#

Australian Early Development Census. (2019). Findings from the AEDC. www.aedc.gov.au/early-childhood/findings-from-the-aedc

Australian Government. (2020). *Closing the Gap Report*. https://ctgreport.niaa.gov.au/sites/default/files/pdf/closing-the-gap-report-2020.pdf

Australian Institute for Teaching and School Leadership (AITSL). (2017). Australian Professional Standards for Teaching. www.aitsl.edu.au/teach/standards

—— (2020). Inclusive education: teaching students with disability. www.aitsl.edu.au/research/spotlight/inclusive-education-teaching-students-with-disability

Buckingham, J., Wheldall, K., & Beaman-Wheldall, R. (2013). Why poor children are more likely to become poor readers: the school years. *Australian Journal of Education*, 57(3), 190–213.

Cain, M. & Fanshawe, M. (2019). Four things students with vision impairment want you (their teachers and friends) to know. The Conversation, 10 June. https://theconversation.com/four-things-students-with-vision-impairment-want-you-their-teachers-and-friends-to-know-115377

Capp, M.J. (2017). The effectiveness of universal design for learning: a meta-analysis of literature between 2013 and 2016. *International Journal of Inclusive Education*, 21(8), 791–807. doi:10.1080/13603116.2017.1325074">

Carrington, S., Berthelsen, D., Nickerson, J., Nicholson, J.M., Walker, S., & Meldrum, K. (2016). Teachers' experiences of inclusion of children with developmental disabilities across the early years of school. *Journal of Psychologists and Counsellors in Schools*, 26(2), 139–154. doi:10.1017/jgc.2016.19

Collins, L.E. (2016). Take a byte: technology for 2e students. *Parenting for High Potential*, 5(2), 16–19.

Cologon, K. (2015). Inclusive education means all children are included in every way, not just in theory. The Conversation, 13 August. https://theconversation.com/inclusive-education-means-all-children-are-included-in-every-way-not-just-in-theory-45237

Cordewener, K.A.H., Bosman, A.M.T., & Verhoeven, L. (2012). Specific language impairments affects the early spelling process quantitatively but not qualitatively. *Research in Developmental Disabilities*, 33, 1041–1047.

Department of Education and Early Childhood Development (DEECD) Victoria. (2012). *Strength-based Approach: A Guide to Writing Transition Learning and Development Statements*. www.education.vic.gov.au/documents/childhood/professionals/learning/strengthbappr.pdf

Department of Education, Employment & Workplace Relations (DEEWR). (2009). *Belonging, Being & Becoming – The Early Years Learning Framework for Australia*. https://docs.education.gov.au/documents/belonging-being-becoming-early-years-learning-framework-australia

Department of Education and Training (DET). (2017). Transition: a positive start to school (resource kit). Victorian Government. www.education.vic.gov.au/Documents/childhood/professionals/learning/Transition-to-School-Resource-Kit.pdf

—— (2019). Education for all. Victorian Government. www.education.vic.gov.au/about/programs/Pages/Education-for-all.aspx

—— (2020a). Understanding learning difficulties. Victorian Government. www.education.vic.gov.au/parents/additional-needs/Pages/learning-difficulties-understanding.aspx

—— (2020b). Making reasonable adjustments. Victorian Government. www.education.vic.gov.au/school/teachers/learningneeds/Pages/reasonable-adjustments.aspx

Devine, A. (2015). *Literacy for Visual Learners: Teaching Children with Learning Differences to Read, Write, Communicate and Create*. Jessica Kingsley Publishers.

Duncan, J., Punch, R., Gauntlett, M., & Talbot-Stokes, R. (2020). Missing the mark or scoring a goal? Achieving non-discrimination for students with disability in primary and secondary education in Australia: a scoping review. *Australian Journal of Education*, 64(1), 54–72.

Early Childhood Australia (ECA). (2016). Code of Ethics. www.earlychildhoodaustralia.org.au/our-publications/eca-code-ethics

Early Learning, Everyone Benefits. (2016). *The State of Early Learning in Australia Report 2016*. Early Learning, Everyone Benefits.

Education Council. (2019). *Alice Springs (Mparntwe) Education Declaration*. www.dese.gov.au/alice-springs-mparntwe-education-declaration

Graham, L., Berman, J., & Bellert, A. (2018). *Sustainable Learning: Inclusive Practices for 21st Century Classrooms*. Cambridge University Press.

Harris, R. (2016). *Trauma-Informed Practice in Education*. Carlton Primary School, Victoria. www.traumainformedpractice.com.au/uploads/2/4/4/4/24444506/trauma_informed_practice_in_education.pdf

Hayes, N., O'Toole, L., & Halpenny, A.M. (2017). *Introducing Bronfenbrenner: A Guide for Practitioners and Students in Early Years Education*. Routledge.

Hyde, M. (2013). Understanding diversity, inclusion and engagement. In M. Hyde, L. Carpenter, & R. Conway (Eds.), *Diversity, Inclusion and Engagement* (pp. 3–13). Oxford University Press.

Jarvis, J.M. (2013). Supporting diverse gifted students. In M. Hyde, L. Carpenter, & R. Conway (Eds.), *Diversity, Inclusion and Engagement* (pp. 297–315). Oxford University Press.

Kearney, E., McIntosh, L., Perry, B., Dockett, S., & Clayton, K. (2014). Building positive relationships with Indigenous children, families, and communities: learning at the cultural interface. *Critical Studies in Education*, 55, 338–352.

Livingstone, R. (2018). Breaking down inclusion barriers and myths. *ACECQA National Education Leader*, 30 April. https://wehearyou.acecqa.gov.au/tag/inclusion

Main, S. & Konza, D. (2017). Inclusive principles and practices in literacy education: inclusive reading practices for Aboriginal and/or Torres Strait Islander students in Australia. *International Perspectives on Inclusive Education*, 11, 177–193. doi:10.1108/S1479-363620170000011011

McCloskey, M. & Rapp, B. (2017). Developmental dysgraphia: an overview and framework for research. *Cognitive Neuropsychology*, 34(3–4), 65–82. doi:10.1080/02643294.2017.1369016

Mueller, C.M. & Dweck, C.S. (1998). Praise for intelligence can undermine children's motivation and performance. *Journal of Personality and Social Psychology*, 75(1). doi:10.1037//0022-3514.75.1.33

Nationally Consistent Collection of Data on School Students with Disability (NCCD). (2019). Broad categories of disability used in the NCCD. www.australiancurriculum.edu.au/media/6100/categories_of_disability.pdf

—— (2020). NCCD and supporting students with disability. www.nccd.edu.au

Oakley, G. (2017). Inclusive principles and practices in literacy education: engaging students in inclusive literacy learning with technology. *International Perspectives on Inclusive Education*, 11, 159–176. doi:10.1108/S1479-363620170000011011

Petrie, P. (2011). *Communication Skills for Working with Children and Young People: Introducing Social Pedagogy*. Jessica Kingsley Publishers.

Pitt, F., Dixon, R., & Vialle, W. (2019). The transition experiences of students with disabilities moving from primary to secondary schools in NSW, Australia. *International Journal of Inclusive Education*, 1–16. doi:10.1080/13603116.2019.1572797

Poed, S., Cologon, K., & Jackson, R. (2020). Gatekeeping and restrictive practices by Australian mainstream schools: results of a national survey. *International Journal of Inclusive Education*, 1–14. doi:10.1080/13603116.2020.1726512

Prior, M. (2013). Language and literacy challenges for Indigenous children in Australia. *Australian Journal of Learning Difficulties*, 18(2), 123–137. doi:10.1080/19404158.2013.840901

Prunty, M. & Barnett, A.L. (2017). Understanding handwriting difficulties: a comparison of children with and without motor impairment. *Cognitive Neuropsychology*, 24(3–4), 205–218. doi:10.1080/02643294.2017.1376630

Roberts, W. (2015). Enabling change through education for children and their families experiencing vulnerability and disadvantage: the understandings of early childhood professionals. *Australasian Journal of Early Childhood*, 40(2), 49–56.

Robinson, S. & Truscott, J. (2014). *Belonging and Connection of School Students with Disability*. Children With Disability Australia. www.cyda.org.au/images/pdf/belonging_and_connection_of_school_students_with_disability.pdf

SPELD Victoria. (2021). Assistive technology. www.speldvic.org.au/assistive-technology

Statman-Weil, K. (2015). *Creating Trauma-Sensitive Classrooms*. National Association for the Education of Young Children (NAEYC). www.naeyc.org/resources/pubs/yc/mnay2015/trauma-sensitive-classrooms

UN General Assembly. (2007). United Nations Declaration on the Rights of Indigenous Peoples. UN General Assembly. www.un.org/development/desa/indigenouspeoples/declaration-on-the-rights-of-indigenous-peoples.html

United Nations. (1989). United Nations Convention on the Rights of the Child. United Nations.

Upton, L., Kezelman, C., Hossack, N., Stavropoulos, P., & Burley, P. (2015). The cost of unresolved childhood trauma and abuse in adults in Australia: A Report for Adults Surviving Child Abuse. *Counselling and Psychotherapy*, November, 146–161.

Vaz, S., Wilson, N., Falkmer, M., Sim, A., Scott,M. , Cordier, R., & Falkmer, T. (2015). Factors associated with primary school teachers' attitudes towards the inclusion of students with disabilities. *PLoS One*, 10(8). doi:10.1371/journal.pone.0137002

Victorian Institute of Teaching (VIT). (2021). Registration categories. www.vit.vic.edu.au/register

Vinson, T., Rawsthorne, M., Beavis, A., & Ericson, M. (2015). *Dropping off the edge 2015*. www.dote .org.au

Vision Australia. (2021). Adaptive technology. www.visionaustralia.org/information/ adaptive-technology

Westwood, P. (2008). *What Teachers Need to Know about Learning Difficulties*. ACER Press. ProQuest Ebook Central. http://ebookcentral.proquest.com/lib/unimelb/detail.action?docID=398377

—— (2015). *Commonsense Methods for Children with Special Educational Needs*. Taylor & Francis Group, ProQuest Ebook Central. http://ebookcentral.proquest.com/lib/unimelb/detail. action?docID=2034023

—— (2018). *Inclusive and Adaptive Teaching: Meeting the Challenge of Diversity in the Classroom* (2nd edn). Routledge. https://doi.org/10.4324/9781351061261

Westwood, P. & Graham, L. (2003). Inclusion of students with special needs: benefits and obstacles perceived by teachers in New South Wales and South Australia. *Australian Journal of Learning Difficulties*, 8(1), 3–15. doi:10.1080/19404150309546718

Woodcock, S. (2013). Trainee teachers' attitudes towards students with specific learning disabilities. *Australian Journal of Teacher Education*, 38(8). http://ro.ecu.edu.au/ajte/vol38/iss8/2

Wormald, C. (2015). Intellectually gifted students often have learning disabilities. The Conversation, 25 March. https://theconversation.com/intellectually-gifted-students-often-have-learning-disabilities-37276

CHAPTER 13

Teaching spelling in context

Lucy Stewart

ANTICIPATED OUTCOMES

After working through this chapter, it is anticipated you will be able to:

- reflect on the importance of spelling development and relevant theories that underpin spelling acquisition
- understand the interrelationships between spelling, oral language, reading and handwriting
- explain key components in spelling development, including auditory, visual and cognitive aspects
- explore the four types of spelling knowledge: phonological, orthographic, morphemic and etymological
- understand typical spelling development in the preschool and primary years
- describe key approaches to teaching spelling in the primary learning environment
- understand the importance of employing a range of teaching approaches for spelling, depending on the developmental stage and needs of each learner
- explain key curriculum, assessment and differentiation approaches to spelling instruction.

Introduction

Many of us may take the ability to spell for granted; however, it is important to remember that spelling is a valuable, but not easily attained, skill. The English writing system can be particularly challenging to learn, although it is generally agreed across languages that learning to read is easier than learning to spell (Bosman & Van Orden, 1997, in Treiman, 2017b).

This chapter unpacks the complexities of learning to spell, including the foundations of knowledge and brain development that must be acquired to support the learning of this skill.

Key issues in spelling development

The importance of spelling

Despite the increased use of digital tools, such as voice-to-text technology, predictive text and spell check, spelling is still an important skill for learners to develop (Graham & Santangelo, 2014). Spelling is central to writing and essential in good communication.

Spelling, grammar and punctuation have all been shown to influence written comprehension in the primary years and acquisition of these skills appears to be a main predictor of success in written comprehension (Daffern, 2017). The broader social and cultural aspects of spelling should also be highlighted. We rely upon our ability to read and write proficiently in our everyday lives and communication with each other, meaning there is disadvantage for those who do not possess competency or ability in these skills (Treiman, 2017b). Learning spelling has been shown to positively impact upon other literacy skills, including the enhancement of reading development, through supporting understanding of the alphabetic principle, phonemic awareness, utilisation of sight words and word reading skills (Graham & Santangelo, 2014; Treiman, 2017a).

Conversely, just as proficient spelling can assist the development of other literacy skills, spelling difficulties can negatively impact on the learner's literacy development. Errors in spelling can make texts challenging to read and devalue the writer's message (Graham & Santangelo, 2014). Difficulties in spelling can particularly effect a developing writer. An increased focus on how to spell a word places greater demands on working memory, leading to cognitive fatigue and the message becoming lost. Over time, this can affect the quality of vocabulary, ideas and written expression, as so much energy is expended on spelling individual words (Daffern, 2017). For learners who experience significant spelling difficulties, this can lead to avoidance of writing and subsequent delays in writing development (Graham & Santangelo, 2014).

Given the value of spelling for clear communication of written messages, and also for other literacy skills, it is important to understand how spelling develops (Treiman, 2017a).

Theories of spelling acquisition

There are a number of theories circulating in educational research in relation to the acquisition of spelling skills (Westwood, 2018). Stage theory, Triple Word Form Theory and integration of multiple patterns are some such examples. Daffern (2017) posits that in order to support children's spelling development, it is necessary to identify how the understanding of spelling is acquired by learners. The perspective that developmental stages exist is still a popular theory. Research increasingly suggests, however, that spelling development is not linear. It has been proposed that 'learning to spell is a process of learning to abstract, apply and interconnect phonological, orthographic and morphological knowledge from the beginning of learning to write' (Daffern, 2017, p. 309).

Stage theory

Stage theory aligns with a cognitive developmental approach in that spelling development occurs over time and in sequence or stages: the learner initially develops spelling knowledge through phonology, followed by orthography and then morphology (Daffern, 2017). Spelling ability progresses through stages in correlation with the developing understanding of the relationship between spoken and written language. The mechanical aspect of spelling, including emergent mark-making, is followed by gradual acquisition and ability to name letters of the alphabet and the sounds that these letters represent. This initial phonological and orthographic understanding is then built upon using increasing phonemic encoding skills, and the rate of skill development is dependent on the instruction the learner receives (Daffern, 2017). These developing spelling patterns (or orthography) are then followed by knowledge of morphology (morphemes are the smallest units of meaning).

Triple Word Form Theory (TWFT)

Triple Word Form Theory (TWFT) builds on stage theory and suggests that, rather than moving through developmental stages of spelling, the working memory and automaticity of the three word forms (phonological, orthographic and morphological) develop spelling competency. There is a trajectory for this development, but it is gradual and complex (Daffern, 2017). When words are stored and analysed using the working memory efficiently, the interrelationships between word forms are mapped through neural transmitters in the brain (Richards et al., 2006, in Daffern, 2017).

TWFT posits that the three word forms are coordinated in the working memory and, as working memory develops, spelling is committed to long-term memory to be coordinated automatically. As the working memory develops throughout the primary years, the increase in functioning assists the efficiency and accuracy of spelling, highlighting the influence of continued spelling instruction and practice in learning to spell (Berninger et al., 2010, in Daffern, 2017).

Integration of multiple patterns (IMP) framework

Treiman and Kessler (2014, in Treiman, 2017b) proposed the integration of multiple patterns (IMP) framework, which seeks to explain the variety of strategies and knowledge that proficient spellers draw upon. These include the spelling of specific words and patterns that can be stored to reference. It is proposed that learners use phoneme-grapheme correspondence and context-based phonological, **graphotactic** and morphological patterns. The term 'patterns' is significant, as IMP also acknowledges that there are exceptions and irregularities in relation to 'rules' of writing systems. By supporting learners to draw upon a range of patterns, learners can speed up the process of learning to spell words, but also decrease the time spent on rules and exceptions (Treiman, 2017b).

Graphotactic: the arrangement of letters and letter patterns to inform spelling rather than pronunciation.

Connection between spelling and other literacy skills

As discussed in previous chapters, the components of literacy are strongly interrelated, with oral language providing the foundation for literacy learning (Mackenzie & Hemmings, 2014). Oral language (expressive and receptive) is essential to the learner's ability to hear and produce sounds (Westwood, 2014). Awareness of the different sounds in words is needed to be able to decode and encode (spell) these words (Mackenzie & Hemmings, 2014). Learners also need to combine hearing and producing sounds with a correlated graphic system in order to understand and communicate written messages (Fellowes & Oakley, 2020). Vocabulary development and comprehension also play a role in the ability to understand and reproduce written texts, and these factors are explored in other chapters (see Chapters 8 and 9).

Successful spelling development relies on the underlying visual, motor, auditory and cognitive processes (Westwood, 2014) and this is explored in the next section.

Underlying processes of spelling development

While theories of spelling acquisition help teachers understand different ways they may observe skill development, there are some important underlying processes that support spelling development. These include the visual and visual-motor aspects of spelling, as well as the auditory, phonological, cognitive and metacognitive aspects (Westwood, 2014).

Visual and visual-motor development

Visual discrimination, visual sequential memory and visual-motor coordination combine to support the development of spelling (Westwood, 2014). It is the visual memory that supports writers to spell words correctly beyond reliance on the use of phonetic spelling (i.e. spelling words how they sound). The ability to visually discriminate between letters and spelling patterns – that is, to notice the differences – is a key skill developed in the early years. These skills also include emerging letter recognition, formation and understanding of print (Puranik et al., 2011).

In addition to differentiating letters and letter patterns, learners need to develop their visual sequential memory – that is, their ability to both remember and store groups of letters (in order) so that they can recall how a word or syllable should look. This assists the learner in identifying errors when reading over their work (Westwood, 2014).

The visual-motor coordination required to handwrite (explored in Chapter 14) can support the development of orthographic knowledge, but automatic and efficient handwriting also enables the writer to focus on the spelling of the words rather than the formation of individual letters (Prunty & Barnett, 2017; Westwood, 2014). When these processes work efficiently, spelling competency is developed. A weakness in any of these visual processes can be a contributing factor to difficulties experienced by a learner (Westwood, 2014).

Auditory and phonological development

Auditory development – that is, the ability to hear spoken words and identify the specific units of sound that make up these words – is essential in being able to decode and encode. Phonological awareness is a broader term that includes the ability to break down the sounds at a sentence level, from words in sentences, to syllables and then individual sounds (or phonemes) (Westwood, 2014). It is this awareness that also enables the learner to hear words that rhyme or start with the same sound, for example.

Phonemic awareness is essential in the development of the interrelationship between written and spoken language (Westwood, 2014). It involves discriminating between individual units of sound (phonemes) (Westwood, 2014). This is then combined with the understanding of how to represent different sounds with the letters and patterns of letters to spell words correctly. Teaching learners to attend to phonemes within words has been shown to be a strong predictor of spelling ability (Mann et al., 2010; Yeung et al., 2013, in Westwood, 2014). Conversely, weakness in the area of phonological and phonemic awareness can correlate with difficulties in reading and spelling development (Westwood, 2014).

In addition to auditory input, oral language and speech play an important role in spelling development. The ability to pronounce words accurately also facilitates correct spelling (Papen et al., 2012, in Westwood, 2015).

Cognitive and metacognitive development

The cognitive and metacognitive development of the learner are literally the 'thinking processes' (Westwood, 2014, p. 48) that enable spelling development. Memory, attention and language comprehension help the learner to use the visual, auditory and kinaesthetic systems when spelling. The brain's ability to combine and organise these different sources is vital in the application of learnt strategies for spelling as well as for making connections between words and how they are represented. Metacognitive development, or thinking about one's own thinking, is a key process in learners being able to self-monitor their spelling inaccuracies.

The development of a range of strategies (including cognitive and metacognitive development) assists the learner to be able to draw upon ways of storing and recalling the spelling of words, and also to check and problem-solve if there is a word they are unsure of. Reliance on a few strategies and rote learning will limit the learner's ability to become a proficient speller (Westwood, 2014).

REFLECTION

1. The interrelationships between literacy skills are evident. Reflect on your current knowledge so far. What parallels can you draw between the skills required for spelling development and the information about literacy that you have read in earlier chapters?
2. How does knowledge of these interrelationships inform your teaching practice?

Developing spelling knowledge

It can be seen that learning to spell is no easy feat, and proficient spellers use a range of strategies and knowledge bases in relation to orthography, phonology, morphology and etymology (Adoniou, 2014; Devonshire & Fluck, 2010; Westwood, 2014). These knowledge areas are explored in the next sections.

Overview of phonological knowledge

Phonological knowledge includes four levels of knowledge in relation to the analysis of sounds in spoken language: word, syllable, onset and rime, and phoneme (Fellowes & Oakley, 2020). Phonological knowledge in spelling relates to the ability to detect, identify and manipulate sounds in words, specifically phonemes and syllables (Fellowes & Oakley, 2020).

Distinguishing between sounds is essential in order to encode spoken word into written form. These sounds consist of syllables (or beats in a word), onset and rime (distinguishing and separating the initial sound of a single syllable word from the rest of the word) and phonemes (the smallest individual sounds in speech) (Tompkins et al., 2019). Learners must draw upon their phonological knowledge to assist spelling and, in order to use letter-sound correlation (the relationship between graphemes and phonemes), orthographic knowledge must be developed in addition to phonemic awareness (Westwood, 2014).

Table 13.1 provides a guide to some of the key terms and examples in this section.

Table 13.1 Mini-glossary: phonological knowledge

Term	Description	Examples
Word awareness	Understanding the difference between a word and a letter	shell, open, fantastic
Syllable	A unit of pronunciation within a word	shell (1 syllable) o.pen (2 syllables) fan.tas.tic (3 syllables)
Onset and rime	Within a syllable the onset includes any consonants before a vowel, the rime is the vowel and consonants after the onset	h-am (h = onset, am = rime) tr-am (tr = onset, am = rime)
Phoneme	Individual speech sounds	cat = /c/, /a/, /t/ shell = /sh/, /e/, /l/

Overview of orthographic knowledge

Orthography refers to the 'the conventional spelling system of a language' (Fellowes & Oakley, 2020, p. 432). Hence, orthographic knowledge is the knowledge of spelling and strategies for encoding words correctly. Understanding how orthography works also involves understanding of concepts of print and alphabetic knowledge.

Concepts of print are essential in reading and writing (and spelling) because they provide the system of rules that underpin written language. This involves the understanding of relationships between written and spoken language, including understanding that sounds are represented as letters, are written together to form words and a space indicates the beginning of a new word.

The knowledge of the 26 letters in the English alphabet in lower case and upper case form allows decoding and encoding using a consistent code. Graphemes, which are the letters of the alphabet (and combinations of letters) that represent one unit of sound (phonemes), are used to spell words. Graphemes can consist of single letters or multiple letters that form one sound (examples are illustrated in Table 13.2) (Fellowes & Oakley, 2020). Letter patterns can also be helpful in learning to spell (e.g. snail, mail, main, pain, wait), as are rules and generalisations that can be learnt to guide how the graphemes are usually arranged in words.

Table 13.2 Mini-glossary: orthographic knowledge

Term	Description	Examples
Graphemes	Letters or combinations or letters of the alphabet that represent one unit of sound (or phoneme)	t = /t/ sh = /sh/
Letter patterns	Letters that can be grouped together as one sound or part of a word (such as a rime)	ail = mail, trail, rail eat = meat, seat, wheat

Overview of morphemic knowledge

Morphemic knowledge refers to the understanding of the smallest meaningful units within words, as distinct from phonemes and syllables, which are units of sound (Fellowes & Oakley, 2020). Morphemes can be used as 'building blocks' to create spelling patterns (Westwood, 2014). Understanding the morphology can be an effective strategy for learners when spelling a word correctly (Treiman, 2017b).

In order to develop this understanding, learners need to recognise that words consist of morphemic units that have meaning. A free morpheme is a word on its own and a bound morpheme can only be part of a word (Westwood, 2014). A word may consist of one morpheme (e.g. skip) or combine morphemes together to create meaning (e.g. love + ly = lovely), where adding the morpheme 'ly' to the word 'love' slightly changes the meaning. Compound words are an example of combining two words (or morphemes) to create a new word (e.g. cupboard) (Fellowes & Oakley, 2020).

Understanding of root words is beneficial to spelling development because these can be applied to multiple words. Morphemes, such as derivational prefixes and suffixes, can be added to base words to create new words (e.g. un + safe = unsafe). Inflectional suffixes can be added to base words to change the word grammatically, such as the tense of the word or to create a plural (e.g. friend + s = friends) (Fellowes & Oakley, 2020). Table 13.3 provides a guide to some of the key terms and examples in this section.

Table 13.3 Mini-glossary: morphemic knowledge

Term	Description	Examples
Morphemes	Smallest units of meaning within words: Free morphemes are single words that can stand alone Bound morphemes can only be part of a word	dog, sick, teach, mother -s as in dogs -ness as in sickness -un as in undone -er as in teacher
Compound words	Two words (or morphemes) written together to create a new word	day, dream = daydream earth, quake = earthquake
Prefix	Added to the beginning of other words to create new words	un- as in unbelievable pre- preview
Derivational suffix	Added to the end of other words to create new words	-ly as in weekly -tion as in attention
Inflectional suffix	Added to the end of words to change the word grammatically but do not create a new word	-ed as in happened -ing as in waiting

Overview of etymological knowledge

Etymological knowledge is the understanding of the origins of words and their changes over time (Fellowes & Oakley, 2020). As many words in English have their origins in other languages, understanding the meanings of these words can assist the learner in understanding the spelling patterns, particularly when the grapheme-phoneme correspondence does not align with consistent rules (Bowers & Bowers, 2017). For example, the knowledge that 'collage' is from a French word can also be applied to 'garage' and 'mirage'. Words or parts of words from Greek (such as 'photo') and Latin (such as 'centum') can support the learner's understanding of the spelling of words like 'photograph' and 'century' (Bowers & Bowers, 2017; Fellowes & Oakley, 2020).

Etymological knowledge, in combination with phonological, orthographic and morphemic knowledge, can provide learners with understanding of the logic of the English spelling system (Bowers & Bowers, 2017).

Stages of spelling development

Despite research suggesting that stage theory may not be the most accurate way to describe the development of spelling, there is evidence that some developmental trajectory exists. When observing spelling development in young learners, it can be helpful to have a guide of stages and approximate ages (Daffern, 2017). The stages in Table 13.4 are loosely grouped by age and features. You will notice there is an overlap in age ranges: this again highlights the difficulty of applying a trajectory approach to spelling.

Table 13.4 Features and examples of spelling development from 3–12 years of age

Stage	Features and examples
Early-emergent spelling: 3–5 years	Learners are experimenting with letter shapes and numerals and directionality of writing. Upper case letters are used more often than lower case letters and there may be some emerging letter-sound correlation towards the end of this stage. Claudia (4 years) has labelled members of her family using the first letters of their names.

Table 13.4 (cont.)

Stage	Features and examples
Emergent spelling: 4–6 years	In this stage, learners display increasing understanding of letter-phoneme (or sound) correspondence. They are able to represent a word using multiple phonemes (e.g. kitten might be 'ktn'). More consonants than vowel sounds are likely to be represented and some common letter patterns or blends might be evident (e.g. 'stop'). The sounding-out strategy and copying words from print in the environment or classroom material may be demonstrated. Miss you are the besd teacher Foundation student (5 years) typing a message to print out using the sounding-out strategy and print in the environment.
Early spelling: 5–7 years	Learners can often overlap with the emergent spelling stage in the first years of school. In the early spelling stage, learners use increasingly accurate phonemic representation in words. Patterns such as consonant blends, short vowel patterns and digraphs (where two letters represent one sound) can be observed. Learners may demonstrate use of high-frequency words that they consistently spell correctly and strategies such as sounding out or 'chunking' (breaking words into smaller parts). Irregular words may be written phonetically (e.g. sed = said) and learners may still experience difficulties in detecting some sounds in words (e.g. wiv = with). Some letter pattern reversals can also be observed (e.g. said = siad, form = from). Billy (6 years) wrote a get well card – 'Dear Miss Lucy. I hoop yu fil bettr'

Table 13.4 (cont.)

Stage	Features and examples
Fluent spelling: 7–10 years	Fluent spellers demonstrate increasing understanding of word structure, including long vowel patterns, r-controlled vowels (vowels followed by the letter 'r'), more complex consonant patterns and diphthongs. Spelling will show phonemes accurately represented by common and increasingly complex letter patterns. Learners begin to apply understandings of spelling patterns to longer, multisyllabic words. Accurate application of morphemic knowledge, including addition of inflectional endings (such as -ed, -ing), use of prefixes and suffixes and understanding of compound words, as well as the ability to distinguish between homophones, will develop. A range of spelling strategies, including analogy, visual memory, sounding out and chunking, will be demonstrated. All letters and syllables will be represented in words, and there may still be some letter order reversals. Alastair (8 years) writing a short story to go with an illustration.
Independent spelling: 11–12 years	Independent spellers demonstrate developing knowledge of etymology in their spelling. This may include understanding of the relationships between spelling and word meanings such as Latin and Greek root words and affixes (e.g. pre-, -able, amphi-). Learners will show use of less common letter patterns, an increasing range of spelling strategies and draw upon a larger 'bank' of words automatically. Learners will apply a variety of spelling patterns, use inflectional suffixes and vowel and consonant alternations. There will also be awareness of incorrectly spelt words and attempts at self-correction. Alastair's (11 years) narrative example includes evidence of self-correction.

Table 13.4 (cont.)

Stage	Features and examples
	Enola was looking at her spicher and found a lot of money in her mum's bed frame. So she made a plan. When she was going to boarding school she asked her driver to let her visit her dad's grave. But the driver did not know she had put her bike and all the things she needed to survive bye her dad's grave. Her plane was to go to the place her brother lest expected her to go. So she was going to London and she was going to disguise her as a lady because her brothers expected her to dress as a boy. Aliyah's (12 years) typed text response example.

Source: Developed from Fellowes & Oakley (2020) and Tompkins et al. (2019).

REFLECTION

1. Why is it important to be aware of the developmental stages in children's spelling acquisition?
2. Reflect on what some of the challenges might be in observing learners' spelling development when using technology.

Key approaches to teaching spelling in context in the primary years

Multisensory learning

Young children learn through their senses, with hands-on materials and by 'doing' (Prashnig, 2008, in Boardman, 2020). This approach to learning does not 'switch off' when children go to school. While much of the research literature focuses on **multisensory learning** for dyslexia and other learning difficulties, this approach is valuable for all learners (Boardman, 2020).

Multisensory learning engages the visual, auditory and kinaesthetic-tactile pathways and helps learners make links between the language they see and hear and the symbols they feel (International Dyslexia Association, 2008). Boardman (2020) noted that a number of studies have highlighted the value of this approach because learners benefited from the variety of experiences provided and the opportunity to learn through more than one of their senses. Rosenthal and Ehri (2011) also noted the benefits for using auditory and visual senses together by reading new words aloud – this appeared to strengthen connections between pronunciation of words and spelling of these words in unfamiliar texts. This also aligns with the development of the underlying visual, motor, auditory and cognitive processes explored earlier in the chapter (Westwood, 2014).

> **Multisensory learning:** employs visual, auditory and kinaesthetic-tactile pathways (or multiple senses) in combination.

While there are many ways to engage multiple senses when learning spelling, some helpful starting points include:

- encouraging learners to say and spell new words aloud as they are writing them
- using finger spelling when 'sounding out' words – assigning each sound to a finger so that the sounds in the word can be counted
- clapping syllables in a word while saying them aloud.

Orthographic mapping

Orthographic mapping involves the connections made between the spelling, meaning and pronunciation of words. Orthographic mapping occurs when learners read particular words and make connections between the written graphemes or spelling patterns and spoken units (phonemes, morphemes or syllables) (Ehri, 2014).

Phonemic awareness and grapheme-phoneme knowledge are needed to support orthographic mapping (Ehri, 2014); through orthographic mapping, it is thought that the brain processes information to increase the learners' sight-word vocabulary. The aim is for learners to read words by sight rather than decoding every single word, as this is exhausting and distracts from the meaning of the text. The same may be applied to spelling (Ehri, 2014).

Authentic, meaningful and purposeful spelling opportunities

As in many areas of learning, and emphasised throughout this book, authentic, meaningful and purposeful learning opportunities are essential. Spelling is no exception. As learners progress through the school years, these authentic opportunities may evolve with the emphasis on learning in context and the role of peers and teachers to mentor and scaffold. If a context such as creating a poster arises through an inquiry, for example, teachers may provide examples and modelling of spelling and relevant vocabulary for learners to build into their own writing.

For younger learners, availability of resources throughout the classroom environment may provide spontaneous opportunities for learners to initiate authentic writing experiences. Drawing also plays a meaningful role in writing and, therefore, spelling. Fostering both drawing and writing can be beneficial for developing the link between oral language and written messages (Adoniou, 2014).

Presence of print in the environment

Environmental print supports young learners' understanding of the purposes of print and symbols used in written language. Specific print resources for spelling can also be provided (Figure 13.1). These could include high-frequency words, word walls, dictionaries (personal or published) and word lists relevant to topics of inquiry (Figure 13.2). Access to computers and iPads can also provide learners with tools to check their spelling or find an unfamiliar word (Westwood, 2014).

Figure 13.1 Example of visual reference for use of double consonants in a Foundation classroom

Figure 13.2 Example of high-frequency words available in the Foundation to Year 2 classroom

Explicit instruction and modelling of encoding strategies

While immersion in rich literacy experiences is valuable for spelling development, such experiences alone will not support all learners (Adoniou, 2014). Explicit instruction and modelling of spelling strategies, as well as opportunities to practise spelling, are essential in educator pedagogy (Treiman, 2018). As discussed previously in this chapter, learners need to develop an understanding of a range of knowledge areas in order to learn to spell effectively.

Research evidence suggests explicit phonics instruction supports early spelling development. Learners can also benefit from explicit instruction and modelling of morphology, etymology and rules alongside phonics in the early and later primary years (Adoniou, 2014; Devonshire & Fluck, 2010; Westwood, 2014).

Knowledge of 'spelling rules' can be helpful for the purposes of proofreading and beneficial for learners with dyslexia (Westwood, 2004). However, the use of 'spelling rules' should be approached with caution due to limited evidence that learning many different (and often complex) spelling rules is best practice. If spelling rules are taught, learners should have a strong foundation in word knowledge (Westwood, 2014).

Learning foci for teaching spelling in context across the primary years

Learning foci for teaching spelling across the primary years should continue developing the phonological, orthographic, morphemic and etymological knowledge of learners in combination with explicit strategies for spelling and continued vocabulary and oral language development.

Some examples of spelling strategies that learners can use to draw upon these knowledge bases include:

- phonetic – spelling based on the sounds in the word
- simultaneous oral spelling – verbalising letter names in sequence
- analogy – using knowledge of a similar known word to spell an unknown word
- syllabification and chunking – breaking words into syllables or chunks to assist in spelling (e.g. Wed.nes.day, fan.tas.tic)
- morphemic – drawing upon knowledge of word meanings, prefixes and suffixes
- mnemonics and memory hooks – using or creating a mnemonic or memory hook to recall tricky words
- dictionary – referring to a dictionary, word wall or other resource to check spelling
- word study – investigations into words and spelling patterns to develop knowledge of word groups that can be applied when needed (Fellowes & Oakley, 2020; Westwood, 2014).

Emergent

The focus in the emergent stage of spelling development should be on phonological and phonemic awareness, highlighting early orthographic knowledge, oral language and vocabulary development. Multisensory approaches, including visual, auditory and kinaesthetic, opportunities are effective (Westwood, 2014). Visual and visual-motor skills can be developed to enable learners to process written words effectively – for example, through colour-coding, underlining or highlighting parts of words. Handwriting is another component in spelling development because smooth, automatic handwriting can increase the focus on the letters and sounds rather than the mechanics of handwriting (Westwood, 2014) – see also Chapter 14.

Teaching phonological and phonemic awareness

Multiple approaches can be applied to the teaching of phonological and phonemic awareness as part of a balanced literacy program. A combination of engaging literacy experiences, particularly involving oral language, and purposeful explicit instruction can best support learners' development of phonological (and phonemic) awareness in the emergent stage (Tompkins et al., 2019).

As discussed in Chapters 4 and 6, appropriate emergent experiences should emphasise the connections between oral and written language in playful ways, such as through wordplay, songs and rhymes (Tompkins et al., 2019; Westwood, 2014). In addition to playful experiences, planned and intentional opportunities for explicit instruction should focus on the development of the learners' understanding of sounds in oral language (Tompkins et al., 2019).

First identifying when words rhyme (e.g. 'Sam' and 'ham') and when they do not rhyme, learners are then encouraged to produce their own rhymes by being given a word and thinking of a word that rhymes with it. Rhymes can become more complex when there are multiple syllables – for example, sta.tion, cre.a.tion; se.ri.ous, mys.te.ri.ous.

Alliteration is an important skill in phonological awareness because it assists the learner to hear and recognise similarities in the initial and final sounds in words. This is another instance where oral language development plays a role. In the initial stages of phonological development, it is important to focus on using auditory skill rather than linking with letter patterns (Hill, 2009). For example, the words 'cat' and 'Christmas' both start with the /k/ sound, even though they are spelt differently, so if sorting is by initial sounds, using the grapheme can cause confusion. Final sound alliteration is also essential to develop so that learners can distinguish between multiple sounds in words (Hill, 2009).

Understanding of onset and rime assists the learner further to distinguish between individual sounds in words, by separating the word into onset (consonant before vowel) and rime (remainder of the word) – for example, 'stamp' can be separated into onset ('st') and rime ('amp').

While there are numerous examples of programs and resources for teaching phonological awareness, some general principles may be helpful:

1. Ensure that learners have strong phonological awareness (word level knowledge), including syllables, rhyme, alliteration, onset and rime, to provide a sound foundation for further spelling skills.
2. Develop phonemic awareness (sound level knowledge) alongside phonological awareness (letter names and phonics).
3. Teach beginning sounds, and then final sounds and medial (middle) sounds.
4. Teach one or two skills at a time, beginning with short sounds and short words.
5. Be aware of the needs of individual children through informal assessment, as this will determine the pace of teaching.
6. Support learners to apply their phonological knowledge in context through their everyday reading and writing experiences.
7. Where possible, small-group instruction is most effective when explicitly teaching phonological skills (Fellowes & Oakley, 2020).

Early primary

Phonemic awareness includes the ability to manipulate sounds within words (Tompkins et al., 2019). To teach phonemic awareness, the focus should include the isolation of sounds within words, orally segmenting sounds and blending sounds as well as manipulating sounds within words (Westwood, 2014). In order to do this, key phonological skills are required, including awareness of syllables, rhyme, alliteration, onset and rime, before building the more complex skills for phonemic awareness. Table 13.5 provides a guide to some of the key terms and examples in this section.

Table 13.5 Mini-glossary: phonemic awareness

Term	Description	Examples
Sound isolation	Isolating different sounds within a word	Cat /c/ – initial sound, /t/ – final sound
Oral segmentation	Segmenting words into phonemes	Shop = /sh/, /o/, /p/ Blend = /b/, /l/, /e/, /n/, /d/
Oral blending	Blending sounds together from graphemes	/b/, /e/, /s/, /t/ = best /t/, /r/, /ee/ = tree
Sound manipulation: • Addition • Deletion • Substitution	Addition of sound to a word Deletion of a sound in a word Substituting a sound in a word with another sound	/s/ + ash = sash milk – /k/ = mil send – substitute /s/ with /b/ = bend

In the early primary years, informal assessment should be used to support the individual levels of spelling development. Learners may still be working in the emergent stage in the first years of primary school. However, moving into early primary school, there are a number of teaching strategies that can be applied. It is essential that educators continue to support learners to apply their spelling knowledge in meaningful contexts; teaching phonics alongside phonological awareness is an effective approach.

Phonics refers to the relationships between phonology and orthography, or the sounds in speech (phonemes) and written spelling patterns (graphemes). The 44 phonemes in English are represented by 26 letters and more than 500 letter combinations can represent these 44 sounds (Tompkins et al., 2019). Many individual letters will have one-to-one correspondence between grapheme and phoneme; however, phonics focuses on the spelling patterns as there are sounds that are spelt in multiple ways (Tompkins et al., 2019) – for example, the long 'a' sound (e.g. as in table) can be represented by 'a', 'ay', 'ai', 'eigh' and 'aigh'.

There is not a universally prescribed order for teaching phonics (although there are programs available that provide a scope and sequence); however, it is important to ensure that these skills are taught explicitly and practised in-context (Westwood, 2014). Initially, teaching the letter-to-sound correspondence, followed by developing the skill to blend the words, is best practice (Westwood, 2014).

As the learner continues to develop the application of simple letter-sound patterns in their spelling, more complex patterns are introduced. In early primary, consonant blends, consonant and vowel digraphs and trigraphs could be introduced. Consonant blends and digraphs (or trigraphs) can be confused. The key difference between them is the number of sounds that can be heard. A consonant blend may have multiple sounds blended together before or after a vowel (e.g. crab, strap; lamp, silk). A digraph is two graphs (or letters) that make one sound as in 'ship', and a trigraph is three graphs (letters) that make one sound as in 'hatch'. Vowel combinations would also be introduced after consonants and short vowels are established. There are many vowel combinations for both short and long sounds, including vowel digraphs (where two vowels represent one sound as in 'meet') and diphthongs (when two vowel sounds glide together – e.g. 'oi' in coin) (Hill, 2009).

It is also important to provide other strategies for spelling irregular words (e.g. 'said', 'could') to enable spelling to become automatic (using a mnemonic is one strategy that could be used). Sometimes these words are grouped as 'sight words'. 'Sight words' are intended to be learnt by 'sight' for the purpose of reading efficiency. These words are often a combination of high-frequency words and irregular words. High-frequency words are commonly occurring words in the English language (e.g. 'that', 'is'). Some of these do follow the phonics code and some are irregular (e.g. 'was', 'said'). The introduction of morphemes would typically be used in spelling development in early primary also. This might include compound words or the use of suffixes such as '-ed' and '-ing' (ACARA, 2018). Table 13.6 provides a guide to some of the key terms and examples in this section.

Table 13.6 Mini-glossary: letter-sound patterns

Term	Description	Examples
Consonant blends	2 letters = 2 sounds 3 letters = 3 sounds	/d/, /r/ as in drip /s/, /c/, /r/ as in scrap
Graph	1 letter = 1 sound	/s/ as in sit
Consonant digraph	2 consonants = 1 sound	/ch/ as in chip, /sh/ as in shop
Vowel digraph	2 vowels = 1 sound	/ai/ as in mail
Trigraph	3 letters = 1 sound	/tch/ as in hatch
Quadgraph	4 letters = 1 sound	/eigh/ as in eight
Diphthong	2 vowels in a single syllable	/oi/ as in coin

The use of single word based activities, such as word sorts, word hunts, missing letters and phoneme frames (or Elknonin boxes), are some of the many examples of how spelling may be modelled and practised explicitly. The important teaching strategy to note is that teaching spelling patterns rather than single unrelated words is likely to be most effective. Teaching irregular words one at a time may be helpful (Fellowes & Oakley, 2020; Westwood, 2014).

Mnemonics can also be used for irregular words or other words that may be confusing. The word 'said' is one that learners often want to use in their writing, but they may not yet possess the knowledge to spell it correctly. The mnemonic 'Snakes And Insects Dance' enables the learner to use the initial sounds of each word in the mnemonic and transcribe them – SAID. There are some well-known examples and learners can also be encouraged to make up their own mnemonics so that they are more meaningful.

Strategies such as these can enable learners to write independently and concentrate on the message they are trying to communicate.

Typically, by the second year of school, phonological knowledge and application through manipulation of sounds for spelling should be proficient. This is dependent on the individual learner and previous phonological learning in the early childhood years (Fellowes & Oakley, 2020). There are a number of other issues that may affect the learner's development of this knowledge, and these are discussed later in the chapter.

Later primary

In the later primary years, further focus is placed on the morphemic and etymological knowledge that underpins spelling. Many of the previously discussed teaching strategies are appropriate to continue with the content and level of this knowledge and can be developed as learners are increasingly able to make connections between base words and derivations of words. The explicit teaching of prefixes and suffixes is related to how well learners are able to apply these accurately and improve their spelling (Devonshire & Fluck, 2010).

Adoniou on teaching courageously

Breadth of vocabulary is a better predictor of students' linguistic capabilities than age is. So teaching spelling through vocabulary, and teaching vocabulary through spelling, is more relevant to planning a spelling program than being restricted by what we think an age group is capable of.

Source: Adoniou (2016, p. 65).

Misty Adoniou writes about seven-year-old learners involved in a program about resilience. Because the word 'courageous' is encountered frequently in these lessons, the learners are introduced to 'how the word's meaning is made through its spelling' (Adoniou, 2016, p. 65). They learn that 'courage' is the base word and comes originally from the French word 'coeur' (heart), thus enriching their understanding of the word. They learn that adding 'ous' turns it into an adjective describing a characteristic that resilient people might have (see Adoniou, 2016, p. 65).

Structured Word Inquiry (SWI) supports the development of spelling that goes beyond grapheme-phoneme correspondence. SWI focuses on developing understanding of words and how they are spelled, by investigating phonology, morphology and etymology in combination (Bowers & Bowers, 2017). SWI engages learners in forming and testing their own hypotheses about why words are spelled in certain ways. Learners benefit from important understandings of phoneme-grapheme correspondence but, additionally, develop understanding of the importance of meaning of words within context and the logic behind the structure of the English spelling system when learning to spell (Bowers & Bowers, 2017).

Continued vocabulary development is essential in the later primary years and, as learners develop increasing skills in reading, this can also be applied to writing. Having the strategies to draw upon and apply more advanced vocabulary is needed for proficient spelling. This is where it is important to continue explicit teaching alongside opportunities for learners to practise spelling (Tompkins et al., 2019). In addition to teaching and modelling spelling strategies, teachers should also model strategies for proofreading and editing (Westwood, 2014).

Learners may also benefit from the continued teaching and practice of generalisations for prefixes and suffixes as well as phonic generalisations for multisyllabic words (such as 'thoughtful', 'straightaway') (ACARA, 2018). Word studies can also be used to understand word origins, including Greek and Latin roots, as well as to practise building morphemic word families (Tompkins et al., 2019).

Differentiating learning

Teaching strategies must be differentiated depending on the developmental levels of each learner. The use of formative assessment to pinpoint learners' current skills and knowledge and where they can develop is not only a paramount part of the planning cycle but is also essential in differentiating the learning for individuals (Westwood, 2004).

A learner's spelling development is not necessarily linear. The range of strategies used increases with age and development, and primary learners may use multiple strategies simultaneously. When teaching spelling strategies, teachers should be monitoring whether learners are utilising strategies efficiently (Westwood, 2014). Part of the educator's role in teaching spelling is monitoring progress and providing learners with feedback on their spelling during writing opportunities. In terms of building strategies, scaffolding and feedback are most helpful during the writing experience rather than correcting work and returning it at a later time (Gentry, 1987, in Westwood, 2014).

Assessment, curriculum and diverse learning needs

Assessment

Authentic and in-context assessment within the classroom environment is considered best practice (Westwood, 2014; see also Chapter 3). The most effective and valid assessment occurs when there is a focus on collecting evidence of the learner's development through what they do, say, make and write (Department of Education, Employment and Workplace Relations [DEEWR], 2009; Griffin, 2020). Spelling can too often be seen as something that is 'tested' rather than emphasised as assessed in the context of communicating a message (Alderman & Green, 2011).

The teacher's observation and analysis of the learner's writing is the most effective way to assess progress. Spelling tests can place pressure on learners, encourage rote learning for short periods of time and devalue the importance of knowing how to spell words in the context of a written message. When a developmental approach to assessment is taken, it allows for the teacher to focus on each learner's developmental level (Griffin, 2020).

316 ENGLISH AND LITERACIES

CASE STUDY 13.1 — Spelling development in a Year 3 learner

Hannah is in Year 3 and has found the transition from Year 2 to Year 3 very challenging. Her parents are concerned, particularly, about her writing development. They express to the teacher that Hannah's spelling is not where it should be and request that she be provided with a list of words every week that she will be tested on in class.

Questions

1. Reflect on this situation. What information might the teacher need to best advise Hannah's parents?
2. Reflect on the idea of providing word lists to test in class. Based on your understanding of best practice, what do you need to consider?

Regular assessment is essential for individual learning as well as for identifying learners experiencing difficulties in order to provide early intervention (Westwood, 2014). While there may be times when a more formal approach is needed to quickly identify areas for target intervention, the most useful tool for the classroom teacher is formative assessment. As such, informal everyday writing samples can provide the most valuable evidence of spelling strategies used by the learner (Westwood, 2014). It is important that when assessing writing samples, teachers are analysing the errors made rather than focusing on a score or whether a word is correct or incorrect (Moats, 2014).

Curriculum links

When viewing the two national curriculum frameworks in relation to spelling, the links to skill development are less explicit than in other areas of literacy. They are integrated within learning and communication outcomes and phonics and word knowledge, which, given the interrelation between these skills, is appropriate.

The Early Years Learning Framework (EYLF) focuses on the transfer of learning from one context to another. As learners begin developing phonological knowledge and understanding symbols and patterns in early childhood, the EYLF plays an important role in this learning continuum. The pedagogical practice outlined in the EYLF aligns with the approach of spelling in context (DEEWR, 2009). Precursors to spelling, including oral language development, phonological and phonemic awareness, understanding of print and that writing contains meaning, are experienced through meaningful and authentic experiences and interactions.

These skills are addressed in the EYLF across a number of learning outcomes. A particular focus is Outcome 5. Some examples of links are provided in Table 13.7.

Table 13.7 Early spelling development – links to the EYLF

Outcome	Examples of specific links to early spelling development
Outcome 5: Children are effective communicators	• Children interact verbally and non-verbally with others for a range of purposes • Children engage in a range of texts and gain meaning from these texts • Children express ideas and make meaning using a range of media • Children begin to understand how symbols and pattern systems work

Source: DEEWR (2009).

The Australian Curriculum highlights the role of phonics and word knowledge in relation to reading, spelling and oral language. The curriculum outlines the development of skills over time, including in the following areas:

- rhyming words, alliteration, syllables and phonemes
- letter-sound correspondence with increasing letter pattern complexity
- onset and rime, phoneme manipulation
- high-frequency words
- morphemic knowledge, including base words, prefixes, suffixes and units of meaning
- homophones and spelling generalisations
- word origins (ACARA, 2018).

Diverse learning needs

Acknowledging the well-established links between oral language and spelling means there will be a number of language-based considerations when planning for and supporting the range of learners in any classroom. These considerations include age, cultural, ethnic and linguistic backgrounds, developmental levels, English as additional language/dialect (EAL/D) learners and Aboriginal and Torres Strait Islander learners.

Additionally, some learning difficulties or disabilities can affect the development of phonological knowledge. Language and auditory issues may have longer-term effects on spelling development. These effects might include articulation disorders (such as cleft palate), expressive and/or receptive language developmental delays, autism spectrum disorder (ASD), auditory processing issues and developmental coordination disorder (DCD) or dyspraxia, which can affect speech as well as physical movement (Devine & Devine, 2015).

It is of particular importance to note that supporting learners with additional needs can often be a case of using effective assessment, differentiated curriculum and quality teaching. In cases of specific language impairment (SLI), research has shown that learners can acquire spelling skills, but this will be at a slower rate than their peers (Cordewener et al., 2012). It has been suggested that this may be due to learners acquiring the prerequisite literacy skills at a slower rate (e.g. oral language development), but also that they may not be receiving effective instruction (Cordewener et al., 2012).

Specific learning disability (SLD) can be highlighted in spelling development. A learner may have developmentally appropriate (or above-average to superior) language development but still find reading, writing and spelling very challenging (Devine & Devine, 2015). Due to the link between handwriting and spelling development, spelling difficulties may be the result of a number of learning difficulties and/or additional needs that can affect handwriting, including attention deficit hyperactivity disorder, ASD and dyspraxia (McCloskey & Rapp, 2017; Prunty & Barnett, 2017; Westwood, 2004).

Ongoing spelling issues may require further support for learners to equitably access learning opportunities. The use of assistive technology, such as keyboarding and voice-to-text options, may be useful tools across age groups (Stevenson & Just, 2014). The use of computer software for spell checking may also be helpful for learners in the later primary years to enable writing composition.

CASE STUDY 13.2 | **Spelling development in a learner diagnosed with a hearing impairment**

Jordan is a learner in Year 1 with a hearing impairment. His family have provided information from his specialists that he experiences 40 per cent hearing loss, which has affected his receptive and expressive language development. Jordan communicates confidently with peers, but some pronunciation issues are evident and his vocabulary development is not at the same level as his peers. Jordan appears to follow instructions and he has also learnt to take cues from others to make sure he keeps up with the rest of the class.

Questions

1. Consider the impact that Jordan's hearing impairment might have specifically on his spelling development, particularly in the first three years of school.
2. Reflect on whether there is additional knowledge you need to seek to provide equitable learning opportunities for Jordan. Would it be beneficial to conduct some in-classroom assessment with Jordan?
3. As a teacher, how would you support Jordan's access to the curriculum in your classroom?

Conclusion

After briefly exploring a number of theories to assist in understanding the complexities of spelling acquisition, this chapter highlighted the importance of spelling development and the key components involved in this. Despite the variance in theories, a typical development of spelling can be seen in the preschool and primary years where learners draw upon their oral language skills and make connections between reading and handwriting skills to develop their spelling.

With all the different terminology used to describe spelling development, teaching spelling may seem daunting. While phonological, orthographic, morphemic and etymological are the key knowledge areas, there are many other important skills and understandings that sit beneath these. Understanding the needs of individual learners through observation and assessment is key in selecting appropriate teaching strategies and approaches.

Bringing it together

1. How does spelling interrelate with other areas of literacy learning?
2. What are the key spelling strategies to support children to develop?
3. Consider what challenges might arise when assessing spelling development in the first years of school.
4. Consider the following scenario. You are teaching in a Year 2 classroom and you are concerned that your learners are displaying a high number of spelling errors in their writing. What steps might you need to take in order to best support them?
5. You are preparing to work with a small group of Year 5 learners, specifically targeting their spelling development. Consider what information you might need to collect and what approaches to teaching you would adopt.

Further resources

Literacy Teaching Toolkit: Phonics (emergent literacy)

This website provides descriptions and resources on the use of phonics, particularly in the emergent/early primary stage. There are downloadable materials, including a summary of basic phonics patterns (graphemes).

www.education.vic.gov.au/childhood/professionals/learning/ecliteracy/emergentliteracy/Pages/phonics.aspx

Spelling It Out

This book provides an excellent discussion of teaching spelling and includes a range of valuable resources. See particularly Appendix 2 Common English morphemes (p. 101); Appendix 3 Ways into words (p. 111); and Appendix 4 Spelling scope and sequence (p. 129).

Adoniou, M. (2016). *Spelling It Out: How Words Work and How to Teach Them*. Cambridge University Press.

Spelling – International Dyslexia Association

This factsheet provides an overview of the commonality of spelling difficulties with information on appropriate accommodations that might be made for learners with dyslexia.

https://dyslexiaida.org/spelling

What should teachers know about spelling?

This article provides some clear examples of how to support phonological, morphemic, orthographic and etymological strategies through prompting questions.

Adoniou, M. (2014). What should teachers know about spelling? *Literacy*, 48(3), 144–154.

References

Adoniou, M. (2014). What should teachers know about spelling? *Literacy*, 48(3), 144–154.

—— (2016). *Spelling It Out: How Words Work and How to Teach Them*. Cambridge University Press.

Alderman, G.L. & Green, S.K. (2011). Fostering lifelong spellers through meaningful experiences. *The Reading Teacher*, 64(8), 599–605. doi:10.1598/RT.64.8.5

Australian Curriculum, Assessment and Reporting Authority (ACARA). (2018). *The Australian Curriculum: English: Version 8.3*. ACARA. www.australiancurriculum.edu.au/english/pdf-documents

Boardman, K. (2020). An exploration of teachers' perceptions and value of multisensory teaching and learning: a perspective on the influence of specialist dyslexia training in England. *Education*, 48(7), 795–806. doi:10.1080/03004279.2019.1653349

Bowers, J.S. & Bowers, P.N. (2017). Beyond phonics: the case for teaching children the logic of the English spelling system. *Educational Psychologist*, 52(2), 124–141. doi:10.1080/00461520.2017.1288571

Cordewener, K.A.H., Bosman, A.M.T., & Verhoeven, L. (2012). Specific language impairments affects the early spelling process quantitatively but not qualitatively. *Research in Developmental Disabilities*, 33, 1041–1047.

Daffern, T. (2017). Linguistic skills involved in learning to spell: an Australian study. *Language and Education*, 31(4), 307–329. doi:10.1080/09500782.2017.1296855

Department of Education, Employment and Workplace Relations (DEEWR). (2009). *Belonging, Being & Becoming – The Early Years Learning Framework for Australia*. https://docs.education.gov.au/documents/belonging-being-becoming-early-years-learning-framework-australia

Devine, A. & Devine, Q. (2015). *Literacy for Visual Learners: Teaching Children with Learning Differences to Read, Write, Communicate and Create*. Jennifer Kingsley Publishers.

Devonshire, V. & Fluck, M. (2010). Spelling development: fine-tuning strategy-use and capitalizing on the connections between words. *Learning and Instruction*, 20, 361–371. doi:10.1016/j.learninstruc.2009.02.025

Ehri, L.C. (2014). Orthographic mapping in the acquisition of sight word reading, spelling memory, and vocabulary learning. *Scientific Studies of Reading*, 18(1), 5–21. doi:10.1080/10888438.2013.819356

Fellowes, J. & Oakley, G. (2020). *Language, Literacy and Early Childhood Education*. Oxford University Press.

Graham, S. & Santangelo, T. (2014). Does spelling instruction make students better spellers, readers and writers? A meta-analytic review. *Reading and Writing: An Interdisciplinary Journal*, 27, 1703–1743. doi:10.1007/s11145-014-9517-0

Griffin, P. (Ed.). (2020). *Assessment for Teaching* (2nd edn). Cambridge University Press.

Hill, S. (2009). *Developing Early Literacy: Assessment and Teaching*. Eleanor Curtain Publishing.

International Dyslexia Association. (2008). *Spelling*. IDA Information Services Committee.

Mackenzie, N. & Hemmings, B. (2014). Predictors of success with writing in the first year of school. *Issues in Educational Research*, 24(1), 41–55.

Mann, T.B., Bushell, D., & Morris, E.K. (2010). Use of sounding out to improve spelling in young children. *Journal of Applied Behaviour Analysis*, 43 (1), 89–93.

McCloskey, M. & Rapp, B. (2017). Developmental dysgraphia: an overview and framework for research. *Cognitive Neuropsychology*, 34(3–4), 65–82.

Moats, L. (2014). What teachers don't know and why they aren't learning it: addressing the need for content and pedagogy in teacher education. *Australian Journal of Learning Difficulties*, 19, 75–91. doi:10.1080/19404158.2014.941093

Prunty, M. & Barnett, A.L. (2017). Understanding handwriting difficulties: a comparison of children with and without motor impairment. *Cognitive Neuropsychology*, 24(3–4), 205–218. doi:10.1080/02643294.2017.1376630

Puranik, C.S., Lonigan, C.J., & Kim, Y.S. (2011). Contributions of emergent literacy skills to name writing, letter writing and spelling in preschool children. *Early Childhood Research Quarterly*, 26(4), 465–474.

Rosenthal, J. & Ehri, L.C. (2011). Pronouncing new words aloud during the silent reading of text enhances fifth graders' memory for vocabulary words and their spellings. *Reading and Writing*, 24, 921–950.

Stevenson, N.C. & Just, C. (2014). In early education, why teach handwriting before keyboarding? *Early Childhood Education Journal*, 42, 49–56. doi:10.1007/s10643-012-0565-2

Tompkins, G., Smith, C., Campbell, R., & Green, D. (2019). *Literacy for the 21st Century: A Balanced Approach*. Pearson Education.

Treiman, R. (2017a). Learning to spell words: findings, theories and issues. *Scientific Studies of Reading*, 21(4), 265–276. doi:10.1080/10888438.2017.1296449

—— (2017b). Learning to spell: phonology and beyond. *Cognitive Neuropsychology*, 34(3–4), 83–93.

—— (2018). Teaching and learning spelling. *Child Development Perspectives*, 12(4), 235–239.

Westwood, P. (2004). *Learning and Learning Difficulties: Approaches to Teaching and Assessment*. Taylor & Francis Group, ProQuest Ebook Central. https://ebookcentral.proquest.com/lib/unimelb/detail. action?docID=652956

—— (2014). *Teaching Spelling: Exploring Commonsense Strategies and Best Practices*. Taylor & Francis Group.

—— (2015). Spelling: do the eyes have it? *Australian Journal of Learning Difficulties*, 20(1), 3–13. doi:10. 1080/19404158.2014.921632

—— (2018). Learning to spell: enduring theories, recent research and current issues. *Australian Journal of Learning Difficulties*, 23(2), 137–152. doi:10.1080/19404158.2018.1524391

CHAPTER 14

Publishing texts
Developing handwriting and keyboarding skills

Lucy Stewart

ANTICIPATED OUTCOMES

After working through this chapter, it is anticipated you will be able to:

- reflect on a brief history of handwriting and the transition to digital technology
- understand typical development of handwriting in the preschool and primary years and the interrelationships between handwriting, keyboarding, oral language and reading
- understand the complex cognitive and physical (or mechanical) developments required in handwriting and keyboarding to be able to produce text successfully
- reflect on the role of keyboarding skills in handwriting development
- describe key approaches to teaching handwriting and keyboarding in the primary learning environment
- identify needs of learners and integrate teaching strategies to support the physical and cognitive skills for handwriting and keyboarding
- explain key curriculum, assessment and differentiation approaches to teaching and learning handwriting and keyboarding instruction.

Introduction

Two decades into the new millennium, the world is changing and evolving faster than ever before. Through digital technology, we have unprecedented access to information and the ability to communicate with others literally at our fingertips through the use of keyboards. Handwritten words have become predominantly typed or even completely replaced by emojis. This chapter focuses on the development of handwriting and keyboarding as a means to express ideas in written form.

The chapter provides a brief history of handwriting development from ancient Egyptian hieroglyphics through to the role of technology and the relevance of handwriting in education in the twenty-first century. An introduction is given to the typical development of handwriting in the preschool and primary years, as well as the critical interrelationships that exist between oral language, reading and handwriting and keyboarding development. The cognitive and physical components involved to support the teaching of handwriting are also discussed. This is followed by key approaches and teaching strategies to support handwriting development. Finally, the chapter examines curriculum and assessment approaches and how the diverse needs of any classroom can be supported through differentiation.

A brief history of handwriting

Some of the earliest examples of writing are ancient Egyptian hieroglyphics. These symbols evolved over time, developing into two cursive forms of writing. The development of these writing systems not only added efficiency to communication but also enabled the discovery of the equivalent of a 'phoneme'. As described in earlier chapters, a phoneme is the smallest unit of sound and is an essential component in spoken and written English language today. 'The invention of writing, which occurred independently in distant parts of the world at many times, even occasionally in the modern era, must rank among mankind's highest intellectual achievements. Without writing, human culture as we know it today is inconceivable' (Tzeng & Wang, 1983, in Wolf, 2008, p. 24).

Maryanne Wolf (2008), in her book *Proust and the Squid*, explores the impact of reading and writing in relation to the systems within the human brain. As part of this, she investigates the history of written language systems from ancient Egypt to the twenty-first century in which, interestingly, we can draw distinct parallels between ancient times and today.

While other cultures continued to develop written language systems, not all were in favour of this human endeavour. Ancient Greek philosopher and teacher, Socrates, vehemently opposed the use of a written language system for fear of the loss of oracy and ways of learning. He believed in the internationalisation of knowledge through the spoken word in conversation, questioning and debate with others. Socrates expressed particular concern about the roles that written words and oral language play in the intellectual life of an individual (Wolf, 2008). He 'passionately advocated for the unique role that oral language plays in the development of morality and virtue in society' (Wolf, 2008, p. 72), perhaps believing that this new written system would endanger the passing on of values and culture between generations.

Fast forward to the twentieth century, and Russian psychologist Lev Vygotsky agreed with Socrates so far as the vital role that social interactions play in the development of language. Vygotsky also observed, however, the value in the process of writing in the development of one's thinking and 'the dialogic capacity of written language' (Wolf, 2008, p. 73).

Travelling further forward to the current day, we see a twenty-first-century society that places value on literacy, although this raises issues of equity for those who do not have access to the written word, whether through barriers of culture, education or disability. What might this imply for learners with dyslexia, for example – are those who cannot read and write not valued members of society?

In a modern-day Australian context, there is also the question of the survival of languages without written form. If a language is not used or recorded, how does it survive? We are seeing the devastating loss of culture and history through the extinction of many Indigenous languages in Australia, further highlighting the role of written language in culture and society.

CASE STUDY 14.1 — The loss of spoken Indigenous languages in Australia

At the time of European settlement in Australia in 1788, over 250 Indigenous Australian languages were spoken. Approximately 160 of these languages are reported to now be spoken and only 13 languages are still acquired by children (Simpson, 2019).

When a language is only (or predominantly) spoken, it is at risk of being lost. An example of this occurred in 2002, when Big Bill Neidjie AO, a Gagadju man, passed away. Bill Neidjie was an activist and advocate for conservation of traditional lands and was heavily involved in the establishment of Kakadu National Park. Bill Neidjie was also the last speaker of the Gadju language. When he passed away, the Gadju language passed away with him (Glynn-McDonald, 2021).

Questions

1. What insight does this information give us about the role of written language systems in perpetuating languages?
2. How might the emphasis on written language systems advantage or disadvantage some cultures?

Wolf (2008) made the observation that Socrates' concerns around the transition from oral to written language mirrored concerns of her own regarding the transition of language to the digital world. Perhaps it is still early days – we are the 'Socrates' of the twenty-first century, venturing into the digital world and unsure about how these new modes of communication will impact upon our knowledge, learning and connections with others. This brings our attention to twenty-first-century learners and the important question: in this digital age, is teaching handwriting still relevant?

Transition to digital technology

The positions of Socrates and Vygotsky are echoed in contemporary literature. Some research suggests that the integration of technology into learning attracts more learners to engaging in writing tasks, while other research suggests that technology interrupts class discussion and student learning (Feng et al., 2019, p. 36). Digital technology is an unavoidable aspect of our daily lives and preparing learners with the skills needed to be successful in using this technology is the prerogative of teachers.

This raises the question of whether handwriting should be a focus in primary teaching, or should the focus shift more to keyboarding as the dominant means to communicate written messages?

REFLECTION

1. What are your thoughts on the impact of written language in relation to equity, social justice and preservation of culture?
2. What are your views on the transition to digital technology? Have you already seen the impact of this in your teaching or on your learners?

Development of writing and handwriting in young learners

The development of handwriting and writing is intertwined for young learners and, as such, they are explored concurrently in this section. Of particular note is the relevance of handwriting in an increasingly digital world and understanding the benefits of handwriting development in the learning of young writers.

Benefits of handwriting in twenty-first-century primary education

Despite the shift towards the use of digital devices, it is essential to consider the role of handwriting in a learner's development. Early handwriting skills have been shown to not only predict school readiness, academic success and writing competency, but they also play a role in the development of specific literacy skills (Daffern et al., 2017). Recent research indicates that the act of handwriting can promote reading, letter recognition, spelling and writing performance (Kiefer et al., 2015).

The benefits of handwriting include the following:

- Handwriting is related to academic achievement and success in school – research has shown that the ability to write in an 'automatic and legible form' (Daffern et al., 2017, p. 78) in the early years of school is a predictor of later writing competency. This may be due to handwriting automaticity enabling the learner to focus more on the planning components of writing rather than the mechanics (Daffern et al., 2017; Medwell & Wray, 2014).

- Handwriting supports the development of letter recognition and memorisation. The kinaesthetic nature of physically forming letters by hand assists the learner in developing automaticity and making letter-sound connections (Longcamp et al., 2005). Motor memory assists in the automaticity of letter formation (through handwriting) (Stevenson & Just, 2014).
- The ability to write one's own name is not only a valuable part of a learner's identity and independence but is also is a predictor of early writing success (Daffern et al., 2017).
- Conversely, poor or illegible handwriting can sometimes correlate with difficulties in spelling and story composition as well as poor self-esteem, lower academic achievement and behavioural problems (Feder & Majnemer, 2007; Feng et al., 2019).

Understanding of purpose in handwriting development

An essential aspect of handwriting and writing development is the understanding of the purpose of writing. To develop this, young learners are exposed to many forms of language from birth. Written language forms will be present in children's environments, including in storybooks, writing in the home and **environmental print** in the community, such as street signs, posters and advertising. Understanding the purpose of writing as communication is fundamental to a learner's development of handwriting as they progress from mark-making to producing letters and words.

Communication that is authentic and meaningful will also support this understanding. 'Writing should be meaningful to children, that an intrinsic need should be aroused in them, and that writing should be incorporated into a task that is necessary and relevant for life' (Vygotsky, 1978, p. 118, in Hill, 2009, p. 298). A learner's name is the perfect starting place for this understanding. A name is meaningful and important for the individual's sense of identity and also to indicate objects and work that belong to them (Raban, 2018).

> **Environmental print:** print (including letters and symbols) in the environment; some examples include house numbers, street signs and logos on advertisements.

Interrelationships between handwriting, writing, oral language and reading

While the focus of this chapter is handwriting and keyboarding, it is necessary to highlight the interrelationships that exist in literacy development, in particular, oral language, reading and writing, as discussed in earlier chapters. Handwriting development is also important for writing development in order for the writer's message to be legible and therefore understood by others.

Oral language

Oral language development supports a learner's ability to understand the grammatical structures and sounds of language as well as vocabulary. Oral language enables learners to communicate their ideas, understand the spoken words of others and is foundational in literacy learning (Dickinson et al., 2010).

Children need to listen to their own speech to work out the sounds they need to write. They then need to find the letters to represent these sounds (Clay, 2005). Oral language also supports the communication of ideas, such as planning written texts (Hill, 2009). This allows learners to share their ideas, provide explanations to accompany their drawings, verbally plan what they will write and create their own stories (Mackenzie & Hemmings, 2014).

Reading

Both reading and writing require the ability to organise and generate ideas, monitor thoughts and problem-solve (Morrow, 2005, p. 205). Broadly speaking, they both involve language, visual information, sound sequence information, word knowledge, composition and motor control to produce symbols (Clay, 2005).

Some examples of specific elements shared by reading and writing include:

- understanding of directionality – moving in a left-to-right direction in English (directionality differs in some other languages – for example, Arabic is written right to left (Department of Education and Training [DET], 2018))
- ability to draw upon language stored in the memory – for example, known words and structures of language
- recognition and creation of visual symbols
- use of visual and sound information together (also known as *graphophonic knowledge* or *graphophonic awareness*)
- ability to hold messages in the mind
- searching, checking and correcting skills (Clay, 2005, p. 20; Kenner, 2004).

Reading and writing also overlap in relation to their purpose – we use both these skills to construct meaning. Writers construct texts to convey their messages, and readers understand meaning by comprehending what has been read (Bromley, 2003, in Morrow, 2005).

Writing

Writing involves a number of processes. Handwriting plays an important role in enabling the writer's message to be legible and therefore understood by others. The early stages of writing development, in particular, evolve concurrently with handwriting development. Children's early understanding of the principles of writing are demonstrated through the marks they make in their developing handwriting.

Stages of early handwriting and writing development

Writing is not only a skill for academic success – it is also an important method of communication. As discussed previously, the understanding of purpose and the ways that language can be used through oral language, reading and writing is necessary, but we also need to consider how writing and handwriting develop. There are a number of different ways of viewing this.

Understandings for early writing

In order to develop the skills and knowledge needed for writing words, learners must develop understanding of the **concepts and conventions of print**. They need to develop

Concepts and conventions of print: the rules of written language, such as direction of print, that enable readers and writers to follow the same system when interacting with text.

graphophonic awareness and have an understanding that letters must be formed a certain way so that they can be understood when read by others (Raban, 2018). Raban (2018) outlined a number of 'writing components' that support early writing development in the early years, including writing as composition, written language versus spoken language, concepts about print and handwriting. These components are interrelated – the first three components are addressed in other chapters. This chapter, however, focuses on handwriting development.

Principles of early writing

Marie Clay (in Hill, 2009) outlined a number of principles of early writing that learners develop in the early writing stages. Some of these include:

- recurring principle – use of repetitive squiggles and lines ('scribbling')
- sign principle – understanding that letters and symbols stand for something, including understanding that a picture is different to a printed word (e.g. the word 'cat' versus an image of a cat – see the example in Figure 14.1)
- flexibility principle – understanding that some symbols are letters and some are not (they might be numbers or mathematical symbols) and that the same letter can be written in different ways (e.g. upper case and lower case letters and different fonts)
- linear principle – this relates to the directionality of writing (in English, language is written left to right in lines across the page, followed by a return sweep)
- spaces between words – understanding that spaces signify the end of one word and the beginning of another.

Figure 14.1 The sign principle

Handwriting development

Later in this chapter, we explore further the physical and cognitive elements of handwriting. First, we provide a broad trajectory of typical handwriting development. Typical handwriting can often be seen to develop in the following way:

- early scribbling with increasing intentionality
- evolving patterns, increasing precision of shapes and then letters
- letter shapes evident in drawings
- print letters by imitation first using vertical strokes, followed by horizontal strokes and then circles
- copying or imitating the shape of a cross
- geometric shape copying – a square and then a circle (this is usually seen in the learner's first year of school) (Feder & Majnemer, 2007).

Stages of writing

There are some features that can be observed in the development of writing, as outlined in Table 14.1. Learners may demonstrate these features concurrently and not necessarily sequentially.

14 PUBLISHING TEXTS: DEVELOPING HANDWRITING AND KEYBOARDING SKILLS 329

Table 14.1 Stages of writing development

Stage	Features	Example
Beginning writing	In the beginning writing stage, drawings begin to communicate a message. Circles or scribbles, numbers and letter-like shapes may be observed.	
Early-emergent writing	Further exploration of the use of symbols to represent words can be observed in the early-emergent writing stage. This can include drawings or letters, and there may be some separation of the drawing and the letter symbols. This is a sign of development as this shows the beginning of 'labelling' images with text.	 'My family' – Claudia, aged 4
Emergent writing	As writing continues to develop, more letter-like shapes can be seen, spaces may be evident between letters and there is some letter-sound correlation. Print begins to show directionality.	

Table 14.1 (cont.)

Stage	Features	Example
Early writing	Early writers will increasingly use invented spelling (or phonetic spelling). A letter may represent a syllable and the use of repeated words, phrases and sentences may be evident. Learners will use upper case and lower case letters and spacing becomes more consistent.	
Transitional writing	Transitional writers demonstrate an increased volume of writing, punctuation is well developed and there is still some repetition as the focus can be on producing more writing.	
Extending writing	In the extending stage, punctuation and writing becomes 'adult-like'. Learners use different text types are dependent on audience and spelling becomes more accurate.	

Source: Developed from Hill (2009).

Understanding the mechanics of handwriting and keyboarding

Handwriting is a complex task that requires the use of fine and gross motor skills in combination with cognitive functions (Feng et al., 2019). Medwell and Wray (2014) described the process of developing handwriting as training the hand and kinaesthetic memory to work together.

There are two components of effective handwriting – fluency and legibility (Feng et al., 2019). *Fluency* refers to the speed with which the letters are formed and *legibility* is the accuracy of the formation of the letters. The 'quality' of handwriting in this sense may also impact on the learner's quality of writing overall (Feng et al., 2019).

It is important for handwriting skills to be explicitly taught and practised because inefficient handwriting may contribute to legibility issues, slow handwriting speed and fatigue or pain during writing (Duiser et al., 2020). Just as handwriting can support writing development, inefficient handwriting can contribute to writing difficulties (Feng et al., 2019).

We have seen what writing and handwriting development look like and how they typically develop. Now we turn to the cognitive and physical processes involved in handwriting development.

Cognitive development

While the act of handwriting can be both cognitively and physically taxing, the physical and cognitive skills must become integrated over time to develop handwriting automaticity. This enables the writer to focus on the substance of what they are writing. A number of cognitive processes are involved in the development of handwriting. One key process is memory.

Medwell and Wray (2014) suggest that we rely on orthographic and memory processes, also known as the ability to recall letter shapes, in order to construct written language. The hand and the memory work together to produce letters and words. The more automatic these memory processes are, the more attention can be devoted to the generation of written ideas (Medwell & Wray, 2014).

Van Galen (1991, in Prunty & Barnett, 2017) highlighted that attention and language were the highest cognitive functions involved in the writing process. This includes 'activation of the intention to write' and the 'semantic retrieval and syntactical construction' of language. This then moves to the process of spelling, including orthographic representation or phoneme-to-grapheme mapping (Prunty & Barnett, 2017, p. 205) – see also Chapter 13.

The brain relies on the working memory to be able to undertake writing. Working memory acts as a short-term storage facility in the brain. It stores information temporarily in order to carry out the processes of planning, handwriting and reviewing compositions (Medwell et al., 2009). If young learners are utilising their working memory primarily to control handwriting, and this may slow down the processes for producing written work, so automaticity of handwriting is essential in supporting overall writing development.

Physical development

The ability to hold a pencil using tripod grip and to control the fine motor movements of the hand required to write are developed during the early childhood years and continue to be consolidated during the first years of school. The motor proficiency required to master the skill of writing includes development of the upper body, specifically the whole arm to provide controlled movement, strength in the whole hand and the use of pincher or pincer movements to enable learners to hold and control writing equipment using a tripod grip (Huffman & Fortenberry, 2011).

It is important in the early years to continue providing opportunities for strengthening the larger muscles of the arms and hands as well as fine motor movements of the fingers. This is necessary to enable the strength, dexterity and control required to manipulate mark-making equipment and to write (Raban, 2018). The developed strength and control of the hand and fingers supports pincer and pincher grip, useful for gripping pencils and pens (Huffman & Fortenberry, 2011). Further, Mackenzie and Spokes (2018b) suggest that:

> Appropriate pencil grasp allows for writing that does not put stress on the hand, arm or shoulder. The creative process of drawing is an important form of expression in its own right, but is also supportive of writing as meaning making, and provides practice in many of the physical and planning skills needed for handwriting. (p. 17)

In order to develop handwriting fluency, it is important for learners to develop the fine motor skills, pencil grip, body positioning and features of letter formation to enable efficient and legible writing, as outlined here and in Figure 14.2:

- mastering the fine motor strength and dexterity to create the lines, shapes, loops and curves to form the upper and lower case letters of the alphabet
- tripod grip – holding the pencil between the thumb and forefinger, the rest of the fingers bent with the pencil resting on them
- body positioning – straight posture with feet flat on the ground, positioning of the hand and arm in relation to the paper
- letter formation – forming upper and lower case letters legibly using correct entry and exit points, directionality of strokes.

The role of keyboarding skills in handwriting development

The use of technology may assist learners who are having physical difficulties with handwriting. Handwriting and keyboarding skills both require the cognitive ability and skill to retrieve information, specifically appropriate letters, and hold them in the memory (Feng et al., 2019). Learners need to be able to develop muscle memory for the motor sequences required to integrate visual and kinaesthetic feedback to produce writing using a keyboard. The more automatic the process of keyboarding, the more the writer is able to focus on the composition rather than the mechanics of typing (Donica et al., 2018). While this skill becomes more useful as learners progress through the school years, it may also be an option for struggling writers.

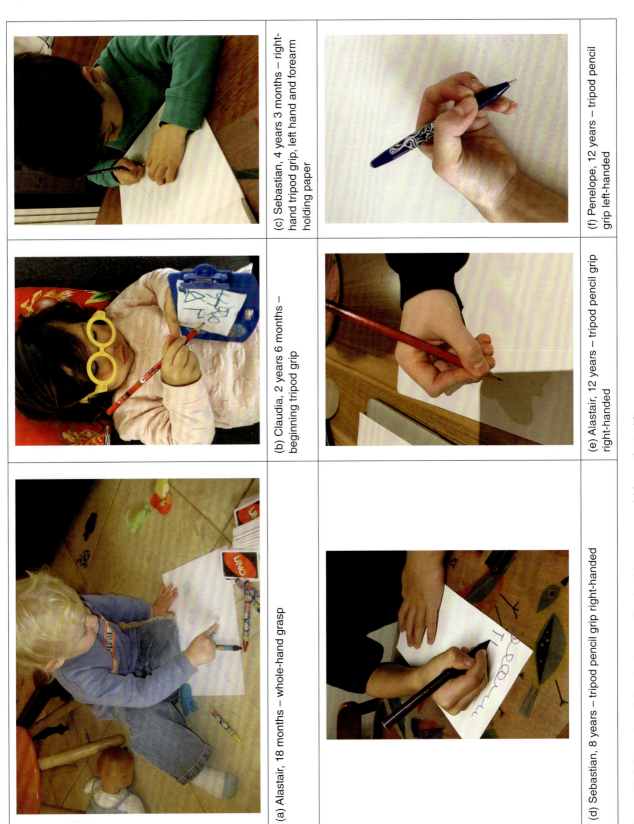

Figure 14.2 Examples of developing pencil grip of learners aged 18 months to 12 years

It should also be noted that many of the motor and visual spatial skills required by handwriting can be applied to the development of keyboarding skills (Mackenzie & Spokes, 2018a). Research support for teaching keyboarding in the early years of primary school has not yet shown the same benefits of handwriting in relation to the development of other literacy skills (Mackenzie & Spokes, 2018a).

In the future, keyboarding (or another form of technology) may become dominant in the classroom, but currently many people use a combination of handwriting and keyboarding, choosing the best tool for the purpose of the task. Learners may have access to keyboards in the home environment and they can be a valuable assistive tool or used as a means for engaging reluctant writers (Mackenzie & Spokes, 2018a). However, before introducing explicit keyboarding instruction, teachers should be mindful of:

- the skills required for keyboarding
- equitable access to keyboard use
- the size of learners' hands as a limitation to effective keyboarding
- appropriateness of programs available for teaching effective keyboarding skills through repetition and correct finger and hand placement.

Key approaches to teaching and learning handwriting and keyboarding in the primary years

Handwriting instruction should be implemented by all educators in the primary learning environment from Foundation to Year 6 (Mackenzie & Spokes, 2018b). The Australian Curriculum includes elements of handwriting development from Foundation, where the focus is on pencil grip, posture and letter formation, to Year 6, when learners should 'develop a handwriting style that is legible, fluent and automatic and varies according to audience and purpose' (Australian Curriculum, Assessment and Reporting Authority [ACARA], 2018). In order for learners to develop the fundamental skills to support handwriting development, a range of approaches can be considered by teachers across the primary years.

Play and multisensory learning

Play can provide valuable and meaningful learning opportunities. Children learn through exploration of their environment by using their senses, navigating their bodies in space and manipulating objects. Earlier in the chapter, we saw the importance of handwriting in providing a kinaesthetic mode for developing other literacy skills; play and multisensory learning opportunities are foundational in this development (Mackenzie & Spokes, 2018b).

Play is a vehicle to experiment, practise, pretend and imagine. Learners can climb, jump, throw and run to develop their larger muscles. They can manipulate objects and tools, paint, engage in sensory play and build towers to develop their fine motor skills. Through dramatic play or role play, they can pretend they are in an office, mimicking adults writing things down and talking on the phone. It is through these types of authentic and engaging playful experiences that young children develop the skills required for writing and begin exploring mark-making, drawing and writing in the early childhood years.

In addition to fine motor development, literacy-rich play provides opportunities for learners to build connections with oral language and written language. Dramatic play with peers allows children to experiment with narrative and provides opportunities for language use, including using longer sentences and more complex syntax (Hill, 2009).

Fine and gross motor development

The development of fine motor skills enables effective mark-making, drawing and writing so that messages are legible to others. While many of these skills will be developed in the early childhood years, it is important to continue to cater for the differing needs of learners, as well as the continued refinement of these skills in the later primary years.

When considering the development of fine motor skills, learning experiences and materials should be provided with the intention of not only building strength in the small muscles of the fingers but also in the larger muscles of the hands and arms. Providing authentic indoor and outdoor experiences, such as dramatic play areas, opportunities for art and design and use of manipulatives and sensory materials, is effective in engaging learners (see Table 14.2).

Table 14.2 Examples of learning experiences to develop core skills needed for handwriting development

Core skill development	Learning experience examples
Upper body and whole arm	• Outdoor play experiences (e.g. catching and throwing a ball, climbing equipment, digging in the sandpit) • Large paintings on easels or murals
Whole hand	• Materials for grasping, squeezing movements, providing some resistance • Playdough, slime, kinetic sand
Pincher grip (pressing forefinger and thumb together in a 'pinching' movement)	• Experiences that involve small objects to pick up and put down • Threading beads, manipulating small objects (e.g. animals in play) • Collecting small items in the environment
Pincer grip (pressing the thumb together with forefinger and middle finger) – particularly important in enabling tripod grip	• Picking up small items with tweezers or tongs • Using pegs, connecting blocks and manipulatives • Possibly using scissors

Drawing to writing

The process of drawing is an 'important form of creative expression and meaning making in its own right' (Mackenzie & Spokes, 2018b, p. 17). The development of writing through drawing aligns with the interrelationship between oral language and handwriting. Drawing allows learners to 'write' their ideas through an already developed skill (drawing) as well as providing stimulus for communicating these ideas verbally. The use of drawing provides a vital link to the use of conventional written language (Mackenzie & Veresov, 2013).

However, it is important not to dismiss drawing as transitional or as a stepping stone for writing development. Adoniou (2014) highlighted the potential benefits of fostering both drawing and writing. Although more research is still needed in this area, it could be hypothesised that, as both systems are used for marking meaning, when both drawing and writing are fostered this may support learners to become even more effective communicators (Adoniou, 2014).

While drawing to writing may not be as structured as explicit instruction, it allows for the development of cognitive skills, such as planning and symbolic representation, and fine motor skills, such as pencil grip. Drawing provides an opportunity to engage with purposeful expression as well as supporting learners to practise the motor skills required for handwriting (Mackenzie & Spokes, 2018b). Initially, drawings may be annotated by an adult using the words of the learner, and then through scaffolding, the learner may add alphabetic code.

Handwriting in the early years of school

Figure 14.3 is an example of drawing supported by writing in the early years of school. This work example is from Sebastian, aged seven years. He has created a poster of a missing spider. It is important to note the formatting that Sebastian has used, including an image with writing. The development of upper and lower case letters is evident, as well as the use of punctuation such as question marks and brackets.

Questions

1. What role might drawing have played in supporting Sebastian's communication of the message in his poster?
2. What does the combination of drawing and picture in this example remind you of?
3. What implicit literacy understandings might this example show?

Figure 14.3 'Missing Spider' poster

Authentic, meaningful and purposeful writing opportunities

Previously in this chapter, we explored the importance of understanding the purpose of writing as fundamental to writing development. In order to continue to develop handwriting, learners must be provided with authentic, meaningful and purposeful writing opportunities to practise these skills.

Play-based experiences can provide these opportunities through the use of engaging materials and experiences that follow the interests of the learner. Socio-dramatic play areas can provide 'real-life' opportunities for drawing and writing authentically through the use of props and writing materials that learners can explore as they may have seen modelled by adults.

Integrating writing into areas of interest such as science, engineering and design provides purposeful opportunities for writing. Learners need to use writing as a means to record data, ideas, observations and predictions.

Encouraging agency in young learners through ensuring writing tasks are meaningful is also important – for example, through supporting learners to write their own names on their work, to create labels and signs in the learning environment, or to make cards for friends' birthdays. It is also beneficial to support learners to write and draw their own stories, make books and then share their work in the learning environment for others to enjoy (Gerde et al., 2016).

Presence of environmental print

Environmental print helps develop children's knowledge of print, including the connection between oral language and writing. Research has shown that learners' writing capabilities are more sophisticated in print-rich learning environments than environments with less print. For environmental print to be effective, it must be meaningful to learners but also used by learners and educators (Gerde et al., 2016).

Print that is meaningful (and accessible) may be in the form of books, posters, work on display, word walls and labels on shelves – these examples can be functional in that they not only provide information, such as where classroom materials belong, but can also support writing development. It is essential that print is related to the interests of the learners and aligns with the learning in the environment.

Co-construction of print in the environment provides opportunities for teacher modelling of handwriting – for example, in a mind map to record ideas learners have brainstormed. Meaningful engagement with print might also occur through using intentional teaching strategies such as modelling, where a learner searches to find a word they would like to use in their writing (Gerde et al., 2016).

Explicit instruction and modelling of handwriting

Two key teaching approaches to handwriting are explicit instruction and teacher modelling. These strategies specifically target the formation of the letters so that handwriting becomes a tool to express ideas rather than a task in itself. Fluent and legible handwriting enables the learner to focus on the composition or writing itself, rather than the motor movements required to produce each letter (Mackenzie & Spokes, 2018b).

Explicit instruction and modelling show correct pencil grip, posture and positioning of writing tools, and modelling accurate letter formation supports learners to develop skills that will not put unnecessary strain on their muscles, restrict movement or cause them to develop inefficient habits. An incorrect pencil grip can slow down the writing process and affect the hand, arm and shoulder. The motor movements required for correct letter formation sequences are essential for developing handwriting efficiency. A letter may look as though it has been formed correctly; however, use of the incorrect starting point will make handwriting more difficult and less fluent (Mackenzie & Spokes, 2018b).

Hand preference is observable at different ages. By the age of five, however, there should be a clear hand preference demonstrated. It is important to be mindful of the hand preference of learners. Explicit instruction and modelling by a right-handed teacher may be quite confusing for a left-handed learner. Left- and right-handed learners will require slightly different instruction, pencil grips and scissors.

Most of the population are right-handed (Cuellar-Partida et al., 2021) so it is important to be aware of some ways of supporting left-handed writers.

- Ensure that left-handed learners sit to the left of the table or next to another left-hander so that writers are not bumping elbows with each other.
- Provide support when using different writing materials because left-handed learners will find their pen or whiteboard marker will be smudged or wiped away as they write, which can be very frustrating.
- Paper positioning and stroke development in letter formation will also be different.

REFLECTION

1. What materials would encourage handwriting and keyboarding development in dramatic play areas such as a cafe, a post office, a building site or a veterinary hospital?
2. How could you integrate multisensory materials throughout the primary school years to support fine motor development?
3. Conduct an audit of your classroom or placement classroom. What examples of environmental print are available? How many of these are handwritten?
4. How might the presence of print differ between early primary and upper primary learning environments?

Teaching and learning for handwriting and keyboarding across the primary years

Teaching letter formation

As previously explored in this chapter, handwriting involves a complex integration of cognitive and physical functions. Teaching handwriting needs to support the development of these functions through explicitly teaching and providing opportunities for regular practice of these skills to enable successful writers (Mackenzie & Spokes, 2018b) – see Table 14.3.

Table 14.3 Explicit instruction and modelling of components of handwriting

Components of handwriting development	Behaviours to support the development of these components
Pencil grip	• Thumb and index finger hold the pencil • Pencil resting on the first joint of the middle finger
Posture	• Feet flat on the floor • Straight back • Non-writing arm resting on table • Non-writing hand to hold paper
Paper placement	• Right-handers – paper to the right of the mid-line of the body, angled slightly to the left • Left-handers – paper to the left of the mid-line of the body, angled slightly to the right
Letter formation	• Correct entry and exit points (where to start the letter and where to finish) • The number of strokes • Whether a letter is completed without lifting the pencil

Source: DET (2002); Mackenzie & Spokes (2018b).

In the initial stages of teaching letter formation, the focus should be on the development of patterns to assist learners to develop control over the muscle movements required to form letters. These include lines (or strokes) vertically and diagonally, anticlockwise and clockwise circles, loops and waves. These movements can begin as larger movements and move to smaller movements (i.e. whole arm to hand to fingers), perhaps by drawing letters in the air, then in sand and then using pencil and paper. Teachers should model these movements and observe the learner's letter formation while they are writing (Mackenzie & Spokes, 2018b).

It is important to teach letter formation in groups of letters (or 'letter families') that are formed in a similar direction – anticlockwise letters, clockwise letters, the 'i' family and the 'u' family – as this assists in forming habits and muscle memory (see Table 14.4). The specific formation of some lower case letters varies between states and territories in Australia. While this can mean that letters will have different entry and exit points, the directionality (and therefore grouping) remains the same.

Table 14.4 Groups of letters ('letter families')

Types of letters	Anticlockwise letters	Clockwise letters	The 'i' family	The 'u' family
Lower case letters	a, c, d, g, q, e, o, f, s	m, n, r, x, z, h, k, p	i, t, l, j	u, y, v, w, b

Source: DET (2002).

In order to support specific development of learners across the primary years, the emergent, early primary and later primary stages of handwriting skill development are discussed in the next sections.

Emergent

The emergent writing stage corresponds with the pre-writing stage: the focus here is on developing the mechanics of handwriting and the links between oral language and reading. Teachers can support writers in the emergent stage using the following teaching strategies:

- Focus on fine motor development – developing strength and ability to manipulate different writing tools.
- Encourage learners to use drawing as a starting point.
- Model and encourage learners to label their drawings with letters representing the first sounds in words.
- Scaffold the understanding of association between letter shapes, letter names and the sounds that they make.
- Begin explicit instruction, particularly focusing on familiar words, such as the learner's own name, and grouping letters by formation (clockwise, anticlockwise, etc.).

Early primary

The early primary stage encompasses Foundation to Year 3. There may be some overlap with the emergent stage, particularly during the Foundation year of school. The following are approximate teaching sequences:

1. Learning correct pencil grip and posture:
   - continued focus on fine motor development and refinement, including smaller and more controlled muscle movements
   - focus on correct tripod pencil grip
   - explicit instruction and encouragement of correct posture and paper positioning for handwriting.
2. Developing basic letter formation:
   - practise handwriting patterns and tracing to develop control and directionality
   - explicit letter formation instruction and modelling of lower case unjoined letters by grouping letters
   - letter formation instruction, including entry and exit points, direction and number of strokes to form the letters
   - model spacing between words, using 'finger spacing' (placing index finger of opposite hand at the end of the last word written to show where to start writing the next word)
   - may include upper case letter formation, with focus on formation from top to bottom with directionality from left to right (as upper case letters are not joined this can be up to the writer, particularly left-handed writers)
   - practise letters using whole-arm movements by drawing them in the air and gradually continue reducing in size.
3. Using a range of writing tools to support handwriting development:
   - provide opportunities to practise letter formation using a range of sensory materials (e.g. playdough, sand, whiteboard markers, chalk and paint)

- provide plain paper, spaced lines and dotted thirds as learners develop control over the size of letter shapes
- spacing of dotted thirds can be reduced as learners develop increasing control over letter formation and sizing
- pencil grips and triangular pencils may be helpful for some writers developing tripod grip – ensure these are appropriate for left-/right-handedness and Years 2 and 3
- focus on consistency and fluency of unjoined upper and lower case letters
- explicit instruction in joining letters together (entry and exit points need to be consolidated to enable joining letters).

Later primary

In the later primary years (Years 4 to 6), the teaching focus becomes legibility, fluency, increase in the range of purposes for handwriting and the use of cursive, or joined, writing. By this stage, automaticity of handwriting is particularly important in order to enable learners to successfully create compositions at a higher level (Medwell et al., 2009). Later in the primary grades, learners can be encouraged to develop their own handwriting style.

In the later primary years, explicit instruction in keyboarding may begin to be beneficial. As in handwriting, posture and positioning are important to ensure comfort and ability and to avoid muscle or eye strain. Stevenson and Just (2014) identify motor learning stages for keyboarding, suggesting that the later primary years are more appropriate to start introducing formal keyboarding instruction than the early years.

Developing keyboarding skills includes locating the letters on the keyboard, using the home keys as a starting point for touch-typing and developing muscle memory to locate the keys. Gradually, learners will improve their muscle memory and increase the speed of typing. It is important to maintain regular practice through meaningful writing opportunities.

Differentiating learning

As in all areas of development, there will be a diverse range of learning needs within any learning environment. In the emergent and early primary stages of handwriting learning, a wide range of fine motor skills, graphophonic awareness and oral language skills may be evident within each classroom. Many learners will continue developing with instruction and scaffolding in a typical trajectory.

Some examples of differentiation for handwriting teaching across the primary years include:

- ensuring a range of writing equipment is available:
  - writing implements in a range of sizes
  - availability of multi-modal resources, such as whiteboard markers, textas, pencils
  - provision of pencil grip resources to support correct grip
  - availability of different writing paper, including a range of sizes and lines (e.g. dotted thirds, blue sky/green grass)
- using explicit instruction and remedial tools (e.g. specialised pencil grips, writing slope board)

- enabling an extended period of drawing to writing
- supporting the use of assistive technology, including speech to text – this is explored later in the chapter.

Assessment, curriculum and diverse learning needs

Assessment

As discussed in Chapter 3, the purpose of assessment is educative: to allow teachers, learners and parents and caregivers to understand the capabilities of learners in their classroom and to scaffold their development accordingly. Effective assessment practices should be authentic and in-context wherever possible (Ewing et al., 2016).

The Early Years Learning Framework (EYLF) highlights the importance of assessment that enables learners to demonstrate their skills authentically and show their true capabilities:

> All children will demonstrate their learning in different ways. Approaches to assessment that are culturally and linguistically relevant and responsive to the physical and intellectual capabilities of each child will acknowledge each child's abilities and strengths, and allow them to demonstrate competence. (Department of Education, Employment and Workplace Relations [DEEWR], 2009, p. 20)

In terms of handwriting, this can be most easily achieved through the collection of handwriting samples that are part of a learner's everyday writing tasks and through observation of the learner engaged in meaningful writing experiences.

Curriculum links

The EYLF focuses on the use of play-based pedagogy and intentional teaching to support children's learning and development:

> Intentional teaching is deliberate, purposeful and thoughtful. Educators who engage in intentional teaching recognise that learning occurs in social contexts and that interactions and conversations are vitally important for learning. (DEEWR, 2009, p. 15)

This pedagogical practice sits closely alongside the idea of meaningful, purposeful and authentic writing opportunities and teacher interactions. The EYLF addresses links with handwriting development across a number of its five outcomes, and some examples are provided in Table 14.5.

Table 14.5 Handwriting development in the EYLF

Outcome	Examples of specific links to handwriting development
Outcome 5: Children are effective communicators	<ul><li>Children interact verbally and non-verbally with others for a range of purposes</li><li>Children engage in a range of texts and gain meaning from these texts</li><li>Children express ideas and make meaning using a range of media</li></ul>

Source: Adapted from DEEWR (2009, p. 39).

The Australian Curriculum integrates language, literacy and literature within the English strand. Key elements of handwriting development are included within the literacy substrand in relation to creating texts (see Table 14.6). Handwriting and clear letter formation are key skills in creating messages that can be interpreted by others.

Table 14.6 Australian Curriculum: English – Literacy F–6, handwriting

Foundation	Year 1	Year 2	Year 3	Year 4	Year 5	Year 6
Produce some lower case and upper case letters using learned letter formations	Write using unjoined lower case and upper case letters	Write legibly and with growing fluency using unjoined upper case and lower case letters	Write using joined letters that are clearly formed and consistent in size	Write using clearly formed joined letters, and develop increased fluency and automaticity	Develop a handwriting style that is becoming legible, fluent and automatic	Develop a handwriting style that is legible, fluent and automatic and varies according to audience and purpose

Source: ACARA (2018).

Diverse learning needs

Some learners may begin to display learning difficulties in the early years of school and it is important to continue documenting and assessing their learning to determine whether early intervention, learning support or referral for assessment is required. Learners with diagnosed additional needs and/or disabilities can find handwriting particularly challenging. Given the complex interrelationship between sensory-motor, visual, language and memory systems, a range of learning difficulties and disabilities can also affect handwriting development (Prunty & Barnett, 2017).

Some examples of learning difficulties that can affect handwriting development include the following:

- language developmental delays (expressive or receptive language), which can result in handwriting difficulties due to the close link between oral language and handwriting
- developmental delays or disabilities related to fine and/or gross motor development
- cognitive disability
- specific language impairment
- specific learning disabilities (including dyslexia and dysgraphia)
- sensory processing disorder
- autism spectrum disorder (ASD)
- attention deficit hyperactivity disorder (ADHD)
- developmental coordination disorder (DCD) (also referred to as dyspraxia) (McCloskey & Rapp, 2017; Prunty & Barnett, 2017).

We have seen the value of handwriting development for a range of literacy skills, particularly writing composition, and it is important to consider equitable access for learners with additional needs. Access for all learners on a regular basis should keyboarding become a required skill is also essential. Keyboarding is recommended for learners in the upper primary years due to the motor development required to be able to use keyboards effectively (Mackenzie & Spokes, 2018a); however, assistive technology may be a useful tool for any age group (Stevenson & Just, 2014). The use of voice-to-text functions can enable learners struggling with handwriting to compose texts and, depending on the program, have their writing read back to them to support any reading difficulties. Additionally, use of technology can positively impact on learning and be beneficial for reluctant writers (Donica et al., 2018).

CASE STUDY 14.2 — Handwriting development in a learner diagnosed with dysgraphia

Lenny is in Year 4 at the local primary school. He has experienced difficulties with reading, handwriting and writing composition since starting school. Lenny and his family were referred to an educational psychologist and a cognitive assessment indicated a specific learning disorder with impairment in reading and written expression. (Impairment in written expression, when a learner experiences difficulties converting spoken sounds and words into written forming letters and has motor or handwriting difficulties, can be referred to as dysgraphia (Dyslexia – SPELD Foundation [DSF] Literacy & Clinical Services, 2020).) Lenny has received some reading intervention over the past 12 months at school and with a private educational specialist, mainly focusing on phonemic awareness and decoding skills. While he has grown in confidence in relation to reading, he still finds writing challenging and will often say he does not know what to write or will report that he has a stomach-ache when he is asked to write. When working in a small group with a teacher to practise handwriting, Lenny will often experience fatigue and discomfort in his hand and forearm.

Questions

1. Consider the impact that this assessment of dysgraphia might have on Lenny in terms of his experience of handwriting in the first years of school.
2. What assessment, approaches and teaching strategies could you employ in the learning environment to specifically support Lenny's handwriting development?
3. As a teacher, how will you support Lenny's access to the curriculum in your classroom?

REFLECTION

1. How might some learning difficulties (such as sensory processing disorder) impact on handwriting development?
2. What might authentic handwriting assessment opportunities look like in the primary years?

Conclusion

Handwriting and keyboarding provide the tools for communicating written messages in the twenty-first century. Despite technological advances that may appear to make handwriting an increasingly redundant skill, handwriting development is still important, especially in enabling literacy development in other areas.

This chapter provided an overview of typical handwriting development throughout the preschool and primary years, as well as the complex combination of cognitive and physical skills needed to produce handwriting. Diversity of learners is a challenge for teachers in all learning environments: the different needs of all writers is just one part of this. However, by having a clear understanding of the factors that influence handwriting development and understanding the range of teaching approaches available, teachers play a vital role in supporting this aspect of development.

This chapter particularly highlighted the importance of differentiation in teaching practices dependent on the developmental and individual needs of each learner. The use of assessment and differentiation approaches can assist teachers in meeting the needs of all of their learners.

Bringing it together

1. How does handwriting support other aspects of literacy learning?
2. What impact might teaching keyboarding rather than handwriting from Foundation have on literacy development?
3. Consider the following scenario. You are working in a Year 1 classroom. You have noticed that most learners are displaying typical handwriting development; however, there are several learners who are reluctant to engage in writing experiences. What might you need to find out about these learners to support their handwriting development?
4. Consider your current placement experience. Are you aware of all the additional learning needs and developmental levels in relation to the handwriting of each learner? If not, how might you find out or assess for this information?

Further resources

Handwriting matters

An interesting perspective on writing development, this article discusses developing handwriting skills as a way to empower learners in their writing development.

Malpique, A. & Pino-Pasternak, D. (2017). To empower students with effective writing skills, handwriting matters. The Conversation, 3 August. https://theconversation .com/to-empower-students-with-effective-writing-skills-handwriting-matters-81949

What is dysgraphia?

The Dyslexia – SPELD Foundation website provides further detail about the specific learning disability in written expression also known as dysgraphia. The site includes how this might be displayed in learners as well as a helpful video identifying the different subtypes of dysgraphia – language-based dysgraphia and motor-based dysgraphia.

Dyslexia – SPELD Foundation (DSF) Literacy & Clinical Services (2020). *What is dysgraphia?* https://dsf.net.au/learning-difficulties/dysgraphia/what-is-dysgraphia

Assessing early writing development

This article discusses the complexities of writing development and how teachers can assess this development. Of particular interest, it explores writing as a set of skills, including the skill of handwriting and the role of drawing within this.

Scull, J.A., Mackenzie, N.M., & Bowles, T. (2020). Assessing early writing: a six-factor model to inform assessment and teaching. *Educational Research for Policy and Practice*, 19, 239–259. doi:10.1007/s10671-020-09257-7

References

Adoniou, M. (2014). Drawing conclusions: what purpose do children's drawings serve? *Australian Art Education*, 36(1), 81–105.

Australian Curriculum, Assessment and Reporting Authority (ACARA). (2018). *The Australian Curriculum: English: Version 8.3.* www.australiancurriculum.edu.au/english/pdf-documents

Clay, M. (2005). *An Observation Survey of Early Literacy Achievement.* Pearson Education.

Cuellar-Partida, G., Tung, J.Y., Eriksson, N., et al. (2021). Genome-wide association study identifies 48 common genetic variants associated with handedness. *Nature Human Behaviour*, 5, 59–70. DOI:10.1038/s41562-020-00956-y

Daffern, T., Mackenzie, N.M., & Hemmings, B. (2017). Predictors of writing success: how important are spelling, grammar and punctuation? *Australian Journal of Education*, 81(1), 75–87. doi:10.1177/0004944116685319

Department of Education, Employment and Workplace Relations (DEEWR). (2009). *Belonging, Being & Becoming – The Early Years Learning Framework for Australia.* https://docs.education.gov.au/documents/belonging-being-becoming-early-years-learning-framework-australia

Department of Education and Training (DET). (2002). *The Teaching of Handwriting* (Revised edn). State of Victoria: Communications Division for the Office of School Education, Department of Education & Training.

—— (2018). *The Teaching of Handwriting: Writing Systems of the World* (Revised edn). State of Victoria: Communications Division for the Office of School Education, Department of Education and Training.

Dickinson, D.K., Golinkoff, R.M., & Hirsh-Pasek, K. (2010). Speaking out for language: why language is central to reading development. *Educational Researcher*, 39(4), 305–310.

Donica, D.K., Giroux, P., & Faust, A. (2018). Keyboarding instruction: comparison of techniques for improved keyboarding skills in elementary students. *Journal of Occupational Therapy, Schools & Early Intervention*, 11(4), 396–410. doi:10.1080/19411243.2018.1512067

Duiser, I.H.F., Ledebt, A., van der Kamp, J., & Savelsbergh, G.J.P. (2020). Persistent handwriting problems are hard to predict: a longitudinal study of the development of handwriting in primary school. *Research in Developmental Disabilities*, 97, 1–10. doi:10.1016/j.ridd.2019.103551

Dyslexia – SPELD Foundation (DSF) Literacy & Clinical Services. (2020). *What is dysgraphia?* https://dsf.net.au/learning-difficulties/dysgraphia/what-is-dysgraphia

Ewing, R., Callow, J., & Rushton, K. (2016). *Language and Literacy Development in Early Childhood*. Cambridge University Press.

Feder, K.P. & Majnemer, A. (2007). Handwriting development, competency and intervention. *Developmental Medicine & Child Neurology*, 49, 312–317.

Feng, L., Lindner, A., Ji, X.R., & Malatesha Joshi, R. (2019). The roles of handwriting and keyboarding in writing: a meta-analytic review. *Reading & Writing*, 32, 33–63. doi:10.1007/s11145-017-9749-x

Gerde, H.K., Goetsch, M.E., & Bingham, G.E. (2016). Using print in the environment to promote early writing. *The Reading Teacher*, 70(3), 283–293. doi:10.1002/trtr.1508

Glynn-McDonald, R. (2021). *First Nations languages*. www.commonground.org.au/learn/indigenous-languages-avoiding-a-silent-future

Hill, S. (2009). *Developing Early Literacy: Assessment and Teaching*. Eleanor Curtain Publishing.

Huffman, J.M. & Fortenberry, C. (2011). Helping preschoolers prepare for writing: developing fine motor skills. *Young Children*, September, 100–102.

Kenner, C. (2004). Living in simultaneous worlds: difference and integration in bilingual script-learning. *International Journal of Bilingual Education and Bilingualism*, 7(1), 43–61.

Kiefer, M., Schuler, S., Mayer, C., Trumpp, N.M., Hille, K., & Sachse, S. (2015). Handwriting or typewriting? The influence of pen- or keyboard-based writing training on reading and writing performance in preschool children. *Advances in Cognitive Psychology*, 11(4), 136–146. doi:10.5709/acp-0178-7

Longcamp, M., Zerbato-Poudou, M.T., & Velay, J.L. (2005). The influence of writing practice on letter recognition in preschool children: a comparison between handwriting and typing. *Acta Psychologica*, 119, 67–69.

Mackenzie, N. & Hemmings, B. (2014). Predictors of success with writing in the first year of school. *Issues in Educational Research*, 24(1), 41–54.

Mackenzie, N. & Spokes, R. (2018a). Handwriting, keyboarding or both? In N. Mackenzie & J. Scull (Eds.), *Understanding and Supporting Young Writers from Birth to 8* (pp. 137–164). Routledge.

—— (2018b). The why, who, what, when and how of handwriting instruction. *Practical Literacy*, 23(1), 17–20.

Mackenzie, N. & Veresov, N. (2013). How can drawing support writing acquisition: text construction in early writing from a Vygotskian perspective. *Australasian Journal of Early Childhood*, 38(4), 22–29.

Malpique, A. & Pino-Pasternak, D. (2017). To empower students with effective writing skills, handwriting matters. The Conversation, 3 August. https://theconversation.com/to-empower-students-with-effective-writing-skills-handwriting-matters-81949

McCloskey, M. & Rapp, B. (2017). Developmental dysgraphia: an overview and framework for research. *Cognitive Neuropsychology*, 34(3–4), 65–82. doi:10.1080/02643294.2017.1369016

Medwell, J., Strand, S., & Wray, D. (2009). The links between handwriting and composing for Y6 children. *Cambridge Journal of Education*, 39(3), 329–344.

Medwell, J. & Wray, D. (2014). Handwriting automaticity: the search for performance thresholds. *Language and Education*, 28(1), 34–51. doi:10.1080/09500782.2013.763819

Morrow, L.M. (2005). *Literacy Development in the Early Years: Helping Children Read & Write* (5th edn). Pearson Education.

Prunty, M. & Barnett, A.L. (2017). Understanding handwriting difficulties: a comparison of children with and without motor impairment. *Cognitive Neuropsychology*, 24(3–4), 205–218. doi:10.1080/02643294.2017.1376630

Raban, B. (2018). Writing in the preschool years. In N. Mackenzie & J. Scull (Eds.), *Understanding and Supporting Young Writers from Birth to 8* (pp. 50–70). Routledge.

Scull, J.A., Mackenzie, N.M., & Bowles, T. (2020). Assessing early writing: a six-factor model to inform assessment and teaching. *Educational Research for Policy and Practice*, 19, 239–259. doi:10.1007/s10671-020-09257-7

Simpson, J. (2019). The state of Australia's Indigenous languages – and how we can help people speak them more often. The Conversation, 21 January. https://theconversation.com/the-state-of-australias-indigenous-languages-and-how-we-can-help-people-speak-them-more-often-109662

Stevenson, N.C. & Just, C. (2014). In early education, why teach handwriting before keyboarding? *Early Childhood Education Journal*, 42, 49–56. doi:10.1007/s10643-012-0565-2

Wolf, M. (2008). *Proust and the Squid: The Story and Science of the Reading Brain*. Icon Books Ltd.

CHAPTER 15

Literacy across the curriculum

Siobhan O'Brien

ANTICIPATED OUTCOMES

After working through this chapter, it is anticipated you will be able to:

- identify literacy as one of the Australian Curriculum seven general capabilities, including the general capability element(s), and how these are designed to be incorporated into planning and teaching
- consider pedagogical approaches for teaching literacy across the curriculum
- locate literacy as a general capability within planning and implementation strategies at the school and classroom level
- explore opportunities for literacy learning beyond the school setting.

Introduction

This chapter will increase your knowledge and awareness of literacy as one of the seven general capabilities in the Australian Curriculum to support your understanding of the function of literacy across the curriculum areas, such as in Science and Humanities and Social Sciences (HASS). The chapter explores the literacy general capability and looks at how it is designed to be incorporated into planning and teaching. It then looks at the use of strategies for writing genres, including the teaching and learning cycle, tiered vocabulary for word knowledge and vocabulary development, as well as some reading strategies for use with technical non-fiction texts. A further consideration for planning and implementation at the school and classroom level is also presented.

Literacy as a general capability in the Australian Curriculum

To achieve a productive and sustainable future within twenty-first-century society, literacy is considered a fundamental and essential skill that is required for all Australians. Literacy is included as one of the Australian Curriculum's seven general capabilities, along with numeracy, critical and creative thinking, digital literacy, personal and social capability, ethical understanding and intercultural understanding. Introduced in Chapter 2, the general capabilities are identified as the essential skills needed for learners to live and work successfully in the twenty-first century (National Curriculum Board, 2009). Gilbert (2019) has found that the general capabilities were designed to act as 'a key part of the curriculum, a dimension standing "alongside" and equivalent in structural terms to disciplinary subject areas' (p. 169). The concept of literacy as a general capability 'involves students listening to, reading, viewing, speaking, writing and creating oral, print visual and digital texts and using and modifying language for different purposes in a range of contexts' (National Curriculum Board, 2009, p. 6). The expectation of state and territory education authorities is that teachers will use the literacy capability to teach and assess learners' progress through judgements on specific knowledge, skills, behaviours and dispositions. Learners are assessed on their ability to apply knowledge and skills in complex and ever-changing circumstances. The Australian Curriculum information for literacy as a general capability includes the nature and scope of the capability, its place in the learning areas and the elements and sub-elements that underpin each learning continuum.

> ### REFLECTION
>
> Literacy is one of the seven general capabilities in the Australian Curriculum. What is the overall function of the general capabilities?

The structure of the literacy general capability

Literacy as a general capability incorporates two overarching processes with interrelated elements. The overarching processes are:

1. comprehending texts through listening, reading and viewing
2. composing texts through speaking, writing and creating (ACARA, n.d.b).

The following elements apply to both of these processes: text knowledge; grammar knowledge; word knowledge; and visual knowledge.

It is important to note that the literacy general capability is apart from the literacy strand located in the English curriculum, but is 'not a separate component of the Australian Curriculum and does not contain new content' (ACARA, n.d.a). Literacy as a general capability presents the aligned aspects of the language and literacy strands covered in the Australian Curriculum: English, meaning that literacy is applied in all other learning areas. Figure 15.1 presents the interrelated elements of the learning continuum of literacy.

To assist teacher planning for learners' development of the general capabilities within classroom learning programs, literacy, as a general capability, is located within the learning continua of each learning area, meaning it sits across all of the subject areas of the Australian Curriculum. The literacy general capability content is identified with the icon shown in Figure 15.2. When the icon is selected, the literacy capability information provides teachers with pedagogical knowledge and strategies that include ways to support learners with word knowledge, the teaching of specific vocabulary and strategies for comprehending and composing texts.

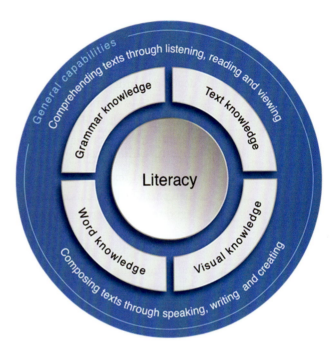

Figure 15.1 The interrelated elements of literacy as a general capability
Source: ACARA (n.d.b).

Figure 15.2 Literacy icon to identify literacy as a general capability
Source: ACARA (n.d.b).

REFLECTION

Literacy as a general capability is structured with two overarching processes: comprehending texts through listening, reading and viewing; and composing texts through speaking, writing and creating (ACARA, n.d.b).

1. How do these processes support the literacy skills of learners?
2. Why do you think these would be an important consideration for planning and learning?

Comprehending texts through listening, reading and viewing

When we consider the element of comprehending texts through listening, reading and viewing, we refer to learners' receptive language and the skills and strategies learners will need to develop in order to interpret spoken, written, visual and multimodal texts. To achieve these aspects, teachers need to provide lessons with strategies where students will learn to read and view texts linked to topic knowledge within the related subject discipline. Teachers must also provide explicit support for the learning of subject-specific and technical vocabulary. An example of this could be a unit or lesson that provides access to subject-specific audio and multimodal texts where the learners listen for information (navigate, read and view) and then participate in classroom activities and discussions (listen and respond to learning area texts) to consolidate (interpret and analyse) their learning.

Composing texts through speaking, writing and creating

The composing texts through speaking, writing and creating element is focused on the development of children's expressive language. This involves providing opportunities to compose different styles and types of texts for a range of purposes within the learning of subject-specific curriculum areas. Such texts can be spoken, written, visual and multimodal, and both formal and informal. Teachers can include group and class discussions to explore and investigate specific learning area topics, and formal and informal presentations and debates within classroom activities.

Four aspects in the literacy general capability

This section presents the four aspects within literacy as a general capability that support the process of comprehending texts through listening, reading, viewing and composing texts through speaking, writing and creating. The aspects are text knowledge, grammar knowledge, word knowledge and visual knowledge.

Text knowledge

Text knowledge relates to the specific teaching and learning of spoken, written, visual and multimodal texts covered within the specific learning areas. For instance, teachers will need to plan for ways to support children to learn specific text structures and sequences so that learners can 'present information, explain processes and relationships, argue and support points of view and investigate issues' (ACARA, n.d.b).

Grammar knowledge

Grammar knowledge considers learners' understanding and skill development of their ability to use grammatical features in the construction of texts. For instance, teachers need to provide support for children to learn and understand the elements and role of sentence structure in composing texts. This includes 'how types of words and word groups convey information to represent ideas' (ACARA, n.d.a).

Word knowledge

Word knowledge involves children learning to understand the specialised and technical vocabulary needed for specific learning topic areas. Teachers plan for strategies to support children to develop skills for acquiring topic vocabulary and also the capacity to spell relevant words accurately.

Visual knowledge

Visual knowledge involves learning about and understanding of visual information. This understanding contributes to meaning and comprehending texts created in topic-specific areas. Teachers plan for strategies to support children to interpret 'still and moving images, graphs, tables, maps and other graphic representations' to support their understanding and evaluation of required learning within curriculum areas (ACARA, n.d.a).

The literacy learning continuum

A literacy learning continuum for each of the above elements is available in a PDF form. The continuum is presented within the following headings: 'Comprehending texts through listening, reading and viewing'; 'Composing texts through speaking, writing and creating elements'; and 'Text knowledge, grammar knowledge, word knowledge and visual knowledge elements'. The stages within the literacy learning continuum are designed to be independent of age and are labelled from Levels 1 to 6. Level 1 is divided into five sub-levels: 1a, 1b, 1c, 1d and 1e. Levels 1a–1d represent the development of early literacy skills with a particular emphasis on communication (ACARA, n.d.c).

REFLECTION

While you review the literacy learning continuum, think about how the learning levels scaffold the needs of the learners. Literacy as a general capability supports the discipline areas of the Australian Curriculum, including HASS, the Arts, Technologies, Health and Physical Education, Mathematics and Science.

1. How would the above elements support this learning?
2. Why do you think this would be an important consideration for teacher planning?

Literacy as a general capability in the learning areas of the Australian Curriculum

In this section, we cover the literacy aspects within the learning areas, or subjects, of the Australian Curriculum Foundation–Year 6/7: HASS, the Arts, Technologies, Health and Physical Education, Mathematics and Science. Each subject is presented and the specific literacy requirements that teachers will need to plan, teach and assess for in order to evaluate each child's understanding are explained.

Humanities and Social Sciences (HASS) (F–6/7)

In HASS, learners develop literacy capability through building 'discipline-specific knowledge on history, geography, civics and citizenship, and economics and business' (ACARA, n.d.b). Teachers support learners to experience a wide range of texts where they will 'pose questions, research, analyse, evaluate and communicate information, concepts and ideas'

(ACARA, n.d.b). As learners participate in an inquiry curriculum, they will 'learn to ask discipline-specific questions and to apply knowledge in discussions and debates' (ACARA, n.d.b).

The Arts

Children use literacy in the Arts to develop, apply and communicate their knowledge and skills as artists and as audience members. Teachers plan teaching and learning activities for children to enhance and extend their literacy skills through discussion, interpretation and the evaluation of their own and others' artworks. Children also learn and use specific Arts terminology as they move through the curriculum.

Technologies

Children develop literacy skills and knowledge within Technologies through the communication of ideas, concepts and proposals. Teachers support learning through providing experiences with reading and interpreting written instructions for technologies. This can include the use of diagrams, procedural writing such as design briefs, and following patterns and recipes. The learning-specific Technologies vocabulary includes terms for concepts, processes and production.

Health and Physical Education

In Health and Physical Education, learners develop literacy capability through the use of specific terminology and communication. They use critical literacy to develop skills as consumers to access, interpret, analyse, challenge and evaluate influences that are present in the fields of Health and Physical Education, such as the media. Children also develop an understanding of the language and science of movement.

Mathematics

Learners develop literacy skills in Mathematics via the technical 'vocabulary associated with number, space, measurement and mathematical concepts and processes' (ACARA, n.d.b). Children also 'use literacy to interpret word problems that contain the language features of mathematics' (ACARA, n.d.b). Teachers support learning via the provision of a range of texts typical to Mathematics, such as calendars and maps.

Science

Literacy capability in Science is covered through the investigation by learners of the world around them. Learners are required to read and compose texts that 'provide information, describe events and phenomena, recount experiments, present and evaluate data' (ACARA, n.d.b). Teachers engage learners with access to resources such as 'charts, graphs, diagrams, pictures, maps, animations, models and visual media' (ACARA, n.d.b). Scientific vocabulary is often technical and includes the teaching and learning of specific terms for concepts and features of the world.

REFLECTION

Teachers will provide lessons with strategies where the children will learn to read and view texts linked to topic knowledge within the related subject discipline. Literacy as a general capability is designed to support the discipline areas of the Australian Curriculum.

Why do you think the information in the curriculum about the literacy general capability would be an important section to access as a part of a teacher's planning?

Planning for Science 'Living Things': literacy as a general capability

CASE STUDY 15.1A

This case study is presented as an ongoing case study within a number of sections of this chapter. It is included to support you with thinking about the applied planning aspects and approaches of literacy across the curriculum.

Your year-level team is planning a Science unit for level 3. The topic is 'Living Things'. This is the first stage of the planning process (subsequent stages for planning will be presented within following sections of this case study). The school-based scope and sequence is available, which gives an outline of the topic and some learning objectives.

At the beginning of the planning meeting, you suggest locating literacy as a general capability and its reference to Science.

Questions

1. What will you need to know about literacy as a general capability within this topic?
2. How would you go about finding this information?

Literacy across the curriculum: strategies and approaches

In this section, we explore strategies and approaches that support aspects of literacy in subject-specific areas. First, a genre approach to literacy is considered, with insights into using language for purposes such as to explain, describe, argue, review or recount. We then look at strategies and approaches for writing, including the teaching and learning cycle for writing and developing vocabulary in subject-specific areas that can be useful for supporting learning.

A genre approach to literacy

A genre approach to literacy was developed from Halliday's functional model of language (Halliday, 1993). The functional model considers the demands of reading and writing and makes provision for, and access to, explicit support. Genre theory sets out to make literacy and language visible and accessible to all, particularly 'for students from non-mainstream groups who might otherwise struggle with the demands of literacy' (Derewianka, 2015, p. 70).

When working within genre theory, teachers need to understand the particular ways in which literacy works in texts across the curriculum and then provide explicit teaching and learning supports that address the capabilities across all years of schooling (Freebody, 2009). Teachers also need to draw learners' attention to the ways in which text genres can build their knowledge and then also demonstrate how language and visual information work together to form information within different curriculum areas (Freebody, 2009). The genre approach to literacy curriculum planning activities involves learners in using language for purposes that explain, describe, argue, review or recount, and the context includes purposeful language for communication that is related to a particular task or unit of work (Derewianka, 2015).

Strategies and approaches for writing

This section explores ways that teachers can support literacy learning within the specific learning areas presented above and with the use of genre theory. We look at the teaching and learning cycle to support genre writing requirements that are included in the Australian Curriculum.

The teaching and learning cycle for writing

The teaching and learning cycle was first introduced in Chapter 9. The cycle is an evidence-based pedagogic approach to support learning and develop children's skills in managing writing across the discipline areas. Using a sociocultural learning theory, the teaching and learning cycle is based on Vygotsky's notion of scaffolding, where children are supported by a more knowledgeable 'other' through modelling and explicit instruction in order to extend their progress (Derewianka, 2015). The cycle includes four key phases that provide support for reading, writing, speaking and listening. These four phases are Phase 1: Building the field or context; Phase 2: Learning about the genre; Phase 3: Supported writing with guided practice; and Phase 4: Independent composition of text. The cycle is used to scaffold learning and knowledge of the required skills within subject-specific areas through supporting the learning with the use of a variety of texts and instructional strategies, including whole-group, small-group, pair and individual work.

The teaching and learning cycle is based on the use of strategies that support reading and viewing of texts and images to build curriculum and field knowledge (Derewianka & Jones, 2016). Within each of the phases of the cycle, the teacher's role is to develop knowledge and skills, then as the learner progresses in becoming competent in the genre, 'the teacher gradually withdraws support and encourages learner independence' (Derewianka, 2015, p. 72).

The four phases of the cycle are not intended to act as a strict sequence. Teachers can move between the phases as needed. The teacher identifies the language demands of the task and teaches the genres through an explicit learning intention and success criteria for each stage of the cycle. The learning is concerned with 'deep learning' of content together with learning the language of the content area. The teacher will also constantly assess progress at each stage of the cycle and respond to identified needs. Figure 15.3 provides an example of an applied version of the teaching and learning cycle.

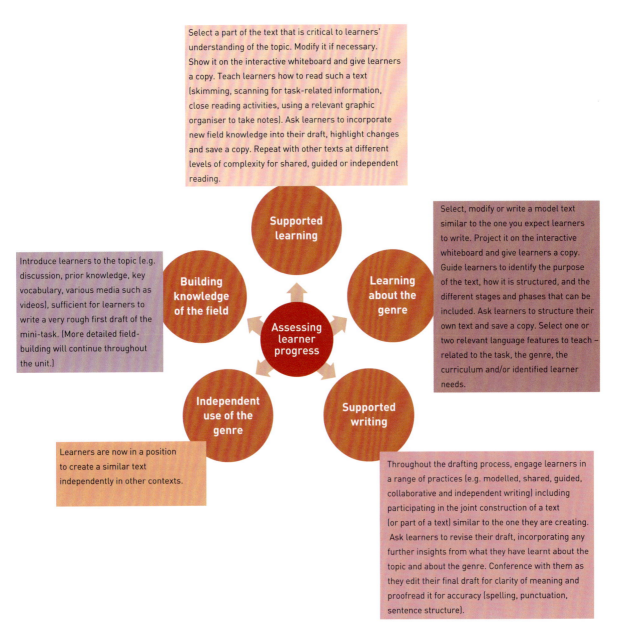

Figure 15.3 The teaching and learning cycle explained
Source: Derewianka & Jones (2016), adapted from Rothery (1994).

Phase 1: Building the field or context

Building the field or context is focused on establishing understanding of the topic or area of study addressed in the literacy capability. Teachers establish prior knowledge, and support learners to increase their discipline-specific and technical understandings (Derewianka & Jones, 2016).

Building the field or context can be returned to as a stage numerous times throughout a unit, and so further knowledge can be presented or co-constructed. Common tasks in this stage include guided discussions, experiments, excursions, mind mapping and vocabulary building, with planned opportunities to use 'subject-specific language in supported and contextualised ways' (Department of Education and Training [DET], n.d.).

Phase 2: Learning about the genre

In the modelling stage, the focus is on the subject-specific genre. This stage includes explicit teaching that examines items such as the language features of text. The role of the teacher is to carefully select extracts and use these with a linguistic focus to teach the key structural features, language features and meanings in relation to the genre. The discipline-specific words will also include 'tier 2 vocabulary', which are words that have been used in multiple contexts or are reflective of the genre. When using a text extract for modelling purposes, teachers can involve the learners in:

- a discussion of the text and its purpose
- annotations highlighting key features relevant to the genre
- highlighting key words, phrases or sentences to support understanding
- 'rearranging cut up parts of a text to reconstruct' (DET, n.d.).

Phase 3: Supported writing with guided practice

Supported writing is an important stage of the teaching and learning cycle, where the focus is on the composition of text. The teacher takes a leading role to guide or jointly construct while shaping understanding. Guidance includes prompts, questions, paraphrasing and thinking aloud in the planning and teaching process as well as guided drafting and editing.

Phase 4: Independent composition of text

When the learners are ready to work on their own texts, independent composition can take place through drawing on their understanding about the genre and language developed through the previous modelling and guided practice. During the independent writing stage, the teacher's role is to guide the composition and provide feedback. For less confident learners, teachers can provide a worked example.

REFLECTION

Review Figure 15.3, 'The teaching and learning cycle explained', and answer the following questions:

1. *Building knowledge of the field.* What are the essential elements of this section?
2. *Supported reading.* How could this element occur in your class? Think about specific needs and differentiation.
3. *Learning about the genre.* How would you go about supporting learners to model and scaffold their learning?
4. *Supported writing.* Joint construction of text is a form of supported writing. How does this strategy build learners' confidence?
5. *Independent use of the genre.* What would the role of the teacher be at this stage?

15 LITERACY ACROSS THE CURRICULUM

Planning for Science 'Living Things': the teaching and learning cycle	CASE STUDY 15.1B

This case study is presented as an ongoing case study within a number of sections of this chapter. It is included to support you with thinking about the applied planning aspects and approaches of literacy across the curriculum.

Your team is planning a science unit on 'Living Things' for level 3. You are now preparing to implement the teaching and learning cycle to support the Science writing genre. Refer to the following questions to guide planning and implementation of the cycle.

Questions

1. What aspects of the teaching and learning cycle do you think will most support knowledge? What is the teacher's role in this process? Think about the writing genre you will teach in the Science unit for your level.
2. How could the teaching and learning cycle support the literacy needs of the learners?

Developing vocabulary in subject-specific areas

Developing vocabulary is another key consideration within literacy as a general capability. Located in the word knowledge element, Konza (2011) explains how 'vocabulary is a key component of reading for meaning. If children know the meaning of a word, they are far more likely to be able to read it and make sense of it within a sentence' (p. 4). When teaching subject areas or topics, teachers need to support learning with the teaching of specific vocabulary. It is also important to make vocabulary teaching and learning explicit. So how can we go about this? There are various teaching strategies that explicitly support the teaching of academic or technical vocabulary. The tiered vocabulary framework is one such approach.

The tiered vocabulary framework

Tiered vocabulary is a framework for categorising words and offers teachers a way to consider the vocabulary that learners may already have prior to the lesson, compared to those words that will need to be introduced.

The framework has three tiers (Figure 15.4), as follows:

- *Tier 1 – familiar everyday words*. Tier 1 words are everyday words familiar to most and are primarily learnt through conversation. These are basic words that most children have learnt through everyday contexts and social interactions. Children from non-English-speaking backgrounds may not have acquired these.
- *Tier 2 – refers to academic vocabulary found in context texts*. Tier 2 words are frequently occurring words that are found across contexts and topics. For example, words such as 'justify', 'expand' and 'predict' appear across the Science and HASS areas. Tier 2 words are important to master understanding of and greatly increase comprehension (Kimberly, 2013).
- *Tier 3 – domain-specific academic vocabulary*. Tier 3 words are specific to subject areas and topics. Learners may not have heard these in common contexts, and these will often need explicit teaching within the subject area.

> **Tiered vocabulary:** a three-tiered framework that is used to categorise words. The framework can support vocabulary development when teaching new concepts and subject-specific terminology.

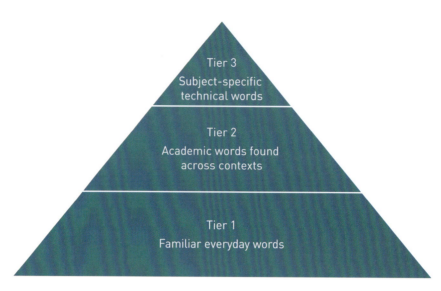

Figure 15.4 Tiered vocabulary

Using tiered vocabulary in the classroom

Tiered vocabulary has practical applications for classroom teaching. When effectively integrated into their practice, the teacher will be able to provide an explicit focus on vocabulary within lesson planning that identifies the important words that are essential or common across subject areas (typically Tier 2 words). The class could also build content vocabulary lists or word walls, with 'should-know words' (Tier 3), 'must-know words' (Tier 2) and 'already-known words' (Tier 1). The learners have access and ownership of word walls and can use them to support their writing and word-based knowledge (Figure 15.5).

Figure 15.5 Example of a tiered vocabulary word wall

REFLECTION

The following questions are designed to prompt your thinking about explicit teaching and learning of vocabulary:

1. How could you go about identifying the required vocabulary within the subject or topic area?
2. How would you make an assessment of what vocabulary learners may or may not already have?
3. How do you then ensure that learners attain an understanding of the required vocabulary to assist them within different academic learning contexts?

15 LITERACY ACROSS THE CURRICULUM 361

| Planning for Science 'Living Things': tiered vocabulary | CASE STUDY 15.1C |

Your team is continuing to plan the Science unit on 'Living Things' for level 3. Using your knowledge of tiered vocabulary, refer to the tiered word list in Table 15.1 and use this template to support your planning of the three-stage process (modified) for the 'Living Things' unit.

Questions

1. What is the required vocabulary that learners will need to know or learn for this topic?
2. What is the teacher's role in this process?
3. How can the tiered vocabulary support the literacy needs of the learners?
4. Where would using the tiered word list occur in the planning process?
5. How would you support learners with using their own version of the tiered word list?

Table 15.1 A template for tiered vocabulary

My tiered word list					
Topic: (for example) Where I live (my community)					
Tier 1 words: Familiar words		Tier 2 words: Key words		Tier 3 words: Technical words	
Word	Meaning	Word	Meaning	Word	Meaning

REFLECTION

1. Why might it be important to unpack the vocabulary and language of a subject area?
2. How can teaching be adapted to take account of the different linguistic needs and strengths of learners?
3. What are some models and planning approaches that would support this?

Strategies and approaches for reading

The teaching and learning cycle: reading strategies and approaches

To support children with their literacy learning across the curriculum, the teaching of reading with explicit pedagogical methods of instruction will ensure that learners are taught how to strategically read specific genre texts. Through this approach, learners will also increase the content knowledge required for specific subject areas. Sometimes this technical reading can be difficult and intensive, with specific styles of texts – for example, a topic on natural disasters, and learning about historical events or scientific concepts.

Derewianka (2015) has applied the teaching and learning cycle to support children's reading and comprehension skills; the 'focus of the teaching learning cycle has typically been on the production of an effective written text' (p. 15); however, it can also be applied to teaching reading (Figure 15.6). The teaching and learning cycle can support the development of the process of reading and viewing of texts and images, through building field knowledge and

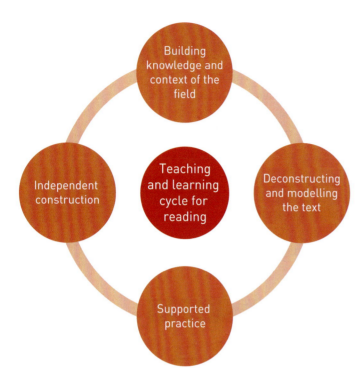

Figure 15.6 The teaching and learning cycle for reading
Source: Adapted from Derewianka & Jones (2016).

Mentor texts: literature that can be used to model forms of writing or specific structures and features. Mentor texts can be studied as exemplars and used as models for a teaching skill.

comprehension via opportunities for learners to engage in conversations and discussion about the language and information presented (Derewianka & Jones, 2016). By being provided non-fiction texts, learners become familiar with the structures and features of different genres, and these can then also be used as springboards to develop their own writing (Dollins, 2016).

Using mentor texts

Mentor texts play an important role in supporting reading proficiency within the teaching and learning cycle. The purpose of using non-fiction mentor texts is to expose learners to various genres and writing styles. Using a selected mentor throughout the teaching and learning cycle will support learners to work within their zone of proximal development along with the support of the more knowledgeable other (DET, 2019; Vygotsky, 1978). This is achieved through explicit instruction strategies where the teacher supports learners to establish field knowledge and informed analysis of texts, and then provides opportunities for guided practice and independent practice (DET, 2019). Identified as a high-impact factor, explicit teaching practice shows learners what to do and then how to do it through guided teacher demonstration and modelling (Hattie, 2012).

Using mentor texts offers a beneficial pedagogical practice for teachers. Teachers can also use the mentor texts as an exemplar in their lessons to help learners with techniques in reading and writing as a pedagogical strategy. Mentor texts can also act as exemplars for the genre of writing the learners need to create, as they provide learners with opportunities to examine authors' craft and observe the structures and features that they can then take into their own writing (Israel, 2008). The use of mentor texts can ensure that learners are exposed to a variety of genre styles and writing features. Through reading, learners immerse themselves in examples of types of texts to observe how authors use specific language and certain features to convey a message (Pytash & Morgan, 2014). Reading non-fiction texts will also support children to think critically and analyse multiple perspectives (Spencer, 2017).

When selecting appropriate mentor texts, teachers need to ensure that the text(s) address the specific genre and are an appropriate level for learning (Pytash & Morgan, 2014). Another important factor is the length of the mentor text, which should be based on what the learners are able to manage or concentrate on within a teaching session. Selecting a text can be timely and challenging; school and local community librarians may be able to offer support with text selection.

Strategies for using mentor texts within the teaching and learning cycle

In this section, we present a number of ways mentor texts can be used in teaching and learning. The strategies are linked to the phases of the teaching and learning cycle (Table 15.2).

Table 15.2 Using mentor texts and the teaching and learning cycle

Strategy	Description
Walk through the book (building the context or field)	In a guided reading group at the first reading of a non-fiction text, encourage the learners to look through the book on their own. Without talking to their peers, ask them to notice how the book is constructed. After a few minutes, ask them to tell you what they noticed.
Close reading (guided practice)	Using non-fiction texts as mentor texts can be reviewed using a strategy called *close reading*. Close reading can occur when a learner conducts a book analysis (Spencer, 2017). When an analysis is conducted, the learner will practise identifying the author's purpose within the text – for example, a learner will be able to identify organisational features and academic vocabulary, and will be able to answer questions about the content and information on the topic (Dollins, 2016).
Examining the text structures and features (guided practice)	After the texts have been introduced, learners can engage in reading from the perspective of a writer, and the teacher's role is to guide the learner to notice how the text is written. Examining the structure helps learners to understand how an author moves from the beginning to the end of the text, using the genre to inform the reader (Pytash & Morgan, 2014), and how the author introduces a topic and then builds on this by presenting further information to the reader. For example, features of an expository text would include the author establishing a clear argument, providing evidence and organising ideas in a logical way while engaging the reader (Spencer, 2017). Through the process of analysing the author's writing, learners will see how an author presents information in a way that is understood by the reader. Examining the structure of texts also supports learners with a base for their own writing.
Text features scavenger hunt (building the field)	Similar to the above activity, this one is a bit more guided. In the planning session, the teacher works through the text and sets up a template of all the items they want the learners to notice in the text – for example, contents page, headings, facts, images, glossary and so on. The template will provide a place where learners can tick off and record the parts they find.
Main idea vs interesting details (guided practice)	During a reading session, an activity such as 'Main idea vs interesting details' will assist the building of note-taking skills. As learners review the text, they will learn to discriminate between important information and other connected but minor information.
Quiz questions (guided practice)	Creating quiz questions from the reading content is a good way to review knowledge. This can be led by either the teacher or the learners.
Topic boxes in classroom libraries (guided or independent practice)	The teacher can prepare classroom bookshelves with an assortment of labelled tubs to hold non-fiction topics. Access to non-fiction books will offer a guide to both locate and display information about topics that have been studied, or topics of interest. It can also include books that have been created by the class.

A further useful strategy for close reading and guided practice is enabling the reader to engage in the reading process of making text connections; this is a strategy that can support the comprehension of text. Nikolajeva (2014) explains how some readers may have limited book knowledge or life experience, which will affect their ability to process information in text form. Making text connections will support comprehension and embed new knowledge. If a learner has no connection to the topic, then understanding will take longer. Knowledge of background and prior experience will be an important factor for planning. Excursions early in the topic are also a good way to build the field and immerse the learners into the area of investigation. For example, if you are teaching a topic on 'The Farm and Farming', some of the children may never have been to a farm or a regional setting. Providing this experience as you begin the topic will lay the foundation and increase engagement. Figure 15.7 provides an example of the making text connections strategy.

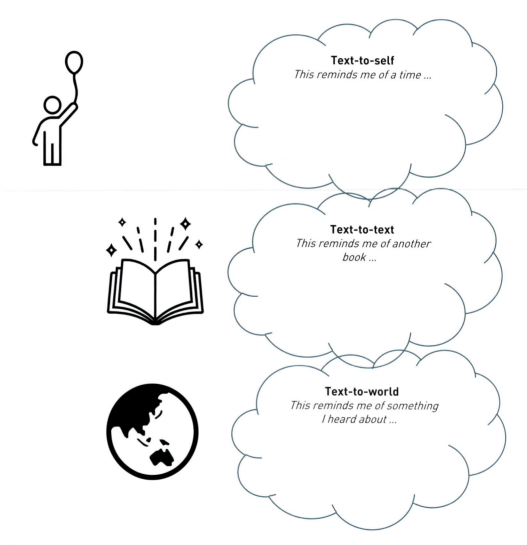

Figure 15.7 Making text connections template for classroom use

Making text connections (i.e. text-to-text, text-to-self and text-to-the-world) can be applied to support readers' understanding and comprehension, particularly when children are not engaged by books. Making text connections activities can also support reluctant readers with ways to make life connections that then scaffold the new knowledge, generating higher levels of engagement (Wilhelm, 1997). Through the making text connections strategy, teachers can support learners to make meaning, a process where they will discover connections to their own experiences. Asking children to draw connections to other factual information, concepts and situations that they have come across guides them to 'pause recall and connect to prior experience, question the author, wonder what the author meant, read ahead, re-read, etc., in an ongoing process of constructing meaning' (Wilhelm, 1997, p. 73).

Graphic organisers also can be used as a strategy to support learning with mentor texts that will assist in the recall of information. Graphic organisers can help with organising information when reading or writing with certain text structures. Table 15.3 provides some suggestions.

Table 15.3 Using graphic organisers as a strategy with mentor texts

Graphic organiser	Text feature	Genre
Venn diagram	Compare and contrast	Persuasive text
Sequence map	Instructional	Procedural
Timeline	Historical	Recount

Planning for Science 'Living Things': reading strategies **CASE STUDY 15.1D**

Your team continues to plan the Science unit on 'Living Things' for level 3. At this stage, you are looking to embed reading strategies that will engage learning. You have located some useful books that can be used as mentor texts.

Some other aspects to consider for the unit content are:

- incorporating Aboriginal and/or Torres Strait Islander perspectives
- addressing the needs of culturally and linguistically diverse (CALD) learners
- holding excursions and/or incursions to engage learning.

Question

Using your knowledge of reading strategies and approaches from the above section, how will your team go about planning for a range of learners with diverse reading needs in a unit of study?

The Australian Curriculum: planning and implementation at the school level

This section presents information on the process of curriculum planning and implementation at the school level. It is most likely that senior teachers will have curriculum planning and implementation as a role within their scope and will work with teams and leadership to ensure that the curriculum and learning expectations are being catered for, as required by their state or territory.

At the school level, most schools will have a set strategy for curriculum planning and implementation. This is usually presented in the form of planning documentation (e.g. scope and sequence, inquiry topics, etc.) that acts as a guide for the whole-school curriculum implementation. Taken from the Australian Curriculum and/or the relevant state or territory curriculum, the school-based planning documents will be in an ongoing process of change and review.

In some schools, a school-wide Australian Curriculum genre planning document may be used to plan the term inquiry topics. Australian Curriculum genre planning documents have been developed by the South Australian Government to support teachers with planning across the curriculum. The genre maps locate the specific genres covered for each of the learning areas in the Australian Curriculum. Table 15.4 provides an example of a genre planning document that incorporates science and genre writing approaches.

Table 15.4 Australian Curriculum genre planning document

Level 1e Typically by the end of Foundation Year	Level 2 Typically by the end of Year 2	Level 3 Typically by the end of Year 4	Level 4 Typically by the end of Year 6
Topic example: The weather	Topic example: Materials	Topic example: Changes to materials	Topic example: Energy
Questions and answers – e.g. questions to guide observations of weather across a term	**Procedures** – e.g. How to make paper	**Procedures** – e.g. How to set up a worm farm	**Procedures** – e.g. How to measure the effect of oxygen on steel.
Statements of observations – e.g. How the ants in our garden respond to different weather	**Descriptions of observations** – e.g. property of materials	**Descriptions of observed objects, living things or phenomena** – e.g. The physical properties of natural materials in our garden	**Information reports using multi-source research** – e.g. Recyclable materials
		Information reports – e.g. Feral predators in our area	
Drawings to represent ideas – e.g. illustrations to accompany observation of ants	**Annotated diagrams** – e.g. From tree to egg carton	**Annotated diagrams that illustrate relationships or processes** – e.g. The lifecycle of a frog	**Investigative reports** – e.g. Effects of heating and cooling metals
		Investigative reports – e.g. How plants provide shelter for animals	
	Sequential explanations – e.g. From tree to egg carton	**Causal explanations** – e.g. How fire affects seed germination	**Causal explanations** – e.g. How oxygen affects steel

Source: Adapted from State Government of South Australia (2014, p. 7).

15 LITERACY ACROSS THE CURRICULUM   **367**

REFLECTION

As a graduate teacher, you will be involved in planning and implementation of the curriculum. Review the State Government of South Australia's Science *Genre Scope and Sequence* document (https://sapsp7.weebly.com/uploads/2/4/7/3/24735495/genre_maps_of_the_australi.pdf) and consider how literacy as a general capability provides a scaffold for learning. For example, refer to level 3 'Living Things'. The genre requires the following writing styles: procedures, descriptions, information/investigative reports, annotated diagrams and causal explanations.

1. How would teacher knowledge and use of the following learning outcomes support the planning process?
   - Comprehending texts through listening, reading and viewing
   - Composing texts through speaking, writing and creating elements
   - Text knowledge, grammar knowledge, word knowledge and visual knowledge elements (ACARA, n.d.b).
2. Is there further pedagogical knowledge you might need to plan for literacy, specifically genre writing, for this unit?
3. How could you go about developing this knowledge?

Whole-school planning process

The curriculum coordinator is often the staff member who will collaborate with other staff to ensure that the planning and implementation is covered across the school in a timely and effective way. Professional learning teams (PLTs) or professional learning communities (PLCs) will also drive and contribute to the ever-evolving planning process. This ensures that all staff are supported and guided within the teaching process.

The year-level term planning is often developed collaboratively by teaching teams who work together planning development for the up-and-coming teaching term. During these discussions, decisions and provisions for future term and weekly planning take place. There are four key questions that you can use for effective planning for teaching and learning:

1. What do we expect our children to learn? (learning intentions)
2. How will we know they are learning? (pre- and post-assessment)
3. How will we respond when they don't learn? (intervention)
4. How will we respond if they already know it? (differentiation) (DuFour, 2004).

REFLECTION

1. As a member of a collaborative team, what would you expect to see when teachers work collectively to plan for learning?
2. How might the four key questions for effective planning for teaching and learning support planning in teams?

There are other examples of school-based curriculum planning that can be considered for planning for literacy across the curriculum. Teaching and Learning in South Australia's video 'Engaging with the Australia Curriculum – History in DECD through Learning Design' (www.youtube.com/watch?v=LkrdSg9qBYo) considers how teachers can engage in the learning design process when planning for learning. There are six key ideas that support the learning design process. These are:

1. What is the intended learning and why is it important?
2. What do we want students to learn and what do they bring (prior knowledge)?
3. What could the intended learning look like at this level?
4. How will learners know if they have achieved the learning outcome and what evidence will enable us to assess the learning?
5. How will we engage, challenge and support learning?
6. What will we do to get there? (Teaching and Learning in South Australia, 2012).

REFLECTION

1. In what ways are the six key ideas of learning design similar or different to the PLT/PLC 'four essential questions'?
2. How important is collaboration among teachers in the planning process?
3. What strategies would you take from the learning design process into your practice for planning within subject areas?

Planning for literacy in the learning areas at the classroom level

Along with an emphasis on planning for the specific literacy demands of different subject areas, all planning needs to engage and support learners at their point of need. To ensure that the lessons and units of work teachers develop engage learners, there are a number of models, strategies, activities and resources that can be introduced. These include pedagogical models such as integrated learning, inquiry learning and experiential learning. While these approaches can be embedded at the school level, teachers can also use these at the classroom and subject area level.

The Victorian Curriculum Assessment Authority (VCAA, n.d.) has developed curriculum planning templates that involve four interrelated layers: school, curriculum area, year level and unit/lesson. Reviewing these will assist you with how to go about planning at the unit/lesson level:

- by year level (https://curriculumplanning.vcaa.vic.edu.au/by-year-level) – across curriculum areas
- by unit/lessons (https://curriculumplanning.vcaa.vic.edu.au/by-unit-lessons) – supports activities and resources for all levels (VCAA, n.d.).

Planning for differentiation through the Building Literacy Capabilities Framework

Differentiation is the process of varying your teaching to meet the needs of all the learners in your class. It involves assessing the educational needs of all learners and then modifying teaching approaches to ensure those needs are met. This can result in grouping learners in different ways within a class and then providing customised instruction or exercises within those groups.

The Building Literacy Capabilities Framework, developed by Kitson (2015), can support the process of differentiation. By working through the three steps of the framework, teachers will be able to identify, address and evaluate the specific needs of learners. The Building Literacy Capabilities Framework can be used alongside the teaching and learning cycle, 'with a range of literacy modes (reading and viewing, writing and creating, speaking and listening)' (Kitson, 2015). The framework includes three stages that classroom teachers need to consider in order for learners to meet the literacy demands of a subject area or topic:

- Stage 1: Identifying literacy demands (the what)
- Stage 2: Building literacy capabilities (the how)
- Stage 3: Reflecting on literacy capabilities (what now) (Kitson, 2015).

Using worked examples, Kitson (2015) demonstrates how teachers can carefully review the aspects of the literacy element stated in the learning continuum. When done well, through planning and selecting learning activities, the point of need for each child is addressed. For Stage 1: Identifying literacy demands (the what), teachers need to carefully identify the 'literacy demands in the texts, activities or assessment they have prepared, the key overarching processes (comprehending and composing) identified, and then associated areas of knowledge (text, grammar, word, visual)' are applied (p. 55).

Next, Stage 2: Building literacy capabilities (the how) can be enacted. This incorporates the required knowledge of the topic or subject area being covered, the context of the teaching and the developmental stage of the learner. Another main factor in this part of the planning is the selection of effective teaching strategies to support and engage the learners. Some children will need more than one style of strategy to reinforce learning and understanding.

In Stage 3: Reflecting on literacy capabilities (what now), teachers need to reflect on and evaluate their teaching and progress. This can be achieved through the use of multiple sources of evidence, such as assessment data, observations (both professional and child) and feedback. In this final stage, teachers are able to provide feedback, reflect on data and plan for the next stage of the learning.

> **Differentiation:** when the teacher tailors the learning instruction to meet the individual needs of learners within each lesson.

Planning for Science 'Living Things': Building Literacy Capabilities Framework

CASE STUDY 15.1E

Your team is still planning the Science unit on 'Living Things' for level 3. Using your knowledge of the DuFour model, and genre writing from the 'Engaging with the Australian Curriculum' video you watched earlier, how do you think the Building Literacy Capabilities Framework (Kitson, 2015) might further support your planning of the 'Living Things' unit? Copy out and use Table 15.5 as a template to consider the three-stage process.

►►

370　**ENGLISH AND LITERACIES**

▶ ▶　**Table 15.5** Planning for literacy as a general capability

Planning for literacy as a general capability			
Activity/Task – Title			
Overarching element (select)			
Comprehending texts through listening, reading and viewing		Composing texts through speaking, writing and creating	
	Stage 1: Identifying literacy demands (the what)	Stage 2: Building literacy capabilities (the how)	Stage 3: Reflecting on literacy capabilities (what now)
Text knowledge			
Grammar knowledge			
Word knowledge (refer to tiered vocabulary)			
Visual knowledge			

Questions

1. What aspects of the Building Literacy Capabilities Framework do you think will most support knowledge? What is the teacher's role in this process? Think about the Science (writing) genres.
2. How will using the Building Literacy Capabilities Framework inform the teaching and learning cycle and support the literacy needs of the children in the planning process?

Learning outside the classroom context: curriculum connections resources

In an increasing technologically driven society, it is important for teachers to consider extending the definition and scope for learning beyond the classroom. Our learning environments are rich with access to 'a diverse range of people, activities and contexts' where learners are able to easily interact in flexible and interchangeable ways, more than any previous generation before them (Ward, 2013, p. 1).

The skills commonly used to enact learning beyond the classroom include learners decoding media messages, sharing ideas and strategies, and making selections about the information they choose to engage with. The use of such technologies requires information literacy. Developing information literacy assists learners with navigating technology formats, including the use of apps, gaming and interactive modalities. This landscape is fast-paced and ever-changing. Learners will regularly communicate with each other online in these forums – for example, with use of the TikTok app and interactive games such as Animal Crossing. As teachers, we can promote this literacy knowledge in the classroom through engaging their learning with formats that require the skills they utilise in their own time. Examples of these might include classroom blogs and interactive games.

Schools encourage further learning within the home setting. This is most often carried out through homework expectations. Some of this learning can be catered for by creating tasks that incorporate a number of curriculum areas. Project-based work, where learners research a topic and make a model or replica to represent their learning, is often something that they will undertake at home. For example, a project may be set on natural disasters and a replica volcano, earthquake or tornado model made at home and brought to school for an exhibition of learning. To support this process, the Australian Curriculum has incorporated curriculum connections, which are further resources developed for teachers to apply across the learning areas. The curriculum connections cover the following themes:

- Consumer and financial literacy
- Food and fibre
- Food and wellbeing
- Multimedia
- Online safety
- Outdoor learning.

Aspects of literacy in the following topics are presented in the next section: Multimedia, Food and fibre, Food and wellbeing and Outdoor learning. They can be used to support learning outside the classroom context, with inquiry and investigations carried out at home. The following curriculum connections include literacy as a general capability to support the progression of learning.

Multimedia

The curriculum connection resource 'Multimedia' is designed to support learners with skills in communication and creating with multimedia in school and wider contexts. Opportunities to use multimedia include communicating through narrative about other people and events, including fiction, through forums such as documentaries, advertising and marketing. This can raise awareness of important cultural, social and policy issues.

Literacy as a general capability is used to support learners with access to members of the community and people with expert knowledge, and to connect with cultural perspectives and traditions from the local and wider environments. Through the skills learnt in multimedia, learners create multimedia using design processes and production skills through performance, arts, texts, songs, film, podcasts, blogs, animation and websites.

Food and fibre

The curriculum connection resource 'Food and fibre' provides a framework to develop understanding of primary industries. Students learn about their environment, and the processes of production surrounding the food they eat and the fibres they use for clothing. Issues of consumption and sustainability are also addressed (ACARA, n.d.a).

Literacy as a general capability is used to support learning with opportunities to research and report their knowledge through communicating ideas and investigating how products, services and environments can change over time. Vocabulary may include technical terms for concepts and processes.

Food and wellbeing

The curriculum connection resource 'Food and wellbeing' is focused on both the nutrition and the preparation of food, and the wellbeing of learners as individuals and also as family members. Children learn skills of independence and ways to connect with others in a community. Literacy as a general capability is used to support learners to communicate ideas and concepts, create design briefs and project outlines, and carry out evaluations through listening, talking and questioning. Learners also read and interpret food labels and follow and make recipes. Vocabulary includes technical terms for specific concepts.

Outdoor learning

The curriculum connection resource 'Outdoor learning' develops skills and understandings that value natural environments and the promotion of sustainable use of these environments.

Literacy as a general capability supports understanding of the language used to describe aspects of the outdoors, including maps, products, resources, information and services (ACARA, n.d.a). Learners develop literacy-specific terminology used in outdoor contexts. They comprehend and compose texts related to outdoor experiences. They express their ideas, opinions and emotions appropriately to be 'critical consumers' who 'interpret, analyse and evaluate the ever-changing knowledge influences' of outdoors environments (ACARA, n.d.a).

Conclusion

In this chapter, we explored literacy as one of the Australian Curriculum's seven general capabilities. We also investigated how literacy can be designed and incorporated into planning and teaching across specific learning areas.

Through looking at some pedagogical approaches for teaching literacy across the curriculum, we have thought about different ways to introduce the skills and knowledge required for specific literacy needs within discipline areas, including genre writing and vocabulary. We also looked at planning and implementation approaches that can be applied at the school, grade and classroom levels.

Bringing it together

1. The literacy general capability is designed to be incorporated into planning and teaching within the specific learning areas of the Australian Curriculum. What pedagogical approaches for teaching literacy across the curriculum are essential to support learning?
2. What planning and implementation strategies at the school and classroom levels can be put in place to ensure that literacy as a general capability is catered for?
3. How can literacy learning across the curriculum areas be catered for in the home context?

Further resources

The Teaching and Learning Cycle Project – VicTESOL

The VicTESOL Teaching and Learning Cycle project 2018 highlights the teaching and learning cycle. Led by Beverly Derewianka, EAL/D teachers developed and implemented a unit of work in a range of educational settings across Victoria.

https://victesol.vic.edu.au/index.php/teaching-and-learning-cycle-project/the-teaching-and-learning-cycle

Literacy across learning in secondary schools

This resource from the National Improvement Hub Scotland contains advice for teachers on how to plan learning and teaching experiences to develop and extend learners' literacy skills. It includes reflective questions to use to develop self-evaluation and inform planning for reading, listening, talking and writing, and PDF documents.

https://education.gov.scot/improvement/learning-resources/literacy-across-learning-in-secondary-schools

Oz Lit Teacher – mentor texts

Riss Leung is an Australian educator and literacy consultant whose blog is based on reviewing a range of texts that can be used to support literacy learning in the classroom.

www.ozlitteacher.com.au

References

Australian Curriculum, Assessment and Reporting Authority (ACARA). (n.d.a). Australian Curriculum: Curriculum connections. www.australiancurriculum.edu.au/resources/curriculum-connections

—— (n.d.b). Australian Curriculum: General capabilities. www.australiancurriculum.edu.au/f-10-curriculum/general-capabilities

—— (n.d.c). Australian Curriculum: The literacy learning continuum. www.australiancurriculum.edu.au/media/3596/general-capabilities-literacy-learning-continuum.pdf

Department of Education and Training (DET). (n.d.). Teaching-learning cycle: reading and writing connections. State Government of Victoria. www.education.vic.gov.au/school/teachers/teachingresources/discipline/english/literacy/readingviewing/Pages/teachingpraccycle.aspx

—— (2019). Literacy Teaching Toolkit. State Government of Victoria. www.education.vic.gov.au/school/teachers/teachingresources/discipline/english/literacy/Pages/default.aspx

Derewianka, B.M. (2015). The contribution of genre theory to literacy education in Australia. In J. Turbill, G. Barton, & C. Brock (Eds.), *Teaching Writing in Today's Classrooms: Looking Back to Looking Forward* (pp. 69–86). Australian Literary Educators' Association.

Derewianka, B.M. & Jones, P. (2016). *Teaching Language in Context* (2nd edn). Oxford University Press.

Dollins, C.A. (2016). Crafting creative nonfiction: from close reading to close writing. *The Reading Teacher*, 70(1), 49–58.

DuFour, R. (2004). What is a 'professional learning community'? *Educational Leadership*, 61(8), 6–11.

Freebody, P. (2009). *Literacy Across the Curriculum*. Commonwealth of Australia.

Gilbert, R. (2019). General capabilities in the Australian Curriculum: promise, problems and prospects. *Curriculum Perspectives*, 39(2), 169–177.

Halliday, M.A. (1993). Towards a language-based theory of learning. *Linguistics and Education*, 5(2), 93–116.

Hattie, J. (2012). *Visible Learning for Teachers: Maximizing Impact on Learning*. Routledge.

Israel, M.A. (2008). Using mentor texts to teach nonfiction writing to third graders. *Language Arts Journal of Michigan*, 24(1), 12.

Kimberly. (2013). No tears for tiers: common core tiered vocabulary made simple. www.valrc.org/learning/sbi/docs/8-Vocabulary-Tiers_a.pdf

Kitson, L. (2015). Building literacy capabilities for comprehension in the curriculum: a framework for teachers. *Literacy Learning: The Middle Years*, 23(1), 54.

Konza, D. (2011). Research into practice. *Understanding the Reading Process*, 1, 1–8. Department of Education and Children's Services, Government of South Australia.

National Curriculum Board. (2009). *National English Curriculum: Framing Paper*. National Curriculum Board.

Nikolajeva, M. (2014). *Reading for Learning: Cognitive Approaches to Children's Literature (Vol. 3)*. John Benjamins Publishing Company.

Pytash, K.E. & Morgan, D.N. (2014). Using mentor texts to teach writing in science and social studies. *The Reading Teacher*, 68(2), 93–102.

Rothery, J. (1994). Exploring literacy in school English (Write it right resources for literacy and learning). Metropolitan East Disadvantaged Schools Program, Sydney.

Spencer, M. (2017). Picture books aren't just for kids! Modeling text structures through nonfiction mentor books. *Voices from the Middle*, 24(4), 74.

State Government of South Australia. (2014). Australian Curriculum Genre Maps. https://sapsp7.weebly.com/uploads/2/4/7/3/24735495/genre_maps_of_the_australi.pdf

Teaching and Learning in South Australia. (2012). Engaging with the Australian Curriculum – history in DECD through Learning Design. www.youtube.com/watch?v=LkrdSg9qBYo

Victorian Curriculum Assessment Authority (VCAA). (n.d). Curriculum planning. https://curriculumplanning.vcaa.vic.edu.au/by-school

Vygotsky, L. (1978). Interaction between learning and development. *Readings on the Development of Children*, 23(3), 34–41.

Ward, L. (2013). Literacy within, across and beyond the curriculum. PETAA Paper. www.petaa.edu.au/w/Teaching_Resources/PPs/PETAA_PAPER_190.aspx?hkey=a72d2150-7399-4f0e-a39d-

Wilhelm, J.D. (1997). 'You gotta be the book': teaching engaged and reflective reading with adolescents. *Adolescence*, 32(127), 754.

CHAPTER 16

Partnerships for literacy

Siobhan O'Brien

ANTICIPATED OUTCOMES

After working through this chapter, it is anticipated you will be able to:
- create a learning culture and understand how parents and caregivers support children's literacy engagement in the home setting
- identify ways to encourage family literacy and parent/caregiver participation in supporting children's reading, including culturally and linguistically diverse (CALD) communities and parents of Aboriginal and Torres Strait Islander learners
- consider resources that will support and encourage parent/caregiver participation in children's reading and literacy development
- review literacy learning beyond the classroom learning context with wider department organisation of literacy support networks, school libraries and external community-based networks.

Introduction

Parents and caregivers play an important and valuable role in supporting their children's literacy engagement. To achieve literacy learning beyond the classroom, a positive school culture is integral to the home and school partnership. Throughout this chapter, you will gain knowledge and understanding of how various partnerships can be involved in supporting literacy learning. Such information is aimed to provide you with the skills and knowledge required in extending support for literacy teaching and learning beyond your learning context. This chapter presents approaches and strategies that will support you in engaging parents and caregivers with their child's literacy development, including school-based approaches and practical strategies that you can implement in your daily teaching practice.

As a classroom teacher, your role is to create a setting where parents and caregivers feel comfortable to enter the school and are welcomed to communicate with teachers and leadership about their child's learning. You will read about how to incorporate ways to connect parents and caregivers within school partnerships and also how to support learning in the home. You will also consider how home literacy practices can have a positive impact on children's learning, both social and academic, in the long term. Specific emphasis on ways to support and engage refugee populations and Aboriginal and Torres Strait Islander peoples are also presented.

Throughout the chapter, we engage with content that considers the benefits of fostering literacy engagement in the home and how effective parent and caregiver engagement will occur when the school culture is based on trust and open communication. The chapter also discusses how school settings can develop a positive learning culture that supports all cohorts of parents and caregivers specific to a school context.

The chapter then explores the wider education department organisation of literacy support networks, including working with professionals such as speech pathologists and school-based literacy specialists. It considers the more recent English/literacy specialisation for graduate teachers. The content also considers the role of school-based libraries and other external community networks such as homework clubs.

Creating a learning culture

For parents and caregivers to become actively engaged in their children's learning, teachers and school leadership teams need to invest in fostering trusting relationships. Merga and Mat Roni (2018) stress the importance of developing and maintaining strong school and home partnerships to ensure increased learning engagement. State and territory education departments across Australia all advocate for engaging parents and caregivers with literacy learning. For instance, the Victorian Department of Education and Training (DET, 2019) has incorporated parents, caregivers and partners within the 'Community Engagement in Learning' (DET, n.d.) section of the Framework for Improving Student Outcomes (FISO). The FISO incorporates eight elements that inform state-wide teaching and learning improvement. The element 'Community Engagement in Learning' includes a continuum that illustrates how an excelling school would work to set high expectations and support teachers to collaborate with learners and parents to develop learning goals and plans. Effective schools ensure high levels of parent and caregiver engagement and involvement through maintaining mutual trust and respect. This is achieved by developing a shared responsibility for the education of the learners at the school. An excelling school initiates programs for parents and caregivers to access so that they are able to co-learn with their children.

Community engagement in learning – parents and caregivers as partners

The parents and caregivers as partners dimension is found within the 'Community Engagement in Learning' element of the FISO (see Table 16.1). The Victorian Department of Education and Training aims for schools to develop collaborative parent and caregiver partnerships where the education of learners is enacted as a shared responsibility.

Table 16.1 Community Engagement in Learning Continuum*

Community engagement in learning – parents and carers as partners			
Essential Element 4	Student voice, leadership, and agency in own learning activated so students have positive school experiences and can act as partners in school improvement		
Essential Element 5	Whole-school approach to health, wellbeing, inclusion and engagement		
Emerging	**Evolving**	**Embedding**	**Excelling**
The school fosters communication and meaningful partnerships with parents and carers			
Parents/carers and families are encouraged to participate in school activities specifically designed to invite parents into the school.	Staff ensure all students, parents/carers and families feel safe, welcomed and supported in the school. Parents/carers are encouraged to participate in and contribute to school activities.	Parents/carers are welcomed as partners into the school community and are involved in decisionmaking activities through mechanisms such as parent associations, committees and school council.	The engagement and involvement of parents/carers with the school is embedded in the school culture.
Home learning connects with school learning			
The school encourages parents/carers and family partnerships as a key strategy to improve student outcomes.	The school provides multiple opportunities for parents/carers and school staff to discuss their respective roles in their children's education. They work together to address the health, wellbeing and learning needs of their children.	The school works with parents/carers to highlight the importance of high expectations and setting challenging goals for their children. It provides advice to parents/carers on how they can support these goals.	Parents/carers uphold positive attitudes to learning and consistently support the school's expectations. They work with teachers in setting high expectations to improve outcomes for all students.

Source: DET (n.d.). © State of Victoria (Department of Education and Training). The full table is available on the Department of Education and Training Victorian Government website (www.education .vic.gov.au/Documents/school/teachers/management/dimension4parentscont.pdf).

> **Questions**
>
> 1. How does a school you know foster communication and meaningful partnerships with parents and caregivers? Refer to the continuum to plot this school's progress as outlined in Table 6.1 – emerging, evolving, embedding and excelling.
> 2. How does the school you know foster home learning connections with school learning? Refer to the continuum to plot this school's progress – emerging, evolving, embedding and excelling.

Developing trusting relationships with parents and caregivers

In some circumstances, fostering trusting relationships can be a challenging process and schools will need to work hard at engaging their community. The Organisation for Economic Co-operation and Development (OECD, 2012) notes that if the emphasis for school staff contacting parents is focused on problems and incidents such as academic or behavioural issues, a negative tone within the school can be created. It is very important, if this emphasis occurs in your setting, that it is addressed as a wider school focus on improvement, so that trusting relationships can be developed. A first approach may be to encourage parents and caregivers who are not comfortable entering the school to become more present. Inviting parents and caregivers to events that celebrate their children's learning could be a good starting point. An effective school-wide policy that celebrates literacy achievement, attainment and enjoyment will offer a strong incentive for parents and caregivers to participate in their child's learning (Colgate & Ginns, 2016).

Another approach is to intentionally extend literacy learning into the home, by introducing parents and caregivers to family literacy activities through policy-driven, evidence-based frameworks. Schools that show a willingness to engage in the wider context in which the child learns and adopt such frameworks increase the literacy achievement of children (Colgate & Ginns, 2016). Implementing a 'family literacy' framework requires teachers and parents or caregivers to work together to support children's learning. Within this framework, teachers provide support tools to explain 'what to do' and 'how to do it'.

Supporting parents and caregivers and school- and home-based literacy

Teachers and school leaders need to create, endorse and maintain a philosophy where literacy is held as the highest priority. To achieve this, school-based policies and teacher practice need to clearly communicate with parents and caregivers to keep them informed about the literacy curriculum. Avenues for communication include online portals with information and tasks for learners, parents and caregivers, social media sites, school-based communication systems and newsletters.

When a school sets high expectations that encourage parents and caregivers to work with teachers to support their child's learning, along with guiding the parents and caregivers with strategies on how to go about implementing ongoing home literacy practices, opportunities for student learning can be increased (Emerson et al., 2012). Emerson and colleagues (2012) have developed a model of parental behaviours, associated with school- and home-based involvement and academic socialisation that supports schools with a way to plan and track their progress of engaging parents and caregivers (see Table 16.2). The model uses a grid to show the type of involvement – school-based, home-based and academic socialisation – with four ways that schools can support parents and caregivers: communication, engagement, learning and parenting. By entering actions into each section, teachers and leadership teams are able to focus their attention on any given area that may need further development. Identifying the types of engagement strategies to support literacy that you and your school will use to engage parents and caregivers will depend entirely on the needs of the school community and be most likely linked to the school literacy improvement areas.

Table 16.2 Parental behaviours associated with school- and home-based involvement

Type of support	School-based involvement	Home-based involvement	Academic socialisation
Communication	Between parents and school personnel	Between parents and children about school	Between parents and children about parental expectations for education and about the value and enjoyment of learning
Engagement	Visiting school for school events, participating in school governance and volunteering at school activities	Helping with school work	Discussing learning strategies with children
Learning	Creating opportunities for parents to become involved in academic and learning activities in the school	Creating an environment at home which is conducive to learning	Linking school work to current events and other topics
Parenting	Building relationships between the school and parents	Taking children to events and places the encourage learning (e.g. museums, libraries)	Fostering educational aspirations and making preparations and plans for the future

Source: Emerson et al. (2012, p. 36). © Australian Council of State School Organisations Ltd.

Family literacy

The practice of family literacy in schools and learning contexts has been shown to create a strong culture of literacy practice in the home (Nutbrown & Hannon, 2003). This occurs when teachers acknowledge and embrace a learner's family cultural background. Then, by communicating to families about how their children's literacy can be supported and developed at home, further learning can be attained as well as creating and maintaining co-learning partnerships.

The ORIM family literacy framework

One tool that teachers and school leaders can use to construct family literacy activities is the ORIM framework (Hannon, 1995). The acronym represents the following components of the framework:

- **O**pportunities: parents and caregivers can provide literacy learning opportunities, such as giving children books and writing materials.

- **R**ecognition: parents and caregivers can provide encouragement by knowing their children's literacy learning goals, and supporting and recognising their achievements in reading and writing.
- **I**nteraction: parents and caregivers can interact through sharing and supporting their children with real-life literacy tasks, such as writing a birthday card.
- **M**odel: parents and caregivers become role models in literacy when children observe them using literacy in everyday life. This can include reading books, following written instructions and writing lists.

This framework is a matrix (see Figure 16.1) made up of the four key roles that parents and caregivers can take on to support the literacy development of their child.

	Environmental print	Books	Writing	Oral language
Opportunities				
Parents and caregivers can provide **R**ecognition				
Interaction				
Model				

The program offered parents and caregivers ways of extending what they did in each cell.

Figure 16.1 The ORIM framework for designing a family literacy program
Source: Hannon (1995).

The ORIM family literacy framework was initially implemented with success in early learning settings; however, the framework also lends itself well to primary learning contexts to underpin school strategic planning and literacy policies through the clear articulation of parent and caregiver engagement strategies (Emerson et al., 2012; Hannon,

1995). Using a theoretical framework such as ORIM assists with the conceptualisation of a family literacy program. At the school level, it actively supports parents' and caregivers' awareness of literacy strategies by providing them with various activities for supporting their children. This will either increase what they are already doing or scaffold their initial stages of interaction. When applying the ORIM framework in your setting, the following questions, phrased by Nutbrown and colleagues (2005), can be applied to each cell:

- 'What can a family literacy programme do here to support parents?'

or

- 'What can parents do to help improve children's experiences in this area of literacy?'
  (pp. 50–54)

Answering these questions will ensure the authenticity and effectiveness of the use of framework (Nutbrown et al., 2005, p. 53).

REFLECTION

1. Are there other ways parents and caregivers could help improve children's experiences of literacy? If so, how could the school communicate this to families?
2. What do you think are the essential features teachers and school leaders need to enact in order to offer a strong community engagement of learning that fosters parents and caregivers as partners?

Australian Professional Standards for Teachers

The Australian Professional Standards for Teachers (APST) include two focus areas at each level of the teaching progression that consider the teacher's role in engaging families (see Table 16.3).

Table 16.3 APST focusing on engaging families

Standard	Graduate	Proficient	Highly Accomplished	Lead
3.7 Engage parents/carers in the educative process	Describe a broad range of strategies for involving parents/carers in the educative process.	Plan for appropriate and contextually relevant opportunities for parents/carers to be involved in their children's learning.	Work with colleagues to provide appropriate and contextually relevant opportunities for parents/carers to be involved in their children's learning.	Initiate contextually relevant processes to establish programs that involve parents/carers in the education of their children and broader school priorities and activities.

Table 16.3 (cont.)

Standard	Graduate	Proficient	Highly Accomplished	Lead
7.3 Engage with the parents/carers	Understand strategies for working effectively, sensitively and confidentially with parents/carers.	Establish and maintain respectful collaborative relationships with parents/carers regarding their children's learning and wellbeing.	Demonstrate responsiveness in all communications with parents/carers about their children's learning and wellbeing.	Identify, initiate and build on opportunities that engage parents/carers in both the progress of their children's learning and in the educational priorities of the school.

Source: Australian Institute for Teaching and School Leadership (AITSL, 2017).

Questions

1. What are some strategies within the APST that would involve parents and caregivers in the educative process with a focus on literacy?
2. As a graduate teacher, how would you work effectively, sensitively and confidentially with parents and caregivers?

Parent and caregiver participation in supporting children's reading

Hannon and colleagues (2006) have found that a child's preschool engagement with literacy experiences has a direct impact on their learning and academic achievement. The more actively the parent or caregiver engages with their child's learning, the greater the child's cognitive growth. It is also acknowledged that regardless of socioeconomic or language background, parents and caregivers who read with their children beyond the early years promote better reading performance in adolescence. In homes with established reading practice, where parents and caregivers read and have positive attitudes towards reading, these attitudes are passed onto their children, who then show higher academic achievement than children from families who do not engage in reading or share positive reading attitudes (Colgate & Ginns, 2016). Merga and Mat Roni (2018) also strongly advocate for parents and caregivers to be engaged in their children's education more broadly. They argue that reading together is imperative to this process while also instilling a lifelong love of reading. Children need to see that reading is a daily activity that provides pleasure and enjoyment. Parents can support their children by acting as positive reading role models through reading aloud, talking to children and posing questions, which will situate reading as a social experience (Nagel & Verboord, 2012; Willingham, 2015). Time spent reading together can include different types of texts or formats, from books and magazines to e-texts. More importantly, sharing and discussing what has been read is valuable and worthwhile as it extends children's comprehension, inference and reading confidence. The Programme for International Student Assessment (PISA) (OECD, 2012) calls for parents to actively read in the home because modelling this practice sets a positive example for children.

As children become older and more independent learners and as their academic requirements change (i.e. they read to learn, as opposed to learning to read), other forms of interaction with their parents will arise. As a part of this process, parents and caregivers need to feel comfortable approaching their child's teacher to ask questions about social and academic development from the onset of the child's schooling.

Sometimes it can be a challenge for teachers and parents to encourage children to read at home, particularly if the family has a diminished attitude towards reading or does not engage in regular reading practice. Some strategies to increase the motivation of children's leisure reading can include ensuring that they comprehend the texts being provided and that high-interest reading material is used to engage them (Willingham, 2015). Schools and libraries can play an important part in this process by making recommendations about quality reading texts.

To summarise, parents and caregivers can engage in the daily practice of reading by:

- talking about books with their children – what they like to read and what topics interest them
- reading together for pleasure at home on a regular basis, as shown in Figure 16.2 – this can also be with e-texts and audio books
- having books on hand in the home – regular library visits can be a cost-effective way to access reading material
- engaging in shared reading – reading aloud and discussing the text can be carried out with children at any age.

The Reading WELL

The Reading WELL (Wellbeing in Everyday Language and Literature) is a home reading program that utilises existing home-school reading routines, enhanced through the use of developmental bibliotherapy. The program was designed for children aged 8–10 and supports children's social and emotional wellbeing through the shared reading of books with a parent and child that cover the themes of resilience, body image and self-esteem (see the The Reading Well blog at https://thereadingwell.blog).

Figure 16.2 Read for pleasure at home on a regular basis

ENGLISH AND LITERACIES

Developmental bibliotherapy

Developmental bibliotherapy: a book-reading framework that offers a process to deal with transitions, challenges and difficult situations that may occur in everyday life (Rozalski et al., 2010).

Developmental bibliotherapy is the process of supporting an individual's wellbeing through shared book reading and reflective discussion (Heath et al., 2005). This is achieved through using books that are specifically selected to cover developmentally appropriate topics and have relevance to a person's life situation.

The developmental bibliotherapy framework can be used by teachers, librarians and parents and caregivers to help children grow and develop self-efficacy and positive wellbeing. By involving parents and caregivers in the process, it positions the discussion in a trusted and supportive space. Through reading and discussion about the topic, the child is able to talk through their emotions. The discussion process can also encourage critical thinking and analysis. To receive the full benefits of bibliotherapy, four stages are integrated into the process of book reading, asking discussion questions and engaging in a follow-up activity (Catalano, 2008; Halstead, 2009):

1. *Identification*: the process of relating to a real or fictional character in a non-threatening way – readers are encouraged to draw on experiences from their own lives.
2. *Catharsis*: when emotional tension or anxiety can be released during the reading – as a character works through a problem, the reader relates, and emotional tension is released.
3. *Insight*: the point where discussion and knowledge come together through follow-up questions and activities based on the reading – supporting the child's awareness that their problems can be addressed or solved through the plausible solutions in the book via the characters and synergy of their own experiences.
4. *Universalisation*: the recognition that our difficulties and sense of difference are not ours alone, but are shared and experienced by others and, initially, the characters in the story.

The discussion questions, prompts and follow-up activities need to be carefully developed and address the four areas of bibliotherapy (Catalano, 2008; Morawski, 1997). Suggested responses to support parents and caregivers can also be prepared as a way to help stimulate children's ideas and to support the parents' understanding in framing a discussion.

Developmental bibliotherapy book selection

Stories that are used for developmental bibliotherapy need to include realistic events, problems and solutions because the selected literature is used as a tool to help young people deal with issues at their particular stage of self-identity, independence and self-esteem (Hynes, 2019; Mankiw & Strasser, 2013; Pardeck & Pardeck, 1998). Each event within the story should offer an opportunity for social skill modelling where the reader can identify and take on the role of the character to practise social and emotional skills.

When selecting a book, the recipient's age, reading level, gender, background, cultural perspectives and interests are important considerations, as well as the moral reasoning level of the child (Cartledge & Kiarie, 2001, in Sullivan & Strang, 2002). The story's duration should be no longer than 30 minutes, so that it can be read within one sitting (Forgan, 2002; Lucas & Soares, 2013). The book selection process needs to be carefully considered. As Hynes (2019) points out, a child's response to a book will take into account the style and presentation of the material because these impact upon children's interest and engagement. Table 16.4 lists some books that could be chosen for a Reading WELL activity.

Table 16.4 A selection of titles for The Reading WELL

Body image titles	Self-esteem titles	Resilience titles
• *Little Miss Jessica Goes to School* (Smith & Blakeley, 2015) • *Messages About Me: Sydney's Story, A Girl's Journey to Healthy Body Image* (Roberts & Webb, 2017a) • *Messages About Me: Wade's Story, A Boy's Quest for Healthy Body Image* (Roberts & Webb, 2017b) • *Minnie and Max Are OK: A Story to Help Children Develop a Positive Body Image* (Calland & Hutchinson, 2017) • *Shapesville* (Mills & Osborn, 2003) • *Stand Tall, Molly Lou Melon* (Lovell, 2001)	• *Better Than You* (Ludwig & Gustavson, 2011) • *I Matter* (Wright, 2016) • *The Invisible Boy* (Ludwig & Barton, 2013) • *The Name Jar* (Choi, 2001) • *The Things Lou Couldn't Do* (Spires, 2017)	• *Allie's Basketball Dream* (Barber, 1996) • *My Two Blankets* (Kobald & Blackwood, 2015) • *Rosie Revere, Engineer* (Beaty & Roberts, 2013) • *Thanks for the Feedback, I Think? My Story about Accepting Criticism and Compliments the Right Way* (Cook, 2013) • *The Girl Who Never Made Mistakes* (Rubinstein & Pett, 2011) • *The Juice Box Bully: Empowering Kids to Stand Up for Others* (Sornson & Dismondy, 2010) • *Those Shoes* (Boelts, 2007) • *My Secret Bully* (Ludwig & Marble, 2005)

The Reading WELL in a family routine — CASE STUDY 16.1

Figure 16.3 Children have busy lives filled with extracurricular activities

In Australia, families have busy lives. Between work commitments and regularly scheduled extracurricular activities for children (Figure 16.3), there can be limited time for families to provide children with a focus on literacy at home. The challenge for teachers is to find ways to encourage and facilitate daily reading and writing activities that happen as a part of the family routine. This includes time to read each day. The following scenario explores how the Reading WELL program can help establish literacy-based activities in the family routine.

Lucy is in Year 2 and her brother Michael is in Year 4. They live with their parents in a suburban area of Sydney. Michael loves sports. He plays and trains for basketball three times a week and has squad swimming training early in the mornings and swimming meets on the weekend. Lucy and Michael also like reading. Sometimes their Mum takes them to the library after school, where they borrow books and comics.

The Reading WELL is in Michael's class this term. He brings home a book about a boy who wants to be a professional basketball player. He reads the book with his Mum and they talk about all the pressures and expectations of professional sports and how the boy in the story trains so hard that he gets injured. Their discussion allows Michael to talk to about how he is very tired the day after training because he doesn't sleep well, which makes it hard to concentrate at school. Through reading the story together, Michael can connect and talk openly to his Mum about how he is feeling. His Mum suggests that he either stops swimming or does one less night of basketball training for a while. She is really pleased that she could have this talk with her son, is surprised by how the book gave her insight into Michael's wellbeing and is satisfied that they could find a solution together.

Questions

1. How did the developmental bibliotherapy process support Michael's wellbeing?
2. Do you think sending books home for parent/caregiver and child shared reading is worthwhile?
3. Do you think the link between home and school partnerships could be strengthened with a program like The Reading WELL?

Funds of knowledge

Funds of knowledge are the essential literacies a family requires for economic, social and ceremonial interactions (González et al., 2005). Barton (2000) explains how a challenge arises when 'socially powerful institutions, such as education, tend to support dominant literacy practices' (p. 12). For instance, the funds of knowledge of children from advantaged classes will include ready access to technologies, learning tools and purposeful support from parents (Feld, 2018). This is reflected in the top quarter of the Australian Index of Community Socio-Educational Advantage (ICSEA) listed on the My School website (Australian Curriculum, Assessment and Reporting Authority [ACARA], 2020b). In contrast, for many Aboriginal and Torres Strait Islander peoples, and migrants from diverse linguistic communities, an entanglement occurs, 'in which the problem is not one of illiteracy, but one of literacy in, English' and their first language. As an outcome, they become compromised because of English dominance (González et al., 2005, p. 64).

Culturally and linguistically diverse (CALD) communities

Our cultural background and experiences can influence the way we learn. The 2016 Australian Bureau of Statistics (ABS) census data indicated that almost half (49%) of Australians are either born overseas (first generation Australian) or have one or both parents born overseas (second generation Australian) (ABS, 2016). The most recent census, held in August 2021, has forecasted further population growth, with the numbers of CALD populations expected to increase. With a national population that is culturally and linguistically diverse, this information is directly reflected in many Australian schools and, as teachers, we need to be aware of the specific context of our CALD communities. The way the school approaches literacy learning may need to be carefully considered in order to support the English-language acquisition of children and their families.

It is also important to acknowledge the aspirant nature of immigrant families, and the value they often place on academic achievement (Gauvain et al., 2000). As a classroom teacher, you can provide a supportive learning environment for children and parents from CALD backgrounds (Emerson et al., 2012). Through a family literacy program, teachers can build the confidence of CALD parents and caregivers by guiding them in ways to increase their own literacy skills, as well as sharing resources and strategies that emulate classroom practice. Schools can hold parent/caregiver sessions with interpreters present to share ways to support families to engage in their children's learning. Such collaborative sessions will also help teachers to understand the families' social and cultural circumstances, their needs and the possible barriers to integrating literacy education at home. To facilitate participation, interpreters and multicultural aides can provide support during information sessions and one-to-one meetings.

The aspects that best assist the home literacy practice of families from CALD backgrounds in supporting language acquisition include the use of bilingual books, reading frequency and parental support and engagement (Chu & Wu, 2010). Therefore, it is essential that teachers are prepared and able to provide parents and caregivers with the tools to engage with literacy in their home. Children can take home the required activities with bilingual instructional support in the family's first language, increasing child and parent/caregiver opportunities to learn English. Through these events, the teacher's efforts to connect and support families will not only be very appreciated but will also establish trust (Villiger et al., 2012).

The emphasis on literacy and home reading for refugee populations

The United Nations High Commissioner for Refugees (UNHCR) defines a refugee as someone who 'has been forced to flee his or her country because of persecution, war or violence. A refugee has a well-founded fear of persecution for reasons of race, religion, nationality, political opinion or membership in a particular social group' (UNHCR, 2020). As a part of the Refugee and Humanitarian Program in 2018–19, Australia has facilitated the transition of around 18 750 vulnerable people from around the world, settling them into communities within the various states and territories (Refugee Council of Australia, n.d.). Schools play a critical role in the transition process because they are often the first point of wider community contact for refugee families. Schools also need to understand and support the refugee experience through identifying their needs in settling into an unfamiliar context. This can be achieved through creating authentic relationships and partnerships that facilitate connections and provide linkages to social services and relevant community organisations (Daniel, 2016). Some of the strategies that have been successful within school communities held at school sites include:

- English classes: English-language teachers provide English classes to parents

- multicultural groups: presentations on parenting, immigration advice, gardening and cooking clubs
- parent information sessions held at the school that strengthen the home school partnerships (Emerson et al., 2012; Victorian Foundation for Survivors of Torture et al., 2016).

Families who have had a refugee experience face a number of challenges and transitions during the settlement process. Adjusting to a completely new way of life can be a daunting experience that involves navigating a new culture, language, finances and education systems as part of the transition. There is also the emotional trauma that families may need to work through, including family separations and disrupted schooling (Matthews, 2008). During the time of transition, Australian schools are a very different place for children with a refugee background – the culture and way of life will be unfamiliar. The transition into their new life can take time. Children's sense of identity, personal development and growth are all essential parts of the process. The new learning environment needs to offer a place where children feel safe in order to become settled (Victorian Foundation for Survivors of Torture et al., 2016).

The APST include a focus area at each level of the teaching progression that considers teachers' roles in supporting children with diverse linguistic, cultural, religious and socio-economic backgrounds (see Table 16.5).

Table 16.5 APST 1.3 is focused on supporting children with diverse linguistic, cultural, religious and socioeconomic backgrounds

Standard 1
1.3 Students with diverse linguistic, cultural, religious and socioeconomic backgrounds

Source: AITSL (2017).

CASE STUDY 16.2

Explicit literacy teaching strategies to meet the needs of learners from diverse language backgrounds

AITSL's video 'Literacy teaching strategies' (www.youtube.com/watch?v=_jWXL_fmhTw&t=2s) explores how specific strategies for teaching literacy can meet the needs of learners from diverse language backgrounds. The school is located in south-western Sydney where the majority of learners come from homes where English is an additional language or dialect (EAL/D). The teacher 'models a lesson for teachers with a year 2 class to demonstrate the importance of developing students' oral language skills as a basis for literacy learning' (AITSL, n.d.). The school has formed close links with the wider community. It runs programs such as TAFE classes for parents, a playgroup for refugee families and a homework centre (AITSL, n.d.).

Watch the video and answer the following question.

Question

What did you notice with regard to reading strategies in the teacher demonstration of the lesson to support the needs of learners from diverse language backgrounds?

Engaging parents and caregivers of Aboriginal and Torres Strait Islander learners

It is vital for schools who have families who identify as Aboriginal and/or Torres Strait Islander within their communities to engage them in the education of their children in order to achieve improved educational outcomes (Emerson et al., 2012). Establishing ongoing discussions about the learning that takes place at school and at home is an essential factor for the success of these relationships. Woodrow and colleagues (2016) explored the notion of learning from an Aboriginal perspective, finding that:

> Aboriginal parents recognised learning Aboriginal culture in the home and community within large extended family groups as the most significant of their children's learning. This learning was described as taking place through land, language, history and story with the concept of respect as an overarching concept linking traditional cultural values and everyday life. (p. 24)

Schools have a role to assist in creating a wider discussion about education and learning within Aboriginal and Torres Strait Islander communities. Importantly, with consideration to schooling and learning for Aboriginal and Torres Strait Islander children, parents have called for a 'higher level of agreement between parents and teachers' (Woodrow et al., 2016, p. 24).

> What we, as Indigenous people, ask of you as teachers of our children is to have high expectations and demonstrate your belief that they can and will succeed. We ask you to honour our cultures, and languages and world views; to commit to including things Aboriginal and Torres Strait Islander in the curriculum; to share good practices with each other and the wider community. We ask you to acknowledge that you may have limited knowledge about Aboriginal and Torres Strait Islander cultures and to develop partnerships with those who know more; to increase parent and caregiver participation within the school, and – critically – to assess the outcomes of Aboriginal and Torres Strait Islander students as a key performance indicator of your teaching program and your teaching. (Buckskin & Price, 2012, p. 288)

Cultural competence

Cultural competence is achieved when appropriate knowledge, behaviours, attitudes, policies and systems that enable education partners to work respectfully, in cross-cultural situations, are applied in the educational setting. To respond to the needs of a culturally diverse population, culturally competent teachers, along with Aboriginal and Torres Strait Islander peoples employed in schools and communities, are required to foster the engagement and participation of families in the learning process. Culturally competent teachers will engage with Aboriginal and Torres Strait Islander children in a way that provides them with the 'opportunity to develop the requisite knowledge, [and] skills' to form their personal identities and strong self-esteem (Buckskin & Price, 2012, p. 277).

Reconciliation NSW includes a guide to culturally competent teaching on its website (Reconciliation NSW, 2021). This presents guidelines that support teachers to develop an understanding of what they should consider when creating teaching programs and how to

Cultural competence: when a person or organisation illustrates appropriate knowledge, behaviours, attitudes, policies and systems to work respectfully in cross-cultural situations. This is required when settings respond to the needs of a culturally diverse population, including Aboriginal and Torres Strait Islander peoples.

provide meaningful learning opportunities for Aboriginal learners. AITSL has a useful video available online about culturally competent teaching (see www.youtube.com/watch?v=oJs-0F8jBFDM); and culturally competent training modules are also offered by a range of organisations, including the Koorie Heritage Trust, in Melbourne, and the Centre for Cultural Competence Australia (CCCA).

Yarning circles

Ungunmerr-Baumann (2002) and Bennet-McLean and Dutton (2004, in Mills et al., 2013) explain that a yarning circle is a part of the oral language tradition of 'Australian Indigenous communities and is sometimes called Dadirri – inner deep listening to the land. The Yarning circle extends from the traditional Murri "Bora" – a circular ceremonial space for communal gathering and sharing' (p. 286). The yarning circle offers an avenue for Indigenous and non-Indigenous learners, teachers and parents to come together. Teachers have also adapted yarning circles to support literacy learning in the classroom and have found them to be effective in opening up shared discussions on themes covered in reading, stimulating writing ideas and as a reflection method (Mills et al., 2013). The Queensland Curriculum and Assessment Authority (QCAA, 2020) has also seen benefits of yarning circles in building respectful relationships and creating harmonious and collaborative ways of communicating.

The APST include a focus area at each level of the teaching progression that considers teachers' roles in promoting reconciliation between Indigenous and non-Indigenous Australians (see Table 16.6).

Table 16.6 APST 2.4 is focused on promoting reconciliation between Indigenous and non-Indigenous Australians

Standard 2
2.4 Understand and respect Aboriginal and Torres Strait Islander people to promote reconciliation between Indigenous and non-Indigenous Australians

Source: AITSL (2017).

Cross-curriculum priorities in the Australian Curriculum

In the Australian Curriculum, Aboriginal and Torres Strait Islander Histories and Cultures is a cross-curriculum priority. Within the English curriculum, Aboriginal and Torres Strait Islander Histories and Cultures is designed to support learners with developing awareness, appreciation of and respect for Aboriginal and Torres Strait Islander peoples. This is achieved through the use of literature and includes storytelling traditions (oral narrative).

The introductory statement of the Aboriginal and Torres Strait Islander Histories and Cultures priority outlines how the Australian Curriculum addresses two distinct needs in Aboriginal and Torres Strait Islander education:

First, that Aboriginal and Torres Strait Islander students are able to see themselves, their identities and their cultures reflected in the curriculum of each of the learning areas, can fully participate in the curriculum and can build their self-esteem. Second, that Aboriginal and Torres Strait Islander Histories and Cultures cross-curriculum priority is designed for all students to engage in reconciliation, respect and recognition of the world's oldest continuous living cultures. (ACARA, 2020a)

The organisation of Aboriginal and Torres Strait Islander Histories and Cultures as a cross-curriculum priority is embedded in the content descriptions and elaborations of each learning area as appropriate. The icon in Figure 16.4 is used for identification of the embedded context.

Figure 16.4 Icon for Aboriginal and Torres Strait Islander Histories and Cultures in the Australian Curriculum
Source: ACARA (2020a).

Literacy learning beyond the classroom learning context

This section provides you with knowledge and understanding of the wider organisation of literacy education in schools and insight into the structures, programs and partnerships in place to support delivery of literacy education in schools. This includes school-based specialist literacy educators and coaches, the AITSL primary specialisation priorities for graduate teachers, literacy support staff, including professional speech therapists, psychologists, occupational therapists, paediatricians and social workers, and the role of libraries (school and community) and homework clubs.

Literacy learning specialists

Australian states, such as Victoria, have recently moved to acknowledge the expertise of their existing staff with the newly appointed role of literacy learning specialists. This role should be provided to an expert teacher with expertise in literacy, knowledge content and pedagogy. A literacy learning specialist is a skilled classroom teacher whose work can incorporate:

- classroom teaching
- demonstration lessons

- observing and providing feedback to other teachers and facilitating school-based professional learning
- developing and promoting school-wide professional learning
- supervising and training pre-service teachers and graduate teachers (DET, 2017).

Literacy learning specialists may also have a blended role of reading specialist and/or literacy coach. The reading specialist role could include reading recovery or reading intervention with learners who require extension or further support with reading (Pletcher et al., 2019).

Literacy learning specialists are effective when they develop trusting relationships. The role's success is steeped in the specialist's ability to communicate, listen, empathise and ask questions. Literacy learning specialists also need to have a clear perspective when they are working with others, and this is determined through the shared goals and objectives that are devised during the instructional conversations (Toll, 2018).

Literacy coaching models

Instructional coaching models in Australian schools have become common, with visible learning and instructional teaching strategies a part of whole-school pedagogical models (Hattie, 2012). For instance, instructional coaching approaches are well established in some states, including Victoria, where approaches include literacy specialists working side-by-side in collaboration with teachers in classrooms. The instructional coaching model is effective when it provides authentic professional development for teachers that is directly related to their individual needs and embedded in day-to-day work (Rennie, 2011).

CASE STUDY 16.3 | **Jenny and the literacy learning specialist meet to plan the Term 2 observation and feedback model**

Jenny is a graduate teacher in her first year. Her school has a literacy learning specialist who is planning to work with her in Term 2. The literacy learning specialist will come in and conduct demonstration lessons that Jenny will observe, and then Jenny will teach using the approaches she has seen while the literacy learning specialist observes and provides feedback on Jenny's teaching. Jenny feels a bit nervous, but also has a good relationship with the literacy learning specialist, and the model is well developed in the school.

Question

What do you think the benefits would be to having the literacy learning specialist supporting Jenny in the classroom?

Instructional conversation: where a coach and coached teacher come together to debrief or share feedback on a teaching session. During the conversation, points of reflection and areas for change are discussed.

Instructional conversations

Following an agreed period of teaching demonstration and/or observation on a pre-decided goal or area of literacy focus, an **instructional conversation** will occur. This acts as a debriefing or feedback session, where points of reflection and areas for change are discussed. This is where the need for trust and open communication comes in – the coach provides the feedback and the coached person receives it. For this conversation to be effective, a number of agreed protocols can be used – with a clear plan in place, the feedback will be specific. The coach will then review and select points from their notes or a recording of the feedback discussions related to the focus of the session and highlight the positive areas of the teacher's practice, as well as some areas for further development that will support progress in the next session. It is important to ensure the tone of these sessions is positive and supportive (Hammond & Moore, 2018).

Jenny and the literacy learning specialist meet to debrief and plan the next steps

CASE STUDY 16.4

Following the targeted observations of Jenny's teaching by the literacy learning specialist, Jenny completes a reflection with guiding questions about her teaching. She then meets with the literacy learning specialist for a debriefing session and to plan the next steps. Jenny is feeling very positive about the experience, and she has enjoyed the opportunity to think critically and reflect on her teaching.

Question

How do you think having the literacy learning specialist supporting Jenny in the classroom might impact on teaching practice and student learning?

Primary specialisation of graduate teachers

As a part of the Initial Teacher Education reform in Australia, AITSL has worked with stakeholders to develop a primary specialisation within the learning areas of Mathematics/numeracy, Science and English/literacy. The features of the English/literacy specialisation are in the context of the APST Graduate stage. Graduates completing their degree with a literacy specialisation will draw on their knowledge of their state or territory curriculum and the Australian Curriculum to work within a school in collaboration with a literacy team to engage in strategies designed to achieve increased outcomes of student literacy learning across the primary curriculum. The key staff in this area will include learning specialists, coaches and professional learning teams.

As an English/literacy specialist at the graduate level, AITSL (2017) states that graduates will have additional depth of understanding within the three domains: (1) expert content knowledge; (2) pedagogical content knowledge; and (3) highly effective classroom teaching in their area of specialisation.

Literacy student support services

Australian education departments offer various student support services. Professionals work within integrated agencies to provide ongoing health and wellbeing-related services to children and families. The student support services include professionals who are trained psychologists, speech pathologists and social workers. This allied health workforce works within schools to focus on providing group-based and individual support of learners and families and can also offer professional development for school staff and the provision of specialised services. For learners to access support, the school needs to arrange for assessment of learning needs and funding is organised by the relevant state or territory education department.

Speech pathology

Speech pathologists work with children in schools to diagnose and treat problems with social communication, speaking and listening, such as stuttering and interpreting language (both written and oral) communication. They also work with learners who have disabilities, including children who have cerebral palsy or are hearing impaired.

Education support staff

Students who are diagnosed with a learning need in a mainstream school will qualify for additional support in the classroom. This education support is provided by school staff. For example, a classroom teacher with a child who has diagnosed learning needs will plan the child's learning and the education support person will assist the teacher to support the child's education needs and meet the agreed goals in their Individual Learning Plan.

School libraries as learning hubs

The Australian Library and Information Association (ALIA) is a professional body that provides support and professional development for school library educators and encourages teacher-trained librarians to obtain qualifications in librarianship to ensure they possess the knowledge to uphold the quality of a twenty-first-century school library. For school libraries to be successful, they need to be considered as valued places of learning by the school community. Schools are encouraged to consider the following advice by Merga (2020), who suggests that school leadership teams need to provide for time for children to access the library for specialist sessions with a qualified librarian within the school week, as well as have open access to the library before, during and after school. Resources and staffing need to be adequate, with provision within school budgets and funding that invests in developing spaces that are conducive to both reading and learning engagement. ALIA (2017) maintains that school libraries can make a valuable contribution to learners' academic achievement when they are accessible and equipped with quality resources.

Homework clubs

Some schools have partnered with philanthropic organisations, such as the Edmund Rice Foundation, to run free out-of-school-hours homework clubs. These sessions are designed to support learners with opportunities for further learning, English-language support, recreation and social skill development. The programs are run with volunteers that include pre-service teachers, senior school students and local community members. School staff can also have a direct presence, offering further value to the program (Mahoney & Siyambalapitiya, 2017).

REFLECTION

As a pre-service teacher, have you considered offering your skills as a volunteer to a local homework club? Conduct a search to see if there are any homework clubs in your area.

Conclusion

This chapter discussed how parents and caregivers play an important and valuable role in supporting their children's literacy engagement and that a positive school culture is integral to the home and school partnership. Literacy learning goes beyond the classroom. The community a school is within needs to establish strong home-school literacy partnerships because these have a positive impact on children's learning, both social and academic, in the long term.

Considerations need to be made in the way schools and classroom settings go about developing a positive learning culture that supports all cohorts of parents and caregivers specific to the school context, including refugee populations and Aboriginal and Torres Strait Islander peoples, with the aim of creating settings where parents are comfortable with entering the school to communicate with teachers about their child's learning. School-based approaches and practical strategies were also presented that are effective in fostering literacy engagement in the home through family literacy programs.

The chapter offered aspects of literacy support provided by the wider education department, school-based roles of literacy specialists and the more recent literacy specialisations for graduate teachers. It also considered the important role of school-based libraries and external community networks such as homework clubs.

Bringing it together

1. Why should schools include parents and caregivers in the role of supporting their children's literacy engagement?
2. How can a teacher go about fostering literacy engagement in the home? How would they achieve this with families who are from:
   - refugee populations
   - Aboriginal and Torres Strait Islander backgrounds?
3. Identify strategies that are responsive to the 'learning strengths and needs of students from diverse linguistic, cultural, religious and socioeconomic backgrounds' (AITSL, 2017).
4. Refer to the APST Graduate focus area 2.4 (AITSL, 2017). What are some ways you can demonstrate broad knowledge of understanding of and respect for Aboriginal and Torres Strait Islander History and Cultures?

Further resources

Aboriginal and Torres Strait Islander education: resources for pre-service teachers

The Respect Relationships Reconciliation (3Rs) resources can be used to support incorporating Aboriginal and Torres Strait Islander content into teaching programs. The 3Rs materials comprise three separate, but interconnected, study modules.

https://rrr.edu.au

Homework clubs

The Centre for Multicultural Youth has a Homework Clubs database that includes over 350 learning support programs across Victoria.

www.cmy.net.au/homework-clubs

Literacy and numeracy tips to help your child every day

The Victorian Government's *Literacy and Numeracy* booklet includes ways for parents and caregivers to help children develop literacy and numeracy skills at home.

www.education.vic.gov.au/Documents/school/teachers/teachingresources/discipline/english/literacy/LiteracyandNumeracyTipstoHelpYourChild_Final.pdf

References

Australian Bureau of Statistics (ABS). (2016). Census reveals a fast changing, culturally diverse nation. www.abs.gov.au/ausstats/abs@.nsf/lookup/MEdia%20Release3#:~:text=The%202016%20Census%20shows%20that,overseas%20(second%20generation%20Australian)

Australian Curriculum, Assessment and Reporting Authority (ACARA). (2020a). Australian Curriculum. Cross-curriculum priorities. www.australiancurriculum.edu.au/f-10-curriculum/cross-curriculum-priorities

—— (2020b). My School. www.myschool.edu.au

Australian Institute for Teaching and School Leadership (AITSL). (n.d.). Literacy teaching strategies – illustrations of practice. www.aitsl.edu.au/tools-resources/resource/literacy-teaching-strategies-illustration-of-practice

—— (2017). Australian Professional Standards for Teachers. www.aitsl.edu.au/teach/standards

Australian Library and Information Association (ALIA). (2017). About school libraries. www.alia.org.au/school-libraries

Barber, B. (1996). *Allie's Basketball Dream*. Lee & Low Books.

Barton, D.P. (2000). Researching literacy practices. In D.P. Barton, M.E. Hamilton, & R. Ivanic (Eds.), *Situated Literacies: Reading and Writing in Context*. (pp. 167–179). Routledge.

Beaty, A. & Roberts, D. (2013). *Rosie Revere, Engineer*. Harry N. Abrams.

Bennet-McLean, D. & Dutton, J. (2004). Delivering the dream: an Indigenous approach to strategic planning. In *Proceedings from the Education and Social Action Conference*.

Boelts, M. (2007). *Those Shoes*. Candlewick.

Buckskin, P. & Price, K. (2012). Engaging Indigenous students: the important relationship between Aboriginal and Torres Strait Islander students and their teachers. In K. Price (Ed.), *Aboriginal and Torres Strait Islander Education: An Introduction for the Teaching Profession* (pp. 164–180). Cambridge University Press.

Calland, C. & Hutchinson, N. (2017). *Minnie and Max Are OK: A Story to Help Children Develop a Positive Body Image*. Jessica Kingsley Publishers.

Cartledge, G. & Kiarie, M.W. (2001). Through literature for children and adolescents. *Teaching Exceptional Children*, 34(2), 40–47.

Catalano, A. (2008). Making a place for bibliotherapy on the shelves of a curriculum materials center: the case for helping pre-service teachers use developmental bibliotherapy in the classroom. *Education Libraries*, 31(1), 17–22.

Choi, Y. (2001). *The Name Jar*. Knopf.

Chu, S.Y. & Wu, H.P. (2010). Understanding literacy practices in culturally and linguistically diverse children's homes. *New Horizons for Learning*, 8(2).

Colgate, O. & Ginns, P. (2016). The effects of social norms of parents' reading behaviour at home with their child. *Educational Psychology*, 36(5), 1009–1023.

Cook, J. (2013). *Thanks for the Feedback, I Think? My Story about Accepting Criticism and Compliments the Right Way*. Boys Town Press.

Daniel, G.R. (2016). Parents' experiences of teacher outreach in the early years of schooling. *Asia Pacific Journal of Education*, 36(4), 559–569.

Department of Education and Training (DET). (n.d.). Community engagement in learning – parents as carers and partners. www.education.vic.gov.au/Documents/school/teachers/management/dimension4parentscont.pdf

—— (2017). *Roles and Responsibilities Teaching Service*. Victorian State Government. www.education.vic.gov.au/hrweb/Documents/Roles_and_responsibilities-TS.pdf

—— (2019). FISO dimension: parents and carers as partners. Victorian State Government. www.education.vic.gov.au/school/teachers/management/improvement/Pages/dimension4parents.aspx#link39

Emerson, L., Fear, J., Fox, S., & Sanders, E. (2012). *Parental Engagement in Learning and Schooling: Lessons from Research. A Report by the Australian Research Alliance for Children and Youth (ARACY)*. Family-School and Community Partnerships Bureau.

Feld, I. (2018). *Parental Involvement and Social Background in Canada and Germany: Limitations and Possibilities of a Comparative Analysis of the Progress in International Reading Literacy Study (PIRLS) 2011*. Waxmann Verlag.

Forgan, J.W. (2002). Using bibliotherapy to teach problem solving. *Intervention in School and Clinic*, 38(2), 75–82.

Gauvain, M., Savage, S., & McCollum, D. (2000). Reading at home and at school in the primary grades: cultural and social influences. *Early Education and Development*, 11(4), 447–463.

González, N., Moll, L., Tenery, M.F., Rivera, A., Rendón, P., Gonzales, R., & Amanti, C. (2005). Funds of knowledge for teaching in Latino households. In N. González, L.C. Moll, & C. Amanti (Eds.), *Funds of knowledge: Theorizing Practices in Households, Communities, and Classrooms* (pp. 89–111). Lawrence Erlbaum Associates Publishers.

Halstead, J.W. (2009). *Some of My Best Friends Are Books: Guiding Gifted Readers from Preschool to High School* (3rd edn). Great Potential Press.

Hammond, L. & Moore, W.M. (2018). Teachers taking up explicit instruction: the impact of a professional development and directive instructional coaching model. *Australian Journal of Teacher Education*, 43(7), 110–133.

Hannon, P. (1995). *Literacy, Home, and School: Research and Practice in Teaching Literacy with Parents*. Psychology Press.

Hannon, P., Morgan, A., & Nutbrown, C. (2006). Parents' experiences of a family literacy programme. *Journal of Early Childhood Research*, 4(1), 19–44.

Hattie, J. (2012). *Visible Learning for Teachers: Maximizing Impact on Learning*. Routledge.

Heath, M.A., Sheen, D., Leavy, D., Young, E., & Money, K. (2005). Bibliotherapy: a resource to facilitate emotional healing and growth. *School Psychology International*, 26(5), 563–580.

Hynes, A.M. (2019). *Bibliotherapy: The Interactive Process. A Handbook*. Routledge.

Kobald, I. & Blackwood, F. (2015). *My Two Blankets* (Illustrated ed.). HMH Books for Young Readers.

Lovell, P. (2001). *Stand Tall, Molly Lou Melon*. Penguin.

Lucas, C.V. & Soares, L. (2013). Bibliotherapy: a tool to promote children's psychological well-being. *Journal of Poetry Therapy*, 26(3), 137–147.

Ludwig, T. & Barton, P. (2013). *The Invisible Boy*. Random House.

Ludwig, T. & Gustavson, A. (2011). *Better Than You*. Knopf Books for Young Readers.

Ludwig, T. & Marble, A. (2005). *My Secret Bully*. Random House.

Mahoney, D. & Siyambalapitiya, S. (2017). Community-based interventions for building social inclusion of refugees and asylum seekers in Australia: A systematic review. *Journal of Social Inclusion*, 8(2), 66–80.

Mankiw, S. & Strasser, J. (2013). Tender topics: exploring sensitive issues with pre-K through first grade children through read-alouds. *YC Young Children*, 68(1), 84.

Matthews, J. (2008). Schooling and settlement: refugee education in Australia. *International Studies in Sociology of Education*, 18(1),31–45.

Merga, M.K. (2020). School libraries fostering children's literacy and literature learning: mitigating the barriers. *Literacy*, 54(1), 70–78.

Merga, M.K. & Mat Roni, S. (2018). Children's perceptions of the importance and value of reading. *Australian Journal of Education*, 62(2), 135–153.

Mills, A. & Osborn, B. (2003). *Shapesville*. Gurze Books.

Mills, K.A., Sunderland, N., & Davis-Warra, J. (2013). Yarning circles in the literacy classroom. *The Reading Teacher*, 67(4), 285–289.

Morawski, C.M. (1997). A role for bibliotherapy in teacher education. *Reading Horizons: A Journal of Literacy and Language Arts*, 37(3), 6.

Nagel, I. & Verboord, M. (2012). Reading behaviour from adolescence to early adulthood: a panel study of the impact of family and education on reading fiction books. *Acta Sociologica*, 55(4), 351–365.

Nutbrown, C. & Hannon, P. (2003). Children's perspectives on family literacy: methodological issues, findings and implications for practice. *Journal of Early Childhood Literacy*, 3(2), 115–145.

Nutbrown, C., Hannon, P. & Morgan, A. (2005). *Early Literacy Work with Families: Policy, Practice and Research*. Sage.

Organisation for Economic Co-operation and Development (OECD). (2012). *Let's Read Them a Story! The Parent Factor in Education*. OECD Publishing. http://dx.doi.org/10.1787/9789264176232-en

Pardeck, J.T. & Pardeck, J.A. (1998). An exploration of the uses of children's books as an approach for enhancing cultural diversity. *Early Child Development and Care*, 147(1), 25–31.

Pletcher, B.C., Hudson, A.K., John, L., & Scott, A. (2019). Coaching on borrowed time: balancing the roles of the literacy professional. *The Reading Teacher*, 72(6), 689–699.

Queensland Curriculum and Assessment Authority (QCAA). (2020). Yarning circles. www.qcaa.qld.edu .au/about/k-12-policies/aboriginal-torres-strait-islander-perspectives/resources/yarning-circles

Reconciliation NSW. (2021). Culturally competent teaching. www.schoolsreconciliationchallenge.org .au/culturally-competent-teaching

Refugee Council of Australia. (n.d.). 2018–2109 federal budget: what it means for refugees and people seeking humanitarian protection. www.refugeecouncil.org.au/wp-content/ uploads/2018/12/2018-2019-Budget-summary.pdf

Rennie, J. (2011). Learning to read: a professional learning journey. *The Australian Educational Researcher*, 38(2), 221–238.

Roberts, K. & Webb, J. (2017a). *Messages About Me: Sydney's Story, A Girl's Journey to Healthy Body Image*. Rising Parent Media.

—— (2017b). *Messages About Me: Wade's Story, A Boy's Quest for Healthy Body Image*. Rising Parent Media.

Rozalski, M., Stewart, A., & Miller, J. (2010). Bibliotherapy: helping children cope with life's challenges. *Kappa Delta Pi Record*, 47(1), 33–37.

Rubinstein, G. & Pett, M. (2011). *The Girl Who Never Made Mistakes*. Sourcebooks.

Smith, J. & Blakeley, J. (2015). *Little Miss Jessica goes to school*. Jessica Smith.

Sornson, B. & Dismondy, M. (2010). *The Juice Box Bully: Empowering Kids to Stand Up for Others*. Nelson Publishing & Marketing.

Spires, A. (2017). *The Things Lou Couldn't Do*. Kids Can Press.

Sullivan, A.K. & Strang, H.R. (2002). Bibliotherapy in the classroom using literature to promote the development of emotional intelligence. *Childhood Education*, 79(2), 74–80.

Toll, C.A. (2018). Progress in literacy coaching success – a dozen years on. *The Clearing House: A Journal of Educational Strategies, Issues and Ideas*, 91(1), 14–20.

Ungunmerr-Baumann, M.R. (2002). Dadirri: inner deep listening and quiet still awareness. Emmaus.

United Nations High Commissioner for Refugees (UNHCR). (2020). What is a refugee? A person forced to flee their country because of violence or persecution. www.unrefugees.org/refugee-facts/what-is-a-refugee

Victorian Foundation for Survivors of Torture, Grant, J., Francis, S. et al. (2016). *School's in for Refugees: A Whole-school Approach to Supporting Students and Families of Refugee Background* (2nd edn). Victorian Foundation for Survivors of Torture Incorporated.

Villiger, C., Niggli, A., Wandeler, C., & Kutzelmann, S. (2012). Does family make a difference? Mid-term effects of a school/home-based intervention program to enhance reading motivation. *Learning and Instruction*, 22(2), 79–91.

Willingham, D.T. (2015). For the love of reading: engaging students in a lifelong pursuit. *American Educator*, 39(1), 4.

Woodrow, C., Somerville, M., Naidoo, L., & Power, K. (2016). *Researching Parent Engagement: A Qualitative Field Study*. The Centre for Educational Research, Western Sydney University.

Wright, L. (2016). *I Matter*. Laurie Wright.

Glossary

Acquisition: a process that occurs largely naturally and unconsciously, via experimentation, and in informal, social settings (Krashen, 1982).

Analytic phonics: an emphasis on larger sub-parts of words (i.e. onsets and rimes, spelling patterns) and phonemes. The starting point is children's known language, but an explicit focus on the components of words, including letter-sound correspondences, follows (Ewing, 2018, p. 11).

Assessment: all informal and formal processes, used by teachers, learners and others, to interpret information about learners' progress. The most important goal of assessment should always be to enhance learning.

Assessment *as* learning: learners self-assess using a range of different assessment strategies, especially in rich tasks, and reflect on their own learning achievements (Earl, 2013). Peer assessment against explicit criteria can also be an important learning experience.

Assessment *for* learning: tasks that are designed to understand learners' current knowledge and skills to enable the teacher to plan future learning activities and experiences that will meet their needs.

Assessment *of* learning: tasks that are designed to ascertain what a learner knows and understands at the end of a sequence of lessons or unit of work. The Australian Curriculum provides expectations for particular year levels in key learning areas.

Authentic or educative assessment: rich and realistic assessment tasks and practices that engage the learner and are linked meaningfully to learning and the curriculum.

BICS: basic interpersonal communication skills.

Bottom-up approach: describes engagements with text that emphasise working from the individual components of language (e.g. sounds, letters or characters, words, and sentences) up to the overall meaning.

CALP: cognitive academic language proficiency.

Children's literature: a broad range of literature such as picture books, verse novels, short stories and plays, visual and multimodal texts such as book trailers and films, and an assortment of non-fiction that help learners be active, constructive and engaged literacy learners.

Cloze activity: the omission of key words or phrases in a text to enable learners to make a meaningful selection.

Concepts and conventions of print: the rules of written language. such as direction of print, that enable readers and writers to follow the same system when interacting with text.

Critical literacy: a questioning and discussing of ideas in a story, podcast, video or game to analyse the attitudes embedded about gender, culture and belief systems.

Cross-curriculum priorities: within the Australian Curriculum, are the skills, knowledge and understandings required to enable effective engagement in a globalised world.

Cultural competence: when a person or organisation illustrates appropriate knowledge, behaviours, attitudes, policies and systems to work respectfully in cross-cultural situations. This is required when settings respond to the needs of a culturally diverse population, including Aboriginal and Torres Strait Islander peoples.

Curriculum: encompasses all the experiences that occur within the school or other learning context. It includes what is intended in syllabus documents (the *intended* or *formal* curriculum), what the teacher implements (the *enacted* curriculum) and what becomes the actuality for the individual learners (the *experienced* curriculum). As well, there are unintended outcomes, often referred to as the *hidden curriculum*.

Decoding: to work out the meaning of words in text, readers combine contextual, vocabulary, grammatical and phonic knowledge effectively (Ewing, 2018, p. 10).

Developmental bibliotherapy: a book-reading framework that offers a process to deal with transitions, challenges and difficult situations that may occur in everyday life (Rozalski et al., 2010).

Developmental theories: suggest children's readiness to engage in reading and writing can be accelerated by 'pre-reading' activities (Barratt-Pugh & Rohl, 2001; Fellowes & Oakley, 2014).

Differentiation: when the teacher tailors the learning instruction to meet the individual needs of learners within each lesson.

Diversity: acknowledging and understanding the uniqueness of every individual, including the dimensions of race, gender, ethnicity and sexual orientation, while, at the same time, valuing our interdependence as human beings.

EAL/D: English as an additional language or dialect.

Elaborated code: a more explicit or formal way of using language so that the language itself stands on its own rather than being tied to a specific context.

Embedded phonics: 'Children are taught letter-sound relationships during the reading of connected text. Since children encounter different letter-sound relationships as they read, this approach will not be a preconceived sequence, but can still be thorough and explicit' (Ewing, 2018, p. 11).

Embodiment: physically representing an idea, concept, emotion or character.

Emergent literacy: an approach that recognises the importance of children's drawing, talking, singing, playing and engaging with images and print, and the connection between these and other forms of communicative practice, such as reading and writing (Rohde, 2015; Strickland, 1990).

Enactment: actioning an event, a moment in time or a character's reaction to a dilemma.

Environmental print: print (including letters and symbols) in the environment; some examples include house numbers, street signs and logos on advertisements.

Etymology: 'The study of the origin and history of words and how their form and meaning changes over time' (Ewing, 2018, p. 10).

Evaluation: an umbrella term that stems from *value* and generally refers to making a judgement or estimation about the worth of something. In education contexts, evaluation is often used to refer to the effectiveness of teachers' strategies, activities and experiences or particular resources.

Expression: the language used for the intended audience.

External norm-referenced testing: compares the results of an individual learner with so-called 'norms' or 'normal' results of a group of learners of the same age or grade.

Formative assessment: plays a pivotal role in the teaching and learning decisions that teachers make. Teachers collect diagnostic information about a learner's needs and abilities (one kind of assessment for learning).

Functional model of language: considers how spoken and written modes of language enable us to understand the world around us in both school and community contexts; the model explores the textual function of language.

Funds of knowledge: the understandings, practices and resources that each learner develops in their home and communities (Moll et al., 1992). This concept is connected to Vygotsky's social development theory.

General capabilities: within the Australian Curriculum, are the essential skills required for learners to live and work successfully in the twenty-first century.

Genre: the social purpose of an oral or written text.

Grapheme: 'A single letter or combination of letters that represent a phoneme. Graphemes occur within morphemes and can represent more than one phoneme. In English, 44 sounds and 26 letters offer more than 120 grapheme choices' (Ewing, 2018, p. 10).

Graphophonic knowledge: 'The knowledge of how letters relate to the sounds of spoken language' (Ewing, 2018, p. 10).

Graphotactic: the arrangement of letters and letter patterns to inform spelling rather than pronunciation.

Hidden curriculum: an unintended consequence within curriculum – for example, a learner who is complimented for sitting quietly may learn that quiet compliance is the desired behaviour.

High-stakes tests: tests where there is much at stake for the learner and the educational institution. Results are made public and tables are constructed that rank and compare learners and their schools. For example,

GLOSSARY 401

in Australia, NAPLAN test scores have been used to compare the results of learners in so-called 'like' schools on the My School website.

Inclusive assessment practices: recognise and honour the diversity of learners and how they learn so that assessment tasks are fair and equitable and do not privilege some learners over others.

Inclusive learning environments: learning environments where all learners feel they belong and are supported socially, emotionally, intellectually and academically.

Infer: extract something from evidence in a text not made explicit. Inferential comprehension is the ability to understand the underlying or deeper meaning(s) of a text as opposed to its literal meaning.

Instructional conversation: where a coach and coached teacher come together to debrief or share feedback on a teaching session. During the conversation, points of reflection and areas for change are discussed.

Intertextuality: the relationships between literary texts.

Joint construction: supports learners to jointly compose a text through both oral interaction with their teacher and peers and by sharing a pen or keyboard in the creation of a text. Also known as *guided writing*.

LBOTE: language background other than English.

Learning: a conscious process that involves some degree of analysis, instruction or explanation (Krashen, 1982).

Literacies: may be defined as the various tools we use for engaging with text.

Maturational theories: argue that children need to reach the required level of maturity before commencing reading and writing instruction (Crain, 2010; Oliveira, 2018

Measure: assign a numerical score, grade or level to a task that has an established scale.

Mentor texts: literature that can be used to model forms of writing or specific structures and features.

Mentor texts can be studied as exemplars and used as models for a teaching skill.

Metacognition: awareness of our thinking and learning skills and processes.

Metalanguage: the language we use to communicate about language. Examples of metalanguage include 'noun', 'conjunction' and 'metaphor'. It is important to ensure all learners have the opportunity to develop metalanguage for different modalities (Kress, 2003; Unsworth, 2006) – for example, the words 'icon' and 'symbol' may be used to discuss visual text.

Microskills: the underlying resources and repertoires we use to read, view, write, listen and speak (Brown, 2001).

Mode: the way that something is communicated – for example, written, spoken or performed. Serafini (2012) refers to this as the 'system of signs created within or across various cultures to represent and express meanings' (p. 153).

Morphology: 'The system-enabling morphemes that combine to represent the meaning of words. Every word is either a base, or a base with another morpheme fixed to it' (Ewing, 2018, p. 10).

Morpho-phonemic: morphemes 'vary widely in their phonological representation across related words. English orthography has evolved to favour consistent representation of morphology over phonology to mark connections in meaning across words' (Ewing, 2018, p. 10).

Multiliteracies: a term coined by the New London Group in the mid-1990s to refer to the many ways in which we engage with the world. 'Multi' means 'many', while literacies are the various tools we use to interpret, utilise, analyse and produce text.

Multimodal: a text that combines two or more modes or ways of communicating information.

Multisensory learning: employs visual, auditory and kinaesthetic-tactile pathways (or multiple senses) in combination.

Nominalisation: the process of turning conjunctions, adverbs, adjectives and verbs into nouns (e.g. *nominalise* (verb); *nominalisation* (noun)).

Norm-referenced tests: compare learners' scores on standardised tests with a so-called representative sample – for example, IQ tests are norm-referenced.

Onset and rime: the first sound in a one-syllable word (the onset) and the sound of the remaining part of the word (the rime) (Ewing, 2018, p. 10).

Oracy: the ability to understand and produce spoken language.

Orthography: the spelling system that represents a language (Ewing, 2018, p. 11).

Passive voice: shifts the focus of the clause by removing the actor – for example, 'Zombies *attacked* …' (active voice) becomes 'The attack *was* by Zombies …' (passive voice).

Phonemes: 'The smallest units of a spoken language which can be combined to form syllables and words. In English, there are at least 44 phonemes but only 26 letters (accents may play a role)' (Ewing, 2018, p. 10).

Phonemic awareness: the ability to focus on, identify and manipulate individual sounds (phonemes) in spoken words (Ewing, 2018, p. 10).

Phonics and word knowledge: the proficiency to identify relationships between letters (the symbols of the written language, graphemes) to the sounds (phonemes) for use with reading and writing (Ewing, 2018, p. 11).

Phonological awareness: the awareness of the sound and structures of language. When developing phonological awareness, children learn to differentiate, identify and locate sounds at the sentence, word, syllable and phoneme (sound) level.

Phonology: 'The system by which speech sounds of a language represent meaning' (Ewing, 2018, p. 11).

Praxis: the meeting point of theory and practice, in which action is informed by theoretical understandings and theoretical understandings are refined and shaped by practice-based evidence.

Print literacy: the knowledge and competencies required to read and write printed text.

Programme for International Student Assessment (PISA): measures 15-year-old students' reading, mathematics, and science literacy every three years.

Recoding: 'Translating sound to print, with no associated meaning. Compare with decoding, … which includes meaning' (Ewing, 2018, p. 11).

Register: the register of a text is made up of the field (what is happening), tenor (who is taking part) and mode (the role of language) (Halliday, 1985).

Restricted code: a very specific way of using language in a particular context, often unique to a small group.

Running record: a diagnostic strategy used to determine a child's use of different knowledge and resources when reading an unknown text.

Salience: the elements of an image that stand out and draw the viewer's attention.

Scaffold: support for learners to achieve a complex task that is gradually removed as learners experience success.

Sociocultural: approaches to literacies that emphasise the importance of the contexts in which texts are produced and interpreted, engage with texts communicated across a range of modalities and platforms, and suggest that literate practices both reflect and shape social and cultural values.

Standardised tests: tests that are administered and scored using the same conditions and protocols (e.g. NAPLAN tests).

Summative assessment: typically occurs at the end of a learning sequence.

Synthetic phonics: a part-to-whole phonics approach emphasising teaching learners to convert letters (graphemes) into sounds (phonemes) (Ewing, 2018, p. 11).

Teaching and learning cycle: the cycle for creating a written text that includes building the field; deconstructing a modelled text; jointly constructing a text; and independently constructing a text.

Temporary instructional detours: points within a lesson or learning experience where conscious attention is given to specific parts of the text or language (Cazden, 1993).

TESOL: teaching English to speakers of other languages.

GLOSSARY 403

Tests: formal, systematic tasks used to gather information about what learners know under strict and uniform conditions. Tests often involve just pencil and paper, but can also be performative.

Text opener, paragraph opener and sentence opener: (theme of clause) are used to create cohesive texts.

Texts: may incorporate many forms for conveying meaning, including print, digital, visual, aural, numerical and kinaesthetic elements.

Think aloud: a strategy where learners share their thought process out loud about a certain point, topic or idea. This supports students with learning concepts being covered in the curriculum.

Tiered vocabulary: a three-tiered framework that is used to categorise words. The framework can support vocabulary development when teaching new concepts and subject-specific terminology.

Top-down approach: describes engagements with text that emphasise working from the overall meaning of text down to the individual components of language, such as sentences, words, sounds, characters or letters.

Vista: a vibrant place where language and literature are an important part of the environmental aesthetics to meet the needs and interests of learners.

Weavings: the 'moments in classroom lessons when explicit connections are made – by teacher or students – across one or another dimension of knowledge' (Cazden, 2006, p. 1).

Zone of proximal development: a term coined by Vygotsky (1978) to describe the distance between a learner's potential development with adult or older more experienced peer support or scaffolding and their developmental level independently.

Phonological knowledge

Term	Description	Examples
Word awareness	Understanding the difference between a word and a letter	shell, open, fantastic
Syllable	A unit of pronunciation within a word	shell (1 syllable) o.pen (2 syllables) fan.tas.tic (3 syllables)
Onset and rime	Within a syllable the onset includes any consonants before a vowel, the rime is the vowel and consonants after the onset	h-am (h = onset, am = rime) tr-am (tr = onset, am = rime)
Phoneme	Individual speech sounds	cat = /c/, /a/, /t/ shell = /sh/, /e/, /l/

Orthographic knowledge

Term	Description	Examples
Graphemes	Letters or combinations or letters of the alphabet that represent one unit of sound (or phoneme)	t = /t/ sh = /sh/
Letter patterns	Letters that can be grouped together as one sound or part of a word (such as a rime)	ail = mail, trail, rail eat = meat, seat, wheat

Morphemic knowledge

Term	Description	Examples
Morphemes	Smallest units of meaning within words Free morphemes are single words that can stand alone Bound morphemes can only be part of a word	dog, sick, teach, mother -s as in dogs -ness as in sickness -un as in undone -er as in teacher
Compound words	Two words (or morphemes) written together to create a new word	day, dream = daydream earth, quake = earthquake
Prefix	Added to the beginning of other words to create new words	un- as in unbelievable pre- as in preview
Derivational suffix	Added to the end of other words to create new words	-ly as in weekly -tion as in attention
Inflectional suffix	Added to the end of words to change the word grammatically but do not create a new word	-ed as in happened -ing as in waiting

Phonemic awareness

Term	Description	Examples
Sound isolation	Isolating different sounds within a word	Cat /c/ – initial sound, /t/ – final sound
Oral segmentation	Segmenting words into phonemes	Shop = /sh/, /o/, /p/ Blend = /b/, /l/, /e/, /n/, /d/
Oral blending	Blending sounds together from graphemes	/b/, /e/, /s/, /t/ = best /t/, /r/, /ee/ = tree
Sound manipulation: · Addition · Deletion · Substitution	Addition of sound to a word Deletion of a sound in a word Substituting a sound in a word with another sound	/s/ + ash = sash milk – /k/ = mil send – substitute /s/ with /b/ = bend

Letter-sound patterns

Term	Description	Examples
Consonant blends	2 letters = 2 sounds 3 letters = 3 sounds	/d/, /r/ as in drip /s/, /c/, /r/ as in scrap
Graph	1 letter = 1 sound	/s/ as in sit
Consonant digraph	2 consonants = 1 sound	/ch/ as in chip, /sh/ as in shop
Vowel digraph	2 vowels = 1 sound	/ai/ as in mail
Trigraph	3 letters = 1 sound	/tch/ as in hatch
Quadgraph	4 letters = 1 sound	/eigh/ as in eight
Diphthong	2 vowels in a single syllable	/oi/ as in coin

GLOSSARY 405

References

Barratt-Pugh, C. & Rohl, M. (Eds.). (2001). *Literacy Learning in the Early Years*. Taylor & Francis.

Brown, H.D. (2001). *Teaching By Principles: An Interactive Approach to Language Pedagogy* (2nd edn). Pearson Education.

Cazden, C.B. (1993). Immersing, revealing, and telling: a continuum from implicit to explicit teaching. Plenary Address, to the Second International Conference on Teacher Education in Second Language Teaching, Hong Kong, 24–26 March.

—— (2006). Connected learning: 'weaving' in classroom lessons. Keynote address, Pedagogy in Practice 2006, University of Newcastle, 18 January.

Crain, W. (2010). *Theories of Development: Concepts and Applications* (6th edn). Pearson Education.

Earl, L. (2013). *Assessment as Learning: Using Assessment to Maximise Student Learning*. Sage.

Ewing, R. (2018). *Exploding SOME of the Myths about Learning to Read. A Review of Research on the Role of Phonics*. NSW Teachers Federation. https://news.nswtf.org.au/application/files/8715/3249/6625/18181_Role_of_Phonics.pdf

Fellowes, J. & Oakley, G. (2014). *Language, Literacy and Early Childhood Education*. Oxford University Press.

Halliday, M. (1985). *An Introduction to Functional Grammar*. Edward Arnold.

Krashen, S. (1982). *Principles and Practice in Second Language Acquisition*. Pergamon Press.

Kress, G. (2003). *Literacy in the Media Age*. Routledge.

Moll, L., Amanti, C., Neff, D., & Gonzalez, N. (1992). Funds of knowledge for teaching: using a qualitative approach to connect homes and classrooms. *Theory Into Practice*, 31(2), 132–141.

Oliveira, P. (2018). Our proud heritage. true then, truer now: the enduring contributions of Arnold Gesell. *Young Children*, 73(3). www.naeyc.org/resources/pubs/yc/jul2018/enduring-contributions-arnold-gesell

Rohde, L. (2015). The comprehensive emergent literacy model: early literacy in context. *SAGE Open*, January-March, 1–11.

Rozalski, M., Stewart, A., & Miller, J. (2010). Bibliotherapy: helping children cope with life's challenges. *Kappa Delta Pi Record*, 47(1), 33–37.

Serafini, F. (2012). Expanding the four resources model: reading visual and multi-modal texts. *Pedagogies: An International Journal*, 7(2), 150–164.

Strickland, D. (1990). Emergent literacy: how young children learn to read and write. *Educational Leadership*, 18–23.

Unsworth, L. (2006). Towards a metalanguage for multiliteracies education: describing the meaning-making resources of language-image interaction. *English Teaching: Practice and Critique*, 1, 55–76.

Vygotsky, L. (1978). Interaction between learning and development. *Readings on the Development of Children*, 23(3), 34–41.

Book list: children's literature

Abdulla, I. (1993). *As I Grew Older*. Omnibus.

Aiken, J. (2019). *Arabel and Mortimer Stories (A Puffin Book)*. Puffin Books.

Allen, P. (1996). *Who Sank the Boat? (Paperstar)* (Illustrated edn). Puffin Books.

Arnold, E.K. & Davick, L. (2019). *What Riley Wore* (Illustrated edn). Beach Lane Books.

Baker, J. (1987). *Where the Forest Meets the Sea*. Walker Books.

Baker, J. (2004). *Home*. Greenwillow Books.

Baker, J. (2010). *Mirror*. Walker Books.

Bancroft, B. (2016). *Remembering Lionsville*. Allen & Unwin.

Barber, B. (1996). *Allie's Basketball Dream*. Lee & Low Books.

Beaty, A. & Roberts, D. (2013). *Rosie Revere, Engineer*. Harry N. Abrams.

Beaty, A. & Roberts, D. (2016). *Ada Twist, Scientist (The Questioneers)* (Illustrated edn). Harry N. Abrams.

Beaty, A. & Roberts, D. (2019). *Sofia Valdez, Future Prez (The Questioneers)* (Illustrated edn). Harry N. Abrams.

Beer, S. (2018). *Love Makes a Family*. Dial Books.

Bell, H. & Martin, M. (2016). *The Marvellous Funambulist of Middle Harbour and Other Sydney Firsts*. University of New South Wales Press.

Bertini, A. (2020). *Where Happiness Hides*. Dirt Lane Press.

Bertini, A., Lamond. M., & Nielson, C. (2020). *Just One Bee*. Dirt Lane Press.

Bin Salleh, R. (2019). *Alfred's War*. Magabala Books.

Blabey, A. (2007). *Pearl Barley and Charlie Parsley*. Puffin.

Blabey, A. (2008). *Pearl Barley and Charlie Parsley* (Illustrated edn). Front Street, Inc.

Blabey, A. (2020a). *Pig the Slob (Pig the Pug)* (Illustrated edn). Scholastic Press.

Blabey, A. (2020b). *Pig the Tourist (Pig the Pug)* (Illustrated edn). Scholastic Press.

Blabey, A. (2021). *The Bad Guys in They're Bee-Hind You! (The Bad Guys #14)*. Scholastic Paperbacks.

Boelts, M. (2007). *Those Shoes*. Candlewick.

Browne, A. (1987). *Gorilla*. Walker Books.

Calland, C. & Hutchinson, N. (2017). *Minnie and Max Are OK: A Story to Help Children Develop a Positive Body Image*. Jessica Kingsley Publishers.

Carroll, D. & Shakespeare, W. (2009). *Stick Figure Hamlet*. CreateSpace Independent Publishing Platform.

Choi, Y. (2001). *The Name Jar*. Knopf.

Constable, K. (2012). *Crow Country* (Original edn). Allen & Unwin.

Cook, J. (2013). *Thanks for the Feedback, I Think? My Story about Accepting Criticism and Compliments the Right Way*. Boys Town Press.

Cooling, W. & Grobler, P. (2010). *All the Wild Wonders: Poems of Our Earth*. Frances Lincoln Children's Books.

Coombes, D. (2019). *Going to the Footy*. Magabala Books.

Cowley, J. (2019). *The Gobbledegook Book*. Gecko Press.

Dahl, R. (1964). *Charlie and the Chocolate Factory*. Puffin.

Dahl, R. (1988). *Matilda*. Puffin.

Davis, A. & Petricic, D. (1999). *The Enormous Potato*. Kids Can Press.

Diaz, J. (2018). *Island Born*. Bloomsbury.

Dreise, G. (2015). *Kookoo Kookaburra*. Magabala Books.

Dreise, G. (2017). *Mad Magpie* (Illustrated edn). Magabala Books.

Dreise, G. (2019). *Cunning Crow*. Magabala Books.

Earls, N. (2015). *New Boy*. Penguin Australia.

Farjeon, E. & Farjeon, H. (2015). *Kings and Queens*. Puffin Books.

Fleming, C. & Kulikov, B. (2013). *Papa's Mechanical Fish*. Farrar, Straus and Giroux (BYR).

Fox, M. (2017). *I'm Australian Too*. Scholastic Australia.

French, J. (2002). *Diary of a Wombat*. Houghton Mifflin.

French, J. & Whatley, B. (2016). *Cyclone!* Scholastic Australia.

Gaines, J. & Swaney, J. (2020). *The World Needs Who You Were Made to Be*. Thomas Nelson.

Gleeson, L. (2012). *Red*. Allen & Unwin.

Gleeson, L. & Blackwood, F. (2006). *Amy and Louis*. Scholastic Australia.

Graham, B. (1992). *Rose Meets Mr Wintergarten*. Walker Books.

Gravett, E. (2019). *Cyril and Pat* (Illustrated edn). Simon & Schuster Books for Young Readers.

Harry, P. (2019). *The Little Wave*. University of Queensland Press.

Harvey, J. (2020). *Alice-Miranda in the Outback: Alice-Miranda 19*. Penguin eBooks.

Hill, A. (1996). *The Burnt Stick*. Puffin.

Horowitz, A. (2021). *Alex Rider: Anthony Horowitz 10 Explosive Missions. Action Adrenaline Adventure*. Walker Books.

Hughes, T. (1968). *The Iron Man*. Faber and Faber.

Janu, T. (2014). *Figgy in the World*. Scholastic Australia.

Janu, T. (2016). *Figgy and the President*. Scholastic Australia.

Jeffers, O. (2005). *Lost and Found*. Harper Collins.

Jennings, P. (2004). *Rascal the Dragon*. Penguin.

Jennings, P. & Gleitzman, M. (1998). *Wicked!* Puffin Books.

Jones, L., Edwards, M., & Bayliss, L. (2015). *The Princess and the Fog: A Story for Children with Depression*. Jessica Kingsley Publishers.

Joyce, W. (2016). *Ollie's Odyssey*. Atheneum/Caitlyn Dlouhy Books.

Karst, P. & Lew-Vriethoff, J. (2018). *The Invisible String* (Illustrated edn). Little, Brown Books for Young Readers.

Kibuishi, K. (2018). *Amulet #1-8 Box Set*. Graphix.

Kilpatrick, K., Ramos Jr, L.O., & Blanco, G. (2019). *When Pencil Met Eraser* (Illustrated edn). Imprint.

King, S.M. (1998). *Henry and Amy*. Scholastic.

Kobald, I. & Blackwood, F. (2015). *My Two Blankets* (Illustrated edn). HMH Books for Young Readers.

Kwaymullina, A. & Tobin, L. (2017). *The Lost Girl*. Walker Books.

Lai, T. (2013). *Inside Out and Back Again* (Reprint edn). HarperCollins.

Lee, A. & McKenzie, H. (2020). *Do Not Open This Book*. Scholastic Press.

Leffler, D. (2016). *Once There Was a Boy*. Magabala Books.

Lester, A. (2005). *Are We There Yet?* (Gift edn). Kane/Miller Book Pub.

Lester, A. (2007). *Isabella's Bed*. Lothian.

Levy, A., Levy, G., & Kaiser, D. (2019). *What Should Darla Do? Featuring the Power to Choose*. Elon Books.

Little Yuin Aboriginal Preschool. (2015). *Our Little Yuin*. Shooting Star Press.

Lovell, P. (2001). *Stand Tall, Molly Lou Melon*. Penguin.

Ludwig, T. & Barton, P. (2013). *The Invisible Boy*. Random House.

Ludwig, T. & Gustavson, A. (2011). *Better Than You*. Knopf Books for Young Readers.

Ludwig, T. & Marble, A. (2005). *My Secret Bully*. Random House.

Lurie, M. (1989). *The 27th Annual Hippopotamus Race*. Penguin.

Luyken, C. (2017). *The Book of Mistakes*. Dial Books.

Mackesy, C. (2019). *The Boy, the Mole, the Fox and the Horse* (Illustrated edn). HarperOne.

Manbullo, K. (2019). *Moli Det Bigibigi*. Pan Macmillan.

Marsden, J. (1997). *Prayer for the 21st Century*. Lothian Books.

McGough, R. (2015). *Poetry Pie*. Puffin Poetry.

McKinlay, M. (2017). *A Single Stone*. Candlewick.

Meade, H. (2011). *If I Never Forever Endeavor* (Illustrated edn). Candlewick.

Meighan, J. (2015). *Fairytales on Stage: A Collection of Children's Plays Based on Famous Fairy Tales (On Stage Books Book 2)*. JemBooks.

Millard, G. & King, S. (2014). *The Duck and the Darklings*. Allen & Unwin.

Miller, Z.P. & Hill, J. (2018). *Be Kind* (Illustrated edn). Roaring Brook Press.

Mills, A. & Osborn, B. (2003). *Shapesville*. Gurze Books.

Minchin, T. (2014). *Storm*. Orion.

Monk, E. (2020). *Bedtime Stories (As Told by Our Dad) (Who Messed Them Up)*. Playscripts Inc.

Morgan, S. & Malibirr, J.W. (2019). *Little Bird's Day*. Magabala Books.

Munson, D. & King, C.T. (2000). *Enemy Pie*. Chronicle Books.

Musa, O. (2014). *Parang*. Penguin Group Australia.

Oliveros, J. & Wulfekotte, D. (2018). *The Remember Balloons* (Illustrated edn). Simon & Schuster Books for Young Readers.

Otoshi, K. (2008). *One* (Later printing edn). KO Kids Books.

Otoshi, K. & Baumgarten, B. (2015). *Beautiful Hands*. Blue Dot Press.

Parish, P. & Siebel, F. (2013). *Amelia Bedelia* (Anniversary edn). Greenwillow Books.

Pascoe, B. (2018). *Dark Emu* (Illustrated edn). Scribe US.

Pascoe, B. (2019). *Young Dark Emu: A Truer History*. Magabala Books.

Pilkey, D. (2021). *Dog Man: From the Creator of Captain Underpants (Dog Man #1)*. Graphix.

Pillans, S. (2022). *Cranky Frankie and the Oceans of Trash*. Van Haren Publishing.

Pugliano-Martin, C. & Pugliano, C. (2008). *Scholastic Greek Myth Plays (Best Practices in Action)* (Illustrated edn). Scholastic Teaching Resources (Teaching Strategies).

Rawlins, D., Potter, H., & Jackson, M. (2018). *Waves*. Walker Books.

Reynolds, P.H. (2003). *The Dot. (Creatrilogy)*. Candlewick.

Reynolds, P.H. (2004). *Ish. (Creatrilogy)*. Candlewick.

Reynolds, P.H. (2012). *Sky Color (Creatrilogy)*. Candlewick.

Roberts, K. & Webb, J. (2017a). *Messages About Me: Sydney's Story, A Girl's Journey to Healthy Body Image*. Rising Parent Media.

Roberts, K. & Webb, J. (2017b). *Messages About Me: Wade's Story, A Boy's Quest for Healthy Body Image*. Rising Parent Media.

Robertson, C. & Shirvington, J. (2020). *Just the Way We Are* (Illustrated edn). ABC Books.

Rodda, E. (2018). *His Name Was Walter*. HarperCollins.

Rubinstein, G. & Pett, M. (2011). *The Girl Who Never Made Mistakes*. Sourcebooks.

Sendak, M. (1963). *Where the Wild Things Are*. Harper & Rowe.

Seymour, J. (2019). *Baby Business*. Magabala Books.

Seymour, J. & Mulgo Watson, L. (2019). *Cooee Mittigar*. Magabala Books.

Smith, J. & Blakeley, J. (2015). *Little Miss Jessica Goes to School*. Jessica Smith.

Solnit, R. (2020). *Cinderella Liberator: Fairytale Revolution*. Vintage Classics.

Sornson, B. & Dismondy, M. (2010). *The Juice Box Bully: Empowering Kids to Stand Up for Others*. Nelson Publishing & Marketing.

Spires, A. (2014). *The Most Magnificent Thing* (Illustrated edn). Kids Can Press.

Spires, A. (2017). *The Things Lou Couldn't Do*. Kids Can Press.

Sternberg, J. & Cordell, M. (2016). *Like Pickle Juice on a Cookie* (Illustrated edn). Harry N. Abrams.

Tan, S. (2000). *The Lost Thing*. Lothian.

Tan, S. (2006). *The Arrival* (Illustrated edn). Arthur A. Levine Books.

Tan, S. (2021). *Eric*. Templar Publishing.

Thiele, C. (2019). *Storm Boy: The Illustrated Story*. New Holland Publishers.

Tullet, H. (2010). *Press Here*. Chronicle Books.

Walliams, D. (2021). *The World's Worst Children 3: Fiendishly Funny New Short Stories for Fans of David Walliams Books*. D. Walliams (Ed.). Harper Collins.

Waters, R. (2021). *Love From Australia* (Illustrated edn). Little Hare Books.

Weston, R.P. (2014). *Prince Puggly of Spud and the Kingdom of Spiff* (Illustrated edn). Razorbill.

Wheatley, N. (1988). *My Place*. Walker Books.

White, E.B. & Williams, G. (2012). *Charlotte's Web* (Illustrated-Media tie-in edn). HarperCollins.

Wieslander, J. (2021). *Mamma Mu simmar*. Natur & Kultur.

Willems, M. (2020). *Don't Let the Pigeon Drive the Bus!* Scholastic Inc.

Williams, M. (1922). *The Velveteen Rabbit*. Simon and Schuster.

Wilson, T. & Wood, L. (2015). *The Cow Tripped Over the Moon*. Scholastic.

Wingfield, E. & Austin, E. (2009). *Living Alongside the Animals – Anangu Way*. IAD Press.

Woods, I. & Scott, K. (2011). *Mamang*. UWA Publishing.

Wright, L. (2016). *I Matter*. Laurie Wright.

Yamada, K. & Besom, M. (2014). *What Do You Do with an Idea?* (9th print edn). Compendium Inc.

Yolen, J., Peters, A.F., & Dunbar, P. (2007). *Here's A Little Poem: A Very First Book of Poetry* (Illustrated edn). Candlewick.

Young, R. & Ottley, M. (2015). *Teacup*. Scholastic Australia.

Zelina, G. & Maczó, H. (2018). *Brave Little Ones*. Independently published.

Index

8 Ways Aboriginal Pedagogy Framework, 85, 262

Aboriginal English, 260
Aboriginal pedagogies, 84–5, 262
Aboriginal peoples
  histories of, lesson example, 60–2
  languages, 63–4, 260, 262
  learning preferences, 389
  texts featuring, 242
  see also Indigenous peoples
Aboriginal and Torres Strait Islander Histories and Cultures cross-curriculum priority, 30–1, 390–1
accountability, assessment, 59
accountable talk, 95–6
acquisition, 112–13
action verbs, 235
active listening, 91
adaptive testing, 35
Adelaide Declaration on Schooling (1999), 30
adjectival prepositional phrases, 240–1
adjustments, reasonable, 288, 290
advance/detail storytelling strategy, 265
adverbial prepositional phrases, 239–42, 244
adverbs, 236
advertising materials, 116
agency, of learners, 258, 263–8, 289, 337
Alfred's War (Bin Salleh), 61–2
Alice Springs (Mparntwe) Education Declaration (2019), 31, 37, 45, 280
All the Wild Wonders: Poems of Our Earth (Cooling and Grobler), 157
alliteration, 311
alphabetic principle, 132
analytic phonics, 139
anti-discrimination, 279–81
appraisal system (tenor), 242–3
apps, 156, 290
Are We There Yet? (Lester), 166
Arrival, The (Tan), 165
Arts learning area, 354
arts-rich strategies, 194–200, 217
  see also drama-rich strategies
assessment
  as learning, 54
  authentic, 49–50, 60–7, 68
  defined, 49
  differentiation and, 315
  ethical, 53–4

EYLF on, 342
for learning, 49
formative. *see* formative assessment
inclusive practices and, 50–1, 287–8
learner involvement in, 54, 56, 146
observation as, 144–5
of learning, 49
oracy, 80–1, 87–8
peer. *see* peer assessment
planning, 57–9, 65–7
reading ability, 144–6
reliability of, 53–4
reporting results of, 55–6
resources, 68
rich tasks for, 55
running records, 145
of self. *see* self-assessment
spelling development, 312, 315–16
strategies, 56–7
subjectivity of, 49
summative, 52–3, 65, 288
timing of, 51–2, 65
of understanding, 188
validity of, 53
work samples, 41, 145
writing development, 342, 346
  see also tests/testing
assistive technology, 288, 290–1, 318, 344
Attenborough, David, 190–1
attendance, 279
audience, 229, 230, 232, 242–3
  see also genre(s)
auditory development, spelling and, 300–1
Austin, Emily Munyungka, 157
Australian Children's Education and Care Quality Authority (ACECQA), 280
Australian Curriculum
  aims/purpose, 32, 44
  bilingual learners and, 250
  cross-curriculum priorities in, 30–1, 32, 390–1
  curriculum connections, 371–2
  design, 30–1
  digital resources and, 45
  EYLF's alignment with, 36–7
  general capabilities, 32, 42, 157, 350
  genre planning document, 366
  on high expectations, 284
  history of, 30–2
  inclusion in, 280

Indigenous cultures in, 30–1, 390–1
learning areas, 351, 353–5, 371–2
planning and implementation of, 365–72
reasonable adjustments in, 290
review of, 32
state/territory implementation of, 31–2
student literacy in, 17
teaching literacy across the, 355–65
  see also literacy general capability
Australian Curriculum, Assessment and Reporting Authority (ACARA), 30, 32, 33, 44
Australian Curriculum: English
  children's literature and, 155, 156–7
  handwriting development in, 334, 343
  Indigenous cultures in, 83
  literature defined in, 157
  National Literacy Learning Progression and. *see* National Literacy Learning Progression
  oracy in, 79–81
  overview, 37–8
  reading in, 127
  spelling development in, 317
  strands, 38–41, 156–7
  understanding and responding in, 181–2
  viewing in, 127
  work samples/portfolios, 41
Australian Institute for Teaching and School Leadership (AITSL), 19, 21, 33, 44, 390, 393
Australian Library and Information Association (ALIA), 394
Australian Professional Standards for Teachers (APST), 250, 281–2, 381–2, 388, 390
authentic assessment, 49–50, 60–7, 68
  see also assessment
autobiographies, literacy, 16
auxiliary verbs, 235

Baby Business (Seymour), 63–4
backward design, 57
Baker, Jeannie, 166, 180, 214
basic interpersonal communication skills (BICS), 251–2
Baumgarten, Brett, 173
Beaty, Andrea, 172

Beautiful Hands (Otoshi and Baumgarten), 173
becoming, in EYLF, 157
'Beginning critical literacy – young children's responses when reading image and text' (NSW, 2021), 18
beginning writing stage, 329
behaviours, 289, 290
being, in EYLF, 157
Bell, Hilary, 166
Belonging, Being & Becoming – the Early Years Learning Framework for Australia (EYLF). *see* Early Years Learning Framework (EYLF)
belonging, in EYLF, 157
benchmarking (assessment), 51
Bertini, Anthony, 165
Besom, May, 172
Best Start Kindergarten Assessment (NSW), 56–7
BICS (basic interpersonal communication skills), 251–2
bidialectalism, 259–60
bilingual learners. *see* EAL/D learners
Bin Salleh, Rachel, 61–2
blogs, 163
book boxes, 162
Book of Mistakes, The (Luyken), 173
book reading, bibliotherapy and, 383–6
BookTrust, 202
bottom-up approach (text engagement), 105, 106, 113, 126
bound morphemes, 303
Bronfenbrenner, Urie, 71, 283
Browne, Anthony, 198
Building Literacy Capabilities Framework, 369–70
building the field. *see* field building
Burnt Stick, The (Hill), 196

CALD (culturally and linguistically diverse) communities, 386–8
see also EAL/D learners
CALP (cognitive academic language proficiency), 251–2
caregivers. *see* parents
catharsis (bibliotherapy stage), 384
chants, 91
child development theories, 71, 103–4
childhood trauma, 276–7, 289–90

children's literature, defined, 155
see also literary texts
Chinese characters, 252
choral reading, 93
circle time, 91
circumstances (adverbials), 239–42, 244
classrooms
language-centred, 263–8
learning beyond, 370–2, 391–4
planning specific to, 368
setting up, 160–3
Clay, Marie, 104
clines, 236
close reading, 363
cloze activities, 186
code breaker role, 133, 254, 257
codes (language development), 72, 230
coding theory, 230
cognitive academic language proficiency (CALP), 251–2
cognitive processes
for spelling development, 301
for handwriting, 331
collaborative approach (learning support), 285–6
collaborative learning, 87, 266
commands, 242
commercial reading programs, 147
communication
behaviour as, 290
ecologies, 117–18
practices. *see* literate practices
skills, 371
social norms of, 89
communities
CALD, 386–8
connecting with, 21, 117–18, 168, 258, 265
literate practices in, 19–23, 117–18
see also parent–school partnerships; literate practices
Community Engagement in Learning continuum (FISO), 21
'Community partnerships to improve literacy' resource (AITSL), 21
composing text element (curriculum), 352
composing texts. *see* texts, creating
compound words, 303
comprehending texts element (literacy general capability), 352

comprehension, of texts
Comprehension Contract and, 264–5
in curriculum, 181–2, 352
inferential, 187, 233–4
spelling development and, 300
teaching and learning cycle for, 361–5
text connections for, 363–5
Comprehension Contract, 264–5
comprehension sub-element (Literacy Progression), 181–2
concept maps, 190
concepts and conventions of print, 327
consonant blends, 312, 313
consonant digraphs, 313
constrained skills (reading), 132
constructivist theories, 88, 137
contexts, 212, 230, 232
see also genre(s); field building
conversations, 74, 95, 165, 183–4, 392–3
see also talk
Cooling, Wendy, 157
Coombes, Debbie, 242
Cow Tripped Over the Moon, The (Wilson and Wood), 173
Cranky Frankie and the Oceans of Trash (Pillans), 157
creating literature (curriculum sub-strand), 40
creating texts. *see* texts, creating
creating texts (curriculum sub-strand), 41
creating texts sub-element (Literacy Progression), 206
creative arts pedagogies, 194–200
creative responses, fostering, 194
creative writing, 199
Creatrilogy series (Reynolds), 172
critical framing, 108
critical literacies, 38, 111, 133, 140
cross-curriculum priorities, 30–1, 32, 390–1
cross-disciplinary learning, 32
cultural competence, 389–90
cultural diversity, in literature, 164
cultural knowledge, literacy and, 253
cultural resources, 250, 254, 258, 262–3, 265–8
culturally and linguistically diverse (CALD) communities, 386–8
see also EAL/D learners
culture, learning, 284, 376–9
see also inclusive learning environments

412   **INDEX**

cumulative learning portfolios, 55
Cunning Crow (Dreise), 164
curriculum
    assessment and. *see* authentic
        assessment
    Australian. *see* Australian
        Curriculum
    authorities, 31–2
    defined, 30
    hidden, 52
    mapping, 109
curriculum connections (Australian
    Curriculum), 371–2
Cyclone (French and Whatley), 197

dance, as text response, 198
Dark Emu (Pascoe), 157
decoding, 136
deconstructing text, 211, 239, 254,
    255–7
derivational prefixes/suffixes, 303
descriptive texts, 220
developing phase (reading
    development), 134
developmental bibliotherapy, 383–6
developmental theories, 104
Diagnostic Assessment Tools for
    English, 87
diagnostic information
    (assessment), 51
dialogue. *see* talk
dialogue circles, 84, 390
Diary of a Wombat (French), 221
differentiation, 315, 341–2,
    369–70
digital inclusion, promoting, 18–19
digital literacy, 18–19, 25
digital technologies
    apps, 156, 290
    assistive, 288, 290–1, 318, 344
    children's literature and, 155–6
    EYLF on, 78
    for literacy development, 290–1,
        370
    reading and, 147
    transition to, 325
digital texts, 13, 14
digraphs, 313
diphthongs, 313
direct teaching, 84, 287
disabilities, 277–8, 291, 317–18,
    343, 344, 346
Disability Discrimination Act 1992,
    277, 280
*Disability Standards for Education
    2005* (the Standards), 280
discrimination, preventing, 279–81
discussion skills, 95

see also conversations
displaying literary texts, 162–3
diversity, 164, 274
    see also EAL/D learners; inclusive
        learning environments;
        learners with additional
        needs
donations, 168
Dot, The (Reynolds), 172
drama, elements of, 195
drama-rich strategies, 68, 195–8,
    201, 211, 224, 238, 265
dramatic play, 335
drawing, 201, 217, 308, 335–6
Dreise, Gregg, 164
Duck and the Darklings, The (Millard
    and King), 198
dysgraphia, 344, 346
dyslexia, 291, 319

e-literature, 155
EAL/D learners
    building on resources of, 250,
        254–7
    classroom practices supporting,
        250–1, 263–8
    defined, 250
    English learning process for,
        251–2
    inclusive environments for.
        see inclusive learning
        environments
    literacy challenges facing, 386
    literacy development for, 252–3,
        278–9
    literacy rates of, 10
    literature engagement of, 254
    readers theatre for, 197
    resources, 269
    teaching strategies, 263–8, 388
Earls, Nick, 164
Early Childhood Australia (ECA)
    Code of Ethics, 280
early childhood education, 36,
    75–9
early-emergent spelling stage, 304
early-emergent writing stage, 329,
    340
early primary years, 79–81, 88–93
early spelling stage, 305, 311–14
early writing stage, 330, 340–1
Early Years Learning Framework
    (EYLF)
    about, 45
    on assessment, 342
    Australian Curriculum's
        alignment with, 36–7
    educational emphasis, 37

on high expectations, 284
on inclusion, 280
lifeworlds as typified in, 157
on literacy development, 127,
    316–17, 342
on literary texts, 157–60
on oracy, 75–9
outcomes, 157–60
structure, 37
ecological systems theory, 71
education, literacy. *see* literacy
    education
education policy. *see* policy,
    education
educative assessment, 49–50, 60–7,
    68
    see also assessment
educators. *see* teachers
8 Ways Aboriginal Pedagogy
    Framework, 85, 262
elaborated code (language use), 72,
    230
Ellis method, 136
embedded phonics, 139
embodiment, 195–6, 198
emergent literacy approach, 104–5
emergent reading stage, 127, 134,
    209
    see also learning to read
emergent spelling stage, 305, 310–11
emergent writing stage, 329, 340–1
enactment, 195, 196–8
engagement, community
    see communities; parent–school
        partnerships.
English (discipline), 37–8, 60–4
    see also Australian Curriculum:
        English; Early Years Learning
        Framework (EYLF)
English (language)
    Aboriginal, 260
    curricular approach to, 39
    language background other than
        (LBOTE), 250
    learning, 74–5, 251–2
    as morpho-phonemic, 132–3
    most common words in, 127
    reading patterns in, 252
    Standard, 260
    see also EAL/D learners
English as an additional language or
    dialect (EAL/D). *see* EAL/D
    learners
English/literacy specialisation, 393
environmental print, 308, 326, 337
environments
    learning, 160–3, 274–9, 288
    natural, 372

INDEX   413

environments (cont.)

   see also inclusive learning environments

Eric (Tan), 166

ethical assessment, 53–4

etymology, 132, 304

evaluation, 59

examining literature (curriculum sub-strand), 40

exclamations, 242

excursions, 364

experiential meanings, field and, 235–42

Experimental World Literacy Program (1966), 8

explanations, 221

explicit instruction

   about, 86, 362

   in handwriting, 337–8, 339

   in keyboarding, 341

   situations requiring, 107, 113

   in spelling, 309, 313

exploratory phase (reading development), 134

expressing and developing ideas (curriculum sub-strand), 39

expression, 213

expressive language, 89

extending phase (reading development), 134

extending writing stage, 330, 341

external norm-referenced testing, 49, 52, 146

factual texts, 218–22, 225, 243

families

   in CALD communities, 386–8

   home literacy engagement, 378–82, 387–8

   Indigenous. *see* Indigenous peoples

   literate practices in, 19–23, 117–18

   oracy role of, 71, 73–5

   school partnerships with. *see* parent–school partnerships

   see also literate practices; parents

family literacy programs, 378–82, 387–8

feedback, 56, 59, 392–3

field, 233, 235–42, 252, 254, 257

field building

   through embodiment, 196

   examples, 61, 63

   for mentor texts, 363

   in teaching and learning cycle, 211, 357

   for text creation, 207

textual understanding and, 183–4

Figgy series (Janu), 164

fine motor development, 335

first language. *see* home/first language

First Nations people. *see* Indigenous peoples

flexibility principle (writing), 328

fluency (handwriting), 331

fluent spelling, 306, 314–15

fluent writing stage, 330, 341

'Food and fibre' curriculum connection, 371

'Food and wellbeing' curriculum connection, 372

formal talks, 95

formative assessment, 51–2, 65, 287–8, 315, 316

Fox, Mem, 164

Framework for Improving Student Outcomes (FISO),

free morphemes, 303

freeze frames (activity), 197

French, Jackie, 197, 221

friendship, books exploring, 184

frozen moments (activity), 197

functional model of language, 38, 355

funds of knowledge, 10, 14, 19, 108, 386

games, making-up, 21

gardens, school, 117

general capabilities, 32, 42, 157, 350

   see also literacy general capability

generalisations, spelling and, 315

genre approach to literacy

   about, 355–6

   for reading, 361–5

   for writing, 356–61

   see also teaching and learning cycle

genre planning document, 366

genre(s)

   defined, 212

   developing understanding of, 212, 358

   grammatical choices and, 229, 230, 232

   predictions facilitated by, 252–3

   references related to, 225

   resources, 246–7

   see also texts

Gesell, Arnold, 103

gifted and talented learners, 278

Gleeson, Libby, 184

globalisation, 32

Going to the Footy (Coombes), 242

Gorilla (Browne), 198

gradual release of responsibility model, 141

Graham, Bob, 193

grammatical features

   choice of, 229, 230, 232, 233–4

   field-related, 235–42

   in informative texts, 218, 220

   mode-related, 243–5

   resources, 246–7

   tenor-related, 242–3

grammatical intricacy, 231

grammatical knowledge, 131, 228–32, 352

grapheme-phoneme knowledge, 308

graphemes, 136, 302, 303

graphic organisers, 189–91, 365

graphophonic knowledge, 131, 133

graphotactic, 299

graphs (letter-sound pattern), 313

'Great Displaced, The' (Musa), 165

Grobler, Piet, 157

grocery shopping, 20, 74

gross motor development, 335

growth mindset, 285

guided reading, 142, 264–5, 363

guided writing. *see* joint construction

hand preference (writing), 338

handwriting

   additional needs affecting, 343–4

   assessment, 342

   benefits, 325–6

   cognitive processes for, 331

   in curriculum, 343

   developmental trajectory, 328

   differentiation for, 341–2

   drawing and, 335–6

   effective, 331

   EYLF on, 342

   history of, 323–4

   keyboarding skills and, 332–4

   letter formation, 339, 340

   mechanics of, 331–3, 339

   play and, 334–5

   purposeful opportunities for, 326, 336–7

   resources, 345–6

   skill development for, 332, 335, 338–42

   spelling development and, 300, 310, 318

   stages, 339–41

414   **INDEX**

teaching approaches, 334–8
writing development and, 325–30
see also writing development
Health and Physical Education learning area, 354
hearing impairments, 318
hidden curriculum, 52
hieroglyphics, 323
high expectations for learners, 284–5
high-frequency words, 127, 309, 313
high-stakes tests, 52–3, 146
see also National Assessment Program – Literacy and Numeracy (NAPLAN)
Hill, Anthony, 196
His Name Was Walter (Rodda), 165
historical recounts, 61–2, 244–5
History (discipline), 60–4
Hobart Declaration on Schooling (1989), 30
home
learning within, 371–2
literacy learning extended into, 378–81, 396
literature exploring, 166
reading at, 147, 382–6
see also family literacy programs
Home (Baker), 166
home/first language
as basis for learning, 230
defined, 250
incorporating, 76
learning to speak and, 74
literacy development in, 252
losing, 252
most common, 76
of Indigenous learners, 259–60
homework clubs, 394, 396
Hughes, Ted, 186
Humanities and Social Sciences (HASS) learning area, 353

'I wonder' questions, 92, 183
I'm Australian Too (Fox), 164
ideas
exposure to new, 86–7
expressing, 77–8
identification (bibliotherapy stage), 384
identity texts, 265–8
If I Never Forever Endeavor (Meade), 173
illiteracy, 135, 276, 277
images, 143, 188
see also visual literacy

imaginative texts, 214–18, 242, 243
inclusive assessment practices, 50–1
inclusive learning environments
aims, 279
barriers, 282–3
benefits, 283
considerations for, 274
creating, 257–9, 261, 283–7
culture of inclusion and, 38, 110–15, 284
defined, 274
documents guiding, 279–81
for EAL/D learners, 257–9
for Indigenous learners, 261
resources, 292
teaching practices supporting, 287–91
independent composition, 62, 212, 358
independent reading, 142, 264–5, 363
independent spelling, 306
Indigenous peoples
classroom inclusivity of, 114–15, 261
cultural resources of, 262–3
curricular focus on, 30–1, 83, 390–1
educational outcomes, 31
engaging families identifying as, 389–91
histories of, lesson example, 60–2, 63–4
languages, 63–4, 76, 259–60, 262, 324
learning preferences, 84, 85, 389
literacy challenges facing, 10, 279, 386
oral narrative culture of, 83–6, 390
pedagogies supporting, 84–5, 262
reading rates of, 10
resilience of, 261
Stolen Generations, 196
stories as culture of, 261
symbol reading of, 135
teacher relationships with, 283
teaching resources related to, 24, 396
texts featuring, 242
trauma and vulnerability of, 276–7
Individual Education Plans (IEPs), 288
inferential comprehension, 187, 233–4
inflectional suffixes, 303

information and communication technologies (ICTs), 78
see also digital technologies
information literacy, 370
information processing theories, 137
informative texts, 218–22, 225, 243
Initial Teacher Education reform, 393
insight (bibliotherapy stage), 384
instructional approaches
see pedagogical approaches; teaching literacies; teaching oracy.
instructional coaching models, 392–3
instructional conversations, 392–3
instructional texts, 221
integration of multiple patterns (IMP) framework, 299
interacting (learning progression sub-element), 83, 181
interacting with others (curriculum sub-strand), 40
interaction, social, 76–7
interpersonal meanings, tenor and, 242–3
interpreting, analysing, evaluating (curriculum sub-strand), 40
intertextuality, 184
Invisible String, The (Karst and Lew-Vriethoff), 165
iPads, 18
Iron Man, The (Hughes), 186
irregular verbs, 235
irregular words, spelling of, 313
Ish (Reynolds), 172

Jackson, Mark, 243
Janu, Tamsin, 164
Jeffers, Oliver, 184, 185
joint construction
examples, 61–2, 207, 214
of historical recounts, 245
implementing, 209–10
resources, 225, 247
in teaching and learning cycle, 211–12, 358
see also teaching and learning cycle
journals
learning, 54
professional, 168
Joyce, William, 184

Karst, Patrice, 165
keyboarding, 332–4, 341, 344

INDEX 415

Kilpatrick, Karen, 173
Kindergarten Development Check
    (Tasmania), 56
King, Stephen Michael, 198
knowledge
    connecting new and existing,
        115–18
    cultural, 253
    funds of. *see* funds of knowledge
    grammatical. *see* grammatical
        knowledge
    language strand, 39
    literacy general capability, 352–3
    literature strand, 40
    morphemic, 303
    orthographic, 302–3
    phonological, 89–90, 300, 302,
        310–11
    reading, 131
    schema theory and, 255
Kookoo Kookaburra (Dreise), 164
Kwaymullina, Ambelin, 233–4, 241

language
    classroom centring of, 263–8
    conditions for learning, 129–30
    cultural access by, 257
    in curriculum, 39, 334
    describing place, 214
    development, 89–90, 112–13,
        228, 230
    diversity of, 76, 165, 250
    English. *see* English (language)
    expressive, 89
    functional model of, 38, 355
    home/first. *see* home/first
        language
    Indigenous, 63–4, 76, 259–60,
        262, 324
    mode continuum of. *see* mode
        continuum
    modelling, 74
    most common non-English, 76
    oral. *see* oral language
    persuasive, 219
    receptive, 89
    repertoires of. *see* linguistic
        resources; literate practices
    social norms and use of, 89
    sociocultural contexts of, 72,
        230
    structure of, 105
    student research on, 258–9
    theories of, 72
language background other than
    English (LBOTE), 250
    see also EAL/D learners

language for interaction (curriculum
    sub-strand), 39
language strand (curriculum), 39
language variation and change
    (curriculum sub-strand), 39
later primary years, 93–6
LAUNCH pedagogical framework,
    170–3
LBOTE (language background other
    than English), 250
    see also EAL/D learners
learner-centred teaching, 287
learners
    agency of. *see* agency, of learners
    assessment involvement of, 54,
        56, 146
    diversity of, 274–9
    EAL/D. *see* EAL/D learners
    as expert, 258
    gifted and talented, 278
    high expectations for, 284–5
    as linguistic ethnographers,
        258–9
    linguistic resources. *see* linguistic
        resources
    literature recommendations from,
        168
    literature reflecting interests of,
        165–6
    remote, 10
    reporting to, 56
    self-esteem, fostering, 194
    support services for, 393–4
    supportive transitions for, 286
    teacher relationship with, 283
    text curation by, 164
    urban, 10
    vulnerable, 276–7, 289–90
learners with additional needs
    assistive technology for, 288,
        290–1, 318, 344
    disabilities and, 277–8, 291,
        317–18, 343, 344, 346
    EAL/D learners. *see* EAL/D
        learners
    examples, 274–5
    gifted and talented learners, 278
    inclusion of. *see* inclusive learning
        environments
    literacy learning and, 275–9
    literacy support for, 317–18,
        343–4
    pedagogical approaches, 287–91
    reasonable adjustments for, 288,
        290
    resources for teaching, 292–3
    support services for, 394

supporting individual, 288–91
    vulnerable learners, 276–7,
        289–90
learning
    acquisition compared to,
        112–13
    approaches to, 307–8
    beyond the classroom, 370–2,
        391–4
    collaborative, 87, 266
    culture, creating, 376–9
    defined, 112
    design process, 287, 368
    differentiation, 315, 341–2,
        369–70
    environments for, 160–3, 274–9,
        288
    goals for, 58, 59
    Indigenous perspectives on, 84–5,
        262, 389
    intentions for, 58, 59, 60, 63, 86
    to read. *see* learning to read
    'sustainable', 283
    two-way, 115, 262
    see also inclusive learning
        environments
learning areas (curriculum), 351,
    353–5, 371–2
    see also literacy general capability
learning difficulties, 317–18, 343
    see also disabilities
learning journals, 54
learning portfolios, 41, 55
learning to read
    approaches, 132, 135–40
    bottom-up process of, 126
    conditions and processes for,
        129–30
    enablers for success in, 128–9
    myths, 148
    non-linear process of,
        139–40
    'readiness' for, 135–6
Leffler, Dub, 237–9
left-handed writers, 338
legibility, 331
legislation, on inclusion, 279–80
Lester, Alison, 166
letter formation, 339, 340
letter recognition, 326
letter-sound patterns, 302, 303,
    313
letters, groups of, 339
Lew-Vriethoff, Joanne, 165
lexical density, 231, 244
lexicogrammar, 72
libraries, school, 394

Life on Our Planet, A
(Attenborough), 190–1
linear principle (writing), 328
linguistic capital, 109
linguistic repertoires. *see* literate
practices
linguistic resources, 250, 255–7,
258, 259, 263–8
see also literate practices
listening
active, 91
speaking and. *see* oracy
listening (learning progression
sub-element), 82
literacies
assessment. *see* assessment
changing definitions of, 7,
12, 79
critical. *see* critical literacies
in curriculum
see Australian Curriculum;
Australian Curriculum:
English
defined, 7
development. *see* literacy
development
digital. *see* digital literacy
family programs for. *see* family
literacy programs
history of, 7–9, 135
as human right, 8
importance of, 8–9, 156
information, 370
as multisited, 20
practices. *see* literate practices
print. *see* print literacy
rates of, 9–10
as social construct, 38
sociocultural approaches to, 19,
107–9
spelling and skills for, 300–1
subject-specific strategies for,
355–65
teaching approaches. *see* teaching
literacies
visual, 17, 18, 239, *see* visual
literacy
see also multiliteracies; reading;
writing
literacy autobiographies, 16
literacy development
for bilingual learners, 252–3
factors affecting, 279
learner difficulties and, 275–9
online games and, 25
phases, 134
technology for, 290–1, 370

theories. *see* theories (literacy
development)
understanding, 105–6, 112–13
literacy education
access and inclusion in, 38, 110–
15, 284
children's literature in. *see* literary
texts
community involvement in, 386
see communities; families
connecting knowledges in,
115–18
current policy objectives, 35–6
EYLF's support of, 75–9
history of Australian, 35
pedagogical approaches. *see*
pedagogical approaches
reasonable adjustments in, 288,
290
sociocultural approaches, 107–9
theories informing. *see* theories
(literacy development)
wider organisation of, 391–4
see also Australian Curriculum:
English; inclusive learning
environments
literacy general capability
about, 42–3, 350
across the curriculum, 355–65
curriculum connections and,
371–2
framework for, 369–70
knowledge in, 352–3
in learning areas, 351, 353–5,
371–2
planning and implementation of,
365–72
processes in, 352
resources, 373
structure, 43, 351, 353
literacy learning cycle. *see* teaching
and learning cycle
literacy learning specialists, 391–3
'Literacy Myth', 8
literacy profiles, 23
literacy strand (curriculum), 40–1
Literacy Teaching Toolkit, 73, 97, 113
literary texts
benefits, 155, 156
classroom organisation of, 160–1,
162–3
curating collections of, 163–7
defining, 155–6
developmental bibliotherapy and,
383–6
digital technologies and, 155–6
diversity in, 164–5, 262

EAL/D learners and, 254–5
in education documents, 155,
156–60
general capabilities and, 157
as grammatical models, 229
home/place in, 166
importance of, 156
LAUNCH framework using,
170–3
picture books, 265
reflecting learner's interests,
165–6
reflective talk encouraged by, 165
resources, 174
staying up-to-date with, 167–9
types, 155–6
see also specific books
literate practices
advantage/exclusion related to,
22, 110–12
in childhood, 21
as co-constitutive, 22
connecting new and existing,
117–18
development of. *see* literacy
development
diversity of, 11, 20
everyday activities involving,
20–1, 74
fluidity of, 20
of Indigenous peoples, 114–15
literacy profiles for, 23
multimodal texts and, 13–15
primary. *see* funds of knowledge
sociocultural understandings of,
11–12, 19–23, 107–9, 110
student research on, 258–9
understanding, 17, 22–3, 105–6,
112–15
see also linguistic resources
literature, 157
see also literary texts
literature circles, 192
literature and context (curriculum
sub-strand), 40
literature strand (curriculum),
39–40, 156–7
litteratus, 7
Little Bird's Day (Morgan and
Malibirr), 236
*Living Alongside the Animals –
Anangu Way* (Wingfield and
Austin), 157
look-say approach (reading), 136
Lost and Found (Jeffers), 184, 185
Lost Girl, The (Kwaymullina), 233–4,
241

INDEX   **417**

Love from Australia (Waters), 166
Lurie, Morris, 218
Luyken, Corinna, 173

Mad Magpie (Dreise), 164
Malibirr, Johnny Warrkatja, 236
Mamma Mu simmar (Wieslander), 165
Marsden, John, 200
Martin, Matthew, 166
Marvellous Funambulist of Middle Harbour and Other Sydney Firsts, The (Bell and Martin), 166
Mathematics learning area, 354
maturational theories, 103
Meade, Holly, 173
meaning-making
  digital tools for, 291
  experiential, field and, 235–42
  EYLF on, 77–8
  interpersonal, tenor and, 242–3
  reading as, 127–8, 137–8
  sociocultural processes of, 127
  textual, 243–5
  see also comprehension, of texts
measurements (assessment), 54
Melbourne Declaration on Educational Goals for Young Australians, 30, 31, 37
memory/memorisation, 326, 331
mentor texts, 362–5, 373
metacognitive processes, 187–8, 301
metalanguage, 105, 208, 228, 229, 259, 266
microskills, 9
middle primary years, 93–6
Millard, Glenda, 198
mind maps, 190
Mirror (Baker), 214
miscue analysis, 145
mnemonics, 313
modality, 236, 242
mode
  about, 233
  complexity of, 13
  defined, 13
  examples, 239, 257
  grammatical features of, 243–5
  questions related to, 254
  register and, 252
  see also multimodal texts
mode continuum, 208–9, 229, 230–1, 266
modelled reading/viewing
  about, 141
  deconstructing text of. *see* deconstructing text

examples, 61, 63–4
parents' role in, 382
reading aloud and, 74, 141
responding to text in, 183
in teaching and learning cycle, 211, 358
text connections and, 184
think aloud strategy, 91–2, 183
modelled spelling strategies, 309, 313
modelled writing/handwriting, 207, 337–8, 339
modelling, peer, 183, 191–2, 193
monitoring (metacognition), 187
Montessori, Maria, 104
Morgan, Sally, 236
morphemes, 303, 313
morphemic knowledge, 303
morphological instruction, 132
morphology, 132
morpho-phonemic, English as, 132–3
Most Magnificent Thing, The (Spires), 173
motor skills, handwriting, 332, 335
movement, as text response, 198
multidisciplinary teams, 286
multiliteracies, 12–15, 107–9
'Multimedia' curriculum connection, 371
multimodal literacy
  autobiographies, 16
multimodal texts, 13–16, 18
  see also visual literacy
'Multiple literacy outcomes' resource (AITSL), 19
multisensory learning, 288, 307–8, 334–5
Musa, Omar, 165
music, as text response, 199
'My Generation' (Musa), 165
My Place (Wheatley), 166
My School website, 33–4, 35, 45, 53, 68

narrative writing, 61–2, 182–3, 215, 265–8
National Assessment Program – Literacy and Numeracy (NAPLAN)
  aims, 35
  controversy around, 34, 53, 146
  examples from, 57
  format, 35
  limitations, 52–3
  overview, 34
National Literacy Learning Progression
  creating texts in, 206

definitions in, 181–2
oracy in, 82–3
overview, 41–2, 80–2, 128
text selection in, 40
National Quality Framework (NQF), 280
National Quality Standard (NQS), 280
natural environments, understanding of, 372
Neidjie, Bill, 324
New Boy (Earls), 164
New Life, A (Nguyen), 257
New Literacy Studies (NLS), 12, 107
New London Group, 12, 107
Nguyen, Mira, 256–7
nominalisation, 209, 218, 237, 244
non-fiction texts, 362–5
norm-referenced tests, 49, 52, 146
note-taking skills, 363
noun groups, 237–9, 244, 245
nutrition, 372

observations (assessment), 144–5
Oliveros, Jessie, 165
Ollie's Odyssey (Joyce), 184
Once There Was a Boy (Leffler), 237–9
online games, 25
online texts, engaging with, 13
onset, 90, 302, 311
oracy
  assessment of, 80–1, 87–8
  at-home strategies, 73–5
  community emphasis on, 20
  in curriculum, 79–81, 181
  defined, 112
  developmental aspects, 72–3
  everyday opportunities for, 74
  EYLF's support of, 75–9
  instructional strategies for, 84, 86–7, 90–6, 266
  key issues, 88–90
  language development and, 89–90
  National Literacy Learning Progression and, 82–3
  prior-to-school development of, 71–5
  resources, 97
  sequence of achievement, 81
  spelling and, 300, 301
  storying and. *see* storying/storytelling
oral blending, 312
oral language
  contextual codes in, 72, 230

418   INDEX

defined, 209
development of. *see* oracy
elaboration on, 229
expressive, 89
literacy learning and, 71, 209, 300
pragmatics of, 89
speech functions, 242, 243
spelling development and, 301, 310–11
writing development and, 326–7
see also mode continuum; phonemic awareness; phonological awareness
oral narrative, 83–6, 390
oral presentations, 192–3
oral segmentation, 312
organisations, literature-promoting, 168
organisers, graphic/semantic, 189–91, 365
ORIM framework, 379–81
orthographic knowledge, 302–3
orthographic mapping, 308
orthography, 132, 302
Otoshi, Kathryn, 173
Ottley, Matt, 188–9
'Outdoor learning' curriculum connection, 372
overt instruction, 107

paper placement (handwriting), 339
paragraph openers, 61, 218
parent–school partnerships
    behaviours fostering, 378–9
    in CALD communities, 386–8
    community engagement continuum for,
    family literacy and, 378–82, 387–8
    home reading programs and, 383–6
    in Indigenous communities, 389–91
    support within, 378–9
    trusting and authentic, 117–18, 258, 265, 283, 378
parents
    assessment and, 54
    behaviours, models of, 378–9
    home literacy engagement, 378–82, 387–8, 396
    oracy role of, 71, 73–5
    reading role of, 382–6
    reporting to, 55, 56
    school partnership with. *see* parent–school partnerships

participants (noun groups), 237–9
partnerships, parent–school. *see* parent–school partnerships
Pascoe, Bruce, 157, 244
passive voice, 218
pattern systems, 78
pedagogical approaches
    Aboriginal pedagogies, 84–5, 262
    arts-rich, 194–200, 217
    as context dependent, 105
    creative arts-based, 194–200
    critical literacy, 38
    for curriculum planning, 368
    direct teaching, 84, 287
    explicit instruction. *see* explicit instruction
    inclusive, 287–91
    LAUNCH framework, 170–3
    learner-centred teaching, 287
    literacy development, 105–6
    multiliteracies framework, 12–15, 107
    reciprocal teaching, 93, 192
    strength-based approach, 284–5
    teaching and learning cycle. *see* teaching and learning cycle
    transformative pedagogy, 112
    see also drama-rich strategies; teaching literacies
peer assessment, 54, 56, 146
peer teaching/modelling, 183, 191–2, 193
pencil grip, 339, 340
perceptual-motor activities, 104
persuasive texts, 222–3, 225, 242, 243
phonemes, 131, 302, 312, 323
phonemic awareness
    defined, 126
    oracy and, 89–90
    reading and, 132
    spelling and, 301, 308
    teaching, 310–12
phonics
    analytic, 139
    defined, 312
    embedded, 139
    reading methods using, 136–7
    synthetic, 137, 139
    teaching, 312–13, 319
    word knowledge and, 39
Phonics Screening Check, 57
phonological awareness, 89–90, 300, 302, 310–11
phonology, 132
physical development, for handwriting, 332, 335

Piaget, Jean, 104
picture books, 265
    see also specific books
Pillans, Sue, 157
place
    language to describe, 214
    literature exploring, 166
planning
    assessment, 57–9, 65–7
    classroom-level, 368
    curriculum connections for, 371–2
    for differentiation, 369–70
    documentation for, 366
    for literacy general capability, 369–70
    oracy, 80–1
    resources, 373
    school-level, 365–72
    templates, 368
play
    dramatic, 335
    literate practices embedded in, 20–1
    storytelling and, 21, 215–16
    writing development and, 334–5, 336
Plus, Minus, Interesting (PMI), 190
poetry, 91, 217, 224
policy, education, 33–6, 280–2
    see also Australian Curriculum; Early Years Learning Framework (EYLF).
portfolios, learning, 41, 55
post-modifiers,
posture (handwriting), 339, 340
Potter, Heather, 243
praxis, 102
Prayer for the 21st Century (Marsden), 200
predictions, 183, 252–3
prefixes, 303
pre-modifiers, 237
prepositional phrases, 239–42
pre-reading activities, 104
presentations, oral, 192–3
Press Here (Tullet), 200
primary years
    early, 79–81, 88–93
    later, 93–6
    middle, 93–6
print
    concepts and conventions of, 327
    environmental, 308, 337
print literacy, 8–10
printing presses, 8
problem-solving teams (PSTs), 285

INDEX 419

process approach (writing), 106, 113

processes (verbal groups), 235–6

professional learning, 286

Programme for International Student Assessment (PISA), 34, 383

pronunciation, 301

protolanguage, 228

puppetry, 198

purpose of text, 212, 213, 229, 230, 232

   see also genre(s); mode

quadgraphs, 313

questions, 92, 183, 242, 254

Rawlins, Donna, 243

reader response theory, 182–3

reader roles/resources, 107, 133, 254, 257

readers theatre, 95, 196–7, 266–8

reading

   assessment of, 144–6

   choral, 93

   close, 363

   commercial programs for, 147

   constrained/unconstrained skills for, 132

   in curriculum, 127, 181

   defining, 126–8

   development, phases of, 134

   genre texts, 143, 361–5

   guided, 142, 264–5, 363

   history of, 7–9, 135

   home, 147, 382–6

   image-interpretation and, 143

   independent, 142, 264–5, 363

   knowledge required for, 131

   learning. *see* learning to read

   meaning-centred view, 127–8, 137–8

   modelled, 61, 63–4, 141

   morpho-phonemic approach to, 132–3

   neurological patterns when, 138

   patterns, 252

   for pleasure, 143, 383

   pre-reading activities and, 104

   process, 131–3

   reader roles in, 107, 133, 254, 257

   'readiness' for, 135–6

   shared, 74, 141–2, 186

   simple view of, 126–7

   teaching. *see* teaching reading

   technology's role in, 147

   as two-way transaction, 182

   writing and, 327

   see also modelled reading/ viewing

reading aloud, 74, 141

Reading Australia website, 201

reading buddies, 186

reading comprehension, 126, 264–5

   see also comprehension, of texts

Reading WELL program, 383–6

reasonable adjustments, 288, 290

receptive language, 89

reciprocal teaching, 93, 192

recoding, 139

Reconciliation NSW, 389

record keeping, assessment, 59

recounts (text type), 61–2, 221–2, 244–5

recurring principle (writing), 328

Red (Gleeson), 184

reflective talk, literature encouraging, 165

reflexivity, 113

reforms, education, 33–5, 393

refugees, 387–8

register (text), 212, 252

relating verbs, 235

relationships

   parent–school. *see* parent–school partnerships

   trauma-informed practice and, 289

   trusting and authentic, 117–18, 258, 265, 283, 378

reliability (assessment), 53–4

Remember Balloons, The (Oliveros and Wulfekotte), 165

remote learners, 10

reporting (assessment), 55–6

responding to literature (curriculum sub-strand), 40

responding to texts. *see* texts, engaging with

restricted code (language use), 72, 230

Reynolds, Peter, 172

rhymes/rhyming, 91, 311

rime, 90, 302, 311

risk-taking, 193

Roberts, David, 172

Rodda, Emily, 165

role models, teachers as, 169

role on the wall (drama strategy), 198

role-play, 21

roles, reader, 107, 133, 254, 257

root words, 303

Rose Meets Mr Wintergarten (Graham), 193

Rosie Revere, Engineer (Beaty and Roberts), 172

routines, 289

running records (assessment), 145

rural learners, 10

salience, 219

saying verbs, 235

scaffolding, 88, 210, 229, 267–8, 356

schema theory, 255

School Drama Companion, 224

school gardens, 117

school libraries, 394

school readiness, 279

schools

   accountability of, 35

   parent partnership with. *see* parent–school partnerships

   planning across whole, 365–72

   refugee support in, 387–8

Science learning area, 354–5, 359, 361, 365, 369

Scootle (digital resource), 45

scripts, learner-created, 266–8

self-assessment, 54, 56, 146

self-esteem, learners, 194

self-regulation, 289

semantic information, 131

semantic organisers, 189–91

sensing verbs, 235

sentence openers, 61, 218, 244–5

sequence maps, 365

sequencing (teaching strategy), 185–6

Seymour, Jasmine, 63–4

shared reading, 74, 141–2, 186

sharing time, 91

shopping, grocery, 20, 74

sight words, 127, 136, 308, 313

sign principle (writing), 328

situated practice, 107

skills (curriculum)

   literacy-related, 40–1

   literature engagement, 39

   multiple exposures to new, 86–7

   phonemic, 39

Sky Color (Reynolds), 172

small-group teaching strategies, 142

social constructivist theories, 137, 182

social disadvantage, poor literacy and, 277

social media, authors', 169

social semiotic theory of language, 72

sociocultural approaches to literacies, 19, 107–9

Socrates, 323
Socratic method, 94
songs, 91
sound isolation, 312
sound manipulation, 312
spaces, between words, 328
speaking. *see* oracy
speaking (learning progression sub-element), 83
specific language impairment (SLI), 317
specific learning disability (SLD), 317
speech functions, 242, 243
speech pathologists, 394
speeches, 95
spelling
    importance of, 298
    independent, 306
    irregular words, 313
    rules of, knowing about, 310
spelling development
    acquisition and, theories, 298–9, 304–7
    additional needs affecting, 317–18
    assessment, 312, 315–16
    authentic opportunities for, 308
    in curriculum, 317
    EYLF on, 316–17
    knowledge areas for, 301–4
    learning foci for, 310–15
    literacy learning and, 300–1
    print resources for, 308
    processes supporting, 300–1
    resources, 319
    stages of, 299, 304–7, 310–15
    teaching approaches for, 307–10
Spires, Ashley, 173
spoken language. *see* mode continuum; oral language
stage theory (spelling acquisition), 299, 304
Standard English, 260
    see also English (language)
standardised tests, 52, 146
    see also National Assessment Program – Literacy and Numeracy (NAPLAN)
statements, 242
still images (activity), 197
Stolen Generations, 196
Storm Boy (Thiele), 165, 184
story maps, 185
storyboards, 185
storybook apps, 156
storying/storytelling
    advance/detail strategy, 265

arts-rich strategies for, 217
drawing and, 217
identity texts and, 265–8
in Indigenous cultures, 83–6, 390
intercultural sharing through, 258, 261, 262
literacy benefits, 73
oral, 83–6, 215
play and, 21, 215–16
strength-based approach, 284–5
Structured Word Inquiry (SWI), 132, 138, 314
students. *see* learners
subtractive bilingualism, 252
success criteria, assessment, 59, 86
suffixes, 303
summarising (metacognition), 188
summative assessment, 52–3, 65, 288
support services, student, 393–4
supported writing. *see* joint construction
surveys, 145
'Sustainable Learning', 283
syllable, 302
symbols, 78
syntactic information, 131
synthetic phonics, 137, 139

tailored testing, 35
talk
    accountable, 95–6
    learning to, 72–3
    as performance, 255
    as process, 255, 259
    reflective, 165
    understanding texts through, 183–4
    see also conversations; oracy
talk moves (teaching tool), 92–3
Tan, Shaun, 165, 166
teachers
    attitudes of, towards inclusion, 282–3
    Code of Ethics for, 280
    cultural competency of, 389–90
    English/literacy specialisation for, 393
    family engagement role, 381–2
    inclusion as responsibility of, 280–1, 388, 390
    learner relationship with, 283
    literacy development role, 38
    as literary role models, 169
    literacy-teaching support for, 391–3

modelling by. *see* modelled reading/viewing
parent partnership with. *see* parent–school partnerships
professional learning for. *see* professional learning
quality regulation of, 33
reading strategies and role of, 140–2
registration and accreditation of, 281–2
TESOL, 251
teaching and learning cycle
    about, 114
    components, 210–12
    defined, 210
    examples, 61–2, 63–4
    genre modelling using, 212
    for reading, 361–5
    resources, 225, 373
    for writing, 356–9
teaching English to speakers of other languages (TESOL), 251
teaching literacies
    across the curriculum, 355–65
    for EAL/D learners, 263–8, 388
    handwriting instruction, 334–8
    instructional coaching for, 392–3
    LAUNCH framework for, 170–3
    literate practices exploration, 17
    multiliteracies framework for, 12–15, 107
    reading instruction. *see* teaching reading
    spelling instruction, 307–15
    theoretical ideas regarding, 102, 103–6
    writing instruction. *see* teaching writing
    see also pedagogical approaches
teaching oracy, 84, 86–7, 90–6, 266
teaching reading
    as balanced and responsive, 139–40
    history, 135
    important considerations, 147
    morphological instruction, 132
    ongoing skill development in, 140
    resources, 149–50
    strategies, 132, 140–2
    teaching and learning cycle for, 361–5
    theoretical influences, 135–40
    see also critical literacies
Teaching Reading in Australia (research project), 135

INDEX   421

teaching writing
  choosing texts for, 213–14
  examples, 207, 214
  imaginative texts in, 214–18, 242
  informative texts in, 218–22, 225
  persuasive texts in, 222–3, 225, 242
  resources, 224–5
  strategies and approaches, 106, 113, 356–61
  teaching and learning cycle, 356–9
  see also teaching and learning cycle
teaching, peer, 183, 191–2, 193
Teacup (Young and Ottley), 188–9
technologies
  assistive, 288, 290–1, 318, 344
  digital. *see* digital technologies
  education categories, 290
  EYLF on, 78
Technologies learning area, 354
temporary instructional detours, 113
tenor, 233, 239, 242–3, 252, 254, 257
TESOL (teaching English to speakers of other languages), 251
tests/testing
  adaptive/tailored, 35
  defined, 49
  high-stakes, 52–3, 146
  norm-referenced, 49, 52, 146
  spelling, 315
  standardised, 52, 146
  see also National Assessment Program – Literacy and Numeracy (NAPLAN)
text analyst role, 133, 254, 257
text connections, 184, 363–5
text decoder role, 133, 254, 257
text knowledge (curriculum), 352
text openers, 61, 218, 244
text participant role, 133, 254, 257
text structure and organisation (curriculum sub-strand), 39
text user role, 133, 254, 257
texts
  advertising materials, 116
  analysing, 133, 233–4, 254, 257
  annotating, 95
  choosing, 213–14, 236, 254, 362
  comparing, 243
  comprehension of. *see* comprehension, of texts
  creating. *see* texts, creating
  in curriculum, 39–40, 181

deconstructing, 211, 239, 254, 255–7
defining, 7, 12, 181, 208
descriptive, 220
digital, 13, 14
engaging with. *see* texts, engaging with
frameworks for engaging. *see* teaching and learning cycle
genre and. *see* genre(s)
imaginative, 214–18, 242, 243
informative, 218–22, 225, 243
instructional, 221
levels of, 234
lexical density of, 231
literary. *see* literary texts
mentor, 362–5, 373
multimodal, 13–15, 18
non-fiction, 362–5
persuasive, 222–3, 225, 242, 243
purpose of, 212, 213
quality of, 147
reading. *see* reading
recounting, 61–2, 221–2, 244–5
writing. *see* writing
texts, creating
  assessment design for, 65–7
  in curriculum, 206, 352
  examples, 214
  resources, 224–5
  teaching and learning cycle for, 356–9
  see also teaching and learning cycle; teaching writing; writing
texts, engaging with
  approaches to, 105–6
  building context/knowledge for, 183–4
  critical approach. *see* critical literacies
  in curriculum, 39–40, 181–2
  'doing a book to death', 200
  examples, 64, 116, 180–1
  in EYLF, 77
  graphic/semantic organisers for, 189–91
  image interpretation and, 143, 188
  knowledge-building through, 254–5
  metacognitive skills for, 187–8
  modelling of. *see* modelled reading/viewing
  online, 13
  oral presentations for, 192–3
  peer-teaching/modelling and, 183, 191–2
  reader response theory and, 182–3

resources, 201–2
  strategies, 182–7, 194–200, 238
  writing for, 199–200
  see also bottom-up approach (text engagement); reading; writing
texts in context (curriculum sub-strand), 40
textual meaning, mode and, 243–5
themes (sentence openers), 244–5
theories (child development), 71, 103
theories (literacy development)
  considerations, 103
  constructivist theories, 88, 137, 182
  developmental theories, 104
  emergent literacy, 104–5
  practice's relationship with, 102
  purposes, 102
  reader response theory, 182–3
  social semiotic theory of language, 72
  spelling acquisition, 298–9, 304
Thiele, Colin, 165, 184
think aloud strategy, 91–2, 183
tiered vocabulary framework, 359–61
timelines, 365
Tiwi culture, 242
Tobin, Leanne, 233–4, 241
top-down approach (text engagement), 106
Tracks to Two-Way Learning website, 115
transformative pedagogy, 112
transformed practice, 108
trans-generational trauma, 276
transitional writing stage, 330, 340–1
transitions, supporting learner, 286
translanguaging, 263–5, 266
trauma-affected learners, 276–7, 289–90
trauma-informed practice, 289–90
trigraphs, 313
Triple Word Form Theory (TWFT), 299
Tullet, Hervé, 200
27th Annual Hippopotamus Race, The (Lurie), 218
two-way learning, 115, 262

unconstrained skills (reading), 132
understanding texts. *see* texts, engaging with
understanding texts sub-element (Literacy Progression), 181

422   INDEX

United Nations
  Convention on the Rights of
    Persons with Disabilities
    2006, 280
  Convention on the Rights of the
    Child, 280, 281
  Declaration on the Rights of
    Indigenous Peoples, 281
  Educational, Scientific and
    Cultural Organization
    (UNESCO), 8, 12
  High Commissioner for Refugees
    (UNHCR), 387
Universal Design for Learning
  approach, 287
universalisation (bibliotherapy
  stage), 384
urban learners, 10

validity (assessment), 53
Velveteen Rabbit, The (Williams),
  184
venn diagrams, 189, 365
verbal groups, 235–6
Victorian Curriculum Assessment
  Authority (VCAA), 368
Victorian Early Years Learning and
  Development Framework
  (VEYLDF), 284
video games, 25
viewing, 126–8, 181, 182
  see also modelled reading/
    viewing; reading
visual arts, 198, 238
visual discrimination, 300
visual knowledge (curriculum), 353
visual literacy, 17, 18, 239
visual-motor development, 300
visual processes, 300
visual sequential memory, 300
visualising (teaching strategy), 92,
  186
vocabulary
  building, 91
  cline for, 236
  Literacy Learning Progression
    and, 128

spelling and development of, 300,
  315
subject-specific, 359–61
tenor and, 242–3, 257
  see also words
vowel digraphs, 313
vulnerable learners, 276–7, 289–90
Vygotsky, Lev, 88, 104, 210, 324

Waters, Ruth, 166
Waves (Rawlins), 243
We Need Diverse Books movement,
  164
weavings (knowledge), 115–17
websites, 13
wellbeing, 372
WestWords (WW), 201
What Do You Do with an Idea?
  (Yamada and Besom), 172
Whatley, Bruce, 197
Wheatley, Nadia, 166
When Pencil Met Eraser (Kilpatrick),
  173
Where Happiness Hides (Bertini), 165
Where the Forest Meets the Sea
  (Baker), 180
whole-class teaching strategies, 142
whole language approach, 105–6,
  113, 138
'whole language plus' approach, 113
whole word method (reading), 136
Wieslander, Jijja, 165
Williams, Margery, 184
Wilson, Tony, 173
Wingfield, Eileen Wani, 157
Wood, Laura, 173
word awareness, 302
word clouds, 191
word knowledge (curriculum), 39,
  352, 359
word studies, 315
word walls/lists, 360–1
words
  compound, 303
  high-frequency, 127, 309, 313
  irregular, spelling of, 313
  root, 303

sight, 127, 136, 308, 313
spaces between, 328
  see also vocabulary
work samples, 41, 145
World War I, lesson example on,
  60–2
writing
  creative, 199
  engaging text through, 199–200
  history of, 7–9, 135, 323–4
  imaginative, 214–18
  independent, 62, 212, 358
  narrative, 61–2, 182–3, 215,
    265–8
  purpose of, 326, 336–7
  reasonable adjustments to, 290
  samples of, as assessment, 316
  spelling development and, 308,
    315
  teaching. *see* teaching writing
  tools for, 340–1
writing development
  assessing, 346
  drawing and, 201, 335–6
  handwriting and, 325–30
  oral language and, 326–7
  play and, 336
  principles of early, 328
  purposeful opportunities for,
    326, 336–7
  reading and, 327
  stages, 328–30
  teaching approaches, 356–9
  understandings for early,
    327–8
  see also handwriting
written language, 208–9
  see also mode continuum
Wulfekotte, Dana, 165

Yamada, Kobi, 172
yarning circles, 84, 390
Young, Rebecca, 188–9
Young Dark Emu: A Truer History
  (Pascoe), 244–5

zone of proximal development, 210

INDEX   423